DESIGN NOW!

DESIGN NOW!

CHARLOTTE & PETER FIELL

TASCHEN

HONG KONG KÖLN LONDON LOS ANGELES MADRID PARIS TOKYO

DESIGNERS

The world of contemporary design is in flux, with no single direction or philosophy enjoying a clear ascendancy. Mass-producible universal designs, consumer objects with a degree of personal customization and limited edition "Design-Art" pieces all jostle for notice in a media-driven world that feeds on novelty rather than on substance.

With this new publication we have set out to counter the pervasive malaise in mainstream design by featuring those practitioners who are true pioneers in their fields. All of them produce work that makes a significant and forward-looking contribution in one or more of the following categories: by expanding the concept of function; by exploiting materials in innovative ways; by pioneering ground-breaking applications of new technologies; or by exploring new aesthetic boundaries.

By surveying the work of 90 leading designers and design-led manufacturing companies from around the world, we also hope to provide an insight into the incredible breadth of contemporary design practice – from lighting and furniture to consumer electronic equipment, transportation, product architecture and environmental design.

Today much of the design/lifestyle press celebrates the "Schlock of the New", prioritizing and celebrating the novelty of an object rather than any merit it might possess. In many cases, so-called design experts seem unable or unwilling to distinguish between wasteful kitsch and objects that are truly innovative and important. Far too frequently their pronouncements recklessly neglect global environmental concerns. Moreover, they appear to have consciously (and probably cynically) taken an opposing stance to the precepts of "Good Design" in the mistaken belief that this is an edgy, avant-garde position. Good Design is a concept based on a rational approach to the design process and encompasses the following criteria: durability, unity, integrity, inevitability and beauty. Good Design is fundamentally about finding better, more efficient solutions that harmoniously balance form, function and materials in order to enhance life and that have an intrinsic value to society. In contrast, the production and promotion of worthless goods can only lead to moral bankruptcy, debasing both creator and consumer. In a recent magazine article, dwarf figurines, Delft dildos and gun-shaped handbags were featured as the latest thing in design. Beyond asking "What the hell is that all about?" we should reflect that if this is the state of contemporary practice then fundamental problems exist within certain areas of the design community.

With this book we have set out to challenge the moral apathy that exists in much mainstream design today by identifying work that is not only original but also meaningful. Many of the designers and design-led companies featured in the following pages are endeavouring to find more sustainable solutions, using a holistic approach to consider all aspects of the design process and its impact on the environment – in short, reinventing the nature of design itself. After all, when you stop and consider the current state of our planet and our behaviour, there really is no alternative but to begin doing the right thing. For a start, the pre-1960s belief in the morality of delayed gratification has been overwhelmingly replaced by an irresponsible and short-termist pursuit of instant pleasure-on-credit. Look, for instance, at examples of consumerist addictions, such as the "stocking stuffer syndrome", in which normally sane people feel an overwhelming compulsion to buy meaningless gimmickry. Often, these decorative knick-knacks and superfluous gadgets are neither needed nor wanted by their recipients – it is just mindless purchasing for the sake of gifting, which, all too soon, ends up as landfill. Furthermore, Westernized societies' "sod-tomorrow-and-have-it-today" ethos is not only burying many in the developed world under mountains of unmanageable debt, but its inherent wastefulness is also contributing to the wrecking of our shared environment, with developing countries most at risk from climate-related catastrophes. Ultimately, the poorest nations will inevitably pay the price for the profligacy of the developed world.

As James Martin points out in his seminal book, *The Meaning of the 21st Century*: "surely our destiny is to build something better than a society with endless, mostly trivial consumer goods. We have created consumer societies on a grand scale. In such societies, a growing number of people are unhappy and seeking therapy, and most of them complain of feelings of emptiness and pointlessness. Extreme consumer societies become devoid of deep values." In fact, we all need to step back, consider our actions and attempt to find simpler ways of living. Everyone needs to consume less and embrace more modest lifestyle choices – it could even make us happier in the long run. Indeed, we can already trace the growth of a new phenomenon of "inconspicuous consumption" whose pared-down austerity and essentialist ethos are the very antithesis of "Bling" culture. In the words of Chris Sanderson, co-founder of the trend-forecasting Future Laboratory, we are moving "out of a period of bling-or-bust spending and into a more reflective and concerned phase of consumption. It's no longer about relaying how fabulous or wealthy or 'arrived' we are. It's not just austerity as an aesthetic. It's as a way of life." This new type of conscience-driven consumerism sees sustainability as the key to the continuation of human civilization. However, we must also be mindful of the vagaries of fashion and not allow sustainability to become this season's must-have fashion accessory, only to be tossed aside when something more eye-catching arrives. Perhaps we should all reflect on Mahatma Gandhi's wise observation that the "Earth provides enough to satisfy every man's need, but not every man's greed", and also his entreaty: "Be the change you want to see in the world."

In this age of technological acceleration, conflicting opinions abound concerning which changes need to be made and how they should be implemented. In the quest for eco-panaceas, technophiles and technophobes share the same goals but propose diametrically opposed ways of getting there – the "Enviro-Luddites" believe we should return to simpler, pre-industrialized ways of living, while the "Techno-Greens" believe that technology will provide the answers to our ecological dilemmas. Probably the real solutions lie somewhere between these two poles. Perhaps the generation of electricity through tidal power as pioneered by Marine Current Turbines (pp. 340–343) offers a perfect example of such an intermediate position, in which appropriate technology is harnessed to the systems of the natural world.

Within the realm of manufacturing, pressure is also growing for the introduction of international quality standards that all products must meet before they can be produced and sold. By allowing the manufacture of gimmicky gift-products and "free" fast-food toys, we are perpetuating a junk culture, and amassing a legacy of wastefulness that will horrify future generations. Our ancestors lovingly made furniture to last generations, yet even five years of good service would be beyond the capabilities of many equivalent modern products. A further legal requirement for companies should involve not only an obligation to limit the amount of packaging, but also to ensure that what remains is recyclable. Ecolean (featured on pp. 156–161) is a shining example of how a manufacturer can reduce the amount of packaging materials without compromising function, while cutting environmental costs still further through the use of biodegradable materials.

There should also be better-tasting carrots and harsher sticks in order to change the output of the car industry. So much could be done by making hybrid or electric cars (such as those produced by NICE or Tesla – see pp. 402–405 and 516–521) tax-free, while at the same time banning SUVs, monster pick-up trucks and sports cars unless they can meet really stringent emissions and fuel-efficiency targets. More than ever, the actions of individuals are having collective and far-reaching repercussions – yes, there is a connection between us driving our cars and rising sea levels…yes, there is a connection between that nice teak garden furniture in the garden center and the deforestation of the Indonesian rainforest…yes, there is a connection between purchasing the very latest mobile phone (even though your old one still works perfectly) and drought-induced famine in Africa. We need to recognize that our still beautiful planet is a web of interwoven connections, which means that we all have the power to change the world for better or for worse. How we choose to live as individuals will not only decide the legacy we bequeath to future generations, but will also determine mankind's destiny.

Many of the designers and manufacturers included here are not only developing more eco-effective solutions, but are also redefining best practice through a holistic approach to problem solving that considers not only every aspect of the design process, but also the environmental impact of products throughout the complete lifecycle loop. These important and vital goals must become central to the world of design and manufacturing, and products that attain the highest standards should be given a globally recognized seal of approval (much like the "kitemark" that used to be awarded by the Design Council in Britain) so that consumers can make educated choices from among the array of apparently similar products on offer. For too long Good Design has been equated with blandness, a serious misconception when the products resulting from this logical approach to design – useful, safe to use and ethically manufactured – are usually the most interesting both in terms of functionality and aesthetics, as many of the examples shown here amply demonstrate.

With the recent ascendancy of computer-aided design and rapid prototyping, designers can quite literally give substance to their dreams in a matter of hours. In fact, rapid prototyping machines that use laser stereo-lithography have in recent years become the high-tech "Easy-Bake Oven" toys of the design industry. This relative ease of making, however, should not lead to a senseless multiplication of whimsical products; instead, these new digital tools should be used to develop more relevant and durable consumer goods. Manufacturers should be encouraged to grasp that doing the right thing can also be a path to riches, as consumers will become increasingly receptive to new products that promise an environmental dividend.

Corporate social accountability has to become a byword for the manufacturing industry, while designers must accept moral responsibility for the objects they create.

Another interesting current in contemporary design has been the blossoming of limited-edition Design-Art. The role of salerooms and galleries in propelling this phenomenon by linking it to the current feeding frenzy in the contemporary fine-art market has been troubling to some. At the same time, Design-Art affords designers the economically unfettered freedom to explore innovative forms, materials and processes. As a movement it also brings architectural and artistic concepts to the realm of design, thereby promoting discussion on the nature of function and our interaction with built environments. The low-volume production that Design-Art implies certainly minimizes its environmental impact and, considering the monetary value of some of these pieces, they are not going to be thrown away in a hurry. Their intrinsic durability must, therefore, be seen as a good thing. The problem, however, is that the development of these often beautiful and highly experimental pieces is beginning to monopolize the time and attention of some of our most creative designers, the very people we need to develop urgent real-world solutions. Despite this, Design-Art is an important aspect of design practice today and we consequently have included in our selection some of the most interesting work that falls within this category – from Marc Newson's Voronoi shelf and Ron Arad's Thick Vac chair, to Zaha Hadid's Vortexx light and Ross Lovegrove's Ginko table. All these limited-edition pieces, which could never have been realized without state-of-the-art CAD software, express the sheer mastery of their form-givers, and are exquisite structural experiments that pull the future into the present.

We have also shown work by designers who are revitalizing notions of handcraft or who are working with "found objects" to create deeply poetic works. Within this grouping, Fernando and Humberto Campana, with their playful and engaging Design-Art furniture, are perhaps the best examples. They show that designing can be a truly hands-on, creative experience, and that approaching the design process with an open, childlike mind can result in unusual objects that forge strong emotional bonds with their users. The Campana brothers also demonstrate that

designers do not always have to take what they do too seriously in order to create innovative work – a fertile imagination is more important. What the Design-Art movement convincingly articulates is that, whether using low-tech or high-tech means of production, it is possible to invest iconic, limited-edition designs with incredible beauty and expressiveness. It also proves that there is a small but very wealthy coterie of collectors prepared to pay a premium price for individuality. In other words, one of the main attractions to buyers is the fact that not everyone else is going to be able to afford these pieces…oh yes, and there is the added allure of speculative investment potential as well.

Contemporary design practice is also being shaped by the rapidly evolving world of materials science. New wonder materials are continually altering the parameters of design possibilities, for example: "frozen smoke" Aerogel (which has the lowest density of any known solid and extraordinary insulating capabilities, as well as pollution absorbing potential) or harder-than-diamond carbon nanotubes (cylinders of carbon atoms with an extraordinary tensile strength and a remarkable resilience to physical impact). Perhaps even more significant, though, is the discovery and isolation of two-dimensional Graphene, which consists of a single atomic plane of carbon atoms in a chicken-wire configuration, and that possesses extraordinary strength as well as being 1000 million times more conductive than copper. This cheap and relatively easily produced material will in the future replace silicon in the manufacture of small, ultra-fast transistors and computer processors, resulting in an exponential increase in computing power. Indeed, the use of Graphene may well leave Moore's Law – which states the processing power of computer chips doubles every eighteen months – looking decidedly conservative. In fact, Graphene is just one of a whole new class of ultra-thin, one-atom-thick materials that are being synthesized, and which promise a new industrial revolution of miniaturized smart products. It is only a matter of time before wearable communications technology becomes so small that it can be safely implanted in the human body. The desirability of implanted smart nano-transponders is, of course, highly debatable, and in so many ways the capabilities of future technologies will refashion our societies along lines that we can only begin to predict. The ethical harnessing of technology – from artificial intelligence to nanotechnology– should be a global concern, because as faster data processing accelerates scientific innovation the potential for harm or benefit increases at the same rate. Now more than ever it is important to make sure that the right choices are made: just because something is a possibility does not mean it should become a reality.

We need a heightened environmental intelligence to tackle the big decisions facing us today. The biosphere is a closed system, so the harmful chemicals produced by industry remain locked within it, even if they are unseen. Industrial production has disturbed the planet's equilibrium, and we need to channel the recuperative energies of the natural world to heal the damage we have wrought. The model of the "American Dream" that has sustained and fuelled our consumerist societies was, from the start, predicated on the notion of conquering nature and extracting as much as possible from it. Private interests, from oil producers and lumber companies to fisheries and mining operations, have remorselessly exploited these resources without sufficiently acknowledging that they constitute our shared and irreplaceable inheritance. Most natural resources are not boundless and because of this our yardsticks for progress are fundamentally flawed – for example, the calculation of GDP (gross domestic product) is based on economic activity, completely disregarding the fact that plundering the earth for financial gain may have devastating, not to mention expensive ecological consequences. Many countries with healthy GDPs, such as Canada or Australia, have economies almost solely based on the extraction of un-renewable resources – yet the full environmental costs of depreciating the natural capital go unaudited and unaddressed.

Rather than pillaging nature for short-term financial gain, we should instead use the systems found in nature as a model for human activity. In their book *Cradle to Cradle: Remaking the Way We Make Things*, William McDonough and Michael Braungart eloquently point out that, "nature operates according to a system of nutrients and metabolisms in which there is no such thing as waste." In fact, the concept of waste has no place in nature because everything is eventually transformed into something useful for the sustaining of life. Designers can benefit greatly from a detailed analysis of natural pro-cesses. For example, once a product has fulfilled its primary function, why should it not go on to have a worthwhile secondary use – packaging could biodegrade into nutrient-rich fertilizers or become useful building blocks for homes.

Our goal should, therefore, be to eliminate the notion of waste in product design, ensuring that once products have reached the end of their first functional life they can either be usefully remanufactured, re-applied or broken down for high-quality recycling of their component parts. In this connection, it is worth bearing in mind that recycling can actually perpetuate our throwaway culture, and can also degrade virgin materials into qualitatively inferior substitutes – usually because too many different materials are used to assemble a product, with the result that they cannot subsequently be easily separated. Another arresting fact is that, on average, a product contains only 5% of the raw materials used for its manufacture and distribution. So what ends up in your garbage bag is actually only a tiny fraction of a much larger picture of consumption and waste. In addition, many of the products that we routinely discard have been designed around the concept of "planned obsolescence" – a practice so repugnant that manufacturers who cynically employ it should be named, shamed and boycotted.

In the knowledge that we all need radically to reduce our eco-footprints, we must insist that products are, instead, designed as intelligently and responsibly as possible. Design must realize its potential to become a powerful and positive problem-solving tool, for the present and for our future. The most sustainable option of all is to re-use existing products or make new products with increased longevity. To this end, the Finnish furniture company Artek, under the design direction of Tom Dixon, has recently instigated their pioneering "2nd Cycle" initiative: a buy-back program that allows institutions, such as schools and hospitals, to swap their old furniture (originally designed by Alvar Aalto in the 1930s) for new versions and then the original vintage furniture with its characterful knocks and scratches is re-sold by Artek into the domestic market. This revolutionary scheme not only perpetuates the idea of design durability, but also ensures that products are not thrown away before their time.

By highlighting those innovators who are plotting a new, ethical course in design, this book is a rallying call not just for designers and manufacturers but also for consumers to act with greater awareness. We must become more mindful of our consumption habits, and suppress our compulsion for things we do not need. Averting global catastrophe demands that we consume less, and that those purchases we really do have to make are the best, most rigorously designed and holistically conceived products available. And a further responsibility for designers and manufacturers is to place such products within the grasp of the many, not just the privileged few. As Nicholas Stern concludes in his influential review of *The Economics of Climate Change*: "There are ways to reduce the risks of climate change. With the right incentives the private sector will respond and can deliver solutions…It is still possible to avoid the worst impacts of climate change, through strong collective action starting from now." We should all acknowledge that the key word in this statement is the last one…NOW!

Editors' note: *We would like to offer our sincere thanks to all those designers, design groups and companies that have contributed to this project, and hope that readers will be inspired as much by their informative personal statements as by their innovative work.*

Die Welt des Designs ist im Wandel begriffen, und es ist nicht abzusehen, welche der verschiedenen Richtungen oder Philosophien sich durchsetzen werden. Unabhängig davon, ob es sich um universelle Massendesignprodukte, um individualisierbare Konsumgegenstände oder um Objekte der „Designkunst" in limitierter Auflage handelt – sie alle wetteifern um die Aufmerksamkeit einer von Medien bestimmten Welt, in der Aktualität mehr zählt als Inhalt. Mit diesem neuen Buch wollen wir der Misere im Mainstream-Design etwas entgegensetzen und jene Designer vorstellen, die sich auf ihrem jeweiligen Gebiet als echte Pioniere erwiesen haben. Sie alle leisten mit ihrer Arbeit einen bedeutenden und zukunftsweisenden Beitrag im Hinblick auf einen oder mehrere der folgenden Aspekte: Erweiterung des Funktionsbegriffs, innovative Verwendung von Werkstoffen, bahnbrechende Anwendungen neuer Technologien oder Erforschung neuer ästhetischer Grenzen. Wir geben einen Überblick über die Arbeit von 90 führenden Designern und designorientierten Unternehmen in der ganzen Welt und hoffen, damit auch die unglaubliche Breite der aktuellen Designpraxis zu veranschaulichen, die von Beleuchtung und Möbeln bis zu elektronischen Geräten, Fahrzeugen, Produktarchitektur und Environmental Design reicht.

Die Design- und Lifestylemagazine widmen heute den Novitäten eines Objekts viel mehr Aufmerksamkeit als seinen Vorzügen. Häufig sind sogenannte Design-experten offenbar nicht fähig oder nicht gewillt, zwischen überflüssigem Kitsch und wirklich innovativen und bedeutenden Objekten zu unterscheiden. Sie lassen in ihren Darstellungen viel zu oft globale Umweltanliegen leichtfertig unter den Tisch fallen. Und anscheinend lehnen sie die Maximen des „Guten Designs" sogar bewusst (und vielleicht in zynischer Weise) ab, in der irrigen Annahme, damit eine allzu radikale Avantgarde-Position einzunehmen. Gutes Design ist ein Konzept, das auf einem rationalen Zugang zum Designprozess beruht und folgende Kriterien umfasst: Beständigkeit, Einheit-lichkeit, Integrität, Zwangsläufigkeit und Schönheit. Bei gutem Design geht es vor allem darum, bessere, effi-zientere Lösungen zu finden, die durch ein harmonisches Gleichgewicht zwischen Form, Funktion und Material zur Verbesserung der Lebensqualität beitragen und einen immanenten Wert für die Gesellschaft darstellen. Die Herstellung und Anpreisung wertloser Güter kann hin-gegen in den moralischen Bankrott führen und Designer wie Konsumenten korrumpieren. In einem kürzlich erschienenen Zeitschriftenartikel wurden Zwergfiguren, Dildos aus Delfter Porzellan und Handtaschen in Pisto-lenform als der letzte Schrei im Design präsentiert. Wenn sich der Zustand der heutigen Designpraxis so darstellt, sollte man sich nicht nur fragen, was das soll, sondern auch darüber nachdenken, ob bestimmte Richtungen in der Design-Community nicht grundlegende Probleme haben.

Mit dem vorliegenden Buch wollen wir der morali-schen Gleichgültigkeit entgegentreten, die heute in vielen Mainstream-Designs zum Ausdruck kommt, indem wir Werke vorstellen, die nicht nur originell, sondern auch sinnvoll sind. Viele der auf den folgenden Seiten zitierten Designer und Unternehmen sind um nachhaltige Lösun-gen bemüht und wenden einen ganzheitlichen Ansatz an, der allen Aspekten des Designprozesses und seinen Aus-wirkungen auf die Umwelt Rechnung trägt – kurz, sie erfinden das Design von Grund auf neu. Wenn wir inne-halten und uns den heutigen Zustand unseres Planeten und unser Verhalten vergegenwärtigen, so bleibt uns aller-dings auch nichts anderes übrig, als endlich anzufangen, das Richtige zu tun. Die bis zu den 1960er-Jahren weit-verbreitete Überzeugung von der moralischen Richtigkeit einer aufgeschobenen Wunscherfüllung ist weitgehend einem verantwortungslosen und kurzsichtigen Streben nach sofortiger Befriedigung auf Kredit gewichen. Man denke nur an Konsumkrankheiten wie den Kaufrausch, bei dem selbst vernünftige Menschen den unwidersteh-lichen Drang verspüren, sinnlose Dinge zu kaufen. Oft landen der derart erworbene Schnickschnack bei Menschen, die ihn nicht brauchen oder gar nicht haben wollen – vieles wird also völlig gedankenlos gekauft, nur um verschenkt zu werden und dann vielleicht allzu schnell als Abfall zu enden. Diese „Wir-pfeifen-auf-die-Zukunft"-Einstellung der westlichen Welt lässt nicht nur viele unter einem Berg von Schulden versinken, die damit verbundene Verschwendung trägt auch zur Zerstörung unserer gemeinsamen Umwelt bei und bürdet den Ent-wicklungsländern das größte Risiko in klimabedingten Katastrophen auf. Letztendlich werden die ärmsten Län-der den Preis für die Unmäßigkeit der entwickelten Welt zahlen müssen.

Wie James Martin in seinem richtungweisenden Buch *The Meaning of the 21st Century* erklärt, sind wir „eindeutig dazu bestimmt, etwas Besseres zu schaffen als eine Gesellschaft mit einer endlosen Folge von meist belanglosen Konsumgütern. Wir haben in großem Stil Konsumgesellschaften errichtet. In solchen Gesellschaften sind immer mehr Menschen unglücklich und suchen therapeutische Hilfe, um einen Weg aus dem Gefühl der Leere und Sinnlosigkeit zu finden. In extrem konsum-orientierten Gesellschaften gehen die inneren Werte ver-loren." Wir sollten also alle einen Schritt zurücktreten, überlegen, was wir tun, und uns um eine einfachere Lebensweise bemühen. Jeder und jede von uns sollte weniger konsumieren und einen bescheideneren Lebens-stil pflegen – auf lange Sicht gesehen könnte uns das sogar glücklicher machen. Tatsächlich sehen wir bereits erste Anzeichen für ein neues Phänomen des „unauffälli-gen Konsums", das mit seiner wirtschaftlichen Einschrän-kung und seinem essentialistischen Ethos geradezu die Antithese zur „Protzkultur" bildet. Nach Chris Sander-son, dem Mitbegründer des Meinungsforschungsinstituts Future Laboratory, sind wir auf dem Weg „aus einer Periode des reinen Wegwerfkonsums in eine Phase des reflektierteren und engagierteren Kaufens. Es geht nicht mehr darum zu zeigen, wie großartig, reich oder ‚angesagt' wir sind. Es handelt sich nicht um Schlichtheit im rein ästhetischen Sinn. Es handelt sich um einen Lebensstil." In diesem neuen, vom Gewissen geleiteten Konsumverhalten gilt Nachhaltigkeit als Schlüssel zum Überleben unserer Zivilisation. Wir müssen uns aber auch über die Launen der Mode im Klaren sein und dürfen nicht zulassen, dass Nachhaltigkeit zum Modeaccessoire dieser Saison wird, nur um wieder beiseitegelegt zu werden, sobald uns etwas Neues ins Auge springt. Vielleicht sollten wir über Mahatma Gandhis weisen Spruch nachdenken, die Erde habe „genug für jedermanns Bedürfnisse, aber nicht für jedermanns Gier", und über seine Aufforderung: „Die Veränderung, die ihr in der Welt sehen wollt, die müsst ihr sein."

In unserer Zeit der beschleunigten technischen Entwicklung gibt es unzählige widersprüchliche Ansichten darüber, welche Veränderungen notwendig sind und wie sie umgesetzt werden können. Auf der Suche nach ökologischen Allheilmitteln verfolgen Verfechter wie Gegner des technischen Fortschritts die gleichen Ziele, ihre Vorstellungen darüber, wie diese zu erreichen wären, stehen einander aber unversöhnlich gegenüber – die „Öko-Maschinenstürmer" sind Verfechter einer Rückkehr zu den einfacheren Lebensweisen der vorindustriellen Zeit, während die „Techno-Grünen" glauben, dass die Technik Lösungen für unser ökologisches Dilemma liefern wird. Die wirklich sinnvollen Lösungen sind wahrscheinlich irgendwo zwischen diesen beiden Polen zu finden. Ein vorbildliches Beispiel für die Verbindung von Technik und Natur ist die Stromerzeugung mittels Gezeitenkraft, bei der die Firma Marine Current Turbines (S. 340–343) eine Vorreiterposition einnimmt.

Auch im Bereich der Fertigung werden zunehmend internationale Qualitätsstandards gefordert, die sämtliche Güter erfüllen müssen, bevor sie produziert und auf den Markt gebracht werden können. Indem wir die Herstellung von nutzlosen Geschenkartikeln und „kostenlosen" Fast-Food-Spielsachen zulassen, halten wir eine Wegwerfkultur aufrecht, die mit ihrer Verschwendung ein schreckliches Erbe für kommende Generationen anhäuft. Während unsere Vorfahren Möbel für mehrere Generationen bauten, beschränkt sich die Lebensdauer vieler vergleichbarer Produkte heute auf kaum fünf Jahre. Die Unternehmen sollten gesetzlich dazu verpflichtet werden, nicht nur

ihre Verpackungen zu reduzieren, sondern auch ausschließlich recyclingfähige Materialien zu verwenden. Die Firma Ecolean bietet eine gute Lösung, um Verpackungsmaterial zu sparen, ohne bei der Funktion Kompromisse zu machen (S. 156–161), zugleich wird die Umweltbelastung durch die Verwendung von biologisch abbaubaren Stoffen weiter gesenkt.

Um die Produktion der Autoindustrie zu verändern, sind weitaus stärkere Anreize und strengere Vorschriften nötig. Es könnte schon viel erreicht werden, wenn Hybrid- oder Elektroautos (wie sie von NICE oder Tesla produziert werden – siehe S. 402–405 und 516–521) steuerfrei wären und gleichzeitig Geländewagen, riesige Pick-ups und Sportwagen verboten würden, sofern sie nicht wirklich strenge Richtwerte hinsichtlich Abgase und Energieeffizienz einhalten. Individuelles Handeln hat mehr denn je kollektive und weitreichende Auswirkungen – ja, es besteht ein Zusammenhang zwischen unseren Autofahrten und dem Ansteigen des Meeresspiegels … ja, es besteht ein Zusammenhang zwischen den schicken Teakmöbeln aus dem Gartencenter und dem Abholzen des indonesischen Regenwalds … ja, es besteht ein Zusammenhang zwischen dem Kauf des allerneuesten Mobiltelefons (obwohl das alte noch tadellos funktioniert) und der dürrebedingten Hungersnot in Afrika. Wir müssen erkennen, dass unser immer noch schöner Planet ein Geflecht von Zusammenhängen ist und wir daher alle die Möglichkeit haben, die Welt zum Besseren oder zum Schlechteren zu verändern. Welche Lebensweise wir als Einzelne wählen, wird nicht nur darüber entscheiden, was für ein Erbe wir künftigen Generationen hinterlassen, sondern unsere Lebensweise wird das Schicksal der Menschheit bestimmen.

Viele der hier vorgestellten Designer und Hersteller entwickeln nicht nur ökologisch effektivere Lösungen, sondern sind dabei, die bewährte Praxis durch ganzheitliche Lösungsansätze neu zu definieren, in denen sie nicht nur alle Aspekte des Designprozesses, sondern auch die Auswirkungen der Produkte auf die Umwelt in ihrem gesamten Lebenszyklus berücksichtigen. Diesen bedeutenden und lebenswichtigen Zielen muss im Design und in der Herstellung ein zentraler Stellenwert eingeräumt werden. Produkte, die den höchsten Standards gerecht werden, sollten ein weltweit anerkanntes Gütesiegel erhalten (ähnlich dem vom britischen Design Council vergebenen Kitemark-Zeichen), damit die Konsumenten aus der Vielzahl von ähnlich scheinenden Produkten eine sachkundige Wahl treffen können. Allzu lange wurde gutes Design mit Farblosigkeit gleichgesetzt, was eindeutig eine Fehleinschätzung ist, sind doch die auf diesem logischen Designansatz beruhenden Produkte nicht nur nützlich, sicher und aus moralisch unbedenklicher Herstellung, sondern in der Regel auch die funktional und ästhetisch interessantesten Objekte, wie viele der Beispiele in diesem Buch deutlich machen.

Seit sich computergestütztes Design und Rapid Prototyping immer mehr durchsetzen, können die Designer ihre Träume buchstäblich innerhalb von einigen Stunden wahr werden lassen. Mit Lasersstereolithografie arbeitende Rapid-Prototyping-Maschinen sind zum leicht zugänglichen Hightech-Spielzeug der Designindustrie geworden. Die relativ einfache Produktionsweise sollte jedoch nicht dazu verleiten, die Zahl absonderlicher Produkte noch zu vervielfältigen. Die neuen digitalen Werkzeuge sollten vielmehr zur Entwicklung wirklich notwendiger und dauerhafter Konsumgüter eingesetzt werden. Unternehmer sollten erkennen, dass man auch reich werden kann, wenn man das Richtige tut, denn die Konsumenten werden zunehmend aufgeschlossener für neue Produkte, die umweltfreundlicher sind. Soziale Verantwortung der Unternehmen muss zu einem Schlagwort der Fertigungsindustrie werden, und die Designer müssen für die Objekte, die sie schaffen, moralische Verantwortung übernehmen.

Eine weitere interessante Entwicklung im aktuellen Design ist die Hochkonjunktur der limitierten Designkunst. Dass Galerien und Verkaufshäuser zur Verstärkung dieses Phänomens beitragen, indem sie den derzeitigen Trend zur Überflutung des Marktes mit zeitgenössischer Kunst bedienen, ist von manchen mit Beunruhigung konstatiert worden. Andererseits räumt die Designkunst den Designern die Freiheit ein, ohne ökonomische Einschränkungen mit innovativen Formen, Werkstoffen und Prozessen zu experimentieren. Zusätzlich führt diese Bewegung architektonische und künstlerische Konzepte im Design ein und fördert damit die Debatte über das Wesen der Funktion und unsere Interaktion mit der Umwelt. Bei kleinen Editionen sind die Umwelteinflüsse

gering, und angesichts ihres oft hohen Geldwerts werden diese Objekte auch nicht unbedacht weggeworfen. Ihre immanente Langlebigkeit muss daher als positiv betrachtet werden. Allerdings ist es bedenklich, dass die Entwicklung dieser oft schönen und äußerst experimentellen Objekte allmählich die gesamte Zeit und Aufmerksamkeit von einigen der kreativsten Designer beansprucht, nämlich genau jener Menschen, die wir brauchen, um Lösungen für akute reale Problemstellungen zu entwickeln. Trotz alledem ist die Designkunst ein wichtiger Aspekt der aktuellen Designpraxis, weshalb wir einige der interessantesten Werke aus dieser Kategorie in unsere Auswahl aufgenommen haben – von Marc Newsons Regal *Voronoi* und Ron Arads Stuhl *Thick Vac* bis zu Zaha Hadids Lampe *Vortexx* und Ross Lovegroves Tisch *Ginko*. In allen diesen in limitierter Zahl produzierten Stücken, die ohne modernste CAD-Software nicht realisierbar gewesen wären, kommt die absolute Meisterschaft ihrer Gestalter zum Ausdruck, und sie stellen erlesene Beispiele struktureller Experimente dar, welche die Zukunft in die Gegenwart holen.

Wir zeigen auch Arbeiten von Designern, die Handwerkliches wieder beleben oder „Fundstücke" zu ausgesprochen poetischen Werken verarbeiten. Die vielleicht besten Beispiele dieser Kategorie sind Fernando und Humberto Campana mit ihren verspielten und fesselnden Möbelstücken zwischen Design und Kunst. Sie zeigen, dass Design eine wirklich praktische, kreative Erfahrung sein kann und ungewöhnliche Objekte mit starker emotionaler Verbindung zu ihren Nutzern entstehen, wenn man sich mit einem offenen, kindlichen Geist auf den Designprozess einlässt. Die Brüder Campana machen auch deutlich, dass Designer nicht immer ernst sein müssen bei dem, was sie tun – um innovativ zu sein, ist eine fruchtbare Fantasie viel wichtiger. Die Designkunst bringt jedenfalls überzeugend zum Ausdruck, dass es möglich ist, ikonenhafte Designobjekte in limitierter Edition mit unglaublicher Schönheit und Ausdruckskraft auszustatten, unabhängig davon, ob die Produktion mit geringem Einsatz von Technik auskommt oder auf hochtechnologischen Verfahren beruht. Sie beweist auch, dass eine kleine, aber sehr reiche Gruppe von Sammlern bereit ist, für Individualität Höchstpreise zu bezahlen. Mit anderen Worten, einer der Hauptanreize für Käufer ist die Tatsache, dass kaum ein anderer Sammler sich diese Objekte wird leisten können ... ach ja, dazu kommt noch ihre Attraktivität als Investition mit Spekulationspotenzial.

Die aktuelle Designpraxis wird auch von den rasanten Fortschritten in der Materialkunde geprägt. Dank neuer Wunderwerkstoffe sind die Parameter der gestalterischen Lösungsmöglichkeiten ständig im Wandel begriffen. Beispiele hierfür sind Aerogel („frozen smoke"), das unter sämtlichen bekannten Festkörpern über die niedrigste Dichte und eine außergewöhnliche Isolierfähigkeit verfügt und überdies Schadstoffe absorbieren kann, sowie Kohlenstoffnanoröhren – Zylinder aus Kohlenstoffatomen, die härter als Diamanten sind und eine imposante Festigkeit gegenüber Zug- oder Druckbeanspruchung aufweisen. Vielleicht noch bedeutender ist die Entdeckung und Isolierung von Graphen, einem nahezu zweidimensionalen Molekular-Gitter mit nur einer Atomschicht, das außergewöhnlich steif und fest ist und eine 1000 Millionen Mal größere Leitfähigkeit besitzt als Kupfer. In der Zukunft wird dieses billige und relativ leicht herstellbare Material an die Stelle von Silizium als Werkstoff für kleine, extrem schnelle Transistoren und Computerprozessoren treten und eine exponentielle Steigerung der Rechenleistung ermöglichen. Durch die Verwendung von Graphen könnte sich sogar das sogenannte *Moore's Law*, wonach sich die Rechenleistung von Computerchips alle 18 Monate verdoppelt, als allzu vorsichtig erweisen. Dabei ist Graphen nur eines der extrem dünnen, aus einer einzigen Atomlage bestehenden Materialien, die heute synthetisch hergestellt werden können und eine neue industrielle Revolution durch intelligente Produkte im Nanobereich versprechen. Es ist nur eine Frage der Zeit, bis tragbare Kommunikationstechnologie so klein sein wird, dass sie problemlos in unseren Körper implantiert werden kann. Wie wünschenswert implantierte intelligente Nanotransponder wirklich sind, ist natürlich sehr umstritten, und wir können erst allmählich erahnen, auf welche Weise die Möglichkeiten der Zukunftstechnologien unsere Gesellschaft verändern werden. Die ethische Absicherung technologischer Entwicklungen – von künstlicher Intelligenz bis hin zu Nanotechnologien – sollte ein globales Anliegen sein, denn je kürzer die Innovationszyklen in der Wissenschaft dank steigender Datenverarbeitung werden, desto größer wird auch das Potenzial für negative Folgen oder nutzbringende Effekte. Es ist heute wichtiger denn je, darauf zu achten, dass die richtigen Entscheidungen getroffen werden: Die Machbarkeit allein bedeutet noch nicht, dass etwas Realität werden sollte.

Wir brauchen deutlich mehr Umweltintelligenz, um in den Fragen, die sich uns heute stellen, die richtigen Entscheidungen treffen zu können. Die Biosphäre ist ein geschlossenes System, in dem die von der Industrie produzierten chemischen Schadstoffe erhalten bleiben, auch wenn sie unsichtbar sind. Die Industrieproduktion stört das Gleichgewicht unseres Planeten, und wir müssen die regenerativen Kräfte der Natur dazu nutzen, den Schaden, den wir ihr zugefügt haben, wiedergutzumachen. Der „American Dream", die treibende Kraft unserer konsumorientierten Gesellschaft, beruhte von Anfang an auf der Idee, die Natur zu erobern und sich diese so intensiv wie möglich zunutze zu machen. Ihre Ressourcen wurden erbarmungslos zugunsten der Einzelinteressen von Ölproduzenten und Holzbetrieben, von Fischerei und Bergbau ausgebeutet, ohne zur Kenntnis zu nehmen, dass sie unser gemeinsames und unersetzbares Erbe darstellen. Die meisten natürlichen Ressourcen stehen nicht unbegrenzt zur Verfügung, und daher sind unsere Maßstäbe für den Fortschritt eklatant falsch – so beruht zum Beispiel die Berechnung des Bruttoinlandsproduktes auf der Wirtschaftstätigkeit und lässt völlig außer Acht, dass die Ausbeutung der Erde zum Zweck der finanziellen Gewinnerzielung verheerende und auch kostspielige ökologische Folgen haben kann. Viele gesunde Volkswirtschaften wie etwa Kanada oder Australien basieren ausschließlich auf dem Abbau nicht erneuerbarer Ressourcen – dennoch wird die Wertminderung des natürlichen Kapitals nirgends beziffert oder erwähnt.

Statt die Natur aus kurzfristigem Gewinnstreben auszuplündern, sollten wir uns ihre Systeme zum Vorbild für unser Handeln nehmen. Wie William McDonough und Michael Braungart in ihrem Buch *Einfach intelligent produzieren* erklären, funktioniert die Natur „nach einem System von Nährstoffen und Metabolismen, in dem kein Abfall vorkommt". In der Natur ist Abfall schon deshalb nicht vorgesehen, weil letzten Endes alles wieder in etwas Lebenserhaltendes verwandelt wird. Die Designer können von der eingehenden Analyse der natürlichen Prozesse sehr viel lernen. Warum sollte zum Beispiel ein Produkt, das seine ursprüngliche Funktion erfüllt hat, nicht eine sinnvolle Weiterverwendung finden – Verpackungsmaterial könnte zu nährstoffreichem Dünger zerfallen oder als Ziegel im Hausbau Verwendung finden.

Unser Ziel sollte daher sein, uns im Produktdesign gänzlich vom Abfall zu verabschieden und sicherzustellen, dass Produkte nach Ablauf ihres ersten Funktionszyklus entweder sinnvoll wiederverwendet werden können oder dass ihre Bestandteile einem hochqualitativen Recycling zugeführt werden. In diesem Zusammenhang sollte man sich allerdings auch vor Augen halten, dass Recycling zum Fortbestand unserer Wegwerfgesellschaft beitragen kann und außerdem reine Stoffe im Recyclingprozess vielfach zu qualitativ minderwertigen Ersatzstoffen abgebaut werden – meist deshalb, weil bei der Herstellung eines Produkts zu viele verschiedene Werkstoffe verwendet werden, die später nicht mehr leicht zu trennen sind. Auffallend ist auch die Tatsache, dass im Endprodukt durchschnittlich nur noch fünf Prozent der für seine Herstellung und Distribution verwendeten Rohstoffe enthalten sind. Was in unseren Müllsäcken landet, ist also nur ein winziger Ausschnitt eines viel umfassenderen, von Ausbeutung und Verschwendung bestimmten Bildes. Überdies basieren viele Produkte, die wir regelmäßig ohne zu überlegen wegwerfen, auf dem Konzept des „eingeplanten Verschleißes" – die Hersteller, die diese üble Methode anwenden, sollten mit Schimpf und Schande belegt und boykottiert werden.

Wohlwissend, dass es notwendig ist, unsere ökologischen Fußabdrücke radikal zu reduzieren, müssen wir darauf bestehen, dass ein größtmögliches Maß an Intelligenz und Verantwortungsbewusstsein für die Gestaltung von Produkten aufgewendet wird. Das Design muss sein ganzes Potenzial ausschöpfen, um ein mächtiges und positives Instrument zur Problemlösung für die Gegenwart und für unsere Zukunft zu werden. Der nachhaltigste Lösungsansatz besteht in der Wiederverwendung vorhandener Produkte oder in der Herstellung von Produkten mit längerer Lebensdauer. Aus diesem Grund hat die finnische Möbelfirma Artek mit Tom Dixon als Chefdesigner kürzlich ihre beispielgebende „2nd Cycle"-Initiative gestartet: ein Rückkaufprogramm, in dem Institutionen wie zum Beispiel Schulen oder Krankenhäuser ihre alten (von Alvar Aalto in den 1930er-Jahren gestalteten) Möbel gegen neue eintauschen können. Die alten Originalmöbel mit ihren stilvollen Schrammen und Kratzern werden dann von Artek auf dem Inlandsmarkt verkauft. In diesem revolutionären Konzept ist nicht nur die Langlebigkeit von Design als Prinzip verewigt, es sorgt auch dafür, dass die Stücke nicht vorzeitig zum Gerümpel kommen.

Dieses Buch stellt jene innovativen Designer vor, die einen neuen, ethischen Kurs im Design einschlagen, und ruft damit nicht nur die Designer und Hersteller, sondern auch die Konsumenten zu bewussterem Handeln auf. Wir müssen viel mehr auf unsere Konsumgewohnheiten achten und den Drang unterdrücken, Dinge zu besitzen, die wir gar nicht brauchen. Um eine globale Katastrophe abzuwenden, müssen wir unseren Konsum einschränken und darauf achten, dass die Produkte, die wir wirklich benötigen, von bester Qualität sind und einen strengen und ganzheitlichen Gestaltungsprozess durchlaufen haben. Die Designer und Hersteller tragen darüber hinaus die Verantwortung, derart hochwertige Produkte der Masse zugänglich zu machen, und nicht nur wenigen Privilegierten. Nicholas Stern kommt in seinem als Stern-Report bekannt gewordenen, viel beachteten Expertenbericht über die Ökonomie des Klimawandels zu folgendem Schluss: „Es gibt Möglichkeiten, die Risiken des Klimawandels zu reduzieren. Mit den richtigen Anreizen reagiert der private Sektor und kann Lösungen liefern. … Es ist immer noch Zeit, die schlimmsten Auswirkungen des Klimawandels zu vermeiden, wenn entschiedenes kollektives Handeln jetzt einsetzt." Wir sollten uns alle darüber im Klaren sein, auf welchem Wort hier die Betonung liegt … JETZT!

Anmerkung der Herausgeber: *Wir möchten allen Designern, Designteams und Designbüros danken, die zu diesem Projekt beigetragen haben, und hoffen, dass die Leserinnen und Leser ihre informativen persönlichen Statements ebenso anregend finden werden wie ihre innovativen Arbeiten.*

Le monde du design contemporain est en fluctuation permanente, sans qu'une direction ou une philosophie puisse se prévaloir d'une claire ascendance sur les autres. Design universel fabriqué en série, objets de consommation courante agrémentés de détails personnalisés et pièces de Design d'art en édition limitée jouent des coudes pour sortir du lot dans une société médiatique qui se nourrit davantage de nouveauté que de substance. Cette nouvelle publication entend contrer le malaise qui envahit le design grand public en présentant des praticiens qui sont de réels pionniers dans leurs domaines. Tous produisent un travail qui apporte une contribution marquante et visionnaire à un ou plusieurs des secteurs suivants : expansion du concept de fonction ; exploitation novatrice des matériaux ; exploitation des nouvelles technologies par l'expérimentation d'applications jusqu'alors inconnues ; ou exploration de nouvelles frontières esthétiques. En suivant le travail de 90 designers et groupes industriels orientés vers le design, dans le monde entier, nous espérons aussi donner un aperçu de l'incroyable ampleur du métier de designer contemporain – des luminaires au mobilier, en passant par l'équipement électronique de consommation courante, le transport, l'architecture et le paysagisme.

Une grande part de la presse spécialisée dans le design et la déco s'accorde aujourd'hui pour célébrer le « Gâchic » et mettre en valeur la nouveauté d'un produit avant de se pencher sur ses éventuels mérites. Dans bien des cas, ces prétendus experts ès design semblent ne pas savoir — ou ne pas vouloir — faire la différence entre du kitsch superflu et des objets réellement novateurs et importants. Bien trop souvent, leurs choix arbitraires négligent imprudemment les questions liées à la préservation de l'environnement. Ils semblent même avoir consciemment (et sans doute cyniquement) décidé de combattre les préceptes du « bon design », convaincus qu'ils sont, à tort, qu'il s'agit d'une position d'avant-garde extrémiste. Le « bon design » est un concept fondé sur une approche rationnelle du processus de création et suppose l'application des critères suivants : durabilité, unité, intégrité, évidence et beauté. Fondamentalement, il s'agit de trouver de meilleures solutions, plus économiques, qui équilibrent harmonieusement forme, fonction et matériaux, donnent du relief à la vie et sont porteuses de valeur ajoutée pour la société. Par contraste, la fabrication et la promotion de biens inutiles ne peuvent provoquer qu'une faillite morale, un avilissement à la fois du créateur et du consommateur. Dans un récent article de magazine, des figurines de nains, des godemichés décorés à la manière de Delft et des sacs à main en forme d'armes étaient présentés comme les dernières nouveautés design. Notre première réaction est de nous demander « Mais qu'est-ce que c'est que ce truc ? », mais la seconde est de nous dire que si le design contemporain en est là, c'est que certains membres de cette communauté souffrent de problèmes profonds.

Avec ce livre, nous voulons partir en guerre contre l'apathie morale qui ronge aujourd'hui une grande part du design conventionnel en mettant en avant des créations originales qui ont aussi du sens. La plupart des créateurs et entreprises de design présentés dans ces pages sont en quête de nouvelles solutions durables avec une approche holistique qui prend en compte tous les aspects du processus de création ainsi que son impact sur l'environnement – en bref, ils réinventent la nature même du design. Rendons-nous à l'évidence, considérons dans quel état est notre planète et observons nos comportements : il n'y a pas d'autre solution que de se mettre à agir dans le bon sens. Pour commencer, l'idée qui prévalait avant les années 1960 selon laquelle le plaisir est plus moral lorsque

son assouvissement est différé a été très largement remplacée par une quête irresponsable et à courte vue du plaisir instantané à crédit. Considérons par exemple ces curieuses addictions consuméristes, comme le « syndrome du fourreur de bas de laine », qui provoque chez des personnes parfaitement saines d'esprit l'achat compulsif de bidules sans intérêt. Ils n'ont souvent ni besoin ni vraiment envie de ces bibelots et gadgets superflus – ils cèdent juste, sans y penser, au plaisir du petit cadeau, qui finira tôt ou tard à la décharge. La philosophie du « un tiens vaut mieux que deux tu l'auras » qui prévaut dans les sociétés occidentalisées ne se contente pas d'ensevelir les régions en voie de développement sous des dettes ingérables, sa religion du gâchis contribue aussi à l'anéantissement de notre environnement commun en participant au développement des pays les plus menacés par les catastrophes liées aux changements climatiques. Au bout du compte, les nations les plus pauvres finiront par payer pour la débauche du monde développé.

Comme le souligne James Martin dans son livre majeur, *The Meaning of the 21st Century* : « Notre destinée est certainement de construire quelque chose de mieux qu'une société saturée de biens de consommation majoritairement futiles. Nous avons créé des sociétés de consommation à grande échelle. Dans ces sociétés, de plus en plus de gens sont malheureux, en thérapie, et la plupart se plaignent d'une sensation de vide, d'à quoi bon. Les sociétés de consommation extrêmes deviennent dépourvues de valeurs profondes. » De fait, nous devons tous faire marche arrière, peser nos actes et tenter de trouver des façons de vivre plus simplement. Nous devons tous consommer moins et adopter des styles de vie plus modestes – ce qui pourrait même nous rendre plus heureux à long terme. Car nous pouvons déjà mesurer la montée en puissance d'un nouveau phénomène de « consommation discrète » dont la philosophie austère et essentialiste se pose en antithèse à la culture « Blingbling ». Comme le dit Chris Sanderson, co-fondateur du précurseur de tendances Future Laboratory, nous sommes en train de « sortir d'une période de dépenses – faut que ça brille » pour entrer dans une phase de consommation plus réfléchie et attentive. Il ne s'agit plus de montrer à quel point on est riche, fabuleux ou – arrivé. Ce n'est pas qu'une austérité érigée en esthétique. C'est une façon de vivre. » Ce nouveau type de consumérisme doté de conscience considère la durabilité comme la clé de l'avenir de notre civilisation. Nous devons cependant aussi prendre garde aux caprices de la mode pour empêcher que la durabilité devienne l'accessoire branché du moment qui sera jeté à la benne dès l'arrivée d'une tendance plus vendeuse. Peut-être devrions-nous tous réfléchir à cette phrase du Mahatma Gandhi : « La Terre donne suffisamment pour satisfaire les besoins de chaque homme, mais pas l'avidité de chaque homme », ainsi qu'à sa prière : « Change comme tu voudrais voir changer le monde. »

En ces temps d'accélération technologique, les opinions contradictoires abondent sur les changements qu'il faudrait opérer et les moyens de les mettre en pratique. Dans cette quête de la panacée écologique, technophiles et technophobes partagent les mêmes objectifs mais proposent des moyens diamétralement opposés pour les atteindre – les « Éco-Ludiques » pensent qu'il faut revenir à des styles de vie plus simples, préindustriels et les « Techno-Verts » que la technologie fournira les réponses à nos dilemmes écologiques actuels. Les vraies solutions sont sans doute à chercher dans l'entre-deux. La production d'électricité par l'utilisation de la force des courants marins, développée par les pionniers de Marine Current Turbines (pages 340–343) offre peut-être l'exemple parfait de cette position intermédiaire où une technologie pertinente est appliquée à des systèmes naturels.

L'industrie est aussi de plus en plus fermement poussée à instaurer des critères de qualité internationaux auxquels devront se conformer tous les produits avant d'entrer en fabrication et d'être mis en vente. En autorisant la fabrication de cadeaux « bidules » et de jouets pour fast-foods, nous perpétuons la culture du jetable et entretenons des amoncellements de déchets qui feront horreur aux générations futures. Nos ancêtres façonnaient avec amour des meubles destinés à durer des générations, tandis que la plupart des produits équivalents actuels ne peuvent que rarement prétendre à une durée de vie supérieure à cinq ans. Les entreprises devraient également s'engager légalement non seulement à limiter les emballages mais aussi à garantir que ceux qui demeurent soient recyclables. Ecolean (présenté pages 156–161) illustre brillamment la façon dont un fabricant peut réduire la quantité d'emballages sans compromettre leur fonction et réduire encore davan-

tage l'impact sur l'environnement en n'utilisant que des matériaux entièrement biodégradables.

Il devrait aussi exister des carottes plus savoureuses et des bâtons plus durs pour obliger l'industrie automobile à changer de stratégie. Tant de choses pourraient changer si les voitures hybrides ou électriques (comme celles fabriquées par NICE ou Tesla – voir pages 402–405 et 516–521) étaient défiscalisées et que dans le même temps les 4x4 et autres tanks et corvettes de la route étaient interdites à moins qu'elles ne puissent atteindre des exigences drastiques en termes d'émissions de gaz et d'économies d'énergie. Plus que jamais, les actes individuels ont des répercussions collectives et d'une grande portée – oui, il existe un lien entre nos bagnoles et la montée du niveau de la mer… oui, il existe un lien entre ce joli salon de jardin en teck et la déforestation des forêts tropicales d'Indonésie… oui, il existe un lien entre l'achat du tout dernier téléphone portable (alors que l'ancien marche encore parfaitement) et la famine et la sécheresse en Afrique. Nous devons comprendre que notre encore si belle planète est un réseau de connections inextricables, ce qui signifie que nous avons tous le pouvoir de changer le monde pour le meilleur ou pour le pire. La façon dont nous choisissons de vivre individuellement va non seulement façonner l'héritage que nous léguerons aux générations futures, mais aussi déterminer le destin de l'Humanité.

Parmi les designers et industriels présents ici, beaucoup conçoivent des produits plus économes et reformulent la pratique de leur métier en abordant la résolution de problèmes d'une façon holistique qui prend en compte non seulement chaque étape du processus créatif mais aussi l'impact écologique des produits d'un bout à l'autre de leur cycle de vie. Ces objectifs cruciaux, vitaux, doivent être placés au cœur du monde du design et de l'industrie ; les produits qui répondent aux exigences les plus élevées devraient être signalés par un label mondial (assez semblable au « kitemark » qu'attribuait autrefois le Design Council en Grande-Bretagne) afin que les consommateurs puissent faire des choix éclairés parmi l'éventail de produits en apparence similaires qui lui est proposé. Le « bon design » a trop souvent été assimilé à la fadeur : grave erreur lorsque les produits résultant de cette approche logique du design – utiles, sûrs et fabriqués de façon éthique – sont généralement les plus intéressants aussi bien en termes de fonctionnalité que d'esthétique, comme le démontrent amplement les exemples présentés ici.

Avec la montée en puissance récente de la création assistée par ordinateur et du prototypage rapide, les designers peuvent presque littéralement donner de la substance à leurs rêves en quelques heures. Les machines de prototypage rapide qui utilisent la stéréo-lithographie au laser sont en fait devenues ces dernières années les joujoux high-tech favoris de l'industrie du design. Cette relative aisance de fabrication ne devrait cependant pas mener à une multiplication insensée de produits saugrenus ; les nouveaux outils numériques devraient au contraire être utilisés pour concevoir des biens de consommation pertinents et durables. Il faut faire comprendre aux fabricants que bien faire les choses peut aussi mener à la fortune, car les consommateurs vont devenir de plus en plus réceptifs aux nouveaux produits qui s'engagent à ne pas nuire à l'environnement. La responsabilité sociale doit être placée au cœur du monde de l'entreprise comme de l'industrie de transformation, et les designers doivent accepter la responsabilité morale des objets qu'ils créent.

Un autre courant intéressant du design contemporain a été l'épanouissement du Design d'art en édition limitée. Les salles de vente et les galeries ont fait progresser ce phénomène en le reliant à la frénésie acheteuse qui anime actuellement le marché de l'art contemporain, ce qui en trouble plus d'un. Dans le même temps, le Design d'art offre aux designers la liberté d'explorer des formes et des méthodes nouvelles, des matériaux novateurs. Ce mouvement fait aussi entrer des concepts architecturaux et artistiques dans le monde du design, encourageant ainsi le débat sur la nature de la fonction et sur notre interaction avec les environnements bâtis. La production mince qu'implique le Design d'art minimise certainement son impact environnemental et, étant donnée la valeur pécuniaire de certaines de ces pièces, elles ne vont pas être jetées à la poubelle tout de suite. Leur durabilité intrinsèque doit par conséquent être considérée comme une bonne chose. Le seul problème est que la conception de ces pièces souvent magnifiques et hautement expérimentales commence à monopoliser le temps et l'attention de certains de nos designers les plus créatifs, ceux-là mêmes dont nous avons besoin d'urgence pour élaborer les solutions réalistes de demain. Le Design d'art reste malgré

cela un aspect important de la pratique actuelle du design et nous avons par conséquent inclus dans notre sélection une partie du travail le plus captivant de cette catégorie – de l'étagère *Voronoi* de Marc Newson à la chaise à bascule *Thick Vac* de Ron Arad, en passant par la table *Vortexx* de Zaha Hadid ou la table *Ginko* de Ross Lovegrove. Toutes ces pièces produites en édition limitée, qui n'auraient pas pu être conçues sans des logiciels de CAO hyper sophistiqués, expriment la maîtrise de leurs pères et sont des expériences structurelles exquises qui font entrer l'avenir dans le présent.

Nous présentons également des designers qui ont une notion vivifiante du travail artisanal ou travaillent à partir d'objets récupérés pour créer des œuvres profondément poétiques. Fernando et Humberto Campana, avec leur séduisant mobilier d'art, sont sans doute les meilleurs exemples de cette tendance. Ils prouvent que le design peut être une expérience créative réellement pratique et qu'aborder le processus créatif avec un esprit ouvert et enfantin peut donner naissance à des objets insolites qui forgent des liens émotionnels forts avec leurs utilisateurs. Les frères Campana prouvent aussi que les designers ne sont pas toujours obligés de prendre leur travail trop au sérieux pour concevoir des produits novateurs – mieux vaut une imagination fertile. Le mouvement du Design d'art démontre clairement, et de façon convaincante, qu'il est possible de donner naissance à des créations emblématiques incroyablement belles et expressives en édition limitée, que l'on utilise des moyens de production artisanaux ou technologiques. Il prouve aussi qu'il existe une coterie de collectionneurs très fortunés prête à payer l'individualité au prix fort. Autrement dit, ce qui attire les acheteurs, c'est notamment que tout le monde ne pourra pas s'offrir ces pièces… Oh que oui, sans oublier qu'elles peuvent aussi représenter un investissement très lucratif.

La pratique contemporaine du design est aussi façonnée par la science des matériaux, en rapide évolution. De nouveaux matériaux prodigieux viennent continuellement modifier les paramètres des possibilités en matière de design, comme par exemple : « la fumée gelée » Aerogel (le solide le moins dense qui existe, également doté d'extraordinaires capacités d'isolation et d'absorption des pollutions), des nanotubes en carbone « plus durs que le diamant » (des cylindres d'atomes de carbone dotés d'une remarquable élasticité et d'une extraordinaire résistance à la traction et à l'impact physique). La découverte et l'isolation du Graphène est peut-être plus marquante encore ; ce cristal bidimensionnel plan en nid d'abeille, dont l'épaisseur est celle d'un atome de carbone, possède une résistance hors du commun et s'est révélé un milliard de fois plus conducteur que le cuivre. Ce curieux métal, relativement facile à produire, est en passe de remplacer le silicone dans la fabrication de petits transistors ultrarapides et de processeurs informatiques, permettant une croissance exponentielle de la puissance des ordinateurs. Il est en effet bien probable que le Graphène fera bientôt passer pour obsolète la Loi de Moore – selon laquelle la puissance des microprocesseurs des puces de silicium proposées sur le marché double tous les dix-huit mois. Et le Graphène n'est qu'un des nombreux matériaux synthétiques de nouvelle génération, ultra-minces, qui annoncent une nouvelle révolution industrielle en microélectronique. Ce n'est plus qu'une question de temps avant que la technologie de communication portable donne naissance à des appareils si miniaturisés qu'ils pourront être implantés en toute sécurité dans le corps humain. L'attrait de nano-transpondeurs en implant est bien sûr tout à fait discutable, mais les capacités technologiques qui sont aujourd'hui à notre portée vont refaçonner nos sociétés suivant des lignes que nous ne pouvons que commencer à deviner. Le monde devrait se soucier d'exploiter la technologie – de l'intelligence artificielle aux nanotechnologies – de façon éthique, parce qu'à mesure que le traitement de plus en plus rapide des données accélère l'innovation scientifique, le danger potentiel augmente autant que les bénéfices potentiels. Il est plus important que jamais de s'assurer que les bons choix sont faits : ce n'est pas parce qu'une chose est possible qu'elle doit être réalisée.

Nous devons acquérir une intelligence approfondie de notre environnement afin de pouvoir prendre à bras le corps les grandes décisions auxquelles nous faisons face aujourd'hui. La biosphère est un système clos, si bien que les produits chimiques nocifs produits par l'industrie y restent prisonniers, même si nous ne les voyons pas. La production industrielle a perturbé l'équilibre planétaire et il est nécessaire de canaliser les énergies de récupération du monde naturel pour réparer les dégâts. Le modèle du « Rêve américain » qui a soutenu et entretenu nos sociétés consuméristes s'est dès le départ construit sur une volonté de dominer la nature et d'en extraire autant de richesse que possible. Ces ressources naturelles ont été impitoyablement exploitées au profit des intérêts privés des producteurs de pétrole, des fabricants de bric-à-brac, des pêcheries ou des exploitants miniers, sans tenir suffisamment compte du fait qu'elles constituent notre héritage commun et irremplaçable. La plupart des ressources naturelles ne sont pas infinies, voilà pourquoi nos critères de progrès sont fondamentalement faussés. Un exemple : le PIB (produit intérieur brut) est calculé en fonction de l'activité économique et ne tient aucun compte du fait que le pillage de la Terre pourrait avoir des conséquences écologiques catastrophiques, y compris financières. Bien que bon nombre des économies jouissant d'un PIB confortable, comme le Canada ou l'Australie, soient presque uniquement basées sur l'extraction de ressources fossiles – le réel coût environnemental de cette dépréciation du capital naturel demeure ignoré ou passé sous silence.

Plutôt que de piller la nature dans le seul souci du profit immédiat, nous devrions utiliser les systèmes observés dans la nature comme modèles pour l'activité humaine. Dans leur livre *Cradle to Cradle : Remaking the Way We Make Things*, William McDonough et Michael Braungart soulignent de façon éloquente que « la nature fonctionne selon un système de nutriments et de métabolismes qui ne connaît pas le gaspillage ». Le concept de gaspillage n'a pas sa place dans la nature parce que tout finit par y être transformé en quelque chose d'utile au maintien de la vie. Les designers peuvent apprendre beaucoup d'une analyse approfondie des processus naturels. Une fois qu'un produit a rempli sa fonction primaire, par exemple, pourquoi n'aurait-il pas ensuite un usage qui vaille la peine – les emballages biodégradables pourraient devenir dans une nouvelle vie des fertilisants nutritifs ou des matériaux de construction.

Nous devons par conséquent avoir pour objectif d'éliminer la notion de gâchis dans la création de produits et nous assurer qu'une fois qu'un produit a terminé sa première vie fonctionnelle il puisse être soit reconstruit et réutilisé, soit démantelé et recyclé. À ce propos, il est important de ne pas perdre de vue que le recyclage peut en fait aussi perpétuer la culture du jetable et peut aussi dégrader des matériaux vierges et les transformer en substituts de qualité inférieure – généralement parce qu'une trop grande variété de matériaux a été utilisée pour constituer le produit, des matériaux qui sont ensuite très difficiles à séparer. Autre aspect intéressant du problème : en moyenne, un produit ne contient que 5 % des matières premières utilisées pour sa fabrication et sa distribution. Ce qui signifie que ce qui finit dans votre poubelle n'est qu'une infime partie des quantités de déchets qui génère notre consommation. Ajoutons qu'un grand nombre des produits que nous mettons régulièrement au rebut ont été conçus en fonction du concept d'« obsolescence planifiée » – une pratique si répugnante que les industriels cyniques qui l'emploient devraient être dénoncés, couverts de honte et boycottés.

Parce que nous savons que nous devons tous drastiquement réduire notre empreinte écologique, nous devons insister pour que les produits soient au contraire conçus de façon aussi intelligente et responsable que possible. Le design doit exploiter totalement son puissant potentiel en matière de résolution des problèmes, dès aujourd'hui et pour notre avenir. L'option la plus viable de toutes est de réutiliser les produits existants ou de fabriquer de nouveaux produits dotés d'une plus grande longévité. Dans cette optique, le directeur du design du fabricant de meubles finlandais Artek, Tom Dixon, a récemment lancé l'initiative « 2nd Cycle », première en son genre : un programme de rachat qui permet aux institutions comme les écoles ou les hôpitaux de remplacer leur mobilier ancien (créé par le designer Alvar Aalto dans les années 1930) par des versions récentes ; Artek revend ensuite ces meubles vintage encore « dans leur jus » sur le marché domestique. Ce procédé révolutionnaire perpétue l'idée d'une durabilité du design tout en assurant que les produits ne seront pas jetés avant l'heure.

En mettant l'accent sur ces créateurs novateurs qui forgent un design nouveau et éthique, ce livre se veut un cri de ralliement, pour que non seulement les designers et les fabricants mais aussi les consommateurs agissent davantage en conscience. Nous devons surveiller nos habitudes de consommation et évacuer notre soif compulsive de choses inutiles. Pour éviter une catastrophe mondiale, il est nécessaire de consommer moins et mieux, en n'achetant que les produits conçus avec le plus de rigueur et de responsabilité à l'égard de la collectivité et de notre environnement. Les designers et industriels ont la responsabilité supplémentaire de mettre de tels produits à la portée du plus grand nombre, et pas seulement de quelques privilégiés. Comme l'écrit Nicholas Stern en conclusion d'un article sur l'économie du changement climatique : « Il existe des moyens de réduire les risques de changement climatique. S'il est encouragé de la bonne manière, le secteur privé relèvera le défi et pourra apporter des solutions… Il est encore possible d'éviter les pires conséquences du changement climatique, si une action collective forte commence dès maintenant. » Soyons tous d'accord pour dire que le mot clé de cette phrase est le dernier… MAINTENANT !

Note des Éditeurs : *Nous voudrions remercier sincèrement tous les designers, ateliers de création et entreprises qui ont contribué à ce projet et espérons que les lecteurs seront autant inspirés par leurs intéressantes déclarations personnelles que par leur travail novateur.*

IIRO A. AHOKAS

"At the moment I am inspired as a designer by the idea that functionality becomes a part of an object only when the object is used, or as a by-product of use. I think that seeing functionality as an inherent part of the object independent of the user was born out of industrial thinking and mass production – the idea that everyone will use a certain object the same way. This gave birth to the linguistic and conceptual perversion, the amusing idea that an object can be impractical. Have you ever seen such an impractical object or design that cannot be used for anything? I haven't. The way I perceive the reality around me, functionality is not an attribute of the object as much as of the person using it. In the best case the objects can find their final shape of existence from an imaginative insight on the part of the viewer or user, their ability to see the invisible and immaterial around us. I like calling design an expedition to new experiences."

„Gegenwärtig bin ich als Designer von der Idee inspiriert, dass Funktionalität nur dann zum Bestandteil eines Objekts wird, wenn das Objekt benutzt wird, oder sie entsteht als Nebenprodukt der Nutzung. Ich denke, die Auffassung von Funktionalität als inhärentem und vom Benutzer unabhängigem Teil eines Gegenstands ist aus dem industriellen Denken und der Massenproduktion entstanden – zusammen mit der Vorstellung, dass jeder einen bestimmten Gegenstand auf dieselbe Art und Weise benutzt. Dies wiederum setzte die linguistische und konzeptionelle Verdrehung in die Welt, die amüsante Idee, dass ein Objekt unpraktisch sein kann. Haben Sie jemals ein unpraktisches Objekt oder Design gesehen, das nicht für irgendetwas verwendet werden kann? Ich nicht. So, wie ich die Realität um mich herum wahrnehme, ist Funktionalität nicht so sehr ein Attribut des Gegenstands als der Person, die ihn benutzt. Im besten Fall erhalten die Objekte ihre endgültige Daseinsform aus dem fantasievollen Verständnis auf Seiten des Betrachters oder Benutzers und aus deren Fähigkeit, das Unsichtbare und Immaterielle um uns herum zu erkennen. Ich nenne Design gern eine Expedition zu neuen Erfahrungen."

« Ce qui m'inspire en ce moment en tant que designer, c'est l'idée que la fonctionnalité ne devient une partie d'un objet que lorsque cet objet est utilisé, directement ou indirectement. Je pense que l'idée selon laquelle la fonctionnalité est une partie inhérente de l'objet, indépendamment de l'utilisateur – tout le monde utiliserait un certain objet de la même manière – est née de la pensée industrielle et de la production en série. Cette façon de penser a débouché sur une perversion linguistique et conceptuelle, la curieuse idée qu'un objet puisse ne pas être pratique. Avez-vous déjà vu un objet ou un design si peu pratique qu'il ne puisse servir à rien du tout ? Moi jamais. De la façon dont je perçois la réalité qui m'entoure, la fonctionnalité est moins un attribut de l'objet que la personne qui l'utilise. Dans le meilleur des cas, les objets parviennent à trouver leur ultime forme d'existence grâce à l'imagination et à la perspicacité du spectateur ou de l'utilisateur, à sa capacité à voir l'invisible et l'immatériel qui nous entoure. J'aime qualifier le design d'expédition vers de nouvelles expériences. »

1

2

IIRO A. AHOKAS

Ahokas
Tilkankatu 7 A 7
00300 Helsinki
Finland
T +358 40 7317070
E iirolle@hotmail.com

BIOGRAPHY

1976 Born in Nurmijärvi, Finland
1992–1995 Higher School Examination, Helsinki Visual Arts High School
1995–1998 BA Ceramics and Glass Design, University of Art and Design Helsinki
1997 Trained at the Arabia Finland Art Department, Arabia, Finland, as Holder of Arabia Foundation Scholarship; Trained at Centro de Formação Profissional para a Industria Ceramica, Caldas da Rainha, Portugal
1998 Trained at Istituto Europeo di Design IED, Milan; Freelance designer, Cristalleria Arnolfo di Cambio, Italy
1998–2001 MA Ceramics and Glass Design, University of Art and Design Helsinki
1998–2001 Freelance consultant, Momentum Helsinki
1999 Freelance designer, SC Sarner Cristal, Uetendorf / Thun, Switzerland; Trainee of Public Administration, University of Art and Design Helsinki UIAH, Finland
2001+ Freelance consultant and project realization assistant, Idea Group Helsinki
2002–2006 Freelance designer, Design House Stockholm
2003–2004 Glass Studio Instructor and Teaching assistant, University of Art and Design Helsinki UIAH
2006+ Fashion photographer, Mugi couture, Berlin
2006+ Freelance designer, Marimekko Corporation, Helsinki
2006–2007 Creative Design Director, Artbar71 GmbH, Berlin
2007-2008 Deputy Lecturer in industrial product design, University of Art and Design Helsinki

RECENT EXHIBITIONS

2004 "The International Exhibition of Glass Kanazawa 2004 in Notojima", Notojima Glass art Museum, Notojima-machi, Ishikawa, Japan; "The International Exhibition of Glass Kanazawa 2004", Kanazawa Korimbo Daiwa, Kanazawa, Ishikawa, Japan; "Nuorten Forum 04 Young Forum", Design Forum Finland, Helsinki; "Finnish Ceramics & Glass Design", Jingdezhen Sanbao Ceramics Museum, China; "Finnish Ceramics & Glass Design", Academy of Art & Design of Tsinghua University, China
2005 "European Academy of the Arts", Universität der Künste Berlin; "Finnish Glass Lives 5", The Finnish Glass Museum, Riihimäki; "Nuorten Forum 04 Young Forum", Kajaani Museum of Art, Finland.
2006 "Lisää uunituoretta, Contemporary Finnish Ceramics", Gallery Elverket, Ekenäs, Finland; "Designpartners 06", Cable Factory, Helsinki; "Design, Meet the User!", Kamp Event Center, Helsinki
2007 "Lisää uunituoretta 2, Contemporary Finnish Ceramics", Åland Museum of Arts, Mariehamn, Finland
2008 Solo exhibition, Finnland-Institut in Deutschland, Berlin

RECENT AWARDS

2003 Grant (x2), The National Council for Design; Grant, The Finnish Cultural Foundation
2005 European Academy of Arts Scholarship – granted by AUDI AG and Universität der Künste Berlin (for living and working nine months in Berlin, Germany); 3rd Prize, "Design, meet the user!" competition launched by Marimekko Corporation and Ornamo
2006 Antti Nurmesniemi Scholarship, Asko Foundation; Grant, The National Council for Design

CLIENTS

Marimekko
Mugi couture

3

4

1–2
TURBULENT
Plastic-coated cotton textile (four colour ways)
2006
Client: Marimekko

3
MORGANA
Soft PVC and silver necklace
2005
Client: self-produced
(one-off)

5

"Functionality is not an attribute of the object as much as of the person using it."

4
KAIKU
Free-blown glass serving spoons
2005
Client: self-produced
(prototype)

5–6
CYBER
Free-blown and silver-mirrored
glass nesting serving vessels
2005
Client: self-produced

6

AIRBUS DESIGN TEAM

"Defining aircraft interior environments which have to satisfy both the operational and brand values of commercial airlines, whilst exceeding the ever more demanding service and product expectations of their passengers is a tough challenge. To achieve this within the restrictive environment of aviation certification requirements and enable the aircraft to provide more than 30 years of daily commercial service is truly remarkable. Drawing on the broad expertise of the Airbus community focused in Hamburg and Toulouse, the 50 strong, internationally based Industrial Design team shapes the cabin of the future under the core brand values of Comfort, Service and Efficiency. To create distinctive and memorable experiences, the Airbus design approach focuses on key product attributes: innovation, modernity, customer focus and ambition. The intelligent application of this Design Language is how Airbus works towards the dream of making flying human. Although the daily challenge of providing innovative customised solutions for more than 400 annual deliveries consumes the majority of design resources, it is with the Cabin Vision mock-ups that Airbus can really show where design can make the difference to the passenger experience. Across a fleet of aircraft ranging from 100 seaters to the revolutionary double-deck A380, the design team uses the evolving Design Language to shape the environment, which showcases the Airline's brand. Harmonizing visionary thinking, cutting edge technology and a wealth of commercial experience, these mock-ups provide test beds for new ideas and drive the expectations of the Airlines, defining the state-of-the-art for the future. The flagships of the mock-up centre in Toulouse, which present six full size aircraft to customers and as many more partial mock-ups, are the 56m A380 and the 20m Long Range Cabin Vision Mock-Ups."

„Flugzeugkabinen zu gestalten, die sowohl den operativen als auch den strategischen Anforderungen kommerzieller Fluggesellschaften gerecht werden müssen, und gleichzeitig die immer anspruchsvolleren Erwartungen der Passagiere im Hinblick auf Service und Produkt zu übertreffen, ist eine große Herausforderung. Dieser innerhalb der restriktiven Zulassungsregularien gerecht zu werden und dabei Flugzeugen mehr als 30 Jahre täglichen Flugdienst zu ermöglichen, ist eine große Aufgabe. Das internationale Industrial Design Team, welches seine Kompetenz sowohl in Toulouse als auch in Hamburg verteilt, konzipiert die Flugzeugkabine der Zukunft gemäß der bedeutendsten Wertetreiber Komfort, Service und Effizienz. Um besondere und unvergessliche Erlebnisse für den Kunden zu schaffen, liegt der Fokus des Airbus Designs auf den wichtigsten Produktmerkmalen Innovation, Modernität, Kundenorientierung und Begehrlichkeit. Mit dem Designansatz möchte Airbus den Traum vom angenehmen und komfortablen Fliegen verwirklichen. Obwohl die tägliche Herausforderung, innovative und kundenspezifische Lösungen für mehr als 400 Auslieferungen jährlich anzubieten, den größten Teil der Design-Ressourcen beansprucht, kann Airbus vor allem mit den „Cabin Vision Mock-Ups" die Bedeutung und Auswirkung des Designs für Passagiere demonstrieren. Für eine ganze Flotte von Flugzeugen, die vom 100-Sitzer bis zum revolutionären A380 reicht, setzt das Design Team die eigens entwickelte Designsprache ein, um der Fluggesellschaft eine optimale Plattform für die Positionierung ihrer Marke anzubieten. Diese Mock-Ups vereinen Visionen, innovative Technologien und einen reichen industriellen Erfahrungsschatz und stehen als Testobjekte für die Umsetzung neuer Ideen zur Verfügung. So steuert Airbus zum einen die Erwartungen der Fluggesellschaften und definiert zum anderen die Technologieanforderungen der Zukunft. Die Aushängeschilder des Mock-Up-Centers in Toulouse, in dem die Kunden sechs Flugzeuge in Originalgröße und einige Teil-Flugzeugkabinen besichtigen können, sind die Modelle des 56m langen A380 und des 20m langen Long Range Cabin Vision Mock-Up."

«Concevoir des aménagements intérieurs pour les avions qui doivent satisfaire à la fois les critères opérationnels et la culture d'entreprise de compagnies aériennes commerciales, tout en dépassant les attentes toujours croissantes des passagers en termes de qualité des services et des produits est un défi de taille. Le relever dans le cadre réglementaire contraignant de l'aviation et rendre l'appareil capable de remplir sa mission quotidiennement pendant 30 années de service commercial relève de la gageure. En s'appuyant sur la vaste expérience des équipes d'Airbus présentes à Hambourg et à Toulouse, l'équipe de création internationale, composée de 50 personnes, façonne la cabine de l'avenir sous les auspices des valeurs fondamentales de la marque : Confort, Service et Efficacité. Pour donner naissance à des expériences spéciales et mémorables, Airbus concentre sa démarche créative sur des impératifs précis : innovation, modernité, prise en compte du consommateur et ambition. En appliquant ce lexique stylistique de façon intelligente, Airbus travaille à réaliser un rêve : rendre le vol humain. Bien que le défi permanent de devancer la demande consume la majorité de nos ressources créatrices (un supplément de plus de 400 appareils livrés en 2006), c'est avec les maquettes imaginées pour la Cabin Vision qu'Airbus parvient réellement à démontrer de quelle manière le design peut faire la différence du point de vue du passager. Sur une flotte d'appareils qui s'étend des avions de 100 passagers au révolutionnaire gros porteur à impériale A380, l'équipe de designers décline le lexique stylistique maison pour façonner l'environnement intérieur, qui doit être la vitrine de chaque compagnie. Parce qu'elles rassemblent harmonieusement pensée visionnaire, technologie de pointe et succès commercial, ces maquettes d'aménagement intérieur sont le banc d'essai des idées nouvelles et expriment les attentes des compagnies en définissant un objectif d'excellence pour l'avenir. Les fleurons de la collection de maquettes Airbus présentée à Blagnac sont celles de l'A380 (longue de 56 mètres) et celle (longue de 20 mètres) de la Long Range Cabin Vision.»

4–8
A350 LONG RANGE CABIN
DESIGN VISION, 2006

"The objective of the Long
Range Cabin Design Vision was
to develop and implement a new,
visionary cabin architecture for
the A350. A platform to proac-
tively support the customer's
operational, brand and service
demands for their passengers.
The approach is driven by three
customer-focused core values:
(1) Comfort – relating to the
spaciousness of the cabin, lighting, high-technology materials
and haptics, environmental control and seat comfort; (2) Services – relating to cabin systems,
entertainment, connectivity,
communication and passenger
guidance; (3) Efficiency – relating to flexibility of space and
cabin reconfiguration. The
Vision Mock-Up is the first
truly holistic approach to cabin
design combining architecture,
lighting, technology and materials into one integrated cabin
package that demonstrates a
design language and philosophy
that can translate through future
aircraft developments."

„Das Designkonzept für die
Kabinen von Langstreckenflug-
zeugen zielte darauf ab, eine
neue und visionäre Kabinenar-
chitektur für den A350 zu entwickeln und in die Praxis umzuset-
zen. Zukunftsweisend und an
den speziellen Kundenbedarf
angepasst, sollte es allen operativen, markenspezifischen und
serviceorientierten Anforderungen gerecht werden, gleichzeitig
aber auch die hohen Erwartungen der Fluggäste erfüllen. Der
Ansatz konzentriert sich auf drei
zentrale Kriterien: (1) Komfort –
im Hinblick auf Geräumigkeit
der Kabine, Beleuchtung, High-
tech-Materialien und haptische
Qualitäten, raumklimatische
Bedingungen und Sitzkomfort;
(2) Service – im Hinblick auf
Kabinensystem, Unterhaltung,
Verbindung, Kommunikation
und Fluggastführung; (3) Effizienz – im Hinblick auf räumliche Flexibilität und Umge-
staltung der Kabinen. Dieses
Modell ist der erste wirklich
ganzheitliche Ansatz im Kabi-
nendesign: Architektur, Beleuchtung, Technologie und
Werkstoffe verbinden sich zu
einem in sich geschlossenen
Kabinenkomplex mit einer
Designsprache und -philoso-
phie, die durch zukünftige Flug-
zeugentwicklungen Wirklichkeit
werden."

« Le but de la Long Range Cabin
Design Vision était de concevoir
et d'installer une architecture de
cabine nouvelle et visionnaire
pour l'A350. Une plateforme qui
réponde activement aux exigences opérationnelles et de service
que la marque nourrit pour ses
passagers. L'approche se structure autour de trois valeurs fondamentales liées à la satisfaction du
consommateur : (1) Confort – ce
qui concerne l'espace dans la
cabine, son éclairage, les matériaux de haute technologie, les
accessoires de contrôle tactile de
l'environnement et le confort
d'assise ; (2) Services – ce qui
concerne le fonctionnement de
la cabine, le divertissement, la
connectique, les systèmes de
communication et les conseils
aux passagers ; (3) Efficacité –
ce qui concerne la flexibilité de
l'espace et les reconfigurations
de la cabine. La maquette Vision
est la première approche réellement holistique de la conception
de cabine combinant architecture, éclairage, technologie et
matériaux en un habillage de
cabine intégré au lexique créatif
particulier, dont la philosophie
peut s'exprimer dans les projets
aéronautiques de l'avenir. »

1
AIRBUS A380–800
Tail section
First flight 2005

2–3
AIRBUS A350–900 XWB
Concept renderings
2006

"Passenger at Heart,
Airline in Mind"

4
AIRBUS A350–900 XWB
Centralised connectivity area:
a dedicated place for passengers
to connect, work and
communicate
2006

5
AIRBUS A350–900 XWB
Main entrance at the heart
of the cabin
2006

6
AIRBUS A350–900 XWB
Lavatory interior
2006

7
AIRBUS A350–900 XWB
Cabin window with
illuminated bezel
2006

8
AIRBUS A350–900 XWB
Lavatory exterior
2006

9
AIRBUS A380–800
First flight 2005

10–11
AIRBUS A380–800
Systems drawings
2005

10

11

AIRBUS DESIGN TEAM

Airbus Headquarters in
Toulouse
1, Rond Point Maurice Bellonte
31707 Blagnac Cedex
France
T +33 5 61933333
www.airbus.com

COMPANY HISTORY

1970 Airbus was officially
formed as a consortium of
France's Aerospatiale and
Deutsche Airbus, a group
of leading German aircraft
manufacturing firms. Shortly
afterwards Spain's CASA joined
the consortium
1974 Airbus Industrie GIE, as
it was known – Groupe d'Intérêt
Economique – moved its headquarters from Paris to Toulouse
1979 British Aerospace
joined Airbus Industrie
2001 Airbus became a single
fully integrated company. The
European Aeronautic Defence
and Space Company (EADS), a
merger of the French, German
and Spanish interests, acquired
80 % of the shares and BAE
Systems, the successor to British
Aerospace, 20 %
2004 In a major reorganisation,
designed to equip the company
to maintain its lead in the industry, Centres of Excellence were
set up to simplify and unify the
design and production-manage-
ment processes
2005 Unveiling of the A380, the
world's largest passenger aircraft

12

12
AIRBUS A380–800
Upper-deck first-class cabins
2005

14
AIRBUS A380–800
Even when closed, adjustable
transparent cabin windows
allow controlled visual
connection to the entire cabin
2005

13
AIRBUS A380–800
Each of the 6 upper-deck
first-class cabins has space for
a separate chair and sofa, which
can be combined to make
a generous L-shape sofa bed
2005

15
AIRBUS A380–800
The integrated upper-deck first-
class cabins, which allow for
discreet airline branding, can
be closed for privacy from the
social area
2005

WERNER AISSLINGER

"It rarely happens that designers create absolutely new product typologies – I mean objects that are an invention in themselves, like the MP3 player some years ago. Many product typologies do not change because the human shape and ergonomics remain constant. So it's not the chair as an archetype for seating that is moving forward. Rather, all the factors around the development and use of chairs are in permanent evolution: new technologies, new materials, space and surroundings, accompanying products and, most important, the habits of users. A vital part of the designer's work, therefore, is the creation of new designs of existing product archetypes. What I am very interested in, however, is the concept of 'prediction': when a product is presented to the market it has to be exciting, absolutely new and somehow mind-blowing. As industrial development periods are sometimes 2, 4 or even 6 years (in the case of the automotive industry) – designers must have the ability to forecast advances in technology and the most appropriate responses in form and use of materials. If you want to make a difference you cannot rely on existing trends – you have to make your own mind up about the future."

„Es kommt selten vor, dass Designer völlig neue Produkttypologien entwickeln – ich meine Objekte, die selbst eine Erfindung sind, wie der MP3-Player vor einigen Jahren. Viele Produkttypen bleiben gleich, weil die menschliche Anatomie und Ergonomie sich nicht verändern. Nicht der Stuhl als Archetyp des Sitzens entwickelt sich weiter – vielmehr sind sämtliche Faktoren, die Nutzung, Entwicklung und Verwendung von Stühlen betreffen, in einem ständigen evolutionären Wandel begriffen: Technologien, Materialien, Räume, Umgebung und benachbarte Produkte, aber vor allem die Gewohnheiten der Nutzer. Ein ganz wesentlicher Teil der Arbeit von Designern besteht daher in der Neugestaltung bestehender archetypischer Produkte. Mein besonderes Interesse gilt dem Thema „Vision". Ein Produkt muss bei der Markteinführung aufregend, absolut neu und völlig überraschend sein. Da die industriellen Entwicklungsperioden zwei, vier oder (im Fall der Autoindustrie) sogar sechs Jahre betragen, müssen Designer die Fähigkeit haben, technische Fortschritte, sowie Materialevolutionen und formale Zukunftstendenzen vorauszusehen. Für relevante Neuerungen kann man sich nicht auf bestehende Trends verlassen, man muss eine eigene Vorstellung von der Zukunft kreieren."

« Il est rare que les designers créent des typologies de produits absolument nouvelles – je veux dire des objets qui sont en eux-mêmes une invention, comme le lecteur MP3 il y a quelques années. Nombre de typologies de produits ne changent pas parce que la forme et l'ergonomie humaines n'évoluent pas. Ce n'est donc pas la chaise en tant qu'archétype de siège qui fait avancer les choses. Ce sont plutôt tous les facteurs qui entourent la réalisation et l'utilisation des chaises qui sont en évolution permanente : les nouvelles technologies, les nouveaux matériaux, l'espace et l'environnement, l'accompagnement des produits et, surtout, les habitudes des usagers. Une partie capitale du travail du designer consiste à créer de nouvelles formes pour les archétypes existants. Ce qui m'intéresse également beaucoup, c'est le concept de ‹ prédiction › : lorsqu'un produit est présenté sur le marché, il doit être excitant, absolument nouveau et hallucinant d'une façon ou d'une autre. Les délais de fabrication industriels étant parfois de 2, 4 ou même 6 années (dans le cas de l'industrie automobile) – les designers doivent être capables de prévoir les avancées technologiques pour trouver les réponses les plus appropriées en termes de forme et d'utilisation des matériaux. Si vous voulez faire la différence, vous ne pouvez pas vous reposer sur les tendances existantes – vous devez vous forger votre propre opinion sur l'avenir. »

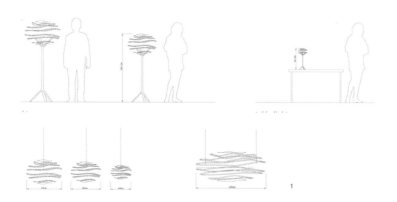

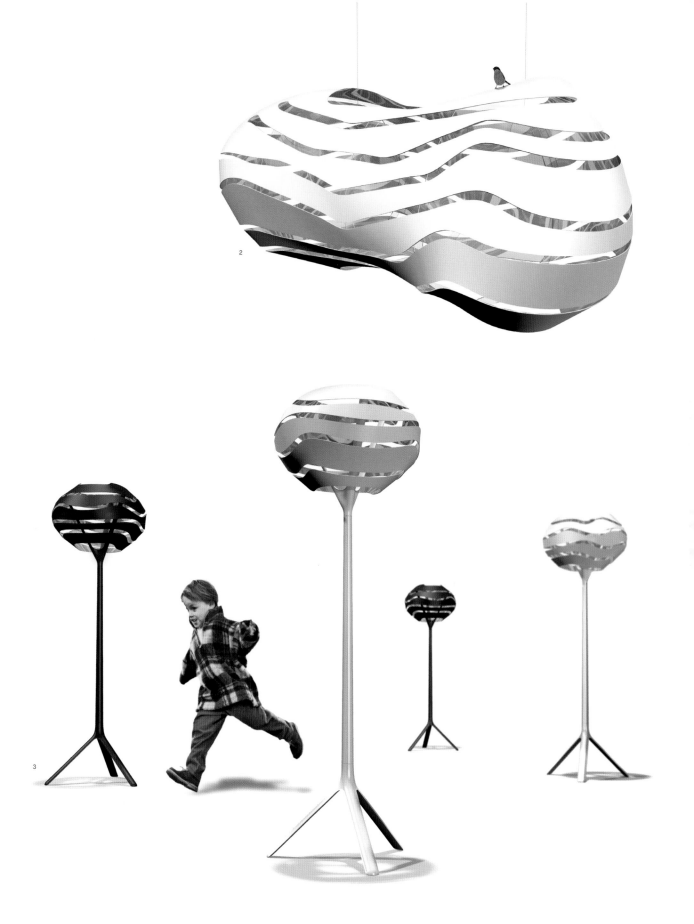

The Tree Light family is a linear and sculptural standing/suspension lighting concept with its aesthetic origin deriving from the abstraction of shapes found in nature. The underlying concept of this series is one stem that forks out into roots and various branches to form the foot and the shade fixtures respectively. The light shade can be seen as an abstraction of a tree-top similar to architectural tree scale models. Its overall form is a sphere, which has been distorted in various planes and constructed of five laser-cut sheet metal strips. The light source, hidden in the top part of the light stem, bounces light inside the shade before it is exited at various, random angles – an intriguing effect due to the mirror-like reflective surface finish of the light shade's interior.

Die Leuchtenfamilie Tree Light besteht aus geradlinigen, skulpturalen Steh-/Pendelleuchten, die ästhetisch aus der Abstraktion von natürlichen Formen abgeleitet sind. Das Konzept dieser Reihe beruht auf einem Stamm, dessen Verzweigungen in Wurzeln und Äste jeweils den Fuß und die Schirmhalterung der Leuchten bilden. Der Leuchtenschirm kann als Abstraktion einer Baumkrone gesehen werden, wie man sie von den in der Architektur verwendeten Baummodellen kennt. Er hat die Form einer in mehreren Wellenlinien durchschnittenen Kugel, die aus fünf lasergeschnittenen Blechstreifen besteht. Die im oberen Teil des Leuchtenstabs verborgene Lichtquelle wirft das Licht in den Schirm, von wo es in mehreren zufällig entstandenen Winkeln austritt – ein verblüffender Effekt, der durch die reflektierende Innenfläche des Schirms hervorgerufen wird.

La famille Tree Light est un système d'éclairage linéaire et sculptural, tantôt posé, tantôt suspendu, dont l'origine esthétique dérive des formes abstraites que nous observons dans la nature. Le concept qui sous-tend cette série est un tronc dont les racines et les nombreuses branches viendraient former des installations en pied ou en ombrage. Ces luminaires sont comme une abstraction de cime, comme des modèles réduits d'arbres architecturaux. Leur forme générale est une sphère, qui a été déformée sur plusieurs plans et se constitue de cinq feuilles métalliques découpées au laser. La source de lumière, cachée dans la partie supérieure du tronc imaginaire, envoie la lumière vers les contours, dont elle fuse ensuite dans diverses directions aléatoires – un effet intrigant est créé par la finition lisse, réfléchissante comme un miroir, choisie pour la surface intérieure de la lampe.

4

1–4
TREE LIGHT
Series of floor, table
and hanging lights
2007
Client: DAB

5
TREE TABLE
Indoor/outdoor occasional table
2006
Client: DAB

5

6

7

8

6–10
LORENZ WATCH
Programme of wristwatches
2006
Client: Lorenz

9

10

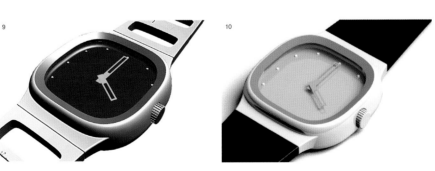

11

"Design is creating
the life of tomorrow –
for me the most exciting
profession."

12

11–12
BOMBAY SAPPHIRE
MODULAR LIGHT CARPET
Communal lighting object
comprising 50 x 50 cm modules
2006
Client: Bombay Sapphire

13–14
SCREENLIGHT
Series of floor and table lights
in 3 sizes
2004–2007
Client: self-generated concept

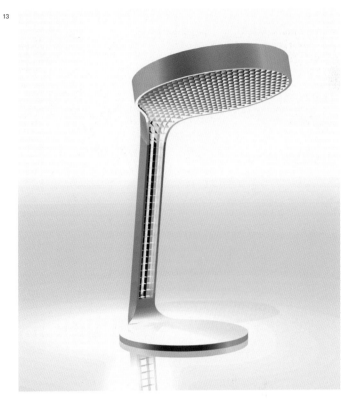

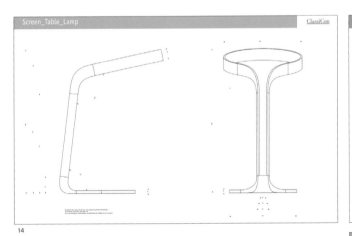

14

41

WERNER AISSLINGER

Studio Aisslinger
Oranienplatz 4
10999 Berlin
Germany
T +49 30 31505400
E studio@aisslinger.de
www.aisslinger.de

BIOGRAPHY

1964 Born in Nördlingen, Germany
1986 History of Art and Communication Sciences, Munich University
1987–1991 Design diploma, Hochschule der Künste, Berlin
1989–1992 Worked as a designer in the offices of Jasper Morrison and Ron Arad in London and of Michele de Lucchi in Milan
1993 Founded Studio Aisslinger in Berlin
1993–1997 Visiting lecturer, Hochschule der Künste, Berlin
1994–1997 Visiting lecturer, Lahti Design Insitute, Finland
1998–2005 Professor of Product Design, Hochschule für Gestaltung, Karlsruhe

RECENT EXHIBITIONS

2006 "Lightwave presentation", Blue Collection of Bombay Sapphire at Lichtwerk Altona, Hamburg; "Loftcube", Eighth Belgrade Triennial of World Architecture; "Second Skin", Zeche Zollverein, Essen; "Loftcube", ArchiSkulptur, Kunstmuseum, Wolfsburg; "Sitzen ist Kunst", Kunstgewerbemuseum, Berlin; "Create Berlin 'Best of Berlin'", as a part of "Red Moscow", Moscow; "5x5 Project-Designers & Producers", Interieur, Design-regio Kortrijk; "FSB", Stilwerk, Berlin
2007 "Second Skin", Vitra Design Museum, Weil am Rhein; "Nature Design", Museum für Gestaltung, Zürich; "Corian: 40 Years/40 Designers", Design Within Reach-Meatpacking/Chelsea Studio, New York and Corian Design Store, Milan; "Suitcases from Berlin – Koffer aus Berlin", M Project Gallery, New York; "Full House", installation, Haus am Waldsee Museum/Design-mai, Berlin; "Loftcube", Fuori Salone, Exanasaldo, Milan; "Design Seating for Design Eating", Fornasarig, Triennale, Milan; "Books", installation, Christuskirche, Passagen Cologne

RECENT AWARDS

2004 Premio Compasso d'Oro award, ADI, Milan; Red Dot Award, Design Zentrum Nordrhein Westfalen, Essen
2005 FX Award UK "Best System Furniture", London
2006 Hotel of the Year, Expo Real, Munich; Red Dot Award, Design Zentrum Nordrhein Westfalen, Essen

CLIENTS

Adidas, Alape, Behr, Biegel, Bombay Sapphire, Böwer, Cappellini, ClassiCon, Crossmobil, Dab, design hotels, Draenert, E-Plus, Ideal Form, Team, Interlübke, Jaguar, Joquer, Jonas & Jonas, Lorenz, Marc O'Polo, Mercedes-Benz, piure, Porro, Purple South, smart-travelling, Stilwerk, Unic Design, Uvex, Viccarbe, View, Vitra, Zanotta, Zeritalia

15–16
GAP
Plywood monoshell
stacking chair
2007
Client: Fornasarig

16

15

17
GLISS
Modular shelving
system
2006–2007
Client: Piure

18
HORIZON
Variable system of low,
high or sideboard case furniture
2006–2007
Client: Piure

17

18

RON ARAD

"I only want to design things that only I can design, things that did not exist before I designed them, things that have enough newness about them, things that rise to the occasion they've created and live up to the promise they claim. Materials, technology, style, culture, needs, surplus, economy, risk, surprise, humour and memory are only some of the ingredients competing for leading roles in the design process. A different mix of ingredients is harnessed for different tasks. At times, ingredients are favoured for a period and then the tasks are invented to suit them. A favourite preoccupation can lead to collections of related objects, united at times by a new material/process, at others by geometry and shape, by an idea about a function, or by some restlessness... or by all combined. Preoccupations also fight each other for quality time but normally cohabit happily; balancing a rotating cantilevered pavilion on an alpine peak at 3000 metres, conniving with scientists to develop vertical negative extrusions, blowing 2 metre diameter balls in aluminium, making them float a foot off the grass, a new way to stack a chair, or going back to an old neglected project that now appears to be urgent. But most recently it is building and materializing the invisible sitter. After years of designing maybe too many chairs, chairs with the best intention to accommodate (ergonomically, comfortably) the unknown sitter, I decided to search for this invisible and yet omnipresent sitter and give him/her a physical presence."

„Ich möchte ausschließlich Gegenstände gestalten, die nur ich gestalten kann. Gegenstände, die es nicht gab, bevor ich sie entworfen habe, Objekte, die genügend Neues bieten, Dinge, die den Ansprüchen, die sie schaffen, gerecht werden und halten, was sie versprechen. Materialien, Technologie, Stil, Kultur, Bedürfnisse, Überschuss, Ökonomie, Risiko, Überraschung, Humor und Erinnerung sind nur einige der Ingredienzien, die um die führende Rolle im Designprozess wetteifern. Sie werden unterschiedlich gemixt, je nachdem, welche Aufgabe sich stellt. Manchmal wird bestimmten Ingredienzien eine Zeit lang der Vorzug gegeben, und man lässt sich entsprechende Aufgaben dafür einfallen. Aus einer Vorliebe können Sammlungen verwandter Objekte entstehen, die manchmal ein neuer Werkstoff/Prozess zusammenbringt, manchmal die Geometrie und Form, die Idee einer Funktion oder eine gewisse Unruhe ... oder auch eine Kombination von allem. Die Vorlieben wetteifern auch um Zeit und Aufmerksamkeit, obwohl sie normalerweise ganz gut miteinander auskommen. Das sieht dann so aus, dass man einen rotierenden freitragenden Pavillon in 3000 m Höhe auf einem Alpengipfel in Balance hält, gemeinsam mit Wissenschaftlern negative vertikale Extrusionen entwickelt, Bälle mit 2 m Durchmesser aus Aluminium bläst und sie 30 cm über dem Boden schweben lässt, eine neue Möglichkeit findet, Stühle zu stapeln, oder sich wieder einem alten Projekt zuwendet, dass plötzlich dringlich zu sein scheint. In letzter Zeit geht es mir darum, dem unsichtbaren sitzenden Menschen Gestalt zu geben. Nachdem ich jahrelang vielleicht zu viele Stühle entworfen habe, Stühle mit der besten Absicht, dem unbekannten sitzenden Menschen einen (ergonomischen, bequemen) Platz anzubieten, habe ich beschlossen, mich auf die Suche nach diesem unsichtbaren und dabei omnipräsenten sitzenden Menschen zu machen und ihn physisch präsent werden zu lassen."

« Je veux seulement créer des choses que je suis seul à pouvoir créer, des choses qui n'existaient pas avant que je les crée, des choses qui sont porteuses de suffisamment de nouveauté, qui s'épanouissent dans l'opportunité qu'elles ont créée et se montrent à la hauteur des ambitions qu'elles affichent. Les matériaux, la technologie, le style, la culture, les besoins, le surplus, l'économie, le risque, la surprise, l'humour et la mémoire sont autant de personnages qui se disputent le rôle principal dans le processus créatif. Ils seront mélangés, comme des ingrédients savamment choisis, en fonction des différentes tâches que l'objet embrassera. Il arrive aussi parfois que les ingrédients soient choisis en amont, en attendant que soient inventées des tâches qui leur conviendraient. Une préoccupation favorite peut donner naissance à des collections d'objets, parfois unis par un nouveau matériau/processus, parfois par la géométrie et la forme, par l'idée que je me fais de leur fonction ou par une certaine impatience... ou par une combinaison de tout cela. Si les préoccupations se battent parfois les unes contre les autres pour obtenir davantage de place, elles cohabitent généralement dans la joie : elles équilibrent un pavillon tournant en porte-à-faux sur un pic alpin à 3000 mètres d'altitude, elles se rendent complices des scientifiques pour pratiquer des extrusions négatives verticales, souffler sur des boules en aluminium de 2 mètres de diamètre de façon à ce qu'elles flottent à une trentaine de centimètres du sol ; elles apportent une nouvelle façon de composer une chaise ou vous ramènent à un vieux projet négligé qui paraît soudain urgent. Aujourd'hui, elles se conjuguent pour construire et matérialiser l'invisible personne assise. Après des années passées à créer (peut-être trop) de chaises, toutes louablement destinées à accueillir (ergonomiquement, confortablement) l'invisible personne assise, j'ai décidé de partir en quête de cette invisible et pourtant omniprésente personne, pour lui donner une présence physique. »

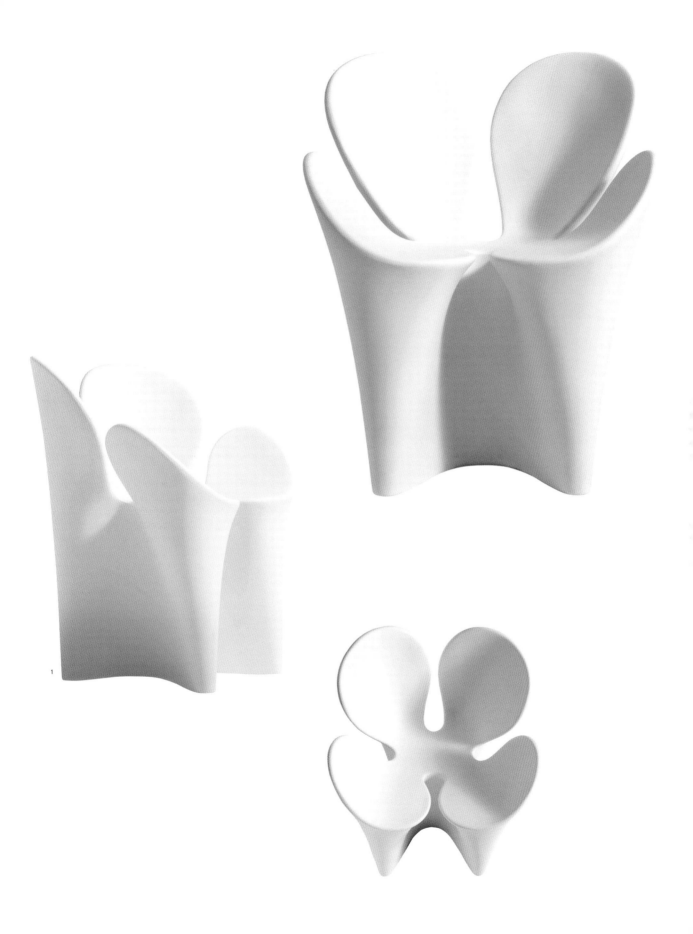

1

2–8
MT SERIES FOR DRIADE,
2005

The MT Series of seating elements was born from experimentation with materials. In this case, rotational moulded two-colour polyethylene. One of Arad's objectives was to dematerialize these chairs by creating unexpected hollows in their form. The very thick polyethylene (approximately 12mm rather than the usual 6mm) is, in fact, clipped on the sides by means of sophisticated "smart" robots that work on five axes, adapting theoretical tracings to real piece dimensions. The MT Series comprises: the MT1 armchair, MT2 sofa and MT3 rocking chair, all of which can be used outdoors, and there are three colour combinations: cream/orange, red/black, blue/light blue. In 2006, the MT Soft series was introduced – upholstered versions of the MT1 and MT2.

Die Sitzelemente der MT-Serie gingen aus Experimenten mit verschiedenen Werkstoffen hervor – in diesem Fall zweifarbiges Polyethylen, das im Rotationsgussverfahren hergestellt wird. Arad hatte sich zum Ziel gesetzt, die Stuhlform durch überraschende Aussparungen aufzulösen. Das außergewöhnlich starke Polyethylen (annähernd 12 mm anstatt der üblichen 6 mm) wurde an den Seiten mithilfe ausgeklügelter „smart robots" ausgeschnitten, die an fünf Achsen wirken und die theoretische Entwurfszeichnung in die Dimensionen des realen Objekts übertragen. Die MT-Serie umfasst den MT1-Stuhl, das MT2-Sofa und den MT3-Schaukelstuhl. Alle Teile sind für den Außenbereich geeignet und in drei Farbkombinationen erhältlich: sand-weiß/orange, rot/schwarz, blau/hellblau. 2006 wurde die MT-Soft-Serie eingeführt, die gepolsterte Versionen der MT1- und MT2-Stühle.

La série MT d'éléments d'assise est née d'une expérimentation de matériaux. Plus précisément d'un intérêt pour le polyéthylène bicolore obtenu par moulage rotationnel. Un des objectifs d'Arad était de dématérialiser ces chaises en créant des creux inattendus dans leur forme. Ce polyéthylène très épais (environ 12 mm, contre les habituels 6 mm) est en fait agrafé sur les côtés à l'aide de robots « intelligents » perfectionnés qui travaillent sur cinq axes pour adapter des tracés théoriques aux dimensions réelles de la pièce. La série MT comprend le fauteuil MT1, le canapé MT2 et le rocking-chair MT3 : ils peuvent tous être utilisés en extérieur et existent en trois combinaisons de couleurs : crème/orange, rouge/noir, bleu/bleu ciel. En 2006 a été lancée la série MT Soft – des versions rembourrées du MT1 et du MT2.

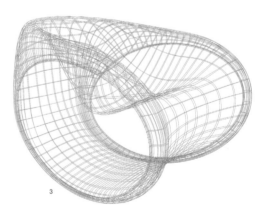

1
CLOVER
Rotational-moulded plastic
monobloc indoor/outdoor
armchair
2007
Client: Driade

2–4
MT ROCKER
Study model, wireframe
drawing and rotational-moulded
plastic indoor/outdoor chair
2005
Client: Driade

"Curious? So am I.
That's why I'm in it."

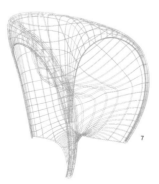

5–7
MT1
Rotational-moulded plastic
indoor/outdoor armchair
and wireframe drawing
2005
Client: Driade

8
MT2
Rotational-moulded
plastic indoor/outdoor sofa
2005
Client: Driade

RON ARAD

62 Chalk Farm Road
London NW1 8AN
United Kingdom
T +44 20 72844963
E info@ronarad.com
www.ronarad.com

BIOGRAPHY

1951 Born in Tel Aviv, Israel
1971–1973 Studied at the Jerusalem Academy of Art
1973 Moved to London, England
1974–1979 Studied architecture at the Architectural Association, London, under Peter Cook and Bernard Tschumi
1981 Established One Off Ltd. (design studio, workshops and showroom) with Caroline Thorman in Covent Garden, London
1989 Founded Ron Arad Associates (architecture and design practice) with Caroline Thorman in Chalk Farm, London
1993 One Off Ltd. incorporated into Ron Arad Associates
1994 Ron Arad Studio (production facility) is established in Como, Italy
1994–1997 Professor of Product Design, Hochschule für Angewandte Kunst, Vienna
1997+ Professor of Furniture Design (later to become Professor of Product Design), Royal College of Art, London
2002 Elected Royal Designer for Industry (RDI) by the Royal Society of Arts, London

RECENT EXHIBITIONS

2000 "Before and After Now", Victoria and Albert Museum, London; "Not Made By Hand Not Made in China", Galeria Marconi, Milan
2001 "Delight in Dedark", Galeria Marconi, Milan
2002 "Two Floors", Galeria Marconi, Milan
2003 "Permetre's la Llibertat", Centre d'Art Santa Monica, Barcelona; "Ron Arad", Galeria Marconi, Milan; "Von Mensch zu Mensch", Sparda Bank, Münster; "Ron Arad Studio Works: 1981-2003", Louisa Guinness Gallery, London; "Ron Arad in der Galerie Stefan Vogdt", Galerie der Moderne, Munich
2004 "Lo-rez-dolores-tabula-rasa", Galeria Marconi, Milan; "Ron Arad Fatto in Italia" as part of the Venice Biennale 9th International Exhibition of Architecture, "Metamorph", Vincenza; "Ron Arad: New Works & Installation", Phillips, de Pury & Co., New York
2005 "Ron Arad: A Retrospective Exhibition", Barry Friedman Ltd, New York; "Designs by Ron Arad", Indianapolis Museum of Contemporary Art; "Paved with Good Intentions" installation, Miami Basel
2006 "Blo-Jobs", Gallery Mourmans, Lanaken, Belgium; "Blo-Glo", Dolce & Gabbana, Metropol, Milan; "There is no solution because there is no problem", 508 West 26 Street, New York (with Barry Friedman Gallery); "The Dogs Barked", de Pury & Luxembourg, Zurich

RECENT AWARDS

2001 Co-winner, Perrier Jouët Selfridges Design Prize, London; Barcelona Primavera International Award for Design; Gio Ponti International Design Award, Denver; Oribe Art & Design Award, Gifu, Japan
2002 Finalist, 2002 World Technology Award for Design
2004 Designer of the Year Award, Architektur & Wohnen
2005 Designer of the Year Award, FX magazine
2006 The Jerusalem Prize for Arts and Letters, awarded by Bezalel Academy of Arts and Design, Israel; 2006 Visionary Award, Museum of Arts & Design, New York

CLIENTS

Alessi, Bonaldo, Cappellini, Driade, Gallery Mourmans, Fiam, Kartell, Magis, Moroso, Serralunga, Swarovski, The Rug Company, Tubor, Vitra International

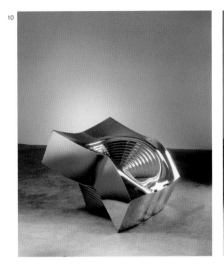

9
WAVY
Thermoformed plastic
stacking chair
2007
Client: Moroso

10
THICK VAC
Polished aluminium armchair
2006
Client: self-produced
(edition of 6)

11
TOM BLOC
Polished aluminium armchair
2006
Client: self-produced
(edition of 6)

12
MT ROCKER
Bronze rocking chair
2005
Client: self-produced
(edition of 2)

13
VOIDO
Rotational-moulded plastic
indoor/outdoor rocking chair
2006
Client: Moroso

DODO ARSLAN

"My philosophy? I am not one of those people who say they know where design is going or even where they want to take it. The only thing I am sure of is that a good product only comes about when there is rapport between the designer and the producer based on mutual esteem and trust, and equally important, when the company has good technical skills and makes good prototypes. I love designing, and apart from that I leave it to others to decide what they think of my work. It is interesting to read what journalists write about my work and see the way they describe the projects. I could talk about my way of working: pencil, pantone, card, wire, foam, rubber, fabric and as little computer as possible. I will add a good dose of enthusiasm, recklessness and laziness. I feel more like a craftsman than a designer. In practice, I do what I did as a kid – but now they pay me to do it! My inspiration is certainly Castiglioni, because of his unpredictability and endless research. His work, and Eames's, fascinate me, especially their innovation and use of materials."

„Meine Philosophie? Ich gehöre nicht zu den Leuten, die behaupten zu wissen, wohin der Weg im Design geht oder wohin sie es lenken wollen. Ich bin mir einer einzigen Sache sicher, nämlich, dass ein gutes Produkt nur dann entsteht, wenn zwischen dem Designer und dem Erzeuger ein gutes Verhältnis der gegenseitigen Wertschätzung und des Vertrauens besteht. Genauso wichtig ist, dass die Firma technisch versiert ist und gute Prototypen herstellen kann. Ich bin Designer aus Leidenschaft, aber abgesehen davon überlasse ich es anderen zu entscheiden, was sie von meiner Arbeit halten. Es amüsiert mich zu lesen, was Journalisten über meine Arbeit schreiben und was ihnen in ihren Artikeln regelmäßig für Fehler unterlaufen. Um etwas über meine Arbeitsweise zu sagen: Bleistift, Pantone, Karton, Draht, Styropor, Schaumgummi, Stoff und so wenig Computer wie möglich. Dazu mische ich eine kräftige Portion Enthusiasmus, Sorglosigkeit und Faulheit. In der Praxis mache ich das Gleiche wie als Kind – aber jetzt werde ich dafür bezahlt! Meine Anregungen beziehe ich sicher von Castiglioni, wegen seiner Unberechenbarkeit und weil er nie aufgehört hat zu forschen. Seine Arbeit fasziniert mich, genauso wie die von Eames, vor allem was ihren innovativen Charakter und die Verwendung von Werkstoffen betrifft."

«Ma philosophie? Je ne suis pas de ceux qui assurent savoir où va le design, ou même où ils veulent l'emmener. La seule chose dont je suis sûr, c'est qu'on ne peut créer un bon produit que s'il existe entre le designer et le fabricant un rapport fondé sur l'estime et la confiance et, tout aussi important, si l'entreprise est techniquement compétente et sait fabriquer de bons prototypes. J'adore le design; pour le reste, je laisse les autres décider de ce qu'ils pensent de mon travail. C'est amusant de lire ce que les journalistes écrivent sur mon travail et de voir les erreurs qui paraissent régulièrement dans leurs articles. Je pourrais parler de ma façon de travailler: crayon, pantone, carton, fil, polystyrène, caoutchouc mousse, tissus et aussi peu d'ordinateur que possible. J'ajouterais une bonne dose d'enthousiasme, d'insouciance et de paresse. J'ai davantage l'impression d'être un artisan qu'un designer. Dans la pratique, je fais ce que je faisais quand j'étais enfant – sauf que maintenant je suis payé pour! Je m'inspire évidemment de Castiglioni, pour son caractère imprévisible et ses recherches actuelles. Son travail, tout comme celui d'Eames, me fascine, en particulier leur nature novatrice et leur utilisation des matériaux.»

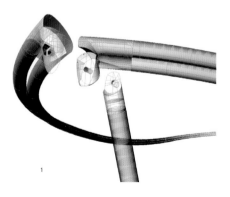

1

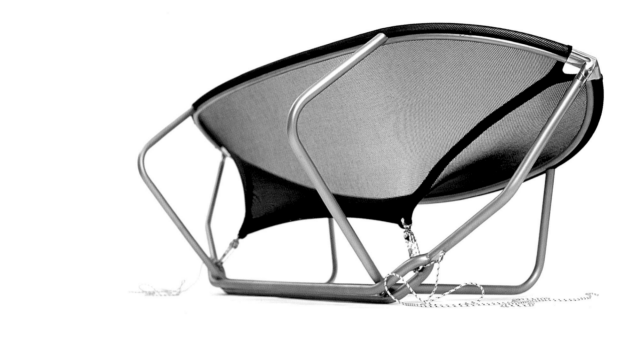

2

LEUDO LOUNGE
COLLAPSIBLE SOFA
PROTOTYPE, 2003

"The frame of this innovative collapsible sofa is constructed of stainless steel, while the hinges are made of aluminium. The self-supporting W2 fabric is by the Quantum Group (supplier to Herman Miller for the Aeron Chair) with reinforcements made of Zenith, a high performance fabric patented by Itam. This fabric 'dress' is stretched with the aid of Harken micro-blocks, products originally made for sailboats. The series of blocks reduce the load required to pretension the seat. Leudo can be used outdoors thanks to its materials (self-supporting fabric prevents perspiration). It weighs 20kg and has a thickness of only 15cm when collapsed, which makes it easy to move and store in the winter."

„Der Rahmen dieses innovativen Faltsofas besteht aus rostfreiem Stahl, die Scharniere sind aus Aluminium gefertigt. Das selbsttragende W2-Gewebe ist ein Produkt der Quantum Group (die auch das Gewebe für den Aeron-Stuhl von Herman Miller liefert), und die Verstärkungen bestehen aus Zenith, einem von Itam patentierten Hochleistungsgewebe. Dieses Gewebe-,Kleid' wird mithilfe von Harken Micro-Blöcken gespannt, die aus dem Segelschiffbau stammen. Dank der Blöcke wird die erforderliche Vorspannkraft reduziert. Das verwendete Material ermöglicht den Einsatz im Außenbereich (selbsttragendes Gewebe wirkt schweißhemmend). Das Sofa wiegt 20 kg und ist zusammengeklappt nur 15 cm breit, es lässt sich also im Winter leicht wegräumen und verstauen."

« Le cadre de ce canapé pliant novateur est composé d'acier inoxydable et ses charnières sont en aluminium. Le tissu ‹ autoportant › W2, une création du groupe Quantum (partenaire de Herman Miller pour sa chaise Aeron), est renforcé d'empièce-ments en Zenith, un tissu hautement performant breveté par Itam. La ‹ jupe › textile est étirée à l'aide de micro-poulies Harken créées à l'origine pour l'accastillage des voiliers. L'accumulation de poulies réduit la charge nécessaire pour tendre l'assise sur les montants du siège. Leudo peut être utilisé en extérieur grâce à ses matériaux (le filet W2 évite la transpiration). Il pèse 20 kg et ne mesure que 15cm d'épaisseur lorsqu'il est plié, ce qui le rend facile à déplacer et à entreposer pour l'hiver. »

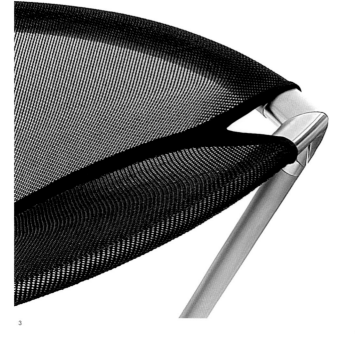

3

4

5

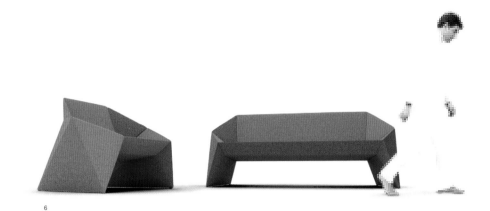

6

"Castiglioni is dead, Magistretti is dead…
and I'm not feeling too good myself!"

1
LEUDO LOUNGE
CAD rendering of collapsible
indoor/outdoor sofa hinges
2003
Client: self-produced
(prototype)

2–5
LEUDO LOUNGE
Collapsible indoor/outdoor
sofa, constructional details
and assembly sequence
2003
Client: self-produced
(prototype)

6
LOWRES
Polyurethane foam sofa
and armchair
2003
Client: SpHaus

7
APPLE
Polyurethane foam
rocking armchair
2004
Client: SpHaus

7

DODO ARSLAN
Via Bolivia 2
20096 Pioltello
Milan
Italy
T +39 02 92169438
E info@arslan.it
www.arslan.it

BIOGRAPHY

1970 Born in Milan, Italy
1989–1993 Worked as a graphic designer at MediaAngle in Milan
1994–1998 Studied industrial design at Istituto Europeo di Design in Milan
1998–1999 Designer, Studio & Partners (Nicholas Bewick, Michele De Lucchi, Torsten Fritze, Emilio Torri) in Milan developing projects for Deutsche Post, British American Tobacco and Zumtobel Staff's Mildes Licht IV, which won the Design Plus Prize
1999–2001 Designer, Continuum (Boston, Milan, Seoul) working for Motorola, Samsung, Hewlett Packard, Elan and Völkl; Samsung Pronta 1200, won the Good Design Award and the KIDA Grand Prize
2002–2003 Worked as a freelance designer
2002–2005 Taught at the Scuola Italiana di Design in Padua
2004 Founded his own studio in Milan
2005–2007 Taught at the Istituto Europeo di Design (in Milan, Turin and São Paulo)

RECENT EXHIBITIONS

2004 "Welltech Award", Museo della Scienza e della Tecnica, Milan
2005 "Tipi Italiani", Design Italia, Milan
2006 "Inside Art", Fondazione Arnaldo Pomodoro, Milan
2006–2007 "Italian Design on Tour 2006/2007" – touring exhibition: New York, Las Vegas, Shanghai, New Delhi, Berlin and London
2007 "New Italian Design", Triennale, Milan

RECENT AWARDS

2004 Art Directors Club Award
2005 Young&Design Award
2006 Mini Design Award; A. De Angelis Young Designers Award

CLIENTS

Alias, Arketipo, Axo Light Guzzini, Lucente, Massimo Lunardon, S.Pellegrino, saporiti italia, SpHaus, VinDesign

8
PILOT
Polyurethane foam lounge chair and ottoman
2007
Client: SpHaus

9–11
LOWRES
Metal skinned edition of sofa, details of metal fabric
2003
Client: self-produced (one-off)

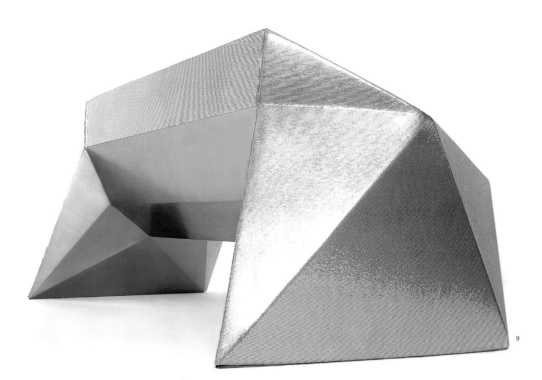

9

10

11

ASKO

"The combination of everyday functionalism, environmental concern and clean, pleasant lines is the principal hallmark of Scandinavian design – and Asko's. The fundamental idea is that carefully designed products should raise people's quality of life. To distinguish ourselves in a market of cluttered, complex and voluptuous designs, we aim for a soft, humanistic minimalism based on the principle of quiet being the new loud. The key elements of Scandinavian design – understated elegance, high quality craftsmanship and natural materials – are reflected in Asko's design language. Much emphasis is also placed on function. We strive to make life easier by offering truly user-friendly interfaces, integration of practical functions and trouble-free, durable products to please people for a long time. Our goal is to provide modular laundry ranges with a discreet but interesting outside, and an extremely functional inside. Whichever solutions appeal to the customer, we hope to contribute to making the laundry area a pleasant, uniform environment – and laundry care a little more enjoyable."

„Die Kombination von Alltagsfunktionalität, Umweltverträglichkeit und klaren, schönen Linien ist das Markenzeichen des skandinavischen Designs – das gilt auch für ASKO. Dahinter steckt der Grundgedanke, dass sorgfältig gestaltete Produkte zur Steigerung der Lebensqualität beitragen sollen. Um auf einem Markt mit überladenen, komplexen und sinnlichen Designs auf uns aufmerksam zu machen, streben wir einen weichen, menschenfreundlichen Minimalismus an, der davon ausgeht, dass Ruhe ein großes Bedürfnis ist. Die entscheidenden Elemente des skandinavischen Designs – zurückhaltende Eleganz, Handwerkskunst von höchster Qualität und natürliche Materialien – kommen in ASKOs Designsprache zum Ausdruck. Der Funktion wird ebenfalls viel Aufmerksamkeit geschenkt. Wir bemühen uns, den Menschen das Leben zu erleichtern, indem wir wirklich benutzerfreundliche Bedienoberflächen, praktische Funktionen und störungsfreie, haltbare Produkte anbieten, die den Menschen lange Zeit Freude machen. Unser Ziel ist es, modulare Waschmaschinenanlagen mit einem unauffälligen, aber interessanten Erscheinungsbild und einem extrem funktionalen Innenleben herzustellen. Welche Lösungen die Kunden auch ansprechen mögen, wir hoffen dazu beizutragen, dass der Raum, in dem die Wäschepflege erledigt wird, eine angenehme, einheitlich gestaltete Umgebung ist – und die Arbeit selbst ein wenig mehr Spaß macht."

« Le design scandinave se définit principalement par un mélange de fonctionnalisme quotidien, de conscience environnementale et de lignes propres et agréables – tout comme Asko. L'idée fondamentale est que les produits conçus avec précision doivent améliorer la qualité de vie des gens. Pour nous distinguer sur un marché où le design est souvent fouillis, complexe, voluptueux, nous visons un minimalisme humaniste tout en douceur, fondé sur le principe que la discrétion est la nouvelle exubérance. Les éléments clé du design scandinave – élégance discrète, fabrication de haute qualité et matériaux naturels – sont présents dans le vocabulaire créatif d'Asko. Nous insistons aussi beaucoup sur la fonction. Nous nous efforçons de faciliter la vie des utilisateurs en leur proposant des interfaces réellement orientées vers leur confort, l'intégration de fonctions pratiques et des produits durables et simples d'utilisation dont ils seront satisfaits longtemps. Notre objectif est de créer des gammes d'électroménager à l'aspect extérieur discret mais intéressant et un intérieur extrêmement fonctionnel. Quelles que soient les solutions que prise le consommateur, nous espérons contribuer à ce que cuisine, salle de bains et buanderies soient des environnements agréables et uniformes – et les travaux ménagers un peu plus plaisants. »

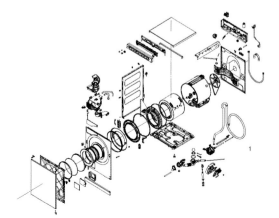

1–2
LINE SERIES
Stainless-steel washing machine
with exploded overview
2007

LINE SERIES STAINLESS
WASHER,
2007

"ASKO offers the only Swan-labelled domestic washer on the market. The Swan is the Nordic symbol awarded to products that are judged to be ecologically aware and environmentally friendly. For a washing machine, this means taking into account the electricity and water consumption, noise levels, rinsing result, and the materials used in construction. The greatest impact on the environment hap-pens when the appliance is being used. ASKO has worked hard to find solutions that reduce consumption of water, electricity and detergent and has top ratings in the European test energy labelling: A+ (energy), A (wash performance) and A (spinning efficiency). It is quiet and all parts over 50 grams are marked for recycling at the end of the machine's useful life."

„ASKO ist der einzige heimische Anbieter einer mit dem ‚Swan Label' ausgezeichneten Wasch-maschine. Der Schwan ist ein skandinavisches Umweltzeichen, das für umweltbewusste und umweltfreundliche Produkte verliehen wird. Die bei einer Waschmaschine beurteilten Kriterien sind Strom- und Wasserverbrauch, Lärmpegel, Waschergebnis und die für die Herstellung verwendeten Mate-rialien. Die meisten Umweltfol-gen entstehen beim Betrieb der Maschine. ASKO bemühte sich um Lösungen, die Einsparungen beim Wasser-, Strom- und Waschmittelverbrauch ermög-lichen: Das europäische Ener-gielabel weist seiner Waschma-schine beste Werte aus: A+ (Stromverbrauch), A (Waschwir-kung) und A (Schleuderleis-tung). Die Maschine arbeitet leise, und alle Bestandteile, die mehr als 50 Gramm wiegen, sind recyclingfähig."

« ASKO propose la seule machi-ne à laver domestique du marché arborant le label du cygne. Le cygne est le symbole accordé dans les pays nordiques aux pro-duits jugés écologiquement res-ponsables et doux pour l'envi-ronnement. Pour une machine à laver, cela signifie une prise en compte de la consommation d'électricité et d'eau, du niveau de bruit, des capacités d'essorage et des matériaux utilisés pour sa construction. L'impact le plus significatif sur l'environnement intervient lorsque l'appareil est utilisé. ASKO a travaillé d'ar-rache-pied pour trouver des solutions qui permettent de réduire la consommation d'eau, d'électricité et de détergent et a obtenu les meilleures notes des tests de qualité européens : A+ (énergie), A (performance de lavage) et A (efficacité d'esso-rage). Elle est silencieuse et toutes les pièces pesant plus de 50 grammes sont aptes à être recyclées à la fin du cycle de vie de la machine. »

3

3
LINE SERIES
Detail of washing machine
detergent compartment
2007

4
LINE SERIES
X-ray drawing of
washing machine
2007

"Scandinavian design with a twist.
But no shout."

5
LINE SERIES
Detail of washing machine Line
Concept™ LC-display linear
user interface
2007

6
LINE SERIES
Washer and tumble dryer
with stainless-steel doors
2007

4

5

ASKO
Asko Cylinda AB
Jung
534 82 Vara
Sweden
T +46 512 32000
E info@asko.se
www.asko.se

COMPANY HISTORY
1950 Self-taught engineer Karl-Erik Andersson founded his own white goods manufacturing company, Junga Verkstäder in Jung, Sweden
1978 Junga Verkstäder was acquired by ASEA. The company name was changed to ASEA Cylinda, later becoming ABB Cylinda after the merger of ASEA with the Swiss Brown Boveri Corporation
1988 The company was acquired by the Finnish company group Asko and renamed Asko Cylinda AB
1996+ Worked in close collaboration with the Propeller design agency in Stockholm
2000 Asko Appliances division acquired by the Italian Antonio Merloni Group

RECENT EXHIBITIONS
2002 "HomeTech Berlin 2002", Berlin; "K/BIS" (Kitchen/Bath Industry Show), Chicago
2003 "iF International Forum Design", Hanover; "K/BIS" (Kitchen/Bath Industry Show), Orlando
2004 "K/BIS" (Kitchen/Bath Industry Show), Chicago
2005 "K/BIS" (Kitchen/Bath Industry Show), Las Vegas
2006 "K/BIS" (Kitchen/Bath Industry Show), Chicago
2007 "K/BIS" (Kitchen/Bath Industry Show), Las Vegas

RECENT AWARDS
2001 Platinum ADEX Award for Design Excellence, Design Journal; 2 x Consumers Digest Best Buy nominations; K/BIS Best of Show Award, Design Journal
2002 K/BIS Best of Show Award, Design Journal
2003 Silver ADEX award for Design Excellence, Design Journal; Nomination, The Grand Award of Design, Sweden; Silver Award – IDEA (Industrial Design Excellence Awards), Industrial Designers Society of America/BusinessWeek; Nomination, iF Award, International Forum Design Hanover
2004 Gold ADEX Award and Silver ADEX Award for Design Excellence, Design Journal; Nomination, Designpreis der Bundesrepublik Deutschland, Germany
2005 Platinum ADEX Award for Design Excellence, Design Journal
2006 2 x Platinum ADEX Awards for Design Excellence, Design Journal; Design Distinction Award – Consumer Products Category, Annual Design Review, I.D. Magazine
2007 Platinum ADEX Award for Design Excellence, Design Journal

YVES BÉHAR

"At its best, design is a reflection of the human ecosystem. More than at any other time, we need designs that are not only new, but that contain a new humanism: embodying the human challenges we face now and those to come. The only thing we have to fear is when, as a species, we don't believe in the future anymore. I am not interested in style, a design signature that is applied to any project or circumstance, but rather what interests me in design work is the communication of ideas through the experience of objects. What I pursue is the fusing of storytelling and form, where the potential for technology and poetry, commerce and culture, merge with the physical world. Today, if design is not ethical, it cannot be beautiful. Usefulness can be about function... but inspiring, resting the soul, creating a sense of wonder and intelligence around one's life is a form of usefulness that goes beyond function. Humanistic design must tap into the 'giving' element of our profession. It must be deeply in tune with the needs to create a sustainable future, deeply connected with emotional needs, deeply self-expressive."

„Das beste Design ist ein Spiegelbild des menschlichen Ökosystems. Mehr denn je zuvor brauchen wir Entwürfe, die nicht nur neu sind, sondern auch einen neuen Humanismus enthalten, das heißt die heutigen und künftigen Herausforderungen an die Menschheit verkörpern. Das Einzige, wovor wir uns fürchten müssen, ist eine Zeit, in der wir als Spezies nicht mehr an die Zukunft glauben. Mich interessiert am Design nicht der Stil, die Handschrift, von der ein Projekt oder eine Sache geprägt ist, sondern die Vermittlung von Ideen durch die Begegnung mit Objekten. Mein Ziel ist die Verschmelzung von Erzählung und Form, das Zusammenführen des technischen und poetischen Potenzials, von Kommerz und Kultur mit der Welt der Körper. Design, das moralisch nicht vertretbar ist, kann in unserer Zeit auch nicht schön sein. Nutzlosigkeit kann etwas mit Funktion zu tun haben ... aber wenn sie inspirierend ist, selig macht und unser Leben mit einem Sinn für Staunen und Intelligenz erfüllt, ist es eine Nutzlosigkeit, die über die Funktion hinausgeht. Humanes Design muss das ‚gebende' Element unseres Berufes erschließen. Es muss vollkommen auf die Notwendigkeit abgestimmt sein, eine nachhaltige Zukunft zu schaffen, zutiefst verbunden mit emotionalen Bedürfnissen, zutiefst dem Selbstausdruck verpflichtet."

« Au mieux, le design est un reflet de l'écosystème humain. Nous avons besoin, aujourd'hui plus que jamais, de créations qui sont non seulement innovantes mais aussi porteuses d'un nouvel humanisme : incarner les défis humains auxquels nous sommes confrontés aujourd'hui et serons confrontés demain. La seule chose que nous avons à craindre, c'est le moment où, en tant qu'espèce, nous ne croirons plus en l'avenir. Je ne me préoccupe pas d'avoir un style, une signature qui serait appliquée à chaque projet et en toute circonstance ; ce qui m'intéresse surtout dans le travail créatif, c'est de communiquer des idées en manipulant des objets. Je recherche une fusion entre récit et forme, où les potentiels technologique et poétique, commercial et culturel se mêlent au monde physique. Aujourd'hui, si le design n'est pas éthique, il ne peut pas être beau. L'utilité peut être affaire de fonction... mais inspirer, reposer l'âme, créer un sentiment d'émerveillement et d'intelligence dans la vie des autres est une autre forme d'utilité qui dépasse la fonction. Le design humaniste doit puiser dans l'élément ‹ donnant › de notre profession. Il doit sincèrement prendre en compte la nécessité de créer un avenir durable, étroitement lié à des besoins émotionnels, être une expression profondément personnelle. »

1

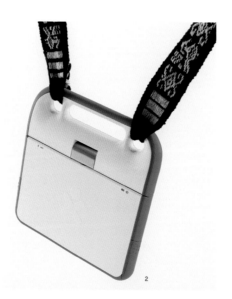

2

1–4
XO
$100 laptop computer
for children, developed in
conjunction with Nicholas
Negroponte and the MIT
Media Lab
2006
Client: OLPC
(One Laptop Per Child)

"One Laptop Per Child, or OLPC, is a non-profit organization committed to bringing technology and education to millions of children in developing countries worldwide. Designed for children and costing only $100, the OLPC XO laptop is a compact, durable, and yet expressive product with a whimsical and tactile richness. The Wi-Fi antennas (also called Rabbit Ears) give the XO a character-like personality, functioning as covers for the laptop's USB ports and as dual latches to close the clamshell. The surrounding coloured bumper is a seal to protect from dust, as well as a tactile ergonomic palm surface: and also integrates the feet on the underside of the laptop. The screen is both a coloured image screen and a high-contrast black and white screen for reading text, even in the sun. In laptop mode, the wide track-pad doubles as a drawing/stencil writing tablet (important for learning to write script letters)."

„One Laptop Per Child (ein Laptop pro Kind) oder OLPC ist eine gemeinnützige Organisation, die sich vorgenommen hat, Millionen von Kindern in Entwicklungsländern mit Technik und Bildung auszustatten. Der eigens für Kinder gestaltete OLPC-XO-Laptop zum Preis von nur 100 US-Dollar ist ein kompaktes, robustes und dennoch ausdrucksstarkes Gerät mit zahlreichen neckischen und taktilen Details. Die Wi-Fi-Antennen (auch Hasenohren genannt) verleihen dem XO so etwas wie eine eigene Persönlichkeit und fungieren auch als Schutzabdeckung für die USB-Anschlüsse und als Gehäuseriegel. Der farbige Rundum-Stoßdämpfer schützt vor Staub, dient als ergonomische Stützfläche für die Hände und nimmt auch die Füße des Laptops auf. Der Bildschirm kann von Farbe auf kontrastreiches Schwarz-Weiß umgeschaltet werden, sodass man auch bei greller Sonne noch gut lesen kann. Im E-Book-Modus funktioniert der breite Trackpad als Schreib- und Zeichenfläche (wichtig, um Buchstaben schreiben zu lernen)."

« L'association ‹ Un ordinateur pour chaque enfant › a pour mission d'apporter la technologie et l'éducation à des millions d'enfants des pays en voie de développement dans le monde entier. L'ordinateur portable XO OLPC ne coûte que 100 $ et a été conçu pour les enfants ; il est compact, durable et pourtant expressif, doté d'une richesse originale et tactile. Les antennes Wi-Fi (aussi appelées ‹ oreilles de lapin ›) donnent au XO une réelle personnalité, cachent les ports USB de l'ordinateur et pivotent pour devenir les loquets qui verrouillent la palourde. Les pare-chocs colorés qui le bordent agissent comme une gaine de protection contre la poussière ; sa surface tactile est aussi un repose-poignet ergonomique et contient un socle encastré sous l'ordinateur. L'écran est à la fois adapté aux images en couleur qu'au noir et blanc, très contrasté, pour lire les textes même en plein soleil. Placé en mode ‹ livre électronique ›, la surface du trackpad double pour former une tablette de travail/dessin/écriture (outil important pour apprendre à écrire les lettres de l'alphabet. »

6

7

5

8

YVES BÉHAR

Fuseproject
528 Folsom Street
San Francisco
California 94105
USA
T +1 415 9081492
E info@fuseproject.com
www.fuseproject.com

BIOGRAPHY

1967 Born in Lausanne, Switzerland
1989–1991 Studied industrial design at Art Center College of Design, Switzerland
1991–1993 B.S. Industrial Design, Art Center College of Design, Pasadena
1992–1995 Designer, Lunar, Palo Alto
1995+ Visiting professor at CCA (California College of the Arts)
1996–1998 Design Leader, frog design, Palo Alto
1999 Founded Fuseproject (integrated design agency) in San Francisco
2005+ Chair of the Industrial Design Department at CCA (California College of the Arts)

RECENT EXHIBITIONS

2004 Solo exhibitions at SFMOMA (San Francisco Museum of Modern Art) and Musée de design et d'arts appliqués contemporains, Lausanne, Switzerland; "Swarovski Crystal Palace", Art Basel Miami Beach, Miami
2005 "Swarovski Voyage Chandelier", JFK International Airport, New York; "Swarovski Crystal Palace", Art Basel Miami Beach, Miami; "Swiss Design Now", Museum of Contemporary Art, Shanghai
2006 "Swiss Design Now", Today Art Museum, Beijing; "Swarovski Crystal Palace", Art Basel Miami Beach, Miami; "Entry 2006 Expo", Essen, Germany; "Swarovski Sparkle, Mini Voyage, Small and Mini Nest", Moss Gallery, New York; "SAFE design takes on risk", The Museum of Modern Art, New York

RECENT AWARDS

2004 National Design Award for Product Design, Cooper-Hewitt National Design Museum, New York; Silver award, D&AD, London; Laureat de la Fondation pour la creation, Switzerland; 2 x Gold, 1 x Silver, 1 x Bronze, 1 x Excellence Awards – IDEA (Industrial Design Excellence Awards), Industrial Designers Society of America/BusinessWeek; 4 x Red Dot Awards, Design Zentrum Nordrhein Westfalen, Essen; 6 x Good Design Awards, Chicago Athenaeum
2005 3 x Red Dot Awards, Design Zentrum Nordrhein Westfalen, Essen; 2 x Gold, 2 x Silver and 2 x Bronze Awards – IDEA (Industrial Design Excellence Awards), Industrial Designers Society of America/BusinessWeek
2006 Gold and Silver Awards – IDEA (Industrial Design Excellence Awards), Industrial Designers Society of America/BusinessWeek; Nomination – Best Products of 2006, Business Week; 2 x iF Awards, Industrie Design Forum Hanover; 2 x Honorable Mentions, CES Consumer Electronics, Las Vegas; Gold Award, NeoCon, Chicago Clients
2007 INDEX Award Grand Prize of Community Design; Best of Category Award, ID Magazine; Gold Award, D&AD; 2x Awards-IDEA Industrial Designers Society of America/BusinessWeek

CLIENTS

Alessi, Aliph, Birkenstock, Cassina, Coca-Cola, Danese, Herman Miller, Hussein Chalayan, Kodak, Magis, Microsoft, MINI, Nike, One Laptop Per Child, Sony, Swarovski, Target, Toshiba

9

INNER LIGHT
Twin ringed self-standing aluminium light sculpture with inner surfaces illuminated by electroluminescent film
2006
Client: self-produced for a travelling UNESCO exhibition on the theme "Love/Why"

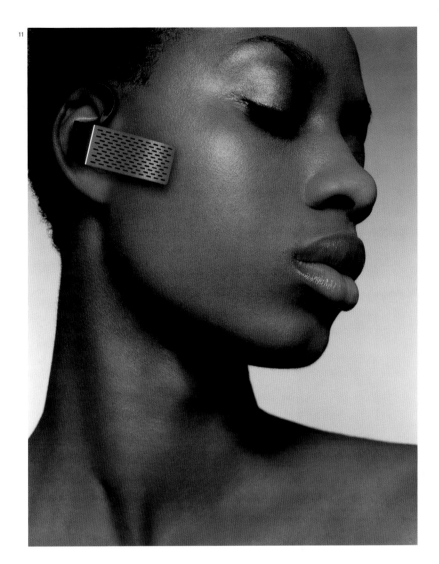

"Design brings stories to life.
Stories bring life to design.
Life brings stories to design."

10–11
JAWBONE AIR
Wireless Bluetooth communication headset with unique voice activity sensor that distinguishes and separates human voice from background noise
2006
Client: Aliph

12
MINI_MOTION
LCD display
wristwatch
2006
Client: BMW/Mini Cooper

MARKUS BENESCH

"My role model from the beginning was Gyro Gearloose (the crazy inventor from Disney comics). I like working as an inventor, always searching for the unknown and unexplored: in technology, aesthetics and perception. I started my career as a cabinetmaker and *trompe l'œil* painter during school when I was 16 years old. Being young and not educated in design I thought if I made furniture or an interior it had to be stunning and innovative in order to satisfy the client. I have a deep respect for the people who are interested in or buy my work, and I don't want to bore them or myself with copies or concepts that already exist. Emphasizing the poetic and innovative side of objects is vital to me. Challenging and reshaping the boundaries of perception and perspective – in a physical and philosophical way – is what stimulates me. The creation and employment of new materials, aesthetics and production technologies are obligatory to my design process. I believe in research, pure curiosity in life and its hidden surprises, as well as in multidisciplinary interaction, rather than following the fashion of the day. Most of all I want to stress the poetic side of design, and to make new functional and aesthetical proposals. Nurture communication and keep/revive that twinkle in your eye!"

„Mein Vorbild war schon immer Daniel Düsentrieb (der verrückte Erfinder aus den Disney-Comics). Ich arbeite gerne als Erfinder, immer auf der Suche nach dem Unbekannten und Unentdeckten: in der Technik, in der Ästhetik und in der Wahrnehmung. Meine Karriere startete ich mit 16 Jahren als Möbeltischler und Trompe-l'Œil-Maler während der Schulzeit. Schon damals fand ich, die Gestaltung von Möbeln und Innenräumen müsse spannend und innovativ sein. Ich habe tiefen Respekt vor den Menschen, die an meiner Arbeit interessiert sind oder sie kaufen, und ich will sie und mich nicht mit Kopien langweilen oder mit Ideen, die es schon gibt. Ich möchte die poetische und innovative Seite der Dinge betonen. Die Grenzen der Wahrnehmung und der Perspektive in Frage zu stellen und neu zu definieren – in physischer und philosophischer Weise – das ist es was mich antreibt. Neue Werkstoffe, ästhetische Ausdrucksformen und Fertigungsverfahren zu entwickeln und einzusetzen ist für meinen Designprozess unerlässlich. Statt der aktuellen Mode zu folgen, glaube ich an die Forschung, die pure Neugierde auf das Leben und seine verborgenen Überraschungen, genauso wie an interdisziplinäre Zusammenarbeit. Vor allem möchte ich die poetische Seite des Designs betonen und neue funktionale und ästhetische Vorschläge einbringen. Kommunikation anregen und ihr Augenzwinkern neu zu beleben oder wiederzufinden."

«Depuis le début, mon modèle etait Géo Trouvetout (l'inventeur fantaisiste de Disney). J'aime travailler comme un inventeur toujours à la recherche de l'inconnu et de l'inexploré : dans la technique, l'esthétique et la perception. J'ai débuté ma carrière comme ébéniste et peintre de trompe-l'œil alors que j'étais encore à l'école, à 16 ans. J'étais jeune et je n'avais pas de culture du design, alors je pensais que si je réalisais un meuble ou un intérieur il devait être stupéfiant et innovant pour satisfaire le client. J'ai un profond respect pour les gens qui s'intéressent ou achètent mon travail et je ne veux ni les ennuyer ni m'ennuyer moi-même avec des copies ou des concepts qui existent déjà. Il est capital pour moi d'insister sur l'aspect poétique et novateur des objets. Ce qui me stimule, c'est de remettre en question et refaçonner les frontières de la perception et de la perspective – physiquement et philosophiquement. La création et l'emploi d'une esthétique, de technologies de production et de matériaux nouveaux sont indispensables à mon processus de création. Je crois à la recherche, à une pure curiosité de la vie et aux surprises qu'elle recèle, ainsi qu'à l'interaction entre disciplines, plutôt que de suivre la tendance du jour. Je veux par-dessus tout accentuer la poésie du design et faire de nouvelles propositions esthétiques et fonctionnelles. Nourrissez la communication et conserver ce clin d'œil!»

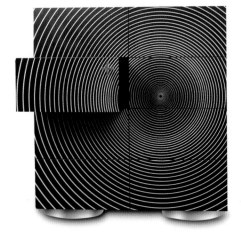

1

1–2
CASSETTIERA DI ALICE
Drawer unit with printed plastic laminate decoration
2005
Client: Memphis

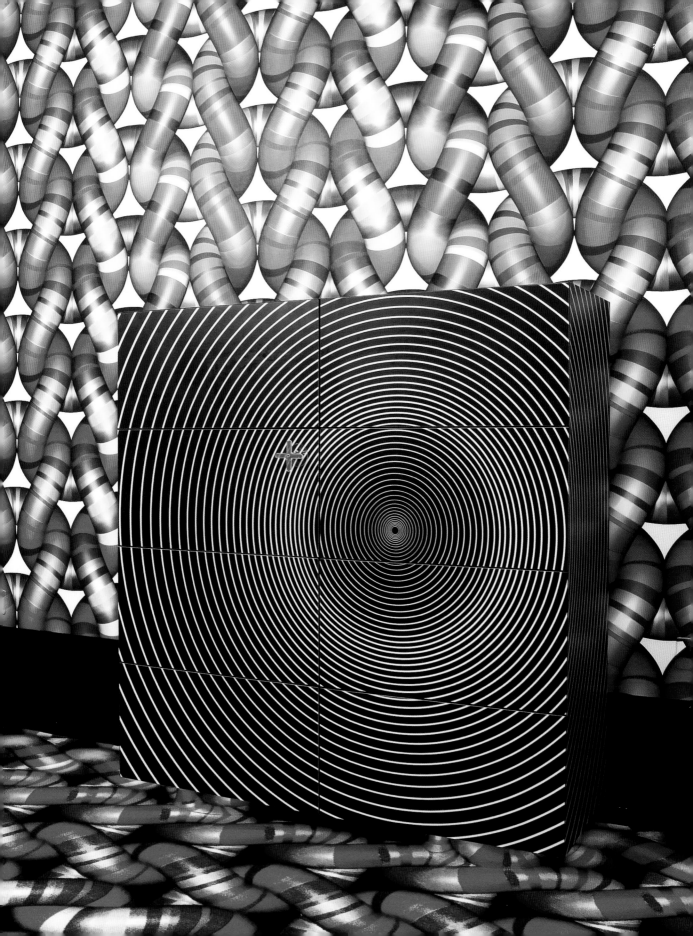

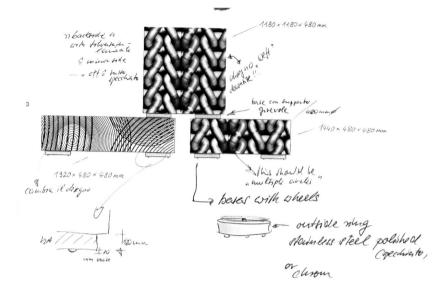

3

1180 × 1180 × 480 mm

1440 × 480 × 480 mm

1320 × 480 × 480 mm

boxes with wheels

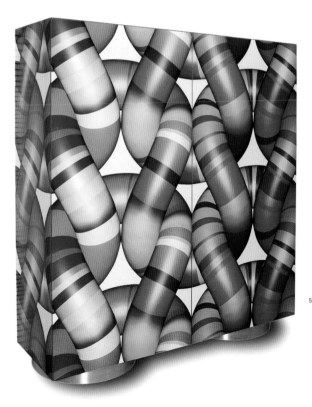

5

4

6

3
UFFICIO DI ALICE
Sketch for large case unit
with printed plastic laminate
decoration
2005
Client: Memphis

4
UFFICIO DI ALICE
Cardboard mock up of case
pieces for La Casa di Alice
exhibition
2005
Client: Memphis

5
CREDENZA DI ALICE
Two-door sideboard with printed
plastic laminate decoration
2005
Client: Memphis

6
UFFICIO DI ALICE
Large case unit with printed
plastic laminate decoration
2005
Client: Memphis

7
TAVOLO DI ALICE
Occasional table with printed
laminate top and polished
stainless-steel legs
2005
Client: Memphis

7

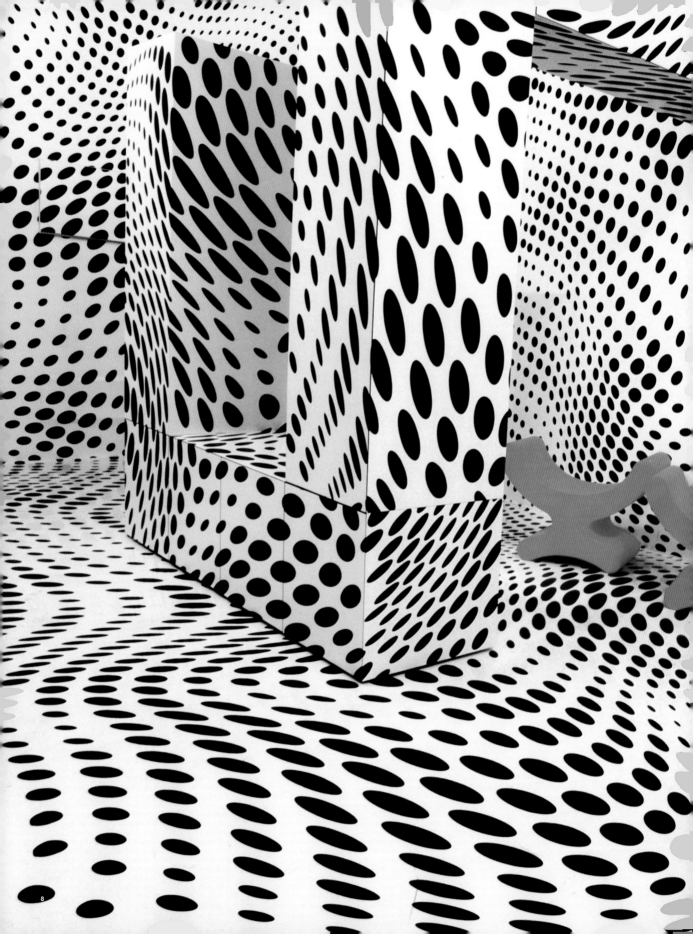

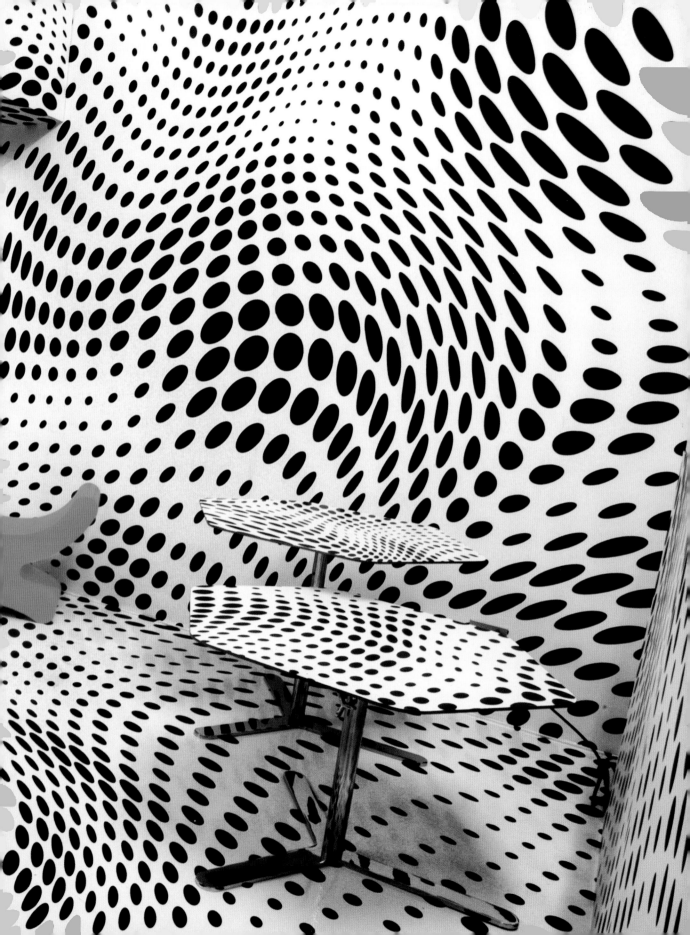

MARKUS BENESCH

Markus Benesch Creates
Via Tiepolo 58
20129 Milan
Italy
Markus Benesch Creates
Mariannenplatz 1
80538 Munich
Germany
T (I) +39 02 70123589
T (D) +49 89 2285262
info@markusbeneschcreates.com
www.markusbeneschcreates.com

BIOGRAPHY

1969 Born in Munich, Germany
1988 Founded own studio, Markus Benesch Creates in Munich
1996 MA Design, Domus Academy, Milan
1996 Founded own brand, Money For Milan
1999 Acquired patents for Silversurfer laminate
2002 Founded Colorflage wallpaper company and brand

RECENT EXHIBITIONS

2004 "Colorflage", Galleria InterNos, Milan; "ISPO", Munich; "Transition Space Edge", E&Y, Tokyo
2005 "La Casa di Alice for Memphis", Galleria Post-Design, Milan; "Dressing Ourselves", Palazzo dalla Triennale, Milan; "Trendstand" (for Elle Decor and Interni), Abitare Il Tempo, Verona
2006 "La Casa di Alice for Memphis", Abitare Il Tempo, Verona; "Colorforce", "Color-flage", "Strip 'n Tease" and "Bauhaus" shows during Milan Design Week
2007 "Architects Hatch", Gallery Maurer, Cologne; "Trendshow Wallpaper", Jannelli & Volpi, Milan; "Tra Decor e Decus", Abet Laminati, Turin and Forum Omegna, Omegna; "The Discovery of Fantabulosa", Jannelli & Volpi, Milan

CLIENTS

Abet Laminati, Benetton, Boscolo, BrainLAB, Colorflage, De Rossi, E&Y, Esselte Leitz, Janneli Volpi, Memphis Milano, Modular, Money For Milan, Mövenpick, Paul Smith, Playlife, Polidesign, Porchet, Rasch, RD Living, Sirpi, Westag, Getalit, Yoox.com

"Stretching and inspiring
the colourful boundaries of design."

9

10

11

8
FLOW DOTS
Furniture, wallpaper and
showroom interior
2005
Client: Colorflage/Rasch

9
TWIST MULTI
Corridor with wallpaper
2005
Client: Colorflage/Rasch

10–11
TURNO – CERENIUM
Revolving case piece with
interchangeable self-applied
magnetic printed plastic
laminate decoration
2006
Client: Money For Milan

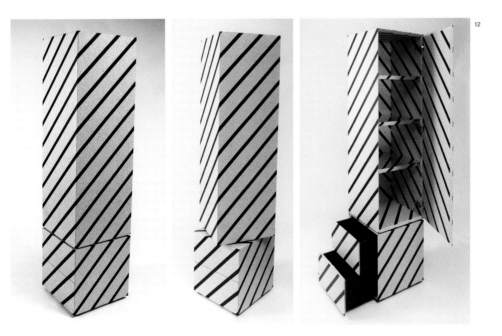

12

12
AH–HIGH
Revolving case piece in
untreated chipboard with
inlaid strips of Corian
2007
Client: Galerie Maurer

STEVEN
BLAESS

"Crucial to my approach is keeping an open mind away from prior expectations. This allows the intuitive to mix with the technological. From out of this arises true design. Every form around us is a product of design whether it is the design of nature or the result of human endeavour. To design with awareness, understanding and passion is how we as individuals choose to leave our legacy and how we will be measured by generations to come."

„Für meine Herangehensweise ist es entscheidend, einen offenen Geist zu haben und frei von jeder Erwartungshaltung zu sein. Dadurch kann sich das Intuitive mit dem Technischen vermischen. Und daraus entsteht wahrhaftes Design. Jede Form, die uns umgibt, ist das Produkt eines Designvorgangs, sei sie nun von der Natur geschaffen oder durch menschliches Bemühen. Wir wollen ein Design hinterlassen, das mit Umsicht, Wissen und Leidenschaft geschaffen wurde, und daran werden wir von künftigen Generationen gemessen werden."

«Conserver une ouverture d'esprit qui s'éloigne des attentes préconçues est capital dans ma démarche. Cela permet à l'intuition de se mêler à la technologie. C'est de cela qu'émerge le vrai design. Toutes les formes qui nous entourent sont le produit d'une création, qu'il s'agisse des créations de la nature ou du résultat d'expériences humaines. Créer du design avec conscience, compréhension et passion est la façon que nous avons choisie, en tant qu'individus, pour laisser notre trace et être appréciés par les générations à venir.»

1

1–3/6
HEXAGONAL BIN SYSTEM
Rotational-moulded plastic bins
and stands for retail display
2004
Client: Naked Grape

2

4–5
MARLI
Stainless-steel bottle opener
based on biomechanical
rotating action of wrist
2005
Client: Alessi

1–3/6

NAKED GRAPE HEXAGONAL
BIN SYSTEM, 2003–2004

This innovative retail interior
was designed for the Australia-
based Naked Grape wine-store
chain. For its Melbourne flag-
ship store the aim was to maxi-
mize the relatively small budget
while creating maximum visual

impact. The store was the
first in Australia to integrate
rotational-moulded plastic,
mass-produced hexagonal display bins for point of sale counters and wine-tasting display
stands.

Diese innovative Verkaufsraum-
einrichtung wurde für die aus-
tralische Weinhandelskette

Naked Grape entworfen. Für
ihren Flagship-Store in Melbourne musste mit einem relativ
kleinen Budget eine maximale
Wirkung erzeugt werden. Dabei
kamen erstmals in Australien im
Rotationsschmelzverfahren hergestellte Kunststoffe für massen-
produzierte, aus sechseckigen
Elementen bestehende Weinre-
gale zum Einsatz, die als Präsen-

tationstresen für Weinverkos-
tung und Verkauf verwendet
werden.

Cette configuration de boutique
novatrice a été conçue pour la
chaîne australienne de mar-
chands de vins Naked Grape.
Pour sa boutique phare de Melbourne, l'objectif était d'optimiser un budget relativement

modeste pour parvenir à un effet
visuel maximal. Ce magasin a
été le premier en Australie à utiliser des plastiques obtenus par
moulage rotationnel pour des
présentoirs hexagonaux destinés
aux comptoirs de vente et des
tables de dégustation.

6

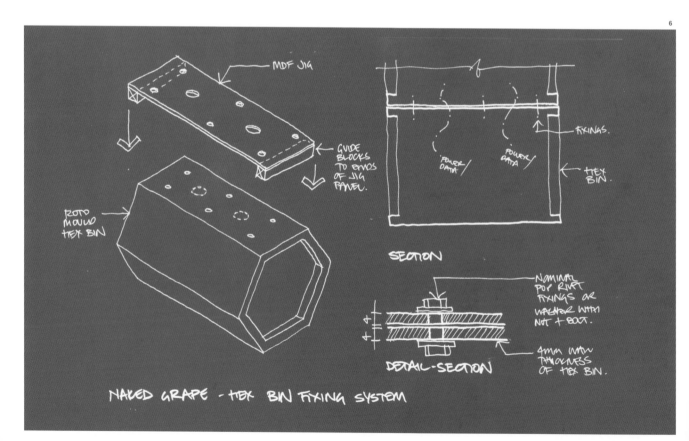

7

7
RECEPTION
Interior design of head
office for international
trading company
2003
Client: Grange Securities

"I approach my work in a holistic manner.
Before any answers are developed I examine each
project from all angles and perspectives."

STEVEN BLAESS

Blaess TM – Design for
Human Environments
Level 1, 16–28 Foster Street
Surry Hills
Sydney
NSW 2010
Australia

PO Box 58041
Dubai
United Arab Emirates

T (GSM) +971 502 806191
E info@blaess.com
www.blaess.com

BIOGRAPHY

1969 Born in Tailem Bend,
South Australia
1992–1993 Woods Bagot
Scholarship for Excellence in
the Study of Interior Design
1994 Bachelor of Design –
Human Environments,
University of South Australia
(Underdale Campus)
2001 Business Management
Certificate, Eastern Suburbs
Business School, Sydney
2002 Design Tutor, University
of New South Wales Australia –
Student design workshop

RECENT EXHIBITIONS

2001 "Reperes – L'Atelier
Renault", Paris; "Salone del
Mobile", Milan
2002 "Tokyo Designers Block",
Japan; "Salon du Meuble",
Paris; "World-Wide", Paris
2003 "Tokyo Designers Block –
Hybrid Objects", Tokyo
2004 "40 Degrees – Design-
mai", Berlin; "Multipli di
Cibo – Salone del Mobile",
Milan
2005 "In Design", Sydney;
"Alessi – Macef", Milan;
"Salone del Mobile", Milan

2006 "Conversation of Things
New", Melbourne, Sydney and
Tokyo

RECENT AWARDS

2000 Finalist, Sydney 2000
Olympic Games Torch Relay
Design
2003 Finalist, Australian Dulux
Colour Awards
2005 Permanent Design
Collection, Powerhouse
Museum Sydney, Australia

CLIENTS

Alessi, Artemide, Edra,
Eiesenmann Nexis, Flos,
Fratelli Guzzini, iGuzzini
illuminazione, La Sala/Sydney,
Mercedes Australian Fashion
Week, Naked Grape Australia,
Samsung USA, Space Island
Group USA, Taymar BHI

RONAN & ERWAN BOUROULLEC

"Our work frequently starts with an encounter with an industrialist, a craftsman, a technique, a material, a machine or a location. The ensuing dialogue acts as a sort of seed-bed for the embryo project. Thus our task is for the most part context-related, embracing the three elements of demand, enterprise and use. In a sense, the procedure resembles what some contemporary artists have styled in-situ art, the end product enshrining a resonance of its intimate surroundings. In the case of a design project, the place is the business, with its background, its philosophy and its know-how. We attempt to integrate these factors into a corporate effort that out performs individual capabilities. Design appears to be a primary function in human society: conceiving objects for users and uses. In concrete terms it means organising materials and production methods to make these items in smaller or greater quantities. In a scenario where being at the cutting edge is a *sine qua non*, technologies are neither temporary nor permanent. Functions, too, develop ceaselessly within society in an almost biological and evolutionary fashion. First and foremost the designer has to understand the present reality and how to manipulate it to make his ideas practicable. He must then force himself to take that extra step, scrutinising the immediate future and thrusting back the boundaries of the possible. With these challenges in mind we try to stamp our work with a distinct character while continuing to respect its future context. Without, of course, forgetting that the consumers of these items are many and diverse. That is why we look for a language that is subtle yet positive, in which formal research retains a primary role."

„Unsere Arbeit beginnt häufig mit einer Begegnung, sei es dass wir auf einen Industriellen, einen Handwerker, einen Werkstoff, eine Maschine oder einen Ort treffen. Der sich daraus ergebende Dialog dient als eine Art Mutterboden, auf dem das Projekt gedeiht. Unsere Aufgabe ist also größtenteils kontextbezogen und vereint die drei Elemente Bedarf, Unternehmen und Verwendung. In gewissem Sinn ähnelt der Vorgang dem, was zeitgenössische Künstler als Kunst vor Ort bezeichnen: Das Endprodukt enthält Anklänge an die unmittelbare Umgebung. Der *Ort* im Fall eines Designprojekts ist das Unternehmen mit seinem Hintergrund, seiner Philosophie und seinem Know-how. Wir versuchen, diese Faktoren in einem gemeinsamen Vorgehen zu bündeln. Design scheint in unserer Gesellschaft einen Hauptzweck zu haben, nämlich Objekte für Anwender und Anwendungen zu konzipieren. Das bedeutet konkret, dass Werkstoffe und Fertigungsverfahren für die Herstellung von Gegenständen in kleineren oder größeren Mengen organisiert werden müssen. In diesem Rahmen, in dem Aktualität eine unerlässliche Bedingung ist, sind Technologien weder universell noch dauerhaft anwendbar. Auch die Funktionen entwickeln sich ununterbrochen in einer fast biologischen und evolutionären Art und Weise. Als Designer muss man vor allem die aktuelle Realität verstehen. Dann muss man sich zwingen, den *einen* Schritt weiter zu gehen, um die unmittelbare Zukunft zu erforschen. Im Bewusstsein dieser Anforderungen versuchen wir, unserer Arbeit einen eigenständigen Charakter zu verleihen, immer mit Bedacht auf ihren zukünftigen Kontext; und natürlich ohne außer Acht zu lassen, dass die Nutzer dieser Objekte zahlreich und unterschiedlich sind. Aus diesem Grund sind wir auf der Suche nach einer Sprache, die subtil und doch selbstbewusst ist und bei der formale Forschung eine vorrangige Rolle spielt."

« Notre travail commence souvent par une rencontre avec un industriel, un artisan, une technique, un matériau, une machine ou un lieu. Le dialogue qui s'installe est comme un terreau dont naîtra le projet. Ainsi, notre travail est le plus souvent inscrit dans un contexte, intégrant une demande, une entreprise et un usage. Dans un certain sens, cette démarche s'apparente à un travail ‹in situ› tel qu'ont pu le définir certains artistes contemporains. Une résonance, à travers l'œuvre produite, du *lieu* précis dans lequel elle s'inscrit. Pour un projet de design, ce *lieu* est une société, avec son histoire, sa philosophie et son savoir-faire. Nous tentons d'intégrer ces données afin d'engager un travail commun qui dépasserait ce que chacun aurait pu faire individuellement. Le design semble être une fonction primaire dans la société humaine : concevoir des objets pour des usagers et des usages. Il s'agit concrètement d'organiser des matériaux et des méthodes de production pour réaliser ces objets en plus ou moins grand nombre. Dans le cadre de cette fonction où la contemporanéité est une donnée fondamentale, les technologies ne sont pas universelles, ni intemporelles. Et les fonctions évoluent sans cesse au sein de la société, de façon quasi génétique. Le designer doit d'abord comprendre la réalité présente et savoir s'en emparer pour rendre ses idées réalisables. Puis, il doit tenter d'aller *au-delà* pour questionner un futur proche et repousser les limites du réalisable. Avec la conscience de ces enjeux, nous tentons d'apporter un caractère fort à notre production, tout en respectant le contexte dans lequel elle va s'inscrire. Sans oublier que les consommateurs qui vont utiliser nos objets sont divers et multiples. C'est pourquoi nous cherchons un langage à la fois subtil et affirmé, dans lequel la recherche formelle a une importance capitale. »

"Our work frequently starts
with an encounter…"

1
ALGUE
Injection-moulded linking
plastic elements that form
web-like curtains or room
dividers
2004
Client: Vitra

2
ASSEMBLAGES
Collection of 5 furniture
pieces with varying finishes,
colours and dimensions
2004
Client: Galerie Kreo

3
STEELWOOD
Indoor/outdoor steel
and wood armchair
2007
Client: Magis

4
ASSEMBLAGES 5
Detail of 3-table assemblage
2004
Client: Galerie Kreo

2

3

4

**RONAN &
ERWAN BOUROULLEC**

ERB – Ronan &
Erwan Bouroullec
23, rue du Buisson Saint-Louis
75010 Paris
France
E info@bouroullec.com
www.bouroullec.com

BIOGRAPHY
RONAN BOUROULLEC

1971 Born in Quimper, France
1991 Industrial Design diploma,
École Nationale Supérieure des
Arts Appliqués et des Métiers,
Paris
1995 Post-graduate diploma,
École Nationale des Arts
Décoratifs, Paris
1995 Began working as a
freelance designer
1996 Taught at the École
Nationale des Beaux-Arts, Nancy
1997 Taught at the École
Nationale des Beaux-Arts, Saint-
Étienne
1999 Established design partnership with his brother, Erwan
2000 Taught at the École
Cantonale d'Art, Lausanne,
and at the École Nissim de
Camondo, Paris

BIOGRAPHY
ERWAN BOUROULLEC

1976 Born in Quimper, France
1999 Diploma, École Nationale
Supérieure d'Arts, Cergy-
Pontoise
1999 Established design partnership with his brother, Ronan

RECENT EXHIBITIONS

2002 "Ronan & Erwan
Bouroullec", Design Museum,
London
2003 "Ronan and Erwan
Bouroullec", Droog Design
Gallery, Amsterdam, The
Netherlands
2004 Solo exhibitions at
Museum of Contemporary Art,
Los Angeles, and the Boijmans
Museum of Art, Rotterdam
2005 "Ronan and Erwan
Bouroullec", Guest of Honor at

International Furniture Fair,
Mobitex, Brno, Czech Republic
2006 "Brothers and Sisters in
Art"; Haus der Kunst, Munich,
and Palais des Beaux-Arts,
Brussels
2007 "The Stitch Room",
installation in the collective
exhibition "MyHome", Vitra
Design Museum, Weil am
Rhein; "North Tiles in Paris",
Kavadrat showroom, Paris;
"Rocs in Buckminster Füller
Dome", Vitra Design Museum,
Weil am Rhein

RECENT AWARDS

2002 "Creator of the Year",
Salon du Meuble, Paris;
"Designer of the Year", Elle
Decoration Design awards,
London
2004 Best Domestic Design:

Outdoor category, Wallpaper
Design Awards
2005 Red Dot Award, Design
Zentrum Nordrhein-Westfalen,
Essen
2006 Honourable Mention in
"Best Restaurant" category,
Travel + Leisure Design Awards
competition; "Designer of the
Year", Elle Decoration Japan

CLIENTS

Cappellini, Galerie Kréo,
Issey Miyake, Kartell, Kvadrat,
Ligne Roset, Magis, Vitra

5

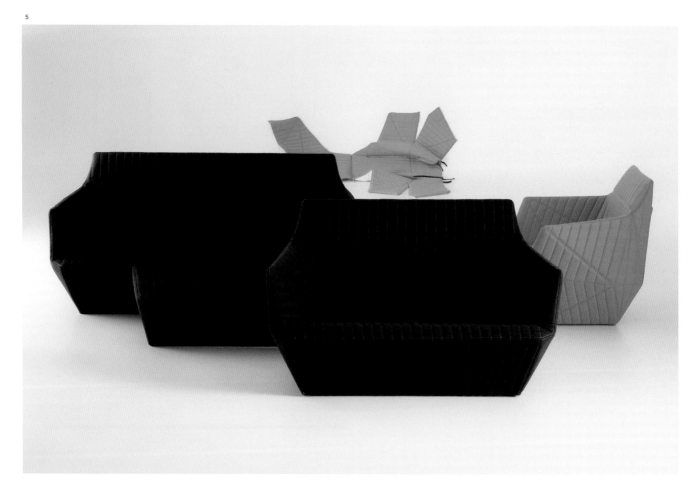

6

7

5
FACETT
Upholstered seating program
of armchair, medium and
large sofa and small and large
footstool with removable
quilted fabric covers
2005
Client: Ligne-Roset

6-7
NORTH TILES
Showroom design comprising
textile walls made of
independent tiles assembled
together via an innovative
folding system
2006
Client: Kvadrat

FERNANDO & HUMBERTO CAMPANA

"Estudio Campana started in 1983 and since its beginning has focused on the research of different kinds of materials, giving preciousness to poor, day-to-day or common materials, and caring not only about creativity in design, but also about expressing Brazilian characteristics. The constant pursuit of new possibilities for materials and things that were disregarded, transformed the studio into an investigative laboratory. Humberto: 'What motivates me is the passion I have for our work. I see what we do as a therapy, as a way of softening the hardness of life – there is no distinction between life and work.' Fernando: 'What motivates me is the ability to express myself, to materialize dreams and my perception of urban life. Another great inspiration is the fact that we have built a vocabulary of signs and fabricating processes without anyone else's influence except the wish to photograph our surroundings and environment, despite the very little tradition of design in Brazil. We are proud to have built and rescued elements of Brazilian culture that were left aside.'"

„Seit den Anfängen von Estudio Campana liegt der Fokus auf der Erforschung unterschiedlicher Werkstoffe. Dabei wollen wir vor allem schlichten oder gewöhnlichen Materialien Kostbarkeit verleihen und nicht nur den kreativen Aspekt von Design betonen, sondern auch brasilianische Besonderheiten zum Ausdruck bringen. Die permanente Suche nach neuen Einsatzmöglichkeiten von Materialien und Dingen, die nicht beachtet werden, hat das Atelier in ein Forschungslabor verwandelt. Dazu Humberto Campana: ‚Was mich motiviert, ist die Leidenschaft, die ich für unsere Arbeit empfinde. Für mich gibt es keine Trennung zwischen Leben und Arbeit.' Und Fernando Campana: ‚Was mich motiviert, ist die Fähigkeit, mich selbst auszudrücken, Träume und meine Vorstellungen von urbanem Leben zu realisieren. Eine weitere wichtige Inspiration ist die Tatsache, dass wir ein Vokabular an Zeichen und Fertigungsabläufen aufgebaut haben, ohne uns dabei von etwas oder jemand anderem beeinflussen zu lassen, nur bestimmt von dem Wunsch, unsere nähere und weitere Umgebung abzubilden, obwohl es kaum eine Designtradition in Brasilien gibt. Wir sind stolz darauf, dass wir achtlos beiseite geschobene Elemente brasilianischer Kultur aufgenommen und gerettet haben.'"

«Estudio Campana a démarré en 1983 et se concentre depuis ses débuts sur la recherche de différents types de matériaux en rendant précieux des matériaux pauvres, quotidiens, banals, en soignant à la fois la créativité et l'expression de caractéristiques purement brésiliennes. La quête constante du potentiel novateur de matériaux et d'objets jusqu'alors méprisés a transformé le studio en laboratoire d'investigation. Humberto : ‹Ce qui me motive, c'est la passion que j'éprouve pour notre travail. Je considère ce que nous faisons comme une thérapie, comme un moyen d'adoucir la dureté de la vie – il n'y a pas de distinction entre vie et travail. › Fernando : ‹Ce qui me motive, c'est la capacité de m'exprimer, de matérialiser des rêves et ma perception de la vie urbaine. Je m'inspire aussi beaucoup du vocabulaire des signes et des processus de fabrication que nous avons créés sans influence extérieure, dans le seul souci de photographier notre environnement et notre cadre de vie malgré la très courte histoire du design brésilien. Nous sommes fiers d'avoir construit et sauvé des éléments de la culture brésilienne qui étaient délaissés. ››»

1

1–3/6
UNA FAMIGLIA
Plastic and wicker triple seating
island
2006
Client: self-produced
(prototype)

1–3/6

UNA FAMIGLIA CHAIR
PROTOTYPE, 2006

The Una Famiglia triple seating island forms part of the Campana's TransPlastic series of chairs and multiple seat units, some of which are intended for serial production. These hybrid designs are meant as ironic comments on the disappearance of traditional outdoor furniture, and the unrelenting rise of the insidious modern plastic equivalent. The natural fibre used in the construction of TransPlastic is a parasitic vine that suffocates trees in northern Brazil, where it is harvested commercially by hand.

Die Dreier-Sitzinsel Una Famiglia entstammt der TransPlastic-Serie der Brüder Campana, die mehrere Sessel und multiple Sitzobjekte umfasst und in Serienproduktion gehen soll. Diese hybriden Entwürfe sind ein ironischer Kommentar zum Verschwinden des traditionellen Mobiliars für den Außenbereich, das unerbittlich von seinem heimtückischen modernen Äquivalent aus Kunststoff verdrängt wird. Hergestellt werden die TransPlastic-Objekte aus den Fasern einer im Norden Brasiliens beheimateten parasitischen Kletterpflanze, die ihren Wirtsbaum regelrecht stranguliert. Zur weiteren Verarbeitung wird sie manuell von den Bäumen geschnitten.

L'assise triple en îlot Una Famiglia fait partie de la collection de chaises et de sièges multiples TransPlastic de Campana, tous destinés à la fabrication en série. Ces créations hybrides sont envisagées comme des commentaires ironiques sur la disparition du mobilier extérieur traditionnel et l'ascension parallèle, implacable et insidieuse, de son équivalent moderne en plastique. La fibre naturelle utilisée pour la fabrication de TransPlastic est une plante grimpante parasite qui asphyxie les arbres dans le nord du Brésil, où elle est récoltée à la main.

3

"Our approach to design centers on revealing the richness of the poorness present in each and every culture we have contact with. We like to look to what everyone else has ignored, to what has not been caught in the glare of globalization."

4

4
BLACK IRON CHAIR
Handcrafted chair in
painted iron rods
2004
Client: self-produced
(limited edition of 20)

5
ROCK BENCH
Handcrafted seating unit
in painted iron rods
2004
Client: self-produced
(one-off)

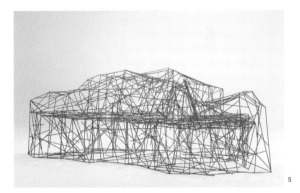

5

6

**FERNANDO &
HUMBERTO CAMPANA**
São Paulo
Brazil
E campana@
campanadesign.com.br
www.campanas.com.br

BIOGRAPHY
FERNANDO CAMPANA

1961 Born in São Paulo, Brazil
1979–1984 BA Architecture, Faculdade de Belas Artes de São Paulo
1983 Instructor – Industrial Design course, XVII Bienal Internacional des Arts de São Paulo
1998 Teacher – Industrial Design course, FAAP (Fundação Armando Alvares Penteado), São Paulo
1999–2000 Teacher, MUBE (Museu Brasileiro de Escultura), São Paulo

BIOGRAPHY
HUMBERTO CAMPANA

1953 Born in São Paulo, Brazil
1972–1977 BA Law, Universidade de São Paulo
1998 Teacher – Industrial Design course, FAAP (Fundação Armando Alvares Penteado), São Paulo

1999–2000 Teacher, MUBE (Museu Brasileiro de Escultura), São Paulo

RECENT EXHIBITIONS

2002 "Never Letting the Poetry Escape", Tel Aviv Museum of Art (TAMA), Tel Aviv
2003 "Campanas", Centro Cultural Banco do Brasil, Brasília; "Campanas", Firma Casa, São Paulo; "Campanas", Lisbon, Portugal; "Campanas Exhibition for Experimental Design", Lisbon, Portugal; "Campanas", Stockholm
2004 "Ideal House", imm cologne 2004, Cologne; "Zest for Life", Design Museum, London; "Tank", Design Museum, London; "Zest For Life", Danish Design Centre, Copenhagen
2005 "Campane di Campana", Moss Gallery, New York; "Campana Brothers", Brazilian Embassy, Tokyo; "Big Bang – Déstruction et Création dans l'art du XXème siècle", Centre George Pompidou, Paris; "100 faces 100 projects", Abitare il Tempo, Bologna
2006 "Il mondo Italiano", Museum Modern Arts Montreal, Toronto, and Museum Mart, Rovereto; "Design, vous avez-dit Design TM?", Lausanne; "Le mouvement des Images", Centre Georges Pompidou, Paris
2007 "TransPlastic", Albion Gallery, London; "Garden Summer Project", Victoria and Albert Museum, London; "My Home", Vitra Design Museum, Weil am Rhein

RECENT AWARDS

2001 Special Prize Award, Museu da Casa Brasileira, São Paulo
2005 Le Prix du Nombre d'Or, Salon du Meuble de Paris; Dim Award – First Prize, Valencia International Furniture Fair; Top of Mind Brazil 2005 Award - design production category, INBRAP (Instituto Brasileiro de Pesquisa de Opinião Pública e Informações Comercials)
2006 Prêmio Top 3 (one of the best three websites in Brazil) – Category iBest Excellence in Design, Academia iBest & Design, Brazil; Award of Excellence – Self-Promotion category (for the website www.campanas.com.br, designed by F/Nazca – Saatchi & Saatchi), 12th Annual Interactive Exhibition, Communications Arts magazine

CLIENTS

Acme, Alessi, Artecnica, Camper, Edra, Fontana Arte, Grendene, Habitart, Magis, Moss Gallery, Museum of Modern Art/New York, Oluce, Teracrea, Venini SPA

7

8

7/9
KAIMAN JACARÈ
Frameless upholstered
seating unit made of several
irregularly shaped elements
2006
Client: Edra

8/10
ASTER PAPPOSUS
Frameless upholstered seating
unit made of two similar
elements placed one on top
of the other
2006
Client: Edra

9

10

CLAESSON KOIVISTO RUNE

"From time to time we've been asked whether we have a philosophy – or a set of rules under which we work. Maybe, possibly, likely – when looking at our work from outside there is some sort of clear line that reads through our projects from the beginning till now...a recognisable design DNA. That's fine. After all we're human beings and if our 'brain children' bear similarities that's to be expected. We all have our individual backgrounds, views and skills that will inevitably influence our work. However, as we see it – from inside – our work is without any clear direction. The only things that are important are to develop, to improve and never to repeat."

„Von Zeit zu Zeit werden wir gefragt, ob wir eine Philosophie haben – oder ein Regelwerk, nach dem wir arbeiten. Vielleicht, möglicherweise, wahrscheinlich – wenn man unsere Arbeit von außen betrachtet, gibt es eine Art Leitlinie, die sich vom Anfang bis heute durch unsere Projekte zieht ... eine wiedererkennbare DNA des Designs. Das ist gut so. Schließlich sind wir menschliche Wesen, und wenn unsere Geistesprodukte untereinander Ähnlichkeiten aufweisen, ist das nicht verwunderlich. Wir alle haben unsere individuellen Hintergründe, Ansichten und Fertigkeiten, die zwangsläufig unsere Tätigkeit beeinflussen. So wie wir es jedoch sehen – nämlich von innen – hat unsere Arbeit keine klare Richtung. Das Einzige, was wirklich wichtig ist: dass man entwickelt, verbessert und sich niemals wiederholt."

«Nous avons été interrogés de temps à autre sur notre éventuelle philosophie – un éventail de règles selon lequel nous travaillerions. Peut-être, possible, probable – lorsqu'on regarde notre travail de l'extérieur, il y a bien une sorte de fil rouge qui parcourt nos projets depuis le début... Une empreinte stylistique aussi reconnaissable qu'un code génétique. Tant mieux. Après tout nous sommes des être humains et il n'est pas si étonnant que nos ‹enfants intellectuels› aient un air de famille. Nous avons tous un passé, des opinions et des talents qui influent immanquablement sur notre travail. Pourtant, de la manière dont nous le percevons – de l'intérieur – notre travail n'a pas de direction précise. La seule chose qui compte est de concevoir, d'améliorer et de ne jamais se répéter. »

1

2

LUNA FOR DUNE, 2005

With Luna, Claesson Koivisto Rune set out to explore the idea of a design as both architecture and furniture – scale and space. What they created can be seen as essentially a sofa – meaning it is constructed like a sofa with a sturdy plywood box frame, padded and upholstered with furniture fabric. Backrests have become walls that curve up from the seat forming a roof in one continuous volume. The dimensions are 5x6 metres, creating a floor area of about 30 m². In the seat and roof, crater-like holes provide places to put your feet and to suspend objects like a pendant lamp or a flat-screen. These voids also break up Luna's volume. The aesthetic is intended to evoke images of the moon's surface and lunar landing modules.

Mit Luna lotet die Designpartnerschaft Claesson Koivisto Rune das Wesen eines Designobjekts als architektonischen Einrichtungsgegenstand – als Dimension und Raum – aus. Ihr futuristisches Objekt kann im Prinzip als Sofa betrachtet werden. Was bedeutet, dass es einen stabilen Schichtholz-Rahmen hat, gepolstert und mit Möbelstoff bezogen ist. Aus den Rückenlehnen wurden allerdings Wände, die sich von der Sitzfläche nach außen wölben und zu einem Dach zusammenwachsen, sodass Luna eigentlich als „selbstständiges Einrichtungsumfeld" mit zirka 30 qm Grundfläche bezeichnet werden sollte. Kraterartige Öffnungen in Boden und Dach geben Räume frei, in die man die Füße stellen und Objekte wie eine Hängelampe oder einen Flatscreen hängen kann. Diese Öffnungen brechen auch die monumentale Einheit von Luna auf. Das ästhetische Konzept soll Bilder von der Mondoberfläche und von Mondlandekapseln evozieren.

Avec Luna, Claesson Koivisto Rune a tenté d'explorer l'idée d'un design qui serait à la fois architecture et meuble – échelle et espace. Ce qu'ils ont créé peut être considéré basiquement comme un canapé, dans le sens où il est construit comme un canapé, avec un coffrage et un cadre en contreplaqué robuste, rembourré et recouvert de tissus d'ameublement. Le dossier est devenu un mur qui s'incurve depuis l'assise pour former une voûte d'un seul tenant. Ses dimensions sont de 5 mètres sur 6 et créent donc une surface au sol de près de 30 m². Dans l'assise et la voûte, des trous semblables à des cratères fournissent des endroits où caler ses pieds et suspendre des objets comme une lampe, ou un écran plat. Ces creux brisent aussi le volume de Luna. Son esthétique veut évoquer les images de la surface de la Lune et de ses modules d'alunissage.

"Can a house be more than a series of rooms?
Or a chair more than a support for sitting?
Our search for this 'more' ingredient, in every project we do,
is at the very heart of our work."

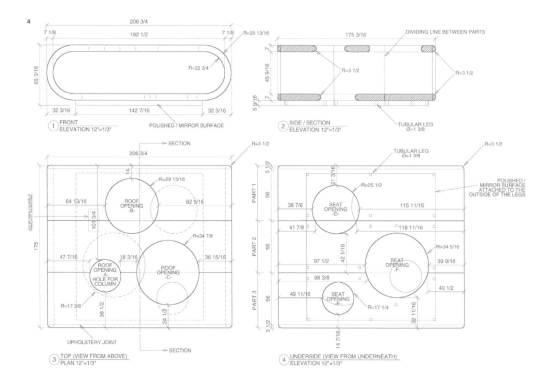

5

1–4
LUNA
Upholstered seating
environment
2005
Client: Dune

5
ALADDIN
Lounge chair with thick
pressed felt seat and back
2006
Client: Paola Lenti

6
WALL
Wall light in sheet metal
with compact fluorescent or
metal halogen lamp
2006
Client: Fagerhult

7
WALL
Wall light in sheet metal with
compact fluorescent or metal
halogen lamp
2006
Client: Fagerhult

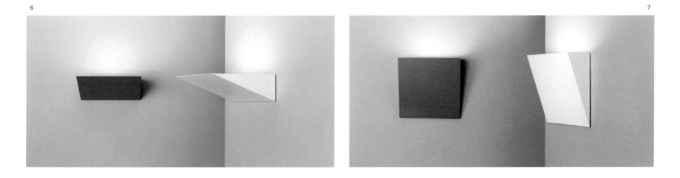

6

7

CLAESSON KOIVISTO RUNE

Claesson Koivisto Rune
Arkitektkontor AB
Östgötagatan 50
11664 Stockholm
Sweden
T +46 8 6445863
E all@ckr.se
www.claesson-koivisto-rune.se

DESIGN GROUP HISTORY

1995 Founded by Mårten Claesson, Eero Koivisto and Ola Rune in Stockholm initially as an architecture design partnership

FOUNDERS' BIOGRAPHIES
MÅRTEN CLAESSON

1970 Born in Lidingö, Sweden
1988 Studied Construction Engineering at Vasa Technical College, Stockholm
1992 Studied Product Design and Architecture, Parsons School of Design, New York
1994 MFA, Konstfack (University College of Arts, Crafts and Design), Stockholm

EERO KOIVISTO

1958 Born in Karlstad, Sweden
1990 Studied at the Stockholm School of Arts

1992 Studied Product Design and Architecture, Parsons School of Design, New York
1993 Studied Architecture and Furniture Design, UIAH – University of Art & Design, Helsinki
1994 MFA, Konstfack (University College of Arts, Crafts and Design), Stockholm
1995 Studied Design Leadership, UIAH – University of Art & Design, Helsinki

OLA RUNE

1963 Born in Lycksele, Sweden
1987 Studied at Stockholm Cutters Academy
1990 Studied at Southwark College of Art & Design, London
1992 Studied Interior and Furniture Design at the Royal Academy of Art, Copenhagen

1994 MFA, Konstfack (University College of Arts, Crafts and Design), Stockholm

RECENT EXHIBITIONS

2002 "Mårten Claesson Eero Koivisto Ola Rune Furniture Design", Totem Tribeca, New York
2003 "Nine Houses", Sfera Exhibition, Kyoto
2005 "Claesson Koivisto Rune – The Models", Röhsska Design Museum, Gothenburg
2006 "Claesson Koivisto Rune", Asplund, Stockholm

RECENT AWARDS

2002 Utmärkt Svensk Form (Excellent Swedish Design) award; Best Interior Object award, Forum Magazine
2004 The Catas Award; Silver Award, Sweden's Top

Interior Design, Forum Magazine
2005 +1 Award for Best Interior Object, Forum Magazine
2006 Chair Design Prize, Elle Deco International Design Awards

CLIENTS

Almedahls, Arflex Japan, Asplund, Boffi, Cappellini, David design, De Vecchi, Dune, E & Y, Fagerhult, Franc franc, Gebrüder Thonet Vienna, Iren Uffici, Italamp, Living, Divani, Lucente, Modus, Muuto, Märta Måås Fjetterström, Nola, Offecct, Örsjö, Paola Lenti, Sedie Friuli di Fornasarig, Sfera, Products, Skandiform, Skruf, Swedese, Väveriet

8

8
GHOST
Cold foam upholstered sofa with Nozag spring system
2006
Client: Offecct

9
SPOOL
Floor light with methacrylate filter in either red, green or blue
2005
Client: Lucente

10
SEESAW
Rocking salt and pepper shakers
2005
Client: De Vecchi

11
ALLROUND
Side chair with beech frame and polyurethane foam upholstery
2005
Client: Sedie Friuli di Fornasarig

9

10

11

KENNETH COBONPUE

"Creating beautiful objects born from a fusion of technology and craft is constant in all my designs. All my works attempt to mix modern manufacturing processes with local techniques while bringing nature indoors. As human beings, we were created to live harmoniously with nature. Everything about my designs reflects nature. A lot of my early work has a transparent characteristic to it because you get that same feeling when you look through the foliage of leaves or a cluster of trees. My designs are created by human hand, not by machine. The materials I use are natural and warm – the forms intentionally organic. Cebu and the surrounding islands provide the inspiration and resources to transform my designs into objects of beauty."

„Die Konstante in allen meinen Designs ist das Herstellen schöner Objekte, die aus der Verbindung von Technologie und Handwerk hervorgehen. Durch alle meine Arbeiten zieht sich der Versuch, moderne Fertigungsverfahren mit lokalen Techniken zu kombinieren. Meine Designs bringen die Natur ins Haus. Als Menschen wurden wir dazu erschaffen, in Harmonie mit der Natur zu leben. Alles an meinen Designs gibt die Natur wieder. Viele meiner frühen Arbeiten zeichnen sich durch Transparenz aus, denn das ist es, was man empfindet, wenn man durch Blattwerk oder eine Baumgruppe blickt. Meine Designarbeiten werden von Menschen, nicht von Maschinen hergestellt. Ich verwende natürliche, warme Werkstoffe und organische Formen. Die Ressourcen und die Inspiration, die ich brauche, um meine Designarbeiten zu schönen Objekten zu machen, beziehe ich von Cebu und den Inseln der Umgebung."

«La volonté de créer de beaux objets nés d'une fusion entre technologie et artisanat est constante dans mon travail. Toutes mes créations tentent de mélanger processus de fabrication modernes et techniques locales. Mes créations apportent la nature à l'intérieur. En tant qu'êtres humains, nous avons été créés pour vivre en harmonie avec la nature. Tout dans mes créations reflète la nature. Une grande partie de mon travail des débuts joue sur la transparence, pour répéter l'impression que l'on a lorsqu'on regarde à travers le feuillage d'un arbre ou d'une haie. Mes créations sont l'œuvre de la main humaine et non d'une machine. Mes matériaux sont naturels et chauds. Mes formes sont organiques. Cebu et les îles environnantes me procurent les ressources et l'inspiration pour faire de mes créations des objets de beauté.»

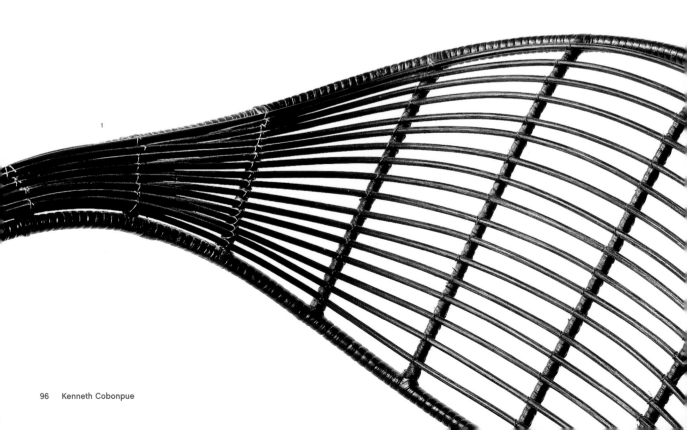

1

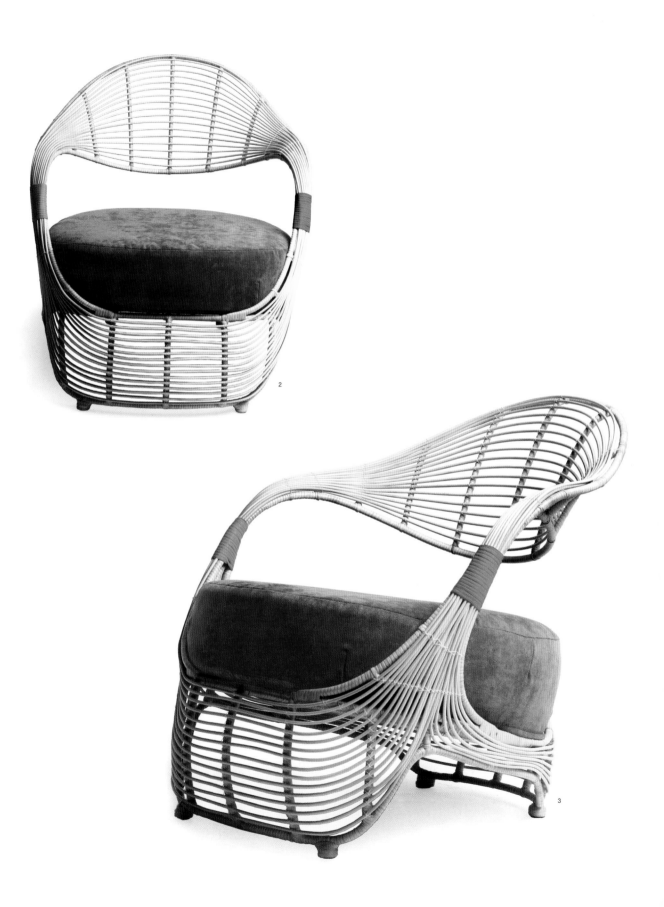

2

3

MANOLO ARMCHAIR, 2006

Inspired by a lady's sandal, the Manolo series of furniture is made of fine natural or stained rattan vines woven over frames of mild steel, then bound with leather strips. The Manolo armchair, club chair, sofa and table are also available as outdoor versions in polyethylene and steel.

Die einer Damensandale nachempfundene Manolo-Serie ist aus dünnen naturbelassenen oder gebeizten Rattanstangen gefertigt. Sie bilden von einem Rahmen aus Schmiedestahl ausgehend ein Geflecht, das mit Lederstreifen zusammengehalten wird. Die Lehnstühle, Klubsessel, Sofas und Tische aus der Manolo-Serie sind in einer Variante aus Polyethylen und Stahl auch für den Außenbereich erhältlich.

Inspirée par un escarpin féminin, la collection de meubles Manolo est constituée de fines tiges de rotin naturel ou teinté, entrelacées sur une structure légère en acier puis attachées avec des liens en cuir. Le fauteuil, le fauteuil club, le canapé et la table Manolo existent aussi pour l'extérieur, en version polyéthylène et acier.

1–3
MANOLO
Easy armchair in fine natural or stained rattan vines
2006
Client: Interior Crafts of the Islands

4

"From the start I was seeking a fresh sensibility to embrace and develop with regard to design. I didn't find it in Milan, or in New York… I found it closer to home, in the tropical island of Cebu."

5

6

7

4
YODA
Sofa section in natural or
stained rattan vines
2006
Client: Interior Crafts
of the Islands

5–7
LOLAH
Sofa and armchair constructed
of rattan poles, detail of
assembly process, detail of
construction
2004
Client: Interior Crafts
of the Islands

KENNETH COBONPUE

3-A General Maxilom Avenue
Cebu City 6000
Cebu
The Philippines
T +63 32 2334045
E info@kennethcobonpue.com
www.kennethcobonpue.com

BIOGRAPHY

1968 Born in Cebu City, The Philippines
1985–1987 MBA – Marketing, University of the Philippines, Diliman, QC
1988–1991 BA Industrial Design, Pratt Institute, New York
1990 Apprenticed at Centro Azur (a leather and wood workshop) in Florence, Italy
1994–1996 Studied Furniture Marketing and Production at the Export Akademie Baden-Württemberg in Reutlingen, Germany
1995 Apprentice in woodworking and cabinetmaking, Firma Decker & Reposa, Germany
1996 Basic Woodworking Machine Course, Holz-Berufsgenossenschaft, Munich
1996 Apprentice in woodworking and upholstery factory Schreinerei, Munich
1996+ Returned to the Philippines to manage Interior Crafts of the Islands, Inc., a furniture design and manufacturing company founded in 1972 by Kenneth's mother Betty Cobonpue, a designer famous for creating new techniques in working with rattan
2001+ Director, Kenneth Cobonpue USA, Washington DC

RECENT EXHIBITIONS

2003–2004 "Life Symphony", Felissimo Design House, New York City, USA
2004 "Design 21 – Why the World Needs Love", travelling exhibition organized by UNESCO and Felissimo Barcelona (Part of Forum Barcelona 2004) – Barcelona, Kobe, Tokyo, New York and Paris
2004–2005 "Kenneth Cobonpue: Idea + Form + Craft", Material Connexion Gallery, New York

RECENT AWARDS

2003 3 x Good Design Awards, JIDPO (Japan Industrial Design Promotion Organization); Ten Outstanding Young Men of the Philippines award
2004 4 x Good Design Awards, JIDPO (Japan Industrial Design Promotion Organization); Perlas Award for Outstanding Cebuano; First Prize winner, Open Design Category, Singapore International Furniture Design Competition
2005 Design for Asia Award, Hong Kong; 2 x Design Excellence Awards, 9th Annual IIDA/Hospitality Design Product Competition; Outstanding Design Prize, 2005 High Point Show, NC

CLIENTS

Interior Crafts of the Islands

8

10

8–10
YODA
Easy chair in natural or stained
rattan vines, detail of material,
details of assembly process
2006
Client: Interior Crafts of the
Islands

CONTINUUM

"At its core, design is a promise between a brand and a person. Understanding the expectations from these encounters and exceeding them is how brands succeed. Identifying the right idea to deliver these encounters is what we do. We strive to define the wants, needs and aspirations of consumers, as well as the context of use – the habits and habitats of the experience. Much of our energy is spent understanding the desired user experience and defining the attributes of that encounter. We marry these real-world insights with business opportunities to ground our design solutions. In the end, it's always about people. Understanding what makes people tick. Revelling in capturing the human beat... constantly growing and challenging... using our learnings to create desire. Great design moves."

„Design ist im Kern das Versprechen einer Marke an einen Menschen. Zu verstehen, welche Erwartungen sich aus solchen Begegnungen ergeben, und sie zu übertreffen, macht den Erfolg von Marken aus. Unsere Aufgabe ist es, die richtige Idee zu finden, die diese Begegnungen vermitteln kann. Es ist uns ein Anliegen, die Ansprüche, Bedürfnisse und Sehnsüchte der Konsumenten genauso wie den Kontext der Verwendung zu definieren – die Gewohnheiten und die Lebensräume, in denen die Erfahrung stattfindet. Wir wenden viel Energie auf, um uns die gewünschte Erfahrung des Konsumenten bei der Verwendung vorzustellen und die Eigenschaften dieser Begegnung zu definieren. Diese faktischen Erkenntnisse bilden in Kombination mit den Geschäftsmöglichkeiten eine fundierte Basis für unsere Designlösungen. Letztendlich geht es dabei immer um Menschen. Darum zu verstehen, was sie bewegt, Freude daran zu haben, ihren Herzschlag einzufangen ..., sich dabei ständig weiterzuentwickeln und alles infrage zu stellen ..., unsere Erfahrungen einzusetzen, um Verlangen zu wecken. Großes Design bewegt."

«Fondamentalement, le design est une promesse scellée entre une marque et une personne. C'est en comprenant les attentes qui résultent de ces engagements et en les dépassant que les marques réussissent. Ce que nous faisons, c'est identifier l'idée qui rendra compte avec justesse de cette rencontre. Nous nous efforçons de définir les besoins, les désirs et les aspirations des consommateurs ainsi que le contexte dans lequel ils s'inscrivent – les habitudes et habitats. Nous consacrons une grande partie de notre énergie à comprendre l'expérience de l'usager que nous ciblons et à définir les conditions de la rencontre. Nous construisons nos solutions design sur le mariage entre ces aperçus du monde réel et des opportunités commerciales. En fin de compte, il s'agit toujours de personnes. Comprendre ce qui fait tiquer les gens. Se plaire à capturer le pouls humain... défi perpétuellement croissant... Utiliser notre savoir pour créer le désir. Le bon design émeut.»

zarafina

1–3
LUXE TEA SERVICE
Tea making suite that regulates and maintains ideal brewing conditions for different types of tea
2004
Client: Zarafina

2

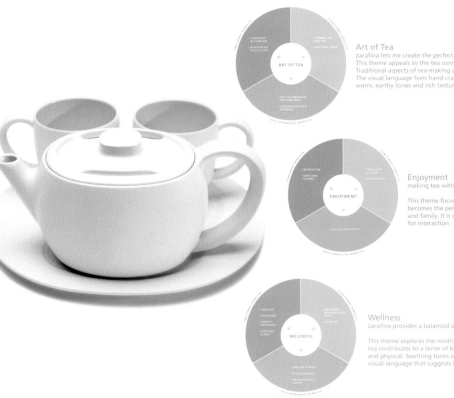

Art of Tea
zarafina lets me create the perfect cup
This theme appeals to the tea connoisseur.
Traditional aspects of tea-making are emphasized.
The visual language feels hand-crafted and features
warm, earthy tones and rich textures.

Enjoyment
making tea with zarafina is fun and easy

This theme focuses on the social aspects of tea. Tea
becomes the perfect means to connect with friends
and family. It is colorful and casual – the perfect catalyst
for interaction.

Wellness
zarafina provides a balanced and healthful lifestyle

This theme explores the meditative aspects of tea –
tea contributes to a sense of balance, both mental
and physical. Soothing tones and natural imagery build a
visual language that suggests harmony and well being.

3

CONTINUUM

1220 Washington Street
West Newton
Massachusetts 02465
USA
T +617 9695400
E info@dcontinuum.com
www.dcontinuum.com

FOUNDER'S BIOGRAPHY
GIANFRANCO ZACCAI

1947 Born in Trieste, Italy
1965–1970 Studied Industrial Design at Syracuse University
1975–1978 Studied architecture at Boston Architectural College
2000 Recognized as a Distinguished Scholar by Syracuse University
Present+ An associate of numerous organizations, institutions and associations including: Industrial Designers Society of America (IDSA); Associazione di Disegno Industriale (ADI); Chairman of the Board, the Design Management Institute (DMI); Board Member & Treasurer, the International Council of Societies of Industrial Design

DESIGN GROUP HISTORY

1983 Founded by Gianfranco Zaccai in Boston
1986 Established sister agency, Continuum Italia in Milan
2000 Established sister agency, Continuum Korea in Seoul

(ICSID); Emeritus Board Member of the International Design Conference in Aspen (IDCA); Board of Advisors to the College of Visual and Performing Arts at Syracuse University and Society of Concurrent Engineers (SOCE); Honorary member of the Australian Academy of Design Board of Directors, The Italy/America Chamber of Commerce and Trade of New England; Board of Governors, The Dante Alighieri Society of Boston

RECENT EXHIBITIONS

2006 "Guangzhou Design Week", China
2007 "Design for the Other 90 %", Cooper Hewitt, New York; "Substance: Diverse Practices from the Periphery", Emmanuel Gallery, Denver

RECENT AWARDS

2005 Top Design of the Year, Grandesign, Italy; Bronze Award, Hatch Awards, The Ad

Club; Merit Award, HOW International Design Competition; Design Distinction winner, Annual Design Review, I.D. Magazine; 3 x Gold, 1 x Silver and 1 x Bronze Awards – IDEA (Industrial Design Excellence Awards), Industrial Designers Society of America/Business Week; 2 x Medical Design Excellence Awards (MDEA), MD&DI (Medical Device & Diagnostic Industry) magazine; International Best of Show, National Paperbox Association's Packaging Competition
2006 Special Merit, Exhibitor Magazine 21st Annual Exhibit Design Awards; Best of Show Award, CES Consumer Electronics, Las Vegas; 4 x Good Design Awards, Chicago Athenaeum; Gold and Silver Awards – IDEA (Industrial Design Excellence Awards), Industrial Designers Society of America/BusinessWeek; Design Distinction Award in Concept category, Annual Design

Review, I.D. Magazine; Medical Design Excellence Award (MDEA), MD&DI (Medical Device & Diagnostic Industry) magazine
2007 Finalist, Design to Improve Life Award, INDEX awards, Copenhagen; Best of Show Award, CES Consumer Electronics, Las Vegas; Special Merit Award, 21st Annual Exhibit Design Awards, Exhibitor Magazine

CLIENTS

American Express, BMW, Boston Medical Technologies, Fluidsense, HTS Biosystems, Johnson Controls, Legrand, LL Bean, Logitech, Master Lock, Mija Industries, Moen Numark Industries, Oster, Photovac, Polaroid, Procter & Gamble, Reebok, Samsung, Sprint, Sunbeam (Zarafina), Target, Zeiss

4

4–5
ELECTRIC WIRING DEVICES
Switch, remote control,
socket and dimmer system
that simplifies user interface
2004
Client: Legrand

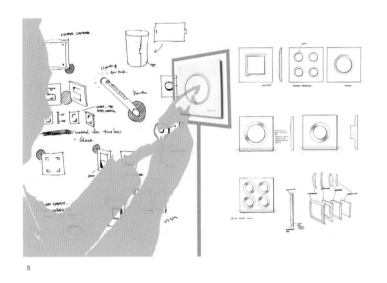

5

"We believe that design
creates a relationship.
The point of contact:
an experience."

6
CENTURION BLACK CARD
Credit card made of titanium
and luxury packaging for
exclusive card member base
2004
Client: American Express

6

MATALI CRASSET

"I'm an industrial designer by training. This is the viewpoint from which I appraise a project and I find the discipline a huge inspiration. I called the exhibition at the mu.dac 'A Sidestep' and I think this totally sums up my philosophy. It's perhaps why I'm fascinated by the new typology in the world of furniture. My present work involves exploring very varied fields, from video clips to graphic charters, collaborating with an artist on a DVD or with a hotel for a dinner service... I approach my work as a series of mental reflections open to the world. I often say I've got fields in my head and I'm cultivating them. I don't have any dream products; my clients' dreams are my incentive."

„Ich bin ausgebildeter Industriedesigner. Bei der Bewertung von Projekten lasse ich mich von dieser Perspektive leiten, und ich finde dabei auch viel Inspiration. Ich habe die Ausstellung im mu.dac ‚Ein Seitenschritt' genannt, und ich finde, das fasst meine Philosophie sehr schön zusammen. Das ist vielleicht der Grund, warum mich die neuen Typologien im Möbeldesign faszinieren. In meiner aktuellen Arbeit wage ich mich in sehr unterschiedliche Bereiche vor, von Videoclips bis hin zu Grafikrichtlinien, von der Entwicklung einer CD in Zusammenarbeit mit einem Künstler oder eines Dinner-Service gemeinsam mit einem Hotel ... Ich betrachte meine Arbeit als einen für alle Welt sichtbaren Reflexionsprozess. Ich behaupte oft, ich hätte Felder im Kopf, die ich bestelle. Ich mache keine Traumprodukte; die Träume meiner Kunden sind meine Motivation."

«Je suis designer industriel de formation. C'est à partir de cet angle de vue, que je réfléchis aux projets qui me sont proposés. la contrainte est ainsi pour moi un fantastique moteur. J'avais appelé l'exposition au mu.dac ‹Un pas de côté› et je pense qu'elle résume assez ma philosophie. C'est peut-être pourquoi je m'intéresse aux nouvelles typologies dans l'univers du mobilier. Mon travail actuel interroge des domaines très variés, de la réalisation d'un clip vidéo à la définition d'une charte graphique, d'une collaboration avec un artiste à un DVD, d'un hôtel à un service de table… Je pense mon travail comme une réflexion ouverte sur le monde. Je dis souvent que j'ai des champs dans la tête et que je les cultive. Je n'ai pas de *dream products*, mon moteur c'est le rêve de mes clients.»

1   2

1
tRANSPLANT ≠ 06
Blown glass vessel with silvered
glass flower elements
2007
Client: Gallery Luisa delle Piane
& Galerie Jacques Dewindt
(limited edition of 20)

2
tRANSPLANT ≠ 02
Blown glass vessel with glass rod
flower elements
2007
Client: Gallery Luisa delle Piane
& Galerie Jacques Dewindt
(limited edition of 20)

3
tRANSPLANT ≠ 01
Blown glass vessel with silvered
glass rod stem elements
2007
Gallery Luisa delle Piane &
Galerie Jacques Dewindt (limited edition of 20)

4
tRANSPLANT
Display of 7 blown glass vessel
variations at the tRANSPLANT
premiere exhibition, Gallery
Luisa delle Piane & Galerie
Jacques Dewindt
2007

1–4
tRANSPLANT SERIES FOR
GALLERIA LUISA DELLE
PIANE, MILAN, 2007

The beautiful and poetic
tRANSPLANT series is an
expression of Matali Crasset's
interest in vegetal forms and
the qualities of structural transparency and clarity. Made of
blown borosilicate glass, each
of the seven models shares
roughly the same base, stem and
structure, while the geometric
flower elements vary in shape
from round, conical to linear.
The tRANSPLANT series is
produced in a limited edition
of 20 examples per model.

In der ansprechenden, poetischen Serie tRANSPLANT
kommt Matali Crassets Interesse
an floralen Formen sowie struktureller Klarheit und Transparenz zum Ausdruck. Alle sieben
aus mundgeblasenem Borosili-
katglas hergestellten Modelle
sind, was den Boden, den
Stamm und die Struktur betrifft, praktisch gleich, ihre
geometrischen Blumenelemente
haben jedoch unterschiedliche
Formen von rund bis konisch
oder linear. Die tRANSPLANT-
Serie wird in einer limitierten
Auflage von 20 Musterstücken
je Modell produziert.

La collection tRANSPLANT,
belle et poétique, est une expression de l'intérêt que porte Matali
Crasset aux formes végétales,
aux qualités de clarté et de transparence de leurs structures.
Constitués de verre de borosilicate soufflé, les sept modèles ont
sensiblement la même base, la
même face postérieure et la
même structure, tandis que la
forme géométrique des éléments
floraux varie du rond au conique
ou au linéaire. La collection
tRANSPLANT est produite en
édition limitée de 20 exemplaires
par modèle.

"Hospitality, generosity, empathy, technology."

5

6

5
ORANGINA LE VERRE
Blown borosilicate glass
drinking vessel
2006
Client: Orangina/Creative
Agent Consultant

6/7
SOUNDSCAPES
General views of Matali Crasset's
solo exhibition at the Cooper
Hewitt National Museum of
Design, New York
2006

7

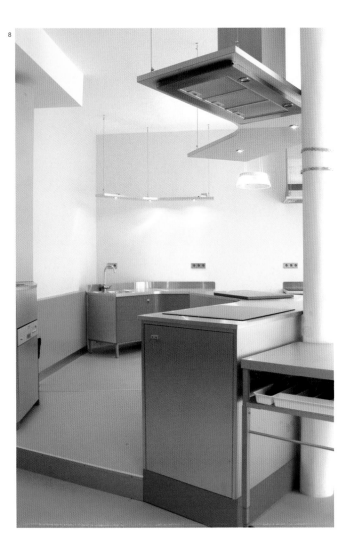

8

9

8/10
CUISINE FRAICH' ATTITUDE
Workshop kitchen interior
2006
Client: Aprifel

9
DÉ(S)LICIEUX
Dessert knife and cake
slice designed for the pâtissier
Pierre Hermé
2007
Client: Forge de Laguiole

MATALI CRASSET

matali crasset productions
26, rue du Buisson Saint-Louis
75010 Paris
France
T +33 1 42409989
E matali.crasset@wanadoo.fr
www.matalicrasset.com

BIOGRAPHY

1965 Born in Châlons-en-Champagne, France
1991 Graduated from Les Ateliers, École Nationale Supérieure de Création Industrielle, Paris, and moved to Milan to work with the designer Denis Santachiara
1993 Returned to Paris and worked in and headed Philippe Starck's design studio prior to working for Thomson Multimedia consumer electronics group
1998 Founded matali crasset productions in Paris

RECENT EXHIBITIONS

2002–2003 Travelling retrospective exhibition – mu.dac (Lausanne), Victoria and Albert Museum (London) and Le Grand Hornu (Belgium)
2004 Solo exhibition, 1st Architectural Biennial, Beijing
2006 "Soundscapes" (solo exhibition), Cooper Hewitt National Design Museum, New York; "Springtherapy"(solo exhibition), SM's, s'Hertogenbosch
2007 tRANSPLANT, Galleria Luisa delle Piane, Milan; "A rebours" (with Peter Halley), galerie Thaddaeus Ropac, Paris

RECENT AWARDS

2000 Étoile de l'Observeur du design 2000, Paris
2002 Baden-Württemberg International Design award
2003 Prix du Nombre d'Or, Salon du Meuble de Paris; ISH award
2004 "International Interior designer of the year", BIDA British Interior design awards, London
2006 Prix du créateur de l'année, Salon du Meuble de Paris; Labels VIA 2006 award, VIA, Paris

CLIENTS

Aprifel/Interfel, Aquamass, Artemide, BHV, Comité Colbert, Cosmit, Cristal Saint Louis, Danese, Decotec, Deknudt Decora, De Vecchi, Domeau & Pérès, Domestic, Domodinamica, Dornbracht, Drugstore Publicis, Dune, Enkidoo, Erreti, Exquise, Fabrica, Felice Rossi, Forges de Laguiole, Grimaldi Forum, Guy Degrenne, Hermès, Hi hotel, Laser, Le Printemps, Lexon, L'Oréal, Orangina, Pierre Hermé, Pitti Immagine, Première Vision Le salon, Restaurant Hélène Darroze, San Lorenzo, Seb/Tefal, Sodebo, Swarosvki, Tarkett Bâtiment, Tendence, Top Mouton, Thomson Multimédia, Who's next…

DEEPDESIGN

"Nature expresses perfection in its forms and processes, which can be at once both very simple and extremely complex. An orange section or a peapod have a structural geometry that upon close examination is captivating. The meeting between formal organicism and functional complexity in nature is spontaneous and perfect, without compromise and simple redundancy, and leads to pure economy of form. When we design we always try to give our best with great discipline and focus our concerns on the solution's relationship with culture. The culture we aspire to lies not only in material and technological expression, but especially also in the conceptual – the transmission of ideas. We consciously imbue our work with cultural meaning. But we are also fascinated by identifying the extraordinary in things that appear to be obvious. Just as in nature, sometimes we only need to accentuate the exceptional."

„Die Natur drückt in ihren Formen und Vorgängen eine Perfektion aus, die zugleich sehr einfach und extrem komplex sein kann. Bei näherer Betrachtung erweist sich die strukturelle Geometrie einer Orangenscheibe oder einer Erbsenschote als bestechend. In der Natur ist das Zusammentreffen von formalem Organismus und funktionaler Komplexität spontan und perfekt, ohne Kompromisse und bloße Redundanz, und führt zur reinen Ökonomie der Form. Wir versuchen, bei unserer Arbeit immer unser Bestes zu geben und sehr diszipliniert vorzugehen. Unser wichtigstes Anliegen dabei ist der kulturelle Bezug unseres Designs. Der von uns angestrebte kulturelle Ausdruck liegt nicht nur im Material und in der Technologie, sondern ganz besonders auch im Konzept – in der Vermittlung von Ideen. Wir erzeugen ganz bewusst kulturelle Bedeutung oder arbeiten damit. Aber wir finden es auch faszinierend herauszufinden, was das Besondere an scheinbar Naheliegendem ist. Genau wie in der Natur müssen wir manchmal nur das Außergewöhnliche hervorheben."

« La nature exprime la perfection dans ses formes et ses systèmes, qui peuvent être à la fois très simples et très complexes. Un quartier d'orange ou une cosse de pois ont une structure géométrique qui devient captivante une fois grossie. La rencontre entre organicisme formel et complexité fonctionnelle qui se fait dans la nature est spontanée et parfaite, sans compromis ou redondance simpliste, et entraîne une pure économie des formes. Lorsque nous créons un objet, nous essayons toujours de donner le meilleur de nous-mêmes avec une grande discipline et de concentrer nos efforts sur la relation qu'entretient notre création avec la culture. La culture à laquelle nous aspirons ne tient pas seulement au matériau et à l'expression technologique, mais aussi beaucoup au concept – à la transmission d'idées. Nous imprégnons consciemment notre travail de sens culturel. Mais nous sommes aussi fascinés par l'identification de l'extraordinaire en toute chose qui semble ordinaire. Tout comme dans la nature, il nous suffit parfois d'accentuer l'exceptionnel. »

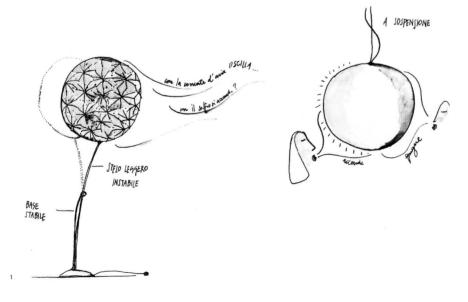

1

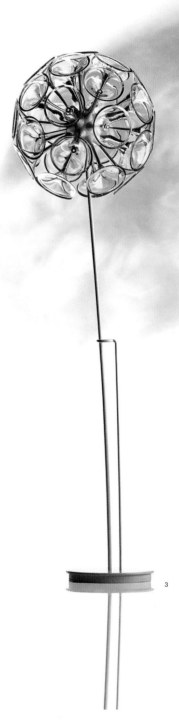

1–5

DANDELION
Floor or hanging light
with sphere of transparent
PMMA flutes
2005
Client: Tecnodelta

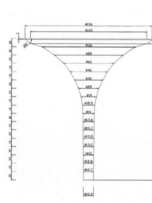

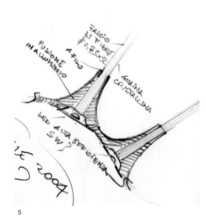

4

5

3

1–5

DANDELION LIGHT FOR
TECNODELTA, 2005

Constructed of aluminium and PMMA techno-polymer, this elegant lighting design draws inspiration from dandelions gently swaying in the wind on their slender, flexible stalks. High-efficiency LEDs illuminate the light's sphere of transparent flutes. The Dandelion is available either as a floor light or a hanging light.

Diese aus Aluminium und PMMA-Technopolymer hergestellte elegante Leuchte bezieht ihre Inspiration von einem Löwenzahn, der sich auf seinen schlanken, biegsamen Stielen sanft im Wind wiegt. Hochleistungs-LED beleuchten die aus transparenten Flöten zusammengesetzte Kugel. Dandelion ist sowohl als Steh- wie auch Pendelleuchte erhältlich.

Constitué d'aluminium et de polymère acrylique, cet élégant luminaire tire son inspiration des pissenlits qui se balancent doucement dans le vent sur leurs tiges creuses et souples. Des diodes très économiques illuminent la sphère de flûtes transparentes. Dandelion existe en lampadaire et en suspension.

6–7
ZELIG
Foodbag in aluminium,
Neoprene and thermo-reflective
tissue
2007
Client: Ventiquattro Sole 24
ORE Magazine

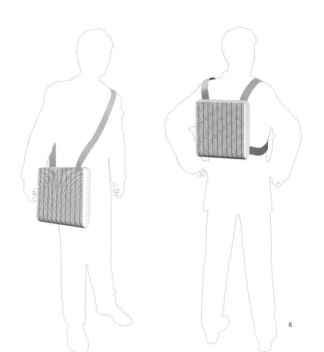

6

7

DEEPDESIGN

Matteo Bazzicalupo
Via Giovanni XXIII, 22
25040 Iseo (BS)
Italy

Raffaella Mangiarotti
Viale Francesco Restelli, 5
20124 Milan
Italy

T (MB) +39 3355894594
T (RM) +39 3338156840
E info@deepdesign.it
www.deepdesign.it

DESIGN GROUP HISTORY

1995 Founded by Matteo Bazzicalupo and Raffaella Mangiarotti in Milan

MATTEO BAZZICALUPO

1966 Born in Parma, Italy
1985–1991 MA Architecture, Politecnico di Milano, Milan
1991–1995 Worked with Arch. Jemmi, Architectural Office
1995–2003 Professor of Industrial Design at Politechnico di Milano and University of Genoa

RAFFAELLA MANGIAROTTI

1965 Born in Genoa, Italy
1984–1990 MA Architecture, Politecnico di Milano, Milan
1991–1994 PhD Industrial Design, Politecnico di Milano, Milan (in collaboration with Sony)
1991–1998 Worked with Marco Zanuso and later worked as design partner with Francesco Trabucco

RECENT EXHIBITIONS

2004 "Salone Satellite", Salone del Mobile, Milan; "Multipli di Cibo, Food Design", Triennale di Milano, Milan
2005 "Design alla Coop", Triennale di Milano, Milan; "ADI Design Index Exhibition", Triennale di Milano, Milan
2006 "www: wonderful water world", Guzzini and S.Pellegrino, Milan; "Sound Design", Fuori Salone, Milan
2007 "Avverati: progetti dal Salone Satellite alla produzione – 10 anni di Salone Satellite", Salone Internazionale del Mobile, Milan; "The New Italian Design", Triennale di Milano, Milan; "ADI Design Index exhibition", Triennale di Milano, Milan

RECENT AWARDS

2001 Young & Design Prize, Salone del Mobile, Milan
2002 Young & Design Prize, Salone del Mobile, Milan
2003 Award, Annual Design Review, I.D. Magazine
2004 New Generation Camera Award, JVC, Japan
2005 Selected for Compasso d'Oro, ADI, Milan

CLIENTS

4 Mariani, Aldo Coppola, Barilla, Castelli Haworth, Coca-Cola, Coin, Comitato Giochi Olimpi Torino 2006, Coop, DaimlerChrysler, Fratelli Rossetti, Giorgetti, Glaxo Smithkline, Guzzini, Imetec, I4 Mariani, Inblu, JVC, Kitchen Aids, Kraft, Suchard, Mandarina Duck, Kimberly-Clark Corp., Matsushita, Misuraemme, Nec, RSVP, San Lorenzo, San Pellegrino, Whirlpool Europe

"Learning from nature, being inspired by materials and technology to express culture through design."

8
SCOPINO
Toilette brush in injection-moulded plastic with a liquid detergent filling
2007
Client: Coop

9
WINDS
Self-standing hairdryer in plastic with rotatable head
2005
Client: self-generated prototype

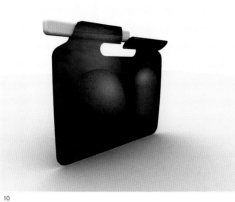

10
BORSAFOLIO
Flat bag in leather and Neoprene
with metal food boxes and cut-
lery holder
2007
Client: Ventiquattro Sole 24
ORE Magazine

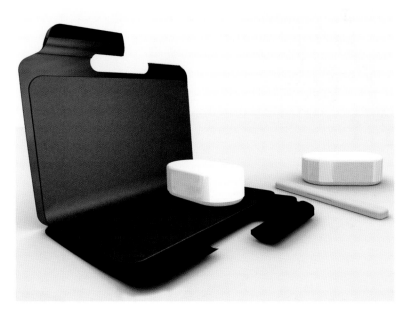

DESIGNAPKIN

"Designapkin is a multidisciplinary product development consulting firm. We find opportunities for clients through strategic market analysis and our unique design process. Our goal is to develop the form of manufactured products. We consider aesthetics, consumer trends, manufacturing processes, costs, functionality, and ergonomics. Using all of these considerations, we create new products that will appeal to consumers and lead to a competitive market advantage for our clients. We work with both entrepreneurs and corporations to bring exciting, new products to life. Our goal is to create new product concepts that can change the way we think about a product. We thrive on the early phases of design where truly profound improvements in a product can be developed."

„Designapkin ist eine multidisziplinäre Consulting-Firma für Produktentwicklung. Wir ermitteln Möglichkeiten für unsere Kunden anhand von strategischen Marktanalysen und unserem einzigartigen Designprozess. Unser Ziel ist es, die Form von industriegefertigten Gütern weiterzuentwickeln. Wir untersuchen Ästhetik, Konsumtrends, Fertigungsverfahren, Kosten, Funktionalität und Ergonomie. Unter Einbeziehung all dieser Aspekte schaffen wir neue Produkte, die bei den Konsumenten gut ankommen und unseren Kunden einen Wettbewerbsvorteil verschaffen. Bei der Realisierung spannender neuer Produkte arbeiten wir sowohl mit kleinen Betrieben als auch mit großen Unternehmen zusammen. Wir streben die Entwicklung neuer Produktkonzepte an, die unsere Betrachtungsweise eines Produkts verändern können. Unser Erfolg liegt in den Anfangsstadien des Designs, in denen noch wirklich grundlegende Verbesserungen eines Produkts entwickelt werden können."

«Designapkin est un cabinet multidisciplinaire de conseil en développement de produits. Une étude de marché stratégique et notre processus créatif unique nous permettent d'offrir des opportunités à nos clients. Notre mission est de concevoir la forme de produits manufacturés. Nous considérons l'esthétique, les tendances de consommation, les processus de fabrication, les coûts, la fonctionnalité et l'ergonomie. À partir de ces considérations, nous créons de nouveaux produits qui séduiront les consommateurs et donneront un avantage concurrentiel à nos clients. Nous travaillons à la fois avec des entrepreneurs et des sociétés commerciales pour donner vie à des produits novateurs et excitants. Notre objectif est de créer de nouveaux concepts qui peuvent modifier notre façon de penser un produit. Nous insistons particulièrement sur les phases les plus précoces du processus, lorsque le produit peut encore véritablement être amélioré.»

1

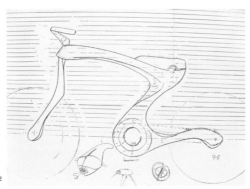

2

SHIFT BICYCLE FOR THE
TAIWAN INTERNATIONAL
BICYCLE DESIGN COMPETI-
TION, 2005

The SHIFT bicycle helps children learn how to ride a bike on
their own. Unlike traditional
training wheels, that simply prevent the bike from tipping, the
SHIFT bicycle requires children
to learn how to balance on their
own. The shifting rear wheels
help balance the bike at slow
speeds. As the child builds up
forward momentum, the wheels
shift inward due to decreased
weight on the rear wheels, thus
causing the balance gradually to
shift from the bicycle to the

child. SHIFT provides more
balance at lower speeds, when
stability is most critical (starting
and stopping), by providing a
larger stance. The SHIFT bicycle features a swinging rear
hub, which allows the rear
wheels to pitch in and out. The
hub allows for the rear wheels
to provide a larger or smaller
stance depending on the amount
of weight on the rear wheels.
An internal belt keeps the drive
train away from the child, thereby helping to prevent possible
injury.

Das Fahrrad SHIFT hilft Kindern, selbstständig das Radfah-
ren zu erlernen. Im Gegensatz
zu den traditionellen Stützrä-

dern, die nur verhindern, dass
das Fahrrad umfällt, lernen die
Kinder auf dem SHIFT, selbstständig das Gleichgewicht zu
halten. Die beweglichen Hinterräder tragen dazu bei, dass das
Kind bei geringem Tempo das
Rad aufrecht halten kann. Wenn
es kräftiger in die Pedale tritt,
gehen die Hinterräder nach
innen, weil nun weniger
Gewicht auf den Hinterrädern
liegt, und das Kind kann zunehmend selbst das Gleichgewicht
halten. Beim langsameren Fahren, das die meiste Stabilität
erfordert (beim Anfahren und
Stehenbleiben), sorgt SHIFT
mit einer größeren Standbreite
für besseren Halt. Hinten hat
das SHIFT-Rad eine bewegliche

Nabe, damit die Hinterräder
schwenkbar sind. Dank dieser
Nabe können die Hinterräder
die Standbreite verändern, je
nachdem, wie viel Gewicht darauf wirkt. Ein innenliegender
Riemen schließt das Getriebe
nach außen hin ab und schützt
das Kind vor Verletzungen.

La bicyclette SHIFT aide les
enfants à apprendre à faire du
vélo tout seuls. Contrairement
aux vélos d'apprentissage traditionnels, dont les petites roues
latérales se contentent d'empêcher le vélo de verser, la bicyclette SHIFT oblige l'enfant à trouver seul son équilibre. Ses roues
arrière mobiles aident à équili-
brer le vélo à allure lente et pivo-

tent pour se rapprocher au sol à
mesure que l'enfant prend de la
vitesse, afin de réduire le poids
qui porte sur elles : le contrôle de
l'équilibre passe ainsi progressi-
vement du vélo à l'enfant. Cette
double roue arrière procure à
SHIFT la stabilité nécessaire à
petite vitesse (au démarrage et à
l'arrêt) en élargissant la surface
d'appui. Le moyeu du vélo
SHIFT oscille pour permettre
aux roues arrière de se rapprocher et de s'écarter de façon fluide en fonction du poids qui leur
est imposé. Une courroie de
transmission interne camoufle
la chaîne pour éviter que les
enfants ne se blessent.

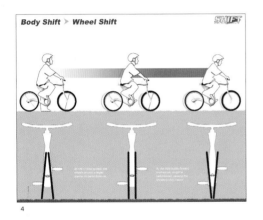

4

SHIFT
Training bicycle for children
2005
Client: self-produced for the
Taiwan International Bicycle
Design Competition

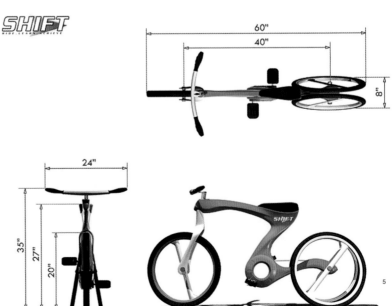

5

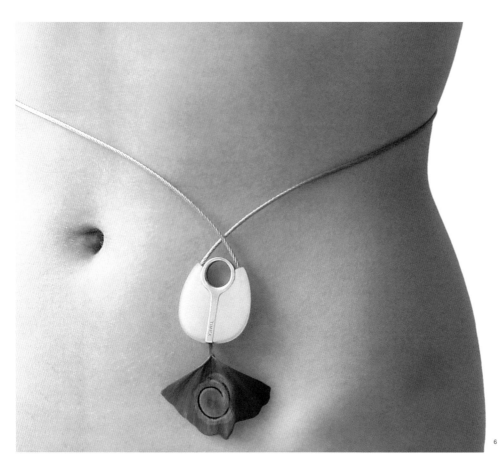

6–8
TIMEX SEASON
Device for measuring and
displaying personal time zone
2005
Client: self-produced concept

6

"Intellectual property
design experts."

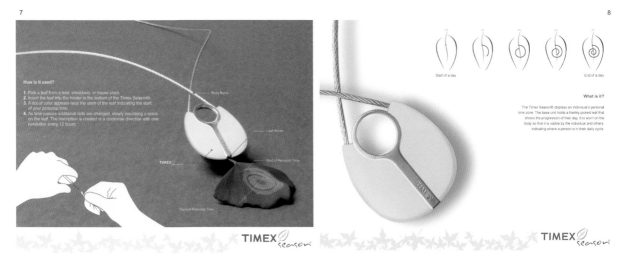

7

How is it used?

1. Pick a leaf from a tree, shrubbery, or house plant.
2. Insert the leaf into the holder in the bottom of the Timex Season®.
3. A dot of color appears near the stem of the leaf indicating the start of your personal time.
4. As time passes additional dots are changed, slowly inscribing a spiral on the leaf. The inscription is created in a clockwise direction with one revolution every 12 hours.

Body Band

Leaf Holder

Start of Personal Time

Current Personal Time

TIMEX Season®

8

Start of a day   End of a day

What is it?

The Timex Season® displays an individual's personal
time zone. The base unit holds a freshly-picked leaf that
shows the progression of their day. It is worn on the
body so that it is visible by the individual and others,
indicating where a person is in their daily cycle.

TIMEX season

TIMEX season

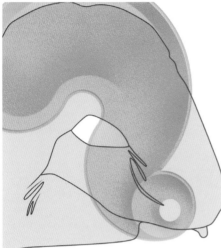

CROSS cushions provide balance in following three elements.

East & West: Elegance of eastern culture meets simplicity of western culture for sophisticated fusion experience.

Values &Functions: Acknowledge traditional values with modern aesthetics that appeals to the general public in macro scale.

Flexibility & Stability: Appropriate weight and pressure distribution to the lower body results stable body posture when sitting crossed leg.

Top view of **CROSS** *in use*

Front view of **CROSS** *in use*

9

DESIGNAPKIN
2472 Gala Court
West Lafayette
Indiana 47906
USA
T +1 765 4919633
E stevevisser@designapkin.com
E scottshim@designapkin.com
www.designapkin.com

DESIGN GROUP HISTORY
2005 Founded by Professor Steve Visser and Professor Scott Shim (of Purdue University) in West Lafayette, Indiana, USA

FOUNDERS' BIOGRAPHIES
PROFESSOR STEVE VISSER
1959
Born in Grand Haven, Michigan, USA
1979–1982 BA Fine Arts, Northwestern College, Orange City, Iowa
1985–1988 MFA Industrial Design, University of Illinois, Champaign/Urbana
1988–1989 Industrial designer, Hari and Associates, Skokie, Illinois
1989–1990 Visiting Assistant Professor, Purdue University, West Lafayette, Indiana
1990–1996 Assistant Professor, Purdue University, West Lafayette, Indiana
1996–1997 Received a Fulbright Scholar award, enabling him to conduct research in industrial design at the University of Art and Design Helsinki
1996–1998 Vice President of the Indiana chapter of IDSA

1996–2006 Associate Professor, Purdue University, West Lafayette, Indiana
2006+ Full Professor, Purdue University, West Lafayette, Indiana

PROFESSOR SCOTT (SEOKBO) SHIM
1971 Born in Seoul, Korea
1992–1995 BFA Industrial Design, University of Illinois, Champaign/Urbana
1995–1997 MA Design Development, Ohio State University, Ohio
1995–1997 Freelance designer, Beyond Design, Chicago
1997–2000 Junior Designer, Daewoo Electronics Design Center, Seoul, Korea
2001–2002 Senior Designer, Daewoo Electronics Design Center, Seoul, Korea
2003+ Assistant Professor, Industrial Design Dept., Purdue University, West Lafayette, Indiana
2003+ Professional Member, IDSA (Industrial Designers Society of America)

RECENT EXHIBITIONS
2003 "2003 Taiwan International Design Competition", Taiwan

Design Center/Taiwan Industrial Development Bureau; International Aluminium Extrusion Conference, ET Foundation
2004 "2004 Taiwan International Design Competition", Taiwan Design Center/Taiwan Industrial Development Bureau
2005 "International Travel Souvenir Design Exhibition", Korea Ministry of Culture & Tourism/Gyeonggi Tourism Organization; "9th International Bicycle Design Competition", Taiwan Design Center/Taiwan Industrial Development Bureau; "2005 Taipei International Cycle Show", Taipei, Taiwan; "Taiwan Design Expo", Taipei, Taiwan
2006 "2006 Consumer Electronics Show", Las Vegas; "Modern Marvels Invent Now Challenge", History Channel and the National Inventors Hall of Fame Foundation; "Bike – The Wheel Story", TELUS World of Science (formerly the Calgary Science Centre), Calgary

RECENT AWARDS
2003 Opus Design Award, International Eyewear Design Competition
2004 Honorable Mention,

Annual Design Review, I. D. Magazine; Award of Excellence
2004 Taiwan International Design Competition
2005 Gold Award, IDEA (Industrial Design Excellence Awards), Industrial Designers Society of America/Business Week; Nomination, Most Amazing Inventions of 2005, Time magazine
2006 Nomination, 100 Best Innovations 2006, Popular Science magazine; Nomination, Most Amazing Innovations 2006, Time magazine; Opus Design Award, International Eyewear Design Competition; Judge's Award, Next Generation PC Design Competition, Microsoft; Opus Design Award, International Eyewear Design Competition

CLIENTS
3M, Apollo Design Technology, Fisher-Price, Klipsch Audio Corp., Omega/Capri Lighting, Proman Products LLC, Samsung Telecommunications, America

9–11
CROSS
Seating cushion for crossed-leg
posture that optimizes ergo-
nomic support
2005
Client: self-produced for the
Interior Design Magazine Future
Furniture Competition

10

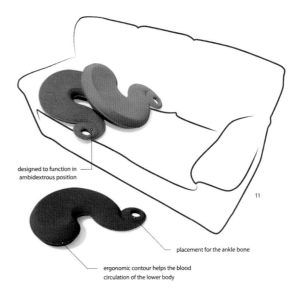

designed to function in
ambidextrous position

11

placement for the ankle bone

ergonomic contour helps the blood
circulation of the lower body

STEFAN DIEZ

"Whatever we invent – stories, plans for the future – we always combine the options we have in a logical, emotional, or any other way to form an idea. For us as designers, the creation of shapes seems to merge with finding more general ideas behind products. Globalisation, division of labour with a resulting network of highly specialized suppliers for services and production facilities create a situation where we can contribute more to a product than its shape. I guess this new, more complex playground will keep us busy for the future."

„Bei allem, was wir uns ausdenken – Geschichten, Pläne für die Zukunft – setzen wir unterschiedliche Möglichkeiten in einen logischen, emotionalen oder anderen Zusammenhang und formulieren so eine Idee. Für uns als Designer scheint dabei das Schaffen von Formen mit dem Finden von grundlegenden Ideen hinter den Produkten zu verschmelzen. Globalisierung und Arbeitsteilung und ein damit einhergehendes Netzwerk hoch spezialisierter Anbieter für Dienstleistungen und Produktionsmöglichkeiten schaffen eine Situation, in der wir zu mehr als der Gestalt eines Produkts etwas beitragen können. Vermutlich werden wir in der nächsten Zeit damit beschäftigt sein, etwas aus diesen neuen, komplexeren Spielräumen zu machen."

«Quoique nous inventions – histoires, projets d'avenir – nous combinons toujours les options qui sont entre nos mains de façon logique, émotionnelle ou autre pour former une idée. Pour les designers que nous sommes, la création de formes semble se confondre avec la découverte de nouvelles idées générales derrière les produits. La mondialisation et la division du travail qui donne naissance à un réseau de fournisseurs hautement spécialisés dans le domaine des services et des capacités de production, créent une situation où nous pouvons apporter au produit plus qu'une forme. J'imagine que ce nouveau terrain de jeu, plus complexe, suffira largement à occuper notre avenir.»

1

3

4

5

1–5
BENT SERIES FOR MOROSO,
2006–07

The Bent series of furniture, comprising a chair, sofa, table and stool, is constructed of laser-cut 3mm perforated sheet aluminium. The idea of bending perforated sheet metal allows shapes that are not manageable in a traditional step-by-step bending process. All the seams of a single piece are bent at the same time with the help of specially engineered templates. Various powder-coated colour options are available.

Die Möbelserie Bent, die Sessel, Sitzbank, Tisch und Hocker umfasst, wird aus 3 mm dickem lasergeschnittenem Aluminium gefertigt, das funktionsbedingt perforiert ist. Die Idee, perforiertes Blech in einem einzigen Arbeitsgang um eigens hergestellte Schablonen zu kanten, lässt geometrische Formen zu, die in einem traditionellen, schrittweise durchgeführten Biegeverfahren nicht möglich wären. Die Serie ist in verschiedenfarbiger Pulverbeschichtung erhältlich.

La collection de meubles Bent, qui comprend une chaise, un canapé, une table et un tabouret, est construite à partir de feuilles d'aluminium de 3 mm perforées et taillées au laser. L'idée de plier des feuilles de métal perforées autorise des formes qui ne peuvent être atteintes par le façonnage progressif habituel. Tous les angles d'une même pièce sont pliés d'un seul mouvement à l'aide de patrons fabriqués sur mesure. La collection peut être habillée de différentes couleurs poudrées.

6
SHUTTLE
Orange squeezer with
perforated swivelling plate
2006
Client: Rosenthal

7–10
SHUTTLE
Range of glass food containers
with air- and watertight soft
rubber tops
2006
Client: Rosenthal

6

7

8

9

10

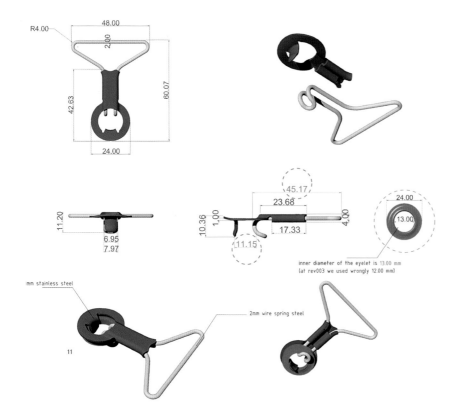

inner diameter of the eyelet is 13.00 mm
(at rev003 we used wrongly 12.00 mm)

mm stainless steel

2mm wire spring steel

11

11
KUVERT
Technical drawing of a carabiner
for travel bags
2006
Client: Authentics

12
KUVERT
Range of lightweight
waterproof semi-coated
polyester fabric travel bags
2006
Client: Authentics

12

"One part of our job is making decisions between options. Finding out what these are is the other part."

14

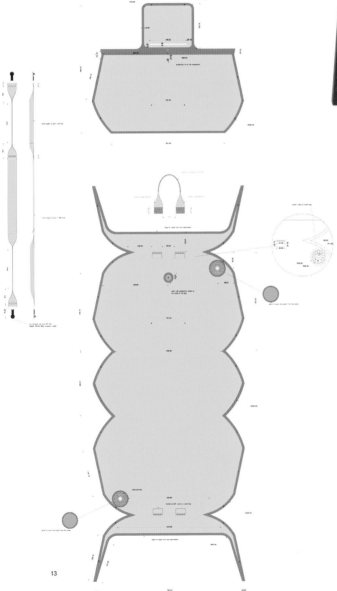

13

13
KUVERT
Technical drawing and
hf-welding pattern of
medium travel bag
2006
Client: Authentics

14
404F
Painted bentwood occasional
chair with armrest integral
to back
2007
Client: Thonet

STEFAN DIEZ

Stefan Diez Industrial Design
Geyerstraße 20
80469 Munich
Germany
T +49 89 20245392
Email@stefan-diez.com
www.stefan-diez.com

BIOGRAPHY

1971 Born in Freising, Germany
1991–1994 Studied Architecture and Cabinet Making in the studio of Ursula Maier and at the University of Stuttgart
1996–2002 Studied Industrial Design at the Academy of Fine Arts in Stuttgart under Richard Sapper and Klaus Lehmann
1998 Design assistant, Richard Sapper's studio in Milan
1999–2002 Design assistant, Konstantin Grcic's studio in Munich
2003 Founded his own design studio in Munich

RECENT EXHIBITIONS

2002 "Spin Off", imm cologne; "Salone Satellite", Milan (exhibited with Christophe de la Fontaine); "Prospects at Terminal-NYC", New York, together with Christophe de la Fontaine; "Vitrinen", Interieur, Kortrijk, Belgium, together with Ayzit Bostan: "wonderwood", Interieur, Kortrijk, Belgium; "Biennale Saint-Etienne", France
2003 "Spin Off Lounge", imm Cologne
2004 "Quality Control" for Porzellan-Manufaktur Nymphenburg, "Designparcours", Munich; Exhibition for Rosenthal Porzellan, "Design-parcours", Bayerisches National-museum, Munich; "Rosenthal Design Award", Pinakothek der Moderne, Munich
2006 "ideal house cologne 06", imm cologne and German Design Council

RECENT AWARDS

2002 Design Report Award, Salone Satellite, Milan
2003 Interior Innovation Award – "best of the best award" – imm cologne; 1st Prize, "Caiazza Memorial Challenge" competition Promosedia, Udine
2004 Gold and Silver "Focus" Awards, Design Center Stuttgart; Nominated "Newcomer of the year 2005", Elle Decoration-Germany; 2 x iF Awards, International Forum Design Hanover; Judges' Award" Best New Furniture Design", Wallpaper magazine; Interior Innovation Award – "best of the best award" – imm cologne
2005 A&W Mentor Award 2005 (selected by Richard Sapper), Architektur & Wohnen, Hamburg; Interior Innovation Award – "best of the best award" – imm cologne; 2 x Red Dot Award, Design Zentrum Nordrhein Westfalen, Essen; Förderpreis der Stadt München, Munich
2006 Interior Innovation Award – "best of the best award" – imm cologne; Designpreis der Bundesrepublik Deutschland; "Focus" Award, Design Center Stuttgart; Materialica Design Award, Munich Expo
2007 Interior Innovation Award – "best of the best award" – imm cologne; Design Plus Award, Ambiente, Frankfurt

CLIENTS

Authentics, Biegel, Elmar Flötotto, Merten, Moroso, Rosenthal, Schönbuch, Thonet, Wilkhahn

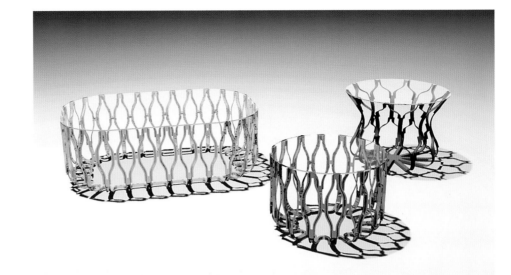

16

17

18

15–17
UPON
Programme of tables, benches
and coatrack in powder-coated
sheet steel laser cut from a single
metal sheet and stretched to
final shape
2007
Client: Schönbuch

18
UPON
Detail of prototype metal
construction
2007
Client: Schönbuch

DING3000

"Our design philosophy cannot be described by a dogma or an 'ism'. The designs come about through a situation, product and customer-oriented design process, which takes place somewhere in between method and magic. The way to the product lies in the search for a new, better, different, unjustly forgotten, humorous idea. The resulting formal and functional elaboration is largely due to this idea. Our work is evidence of the pleasure we take in challenging materials, products and not least people's behaviour. Often we question available solutions and popular assumptions and proceed in a way that is contradictory to them. As a result, we continually make wonderful discoveries off the beaten track."

„Unsere Designphilosophie lässt sich nicht durch ein Dogma oder einen ‚Ismus' beschreiben. Die Entwürfe entspringen einem situations-, produkt- und kundenbezogenen Designprozess, der sich im Spektrum zwischen Methodik und Magie abspielt. Der Weg zum Produkt führt über die Suche nach einer neuen, einer besseren, einer anderen, einer zu Unrecht vergessenen, einer humorvollen Idee. Die formale und funktionale Ausarbeitung ist dieser Idee in hohem Maße verpflichtet. Unsere Arbeiten zeugen von der Freude, die wir an der Auseinandersetzung mit Materialien, Produkten und nicht zuletzt dem Verhalten der Menschen haben. Häufig stellen wir vorhandene Lösungen und gängige Annahmen infrage und begeben uns in Widerspruch zu ihnen. Dadurch machen wir abseits der ausgetretenen Pfade immer wieder wundersame Entdeckungen."

«Aucun dogme ou mot en ‹isme› ne peut décrire notre philosophie du design. Le design se façonne en fonction des situations, des produits, des processus créatifs orientés vers le consommateur, quelque part entre la méthode et la magie. Pour arriver jusqu'au produit, il faut partir en quête d'une idée nouvelle, meilleure, différente, injustement oubliée, humoristique. La perfection formelle et fonctionnelle qui en résulte provient largement de cette idée. Notre travail est la preuve du plaisir que nous prenons à manipuler des matériaux, des produits, et aussi des personnalités difficiles. Nous remettons souvent en question les solutions habituellement disponibles et les idées reçues et procédons de façon à les contredire. C'est ainsi que nous faisons régulièrement des découvertes magnifiques en dehors des sentiers battus.»

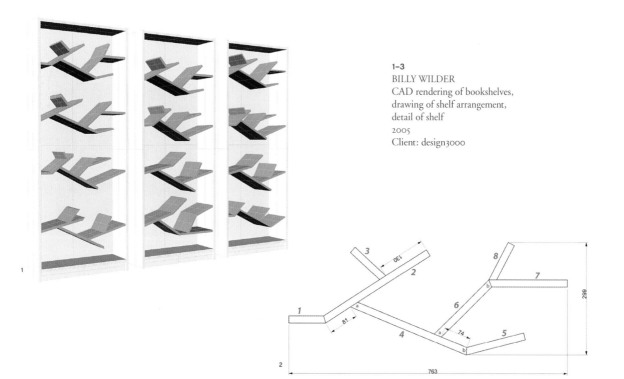

1–3
BILLY WILDER
CAD rendering of bookshelves,
drawing of shelf arrangement,
detail of shelf
2005
Client: design3000

BILLY WILDER BOOK-
SHELVES FOR DESIGN3000,
2005

35 million units of Ikea's famous
Billy bookcase have been sold
worldwide – making it the
world's biggest seller when it
comes to shelving. Following
the slogan "pimp my billy"
ding3000 have devoted their
creativity to redesigning this
classic Ikea piece. Their Billy

Wilder unit, constructed of
painted MDF, meets one's
primary expectation of a shelf –
to be able to put everything in
order. It is meant as a playful
approach to the subject "our
daily mess" and serves as an
interim storage place for unsort-
ed books, magazines and news-
papers. The wildly growing rack
makes Billy "wilder".

Ikeas berühmter Bücherschrank
Billy ist weltweit 35 Millionen

Mal verkauft worden, was ihn
zum Spitzenreiter unter den
Regalen macht. Frei nach dem
Wahlspruch „Pimp my Billy"
ließen die Designer von
Ding3000 ihre kreativen Mus-
keln spielen und möbelten den
Einrichtungsklassiker fantasie-
voll auf. Der Billy Wilder aus
lackiertem MDF packt ein Problem unseres Lebens – Ordnung zu schaffen – auf spielerische Weise an. „Unser
alltägliches Chaos" aus unsor-

tierten Büchern, Magazinen und
Zeitungen kann nunmehr in
dieser Ablage zwischengelagert
werden. Der kreuz und quer
wachsende Regalboden macht
Billy „wilder".

La célèbre étagère Billy d'Ikea
s'est vendue à 35 millions
d'exemplaires – ce qui fait d'elle
le modèle le plus vendu dans le
monde. Sous le slogan « retape
ton Billy » ding3000 a consacré
sa créativité à reformuler ce clas-

sique d'Ikea. Leur pièce Billy
Wilder, constituée de plaques
d'aggloméré, correspond à ce
que chacun attend d'une
étagère – on peut tout y ranger.
Elle a été conçue comme un
commentaire amusé de « notre
bazar quotidien » et sert de lieu
d'entreposage temporaire pour
les livres, les magazines et les
journaux orphelins. Cette accumulation sauvage fait naître un
Billy « plus sauvage ».

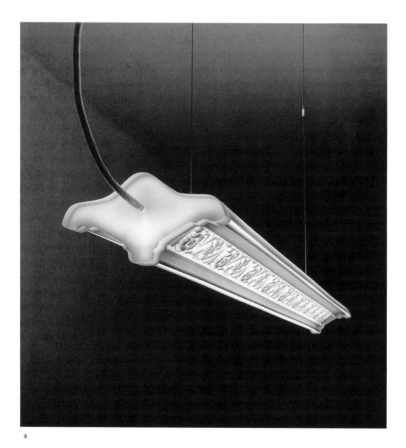

4

STUCKLEUCHTDING
Hanging light in acrylic
and styrofoam with
twin fluorescent tubes
2005
Client: self-produced

5

"It is both a challenge and a delight
to make wishes, dreams and ideas come
true every day."

6/7
CHARGE BOX
Wall-mounted or freestanding
powder-coated sheet steel and
felt cable management container
2007
Client: Konstantin Slawinski

8
TEHERAN
Table light with plastic shade
2006
Client: self-produced

11

10

9

9
CORONA
Plastic wall clock with
fluorescent rear surface that
produces a corona effect
2006
Client: Authentics

10
ABROLLDING
Cast metal dispenser
2005
Client: Troika

DING 3000

Braunstraße 28
30169 Hannover
Germany
T +49 511 91199436
E info@ding3000.com
www.ding3000.com

DESIGN GROUP HISTORY

2005 Founded by Sven
Rudolph, Ralf Webermann and
Carsten Schelling in Hanover

FOUNDERS' BIOGRAPHIES
SVEN RUDOLPH

1978 Born in Kassel, Germany
1998 Internship, OGC (packaging design company), Johannes-
burg, South Africa
1999 Studied product design at
Fachhochschule Hannover
(University of Applied Sciences
and Arts)
2002 Studied product design
at University of Hefei, China

2002–2003 Studied product
design at HFG Karlsruhe,
Germany
2003–2004 Internship,
Vogt+Weizenegger, Berlin
2005 Diploma – product design,
Fachhochschule Hannover
(University of Applied Sciences
and Arts)

RALF WEBERMANN

1972 Born in Westerstede,
Germany
1998 Worked as cabinetmaker foreman
2002 Studied product design
at University of Hefei,
China
2004 Diploma – product
design, Fachhochschule
Hannover (University of
Applied Sciences and Arts)

CARSTEN SCHELLING

1977 Born in Stuttgart,
Germany
1999 Studied product design at
Fachhochschule Hannover
(University of Applied Sciences
and Arts)
2002 Studied product design at
University of Hefei, China –
Project cooperation with ESAD
Reims, France
2003 Studied product design
and typography at the Univer-
sity of Technology, Sydney,
Australia
2003–2004 Internship,
Marcel Wanders Studio,
Amsterdam, The Netherlands
2005 Diploma – product design,
Fachhochschule, Hannover
(University of Applied Sciences
and Arts)
2005–2006 Designer, Marcel
Wanders Studio, Amsterdam,
The Netherlands

RECENT EXHIBITIONS

2005 "Talents", Tendence
Lifestyle, Frankfurt; "Salone
Satellite", Salone del Mobile,
Milan; "Inspired by Cologne",
imm cologne
2006 "form2006", Tendence
Lifestyle, Frankfurt; "DMY06",
Designmai Youngsters, Berlin,
"Dreimal Möbelglück", Vienna
2007 "Silver Design",
Shop der Generationen, Berlin
"Design Plus Exhibition", Ambi-
ente, Frankfurt

RECENT AWARDS

2005 Designpreis Rheinland-
Pfalz, Netzwerk für Design und
Kommunikation Rheinland-
Pfalz; iF Award, International
Forum Design Hanover
2006 Good Design Award,
JIDPO (Japan Industrial Design
Promotion Organization); iF
Award, International Forum

Design Hanover; Promotional
Gift Award (PGA), WA Verlag,
Cologne; Nomination, Design-
preis Deutschland, Bundes-
republik Deutschland
2007 Design Plus Award,
Ambiente, Frankfurt,
Red Dot Award, Design
Zentrum Nordrhein Westfalen,
Essen

CLIENTS

Authentics, Corpus Delicti,
Design3000, Esprit, Fussi,
Deluxe, Konstantin Slawinski,
Magazin, Pension für Produkte,
Pulpo, Sompex,
Style Foundation, Troika,
Wilkhahn

TOM DIXON

"Some days I work as a designer, but the bits that really interest me are the invention, engineering and marketing rather than the actual process of designing. I think that effective designers tend to be interested in the whole chain. Robin Day, Verner Panton and all those people really felt that they were going to change everything through design. It's a very humbling way to look at it. I think designers now are more concerned about the shape of the object and their own personal evolution within it. And I think a good designer is somebody who manages to put together all the elements – an understanding of materials and a belief in improving functionality – then puts the shape on last as a result of all those experiments. I'm a designer very occasionally. I tend to be on the periphery, occasionally popping out a product which is designed mainly through an interest in materials and technologies."

„An manchen Tagen arbeite ich als Designer, aber was mich wirklich interessiert, mehr als der tatsächliche Designprozess, ist die Innovation, die Technik und die Vermarktung. Ich glaube, erfolgreiche Designer sind meist an der gesamten Abfolge interessiert. Robin Day, Verner Panton und diese Leute dachten wirklich, sie würden durch Design alles verändern. Es so zu sehen, macht ganz klein. Ich finde, heute geht es den Designern mehr um die Form des Objekts und ihre persönliche Weiterentwicklung an diesem. Ich glaube, dass ein guter Designer alle Elemente unter einen Hut bringen kann – die Kenntnis der Werkstoffe und den Willen, die Funktionalität zu verbessern –, und zum Schluss findet er durch seine Experimente zur Form. Ich bin nur gelegentlich ein Designer. Ich bewege mich eher an der Peripherie und bringe ab und zu ein Produkt heraus, das seine Gestaltung vorwiegend meinem Interesse an Materialien und Technologien verdankt."

«Certains jours, je fais un travail de designer, mais ce qui m'intéresse réellement, plus que le design pur, c'est l'invention, l'ingénierie et la commercialisation. Je pense que les designers efficaces ont tendance à s'intéresser à toute la chaîne de production de l'objet. Robin Day, Verner Panton et tous ces gens-là avaient vraiment le sentiment qu'ils allaient tout changer grâce au design. C'est une manière de voir les choses qui impose le respect. Je pense que les designers d'aujourd'hui s'inquiètent davantage de la forme de l'objet et de la façon dont ils font évoluer grâce à lui. Et je pense qu'un bon designer est quelqu'un qui réussit à réunir tous les éléments – une intelligence des matériaux et une foi dans l'amélioration de la fonctionnalité – et n'apporte la forme qu'en dernier, comme le résultat de ces expériences. Je ne suis designer que très occasionnellement. Je me promène plutôt à la périphérie du métier, et de temps à autre je sors un produit qui a été principalement créé à partir de mon intérêt pour les matériaux et la technologie.»

1–3
BAMBU
Tandem seating unit in moulded bamboo laminate, details of lap joins
2006
Client: Artek

4

5

6

4–6
BAMBU
Chair in moulded bamboo laminate, drawing of constructional detail, chair profile
2006
Client: Artek

1–10

BAMBU SERIES FOR ARTEK,
2006

Describing this robust, technologically advanced and sustainable series of furniture designs Tom Dixon says, "With Bambu we hope to demonstrate our commitment to innovation in natural materials, leading to superior furniture, fit for the 21st century".

An extraordinary plant, used for millennia as a resource for food, wine, building material and fuel, bamboo is a material with many remarkable qualities. It has for example twice the compressive strength of concrete and the same tensile strength-to-weight ratio as steel.
The Bambu series elegantly exploits this versatile, fast-growing renewable and incredibly strong material with modern moulding technology. Three years of investment into research and development has led to this remarkable collection of chairs and tables.

Zu dieser robusten, technisch innovativen und nachhaltigen Möbelserie sagt Tom Dixon: „Mit Bambu möchten wir unser Engagement für Innovation mit natürlichen Materialien demons-trieren und die Möglichkeit, damit Möbel von allerhöchster Qualität zu schaffen, Möbel für das 21. Jahrhundert."
Bambus, eine außergewöhnliche Pflanze, die jahrtausendelang als Ressource für Nahrung, Getränke, Bau- und Brennstoffe diente, ist ein Material mit vielen hervorragenden Eigenschaften. Zum Beispiel weist er eine doppelt so große Druckfestigkeit wie Beton auf und das gleiche Verhältnis von Zugfestigkeit und Gewicht wie Stahl. In der Serie Bambu wird dieses vielseitige, rasch nachwachsende und unglaublich solide Material mittels moderner Formverfahren zu eleganten Möbelstücken verarbeitet. Drei Jahre mussten in die Forschung und Entwicklung investiert werden, um diese bemerkenswerte Kollektion aus Stühlen und Tischen zu verwirklichen.

Tom Dixon décrit ainsi cette collection de meubles durables et robustes, fruits d'une technologie avancée : « Avec Bambu, nous espérons montrer combien nous sommes engagés dans la recherche sur les matériaux naturels, qui nous permet de créer un mobilier de haute qualité adapté au XXIe siècle ». Végétal utilisé depuis des millénaires pour fournir nourriture, vin, matériaux de construction et carburant, le bambou est un matériau doté de qualités extraordinaires. Son taux de résistance à la compression est deux fois supérieur à celui du béton et il résiste aussi bien à la traction que l'acier. La collection Bambu exploite avec élégance ce matériau plein de ressources, solide et renouvelable, grâce aux techniques modernes de moulage. Il a fallu trois années de recherche et de développement pour donner naissance à cette remarquable collection de chaises et de tables.

7–8
BAMBU
Programme of tables in
moulded bamboo laminate
2006
Client: Artek

7

8

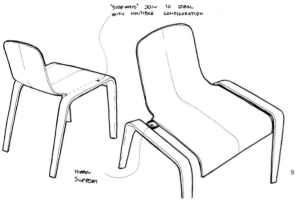

"SIDEWAYS" JOIN TO DEAL
WITH MULTIBLE CONFIGUERATION

HIPPEL
SUPPORT

9

9
BAMBU
Sketch of moulded bamboo
laminate chair's construction
2006
Client: Artek

10
BAMBU
Dining table and chairs in
moulded bamboo laminate
2006
Client: Artek

10

12

13

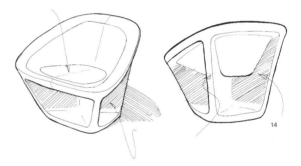

14

"I like to try and approach each project as a naïve outsider… I work better when I am not encumbered with preconceptions."

15

11–13
EPS
Single-form expanded
polystyrene lounge chairs on
display in Trafalgar Square,
London, installation
2006
Client: self-production/EPS
Packaging Group
(limited edition of 500)

14–16
EPS
Single-form expanded
polystyrene lounge chair,
drawings, mould and
prototypes
2006
Client: self-production/EPS
Packaging Group
(limited edition of 500)

16

TOM DIXON

4 Northington Street
London WC1N 2JG
United Kingdom
T +44 20 74000500
E info@tomdixon.net
www.tomdixon.net

BIOGRAPHY

1959 Born in Sfax, Tunisia
1963 Moved to England and subsequently educated in London
c.1980 Briefly studied at Chelsea School of Art, prior to playing bass guitar in the band Funkapolitan and teaching himself welding
1995 Established Space (a creative think-tank and shop) in London
1998–2004 Head of Design, Habitat
2000 Awarded OBE by Her Majesty The Queen
2002 Founded own eponymous design company with business partner David Begg
2004 Teamed up with Proventus, the Swedish-based private investment company, to establish Design Research, which includes Artek, the iconic modernist company created in 1935 by Alvar Aalto in Finland
2007+ Creative director for Artek and Tom Dixon, as well as non-executive Creative Director on the Habitat board

RECENT EXHIBITIONS

2005 "London Design Festival: Bombay Sapphire Stretch Installation", London; "Salone del Mobile", Milan; "imm cologne", Cologne; "100% Design", London
2006 "Designer of the Year", Design Museum, London; "London Design Festival: Grab a Chair Installation", London; "Salone del Mobile", Milan; "100% Design", London
2007 "Salone del Mobile", Milan

RECENT AWARDS

2005 Best International Lighting Design Award, Elle Decoration, London; "UK Designer of the Year", Elle Decoration, London
2006 Nomination, Designer of the Year Award, Design Museum, London; Best New Accessory Award, Elle Decoration, London
2007 "Best Lighting in Show", Editors Awards, ICFF, New York

CLIENTS

Artek, Habitat, Lacoste, London Design Embassy/London ICA, Myla, Soho House, Sony, Swarovski

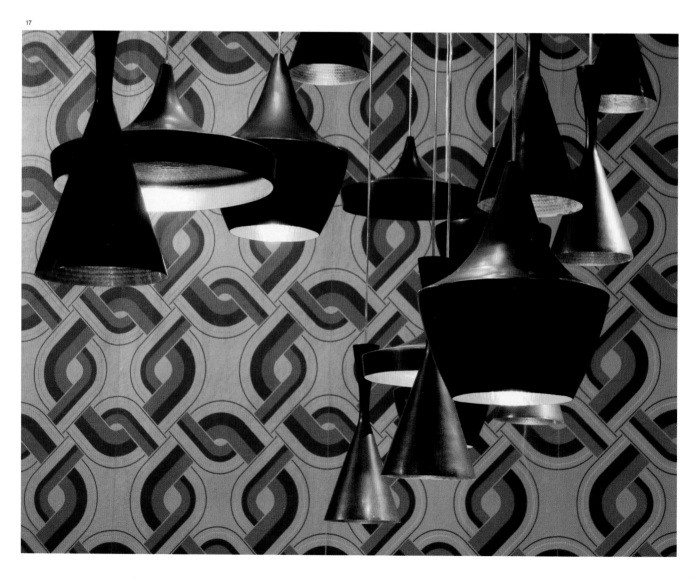

18

17–18
BEAT
Programme of hand-beaten and
patinated brass hanging lights
2007
Client: self-produced prototypes

JAMES DYSON

"At Dyson, we take an iterative approach to design. Inspired by Thomas Edison, the engineers make lots of tiny step-by-step changes. This is the only way to make sure a change improves a design before going on to the next stage. You can't be in a hurry. Invention isn't a flash of inspiration; it's a rigorous and scientific process. Innovation takes time, persistence and obsession. It took me over 5,000 prototypes before I perfected Dual Cyclone™ technology. Engineering and design aren't separate disciplines. Our machines evolve as part of a holistic design process. The technology on the inside informs the way it should look on the outside. Aesthetics should be a by-product of the design, not the other way around. Everything on a Dyson vacuum cleaner has a purpose. Its distinctive look is determined by the functionality, first and foremost. The clear bin isn't an artistic statement. It just shows you when you need to empty it. There is no extraneous window-dressing. Purpose prevails."

„Bei Dyson gehen wir schrittweise an Design heran. Inspiriert von Thomas Edison nehmen die Ingenieure winzige Veränderungsschritte vor. Das ist die einzige Methode, um sicherzustellen, dass eine Veränderung ein Design verbessert, bevor es in die nächste Entwicklungsphase geht. Man kann es nicht überstürzen. Eine Erfindung ist kein Gedankenblitz, es ist ein exakter und wissenschaftlicher Prozess. Innovation braucht Zeit, Beharrlichkeit und Leidenschaft. Es kostete mich über 5000 Prototypen, bevor ich die Dualzyklon-Technologie für Staubsauger perfektioniert hatte. Technik und Design sind keine getrennten Bereiche. Unsere Geräte entwickeln sich aus einem ganzheitlichen Gestaltungsprozess, bei dem die innere Technik die äußere Optik definiert. Die Ästhetik sollte ein Nebenprodukt des Designs sein, nicht umgekehrt. Alles an einem Dyson-Staubsauger hat einen praktischen Zweck. Sein charakteristisches Aussehen wird zu allererst von der Funktionalität bestimmt. Der durchsichtige Staubbehälter ist kein künstlerisches Statement. Vielmehr erkennt man so, wann man ihn leeren muss. Es gibt kein überflüssiges Schnickschnack. Zweckmäßigkeit siegt."

«Chez Dyson, nous abordons le design de façon itérative. Les ingénieurs, s'inspirant de Thomas Edison, effectuent toute une série de minuscules changements progressifs. C'est la seule manière de s'assurer qu'un changement améliore une création avant de passer à l'étape suivante. Impossible d'être pressé. L'invention n'est pas un éclair d'inspiration; c'est un processus scientifique rigoureux. L'innovation nécessite temps, persévérance et obsession. Il m'a fallu plus de 5000 prototypes pour parfaire la technologie du double cyclone. L'ingénierie et le design ne sont pas des disciplines séparées. Nos machines évoluent dans le cadre d'un processus de création holistique, où la technologie, interne, façonne leur apparence extérieure. L'esthétique ne devrait être qu'une conséquence indirecte du design et non le contraire. Sur un aspirateur Dyson, chaque élément a une fonction. Son allure particulière est déterminée avant tout par la fonctionnalité. Le réservoir transparent n'est pas une prise de position artistique. Il permet juste de voir à quel moment il faut le vider. Pas de fioritures superflues. La fonction prime.»

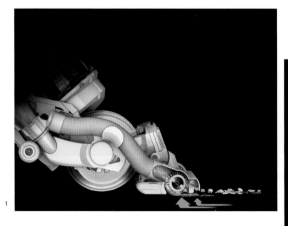

1

2

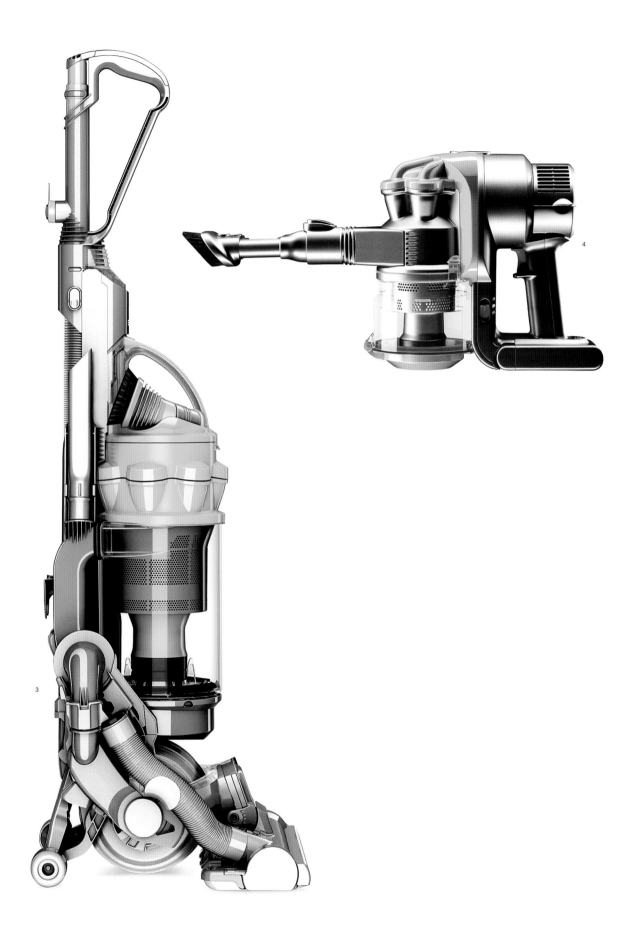

1–3/5
DC15, 2005

"Dyson engineers developed a vacuum cleaner that sits on top of a ball giving it maneuverability that has never been seen before. DC15 The Ball™ quickly zigzags around furniture and obstacles in the home. It is the biggest step-change to vacuum cleaners since Dyson introduced its no-loss-of-suction Dual Cyclone™ in 1993. The DC15 took three years to develop and has 182 patents. With just a small turn of your wrist, you can easily steer the cleaner – changing direction at will. The motor is in the ball giving it a lower centre of gravity, which makes it light and maneuverable in use."

„Um die Manövrierfähigkeit von Staubsaugern zu verbessern, haben die Ingenieure von Dyson ein Modell entwickelt, das auf einem Ball gelagert und dadurch besonders gut schwenkbar ist.

Mit einer nie zuvor gesehenen Wendigkeit kurvt DC15 The Ball™ behände um alle Möbel und Hindernisse in der Wohnung, was für Dyson den größten Entwicklungsschritt seit der Präsentation der Dual-Cyclone™-Technologie im Jahr 1993 darstellt, die seither für konstante Saugkraft sorgt. Die Entwicklung des DC15 nahm drei Jahre in Anspruch, und es wurden dafür 182 Patente erteilt. Der Staubsauger lässt sich mit einer leichten Drehung des Handgelenks mühelos lenken und in jede beliebige Richtung bewegen. Der Motor befindet sich im Ball, sodass der Schwerpunkt tiefer sitzt, was dem Gerät eine enorme Wendigkeit verleiht."

« Cet aspirateur conçu par les ingénieurs de Dyson repose sur une boule qui le rend plus manœuvrable qu'aucun autre avant lui. DC15 The Ball™ se faufile prestement entre les meubles et les obstacles de la maison et pour Dyson il s'agit de l'avancée la plus importante depuis le lancement du système d'entretien de l'aspiration Dual Cyclone™, en 1993. Il a fallu trois ans et 182 brevets pour élaborer le DC15. Un léger tour de poignet suffit pour faire avancer l'appareil et le faire changer de direction à volonté. Le moteur se trouve dans la boule, ce qui fait baisser le centre de gravité de l'aspirateur et le rend ainsi plus léger, et donc plus facile à manœuvrer. »

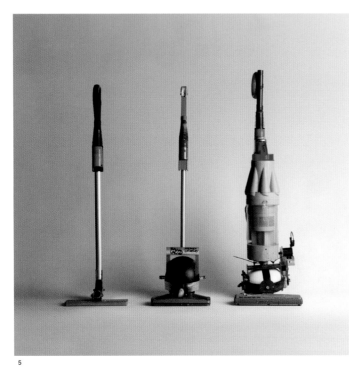

5

1
DC15
Detail of upright vacuum cleaner motorized brush bar and ball mechanism with internal motor
2005

2
DC15
Detail of upright vacuum cleaner Dual Cyclone™ element
2005

3
DC15
Upright vacuum cleaner with ball mechanism for increased maneuverability
2005

4
DC16
Cordless handheld vacuum cleaner incorporating Root Cyclone™ technology
2005–06

6

7

8

9

5
DC15
Progression of prototypes of upright vacuum cleaner with ball mechanism
2005

6
DYSON DIGITAL MOTOR
Exploded view of the fastest, lightest and highest-power density motor ever developed for domestic appliances – used in the Dyson Airblade hand dryer
2006

7
DYSON DIGITAL MOTOR
Detail of turbocharger style-3D impeller made of PEEK™ that spins at 1666 revolutions per second
2006

8–9
AIRBLADE
Energy-efficient hand dryer with a unique drying action that blows a wafer-thin sheet of air onto hands at 400 mph (640 kmph)
2006

JAMES DYSON
Dyson Ltd.
Tetbury Hill
Malmesbury
Wiltshire SN16 ORP
T +44 1666 827200
press.office@dyson.com
www.dyson.co.uk

BIOGRAPHY
1947 Born in Norfolk, England
1965–1966 Studied at the Byam Shaw School, London
1966–1970 MA industrial design, Royal College of Art, London
1970–1974 Worked for Rotork, Bath – an engineering firm where he managed the new Marine Division
1974–1979 Developed the "Ballbarrow", which replaced the wheelbarrow's traditional wheel with a ball
1979–1984 Developed "Dual Cyclone™" vacuum cleaner
1993 Established Dyson Appliances, Chippenham, Wiltshire
1995 Elected Fellow of the Chartered Society of Engineers
1997 Wrote "Against The Odds: An Autobiography" co-authored by Giles Coren

2007 Awarded Knighthood in New Year Honours, UK

RECENT EXHIBITIONS
Since 2000 Dyson has exhibited at the following institutions: Science Works Museum (House Secrets Exhibition), Melbourne; Powerhouse Museum, Sydney; Museum für Angewandte Kunst (MAK), Vienna; Technopolis, Mechelen, Belgium; Dansk Design Centre, Copenhagen; Kunstindustrimuseet, Copenhagen; Centre Georges Pompidou, Paris; Cité des Sciences et de l'Industrie, Paris; Musée d'Art Moderne, Saint-Étienne; Museum für Angewandte Kunst, Cologne; Neue Sammlung Pinakothek der Moderne, Munich; Boijmans Museum, Rotterdam; Museum van de Twintigste Eeuw, Hoorn,

The Netherlands; Hawke's Bay Museum, New Zealand; Museo do Design, Lisbon; Museo de les Arts Decoratives, Barcelona; Museum für Gestaltung, Zurich; Science Museum, London; Victoria and Albert Museum, London; Design Museum, London; Magna, Sheffield; The Ironbridge Gorge Museum, Shropshire; Chicago Athenaeum, Chicago; Metropolitan Museum of Art, New York; Design Center, Philadelphia University; San Francisco Museum of Modern Art; The Museum of Modern Art (MoMA), New York

RECENT AWARDS
2004 Wiltshire Business of the Year Award – Winner; Judge's Award, Homes and Gardens Classic Design Awards;

Outstanding Excellence award, Wiltshire Business Awards; Giant Of Design (G.O.D.), Annual House Beautiful Awards; Best Appliance, Home Beautiful Magazine Awards, Australia; British Consul – General Award, voted for by British-American Chamber of Commerce; Best Design Award, Japan; PLUS X Award, "Innovation, design and ease of use" category, Germany; Design for Asia Award
2005 PLUS X Award, "Innovation, design and ease of use" category, Germany
2006 Bottom Line Design Award, USA; The Queen's Award for Enterprise (International Trade category), UK

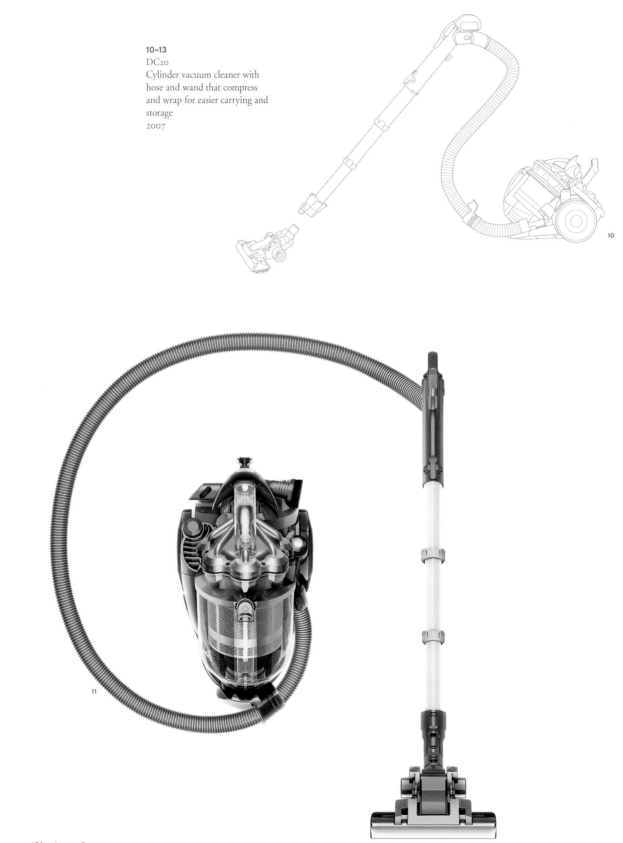

10–13
DC20
Cylinder vacuum cleaner with
hose and wand that compress
and wrap for easier carrying and
storage
2007

10

11

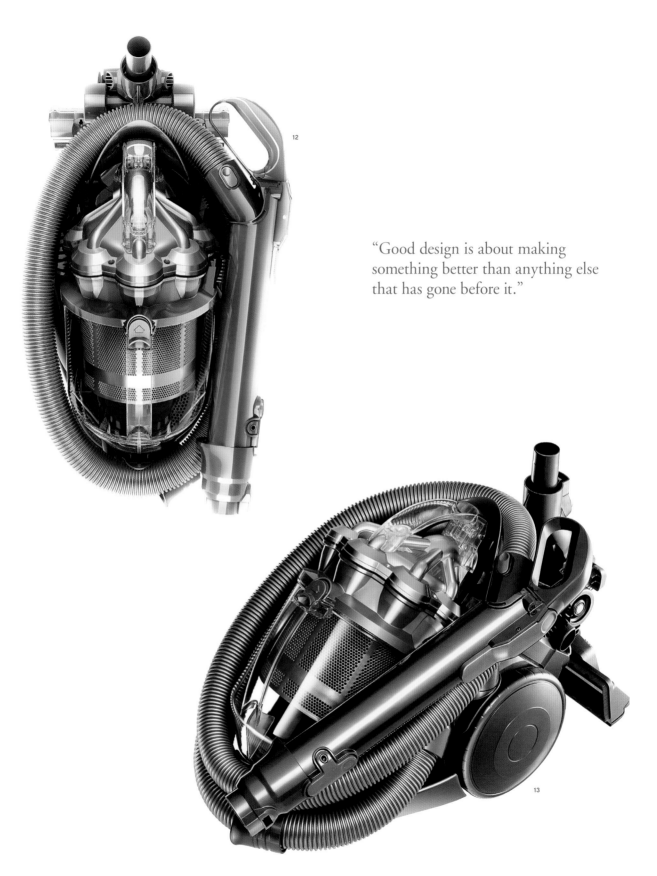

"Good design is about making something better than anything else that has gone before it."

12

13

ECOCATS

"When it comes to powerboats, environmentally speaking, one thing is very clear: one hull bad, two hulls good. Ecocats' design philosophy is to use computer and materials technology to create powerboats that offer hugely reduced fuel consumption (67%) and two-thirds less wash. Wash is the wave-like effect created by passing boats that damages riverbanks and shores, causing subsequent silting as mud and sand falls to the river or sea floor. Initially developed by professional sailing catamaran builders who wanted to use their skills to design and build environmentally-friendly motorboats, Ecocats' design approach reduces the environmental impact of both commercial and pleasure boats by going back to first principles: the less power needed to move a boat, the less environmental damage will be done. With their 'wave-piercing' hulls, these state-of-the-art catamarans are crafted from one of the lightest and strongest modern composite materials available – Kevlar. This combination of knife-like hull form and low-weight-to-strength ratio enables the boats to glide silently through the water without large engines or the noise and fuss of conventional motor craft. With their twin-hulled design they also have the added benefit of being more stable than traditional mono-hulls and also have larger open-decks. Initially working with government and commercial customers buying patrol boats and passenger ferries, the company is now branching out into the leisure yachts the founders have long dreamt of creating."

„Wenn es um Powerboote geht, ist in ökologischer Hinsicht eines völlig klar: Ein Schiffsrumpf ist schlecht, zwei Schiffsrümpfe sind gut. Die Designphilosophie von Ecocats besteht darin, mithilfe von Computer- und Materialtechnologie Powerboote zu entwickeln, die einen enorm verringerten Treibstoffverbrauch (67 %) haben und zwei Drittel weniger Kielwasser bedingen. Kielwasser ist die von Booten erzeugte Wasserwelle, die Flussufer und Küsten schädigt und in der Folge eine Verschlammung verursacht, da Schlamm und Sand auf den Grund des Gewässers absinken. Das Design von Ecocats war ursprünglich von professionellen Segelkatamaran-Konstrukteuren, die ihre Fertigkeiten an der Gestaltung und dem Bau umweltfreundlicher Motorboote erproben wollten, entwickelt worden. Es verringert die Umweltbelastung durch Handels- oder Freizeitschiffe, indem es grundlegende Prinzipien anwendet: Je weniger Kraftstoff benötigt wird, um ein Schiff zu bewegen, desto geringer ist die Umweltbelastung. Diese nach dem neuesten Stand der Technik entwickelten Katamarane mit ihren Wellen durchschneidenden Rümpfen werden aus einem der leichtesten und robustesten Verbundwerkstoffe gefertigt, den es gibt: Kevlar. Die Kombination aus messerscharfem Rumpf und dem im Verhältnis zur Stärke geringen Gewicht ermöglicht es den Booten, geräuschlos durchs Wasser zu gleiten, ohne ausladende Triebwerke und den Lärm konventioneller Motorboote. Durch ihre Doppelrumpf-Gestaltung sind die Boote stabiler als traditionelle Mono-Rumpf-Boote und verfügen zudem über großzügigere offene Deckflächen. Ecocats war ursprünglich für Kunden aus Regierungs- und Wirtschaftskreisen tätig, die Patrouillenboote und Fährschiffe in Auftrag gaben. Nun weiten die Firmengründer ihre Tätigkeit auf Freizeitjachten aus, von deren Gestaltung sie schon lange geträumt haben."

«Pour ce qui est des hors-bord, d'un point de vue environnemental, une chose est très claire: une coque mauvais, deux coques bon. Notre philosophie est d'utiliser l'ordinateur et la technologie des matériaux pour créer des hors-bord qui consomment infiniment moins d'essence (67%) et laissent un sillage aux deux tiers moins important. L'effet de remous occasionné par le passage des bateaux à moteur endommage et érode les rives fluviales et les côtes, ce qui provoque des glissements de terrain sablonneux ou boueux dans l'eau. Développé à l'origine par des architectes navals spécialisés dans la fabrication de catamarans à voile qui ont voulu mettre leurs compétences au service de la création de bateaux à moteur rapides et écologiques, Ecocats contribue à réduire l'impact sur l'environnement des bateaux commerciaux et de loisirs en revenant aux principes de base: moins on a besoin d'énergie pour déplacer un bateau, moins il est nuisible pour la nature. Avec leurs coques ‹fendeuses de houle›, ces catamarans exceptionnels sont constitués d'un des matériaux composites modernes les plus légers et solides qui existe – le Kevlar. Cette combinaison entre étraves affûtées et faible ratio poids/résistance permet à ces navires de glisser silencieusement sur l'eau sans avoir recours à de gros moteurs, encombrants et bruyants. Leur silhouette à double coque les rend également plus stables que les traditionnels monocoques et les dote de ponts ouverts plus spacieux. La compagnie a démarré en vendant des bateaux de patrouille et des ferries à des entreprises publiques et privées et se diversifie aujourd'hui en se lançant dans les yachts de loisirs que ses fondateurs rêvaient de créer depuis bien longtemps.»

1–2
10 m HARBOUR
 PATROL BOAT
Low-wash catamaran launch
at 16 knots on River Thames
and demonstrating offshore
capability
2006

Fuel consumption of the Ecocat 10m Harbour Patrol Boat is 67% less than other patrol boats. Wash is also reduced by two-thirds. According to the Port of London Authority, for whom the boat was designed and built, "Each Ecocat patrol boat will save 3,660 litres of fuel a year. With a litre of diesel producing 2.7kg of carbon dioxide, that represents almost 10 tonnes of CO_2 per boat annually." The Ecocat Harbour Patrol Boat is also more stable and has a bigger and more secure deck than other designs. In addition, it enables recovery from the water through its side doors, and at half the draught of monohulls (40cm) it can operate closer to shore. The boat's hulls and deck are constructed entirely of monolithic Kevlar composite, which is 20 times stronger than steel weight for weight. The correct mix of impact resistance, panel strength and light weight have enabled full commercial certification by the UK Maritime Coastguard Agency while radically improving performance over previous craft. Top speed: 30kts, weight: 3.8tonnes, maximum personnel rescue capability: 30.

Das 10 m lange Hafenpatrouillenboot des Bootsbauers Ecocats hat gegenüber anderen Wasserfahrzeugen dieser Klasse einen um 67 Prozent geringeren Treibstoffverbrauch. Auch das Kielwasser wird um zwei Drittel reduziert. Jedes der für die Port of London Authority entwickelte und gebaute Ecocats-Patrouillenboote ermöglicht der Hafenbehörde zufolge „eine Treibstoffersparnis um 3.660 Liter pro Jahr. Bei einer Kohlendioxidemission von 2,7 kg pro 1 Liter Diesel entspricht das fast 10 Tonnen CO_2 pro Boot und Jahr." Das Ecocats-Modell ist dabei stabiler und bietet mit seinem großzügigeren Deck mehr Sicherheit als andere Designs. Darüber hinaus machen die seitlichen Einstiegsluken die Bergung aus dem Wasser einfacher, und mit einem im Vergleich zu Einrumpfbooten halb so niedrigen Tiefgang (40 cm) kann das Ecocats-Boot auch näher am Ufer operieren. Die beiden Rümpfe und das Deck sind in monolithischer Bauweise aus Kevlar-Verbundwerkstoff gefertigt, der bei gleichem Gewicht 20-mal härter als Stahl ist. Die richtige Mischung aus Stoßfestigkeit, Plattenstärke und Leichtigkeit wurde von der UK Maritime Coastguard Agency für den kommerziellen Einsatz zertifiziert; aber auch in der Performance wurden gegenüber früheren Schiffen enorme Fortschritte erzielt. Höchstgeschwindigkeit: 30 Knoten, Gewicht: 3,8 Tonnen, Fassungsvermögen bei Rettungseinsätzen: 30 Personen.

Le bateau de patrouille portuaire Ecocat de 10 m consomme 67 % moins de carburant que les autres bateaux de police maritime du marché. D'après les autorités portuaires de Londres, pour lesquelles ce bateau a été conçu et fabriqué, « chaque bateau de patrouille Ecocat économisera 3660 litres d'essence par an. Un litre de diesel produit 2,7 kg de dioxyde de carbone, ce qui représente presque 10 tonnes de CO2 par bateau et par an. » Le bateau de patrouille Ecocat est aussi plus stable et jouit d'un pont plus vaste et plus sûr que ses concurrents. De plus, il permet de remonter des personnes de l'eau par les portes latérales et sa ligne de flottaison, deux fois plus basse que celle des autres monocoques (40 cm), lui permet d'opérer plus près de la côte. La coque et le pont du bateau sont entièrement constitués de composite monolithique Kevlar, un matériau 20 fois plus solide que l'acier à poids égal. Le juste mélange de résistance à l'impact, de robustesse et de légèreté a permis à l'Ecocat d'obtenir de l'Agence maritime des Garde-Côtes du Royaume-Uni un certificat de commercialisation complet. Ses performances dépassent largement celles de ses prédécesseurs : vitesse de pointe à 30 nœuds, poids 3,8 tonnes, capacité maximum de 30 secouristes.

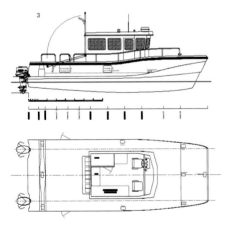

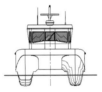

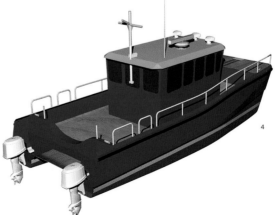

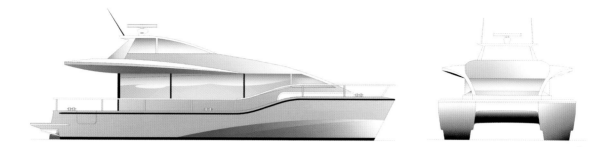

5

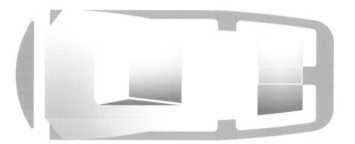

"To make a green motorboat, add another hull."

3–4
10 m HARBOUR PATROL
BOAT
Drawings and CAD renderings
2006

5
15 m YACHT
Low-wash catamaran power
yacht
2006

6
ROUND BRITAIN CIRCUM-
NAVIGATION PROPOSAL
Solar/fuel cell and wind-
powered trimaran concept
2005

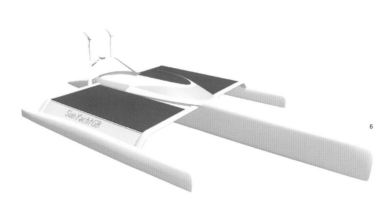

6

ECOCATS
6 Enterprise Court
Marine Drive
Torpoint
Cornwall PL11 2EH
United Kingdom
T +44 20 73625089
E henry.mayhew@ecocats.com
www.ecocats.com

COMPANY HISTORY
2000 Founded by Andy Fox
(Master Boat Builder) and
Derick Reynolds (Boat Designer) in Cornwall, England to
commercialize their design of
the first Ecocat powerboat
2002 Investor Henry Mayhew
joins company as Managing
Director
2007 Company establishes new
design and production facility in
Al Khobar, Saudi Arabia

RECENT EXHIBITIONS
2004 "London Boat Show",
ExCel Exhibition Centre, London
2005 "Gulf International Boat
Show", Dubai; "Seawork 2005
International", Port of
Southampton
2006 "Seawork 2006 International", Port of Southampton
2007 "Seawork 2007 International", Port of Southampton;
"Workboat", Glasgow Exhibition Centre

RECENT AWARDS
2006 Sustainable Products and
Services Trophy, Cornwall Sus-
tainability Awards
2007 RINA–Lloyd's Register
Ship Safety & Environment
Award, RINA (Royal Institution
of Naval Architects) and Lloyd's
Register of Shipping, London;
Featured, "Significant Small
ships 2006" publication, RINA
(Royal Institution of Naval
Architects)

CLIENTS
Port of London Authority,
The Boat Race Company
(Oxford vs Cambridge
University boat race),
Trentham Leisure Ltd

ECOLEAN

"Ecolean offers a packaging material based on calcium carbonate, or chalk as it is commonly known. Our task is to supply efficient packaging solutions with minimal environmental impact. We use our key technology of mixing calcium carbonate with plastics to create efficient packaging solutions for distribution of food. Sustainable packaging is a conception best defined as a packaging with a lifecycle that can sustain unmodified for many generations without exhausting any natural resources. The design of the Ecolean packaging system is efficient in materials, processing, waste and has the great effect of saving energy and water."

„Ecolean bietet ein Verpackungsmaterial an, das auf Calciumcarbonat, gemeinhin als Kalk bekannt, basiert. Unsere Aufgabe ist es, effiziente Verpackungslösungen mit minimaler Umweltbelastung herzustellen. Mithilfe unserer Schlüsseltechnologie, bei der Calciumcarbonat mit Kunststoffen vermischt wird, erzeugen wir effiziente Verpackungen für Lebensmittel. Als nachhaltige Verpackungsmaterialien lassen sich am besten solche definieren, deren Lebenszyklus über viele Generationen unverändert bleiben kann, ohne dass natürliche Ressourcen erschöpft werden. Das Design des Ecolean-Verpackungssystems ist in Bezug auf Material, Verarbeitung und Abfallproduktion effizient und spart Energie und Wasser."

«Ecolean propose un matériau d'emballage élaboré à partir de carbonate de calcium, plus couramment connu sous le nom de craie. Notre tâche est de fournir des solutions d'emballage ayant un bon rendement mais un impact minime sur l'environnement. Nous utilisons pour cela une technologie particulière qui consiste à mélanger le carbonate de calcium avec des plastiques pour créer des emballages aptes à la distribution de nourriture. Notre concept d'emballage durable est celui d'un emballage dont le cycle de vie peut durer sans dégradation sur plusieurs générations sans épuiser les ressources naturelles. Le système d'emballage d'Ecolean est adapté en termes de matériaux, de conception et de déchets et a pour autre effet positif d'économiser de l'énergie et de l'eau.»

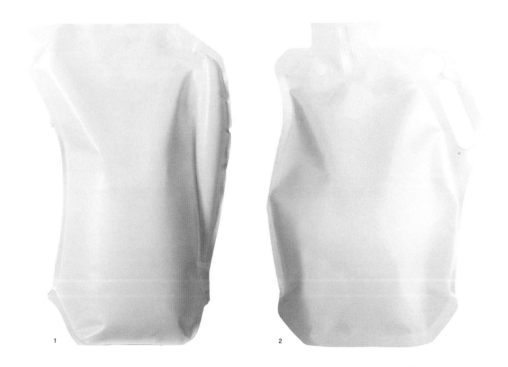

1   2

4

1–2
LA (LEANAIR) 1000
AND LB (LEANBASE) 1000
Two basic forms of Calymer low
environmental impact packages
2003

3
LA (LEANAIR) 1000
Calymer low environmental
impact milk packaging with
printed graphics for Bannister,
Australia
2005

4
CALYMER MATERIALS
Calcium carbonate (natural
chalk) in raw state, pulverized
and granulated, and granulated
plastic (PE and PP) binding
agent

1–5
ECOLEAN CALYMER
PACKAGING, 2003

"Ecolean® packages are made of
Ecolean Calymer™ material,
which consists of 40% calcium
carbonate – natural chalk – and
polymers as a binding agent.
This provides a package material
that is flexible and tough, perfect for dairy products, but also
a material with exceptional environmental properties. After dis-
posal, the calcium carbonate is
returned to nature and the binding agent is transformed into
water vapour and carbon dioxide
(as for all incinerated material)
after complete degradation, e.g.
after incineration. The Ecolean
Calymer material is not only a
resource-efficient material with
low environmental impact, but
also a new packaging material
with improved organoleptic
properties. It will preserve the
freshness and protect your products longer."

„Der Grundstoff von Ecolean®-
Verpackungen ist Ecolean Caly-
mer™, das zu 40 Prozent aus
Calciumcarbonat – in der Natur
vorkommender Kalk – und
Polymeren als Bindemittel
besteht. Das sehr flexible und
feste Verpackungsmaterial bietet
für verschiedene Anforderungen
optimale Lösungen und hat
zugleich außergewöhnliche
Umwelteigenschaften. Wird das
Material entsorgt, kehrt das Calciumcarbonat in die Natur
zurück, und das Bindemittel zer-
fällt im endgültigen Abbaupro-
zess, zum Beispiel bei der Müll-
verbrennung, zu Wasserdampf
und Kohlendioxid. Ecolean
Calymer ist nicht nur ein res-
sourceneffizientes Material mit
geringer Umweltbelastung, neu
an diesem Verpackungsmaterial
sind auch seine verbesserten
organoleptischen Eigenschaften.
Die darin verpackten Produkte
werden geschützt und bleiben
länger frisch."

« Les emballages Ecolean® sont
constitués de Calymer™, un
matériau breveté par Ecolean
composé à 40% de carbonate de
calcium – la craie naturelle –
et de polymères comme agents
liants. Ce mélange produit un
matériau d'emballage à la fois
souple et résistant, parfaitement
adapté à la variété des problèma-
tiques d'emballage et aussi
exceptionnellement peu nocif
pour l'environnement. Après utilisation, le carbonate de calcium
retourne à la nature et l'agent de
liaison est transformé en vapeur
d'eau et en dioxyde de carbone à
l'issue de son processus de dégradation, notamment après inciné-
ration. Le Calymer d'Ecolean est
non seulement un matériau économe en ressources mais aussi
un matériau dont l'impact sur
l'environnement est minime et
un nouveau matériau d'emballage aux meilleures propriétés
organoleptiques. Il préservera la
fraîcheur de vos produits plus
longtemps. »

"We develop, manufacture and market highly functional and cost-efficient packaging solutions with low environmental impact for the international food industry."

5

6

5
LA (LEANAIR) 1000
Drawing showing packaging
structure

6–7
EL2/EP2
Automatic flexible filling and
packing machine for packaging
liquid food products into LA
(LeanAir) packages
2003

7

ECOLEAN
Ecolean AB
Kielergatan 48
25232 Helsingborg
Sweden
T +46 42 4504500
E info@ecolean.se
www.ecolean.com

COMPANY HISTORY
1996 Founded by Åke Rosen in Helsingborg, Sweden; subsequently opened production sites in Helsingborg, Sweden and Tianjin, China and marketing companies in China, Bulgaria, Russia, Italy and Poland
2001 Hans Rausing became the major stakeholder in the company

RECENT EXHIBITIONS
2006 "Anuga Foodtec", Cologne

RECENT AWARDS
2003 Gold award, Prize-Pack 2003 awards, BalkanPac Exhibition, Sofia, Bulgaria
2004 First Prize, PakStar 2004 awards, Polish Packaging Research and Development Center

2006 Gold Award for Innovation, The Dairy Industry of Australia Awards (Bannister Downs Farm); Silver award and Yellow Pencil, D&AD, London (Daylesford Organic)

9

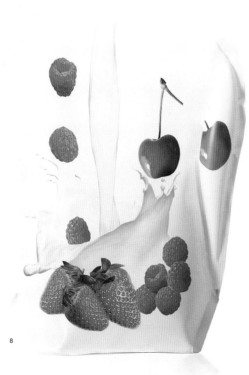

8

10

8–10
LA (LEANAIR) 200,
500 SLIM and 1000
Calymer low environmental
impact milk packages with
printed graphics
2003

11
LA (LEANAIR) 1000
Calymer packaging is opened by
tearing or cutting a slit at the top
of the container and then poured
while gripping the package's
integral air handle

[ECOSISTEMA URBANO] ARQUITECTOS

"Ecosistema Urbano is an open system, dedicated to architectural research and design. It is characterized by a heightened sensitivity towards ecology and a commitment to sustainable cities and a sustainable planet. In contrast with passive architectural theory and opinion, Ecosistema Urbano takes an active role, starting from a critical and propositional look at reality, then using this position as a project guideline. Architects should stop thinking exclusively in terms of materiality. Man creates artificial conditions, and he configures environments that can also be architecture. The use of non-tangible materials is as important as tangible material. The contemporary architect is a manager who optimizes the available budgetary and energy resources. Ecosistema Urbano attempts to use architecture as a preventive tool, because to prevent is a more sustainable approach than to cure...that includes the dimension of time as a project component. The strategy should provide capacity for anticipation, including the eventual expiration date. The design should be able to be dismantled when necessary and its manufacture should be regarded as a reversible process. It should be created with the construction and dismantling processes in mind. The life of a structure must be taken into consideration so that it is designed with the economy of its media in mind. Establishing priorities directed at obtaining the maximum with the minimum, in terms of sustainability not in terms of minimalism... for spontaneity and freedom. Architecture designed from reality and not from some vision of utopia."

„Ecosistema Urbano ist ein offenes System, konzipiert für die Forschung und Gestaltung im Bereich Architektur. Es zeichnet sich durch eine erhöhte Sensibilität für Ökologie sowie ein Engagement für nachhaltige Städte und einen nachhaltigen Planeten aus. Im Gegensatz zu passiver Architekturtheorie und Kritik nimmt Ecosistema Urbano eine aktive Rolle ein, beginnend bei einem kritischen und unvoreingenommenen Blick auf die Wirklichkeit und der anschließenden Umsetzung dieser Position in eine Projektrichtlinie. Architekten sollten aufhören, ausschließlich in materiellen Begriffen zu denken. Der Mensch schafft künstliche Bedingungen, und er konfiguriert seine räumliche Umgebung auf eine Art, die ebenfalls Architektur sein kann. Die Verwendung unstofflicher Materialien ist genauso wichtig wie die stofflicher Materialien. Der zeitgenössische Architekt ist ein Manager, der die verfügbaren Ressourcen an Budget und Energie optimiert. Ecosistema Urbano sucht Architektur als Präventivmaßnahme einzusetzen, denn vorzubeugen ist ein nachhaltigerer Zugang als zu heilen ... das schließt die Zeitdimension als Projektkomponente mit ein. Diese Strategie sollte Raum für Antizipation lassen, einschließlich des möglichen Ablaufdatums. Das Design sollte zerlegbar sein, wenn nötig, und seine Herstellung sollte als ein reversibler Prozess betrachtet werden. Die Gestaltung sollte im Hinblick auf den Konstruktions- und Dekonstruktionsprozess erfolgen. Die Lebensdauer einer Konstruktion muss in Betracht gezogen werden, sodass sie mit Rücksicht auf die Ökonomie ihres Mediums gestaltet wird. Priorität sollte sein, das Maximum mit einem Minimum zu erreichen, im Sinne der Nachhaltigkeit, nicht im Sinne des Minimalismus ... für Spontaneität und Freiheit. Architektur, die aus der Realität gestaltet wird und nicht aus irgendeiner utopischen Vision."

« Ecosistema Urbano est un système ouvert dédié à la recherche et à la création architecturales. Il se caractérise par une sensibilité accrue à l'égard de l'écologie et un engagement en faveur de villes et d'une planète viables. Contrairement aux théories et opinions architecturales passives, Ecosistema Urbano joue un rôle actif, en posant sur la réalité un regard critique et propositionnel selon l'axe duquel chaque projet s'organise. Les architectes devraient cesser de ne penser qu'en termes matérialistes. L'homme crée des conditions artificielles et configure des environnements qui peuvent aussi être de l'architecture. L'utilisation de matériaux intangibles est aussi importante que celle de matériaux tangibles. L'architecte contemporain est un gestionnaire qui optimise les ressources budgétaires et énergétiques à sa disposition. Ecosistema Urbano veut utiliser l'architecture comme un instrument de prévention – parce que prévenir est plus durable que guérir – qui tienne compte de la dimension temporelle dans l'élaboration du projet. La stratégie doit permettre d'anticiper, y compris la date éventuelle d'expiration. Le design doit pouvoir être démantelé si nécessaire et sa fabrication doit être abordée comme un processus réversible. Le designer doit garder à l'esprit les processus de construction et de démantèlement. La vie d'une structure doit être prise en considération pour être élaborée de façon à optimiser sa matière. Établir des priorités afin de tirer le maximum du minimum, en termes de durabilité, pas de minimalisme... pour conserver spontanéité et liberté. Une architecture créée à partir de la réalité et pas d'une quelconque vision d'utopie. »

ECO-BOULEVARD OF VALLE-
CAS FOR MADRID CITY
COUNCIL, 2004–2005

Eco-boulevard is the competi-
tion-winning design for a public
work on the main street of the
Madrid suburb of Vallecas.
With the competition goals
being to generate places for
social activity and to adapt an
open space from a bioclimatic
perspective, Ecosistema Urbano
devised an innovative and whol-
ly sustainable solution. Three
cylindrical pavilions or "air
trees", each with a diameter of
about 20 metres and a slight hol-
low at their base to accommodate urban park-like activities,
have been sited in the middle of
the boulevard. The façade of
each structure varies: the first is
formed by 16 hemispherical air
columns covered with a thermal
fabric, while its interior is clad
with vegetation; the second is

covered with vegetation both
inside and out; the third is covered in a green fabric with a
video projection wall on its
internal surface. Easily erected
and dismantled, the air trees are
light and energy self-sufficient
through the use of solar photovoltaic systems. Evaporation and
transpiration plants provide air
conditioning – water pumped
into tanks at the top of each
cylinder is redistributed to the
lower layers where it is vapor-
ized, thus reducing the temperature by eight to ten degrees in
the sunken meeting areas.

Der Eco-Boulevard ging als Sie-
ger aus einem Wettbewerb zur
Gestaltung einer Freifläche auf
einer Hauptstraße im Madrider
Stadtteil Vallecas hervor. Die
Aufgabenstellung des Wettbe-
werbs, Freiräume für soziale All-
tagsaktivitäten aus einer biokli-
matischen Perspektive zu
gestalten und neu zu definieren,

löste das Architektenteam Ecosistema Urbano mit einem innovativen und umweltverträglichen
Konzept. Man platzierte in der
Mitte des Boulevards drei zylin-
drische Pavillons von zirka 20 m
Durchmesser, „Air trees" genannt, deren Fundamente leicht
abgesenkte urbane Erholungs-
räume umschließen. Die Bau-
werkshüllen bestehen aus 16
hemisphärischen, mit Thermo-
folie bespannten Luftsäulen und
sind unterschiedlich gestaltet:
Während beim ersten Zylinder
nur die Innenfläche bepflanzt
wurde, ist der zweite innen
wie außen begrünt; der dritte
Zylinder wiederum ist mit grü-
ner Folie bespannt und an der
Innenseite mit einer Videopro-
jektionsfläche ausgestattet. Die
einfach zu errichtenden und
abbaubaren „Air trees" sind
leicht und luftdurchlässig und
durch den Einsatz einer Photo-
voltaikanlage auch energieau-
tark. Ein Evaporations- und

Transpirationssystem sorgt für
die Klimatisierung: Wasser wird
in Reservoirs oben auf den
Zylindern gepumpt, zerstäubt
und wieder nach unten ver-
sprüht, was die versenkten Auf-
enthaltsräume zu einer um acht
bis zehn Grad kühleren Zone
macht.

L'Eco-boulevard est le projet qui
a été retenu par le conseil muni-
cipal de Madrid pour la rue
principale de la ville de Vallecas,
banlieue de la capitale espagnole.
L'objectif de cette compétition
était de créer des lieux d'activité
sociale en concevant un espace
ouvert dans une perspective bio-
climatique, et Ecosistema Urbano a trouvé une solution novatrice et totalement durable. Trois
pavillons cylindriques d'environ
20 mètres de diamètre, des
« arbres d'air » au creux desquels
viennent s'installer des activités
de loisirs, ont été installés au
milieu du boulevard. Chaque

pavillon a une façade différente :
le premier est constitué de 16
colonnes d'air hémisphériques
couvertes de tissu thermique
tandis que l'intérieur est tapissé
de végétation ; le deuxième est
recouvert de végétation dedans
et dehors ; le troisième est tapissé d'un tissu vert à l'extérieur
et d'une surface de projection
vidéo à l'intérieur. Facile à monter et à démanteler, les arbres
d'air sont légers et énergétiquement autosuffisants grâce à l'utilisation de panneaux solaires
photovoltaïques. L'air condition-
né est apporté par des installations d'évaporation et de transpiration – l'eau remplit des
réservoirs situés en haut de
chaque cylindre pour être redis-
tribuée aux niveaux inférieurs où
il est vaporisé, ce qui réduit la
température ambiante de huit à
dix degrés dans les zones de rencontre en contrebas.

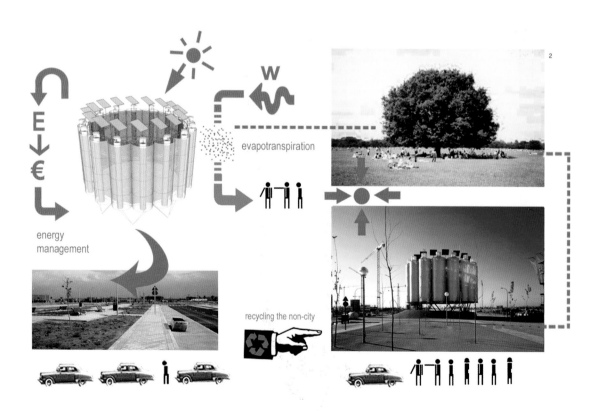

energy
management

evapotranspiration

recycling the non-city

3

"[Ecosistemo Urbano] is an architecture and engineering team that focuses on the research and ecological design of new architecture projects that understand sustainable development as a resource for innovation and enthusiasm."

4

5

1
AIR TREE
Detail of first solar-powered bioclimatic pavilion for the Eco-Boulevard of Vallecas
2004–2005
Client: Madrid City Council

2
AIR TREE
Process diagram of solar-powered bioclimatic pavilion

3–5
AIR TREE
First solar-powered bioclimatic pavilion for the Eco-Boulevard of Vallecas and details of air columns and public seating
2004–2005
Client: Madrid City Council

COMPONENTS:

[1] Photovoltaic panels

[2] Wind catcher

[3] Cooling system

[4] Ventilation pipes

[5] Air difusser

[6] Tightened galvanized steel mesh. Climbing plants support

[7] Green wall of climbing plants

[8] Lighting system. Fiber optics

[9] Exterior thermal shield

[10] Circular bench. Recycled plastic pieces

[11] Artificial topography and continuous paving made of recycled tires

[12] Densification of existing tree grid

[13] Superficial interventions within the existing urbanization (backfill, paint, etc.)

6

8

7

6–7
AIR TREE
Components of first solar-powered bioclimatic pavilion and view at night

8
AIR TREE
View of the Eco-Boulevard of Vallecas with second solar-powered bioclimatic pavilion in foreground
2004–2005
Client: Madrid City Council

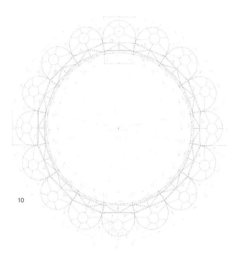

9
ECO-BOULEVARD
OF VALLECAS
CAD rendering showing
position of three cylindrical
pavilions
2004–2005
Client: Madrid City Council

10–11
AIR TREE
Plan and axonometric drawings
of first solar-powered bioclimatic
pavilion for the Eco-Boulevard
of Vallecas

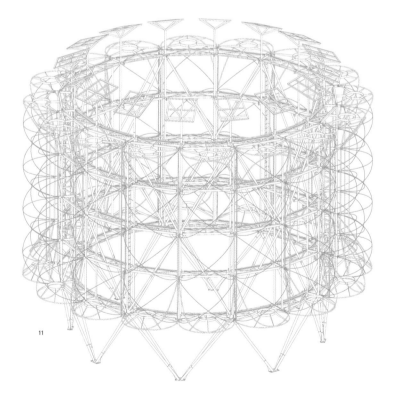

[ECOSISTEMA URBANO] ARQUITECTOS

Estanislao Figueras 6
28008 Madrid
Spain
T +34 915591601
info@ecosistemaurbano.com
www.ecosistemaurbano.com

DESIGN GROUP HISTORY
2000 Founded by Belinda Tato and Jose Luis Vallejo in Madrid
2004 Diego García-Setién joins office
2005 Constantino Hurtado joins office

PARTNERS' BIOGRAPHIES
BELINDA TATO
1971 Born in Madrid, Spain
1990–1999 Studied Architecture at Universidad Politécnica de Madrid
1996–1997 Studied Architecture at The Bartlett School of Architecture – University College London

JOSE LUIS VALLEJO
1971 Born in Bilbao, Spain
1990–1999 Studied Architecture at Universidad Politécnica de Madrid
1996–1997 Studied Architecture at The Bartlett School of Architecture – University College London

DIEGO GARCÍA-SETIÉN
1974 Born in Madrid, Spain
1993–2000 Studied Architecture at Universidad Politécnica de Madrid
1997–1998 Studied Architecture at Istituto Universitario di Architettura di Venezia (Venice)

CONSTANTINO HURTADO
1971 Born in Madrid, Spain
1989–1995 Studied Engineering at Universidad Politécnica de Madrid
1996–2007 Studied Architecture at Universidad Politécnica de Madrid

RECENT EXHIBITIONS
2006 "Monoespacios 8", COAM (Colegio oficial de arquitectos de Madrid), Madrid; "Freshmadrid.com", Madrid, Barcelona, Bogota, Brussels and Dublin; "9ª Muestra de jóvenes arquitectos de la Fundación Camuñas", Madrid and Alicante; "Biennial Awards, Architects Association of Asturias", Gijón; "Europan 8 awards", Madrid, Maribor (Slovenia), Dordrecht (The Netherlands); "Hibrids 2.0" COAC (Col·legi d'Arquitectes de Catalunya), Gerona and Las Palmas; "Philadelphia Urban Voids", Philadelphia
2007 "Construir, Habitar, Pensar", IVAM, Valencia and various venues in Latin America; "Mies van der Rohe European Prize" exhibition, Barcelona; "Ecoboulevard", Museum El Croquis, Madrid; "Technology, Steel and Construction", COAC, Barcelona; "Horizons – Madrid Social Housing", Royal Institute of British Architects, London; "Intermediae 2.0", Madrid
2008 "Spanish Pavilion", Zaragoza Expo 2008

RECENT AWARDS
2005 3rd Prize, Competition for Ies Son Fangos, Manacor, Mallorca (an educational institute); Award for Constructed Project, Architectural Association of Asturias; European Acknowledgement Award, Holcim Foundation for Sustainable Construction
2006 1st Prize, EUROPAN 8, Maribor, Slovenia; 2nd Prize, International Competition for the Revitalization of Philadelphia; Madrid Award, Enor Foundation; European Acknowledgement Award, Holcim Foundation; 1st Prize Award for Sustainable Construction, Forestalia, Galicia; Mention, 9th Muestra de Arquitectos Jóvenes Espanoles 2005, Fundación Camuñas; Honourable mention, Asprima Awards; Honourable mention, Municipality of Madrid Urbanism Awards; Honourable mention, Architectural Association & EES's Environmental Tectonics Competition, London; Honourable mention, ITC Tubular Awards, Madrid; Honourable Mention, Architectural Association and the Environments, Ecology and Sustainability Research Cluster Award, London
2007 Honourable mention, Architectural Exhibition Award; Honourable mention, Intermediae Competition, Madrid; Finalist for the European Union Prize for Contemporary Architecture, Mies van der Rohe Award for "Emerging European Architect"

CLIENTS
AENA, Ayuntamiento de Madrid/Municipality of Madrid, Arcelor, Biosfera, Caja Madrid, INECO, Ministerio de Medio, Ambiente/Spanish Ministry of Environment, Universidad Politécnica de Madrid

12–13/16
STREET ECO-FURNITURE
Photo-luminescent public seating units made of moulded recycled PET, water and photo-luminescent resin proposed for the Zaragoza Expo 2008
2007
Client: self-produced concept

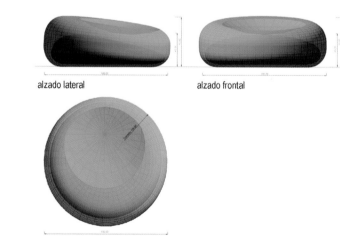

alzado lateral   alzado frontal   12

planta

13

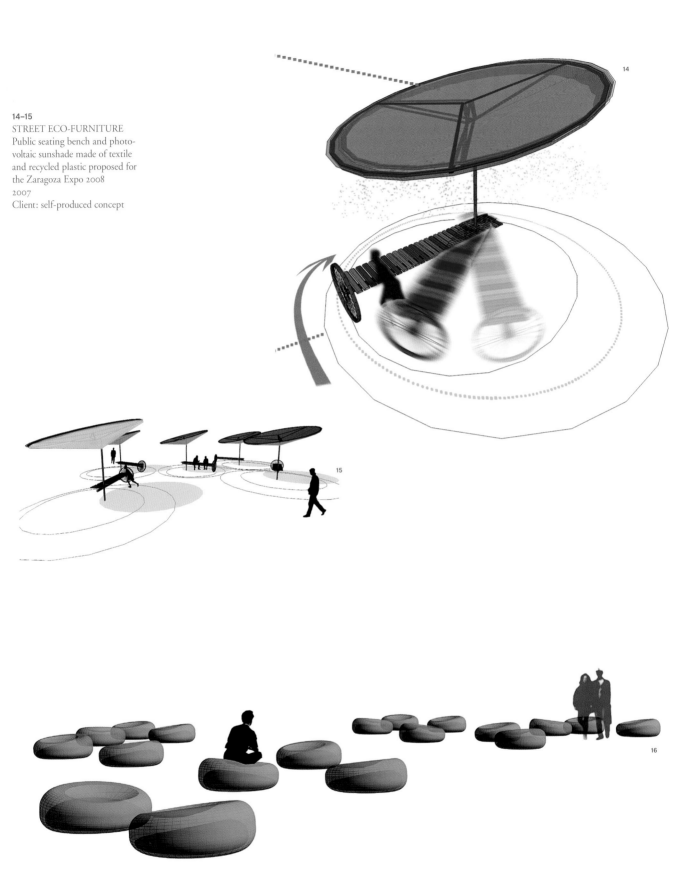

14–15
STREET ECO-FURNITURE
Public seating bench and photovoltaic sunshade made of textile
and recycled plastic proposed for
the Zaragoza Expo 2008
2007
Client: self-produced concept

ECOTRICITY

"Ecotricity believes that wind turbines make good neighbours. The cutting edge of technology and symbols of a greener future, they are moving pieces of art rather than industrial machines. Ecotricity's technology partner Enercon is the pioneer of the world's leading direct drive, variable speed wind technology. The E-70 Wind Turbine is based on a design by the award-winning British architect Norman Foster. The E-70 is much quieter and more efficient than its predecessors, making it ideally suited to urban as well as rural locations. Ecotricity operates a wide range of projects, all of them examples of its good neighbour policy; a marriage of good design, good technology and committed ownership. Our single turbine at Green Park, Reading, is Europe's most 'seen' wind turbine to date. Approximately 100,000 people pass this spot every day, people who may have never seen modern windmills before. Ecotricity have more landmark projects in the pipeline. Permission has been granted for a wind turbine to be constructed at Manchester City Football Clubs' Sportcity stadium. It will be one of the UK's largest landbased turbines and make MCFC the only sporting arena in the world to have its own green energy supply."

„Ecotricity ist davon überzeugt, dass Windkraftanlagen gute Nachbarn sind. Die technisch innovativen Symbole einer umweltfreundlicheren Zukunft sind eher bewegliche Kunstwerke als Industriemaschinen. Enercon, der technische Partner von Ecotricity, ist Pionier in der weltweit führenden Windkrafttechnologie mit Direktantrieb und variabler Drehzahl. Die Windkraftanlage E-70 basiert auf einem Entwurf des preisgekrönten britischen Architekten Norman Foster. Die E-70 ist wesentlich leiser und effizienter als ihre Vorgängermodelle und eignet sich damit ideal sowohl für urbane als auch für ländliche Umgebungen. Ecotricity betreibt eine ganze Palette von Projekten, die als Beispiel für eine Politik der guten Nachbarschaft gelten können und gutes Design mit hochwertiger Technologie und Eigentümerengagement verbinden. Unser Windrad in Green Park, Reading, ist bis heute das meistbeachtete in Europa. Täglich kommen rund 100 000 Menschen daran vorbei, Menschen, die vielleicht noch nie eine moderne Windmühle gesehen haben. Ecotricity hat weitere markante Projekte in Planung. Für die Errichtung einer Windkraftanlage im Sportcity-Stadion des Fußballvereins Manchester City wurde die Baugenehmigung erteilt. Es wird eine der größten Anlagen in Großbritannien auf dem Festland sein und das Stadion zur weltweit einzigen Sportarena mit eigener umweltfreundlicher Energieversorgung machen."

«Ecotricity pense que les éoliennes font de bonnes voisines. À la pointe de la technologie, ces symboles d'un avenir plus vert sont davantage des œuvres d'art en mouvement que des machines industrielles. Le partenaire technologique d'Ecotricity, Enercon, est le pionnier de la principale technologie énergétique fondée sur la vitesse variable du vent. La forme de l'éolienne E-70 a été conçue par le célèbre architecte britannique Norman Foster. La E-70 est bien plus silencieuse et efficace que ses ancêtres et convient donc aussi bien aux zones urbaines que rurales. Ecotricity s'occupe d'un large éventail de projets, qui illustrent tous sa politique de bon voisinage; un mariage de bon design, de bonne technologie et de propriété engagée. Notre unique turbine de Green Park, à Reading, est l'éolienne la plus ‹vue› d'Europe à ce jour. Quelque 100 000 personnes passent devant elle chaque jour, des gens qui n'ont peut-être jamais vu de moulin à vent moderne auparavant. Ecotricity a encore bien des projets grandioses dans ses tuyaux. Permission vient de nous être donnée d'installer une éolienne pour le stade de la ‹Cité du Sport› du Club de football de Manchester. Elle sera la plus grande éolienne construite sur le territoire britannique et fera du Manchester City Football Club la seule installation sportive au monde à posséder son propre système d'alimentation en énergie verte.»

1

1–5
E-70 WIND TURBINE, 2004

Ecotricity's founding aim was to change the way electricity was made, by stimulating a mass market for a new kind of electricity – the "green" kind. In doing so they created the world's first "green" electricity company. Today, the company continues to be a sector pioneer, from wind park design to the delivery of clean, green energy to customers across the UK. Ecotricity owns and maintains 27 wind turbines on 11 parks around the UK and are the biggest independent supplier of homes in the UK, supplying over 24,000 business and domestic properties. One in ten of the wind projects operating in the UK today were planned and built by Ecotricity, and the company invests more per customer in new renewable energy than any other electricity supplier – in fact more than all of them combined – a total of £17 million so far and a planned £24 million in 2007.

Ecotricity wurde mit dem erklärten Ziel gegründet, die Stromerzeugung durch Belebung eines Massenmarktes für eine neue Form der elektrischen Energie – der Ökoenergie – zu verändern. Bei diesem Versuch ist das erste „grüne" Elektrizitätsunternehmen entstanden. Die Firma ist bis heute ein Pionier auf diesem Sektor, sowohl hinsichtlich des Designs von Windparks als auch der Versorgung von Kunden mit Ökoenergie im gesamten Vereinigten Königreich. Ecotricity besitzt und betreibt 27 Windkraftanlagen in elf Parks in ganz Großbritannien. Als größter unabhängiger Energielieferant des Landes versorgt Ecotricity mehr als 24 000 Unternehmen und private Haushalte. Jedes zehnte existierende Windkraftprojekt in Großbritannien wurde von Ecotricity geplant und errichtet. Die Firma investiert pro Kunden mehr als jeder andere Stromanbieter in erneuerbare Energie – sogar mehr als alle anderen zusammen: Insgesamt 17 Millionen Pfund waren es bis dato, und für 2007 sind weitere 24 Millionen Pfund geplant.

L'objectif fondateur d'Ecotricity était de modifier la façon dont l'électricité est produite en encourageant un marché mondial de masse à se saisir d'une nouvelle forme d'électricité – la ‹ verte ›. Ils ont ainsi créé la première entreprise d'électricité ‹ verte › du monde. L'entreprise a toujours un rôle pionnier dans le secteur, de la création de parcs éoliens à la distribution d'une énergie propre et écologique à ses abonnés britanniques. Ecotricity possède et entretient 27 éoliennes dans 11 parcs situés au Royaume-Uni, ce qui en fait le plus important fournisseur d'électricité domestique indépendant du Royaume-Uni, avec plus de 24 000 abonnés, commerciaux ou particuliers. Un projet éolien sur dix au Royaume-Uni a été élaboré et mis en place par Ecotricity, qui investit davantage en énergie renouvelable neuve par abonné que tout autre fournisseur d'électricité – même davantage que l'ensemble de nos concurrents réunis – soit 25 millions d'euros au total, et prévoit d'en investir 35 millions en 2007.

1	Main carrier	5	Rotor hub
2	Yaw motors	6	Rotor blade
3	Ring generator		
4	Blade adaptor		

3

1
ENERCON E-70
Construction of 2MW wind turbine nacelle in Dundee, Scotland
2006
Client: Michelin

2
ENERCON E-66
1.5MW wind turbine in Dagenham, England
2004
Client: Ford

3
ENERCON E-70
Diagram of 2MW wind turbine drive train, generator and rotor hub assembly

4
ENERCON E-70
Detail of 2MW wind turbine tubular steel tower

4

"We use good design and planning to harness the power of nature, generating new energy and helping the fight against climate change."

5
ENERCON E-70
Detail of 2MW wind turbine

6–8
ENERCON E-70
Construction of 2MW wind turbine in Dundee, Scotland
2006
Client: Michelin

5

6

7

8

ECOTRICITY
Axiom House
Station Road
Stroud
Gloucestershire GL5 3AP
United Kingdom
T + 44 1453 756111
E info@ecotricity.co.uk
www.ecotricity.co.uk

COMPANY HISTORY
1995 Founded by Dale Vince (b.1961) in Stroud, England
2001 Dale Vince is named "Entrepreneur of the Year 2001" by Ernst & Young Entrepreneur of the Year Program
2004 Dale Vince is awarded an OBE in the New Years Honours List for services to the Environment and to the Electricity Industry

RECENT AWARDS
2000 The Queen's Award for Enterprise; Award for Business Innovation – Utility Industry Achievement Award
2005 South East Renewable Energy Award for Wind Energy

CLIENTS
Co-op, Ford, Manchester City Football Club, Michelin, Prudential Ltd., Sainsbury's, The Bristol Port Company

ELEGANT EMBELLISH-MENTS

"Elegant Embellishments was formed in 2006 to investigate and develop new materials and methods for the quick modification of existing buildings and spaces. These modifications are used to 'tune' buildings, converting previously inert surfaces into active surfaces that can meet new challenges set by a rapidly changing world. A key interest of our work is the visual articulation of innovative technologies that have the potential to alleviate the ecological impact of cities but often require a re-examination of current practices, in particular the slow institutional processes of architecture. Existing applications of such new technologies often aim at visual integration with conventional building materials, but miss their potential as catalysts for behavioral change and public discussion. Our first functioning product is a decorative architectural tile that is cheap to install and that can effectively reduce air pollution from traffic in cities when installed near traffic ways or on building façades. Utilizing computer-based manufacturing techniques, these tiles increase the effect of the underlying technology while also creating visually striking installations that highlight the problems of air pollution and its possible solutions."

„Elegant Embellishments wurde 2006 gegründet, um neue Materialien und Methoden zur raschen Modifikation bestehender Gebäude und Räume zu untersuchen und zu entwickeln. Diese Veränderungen dienen dazu, Gebäude ‚anzupassen', indem bislang inaktive Flächen in aktive verwandelt werden, die den neuen Anforderungen einer sich rapide verändernden Welt gerecht werden können. Ein Hauptaugenmerk unserer Arbeit ist die visuelle Artikulation von innovativen Technologien, die das Potenzial haben, die ökologischen Auswirkungen von Städten zu reduzieren, jedoch oft eine Überprüfung der gängigen Praxis erfordern, insbesondere der langsamen institutionellen Prozesse der Architektur. Bestehende Anwendungen dieser neuartigen Technologien streben oft nach visueller Integration mit herkömmlichen Baustoffen. Dabei wird ihr Potenzial als Katalysatoren für verändertes Verhalten und öffentlichen Diskurs übersehen. Unser erstes realisiertes Produkt ist eine dekorative Kachel, die billig im Einbau ist und die Luftverschmutzung durch den Verkehr deutlich reduzieren kann, wenn sie in der Nähe von Straßen oder an Gebäudefassaden angebracht wird. Durch den Einsatz neuester computerbasierter Produktionsverfahren erhöhen diese Kacheln den Wirkungsgrad der zugrunde liegenden Technologie und ergeben zugleich optisch eindrucksvolle Installationen, die die Aufmerksamkeit auf die Probleme der Luftverschmutzung und mögliche Lösungsansätze lenken."

« Elegant Embellishments a été créé en 2006 pour rechercher et développer des méthodes et des matériaux nouveaux permettant de modifier rapidement des immeubles et espaces existants. Ces modifications sont utilisées pour ‹tuner› des immeubles, changer des surfaces autrefois inertes en zones actives prêtes à relever les nouveaux défis imposés par un monde qui évolue vite. Une des choses qui nous intéressent le plus dans notre travail est l'articulation d'expressions visuelles de technologies innovantes qui ont le potentiel d'atténuer l'impact écologique des villes mais nécessitent souvent un réexamen des pratiques actuelles, en particulier des délais institutionnels, trop longs dans l'architecture. Les applications existantes de telles technologies ont souvent pour objectif une intégration visuelle dans les matériaux de construction traditionnels. Mais ce faisant, elles passent à côté de leur potentiel en tant que catalyseurs des changements comportementaux et du débat public. Notre premier produit réussi est une tuile architecturale décorative qui a l'intéressante propriété de réduire significativement la pollution atmosphérique provenant du trafic automobile en ville lorsqu'il est installé près des axes routiers ou façades des immeubles. Avec l'aide des dernières techniques de fabrication assistées par ordinateur, ces carreaux accentuent l'effet de la technologie qui les sous-tend tout en créant des installations qui mettent en lumière les problèmes liés à la pollution atmosphérique et leurs solutions possibles. »

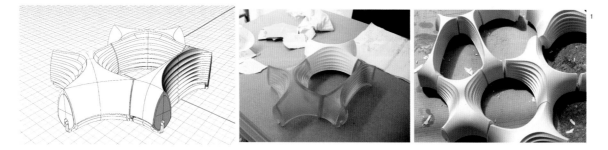

1

1–5

PROSOLVE 370E,
2006

Targeting pollution created by vehicular combustion, Prosolve 370e tiles engage the inevitable context of cities and urban areas, converting previously inert surfaces to active surfaces. The tiles, which are modular in structure and coated in superfine titanium dioxide, utilize an elegant photo-catalytic process to reduce air pollution. Inspired by the fractal nature of sponges and corals, their increased surface area enhances the performance of the TiO2 technology in its omni-directional reception of light. Emissions from combustion engines are identified as the largest source to air pollution in cities, their effect compounded by urban form. Urban motorways, tunnels, car parks, street canyons and underpasses trap pollution in high concentrations. When positioned near pollutant sources, previously polluted spaces are improved in terms of air quality and visual appeal and re-appropriated for safe pedestrian use.

Die Kachel Prosolve 370e hat die Luftverschmutzung durch Verbrennungsmotoren im Visier und greift in den Kontext von Städten und urbanen Räumen ein, um Aktivität zu schaffen, wo vorher nur starre Flächen waren. Die modular zusammen-setzbaren und mit extrem feinem Titandioxid beschichteten Kacheln nutzen einen eleganten photokatalytischen Prozess zur Reduktion der Luftverschmutzung. Ihre erhöhte Oberfläche, die der fraktalen Struktur von Schwämmen und Korallen abge-sehen wurde, verbessert durch ihre omnidirektionale Lichtauf-nahme die Effizienz der TiO2-Technologie. Autoabgase gelten als die größte Quelle von Luft-verschmutzung im urbanen Umfeld, und die städtebau-lichen Gegebenheiten verstär-ken ihre Wirkung noch. Stadt-autobahnen, Tunnels, Garagen, Straßenschluchten und Unter-führungen fangen Schadstoffe in hohen Konzentrationen ein. Wenn man die Kacheln in der Nähe von Verschmutzungsquel-len montiert, wird eine Verbes-serung der Luftqualität erzielt, die Umgebung wird attraktiver und Fußgänger können sich wieder bedenkenlos darin bewegen.

En se concentrant sur la pollution émise par les moteurs à combus-tion, Prosolve 370e se saisit du contexte inéluctable des villes et des zones urbaines et convertit des surfaces jusqu'à présent inertes en surfaces actives. Cette sculpture modulaire, réalisée en céramique revêtue de dioxyde de titane, participe à la réduction de la pollution atmosphérique grâce à un processus sophistiqué de photocatalyse moléculaire. In-spirée de la structure fractale des éponges ou des coraux, leur importante zone de surface démultiplie la performance de la technologie TiO2 grâce à une réception omni-directionelle de la lumière. Les émissions de gaz d'échappement ont été identi-fiées comme étant la principale source de pollution atmosphé-rique en zone urbaine, leur effet étant accentué par la conforma-tion des villes. Les boulevards, tunnels, parkings, rues encais-sées et passages souterrains emprisonnent la pollution et provoquent sa concentration. Lorsque le dispositif est placé à proximité de sources de pollu-tion, il améliore la qualité de l'air et l'aspect des lieux où la pollution était jusqu'alors gênan-te et permet ainsi une réappro-priation de ces lieux par les pié-tons, en toute sécurité.

3

"Building tuning"

1
PROSOLVE 370E
Wireframe drawing,
rapid prototype and casts
of pollution-filtering tiles
2006
Client: self-produced

2
PROSOLVE 370E
Pollution-filtering tile
cladding system
2006
Client: self-produced

3
PROSOLVE 370E
Proposed installations
of pollution-filtering tile
cladding system
Client: self-produced

4
PROSOLVE 370E
Collage of pollution-filtering
tiles at Neukölln, Berlin
S-Bahn station entrance
2006
Client: self-produced

4

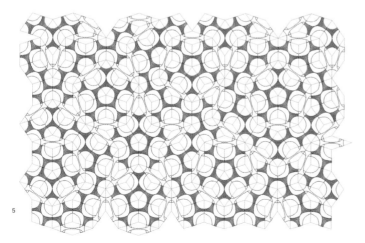

5

5
PENROSE PATTERN
The underlying grid the
Prosolve 370E is based on
was developed by physicist
Roger Penrose, in an attempt
to tile a surface with five-fold
symmetry. The pattern is
aperiodic, and is achieved
with only two parts.

ELEGANT EMBELLISHMENTS
Top Floor
100 de Beauvoir Road
London N1 4EN
United Kingdom

Schliemannstraße 35
10437 Berlin
Germany

T (UK) +44 7951 909898
T (D) +49 177 1560192
info@elegantembellishments.net
www.elegantembellishments.net

DESIGN GROUP HISTORY

2006 Co-founded by Allison Dring and Daniel Schwaag in London

FOUNDERS' BIOGRAPHIES
ALLISON DRING

1974 Born in San Diego, USA
1992–1998 Bachelor of Architecture, University of Arizona, Tuscon
1999–2000 MArch, The Bartlett School of Architecture, University College London – studied under Prof. Peter Cook
2000–2001 Unit Tutor, The Bartlett School of Architecture, University College London, with François Roche
2000–2001 Freelance Designer working for among others, Block, Oliveira Rosa, Softroom Architects and FIFA
2002–2005 Senior Designer, Urban Salon Architects

DANIEL SCHWAAG

1972 Born in Detroit, USA
1992–1997 BSc Architecture, University of Virginia, Charlottesville, VA
1999–2000 MSc Urban Design, The Bartlett School of Architecture, University College London – studied under Prof. Colin Fournier
1999–2001 Diploma in Architecture, The Bartlett School of Architecture, University College London

2001–2004 Freelance Designer and Illustrator for among others, Urban Salon Architects, Glas Architects and Ove Arup
2002–2005 Visiting Critic, Cambridge University, Architectural Association, London Metropolitan University
2005–2006 Module Tutor, London Metropolitan University
2005 Part II Architect, Glas Architects

RECENT EXHIBITIONS

2006 "London Architecture Biennale", Clerkenwell, London; "100% Detail", Earl's Court, London
2007 "Digitalability", Designmai, Berlin

CLIENTS

CABE,
Middlesborough City Council,
Millennium Chemicals,
Science Museum/London,
Studio Egret West for Urban Splash

6

PHOTOCATALYSIS
Diagram of valence band showing the molecular process of photocatalytic titanium dioxide: excited by UV light, an electron jumps from a valence band to a conduction band.

Once excited to the conduction band, oxygen and water are reduced to form superoxide anions and hydroxyl radicals, which together with the remaining electron hole have a strong ability to decompose organic matter and pollutants.

6

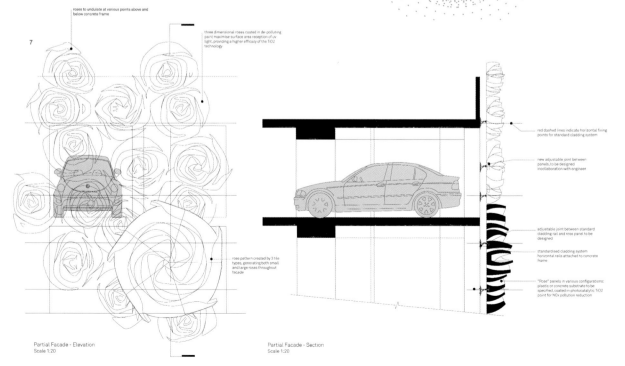

7

roses to undulate at various points above and below concrete frame

three dimensional roses coated in de-polluting paint maximise surface area reception of uv light, providing a higher efficacy of the TiO2 technology

rose pattern created by 3 tile types, generating both small and large roses throughout facade

Partial Facade - Elevation
Scale 1:20

Partial Facade - Section
Scale 1:20

red dashed lines indicate horizontal fixing points for standard cladding system

new adjustable joint between panels, to be designed incollaboration with engineer

adjustable joint between standard cladding rail and rose panel to be designed

standardised cladding system horizontal rails attached to concrete frame

"Rose" panels in various configurations; plastic or concrete substrate to be specified, coated in photocatalytic TiO2 paint for NOx pollution reduction

8

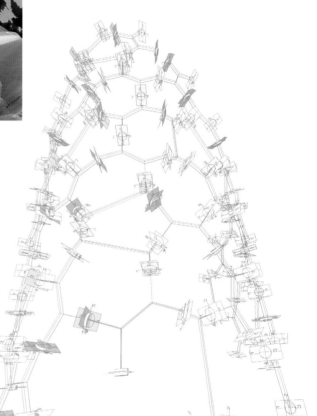

9

7
CAR PARK
Section showing pollution-
filtering photocatalytic TiO2
elements employed in a deco-
rative façade of a car park in
Northern England
2006
Client: Egret West for Urban
Splash

8
LAB06
Installation of pollution-filtering
TiO2 elements around a tree
at the London Architecture
Biennale
2006
Client: self-produced

9
LAB06
Cylindrical Penrose application
around a tree, joint study

10
LAB06
Casts of various TiO2 pollution-
filtering elements

10

ELIUMSTUDIO

"Our objectives are: to develop both a strong design concept and a strong design image and to create objects with real significance. Our philosophy is: Lightness expressed in terms of Liberty, Mobility, Ecology, Technology and Economy. We are actively creating international design (the complete interaction between cultural, artistic, scientific, technical and economic elements). Human sciences are a crucial part of our vision. Beyond technological innovation, we also seek to offer a seductive and highly expressive form of design."

„Unsere Ziele sind: ein aussagekräftiges Designkonzept ebenso wie ein aussagekräftiges Designimage zu entwickeln und wirklich bedeutsame Objekte zu schaffen. Unsere Philosophie ist: Leichtigkeit im Sinne von Freiheit, Mobilität, Ökologie, Technologie und Ökonomie. Wir schaffen aktiv internationales Design (die umfassende Interaktion zwischen kulturellen, künstlerischen, wissenschaftlichen, technischen und wirtschaftlichen Elementen). Die Humanwissenschaften sind ein entscheidender Bestandteil unserer Vision. Jenseits der technischen Innovation streben wir auch eine verführerische und stark expressive Form von Design an."

«Nos objectifs sont: de développer à la fois un concept fort et une image forte et de créer des objets qui ont une réelle signification. Notre philosophie est: Légèreté exprimée en termes de Liberté, de Mobilité, d'Écologie, de Technologie et d'Économie. Nous participons activement à un design international basé sur l'interaction culturelle, artistique, scientifique, technique et économique. Les sciences humaines jouent un rôle capital dans notre approche. Au-delà de l'innovation technologique, nous tentons aussi de proposer une forme de design séduisante et hautement expressive.»

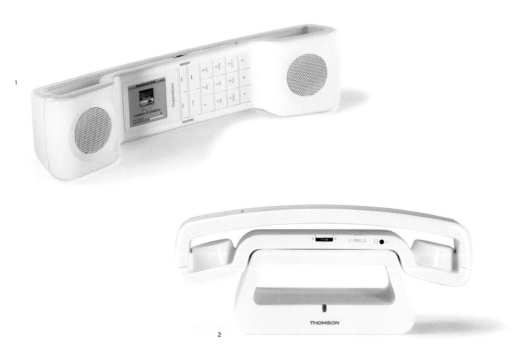

1

2

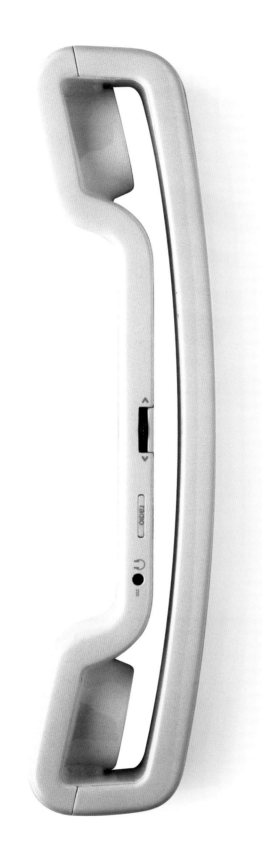

1–3
THOMSON T2007
Residential DECT cordless
telephone for Internet radio
streaming and high-quality
sound Internet telephony
2006
Client: Thomson

4
THOMSON T2007
Exploded diagram of residential
DECT cordless telephone
2006
Client: Thomson

5
FOAM RADIO
AM-FM radio in aluminium
encased in polyurethane foam
2005
Client: Lexon

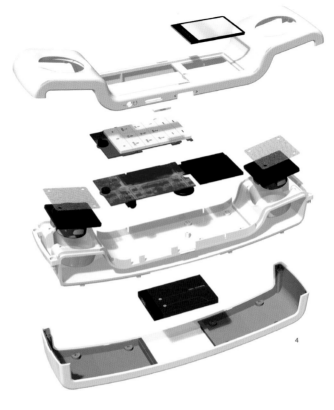

4

5

"To create objects with real significance."

6

7

6
PIPE LIGHT
LED task light in
aluminium with transformer
housed in base
2005
Client: self-produced concept

7
GALAXY
Programme of small
electronic devices (flashlight,
calculator, alarm clock and
external pen hard drive)
in ABS and polycarbonate
2006
Client: Lexon

8
GRAVEL IN POCKET
WiFi media player that fits in palm of hand and plays music and video on demand at the click of one button
2006
Client: Commodore

ELIUMSTUDIO

166, boulevard du Montparnasse
75014 Paris
France
T +33 1 42795752
E mail@eliumstudio.com
www.eliumstudio.com

DESIGN GROUP HISTORY

2000 Founded by Marc Berthier, Pierre Garner, Frédéric Lintz, Elise Berthier and Gilles Caillet in Paris as the successor of Design Plan Studio, which had previously been established in 1985
2001 Eliumstudio launch (event held at VIA Gallery, Paris: "Le Design de la légèreté")

FOUNDERS' BIOGRAPHIES
MARC BERTHIER

1935 Born in Compiègne, France
1955–1959 Studied at ENSAD (École Nationale Supérieure des Arts Décoratifs), Paris
1963–1965 Worked as Architect with various agencies

1966–1999 Established and ran design studio for Les Galeries Lafayette department store, Paris
1967 Organized "Domus Formes Italiennes" exhibition in Galeries Lafayette, Paris – with the Domus magazine team
1970 Established his own design and architecture studio in Paris
1985 Established Archi Plan Studio and Design Plan Studio in Paris
1986 Awarded Le grand prix National de la Création Industrielle (Ministère de la Culture, France)
1985–2000 Teacher and Unit Director, ENSCI (École Nationale Supérieure de Création Industrielle), Paris
1992 Elected "Chevalier des Arts et des lettres"
2001+ Eliumstudio partner

PIERRE GARNER

1968 Born in Toulouse, France
1989–1995 Studied at ENSCI (École Nationale Supérieure de Création Industrielle), Paris

1995–1998 Worked as designer for various studios in Paris
1999–2000 Worked as designer at Design Plan Studio, Paris
2001+ Eliumstudio partner

FRÉDÉRIC LINTZ

1971 Born in Rennes, France
1989–1994 Studied at ENSCI (École Nationale Supérieure de Création Industrielle), Paris
1995–1996 Worked as designer for various studios in Paris
1997–2000 Worked as designer at Design Plan Studio, Paris
2000+ Teaches at ENSCI (École Nationale Supérieure de Création Industrielle), Paris
2001+ Eliumstudio partner

ELISE BERTHIER

1965 Born in Boulogne, France (daughter of Marc Berthier)
1982–1985 Studied Graphic Design at Charpentier Academy, Paris
1986 Studied Art at American Academy, Paris and Florence

1987–1990 Studied Fashion Design at the Berçot Studio School, Paris
1991–1995 Freelance Fashion Designer, France and Italy
1995–2000 Worked as designer at Design Plan Studio, Paris
2001+ Eliumstudio partner

GILLES CAILLET

1977 Born in Arras, France
1997–2001 Studied at ENSCI (École Nationale Supérieure de Création Industrielle), Paris
2001–2002 Designer, Starck Studio, Paris
2002+ Eliumstudio designer

RECENT EXHIBITIONS

2004 "Capitale Européenne de la Culture", Lille
2005 "Reopening Exhibition", The Museum of Modern Art, New York; "D.Day, Le Design Aujourd'hui", Centre Georges Pompidou, Paris; "Reopening Exhibition", Musée des Arts Décoratifs, Paris

RECENT AWARDS

2000 New York Accent Design Award, USA
2001 Buenos Aires Design Award, Argentina
2004 London Design Festival Award, England
2006 Red Dot Award, Design Zentrum Nordrhein Westfalen, Essen

CLIENTS

Alcatel, AOL, Arno, Back Design, Bell&Ross, Calor, Calvin Klein, Cinna, Combi Co., Commodore, Cousteau sp.350, Dé Signe, DKNY, Fujitsu, Hedworth Ltd, Hermès, iGuzzini, International 14, Inventel, Italarredo, Knoll, Lexon, L'Oréal, Magis, Quid Novi, RATP, Rowenta, Seb, Seiko, Tanita Co, Thomson, TOTO Co, Villa Tosca

9
TAO
Transparent polycarbonate
side chair
2006
Client: self-produced concept

10
EXPERT SLATE DG9040
High-pressure (5 bar) 100g/min
continuous steam generating
iron in polypropylene
2005
Client: Rowenta

9

10

JOZEPH FORAKIS

"The idea of 'Progress' is out; 'Evolution' is our future. Evolution can be expressed, but it's not a particular 'style' or a 'language'. I want products to be like highly evolved organisms resulting from holistic thought processes. Every project has its own 'DNA-code' to be discovered, derived from the consideration of its distinctive context. Its 'language' is the result of balancing these unique factors – like a balanced ecosystem. Natural phenomena and structures inform my thinking, while I avoid 'Biomorphic' design, which often superficially mimics nature without learning from its way of achieving balance. The emerging 'Interactive Society' is giving birth to a new 'Behavioral Design', which is driven by the creation of actions and gestures in Time – beyond traditional concepts of forms and materials in Space. The design of a gesture can define the object. A gesture can be as iconic, functional, beautiful, elegant, poetic and meaningful as an object."

„Der ‚Fortschrittsgedanke' ist out. Die Zukunft heißt ‚Evolution'. Evolution lässt sich ausdrücken, aber nicht in einem bestimmten ‚Stil' oder einer bestimmten ‚Sprache'. Meiner Vorstellung nach sollen Produkte wie hoch entwickelte Organismen sein, die auf ganzheitlichen Denkprozessen beruhen. Jedes Projekt hat seinen eigenen ‚DNA-Code', den es zu entdecken gilt und der sich aus seinem unverwechselbaren Kontext herleitet. Seine ‚Sprache' entsteht, wenn ein Gleichgewicht zwischen diesen einzigartigen Faktoren gefunden wird – wie in einem ausgewogenen Ökosystem. Ereignisse und Strukturen, die in der Natur vorkommen, fließen in mein Denken ein, wobei ich allerdings nichts mit ‚biomorphem' Design zu tun habe, das die Natur oft nur oberflächlich nachahmt, ohne von ihr zu lernen, wie sich ein Gleichgewicht herstellen lässt. Die sich abzeichnende ‚interaktive Gesellschaft' schafft ein neues ‚Verhaltensdesign', das sich an Handlungen und Gesten in der ZEIT orientiert – jenseits traditioneller Konzepte von Formen und Werkstoffen im RAUM. Das Design einer Geste kann das Objekt definieren. Eine Geste kann genauso ikonisch, funktional, schön, elegant, poetisch und bedeutungsvoll sein wie ein Objekt."

« L'idée de ‹ Progrès › est derrière nous ; notre avenir, c'est ‹ l'Évolution ›. L'Évolution peut être exprimée, mais elle n'est ni un ‹ style › ni un ‹ langage › particuliers. Je veux que les produits soient comme des organismes très évolués résultant de cheminements de pensée holistiques. Chaque projet a son propre ‹ code ADN ›, qui doit être découvert en dehors de toute considération contextuelle. Son ‹ langage › découle de l'équilibre entre des facteurs uniques et particuliers – comme un écosystème équilibré. Les phénomènes et structures naturels nourrissent ma réflexion mais j'évite le design ‹ biomorphique ›, qui singe souvent la nature de façon superficielle sans chercher à savoir comment elle parvient à un équilibre. La ‹ société interactive › émergeante donne naissance à un nouveau ‹ design behavioriste ›, qui se caractérise par la création d'actions et de gestes dans le Temps – au-delà des concepts traditionnels de forme et de matériaux dans l'Espace. La création d'un geste peut définir l'objet. Un geste peut être aussi emblématique, fonctionnel, beau, élégant, poétique et signifiant qu'un objet. »

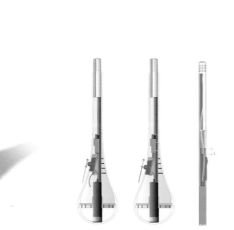

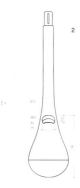

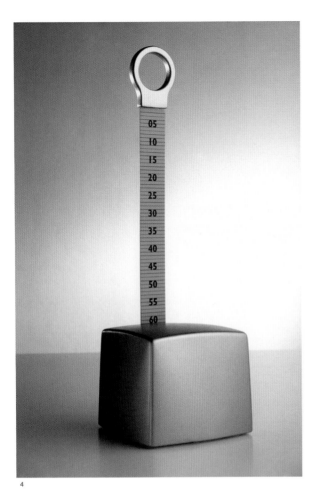

4

1–2
FLARE
Self-balancing gas lighter
in shock-resistant ABS
with Chromaflair colour-
shifting pigments
2006–2007
Client: Kikkerland

3
DEWBERRY WATER
FILTRATION PITCHER
Domestic water filtration
and purification container in
transparent polycarbonate
2006–2007
Client: Dewberry

4–7
TAPE TIMER
Kitchen timer in cast aluminium
with tape that when pulled
winds the internal clock
mechanism and shows 60-
minute time increments
2004
Client: Kikkerland

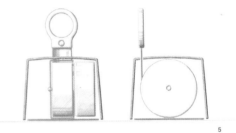

5

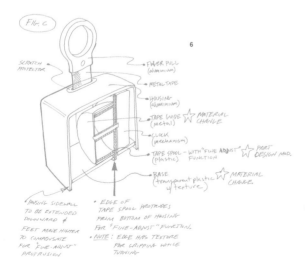

6

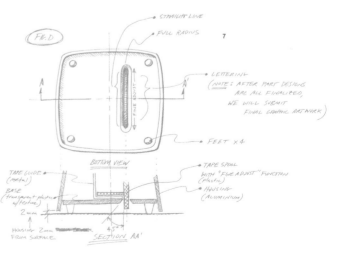

7

"Designs are like aphorisms.
I strive for a certain inevitability;
an authenticity, simplicity
and clarity – without imposing
particular forms."

8

8–9
CALDER
Lounge chair with injection-
moulded single-form seat and
frame of elliptical profiled
aluminium tubing bent in a
single continuous line
2006–2007
Client: Gebrüder Thonet

9

JOZEPH FORAKIS
Via Canonica 67
20154 Milan
Italy
T +39 02 83240543
E info@forakis.com
www.forakis.com

BIOGRAPHY

1962 Born in New York, USA
1985 BFA Industrial Design, Rhode Island School of Design, Providence, USA
1992 MA Industrial Design, Domus Academy, Milan
1993 Began his design consulting activities in Milan
1993–1997 Program Manager, DARC (Domus Academy Research Center), Milan
1994+ Teacher and Lecturer, Domus Academy, Milan
1999–2002 European Design Director, Motorola USA
2002+ Founded "jozeph forakis ... design" studio in Milan

RECENT EXHIBITIONS

2003 "Jozeph Forakis: 10 years of Design in Italy", ADI (Italian Design Association), Rome
2004 "Jozeph Forakis: 10 years of Design in Italy", Felissimo Design House, New York
2005 "Design Korea 2005", Seoul; "International Design Biennial", Saint-Étienne
2006 "BIO.20 – 20th Biennial of International Design", Ljubljana, Slovenia

RECENT AWARDS

2003 Silver iF Award, International Forum Design Hanover
2005 Good Design Award, Chicago Athenaeum; Best Products award, Wired Magazine Best Products

CLIENTS

Arper, EmmeBi, Epson, Foscarini, Gebrüder Thonet, Kikkerland Design, LG Electronics, Magis, MK Kitchen Design, Motorola, Nava Design, Nemo, New Media Life, Panasonic, Philips, Rotring, Samsung, Sharp, Swarovski, Swatch, Tecno

10–13
CLOUD
Task light with aluminium arm and base and translucent polycarbonate diffuser containing a projector screen that concentrates light on to a plane
2005
Client: Foscarini

10

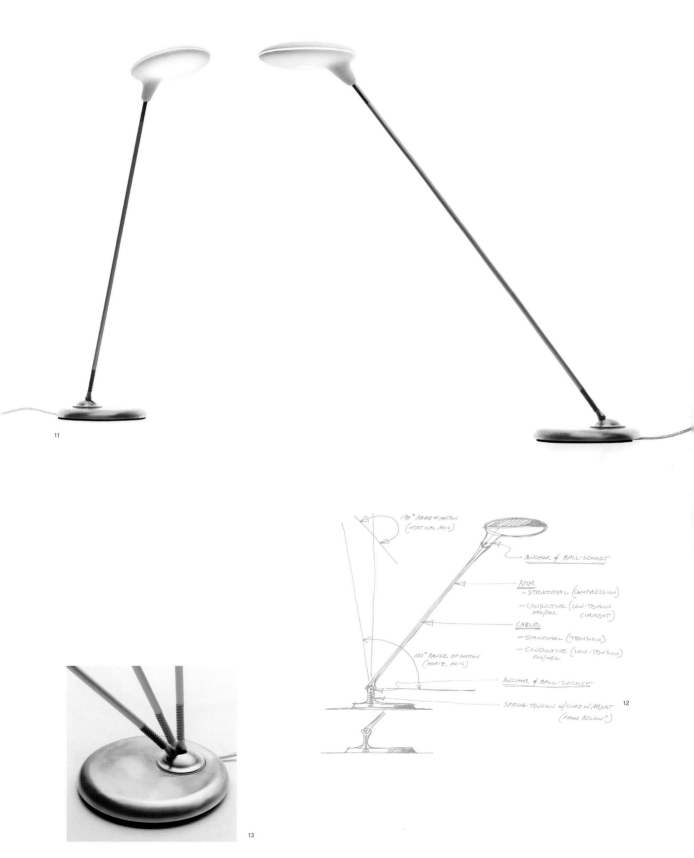

11

170° RANGE OF MOTION
(VERTICAL AXIS)

ANCHOR & BALL-SOCKET

ARM
— STRUCTURAL (COMPRESSION)
— CONDUCTIVE (LOW-TENSION
NEG./POS.   CURRENT)

CABLE
— STRUCTURAL (TENSION)
— CONDUCTIVE (LOW-TENSION
POS./NEG.

100° RANGE OF MOTION
(HORIZ. AXIS)

ANCHOR & BALL-SOCKET

SPRING-TENSION W/SCREW ADJUST   12
(FROM BELOW?)

13

NAOTO FUKASAWA

"Sometimes something is so normal that I am asked, 'So, what part of this has actually been designed?' To which I respond, 'OK, so you don't want it?' Whereupon the answer is, 'No, no, we want it, we need it'. I have a deep interest in the kind of 'normal' that can be overlooked when one gets caught up in 'design'."

„Manchmal ist etwas so normal, dass ich gefragt werde: ‚Was wurde daran nun wirklich *gestaltet*?' Dann antworte ich: ‚Das heißt, Sie wollen es nicht?' Worauf die Antwort lautet: ‚Nein, nein, wir wollen es, wir brauchen es.' Mein Interesse gilt jener Art von ‚normal', die übersehen werden kann, wenn man am ‚Design' hängen bleibt."

«Il arrive parfois qu'une chose soit si normale qu'on me demande : ‹Alors, quel élément a réellement été *design* ? › Question à laquelle je réponds : ‹OK, donc vous n'en voulez pas ? › Ce à quoi on me répond : ‹Si, si, nous en voulons, nous en avons besoin. › J'ai un profond intérêt pour le genre de ‹normal› qui peut être perdu de vue lorsqu'on se laisse trop prendre au jeu du ‹design›. »

1
INFOBAR 2
Concept model of mobile telephone with magnesium flame plastic body
2006
Client: au KDDI

2
ITIS
Low-energy LED table light with zamak base, painted metal stand and lamp head, and transparent polycarbonate diffuser
2006
Client: Artemide

"Normal, not special.
Transforming an object into something
in harmony with modern life without harming
the familiar relationship people already
have with said object.
This is the concept of 'normal'."

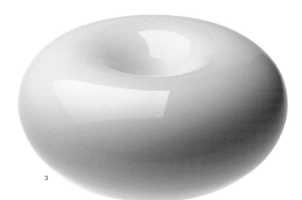

3

4

3
HUMIDIFIER
Humidifier in injection-
moulded polypropylene and
polycarbonate
2003
Client: Plus Minus Zero ± 0

4
CLOUD
Polyurethane foam-upholstered
sofa with tubular-steel frame
2006
Client: B&B Italia

5
PADELLA
Fluorescent ceiling light and
suspension light with die-cast
aluminium body and opalescent
methacrylate diffuser
2007
Client: Artemide

6
NANOCARE
Hair dryer in injection-moulded
ABS
2006
Client: Matsushita Electric
Industrial Co. Ltd.

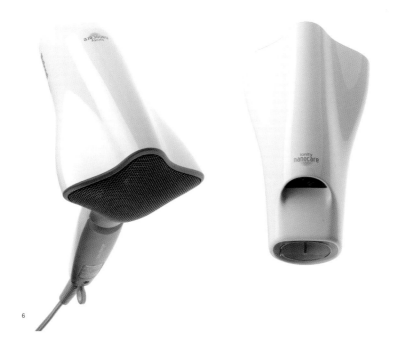

7

NAOTO FUKASAWA

Naoto Fukasawa Design
4F Jingumae 5-17-20
Shibuya-Ku
Tokyo 150-0001
Japan
www.naotofukasawa.com

BIOGRAPHY

1956 Born in Yamanashi
Prefecture, Japan
1980 Graduated in Product
Design from Tama Art University
c.1980–1988 Designer, Seiko-
Epson Corp., Japan
1989 Designer, ID two,
San Francisco (later to become
IDEO)
1996 Returned to Japan
and established IDEO design
office in Japan
1996–2002 Design Director,
IDEO, Japan
2003 Founded his own design
office, Naoto Fukasawa Design,
joined the advisory board of
the company MUJI and
established his own production
brand "±o"

2005 Founded Super Normal
with Jasper Morrison
2007+ Lecturer in product
design departments at
Musashino Art University and
Tama Art University, Tokyo

RECENT EXHIBITIONS

2003 "Visualogue 2003 –
Icograda Congress", Nagoya
Congress Center, Nagoya;
"Without Thought", Muji,
Tokyo
2004 "Without Thought, Trash-
cans", Matsuya Design Gallery,
Tokyo; "Japanese Design Today
100", Kawasaki City Museum,
Kanagawa, Japan; "Things we
think exist but don't" (solo exhi-
bition), The Watari Museum of
Contemporary Art, Tokyo;
"Interieur Biennale – Design
Anatomy", Kortrijk, Belgium;
"Danese Milano – Simple
Avant-Garde", Imoaraizaka
5days-gallery, Tokyo; "Fusion –
Architecture + Design in Japan",
The Israel Museum, Jerusalem;
"Haptic – Takeo Paper Show

2004", Spiral Garden & Hall,
Aoyama, Tokyo; "Design 21 –
Why Love?" travelling exhibi-
tion organized by UNESCO &
Felissimo Corporation, Forum
Barcelona, Barcelona, Kobe;
"Roppongi Crossing – New
Visions in Contemporary Japan-
ese Art 2004", Mori Art Muse-
um, Tokyo, Japan
2005 "Snoopy Life Design"
travelling exhibition, Tokyo,
Japan; "T-room project – Alter-
native Paradise", 21st Century
Museum of Contemporary Art,
Kanazawa, Japan; "Gwangju
Design Biennale 2005", Kim-
daejung Convention Center,
Korea; "Without Thought
Coin", D&Department, Tokyo;
"Under a Tenner – What is
good design?", Naoto Fukasawa
selection exhibition amongst
others, Design Museum
London
2006 "Shanghai biennale –
Emergency exit light", Shanghai
Art Museum, Shanghai";
"Design with Respect", Matsuya

Ginza Exhibition Hall, Tokyo;
"Super Normal" travelling exhibition with Jasper Morrison,
Axis Gallery, Tokyo, and twenty-
twentyone, London; "Without
Thought, Breakfast", Gallery Le
Bain, Tokyo; "Swarovski Crystal
Palace", Salone del Mobile,
Milan; "London Design Festival" and "100% DESIGN
2006", London; "Stockholm
Furniture Fair" (guest of honour); "Stockholm International
Fairs", Stockholm
2007 "Ideal House 07", imm
cologne; "Super Normal", Triennale, Milan

RECENT AWARDS

2002 4 x Good Design Awards,
JIDPO (Japan Industrial Design
Promotion Organization);
Design Week Award, UK
2003 5 x Good Design Awards,
JIDPO (Japan Industrial Design
Promotion Organization);
Mainichi Design Award, Japan
2004 Design for Asia Award,
Hong Kong; 3 x Good Design

Awards, JIDPO (Japan Industrial
Design Promotion Organization
2005 5th Oribe Award, Gifu
Prefecture, Japan; 5 x Good
Design Awards, 1 x Good
Design Gold Award, JIDPO
(Japan Industrial Design
Promotion Organization); 3 x iF
Awards, 1 x Gold Award,
International Forum Design
Hanover
2006 4 x Good Design Awards,
JIDPO (Japan Industrial Design
Promotion Organization)
2007 Red Dot Award, Design
Zentrum Nordrhein Westfalen,
Essen

CLIENTS

Artemide, au KDDI, B&B Italia,
Boffi, Danese, Issey Miyake,
Magis, Matsushita Electric
Industrial Co. Ltd.,
Plus Minus Zero ±o,
Swedese, Shachihata, Ryouhin
Keikaku (MUJI), Vitra, Driade

8

7
DÉJÀ-VU
Dining chair in polished extruded aluminium with optional
ABS or wood veneer for reverse
of back or fabric covering for
seat and back
2006
Client: Magis

8–9
DÉJÀ-VU
Range of tables in polished
extruded aluminium with
optional painted MDF or wood
veneered tops
2006
Client: Magis

9

CHRISTIAN GHION

"I define myself as a 'one hundred percent designer'. Even if architecture is far from foreign to me, my purpose is to reinterpret furniture archetypes with the assistance of innovative shapes and materials. From a stay in Japan I returned with a great interest in moulded wood shapes, which I use as complements to synthetics materials. I'm also inspired by Andy Warhol's Pop Art and the designs by Pierre Paulin in the sixties. As an architect, I am crazy about Frank O. Gehry's work. Artists like Bill Viola or James Turrell also influence me. I try to revolutionize the use of furniture but also like to use clichés by reinterpreting them. My dream is to make design truthful and accessible to the public at large, to find a middle ground between Ikea and the art gallery. After the Starck and Putman generation, we can see in France the new generation emerging who are giving a new direction and a new vision of design, more kindly, more sensitive and not so demonstrative. I'm quite proud to belong to what we call today 'the French touch'. It's the reflection of one generation and an attitude towards our profession."

„Ich sehe mich als ‚hundertprozentigen Designer'. Architektur ist mir keineswegs fremd, aber mein eigentliches Ziel ist, Grundtypen von Möbeln mithilfe von innovativen Formen und Werkstoffen neu zu interpretieren. Von einem Aufenthalt in Japan habe ich ein intensives Interesse an Holzformen mitgebracht, die ich mit synthetischen Materialien kombiniere. Auch Andy Warhols Pop-Art und die Designs von Pierre Paulin aus den 1960er-Jahren dienen mir als Inspiration. Als Architekt bin ich ganz vernarrt in Frank O. Gehrys Arbeit. Ebenso üben Künstler wie Bill Viola oder James Turrell Einfluss auf mich aus. Ich versuche, die Verwendung von Möbeln zu revolutionieren, greife aber auch gern auf Klischees zurück und interpretiere sie neu. Mein Traum ist, ehrliches Design zu schaffen, das für die Allgemeinheit zugänglich ist, einen Mittelweg zwischen Ikea und der Kunstgalerie zu finden. Nach der Ära von Starck und Putman tritt in Frankreich eine neue Generation in Erscheinung, die dem Design eine neue Richtung und eine neue Vision gibt, eine, die freundlicher, sensibler und nicht so demonstrativ ist. Ich bin ziemlich stolz darauf, ein Teil dessen zu sein, was wir heute ‚die französische Note' nennen. Es ist das Abbild einer Generation und eine bestimmte Einstellung zu unserem Beruf."

« Je me définis comme un ‹ designer à cent pour cent ›. Même si l'architecture est loin de m'être étrangère, mon but est de réinterpréter des meubles archétypaux en m'aidant de formes et de matériaux innovants. Depuis un séjour au Japon, j'ai une passion pour le bois moulé façonné, que j'utilise en complément de matériaux synthétiques. Je m'inspire aussi du Pop Art d'Andy Warhol et des créations de Pierre Paulin dans les années 1960. En tant qu'architecte, je suis fou du travail de Frank O. Gehry. Des artistes comme Bill Viola ou James Turrell m'ont aussi influencé. J'essaie de révolutionner les usages mobiliers mais j'aime aussi utiliser des clichés pour les réinterpréter. Mon rêve est de produire honnêtement un design accessible au grand public, de trouver un juste milieu entre Ikea et la galerie d'art. Après la génération Starck et Putman émerge en France une nouvelle génération qui donne une nouvelle direction et une nouvelle vision au design, plus douce, plus sensible et moins démonstrative. Je suis assez fier d'appartenir à ce qu'on appelle aujourd'hui la ‹ French touch ›. C'est le reflet d'une génération et de son attitude à l'égard de la profession. »

1

1
SWEETHEART
Teapot in white ceramic
2007
Client: Gaia & Gino

2
FULLMOON
Water jug in stainless steel with wood handle
2007
Client: Gaia & Gino

CHRISTIAN GHION
156, rue Oberkampf
75011 Paris
France
T +33 1 49290690
E ghion@christianghion.com
www.christianghion.com

BIOGRAPHY
1958 Born in
Montmorency, France
1983 BA Law, University
of Paris XIII, France
1984 Diploma,
École du Louvre, Paris
1986–1987 Post-diploma studies, ECM (Étude et Création de
Mobilier)/ ENSCI (École
Nationale Supérieure de Création Industrielle), Paris
1986–1987 Taught at the École
des Beaux-Arts of Saint-Étienne,
Reims and Rennes
1988–1997 Worked in
collaboration with the architect
Patrick Nadeau
1998 Established his own
design office in Paris

RECENT EXHIBITIONS
2003 "Design Lab –
Researches", Salon du Meuble,
Paris
2004 "Le Verre, des créateurs
aux industriels" Espace
Landowski, Boulogne-
Billancourt
2005 "Le luxe français s'expose
en Chine", Comité Colbert,
Shanghai

RECENT AWARDS
2006 Elected "Chevalier des
Arts et des Lettres", Ministère
de la culture et de la
communication (French
Ministry of Culture)

CLIENTS
Cappellini, Chantal Thomass,
Christian Dior, Daum, Driade,
Ercuis, Gaia & Gino,
Galerie Cat Berro,
Jean-Charles de Castelbajac,
Louis Vuitton,
Mobilier National,
Nicolas Feuillatte,
Pierre Gagnaire, Salviati,
Sawaya & Moroni, XO

3

4

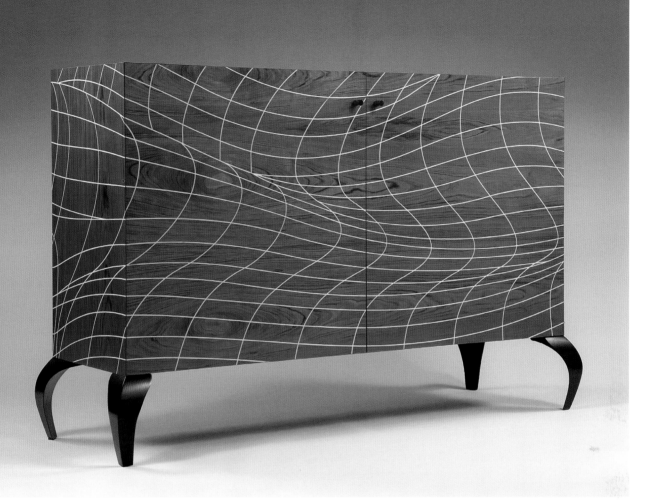

5

"Design… a question of subtlety,
proportions, vibrations
and a supplement of soul."

STEFANO GIOVANNONI

"Jean Baudrillard's writings and his theories on goods and the consuming society were determinant points for my formation as a designer. I have tried to apply them in a rigorous and effective way, considering the market at the centre of my work and the quality of a product directly proportional to its impact on the market. I have always thought that, for an industrial product, like for a television show, the 'audience' was the determining factor – 'audience' being the diffusion of the product itself and not only of its image. I've tried to move the traditional approach to design based on language and composition towards communication, with products characterized by strong, immediate and recognizable icon signs. So I recovered the figurative language that the Modern Movement had relegated to the spheres of kitsch including the potential connection to popular culture. I always have lots of doubts and few certainties; instead of considering the marketing as an obstacle to creativity, I often request its collaboration to test my products. I think that looking at Design from an economical point of view allows us to have a less subjective vision, more transparent and less ideological."

„Jean Baudrillards Schriften und seine Theorien über Waren und die Konsumgesellschaft waren bestimmend für meinen Werdegang als Designer. Ich habe sie auf rigorose und wirksame Weise anzuwenden versucht, indem ich den Markt in den Mittelpunkt meiner Arbeit gestellt und die Qualität eines Produktes als direkt proportional zu seiner Marktwirkung betrachtet habe. Meiner Ansicht nach ist der bestimmende Faktor für ein industrielles Erzeugnis genau wie bei einer Fernsehshow das ‚Publikum', wobei ‚Publikum' die Verbreitung des Produkts selbst und nicht nur seines Bildes meint. Ich habe versucht, den traditionellen, auf Sprache und Komposition beruhenden Ansatz im Design in Richtung Kommunikation zu bewegen, mit Produkten, die sich durch markante, direkte und erkennbare Symbole auszeichnen. Damit habe ich die bildliche Sprache zurückgeholt, die die Moderne in den Bereich des Kitsches verbannt hatte, ebenso wie die potenzielle Verbindung zur Popkultur. Ich habe immer eine Menge Zweifel und wenig, dessen ich mir sicher bin. Statt das Marketing als Hemmschuh für die Kreativität zu sehen, arbeite ich oft mit dieser Disziplin zusammen, um meine Produkte zu testen. Ich bin der Ansicht, dass ein ökonomischer Blick auf das Design uns eine weniger subjektive, transparentere und weniger ideologische Sichtweise eröffnet."

«Les écrits et les théories de Jean Baudrillard sur les biens et la société de consommation ont été déterminants dans ma formation de designer. J'ai essayé de les appliquer de façon rigoureuse et efficace, en plaçant le marché au centre de mon travail et en partant du principe que la qualité d'un produit est directement proportionnelle à son impact sur le marché. C'est ce que j'ai toujours pensé à propos des produits industriels : pour une émission de télévision par exemple, ‹l'audience› est le facteur déterminant – l'audience du design se mesure par la diffusion du produit lui-même et pas seulement de son image. J'ai tenté de faire évoluer la façon habituelle d'approcher le design à partir du langage et de la composition pour le rapprocher de la communication, avec des produits qui se caractérisent par des symboles forts et immédiatement reconnaissables. J'ai ainsi renoué avec le langage figuratif que l'École Moderne avait relégué dans la sphère du kitsch, y compris dans ses liens possibles avec la culture populaire. J'ai toujours beaucoup de doutes et peu de certitudes ; plutôt que de considérer le marketing comme un obstacle à la créativité, je l'utilise souvent pour tester mes produits. Je pense que considérer le design sous un angle économique nous permet d'avoir une vision moins subjective, plus transparente et moins idéologique. »

1

TIMESPHERE WIRELESS
PROJECTION CLOCK FOR
OREGON SCIENTIFIC, 2006

"TimeSphere Wireless Projection Clock is the first of this kind in the world to feature a mobile wireless time projection unit. The radio-controlled spherical unit can project and illuminate the time anywhere and whenever you want. Just place the sphere on the base unit to recharge its batteries and then position it where and how you desire to suit your individual life and style. Precision timekeeping is maintained with the base unit, which displays both the time and the indoor temperature on a red backlit touch screen. Touch screen technology is also ingeniously used to adjust alarm, time and temperature settings, while simply pressing the top of the main unit will activate the snooze function."

„Die Projektionsfunkuhr Time-Sphere ist die erste ihrer Art, die mit einem mobilen kabellosen Projektionsteil ausgestattet ist – basisunabhängig wirft hier eine Kugel die Zeit an die Wand oder jede andere beliebige Fläche. Die Kugel wird lediglich zum Aufladen der Batterien auf die Basiseinheit gelegt und kann anschließend platziert werden, wo immer es den eigenen Erfordernissen, Wünschen und stilistischen Präferenzen entgegenkommt. Für eine präzise Zeitangabe sorgt die automatische Synchronisation mit der Basis, die auf einem Touchscreen mit roter Hintergrundbeleuchtung nicht nur die Zeit, sondern auch die Innentemperatur anzeigt. Darüber hinaus wurde die Touchscreen-Technologie auf raffinierte Weise für die Alarm-einstellung, die Zeit- und Temperaturanzeige sowie die Schlummerfunktion eingesetzt, die einfach durch Drücken auf die Basiseinheit aktiviert wird."

« Le réveil à projection sans fil TimeSphere est le premier au monde à proposer une unité mobile sans fil de projection de l'heure. Ce module sphérique radiocommandé peut projeter l'heure en lumière en tout endroit et à tout moment. Il suffit de placer la sphère sur sa base pour recharger sa batterie puis de la placer à l'endroit de votre choix, comme vous désirez qu'il s'accorde à votre style de vie. La précision horaire est assurée grâce à la base, qui donne à la fois l'heure et la température intérieure sur un écran tactile à rétro-éclairage rouge. La technologie des écrans tactiles est aussi astucieusement utilisée pour régler heure, température et alarme tandis qu'une simple pression sur le sommet de l'unité principale active la fonction d'arrêt momentané. »

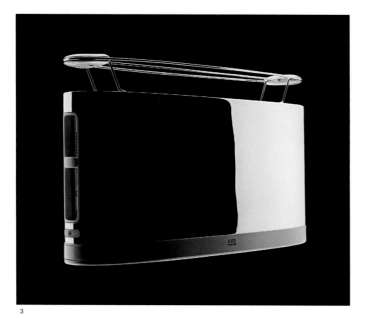

3

4

5

6

1
TIMESPHERE
Wireless LCD projection clock
2006
Client: Oregon Scientific

2
WEATHERBOX
Wireless 12- to 24-hour weather
forecast and indoor/outdoor
temperature and humidity LCD
display unit
2006
Client: Oregon Scientific

3–4
SG68
Stainless-steel toaster with bun
warmer
2006
Client: Alessi

5–6
FIRST
Single-form stacking chair and
dining table in air-moulded
polypropylene (table with tops
either in MDF or oak veneer)
2007
Client: Magis

7

8

"The quality of an industrial product is directly proportional to its impact on the market."

9

STEFANO GIOVANNONI

Giovannoni Design
Via Stendhal 35
20144 Milan
Italy
T +39 02 47719280
T +39 02 48703495
E studio@stefanogiovannoni.com
www.stefanogiovannoni.com

BIOGRAPHY

1954 Born in La Spezia, Italy
1978 Graduated in Architecture, Università degli Studi, Florence
1979–1991 Taught and conducted research at the Facoltà di Archittetura, Università degli Studi, Florence
1989–1991 Master-professor, Università del Progetto, Reggio Emilia
1989–2005 Master-professor, Domus Academy, Milan
1985–1989 Collaborated with Guido Venturini under the name King Kong Productions, Milan
1989 Founded his own studio in Milan

RECENT AWARDS

2003 Design Plus award, Ambiente, Frankfurt; ISH award, ISH, Frankfurt

CLIENTS

3M, Alessi, Cedderoth, Deborah, Fiat, Flos, Hannstar, Helit, Henkel, Inda, Kokuyo, Laufen, Lavazza, Magis, Oras, Oregon Scientific, Seiko, Siemens, Toto, NEC, NTT Docomo

7–9
PANDA ALESSI
The result of a collaboration between Alessi and Fiat, this project was based on the use of colour and on creating a sharp communicative impact, while maintaining substantial respect for the inherent design of the Panda car
2004
Client: Fiat/Alessi

10
PIRIPICCHIO
Battery-operated clothes shaver in polycarbonate with detachable fluff container
2005
Client: Alessi

11
BODY SCALES
LED-display weighing scales in stainless steel with transparent PMMA protective shell
2005
Client: Alessi

10

11

EMILIANO GODOY

"Every material, every colour, every shape is a signifier. The pieces I design with them are going to have a meaning, the result of my reality as the designer combined with the viewpoint of the spectator. I can try, but only try, to control how the pieces are read by finding out where each element comes from and where it will go as a result of my intervention. We designers are creating images that suggest possible paths and scenarios. I seek to work with a visual language that speaks about a future place I want to reach, as an individual, as a society, as a way of understanding the world."

„Jeder Werkstoff, jede Farbe, jede Form hat etwas zu sagen. Die Objekte, die ich damit gestalte, bekommen eine Bedeutung, die sich aus der Kombination meiner Wirklichkeit als Designer mit dem Standpunkt des Betrachters ergibt. Ich kann versuchen, aber eben nur versuchen, zu kontrollieren, wie die Stücke gelesen werden, indem ich herausfinde, woher jedes Element kommt und wohin es als Ergebnis meiner Intervention gehen wird. Wir, die Designer, schaffen Bilder, die mögliche Wege und Szenarios aufzeigen. Ich für meinen Teil arbeite mit einer Bildersprache, die von einem Ort in der Zukunft erzählt, den ich erreichen will, als Individuum, als Gesellschaft, als Möglichkeit, die Welt zu verstehen."

«Chaque matériau, chaque couleur, chaque forme est un signifiant. Les pièces que je conçois avec eux vont avoir un sens, qui résultera de la combinaison entre ma réalité de designer et le point de vue du spectateur. Je peux essayer, mais seulement essayer, de contrôler la façon dont les pièces seront lues en découvrant d'où vient chaque élément et où il se trouvera après mon intervention. Nous, les designers, créons des images qui suggèrent des routes, des scénarios possibles. Je cherche à travailler avec un langage visuel qui parle d'un endroit futur que je veux atteindre, comme un individu, comme une société, comme une manière de comprendre le monde. »

1

2

1–3
WEIDMANN CHAIR
Side chair with single-form seat and back made of moulded Maplex supported on tubular stainless-steel frame
2005
Client: Weidmann (prototype)

4

5

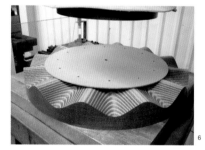

6

1–9
WEIDMANN CHAIR,
MODULAR STORAGE UNIT
AND WALL CLOCK FOR
WEIDMANN, 2005

The Weidmann chair, Modular Storage Unit and Wall Clock form part of a project undertaken in collaboration with Erika Hanson for Weideman, a worldwide leader in fiber products manufacturing and engineering. Each of these products is constructed of Maplex – a sustainable, extremely dense, all-natural building material with long, high-quality fibers. Maplex is made from an entirely renewable resource: softwood fibers from certified sustainably managed forests. Stronger and more formable than birch plywood, Maplex is manufactured without the use of bleach, binders, formaldehyde, petroleum-based products or other off-gassing additives. As a result, it's 100 % non-toxic and biodegradable. Weidmann has also used coating products that protect Maplex, add colour and increase resistance to stains and abrasions, but do not affect its biodegradability.

Stuhl, Aufbewahrungseinheit und Wanduhr entstammen einem umfangreichen Designprojekt für Weidmann, einem weltweit führenden Unternehmen im Bereich der Zellstoffproduktion und -verarbeitung, und wurden mit Erika Hanson entworfen. Alle Objekte werden aus Maplex gefertigt, einem umweltverträglichen, extrem dichten und naturbelassenen Werkstoff mit langen, hochwertigen Fasern. Der Werkstoff selbst wird aus einer erneuerbaren Ressource hergestellt: Weichholzfasern, die aus Bäumen von nachhaltig bewirtschafteten Wäldern gewonnen werden. Maplex ist härter, kann leichter geformt werden als Birken-Schichtholz und wird ohne Anwendung von Bleichverfahren und Einsatz von Bindemitteln, Formaldehyd, Produkten auf Erdölbasis oder anderen ausgasenden Zusätzen produziert. Maplex ist also 100 Prozent schadstofffrei und biologisch abbaubar. Weidmann hat auch verschiedene Beschichtungsprodukte entwickelt, die den Werkstoff schützen, farblich verändern sowie widerstands- und strapazierfähiger machen, seine biologische Abbaubarkeit aber nicht beeinträchtigen.

La chaise, l'unité modulaire de rangement et la pendule Weidmann (créées en collaboration avec Erika Hanson) font partie du projet entrepris pour Weideman, leader mondial de la conception et de la transformation de fibres. Ces produits sont constitués de Maplex – un matériau de construction totalement naturel, durable et extrêmement dense doté de fibres longues et de haute qualité. Le Maplex est composé à partir d'une ressource entièrement renouvelable : des fibres de bois tendre issues de forêts dont la gestion durable est certifiée. Plus solide et souple que le contreplaqué de bouleau, le Maplex est fabriqué sans décolorants, sans liants, sans formaldéhyde, et sans produits à base de pétrole ou autres additifs à forte teneur en gaz nocifs. Il est donc non toxique et biodégradable à 100%. Weidmann a également conçu des produits de revêtement qui protègent le Maplex, lui ajoutent de la couleur et améliore la résistance aux taches et à l'usure sans affecter sa biodégradabilité.

4–6
CLOCK
Wall clock made of moulded
Maplex (designed with Erika
Hanson)
2006
Client: Weidmann (prototype)

7–9
STORAGE UNIT
Modular storage unit made
of moulded Maplex with
eco-friendly protective
coloured coating (designed
with Erika Hanson)
2005
Client: Weidmann (prototype)

8

7

9

11

10

10–12
PIASA
100% biodegradable "knitted"
wood self-supporting room
divider
2005
Client: PIRWI

EMILIANO GODOY

Godoylab
Córdoba 1-A
Roma Norte, 06700, DF
Mexico City
Mexico
T +52 55 2072777
E info@godoylab.com
www.godoylab.com

BIOGRAPHY

1974 Born in Mexico City, Mexico
1997 BA Industrial Design, Universidad Iberoamericana, Mexico City
2003 Furniture design program, Danish Design School, organized by DIS (Denmark's International Study program), Copenhagen
2002 Fulbright scholarship for graduate studies, New York–Mexico City
2004–2005 MID with distinction – Industrial Design, Pratt Institute, New York City
2004 Founded own design studio in Mexico City
2004+ Teaches sustainable design and drawing classes for undergraduate industrial design program at ITESM, Mexico City
2005+ Teaches sustainable design at UNAM's Center for Industrial Design Research, Mexico City
2005+ Staff editor, Arquine (architecture and design magazine)
2006+ Member of the design collective NEL
2006+ Design director, PIRWI, Mexico City

RECENT EXHIBITIONS

2003 "Ambiente", Frankfurt; "Holanda 2003", Amsterdam; ICFF (International Contemporary Furniture Fair), New York
2004 ICFF (International Contemporary Furniture Fair), New York; "Brooklyn Designs", St Ann's Warehouse and the Brooklyn Designs Gallery; "Indispensable Trashcan", Galapagos, New York; "The Importance of Being Earnest", Sustainable Living, New York; "Living Spaces", Volume, New York; "Designers Market", with the Latin American Design Foundation, Eindhoven, The Netherlands
2005 "Holanda 2005", Amsterdam; ICFF (International Contemporary Furniture Fair), New York; "Diseño Muerto", Galería de Arte Mexicano, Mexico City; "Un papel para todos", group show organized by Original Múltiple, Mexico City; "Matrimonios Caprichosos", Ludens, Mexico City; "Se vende diseño", Galería Mexicana de Diseño, Mexico City; "Materia Prima", Ludens, Mexico City; "International Furniture Design Award", Asahikawa Furniture Center, Asahikawa, Japan
2006 ICFF (International Contemporary Furniture Fair), New York; "Import/Export, de Cambios e Intercambios", Museo Franz Mayer, Mexico City; "Las tres en verano", with the NEL collective, Galería Mexicana de Diseño, Mexico City; NEL booth, Salone Satellite, Salone del Mobile, Milan

RECENT AWARDS

2001 Honorable mention, Primer Bienal de Diseño del INBA, Mexico City; Scholarship for cultural projects, FONCA (Fondo Nacional para la Cultura y las Artes), project matatena.com, Mexico City
2002–2004 Scholarship for graduate studies, CONACYT, Mexico City
2005 Bronze Leaf – International Furniture Design Award, Asahikawa, Japan; Conduit Artist Project Award, Columbia County Council on the Arts, Greene County Council on the Arts and New York State Council on the Arts (NYSCA)

CLIENTS

Aurelio López Rocha, CCNS, Frito Lay/Sabritas, Gamesa Holland Chemical International (HCI), Lacoste, Metrobus, Museo de la Ciudad de México, Peñafiel, Pepsico, Pipeline Integrity International (PII), Pipetronix, PIRWI, Weidmann, WESCO Distribution

12

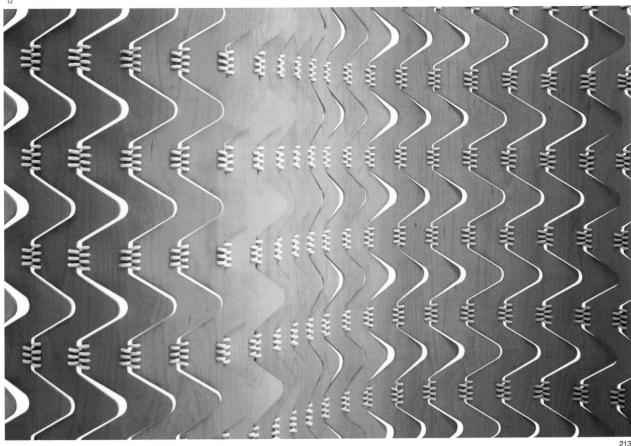

KONSTANTIN GRCIC

"Since today we talk about 'designing life' it perfectly illustrates the significant evolution that has taken place from a specialized discipline to a much broader idea of what design encompasses. What strikes me is the largely positive notion design relishes outside the commercial context. In the domains of services and facilities design is considered to be smart, producing intelligent solutions to the specific demands of a situation. In comparison to this, a lot of product design is seen to have lost its integrity and original virtues to the marketing interests of the large corporations. As the fundamentals of social and ecological issues become ever more sensitive to modern industry we need to rebuild a culture of products that 'make sense'. The relevance a product has to our life lies not only in its use, but also in how it is made, what it is made of and where it is made... and finally who disposes of it and how?"

„Wenn wir heute davon sprechen, das ‚Leben zu designen', so drückt das die markante Entwicklung von einer Spezialdisziplin zu einer viel umfassenderen Vorstellung dessen, was Design alles sein kann, sehr zutreffend aus. Bemerkenswert finde ich das weitgehend positive Image, das Design außerhalb des kommerziellen Kontextes genießt. Im Bereich von Dienstleistungen und Einrichtungen gilt Design als clever und geeignet, intelligente Lösungen für die spezifischen Anforderungen einer Situation zu liefern. Dem Produktdesign hält man hingegen vielfach vor, seine Integrität und seine ursprünglichen Vorzüge den Marketinginteressen großer Konzerne geopfert zu haben. Da soziale und ökologische Fragestellungen für die Industrie immer relevanter werden, müssen wir wieder eine Kultur von Produkten errichten, die einen ‚Sinn' haben. Die Relevanz, die ein Produkt für unser Leben hat, besteht nicht nur in seiner Verwendung, sondern auch darin, wie es entstanden ist, woraus und wo es hergestellt wurde ..., und schließlich in der Frage, wer es auf welche Weise entsorgt."

«Le fait que nous parlions aujourd'hui de ‹designer la vie› illustre parfaitement l'évolution importante qui a vu passer le design d'une discipline spécialisée à un champ beaucoup plus vaste. Ce qui me frappe, c'est l'image largement positive dont jouit le design en dehors du contexte commercial. Dans le secteur des services et des équipements, le design est apprécié pour son art de produire des solutions intelligemment adaptées aux exigences spécifiques d'une situation. En comparaison, le public juge que le design produit a pour une large part perdu son intégrité et ses vertus originelles au profit des intérêts commerciaux des multinationales. Alors que les principes sociaux et écologiques fondamentaux deviennent de plus en plus sensibles dans l'industrie moderne, il est nécessaire que nous reconstruisions une culture du produit qui ‹ait un sens›. Le sens qu'un produit prend dans notre vie tient non seulement à l'usage qui en est fait mais aussi à la manière et à la matière dont il est fait, à l'endroit dont il vient... et enfin à qui en dispose au bout du compte, et comment?»

1

3-6
CHAIR_ONE PUBLIC
SEATING SYSTEM 2 FOR
MAGIS, 2006

The Chair_One Public Seating
System 2 is based on Konstantin
Grcic's earlier Chair_One series
for Magis. The seat elements are
constructed like a football: a
number of flat planes assembled
at angles to each other, creating
the three-dimensional form.

Their structural logic is compelling. Made of die-cast aluminium treated with sputter
fluorinated titanium and painted in polyester powder, the
Chair_One Public Seating System 2 is suitable for both indoor
and outdoor use.

Die Chair_One-Stühle für den
öffentlichen Raum basieren auf
der zu einem früheren Zeitpunkt
von Konstantin Grcic für Magis

gestalteten Chair_One-Reihe.
Die Sitzelemente sind wie ein
Fußball aufgebaut: Mehrere Flächen werden im Winkel zuein-
ander angeordnet, sodass eine
dreidimensionale Form entsteht.
Ihre strukturelle Logik ist bestechend. Die Chair_One-Stühle
für den öffentlichen Raum sind
aus Druckgussaluminium gefertigt, das mit fluoriertem Titan
und Polyesterlackierung oberflä-
chenbehandelt ist, und können

sowohl im Innen- wie im
Außenbereich verwendet
werden.

Le Système d'assise pour les
lieux publics Chair_One est
basé sur la série Chair_One
précédemment créée par Konstantin Grcic pour Magis. Les
sièges sont construits comme un
ballon de football : un grand
nombre de facettes qui s'assem-
blent les unes aux autres par les

angles pour créer un forme tri-
dimensionnelle. Leur logique
structurelle est fascinante.
Constitués d'aluminium moulé
sous pression, traité par projection de titane fluoré et peint à la
poudre de polyester, les sièges du
Chair_One Public Seating System sont utilisables à l'intérieur
comme à l'extérieur.

1–2
STOOL_ONE
Indoor/outdoor barstool in
powder-coated die-cast and
extruded aluminium
2006
Client: Magis

3–6
CHAIR_ONE PUBLIC
SEATING SYSTEM 2
Indoor/outdoor beam seating
system in powder-coated die cast
and extruded aluminium with
optional table in HPL laminate
2006
Client: Magis

"I always strive to make
things simple... but they should
never be too simple."

3

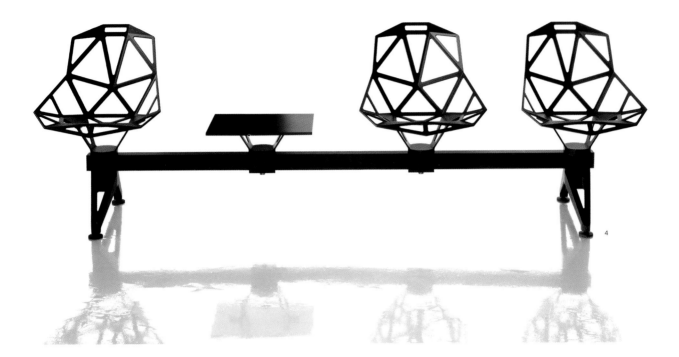

4

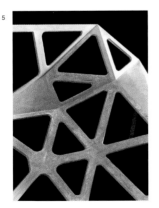

5

6

7
KB7020
Electric blender with keypad in
die-cast aluminium and glass
2006
Client: Krups

8
KA850 PREP EXPERT
1100W 3-speed food processor
in ABS, SAN, glass and stainless
steel
2006
Client: Krups

7

8

KONSTANTIN GRCIC

Konstantin Grcic Industrial
Design
Schillerstraße 40
80336 Munich
Germany
T +49 89 55079995
E office@konstantin-grcic.com
www.konstantin-grcic.com

BIOGRAPHY

1965 Born in Munich,
Germany
1985–1987 Cabinetmaking,
John Makepeace School for
Craftsman in Wood, Parnham
College, Dorset
1988–1990 MA – Industrial
Design, Royal College of Art,
London
1990 Worked in the design
office of Jasper Morrison in
London
1991 Founded his own design
office in Munich

RECENT EXHIBITIONS

2003 "The Origin of Things",
Museum Boijmans Van Beunin-
gen, Rotterdam; "La Forza delle
Cose – Tradizione Valdostana e
Design", Chiesa di San Lorenzo,
Aosta
2005 "European Design Show
2005", Design Museum,
London
2006 "Konstantin Grcic
Industrial Design – Parade",
Boijmans van Beuningen,
Rotterdam; "Konstantin Grcic
Industrial Design – On/Off",
Haus der Kunst, Munich;
"Konstanin Grcic Industrial
Design – High/Low",
Garanti Galeri, Istanbul
2007 "Konstantin Grcic
Industrial Design – This Side
Up", Museum für Gestaltung,
Zurich

RECENT AWARDS

2004 Nombre d'Or, Salon du
Meuble, Paris, France; Design
Plus Award, Ambiente, Frank-
furt; Nomination, Compasso
d'Oro award, ADI, Milan
2005 Blueprint Best Product
Award, 100% Design, London;
Good Design Award, Chicago
Athenaeum; Silver iF Award,
International Forum Design
Hanover
2006 Gold iF Award, Interna-
tional Forum Design Hanover;
Best Product Award, imm,
Cologne; Silver Medal, Design-
preis Deutschland, Bundesre-
publik Deutschland
2007 Silver Medal, Designpreis
Deutschland, Bundesrepublik
Deutschland; Designer de l'Année, Salon NOW! design à
vivre, Paris; Designer of the
Year, imm cologne (sponsored
by Architektur & Wohnen)

CLIENTS

Agape, Authentics, Biegel,
Böwer, Cappellini,
Chi Ha Paura…?, Classicon,
Colombo Design, Cor Unum,
Driade, Flos, Iittala, Krups,
Lamy, Magis, Moormann,
Moroso, Montina International,
Muji, Plank, Porzellan-
Manufaktur Nymphenburg,
SCP, Teracera,
Thomas/Rosenthal,
Whirlpool Europe,
Wireworks

9
MIURA TABLE
Indoor/outdoor tilt-top bistro
table in powder-coated steel
2007
Client: Plank

10
TOP
25 litre waste bin in
injection-moulded ABS
and polypropylene
2007
Client: Authentics

11
BUGGY
Gas-lift swivelling chair on
5-star pedestal base with seat in
blow-moulded polypropylene
and base in epoxy resin painted
steel tube
2007
Client: Magis

GRO DESIGN

"Balancing analysis and imagination, we follow a process of: observing and testing products on the market; thinking about the product's potential and imagining scenarios that would engage users; creating a project framework in which designers can exchange thoughts and concept ideas; developing and selecting the design identity through a series of conceptual design workshops; refining the design identity through a range of models and CAD studies; and then realizing the final design. Over the years, the combination of high-level strategic design exercises and regular production projects has enabled us to fine-tune our approach and execution."

„Unser zu gleichen Teilen auf Analyse und Fantasie beruhender Designprozess läuft folgendermaßen ab: Beobachtung und Untersuchung von markteingeführten Produkten; Nachdenken über das Potenzial des Produkts und Entwicklung von Szenarios, die Benutzer einbeziehen; Schaffung eines Projektrahmens, in dem die Designer Meinungen und Ideen austauschen können; Entwicklung und Festlegung der Designidentität in einer Reihe von Konzeptsitzungen; Präzisierung der Designidentität durch Modelle und CAD-Studien; schließlich Realisierung des fertigen Designs. Durch die jahrelange Kombination von anspruchsvollen Aufgaben in strategischem Design mit regulären Produktionsprojekten sind unsere Methoden und Prozesse sehr ausgefeilt."

« En équilibrant analyse et imagination, notre démarche suit les étapes suivantes : observer et tester des produits présents sur le marché ; penser au potentiel du produit et imaginer des scénarios qui sollicitent les usagers ; créer une structure de projet dans laquelle les designers peuvent échanger pensées et concepts ; concevoir et sélectionner l'identité stylistique à travers une série d'ateliers de design conceptuels ; peaufiner l'identité design grâce à une série de modèles et d'esquisses en CAO ; et, pour finir, réaliser le produit final. Au fil des années, la combinaison entre exercices stratégiques de design de haut niveau et projets de production classiques nous a permis de parfaire notre approche et notre exécution. »

1

1–3
SCOOT
Lithium ion battery-powered
electric scooter
2005
Client: self-produced concept

2

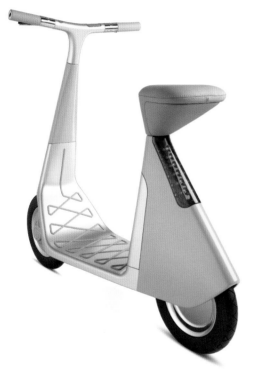

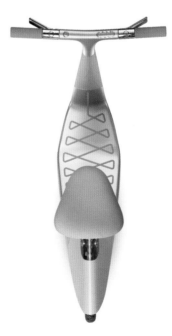

SCOOT ELECTRIC
MOBILITY FOR
ELECTROSCOOT, 2005

Incorporating recent advances in
lithium ion battery technology
and performance, Scoot offers a
clean, quiet solution for daily
travel needs. It was designed for
people who want a product that
offers style and simplicity. With

a range of 40-50 km, Scoot's
lightweight removable battery
can be fully charged in 6 hours.
It is cheap to run – 50 Euro-
cents per 50 km. Limited to
30 km/h, Scoot is classified as
a bicycle so no registration plate
is necessary.

Der Elektroroller Scoot nutzt die
aktuellen technischen Fortschritte und Leistungsverbesserungen

der Lithiumionenbatterie und
stellt eine saubere, geräuscharme
Lösung für den täglichen Fahr-
bedarf dar. Er wurde für Menschen entworfen, die sich ein
stilvolles und doch einfaches
Produkt wünschen. Die heraus-
nehmbare Leichtbatterie hat eine
Reichweite von 40–50 km und
kann in sechs Stunden vollständig aufgeladen werden. Der
Scooter ist billig im Betrieb –

50 km schlagen mit nur 50 Cent
zu Buche. Mit einer Höchstgeschwindigkeit von 30 km/h
gilt der Roller als Fahrrad, eine
Zulassung ist daher nicht erforderlich.

Scoot incorpore les récentes
avancées technologiques et qua-
litatives en matière de batteries
lithium-ion pour proposer une
solution de transport quotidien-

ne propre et silencieuse. Il a été
créé pour les personnes à la
recherche d'un produit à la fois
stylé et simple. Dotée d'une portée de 40 à 50 km, la batterie
amovible légère se recharge
entièrement en six heures. Il est
économique – 50 centimes d'euros pour 50 km. Limité à 30 km/
h, Scoot est classé parmi les
vélos, aucune plaque d'immatri-
culation n'est donc nécessaire.

4

4
NOKIA 5300 XPRESSMUSIC
Mobile telephone MP3 player
with dedicated music playing
keys integrated in elastomer grip
2006
Client: Nokia

5–6
BOOM BAG
Designed as an accessory for
iPods and other mobile music
players, the Boom Bag is made
of durable and weatherproof
speaker fabric. Housing a full-
range speaker and rechargeable
battery, it is easy to carry and
protects the MP3 player from
the elements.
2007
Client: self-produced
concept

5

6

"We strive to create
well thought-out products
with personality and soul."

GRO DESIGN
Bergstraat 36
5611 JZ Eindhoven
The Netherlands
T +31 40 2960763
E office@grodesign.com
www.grodesign.com

FOUNDERS' BIOGRAPHIES
ROLAND BIRD
1967 Born in Hertfordshire,
England
1987–1991 BA Design for
Industry, Newcastle
1991–1999 Designer/Senior
designer, Philips Design,
Eindhoven
1995–1996 Core-team member,
"Vision of the Future", Philips
Design, Eindhoven
1996–1999 Senior design consultant, Philips Design – Strategic Design Group, Eindhoven

DESIGN GROUP HISTORY
1999 Founded by Roland Bird,
Graham Hinde and Roger
Swales in Eindhoven, The
Netherlands

GRAHAM HINDE
1960 Born in London, England
1980–1983 BA Furniture and
Related Product Design,
Kingston Polytechnic, England
1984–1985 Junior designer,
Philips Design – Television
Group, Croydon UK,
1985–1989 Designer, Philips
Design – Television Group,
Eindhoven
1989–1991 Senior designer,
Philips Design – Audio Group,
Eindhoven
1991–1993 Senior designer,
Philips Design – Multi-Media
Group, Eindhoven
1993–1995 Senior designer,
Philips Design – Telephony
Group, Eindhoven
1995–1996 Core-team member,

"Vision of the Future", Philips
Design, Eindhoven
1996–1999 Senior design consultant Philips Design – Strategic
Design Group, Eindhoven

ROGER SWALES
1966 Born in Bridgnorth,
Shropshire, England
1985–1988 BA Industrial
Design, Bristol University f Arts
1988–1989 Junior designer,
Pentagram, London
1989–1991 Designer, Philips
Design – High-End Television
Group, Eindhoven
1995–1996 Core-team member,
"Vision of the Future", Philips
Design, Eindhoven
1996–1999 Senior design
consultant, Philips Design –

Strategic Design Group,
Eindhoven

RECENT EXHIBITIONS
2006 Zona Tortona/Design
Week, Milan; ICCF Design
Week, New York; Design Week,
Kortrijk; "Dutch design", Palace
Garden exhibition, The Hague;
Amsterdam Design Week,
Amsterdam; Design Week,
Eindhoven; "Via Milan – New
Dutch Design", Amsterdam
2007 European Parliament,
Brussels

CLIENTS
Grohe, Grolsch, Microsoft,
Nokia, Oce, Philips, Samsung,
Sara Lee, Unilever

ALFREDO HÄBERLI

"I try to unite tradition with innovation, joy and energy in my design work. My products should be playful and soulful in defiance of a world of bland merchandise, effective where other goods fall down on the job. They should prove that fine design can be complex in its variety of functions, but doesn't have to be complicated. My creations have a clear, rational base, the results of my orientation and training, but they also have a fragile, emotional, even poetic quality that stems from my openness and my culturally diverse upbringing. And there is always a concept of lightness, transparency, movement, a slight touch of mystery and a certain affinity to artistic works."

„Ich versuche, in meiner Designarbeit Tradition mit Innovation, Freude und Energie zu verbinden. Meine Produkte sollen spielerisch und gefühlvoll sein, um der langweiligen Warenwelt etwas entgegenzusetzen und da Effizienz zu zeigen, wo andere Güter versagen. Sie sollen beweisen, dass hochwertiges Design komplex in der Vielfalt seiner Funktionen sein kann, ohne notwendigerweise kompliziert zu sein. Meine Kreationen haben eine klare, rationale Basis, beruhend auf meiner Ausrichtung und Ausbildung, aber sie haben auch eine fragile, emotionale, sogar poetische Qualität, die von meiner Offenheit und meinem Aufwachsen in mehreren Kulturen herrührt. Außerdem ist da immer ein Konzept von Leichtigkeit, Transparenz, Bewegung, ein Hauch von Geheimnis und eine gewisse Affinität zu künstlerischen Werken."

« J'essaie d'unir tradition et innovation, joie et énergie dans mon travail créatif. Mes productions doivent être ludiques et profondes au mépris d'un monde de marchandises fades, efficaces quand d'autres produits ne tiennent pas leurs promesses. Elles doivent démontrer qu'un bon design peut être complexe par la variété de ses fonctions sans devoir forcément être compliqué. Mes créations ont une base claire, rationnelle, qui résulte de mon orientation et de ma formation ; mais elles ont également quelque chose de fragile, d'émotionnel, de poétique même, qui vient de mon ouverture d'esprit et de mon éducation culturellement variée. Et il y a toujours une notion de légèreté, de transparence, de mouvement, une petite touche de mystère et certaines affinités avec les œuvres artistiques. »

4

1–4/8

TAORMINA SEATING
SYSTEM FOR ALIAS, 2006

The Taormina chairs are based
on a stove-enamelled steel structure. Their monocoque shells are
constructed of HiREK solid
polymer and padded with CFC-
free expanded polyurethane
foam. The removable fabric covers come in a range of colours
and four base options are available: 4-leg, sled, 4-leg with cast-
ers and 5-star swivelling gas-lift.

Die Stühle der Taormina-Serie
haben ein Gestell aus einbrenn-
lackiertem Stahl. Ihre selbsttra-
genden Schalen bestehen aus
HiREK-Solid-Polymer und sind
mit FCKW-freiem flexiblem
Polyurethanschaum gepolstert.
Die abziehbaren Stoffbezüge
sind in verschiedenen Farben
erhältlich, und es gibt vier
Gestellvarianten: vierbeinig,
Stützschienen, vierbeinig mit
Laufrollen sowie ein Stuhl mit
regulierbarer Sitzhöhe und Fuß-
kreuz auf Rollen.

Les chaises Taormina reposent
sur une structure en acier
émaillée au four. Leurs coques
unifiées sont composées de
HiREK, un polymère très dense,
qui est recouvert de mousse de
polyuréthane expansée sans chlo-
rofluorocarbures. Les housses de
tissus amovibles sont disponibles
en un grand nombre de couleurs
pour quatre options de base :
4-pieds, à glissière, glissière
lounge et 4-pieds avec roulettes.

"Design is what you see
when you close your eyes…
observing is the most beautiful way
of thinking…
design is taking a thought-line
for a walk."

5
PLEIN AIR CHAIR 270
Indoor/outdoor upholstered
side chair with stove-enamelled
steel rod frame
2007
Client: Alias

6
PLEIN AIR ARMCHAIR 271
Indoor/outdoor upholstered
armchair with stove-enamelled
steel rod frame
2007
Client: Alias

7
PLEIN AIR TABLE 090281
Indoor/outdoor table with
circular polymer top on stove-
enamelled tubular steel frame
2007
Client: Alias

ALFREDO HÄBERLI

Seefeldstrasse 301a
8008 Zurich
Switzerland
T +41 44 3803230
E studio@alfredo-haeberli.com
www.alfredo-haeberli.com

BIOGRAPHY

1964 Born in Buenos Aires, Argentina
1977 Moves with family to Switzerland
1980–1984 Trains as a super-structure draughtsman and attends vocational college in Zurich
1986–1991 Degree in industrial design at the Höhere Schule für Gestaltung Zurich; awarded the school's Diploma Prize
1988 First collaborative project with the Museum für Gestaltung Zurich; since 1988 has designed and curated numerous exhibitions at the museum
1989 Gained practical experience at Siemens, New York and at the Product Development Department of Roericht, Ulm, Germany
1991 Launched career as freelance designer; IKEA Foundation grant for a project in the field of "Ecology in Draft Form", together with Martin Huwiler and Christophe Marchand
1994 Awarded the Achievement Prize of the Höhere Schule für Gestaltung Zurich, together with Christophe Marchand
2000 Founded Häberli Design Development Atelier in Zurich
2004 Guest professor at the Hochschule für Gestaltung Zurich

RECENT EXHIBITIONS

2002 "Sketching My Own Landscape", Asplund, Stockholm
2003 "Denkblasen", Abitare, Chur; "Zwischenwelten", (Between Worlds) travelling exhibition – Teo Jacob, Solothurn/Zurich/Bern
2004 "Now! – Designer de l'année 2004", Maison & Objet, Paris; "Shootingstars", Designmai, Berlin "New Designs by Alfredo Häberli for Classicon", Via Manin 15, Milan, Italy
2005 "Mini Event", Zurich; Bubenzimmer, Neue Räume, Zurich
2006 "The In-Betweens/CH+ Design" (guest of honour), Interieur06, Kortrijk, Belguim
2007 "Neue Räume" & "Lebensart", Wittgenstein, Munich
2008 Solo exhibition, Museum of Design, Zurich

RECENT AWARDS

2004 Now! – Designer de l'année, Maison & Objet, Paris
2005 Design Preis Schweiz, Bern

CLIENTS

Alias, Bd Ediciones de Diseño, Camper, Cappellini, Classicon, Iittala, Joop!, Kvadrat, Luceplan, Moroso, Offecct, Volvo

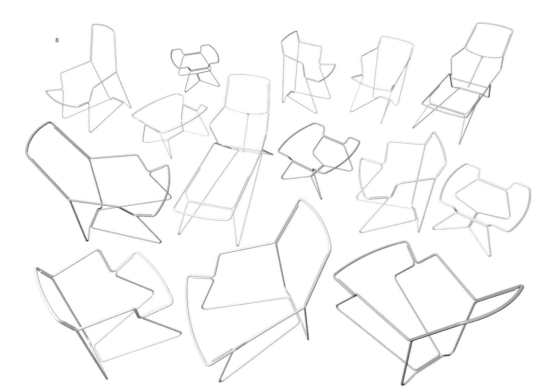

8

10–11
SKATE
Polyurethane foam-upholstered sectional-seating system with steel frames
2005
Client: Moroso

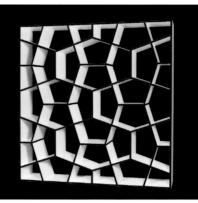

9

10

8
PLEIN AIR
Chair and table frame/base
variations
2007
Client: Alias

9
PATTERN
Bookcase constructed of satin
white or silver aluminium sandwich panels with black edges
2006
Client: Quodes

11

ZAHA HADID

"My Seamless furniture collection is an excellent embodiment of our built manifesto towards the potential for a new language of design and architecture, which is driven by the latest in digital design processes and the most cutting edge manufacturing techniques. With the overall conception of the designs ultimately driven by the new possibilities created by significant technological advancements in three dimensional design software, as well as our inherent desire to test and engage with the very latest manufacturing capabilities, the result is a dialogue of complex curvilinear geometries and detailed ergonomic research that provides the opportunity for us to reinvent the balance between furniture and space. These unique pieces are an obvious evolution of the architectural language explored by my practice: soft meets sharp, the combination of convex and concave, and a sculptural sensibility that impacts on our self-conception as bodies."

„Meine Möbelkollektion Seamless ist das Werk gewordene Manifest einer neuen Design- und Architektursprache, die ihr Potenzial aus dem Neuesten, was es an digitalen Designprozessen gibt, und aus den innovativsten Fertigungstechniken bezieht. Mit der Gesamtkonzeption des Designs, das letztlich auf die durch signifikante Fortschritte der 3D-Designsoftware geschaffenen neuen Möglichkeiten zurückgeht, und mit unserem Anspruch, die allerneuesten Fertigungstechniken auszuprobieren und anzuwenden, stellt diese Möbelkollektion einen Dialog von komplexen Kurvengeometrien und detaillierten ergonomischen Untersuchungen dar. Er ermöglicht uns, das Gleichgewicht zwischen Möbel und Raum neu zu erfinden. Diese Unikate sind eine folgerichtige Weiterentwicklung der Architektursprache, die in meinem Büro erprobt wird: Weich trifft auf Scharf, die Kombination von Konvex und Konkav und eine plastische Sensibilität, die unsere Selbstwahrnehmung als Körper beeinflusst."

«Ma collection de meubles Seamless (sans heurts, en douceur, homogène) est un manifeste en volume de ce que pourrait être un langage neuf pour le design et l'architecture, établi à partir du dernier cri en matière de processus de création numériques et de techniques de fabrication. La conception générale des créations étant en fin de compte élaborée grâce aux nouvelles possibilités nées d'avancées technologiques importantes dans les logiciels de création en trois dimensions, et grâce à notre désir de nous investir dans les toutes dernières potentialités industrielles, la collection de mobilier qui en résulte est un dialogue entre une complexe géométrie curviligne et une recherche ergonomique poussée qui nous offre la possibilité de réinventer l'équilibre entre mobilier et espace. Ces pièces uniques représentent une évolution évidente du langage architectural, après investigation de la part de mon équipe : le doux rencontre l'anguleux, le convexe se mêle au concave pour doter chaque pièce d'une sensibilité sculpturale qui influe sur la conception que nous avons de nos propres corps.»

1

2

4

1–3/5
VORTEXX
Glass fibre-reinforced polyester
suspended ceiling light with
internal translucent acrylic
diffuser and RGB PowerLED
modules
2005
Client: Sawaya & Moroni

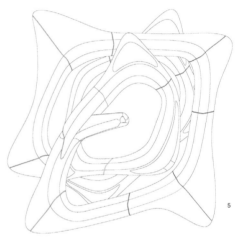

5

4
VORTEXX
Detail showing RGB
PowerLED-generated light
colour modulations
2005
Client: Sawaya & Moroni

6
VORTEXX
Suspended ceiling lights in Zaha
Hadid's installation at the 2007
imm cologne fair

1–6
VORTEXX SUSPENDED
CEILING LIGHT (WITH
PATRIK SCHUMACHER)
FOR SAWAYA & MORONI,
2005 (MANUFACTURED BY
ZUMTOBEL, 2006)

Fluidity and seamlessness are
conceptual terms that best
describe the appearance of this
large chandelier. Its complex
curvilinearity follows a double
helix connecting its beginning to
its end and therefore forms an
endless ribbon of light. In plan
the object resembles a star with
its protrusions pointing out-
wards from the centre, emphasizing an imaginary centrifugal
force. Two transparent acrylic
light spirals are inscribed in the
chandelier's otherwise opaque
surface. A recessed LED light

strip provides animated and pro-
grammable light sensations.
Direct as well as indirect light
can be optionally emitted to the
environment. Consequently different lighting atmospheres may
be created by the user in order
to match the specific space in
which the chandelier is installed.
This new interior design language is fuelled by advanced
digital design possibilities and
manufacturing methods such as
CNC-milling and 3D printing.
The user is invited to explore
creatively its interactive qualities
and respond to its unfamiliar
aesthetics.

Nahtloses Fließen ist das Designkonzept, das diesen eindrucks-
vollen Luster am treffendsten
beschreibt. Seine kompliziert
geschwungene Linie folgt einer

Doppelhelix, die sich zu einem
durchgehenden, endlosen Licht-
band formt. Im Grundriss
ähnelt das Objekt einem Stern
mit seinen vom Mittelpunkt
wegstrebenden Zacken, wo-
durch der Eindruck einer imagi-
nären Zentrifugalkraft noch verstärkt wird. Zwei spiralförmige
Lichtstränge aus transluzentem
Acryl wurden in die ansonsten
opake Oberfläche eingesetzt.
Durch LED-Lichtbänder im
Inneren können unterschiedliche
Lichtstimmungen geschaffen
und programmiert werden.
Optional kann direkt oder indi-
rekt abstrahlendes Licht erzeugt
werden. Das Lichtspiel lässt sich
individuell an den Raum anpas-
sen, in dem der Luster installiert
wird. Diese neue Designsprache
in der Innenraumgestaltung ist
stark beeinflusst von den faszi-

nierenden Möglichkeiten des
digitalen Designs und von Fertigungstechniken wie CNC-
gesteuerten Fräsrobotern und
3D-Printing. Der Benutzer ist
aufgefordert, das interaktive
Potenzial des Objekts kreativ
auszuloten und auf seine ungewöhnliche Ästhetik zu reagieren.

Fluidité et homogénéité sont les
termes conceptuels qui décrivent
le mieux l'aspect de ce grand
lustre. Sa structure curviligne et
complexe suit une double hélice
dont le début est relié à la fin, ce
qui forme un ruban lumineux
continu. Sur plan, l'objet ressemble à une étoile dont les
saillies pointent du centre vers
l'extérieur pour mettre l'accent
sur une force centrifuge imaginaire. Deux spirales lumineuses
d'acrylique transparent s'inscri-

vent dans la surface opaque du
lustre. Une bande de diodes élec-
troluminescentes encastrées produit des sensations lumineuses
animées et programmables. La
lumière peut être diffusée de
façon directe ou indirecte dans
la pièce. Différentes atmo-
sphères d'éclairage peuvent par
conséquent être créées par l'usager en fonction de l'espace dont
il dispose et du volume dans
lequel s'inscrira le lustre. Ce
nouveau lexique décoratif se
nourrit des nouvelles possibilités
de création numérique et de
méthodes industrielles comme le
crénelage CNC et l'impression
en 3D. L'usager est invité à
explorer de façon créative ses
qualités interactives et à établir
un dialogue avec son aspect
inhabituel.

7
FLOW
Large (1.2 and 2.0 metre high)
vases in rotational-moulded
polyethylene (designed with
Patrik Schumacher)
2007
Client: Serralunga

7

8

8–11
Z.ISLAND
Two freestanding kitchen
islands, modular wall-panel
system and shelving system
in thermoformed Corian for

installation at the 2006 Milan
Furniture Fair (designed with
Patrik Schumacher)
2005–2006
Client: DuPont Corian

9

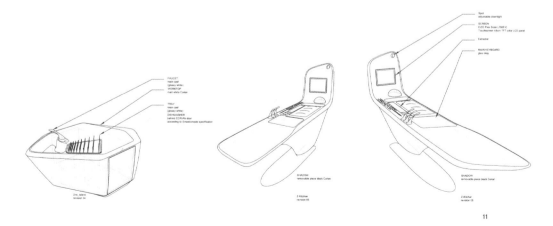

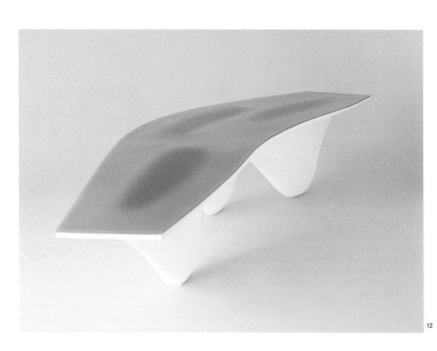

"My exploration
into a world
of seamless fluidity"

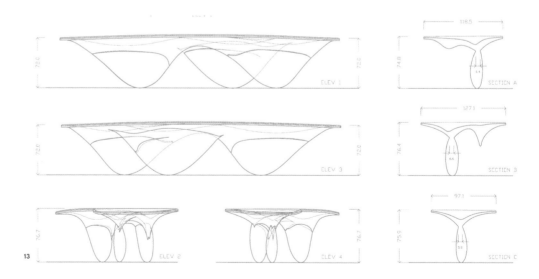

14

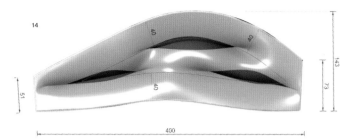

400

51

143

73

40

40

40

12–15
AQUA TABLE
Table with single-form monolithic base in gloss-finish
polyurethane and top in
translucent silicon gel with
non-slip surface
2005
Client: Established & Sons

15

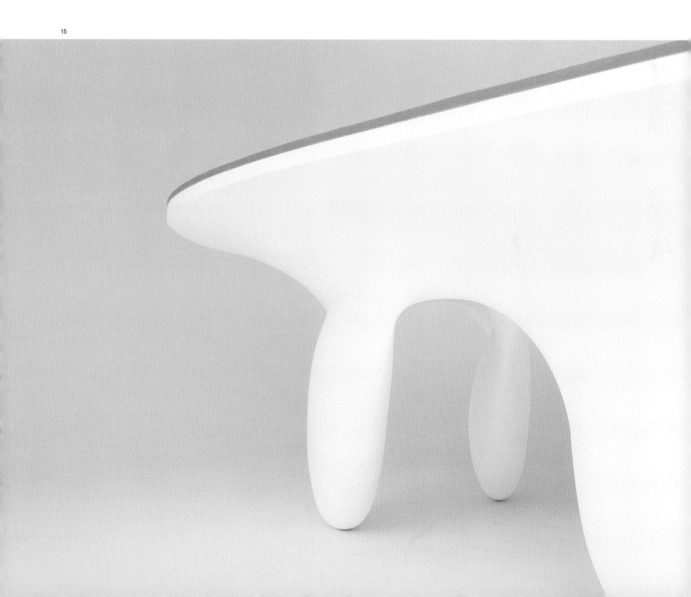

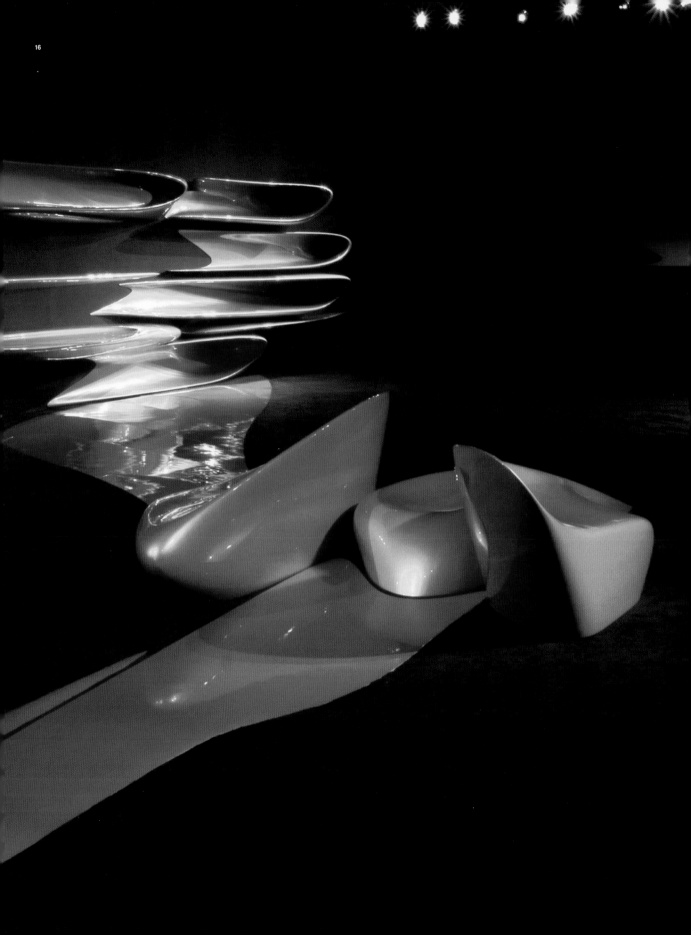

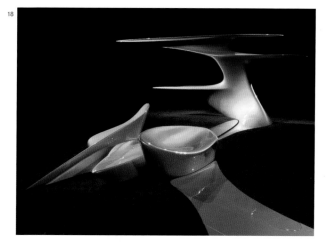

17

16–19
DUNE FORMATIONS
Collection of wall shelving units,
tables, benches and an artificial
tree in metal and polyester
resin with polyurethane lacquer

finish (designed with Patrik
Schumacher)
2007
Client: David Gill Galleries
(limited edition of 8 per design)

19

ZAHA HADID

Zaha Hadid Architects
10 Bowling Green Lane
London EC1R 0BQ
T +44 207 2535147
E press@zaha-hadid.com
www.zaha-hadid.com

BIOGRAPHY

1950 Born in Baghdad, Iraq
1972 Enrolled at the Architectural Association, London, after taking a mathematics degree at the American University of Beirut
1977 Diploma Prize, Architectural Association, London
1977 Partner, Rem Koolhaas' Office for Metropolitan Architecture (OMA)
1980–1988 Taught at the Architectural Association, London
1980 Established her own architectural office in London
1982 Won the competition to build The Peak, a spa in Hong Kong (unbuilt)
1987–Present Kenzo Tange Chair at the Graduate School of Design, Harvard University; the Sullivan Chair at the University of Chicago School of Architecture; guest professorships at the Hochschule für Bildende Künste in Hamburg, the Knolton School of Architecture, Ohio and the Masters Studio at Columbia University, New York and visiting Professor of Architectural Design at Yale University, New Haven, Connecticut. In addition, she has been made Honorary Member of the American Academy of Arts and Letters and Fellow of the American Institute of Architecture
1993 Completed her first built work, the Vitra Fire Station, Weil am Rhein, Germany
2001+ Professor of Architecture, Universität für Angewandte Kunst (University of Applied Arts), Vienna

RECENT EXHIBITIONS

2006 "Zaha Hadid" at the Solomon R Guggenheim, New York
2007 "Ideal House Cologne", imm cologne; "Dune Formations", Scula dei Mercanti, Venice Biennale; "Zaha Hadid: Architecture & Design" at the Design Museum London

RECENT AWARDS

2002 Commander of the British Empire (CBE)
2003 Mies van der Rohe Award
2004 Pritzker Architecture Prize, Hyatt Foundation (first woman to be awarded this prestigious prize)
2005 Honorary Fellow of Columbia University, New York; Deutsche Architecture Prize "Building of the Year" (BMW Central Building); Finalist for the RIBA Stirling Prize (BMW Central Building); UK Gold Medal for Design, International Olympic Committee (Bergisel Ski Jump); Austrian Decoration for Science and Art, Vienna; Designer of the Year, Design 05 Miami
2006 Honorary Doctorate, Yale University; Honorary Doctorate, American University of Beirut; RIBA Medal, European Cultural Building of the Year (Phaeno Science Center); RIBA Jencks Award; Leading European Architects Forum Award for Best Structural Design (Phaeno Science Center); Finalist for the RIBA Stirling Prize (Phaeno Science Center)
2007 AIA UK Chapter Award for Excellence (Maggie's Centre Fife); Finalist for the Mies van der Rohe Award for European Architecture (Phaeno Science Center); Thomas Jefferson Foundation Medal in Architecture, USA; Scottish Design Awards, Best Public Building Award (Maggie's Centre, Fife); London Design Medal, Outstanding Contribution for Design

CLIENTS (PRODUCT DESIGN)

Established & Sons, B&B Italia, David Gill Galleries, DuPont Corian, Louis Vuitton, Sawaya & Moroni, Serralunga

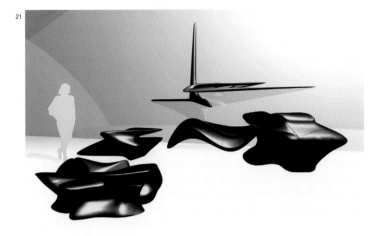

20
CREST
Chaise longue from the
Seamless Collection in polyester
resin with polyurethane
lacquer finish
2006
Client: Established & Sons
(limited edition of 8)

21
COMPUTER RENDERING
OF SEAMLESS COLLECTION
PIECES
2006
Client: Established & Sons

22
COMPUTER RENDERING
OF NEKTON
Set of four interlocking low
stools from the Seamless
Collection in polyester resin
with polyurethane lacquer
finish
2006
Client: Established & Sons
(limited edition of 12)

JAIME HAYON

"For quite some time I didn't know what I was. Furniture designer? Artist? Graphic designer? Ultimately, however, I found out that such designations are not the point. I'm here to tell stories with my pieces of furniture. The story you tell with a collection is important, because it can make it strong and coherent. The story doesn't have to be based on reality; it can be a complete fantasy as long as people can recognize themselves in it. Designers can make the world into a theatre. They can make life a lot more fun. The only things that hold us back, unfortunately, are money and conservatism. Quality is another of my obsessions… the lasting impression made by these projects is that of a serious devotion to well-made things and a return to the golden years of luxury… you need to discuss your work and to ask others what they think. Only through conversation can you get where you want to be. And while you're talking about your work, you're educating others: clients, marketing people, manufacturers – even yourself. The designs from a collection are part of an ongoing story. Pieces that are part of the limited collection can be used as the basis for new designs, applications and experiments with materials. That's what really gives the designs their value and what a manufacturer profits from."

„Ziemlich lange wusste ich nicht, was ich war. Möbeldesigner? Künstler? Grafiker? Schließlich fand ich heraus, dass es nicht um solche Kategorisierungen geht. Ich bin hier, um mit meinen Möbelstücken Geschichten zu erzählen. Die Geschichte, die mit einer Kollektion erzählt wird, ist wichtig, denn sie trägt zur Aussagekraft und Kohärenz der Kollektion bei. Die Geschichte muss nicht auf Tatsachen beruhen: Sie kann reine Fantasie sein, solange sich die Menschen darin wiedererkennen können. Designer können die Welt in ein Theater verwandeln. Sie können das Leben lebenswerter machen. Was uns – leider – zurückhält, sind einzig und allein Geld und konservative Einstellungen. Ich bin außerdem besessen von dem Anspruch auf Qualität … damit hinterlässt man den nachhaltigen Eindruck, dass es hier jemandem ernsthaft um gut Gemachtes und die Rückkehr in ein goldenes Zeitalter des Luxus ging … man muss über seine Arbeiten diskutieren und andere nach ihrer Meinung dazu fragen. Nur durch Gespräche erreicht man sein Ziel. Und während man über seine eigene Arbeit spricht, informiert man die anderen: Kunden, Marketingleute, Hersteller – sogar sich selbst. Die Designs einer Kollektion sind Bestandteile einer offenen Geschichte. Stücke aus einer begrenzten Kollektion können als Ausgangsbasis für neue Designs, Anwendungen und Versuche mit anderen Werkstoffen verwendet werden. Das macht ihren wahren Wert aus und ist das, wovon ein Hersteller profitiert."

«Pendant un bon moment, je n'ai pas su qui j'étais. Créateur de meubles? Artiste? Graphiste? Pourtant, au bout du compte, j'ai découvert que ce ne sont pas les étiquettes qui comptent. Je suis là pour raconter des histoires avec mes meubles. L'histoire que l'on raconte avec une collection est importante, parce qu'elle peut la rendre forte et cohérente. L'histoire ne se fonde pas forcément sur la réalité; il peut s'agir d'un fantasme tant que les gens peuvent s'y reconnaître. Les designers peuvent faire du monde un théâtre. Ils peuvent rendre la vie bien plus amusante. Les seules choses qui nous retiennent, malheureusement, sont l'argent et le conservatisme. La qualité fait également partie de mes obsessions… L'impression que laissent ces projets est celle de choses bien réalisées et d'un retour à l'âge d'or du luxe… Il faut remettre son travail en question et demander aux autres ce qu'ils en pensent. Seule la conversation peut nous amener où nous voulons aller. Et pendant que nous parlons de notre travail, nous éduquons les autres: les clients, les commerciaux, les fabricants – et nous-même. Les éléments d'une collection font partie d'une histoire en cours. Certains peuvent être utilisés comme base pour de nouvelles créations, de nouvelles applications et expérimentations de matériaux. C'est ce qui donne réellement aux créations leur valeur et ce dont un fabricant peut tirer bénéfice.»

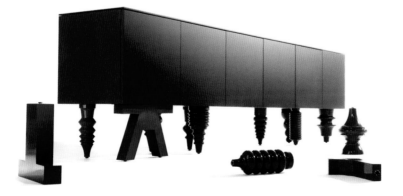

1
MULTILEG CABINET
Sideboard from the Showtime
Collection in lacquered MDF
with interchangeable legs
2006
Client: BD Ediciones de Diseño

2
JOSEPHINE M
Table light with porcelain body
2004
Client: Metalarte

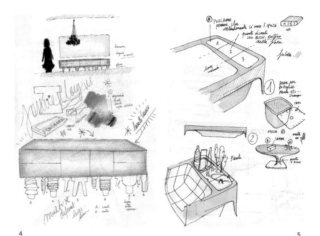

"Design is a platform I use
to make my dreams come true."

3
DOUBLE POLTRONA
Sofa from the Showtime
Collection in plastic and leather
2006
Client: BD Ediciones
de Diseño

4
MULTILEG CABINET
Drawing of sideboard from
the Showtime Collection in
lacquered MDF with inter-
changeable legs
2006
Client: BD Ediciones
de Diseño

4

5

6

5
AQH5 BATH
Drawing of bath and accessories
from the AQHayon Collection
2006
Client: Artquitect

7
AQH5 BATH
Bath from the AQHayon
Collection
2006
Client: Artquitect

6
KUBOKUBE & HALO
MIRROR
Smoked tempered glass
sideboard with lacquered MDF
inner cabinets and circular mirror with lacquered wood frame
2006
Client: Pallucco

7

8

8
FUNGHI
Family of ceramic table lights
2006
Client: Metalarte

9
SEAU
Champagne bucket in
moulded Surlyn
2006
Client: Piper-Heidsieck

9

JAIME HAYON
Hayon®StudioBCN
Muntaner 88 – 2°1a
08011 Barcelona
Spain
T +34 93 5321776
E info@hayonstudio.com
www.hayonstudio.com

BIOGRAPHY
1974 Born in Madrid, Spain
1993–1996 Studied industrial
design at Instituto Europeo di
Design, Madrid
1996–1997 Studied at the
ENSAD (École Nationale
Supérieure des Arts Décoratifs),
Paris
1997 Began working as a
researcher for Fabrica, Treviso
(Benetton Group's communication research centre)
1998 Appointed head of
design, Fabrica, Treviso
2004 Founded his own
design office

RECENT EXHIBITIONS
2003 "Mediterranean Digital
Baroque", David Gill Gallery,
London
2005 "Tank", Design Museum,
London; "Mon Cirque" travel-
ling installation, Barcelona,
Minneapolis, Lisbon, Paris,
Cologne
2006 "Stage" (solo exhibition),
Aram Gallery, London;
"Animal Magic", Vessel Gallery,
London
2007 "Pixel Ballet", Bisazza,
Superstudio Piu, Milan; "Stage
Holland", Vivid Gallery,
Rotterdam; "Stage Madrid",
Casa Pasarela Ifema Parque
Ferial Juan Carlos I, Madrid

RECENT AWARDS
2006 Wallpaper Award – one of
the 10 breakthrough creators
worldwide; Elle Decoration
International Award; Icon
Magazine Best Show award for
the 2006 London design week

CLIENTS
Artquitect Edition,
BD Barcelona, Bisazza,
Camper, Lladro, Metalarte,
Pallucco, Piper-Heidsieck,
Swarovski

SAM HECHT

"Many people who go about their daily life are oblivious to the fact that everything they see, hear, touch or smell has a profound effect on their temperament. The city, the building, the room, the chair, the table – they are all interconnected and equally influential. I'm surprised that this simple idea is often, either neglected, not involved, forgotten or misunderstood. Consequently we become oblivious to subtlety and simplicity, because our receptors are challenged by an ever-greater dependence on marketplace 'wow' factors. A consumer may not know all reasons for desiring an object – but nevertheless, desire is there. The foundation for this desire is discovered with use and the appreciation acquired over time. Through the work of our studio, we acknowledge that all things are dependant on each other. Rather than seeing contemporary life through an outdated Renaissance model, where everything is independent, self-contained and focused towards the human, we see that everything affects and communicates with each other. It means seeing the world without imagining we can control it all. Imagine designing a printer or a coffee maker, for the room that it sits in, the table that it is on, or the person operating it. This idea allows the evacuation of superfluous functions, and the abandonment of complexity, because it acknowledges what already exists, and doesn't see a need for duplication or replication. The environment for an object, as much as its use, determines its form and content."

„Viele Menschen nehmen in ihrem Alltag nicht wahr, dass alles, was sie sehen, hören, spüren oder riechen, sich sehr deutlich auf ihr Gemüt auswirkt. Die Stadt, das Gebäude, das Zimmer, der Stuhl, der Tisch – sie alle sind miteinander verbunden und entfalten gleichermaßen eine Wirkung. Ich bin oft erstaunt, dass dieser einfache Gedanke häufig entweder vernachlässigt, nicht berücksichtigt, vergessen oder missverstanden wird. Wir werden folglich auch unempfänglich für Feinheit und Einfachheit, weil unsere Sinnesorgane immer mehr auf die ‚Wow-Faktoren' des Marktes reagieren. Konsumenten wissen nicht immer ganz genau, warum sie ein Objekt haben wollen – doch das Verlangen ist da. Die Grundlage des Verlangens wird bei der Verwendung klar, und mit der Zeit lernt man, das Objekt zu schätzen. Durch die Arbeit unseres Büros bringen wir unsere Überzeugung zum Ausdruck, dass alles voneinander abhängig ist. Statt das heutige Leben an einem überholten Renaissance-Vorbild zu messen, in dem alles unabhängig, autark und auf das Menschliche ausgerichtet ist, sind wir der Ansicht, dass sich alles gegenseitig beeinflusst und alles mit allem kommuniziert. Das ist eine Weltsicht ohne die Vorstellung, dass man alles kontrollieren kann. Stellen Sie sich vor, einen Drucker oder eine Kaffeemaschine für den Raum zu gestalten, in dem sie untergebracht sein werden, für den Tisch, auf dem sie stehen werden, oder für den Menschen, der sie bedienen wird. Dieser Gedanke ermöglicht es, auf unnötige Funktionen und Komplexität zu verzichten, da Vorhandenes zur Kenntnis genommen wird und keine Notwendigkeit besteht, etwas zu duplizieren oder zu wiederholen. Die Umgebung eines Objekts ist genauso bestimmend für seine Form und seinen Inhalt wie seine Verwendung."

« Dans leur vie quotidienne, beaucoup de gens oublient que tout ce qu'ils voient, entendent, touchent ou sentent a un profond impact sur leur tempérament. La ville, l'immeuble, la pièce, la chaise, la table – sont tous liés entre eux et d'une influence égale. Je suis souvent surpris que cette idée simple soit le plus souvent négligée, écartée, oubliée ou mal comprise. C'est ainsi que nous perdons d'esprit la subtilité et la simplicité, parce que nos récepteurs sont déstabilisés par une dépendance toujours croissante aux facteurs ‹ouah› qui règne sur le marché. Un consommateur peut ne pas connaître toutes les raisons qui le poussent à désirer un objet – et pourtant, le désir est bien là. Les bases de ce désir se découvrent à l'usage, grâce à l'œil que l'on acquiert avec le temps. Notre travail au sein du studio nous permet de vérifier que toutes les choses dépendent les unes des autres. Plutôt que de voir la vie contemporaine à travers un modèle Renaissance obsolète où toute chose se construit indépendamment de ce qui l'entoure et du seul point de vue humain, nous constatons que toute chose agit et communique. C'est regarder le monde sans imaginer que nous pouvons le contrôler totalement. Imaginer, lorsque l'on crée une imprimante ou une machine à café, la pièce dans laquelle elle sera installée, la table sur laquelle elle sera posée, la personne qui s'en servira. Cette idée permet d'évacuer les fonctions superflues et d'abandonner la complexité parce qu'elle met en évidence ce qui existe déjà et n'implique ni duplication ni réplication. L'environnement d'un objet, tout autant que son usage, détermine sa forme et son contenu. »

1–4
PICTUREMATE 240
Digital photo printer in
injection-moulded ABS
2006
Client: Epson

1–4

PICTUREMATE 240 PRINTER
FOR EPSON, 2006

"Representing a significant shift
in design approach for Epson,
Industrial Facility created a
small home printing unit that is
portable and beyond peripheral.
With liberating features such as
battery power, integral handle
and adjustable LCD screen, this
home printer takes up a position
of complete domestic use,
instead of migrated office
machinery. The lid acts both as
protective cover and paper tray;
the paper exit door reveals camera card inputs. In this design,
the domestic landscape informs
the product with technology presented as liveable and simple."

„Industrial Facility hat einen
kleinen tragbaren Drucker für
zu Hause gestaltet, der mehr ist
als ein Peripheriegerät und der
eine markante Veränderung in
der Designphilosophie von
Epson darstellt. Ein optionaler
Akku, der integrierte Griff und
der einstellbare LCD-Schirm
sorgen für Unabhängigkeit, und
die Gestaltung ist nicht auf den
Anschluss von Bürogeräten
abgestimmt, sondern ausschließlich auf die Verwendung im pri-
vaten Bereich ausgerichtet. Die
obere Klappe ist Schutz und
Papierkassette zugleich; hinter
der Verschlussklappe des Papier-
ausgangs verbergen sich die Slots
für die Speicherkarten der
Kamera. Der private Lebens-
raum hat Pate gestanden bei der
Gestaltung dieses Produkts, das
sich mit einfacher Technik problemlos in den Alltag einfügt."

« Pour marquer une importante
évolution du design d'Epson,
Industrial Facility a créé une
petite imprimante domestique
portable qui fonctionne aussi
sans être reliée à un ordinateur.
Grâce à des équipements libéra-
teurs comme son alimentation
sur batteries, sa poignée intégrale
et son écran LCD réglable, cette
imprimante devient un objet
domestique à part entière au lieu
d'être un simple transfuge de la
vie de bureau. Le couvercle sert
à la fois d'étui protecteur et de
boîte de stockage pour le papier ;
le clapet de sortie du papier
révèle les données contenues
dans les cartes image. Dans ce
design, l'environnement domestique influe sur le produit grâce
à une technologie présentée de
façon simple et facile à vivre. »

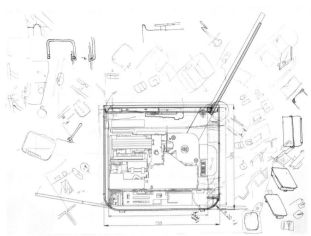

3

5

5–6
FAN
Floor fan in injection-moulded
ABS and steel with remote
control
2006
Client: Muji

6

"Design is about enjoying risk.
Give me a design that involves no risk
and you give me a copy."

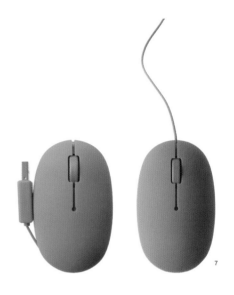

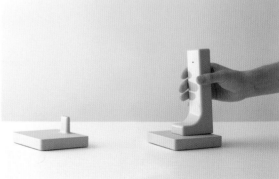

7
MOUSE TRAP
Optical computer mouse in
injection-moulded ABS
2005
Client: Lexon

8–9
CORDLESS PHONE
Cordless telephone and base unit
in injection-moulded polymer
2006
Client: self-generated concept

10–11
LITTLE DISK PROGRAM
Family of media drives in
injection-moulded ABS
2007
Client: LaCie

SAM HECHT

Industrial Facility
Clerks Well House
20 Britton Street, 3rd Floor
London EC1M 5UA
T +44 20 72533234
E mail@industrialfacility.co.uk
www.industrialfacility.co.uk

BIOGRAPHY

1969 Born in London, England
1988–1989 Foundation course, Hornsey School of Art, London
1989–1991 BA Industrial Design, Central St. Martin's College of Art and Design, London
1991–1993 MA Industrial Design, Royal College of Art, London
1993 Apprenticeship, David Chipperfield Architects, London
1994–1999 Designer, IDEO Offices, San Francisco and Tokyo
1999 Head of Industrial Design, IDEO, London
2002 Co-founded Industrial Facility design office with architect Kim Colin

RECENT EXHIBITIONS

2003 "Sam Hecht and Ron Arad – The artist and engineer", Now! Design à vivre, Paris
2004 "Haptic", Spiral Gallery, Tokyo; "European Design Show", Design Museum, London
2005 "Found/Made/Thought" (Industrial Facility retrospective), Israel Museum, Jerusalem; "Object of Conversation", Galerie Kreo for Le Bon Marche, Paris; "Hearwear", Victoria and Albert Museum, London; "Under a Tenner", Design Museum, London; "Import/Export", Victoria and Albert Museum, London
2006 "Tank", Design Museum, London; "Love & Money", Ozone Gallery, Tokyo
2007 "25 Designers/25 Designs", Design Museum, London

RECENT AWARDS

2004 Good Design Award, JIDPO (Japan Industrial Design Promotion Organization); Red Dot Award, Design Zentrum Nordrhein Westfalen, Essen; FX Design Award, London
2005 Gold iF Award, International Forum Design Hanover: Good Design Award, JIDPO (Japan Industrial Design Promotion Organization); Design Plus Award, Ambiente, Frankfurt
2006 Gold iF Award, International Forum Design Hanover; Design Plus Award, Ambiente, Frankfurt; Good Design Award, JIDPO (Japan Industrial Design Promotion Organization)
2007 Gold iF Award, International Forum Design Hanover; Honorary Award for Design Medium, Material Connexion and I.D. Magazine; Pen Japan award; Good Design Award; JIDPO (Japan Industrial Design Promotion Organization)

CLIENTS

Epson, Established & Sons, France Telecom, Habitat, Harrison Fisher, IDEA International, KitchenAid, LaCie, Lexon SA, Magis, Muji, National Japan, Panasonic, RNID, Seiko, Steelcase, Takeo, Taylors Eye Witness, Yamaha, Whirlpool

12

13

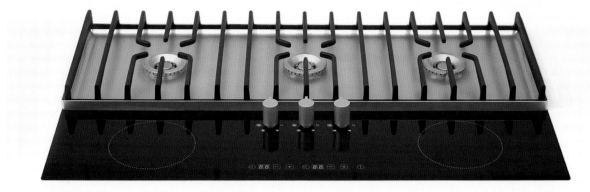

14

15

14–15
STEP
Cooktop with induction and
gas sources in glass and stainless
steel
2006
Client: KitchenAid

16
IF4000
Fully forged hi-carbon
stainless-steel chef's knife and
magnetic knife rack
2006
Client: Taylors Eye Witness

16

12–13
COFFEE MAKER
Automatic coffee maker in
injection-moulded polypropylene and vacuum-formed
stainless steel
2006
Client: Muji

INDIO DA COSTA

"To quote Tom Jobim (*Wave*, 1967), 'So close your eyes, for that's a lovely way to be aware of things your heart alone was meant to see...' Our goal is to imbue objects with a Brazilian sensuality and a Swiss precision. A timeless, sensual and joyful approach to life and design inspires our brand to pursue the wellness of people, through the use of products, services and the experiences they provide. We love to solve people's problems and enhance their lives through remarkable design. We love, care and respect our home planet, and therefore every project becomes an opportunity for sustainability. We love to flow freely around cultures, speaking a fluent eco-tech design language. We think that's a lovely way to be."

„Um den brasilianischen Sänger und Komponisten Tom Jobim mit seinem Lied *Wave* (1967) zu zitieren: ‚So schließe deine Augen, denn es ist eine schöne Art, der Dinge gewahr zu werden, die allein dein Herz sehen sollte ...' Unser Ziel ist es, Objekte mit einer brasilianischen Sinnlichkeit und einer schweizerischen Präzision zu imprägnieren. Ein zeitloser, sinnlicher und freudiger Zugang zum Leben und Design inspiriert unsere Marke. Wir streben nach dem Wohlbefinden der Menschen, die die Produkte und Dienstleistungen nutzen und erfahren. Wir lösen gern die Probleme von Menschen und bereichern deren Leben durch ungewöhnliches Design. Wir lieben, pflegen und respektieren unseren Heimatplaneten, und deshalb wird jedes unserer Projekte zu einer Chance für Nachhaltigkeit. Wir lieben es, uns frei zwischen den Kulturen zu bewegen und eine fließende öko-tech Designsprache zu verwenden. Wir finden, das ist eine schöne Art des Seins."

«Pour citer Tom Jobim (*Wave*, 1967), ‹Alors ferme tes yeux, car c'est une jolie façon de prendre conscience des choses que seul ton cœur devait voir... › Notre objectif est d'imprégner les objets d'une combinaison de sensualité brésilienne et de précision suisse. Une approche intemporelle, sensuelle et joyeuse de la vie et du design pousse notre marque à procurer aux gens du confort grâce à des produits, à des services ou à des expériences. Nous adorons résoudre les problèmes des gens et embellir leur vie grâce à des créations qui sortent de l'ordinaire. Nous aimons, soignons et respectons notre planète mère : c'est pourquoi chaque projet devient une occasion de créer durablement. Nous adorons voguer librement parmi les différentes cultures et parlons avec aisance la langue internationale du design éco-technologique. Nous trouvons belle cette façon d'être. »

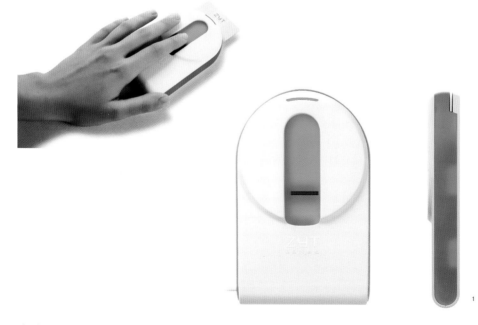

1

3

1
ZYT COMBO
Biometric smart card reader in
injection-moulded polymer
2006
Client: Taua Biomática

2
SMARTDOOR
Biometric door security system
in brushed stainless steel
2007
Client: I-House

3–5
SMARTHYDRO
Hydro massage bath in moulded
polymer, acrylic and aluminium – water temperature, water
level, bathing additives, different
hydro-massage settings,

light intensity and other parameters can be activated remotely
via a mobile telephone or the
Internet
2005
Client: I-House

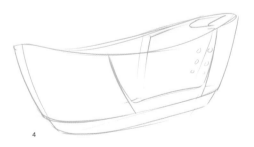

4

5

> "Simplicity, sensuality and precision."

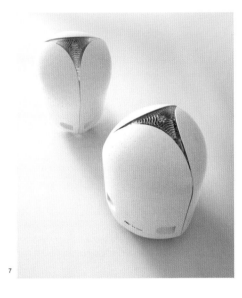

7

6

6
SPIRIT
Remote control for Spirit fan, in injection-moulded polymer
2005
Client: Spirit

7
AIRFREE P80
Portable, non-ozone emitting air purifier in injection-moulded polymer with unique ceramic core and incineration chamber filtering technology
2005
Client: Airfree

INDIO DA COSTA

Indio da Costa Product Design
R Pinheiro Guimarães 101,
Botafogo
Rio de Janeiro
Brazil

Indio da Costa Product Design
PO Box 4756
Walnut Creek
California 94596
USA

T (BR) +55 21 25379790
T (USA) +1 925 9352497
E icd@indiodacosta.com
www.indiodacosta.com

BIOGRAPHY

1969 Born in Rio de Janeiro, Brazil
1987–1989 Studied Industrial Design at the Faculdade da Cidade, Rio de Janeiro
1990–1993 BSc (Hons) Product Design, Art Center College of Design (Europe), La Tour-de-Peilz, Switzerland
1991 Art Center College of Design (USA) International Exchange Program
1992 Design internships at Bértrand Barré Design, Paris and Jacob Jensen Design, Denmark
1994 Industrial designers, NCS Design, Rio de Janeiro
1995 Industrial designer, Neumeister Design, Munich
1995 Founded his own design firm, Indio da Costa Arquitetura e Design in Rio de Janeiro in association with an already established architecture studio
2001 Founded the Indio da Costa Design studio in Rio de Janeiro and São Paulo

RECENT EXHIBITIONS

2000 "Mies van der Rohe Award for Latin America" (Exhibition of 10 Finalists), Museum of Modern Art, New York; "International Biennial of Design", St.Étienne
2004 "Mostra BrasilFazDesign", Milan and São Paulo

RECENT AWARDS

2004 iF Award, International Forum Design Hanover; 3 x Mostra BrazilFazDesign Awards, São Paulo; Premio Museu da Casa Brasileira award, São Paulo; Brasil Award, POPAI (Point of Purchase Advertising International), São Paulo
2005 2 x iF Awards, International Forum Design Hanover; 2 x Red Dot Awards, Design Zentrum Nordrhein Westfalen, Essen; 1st Prize – electronics catagory, Premio Museu da Casa Brasileira award, São Paulo
2006 2 x Nominees, Designpreis, Design Award of the Federal Republic of Germany; Honorable Mention, I. D. Magazine Design Award; Honorable Mention, Premio Museu da Casa Brasileira award, São Paulo
2007 Nominee, Designpreis Design Award of the Federal Republic of Germany, German Design Council/Rat für Formgebung; 1st Prize, Design Top XXI Arc Design, Associação Brasileria de Empresas de Design, São Paulo

CLIENTS

3M, Airfree, Aladdin, Ambev, Brudden, CHL, City of Rio de Janeiro – Planning and Development Institute, Coca-Cola, Compactor, GE Appliances (General Electric), Groupe Seb (Arno), I-House, Intelbras, Itautec, JCDecaux, Legrand, L'Occitane, Mabe, O Boticário, Orla Rio, Papaiz, Spirit, Springer Carrier

INTELLIGENT ENERGY

"Intelligent Energy is an international fuel cell power systems company, with a range of leading fuel cell, fuel processing, desulphurisation and hydrogen generation technologies. The company is focused on the provision of cleaner power and carbon abatement technologies. Fuel cells work by means of chemical reactions. The type of fuel cell that has been developed by Intelligent Energy is the Proton Exchange Membrane (PEM) fuel cell. Each fuel cell is a multi-layered sandwich of plates and MEAs (Membrane Electrode Assemblies), in which the MEA acts as a catalyst during an electro-chemical reaction, producing water and electricity from hydrogen and oxygen. The water by-product is completely pure and can be evaporated, drained or drunk. PEM fuel cells are highly efficient, low-temperature devices suitable for a wide range of applications, from battery replacement and automotive use to domestic heat and power generation. Intelligent Energy's business model is to partner with leading companies globally in the transportation, oil and gas, aerospace, defence and stationary and portable power markets, looking for a power source that is both clean and efficient. Intelligent Energy's proprietary fuel cell power systems and underlying technologies are characterised by high performance, the use of multifunctional low-cost components designed for manufacturing and much simpler systems, resulting in fuel cell systems of reduced size, cost and complexity. The company's fuel processing and hydrogen generation platforms are fuel-flexible, providing hydrogen from a range of both conventional fossil fuel and sustainable fuel feedstocks."

„Intelligent Energy ist ein internationaler Hersteller von Brennstoffzellensystemen und führend in der Entwicklung von Brennstoffzellen und Technologien für Energieumwandlung, Entschwefelung und Wasserstoffproduktion. Der Schwerpunkt der Firma liegt auf der Entwicklung von Technologien zur Gewinnung sauberer Energie und Reduktion der Kohlenstoffemissionen. Brennstoffzellen funktionieren auf der Basis von chemischen Reaktionen. Intelligent Energy hat die Protonenaustauschmembran-Brennstoffzelle (PEMFC) entwickelt. Jede Brennstoffzelle ist aus sandwichartig geschichteten Platten und MEAs (Membran-Elektroden-Einheiten) zusammengesetzt, wobei die MEA als Katalysator für eine elektrochemische Reaktion fungiert, bei der aus Wasserstoff und Sauerstoff Wasser und Strom erzeugt werden. Das Nebenprodukt Wasser ist absolut sauber und kann verdampfen, abgeleitet oder sogar getrunken werden. PEM-Brennstoffzellen sind höchst effiziente Systeme mit geringer Wärmeentwicklung und vielfältigen Einsatzmöglichkeiten, zum Beispiel als Batterieersatz im Fahrzeugbereich, für die Beheizung von Häusern und zur Stromerzeugung. Auf der Suche nach einer ebenso sauberen wie effizienten Energiequelle verfolgt Intelligent Energy ein Geschäftsmodell, das sich auf die weltweite Zusammenarbeit mit führenden Unternehmen in den Bereichen Transport, Öl und Gas, Luftfahrt, Verteidigung sowie stationäre und netzunabhängige Energieversorgung stützt. Die firmeneigenen Brennstoffzellensysteme und die ihnen zugrunde liegenden Technologien zeichnen sich durch besondere Leistungsfähigkeit, die Verwendung von multifunktionalen und kostengünstigen, eigens für die Fertigung konzipierten Komponenten und wesentlich vereinfachte Systeme aus, sodass kleinere, billigere und einfachere Brennstoffzellen angeboten werden können. Die Systeme zur Energieumwandlung und Wasserstoffgewinnung funktionieren mit verschiedenen Brennstoffen und erzeugen Wasserstoff aus einer Reihe fossiler Brennstoffe und erneuerbarer Rohstoffe."

«Intelligent Energy est une société internationale pionnière des systèmes de production d'énergie avec piles à combustible, qui propose tout un éventail de technologies de pointe: piles, traitement des combustibles, désulfuration et synthèse de l'hydrogène. La société se consacre à la production d'une énergie plus propre et aux technologies limitant les émissions de carbone. Les piles à combustible fonctionnent par réaction chimique. Intelligent Energy développe des piles à membrane d'échange de protons (PEMFC). Chacun de ces générateurs est un sandwich de plaques et de membranes électrolytes polymères (MEA) qui agissent comme catalyseurs de la réaction électrochimique et permet de produire de l'eau et de l'électricité à partir d'hydrogène et d'oxygène. L'eau ainsi produite est pure et peut être évaporée, puisée ou bue. Les PEMFC sont des générateurs très efficaces, à basse température, qui peuvent avoir une large variété d'applications, et notamment remplacer les piles polluantes dans l'industrie automobile, le chauffage domestique ou la production d'énergie. La démarche commerciale d'Intelligent Energy est de s'associer avec les plus importantes entreprises mondiales dans les secteurs du transport, du pétrole, du gaz, de l'espace, de la défense, des générateurs fixes et portables, pour développer une source d'énergie propre et rentable. Les systèmes PAC d'Intelligent Energy et les technologies qu'ils mettent en pratique sont hautement performantes, utilisent des composants multifonctionnels peu chers conçus pour être transformés: nos systèmes sont à la fois plus petits, moins chers et plus simples. Les plate-formes de transformation de combustible et de production d'hydrogène sont énergétiquement souples et utilisent à la fois les combustibles fossiles conventionnels et des réserves de combustibles durables. »

1

2

3

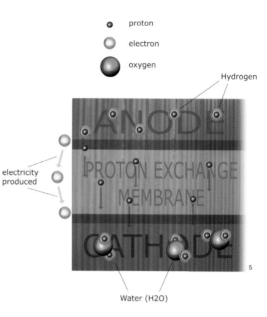

proton

electron

oxygen

Hydrogen

ANODE

PROTON EXCHANGE MEMBRANE

CATHODE

electricity produced

Water (H2O)

5

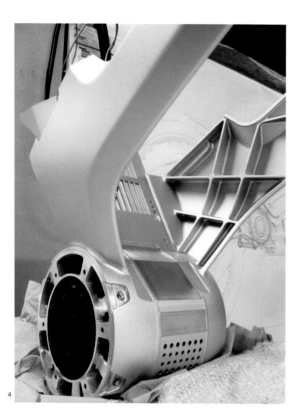

4

1
ENV
Fuel-cell motorcycle
showing two monochromatic
colourways: black supergloss
and iridescent white
2005

2–3
CORE FUEL CELL
PEM (Proton Exchange
Membrane) 1kW hydrogen
fuel cell generator in black and
iridescent white colourways
with diagram showing fuel cell
integration at the heart of the
motorcycle
2005

1–9
ENV (EMISSIONS NEUTRAL
VEHICLE) DESIGNED BY
SEYMOURPOWELL, 2005

The ENV is the world's first
purpose-built, fuel-cell motorcycle. Designed and engineered
around Intelligent Energy's
world-beating CORE fuel cell,
the ENV demonstrates the real,
everyday applicability of fuel cell
technology. The CORE, which
is completely detachable from
the bike, is a radically compact
and efficient fuel cell, capable
of powering anything from a
motorboat to a small domestic
property. The ENV is lightweight, streamlined and aerody-
namic and boasts a performance
that outreaches any existing electrical bike. In an urban or off-
road environment, it can reach
speeds of 50 mph. It is also vir-

tually silent and its emissions are
almost completely clean. On a
full tank, the ENV can be used
continually for up to four hours
without any need for refuelling.
The bike can also be used by
riders of any skill level thanks to
its simple controls that employ a
throttle directly linked to the
applied power. The bike has no
gears and is strictly defined as a
motorbike, although it feels to
riders more like a very quick and
responsive mountain bike.

Das ENV ist das erste spezialgefertigte Motorrad mit Brennstoffzellenantrieb. Es wurde für
die von Intelligent Energy entwickelte, weltweit einzigartige
CORE-Brennstoffzelle konzipiert und gebaut und ist der
Beweis dafür, dass die Brennstoffzelle eine alltagstaugliche
Technologie darstellt. Das

CORE genannte Herz des Fahr-
zeuges ist die komplett heraus-
nehmbare Brennstoffzellenein-
heit, die sich durch radikale
Kompaktheit und Effizienz aus-
zeichnet und alles vom Motor-
boot bis zum kleinen Eigenheim
mit Energie versorgen kann.
Dank seiner leichten, stromlinienförmigen und aerodynami-
schen Bauweise ist das ENV
leistungsfähiger als alle bisheri-
gen Motorräder mit Elektro-
antrieb. In der Stadt wie im
Gelände erreicht es Geschwin-
digkeiten von bis zu 80 km/h.
Es ist praktisch lautlos und weitgehend schadstofffrei. Voll gela-
den kann das ENV bis zu vier
Stunden durchgehend ohne
Nachladen betrieben werden.
Dank seiner einfachen Steue-
rung über einen direkt mit dem
Strom-Leistungsregler verbunde-
nen Gasdrehgriff ist das Bike

außerdem für Fahrer aller Klas-
sen geeignet. Es hat keine Gang-
schaltung und entspricht exakt
der Definition eines Motorrads,
obwohl das Fahrgefühl eher an
ein sehr schnelles und sensibles
Mountainbike erinnert.

L'ENV est la première moto au
monde fonctionnant avec des
piles à combustible. Conçue et
réalisée autour de la révolutionnaire pile à combustible CORE
d'Intelligent Energy, l'ENV fait
la preuve de l'applicabilité
concrète et quotidienne de la
technologie des piles à combustible. La pile CORE, totalement
amovible, est extrêmement compacte et économe en énergie, et
capable de propulser n'importe
quoi, du bateau à moteur au
petit objet domestique. L'ENV
est légère, carénée et aérodynamique et peut se vanter de per-

formances qui dépassent celles
de toutes les autres motos électriques du marché. En ville ou
en campagne, elle peut atteindre
la vitesse de 80 km/h. Elle est
aussi quasiment silencieuse et ses
émissions quasiment propres.
Une fois le plein fait, l'ENV
peut être utilisée sans interruption pendant *quatre heures* sans
qu'il soit nécessaire de la recharger. La moto peut aussi être utilisée par des conducteurs de tous
niveaux grâce à des commandes
simples qui utilisent un accé-
lérateur qui s'adapte à la puissance appliquée. Elle n'a pas de
vitesses et porte l'étiquette de
motocyclette alors que ses utilisateurs ont davantage l'impression de chevaucher un VTT
exceptionnellement rapide et
sensible.

4
ENV
Bike frame constructed of
hollow-cast aircraft grade
aluminium
2005

6–8
ENV
First frame assembly and construction of prototype
2005

5
CORE FUEL CELL
Diagrame showing PEM fuel
cell chemistry

9
HYDROGEN
GENERATION SYSTEM
Schematic illustrating Intelligent
Energy hydrogen generation
system – starting with multi-fuel
input, processed via a scalable
Hestia reformer unit, which
then feeds pure hydrogen into
a fuel cell-powered CHP unit or
directly to another fuel
cell-powered application (in
this example the ENV motorcycle).

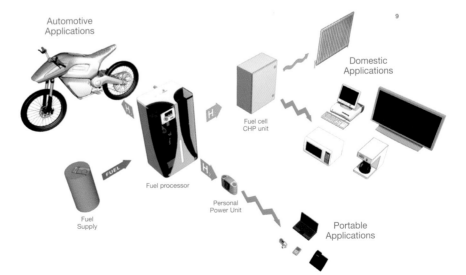

Automotive
Applications

Domestic
Applications

Fuel cell
CHP unit

Fuel processor

Personal
Power Unit

Portable
Applications

Fuel
Supply

INTELLIGENT ENERGY

42 Brook Street
Mayfair
London W1K 5DB
United Kingdom
T +44 20 79589033
E unitedkingdom@intelligent-energy.com
www.intelligent-energy.com

COMPANY HISTORY

2001 Intelligent Energy was formed, having emerged from one of the most established research teams working on fuel cell technologies anywhere in the world. That team, based at Loughborough University in the UK, had been working since 1988 on PEM fuel cell development.

2003 Intelligent Energy acquired Element One Enterprises (a team of experts working in the field of hydrogen generation and fuel processing in America)

2004 Intelligent Energy acquired MesoFuel Inc, which develops micro-devices for the conversion of liquid and gaseous hydrocarbons into pure hydrogen for storage and use in PEM and other fuel cells.

2005 Intelligent Energy ranked 3rd in the Sunday Times Tech 100 league table of the top 100 privately-owned technology companies in the UK

2006 Awarded status of WEF Technology Pioneer 2006 by the World Economic Forum (one of only 36 advanced technology companies worldwide)

2007 Intelligent Energy and the Suzuki Motor Corporation form partnership to develop prototype hydrogen fuel cell motorcycles using Intelligent Energy's advanced fuel cell power systems

RECENT EXHIBITIONS

2004 "Group Exhibit Hydrogen + Fuel Cells Hanover Fair", Hanover

2005 "FC Expo 2005", Tokyo Big Site, Tokyo; "Group Exhibit Hydrogen + Fuel Cells Han-nover Fair", Hanover; "Grove Fuel Cell Symposium", QE2 Conference Centre, London; "Fuel Cell Seminar", Palm Springs Convention Center, Palm Springs

2006 "Expo 2006", Tokyo Big Site, Tokyo; "National Hydrogen Association", Long Beach Convention Center, Long Beach; "3rd HFP General Assembly, Exhibition and Drive", Parc du Cinquantenaire, Brussels

2007 "FC Expo 2007", Tokyo Big Site, Tokyo; JSAE (Japanese Society of Automotive Engineers) Expo, Yokohama

RECENT AWARDS

2005 Tech Track 100 Research & Development Award, The Sunday Times, UK; Technology Pioneer Award, World Economic Forum, Geneva; Best of What's New 2005 Award – General Innovations Category, Popular Science magazine; Carmen's Company Award of Merit, The Worshipful Company of Carmen, London

2006 Finalist, 2006 World Technology Awards; Finalist, First Choice Responsible Tourism Award; Gold Award – IDEA (Industrial Design Excellence Awards), Industrial Designers Society of America/BusinessWeek; Microsoft Tech Track Research and Development Award

CLIENTS

Boeing
PSA Peugeot Citroën
Suzuki

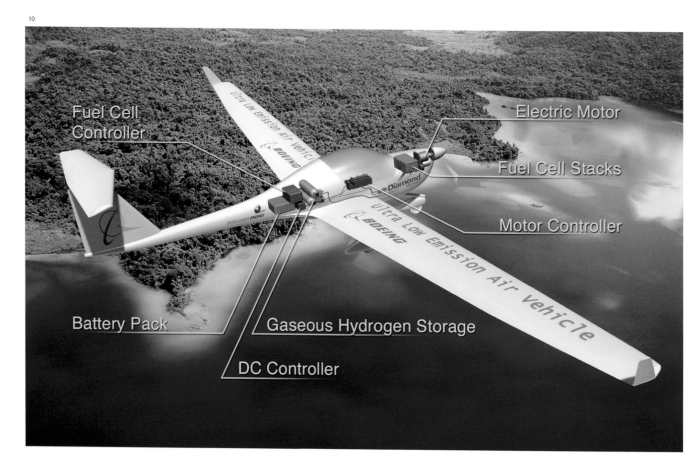

Fuel Cell Controller

Electric Motor

Fuel Cell Stacks

Motor Controller

Battery Pack

Gaseous Hydrogen Storage

DC Controller

11

"Bringing tomorrow's vision of a cleaner future into today's world."

12

10
ULTRA LOW EMISSION
AIR VEHICLE
Proposed first-ever hydrogen
fuel cell aircraft, developed in
collaboration with Boeing
2006–2007

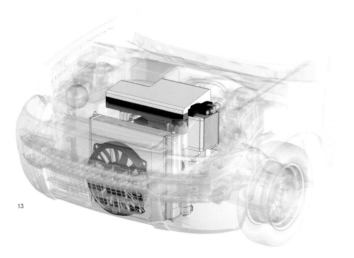

13

11
PSA PEUGEOT CITROËN
Vehicle in which Intelligent
Energy 10kW PEM hydrogen
fuel cell will be integrated
2007

12–13
10KW PEM FUEL CELL
Automotive hydrogen fuel
cell generator developed by
Intelligent Energy for use in
PSA Peugeot Citroën's fuel
cell cars with schematic
showing its integration
2007

JAMES IRVINE

"One of the problems designers have is that they are very often cornered into designing inside rather perverse market criteria. All too often this means we are presented with products which relate more to how a company sees itself, in direct competition with others, rather than to a normal consumer's needs. Competition has set up a kind of 'let's get weirder' syndrome. The companies look at each other and then go one step further to get noticed. But the step further is usually in the weird direction rather than coming down to earth. I guess I am lucky because being freelance I don't have to perform the game. People come to me because they know what they might get. I think as a freelancer one has the privilege to design out of the loop. For me this means that I can design something, which I hope is fairly normal. The strange thing is that normal today has become unusual."

„Eines der Probleme von Designern ist, dass sie häufig gezwungen sind, innerhalb ziemlich verrückter Marktkriterien zu gestalten. Das bedeutet allzu oft, dass uns Produkte präsentiert werden, die mehr damit zu tun haben, wie sich ein Unternehmen im direkten Wettbewerb mit anderen selbst sieht als mit gewöhnlichen Konsumentenbedürfnissen. Diese Konkurrenzsituation hat ein ‚Lasst uns noch verrückter werden'-Syndrom erzeugt. Die Firmen beobachten sich gegenseitig und gehen dann immer noch einen Schritt weiter, um sich von anderen abzuheben. Aber dieser eine Schritt geht meist in eine absurde statt sachliche Richtung. Ich schätze mich glücklich, da ich als Freiberufler nicht an diesem Spiel teilnehmen muss. Die Leute kommen zu mir, weil sie ungefähr wissen, was sie von mir bekommen. Ich finde, als Selbstständiger hat man das Privileg, außerhalb eines geschlossenen Systems zu arbeiten. Für mich bedeutet das, etwas gestalten zu können, von dem ich hoffe, dass es ziemlich normal ist. Das Merkwürdige ist, dass das Normale heute außergewöhnlich geworden ist."

«Un des problèmes que rencontrent les designers est qu'ils voient souvent leur travail cantonné par des critères de marché plutôt pervers. Bien trop souvent, cela signifie que nous sommes associés à des produits qui sont plus proches de la façon dont l'entreprise se perçoit, en concurrence directe avec les autres, que des besoins d'un consommateur normal. Cette concurrence a installé une espèce de course à ‹qui sera le plus bizarre. Les entreprises se surveillent les unes les autres et vont un peu plus loin que leurs concurrentes pour être remarquées. Mais ce pas en avant s'oriente généralement dans la direction bizarre plutôt que de revenir sur Terre. J'imagine que j'ai de la chance, parce que travailler en freelance m'autorise à ne pas jouer ce jeu. Les gens viennent me trouver parce qu'ils savent ce qu'ils pourront obtenir. Je pense qu'un créateur indépendant a le privilège de faire un design qui ne soit pas branché. Pour moi, cela signifie que je peux créer un design d'apparence relativement normale. Ce qui est étrange, c'est qu'aujourd'hui le normal est devenu inhabituel. »

1

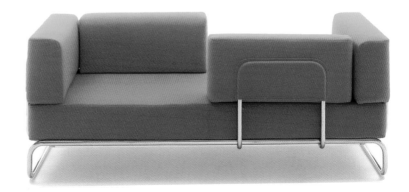

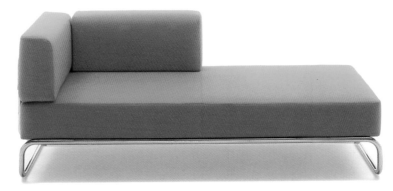

6

1
ZP02
Indoor/Outdoor bench with
stainless-steel frame and seat and
back in 100% recycled plastic
2005
Client: Coro

2
S5000
Foam upholstered sofa on
tubular steel frame with
adjustable back elements
2006
Client: Thonet

3
BOX
Multifunctional, stackable and
swivelling storage units in 8 mm
thick fibreboard, available in
three configurations
2006
Client: MDF

4–6
SMOOTH
Furniture handles in alumi-
nium-zinc-magnesium alloy
2006
Client: Pamar

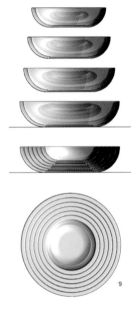

7–9
BOWLS
Set of six nesting bowls in
stainless steel
2006
Client: WMF

10
ANYWAY
Ink-jet printer, scanner and
copier (designed with Alberto
Meda)
2005
Client: Olivetti

JAMES IRVINE
Via Vigevano 8
20144 Milan
Italy
T +39 02 89059980
E info@james-irvine.com
www.james-irvine.com

BIOGRAPHY
1958 Born in London, England
1978–1981 BA (Hons)
Product Design, Kingston
Polytechnic, London
1981–1984 MA Furniture
Design, Royal College of Art,
London
1984–1992 Designer,
Olivetti design studio,
Milan
1987 Designer, Toshiba
Design Centre, Tokyo

1988 Established his own design
studio in Milan
1992–1998 In parallel to private
practice, partner, Sottsass
Associati, Milan
2004 Elected Royal Designer for
Industry by the Royal Society
of Arts, London and was Guest
of Honour at Interieur fair,
Kortrijk
2005–2007 Professor for
Industrial Design, Hochschule
für Gestaltung, Karlsruhe

RECENT EXHIBITIONS
2003 "Vitamin Bar –
De-Lighted by Corian®", Milan
2004 "Design Anatomy"
Kortrijk

RECENT AWARDS
2000 iF Award, International
Forum Design Hanover
2006 iF Gold Award, International Forum Design Hanover
2007 Honorary Doctorate in
Design, Kingston Polytechnic

CLIENTS
Alfi, Alias, Artemide,
B&B Italia, Canon, Coro,
Duravit, Foscarini, LG,
Magis, MDF Italia, Muji,
Olivari, Olivetti, Pamar,
Phaidon, Ströer, Thonet,
Whirlpool, WMF

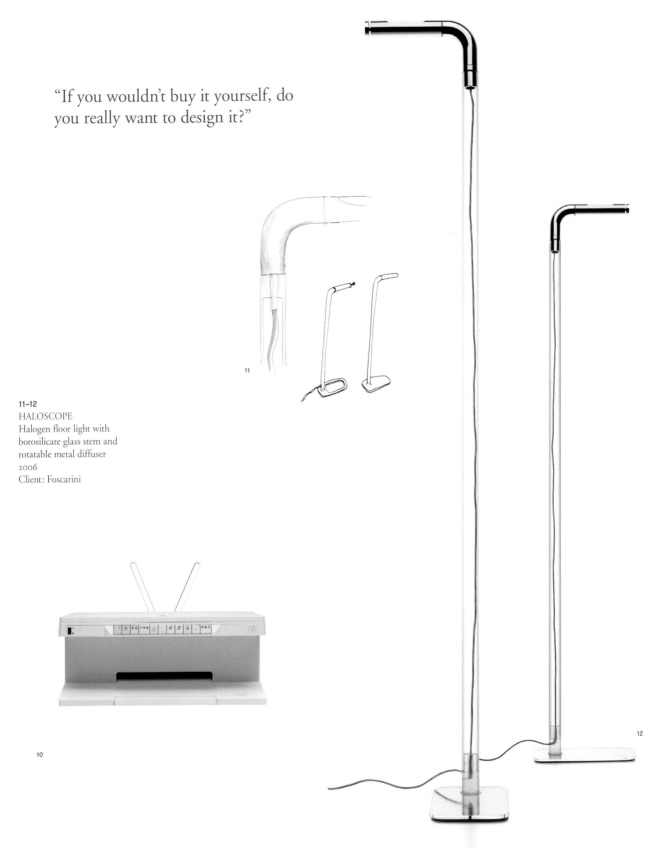

"If you wouldn't buy it yourself, do
you really want to design it?"

11–12
HALOSCOPE
Halogen floor light with
borosilicate glass stem and
rotatable metal diffuser
2006
Client: Foscarini

11

10

12

TOYO ITO

"Things in the natural world are changing constantly. Like that, humans are always moving, too. For me, to design is nothing else but to freeze this active state directly."

„Die Dinge in der natürlichen Welt verändern sich ständig. Ebenso sind auch die Menschen permanent in Bewegung. Für mich bedeutet Design nichts anderes, als diesen aktiven Zustand unmittelbar zu verewigen."

«Les choses du monde naturel évoluent constamment. De la même manière, les humains évoluent aussi en permanence. Pour moi, faire du design n'est rien d'autre que de geler cette évolution.»

1

2

4

1

MAYUHANA PE101
Hanging light in wound glass
fibre and aluminium
2007
Client: Yamagiwa

2

MAYUHANA SE120
Floor light in wound glass fibre
and aluminium
2007
Client: Yamagiwa

3

MAYUHANA SE121
Floor light in wound glass fibre
and aluminium
2007
Client: Yamagiwa

4

MAYUHANA SE118
Floor light in wound glass
fibre and aluminium
(available in two sizes)
2007
Client: Yamagiwa

1–4

MAYUHANA SERIES FOR
YAMAGIWA, 2007

The elegant Mayuhana lights are
created by reeling string around
a mould, in the same way silk
thread is spun from a cocoon.
The softness of the light emitted,
reminiscent of that cast by traditional Japanese portable paper
lanterns (*Bonbori*), is enhanced
by the light coming through the
Mayuhana series' double and

triple wound shells. According
to Yamagiwa, the manufacturer
of the lights, this illumination
brings to mind the image of
the light depicted in Junichiro
Tanizaki's "In Praise of Shad-
ows" (*In-ei Raisan*) – an essay
that expresses a love for the traditions and remnants of the
past.

Die eleganten Leuchten der
Mayuhana-Serie entstehen,
indem ein Faden um eine Form

gewickelt wird, also in derselben
Weise, wie eine Seidenraupe
einen Kokon um sich herum
spinnt. Sie verströmen ein wei-
ches, gedämpftes Licht, das an
traditionelle japanische Handla-
ternen aus Papier (Bonbori)
erinnert, wobei die Wirkung
durch die doppelt und dreifach
gewickelten Lampenschirme
noch gesteigert wird. Laut
Yamagiwa, dem Hersteller der
Mayuhana-Serie, transportiert
diese Art der Beleuchtung auch

jenes ästhetische Bild von Licht,
das Junichiro Tanizaki im „Lob
des Schattens" („In'ei raisan")
gezeichnet hat – einem Essay,
der seine Liebe zur traditionellen
Kultur und den letzten verblie-
benen Zeichen der Vergangenheit zum Ausdruck bringt.

Les élégantes lampes Mayuhana
sont créées en enroulant de la
corde autour d'un moule comme
la soie se dévide du cocon. La
douceur de la lumière qu'émet-

tent celles de la collection Mayuhana à double ou triple sphère
est une réminiscence de celle que
diffusent les lanternes de papier
traditionnelles du Japon (Bonbori). Selon Yamagiwa, le fabricant de ces luminaires, cet éclairage rappelle aussi la lumière
décrite par Junichiro Tanizaki
dans *Éloge de l'ombre* (In-ei Raisan) – un essai sur l'amour des
traditions et des vestiges du
passé.

5–6
SENDAI
Bookshelves with wood
structure and varnished
safety glass
2005
Client: HORM

7–8
RIPPLES
Bench in plywood composed of
six different types of heartwood
2005
Client: HORM

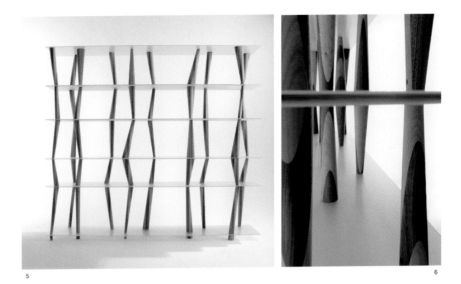

5

6

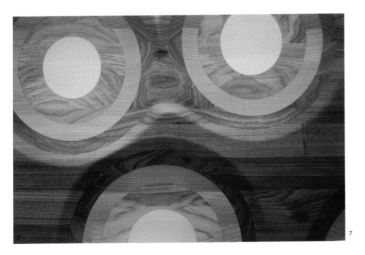

7

"Good design means not to design,
not to make shapes deliberately."

8

9

10

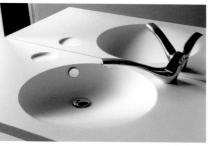

11

9–10
KU
15-piece white porcelain
tableware set
2006
Client: Alessi

11
PART OF TOYO ITO BATH-
ROOM COLLECTION
Washbasin in Corian
and tap in stainless steel
2006
Client: Altro

TOYO ITO

Toyo Ito & Associates,
Architects
Fujiya Bldg. 1-19-4
Shibuya Shibuya-ku
Tokyo 150-0002
Japan
T +81 3 34095822
www.c-channel.com/c00088/

BIOGRAPHY
1941 Born in Seoul, Korea
(Japanese national)
1965 Graduated from Department of Architecture, The
University of Tokyo
1965–1969 Worked at
Kiyonori Kikutake Architects
and Associates
1971 Started his own studio,
Urban Robot (URBOT) in
Tokyo
1979 Changed studio's name to
Toyo Ito & Associates, Architects

RECENT EXHIBITIONS
2002 Venice Biennale, 8th
International Architecture
Exhibition, "NEXT", Venice
2004 Venice Biennale, 9th
International Architecture
Exhibition "METAMORPH",
Venice
2005 "TOYO ITO made IN
ITALY", Museo Nacional Bellas
Artes, Santiago, Chile
2006 "Toyo Ito: The New Real
in Architecture", Tokyo Opera
City, Tokyo
2007 "Toyo Ito: The New Real
in Architecture", Sendai
Mediatheque, Miyagi, Japan
and The Museum of Modern
Art, Kamakura & Hayama,
Japan

RECENT AWARDS
2000 The Arnold W. Brunner
Memorial Prize in Architecture,
American Academy of Arts
and Letters; Accorded the Title
"Academician" from The Inter-
national Academy of Architecture
2001 Grand Prize of Good
Design Award for Sendai
Mediatheque, Japan Industrial
Design Promotion Organization
2002 World Architecture
Awards 2002, Best Building in
East Asia for Sendai Media-
theque Grand Prize – Good
Design Award, Japan Industrial
Design Promotion Organization
2003 Honorary Diploma of the
Architectural Association, Lon-
don; Architectural Institute of
Japan Prize
2004 Compasso d'Oro award,
ADI, Milan
2005 Royal Gold Medal, The
Royal Institute of British Archi-
tects, London; Public Building
Award for Sendai Mediatheque

CLIENTS
Akita Prefecture, Brugge 2002,
Escofet, Fondation Cognacq-Jay,
Fukuoka City, Holpaf B.V.,
HORM, K. Mikimoto & Co.
Ltd., Kakamigahara City,
Mapletree Investments Pte. Ltd.,
Matsumoto City, Sapporo
Breweries, Sendai City, Serpen-
tine Gallery, Studio 3 Grupo,
Tama Art University Urban
Development Corporation,
Yamagiwa

12–13
NAGUISA
Outdoor public seating system
in reinforced cast stone
2005
Client: Escofet

JONATHAN IVE & APPLE DESIGN TEAM

"We try to design and develop simple solutions for extremely complex problems. We are inquisitive, always learning and utterly consumed with the integrity of how something is made. The design team enjoys being part of a broader development community at Apple."

„Wir versuchen, einfache Lösungen für äußerst komplexe Probleme zu gestalten und zu entwickeln. Wir sind wissbegierig, lernen immer dazu und sind intensiv mit der Frage beschäftigt, wie etwas gemacht wird. Das Design Team hat Freude daran, Teil einer größeren Entwicklungsgemeinschaft bei Apple zu sein."

«Nous essayons de concevoir et de fabriquer des solutions simples pour des problèmes extrêmement complexes. Nous sommes curieux, toujours en cours d'apprentissage et profondément soucieux de la façon dont une chose se fabrique dans son intégralité. L'équipe de design est heureuse de faire partie d'une plus vaste communauté créatrice au sein d'Apple.»

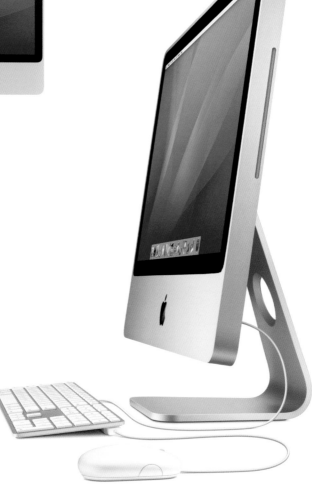

3

1–2
iPHONE
New generation mobile phone
that syncs with PC or Mac
computers to optimize calling,
texting, emailing, surfing,
listening, and watching
2007

3
iMAC
New generation all-in-one
desktop computer with
20" or 24" widescreen LCD
display encased in
aluminium and glass
2007

1-2
iPHONE FOR APPLE, INC.,
2007

"The iPhone combines three
products – a revolutionary
mobile phone, a widescreen iPod
with touch controls, and a
breakthrough Internet communications device with desktop-
class email, web browsing,
maps, and searching – into one
small and lightweight handheld
device. iPhone also introduces an
entirely new user interface based

on a large multi-touch display
and pioneering new software,
letting you control everything
with just your fingers. So it ush-
ers in an era of software power
and sophistication never before
seen in a mobile device, completely redefining what you can
do on a mobile phone."

„Das iPhone vereinigt drei Produkte zu einem kleinen und
leichtgewichtigen Handgerät:
ein revolutionäres Mobiltelefon,
einen berührungssensitiven iPod

mit Breitbild-Display und ein
fortschrittliches Internet-Kom-
munikationsgerät mit E-Mail,
Web-Surfen, Kartendienst und
Suchfunktion. Das iPhone ist
auch mit einer völlig neuen
Benutzeroberfläche ausgestattet,
das auf einem großen Multi-
Touch-Display und einer innovativen neuen Software basiert
und sich einfach durch Finger-
berührungen bedienen lässt. Es
leitet somit eine neue Ära in der
Geschichte des produktiven und
innovativen Softwaredesigns ein

und schöpft das Potenzial mobi-
ler Geräte in einem Ausmaß aus
wie niemals zuvor: mit der Neu-
erfindung des Mobiltelefons."

« L'iPhone combine trois produits — un téléphone portable
révolutionnaire, un iPod grand
écran à contrôle tactile et un
outil pionnier de communication par Internet avec services de
messagerie électronique, cartes,
navigation et recherche dignes
d'un ordinateur — en un seul
appareil léger et maniable. Le

iPhone inaugure également une
toute nouvelle interface utilisateur basée sur un important dispositif tactile interactif et un
logiciel novateur qui vous permet de tout contrôler du bout
des doigts. Il nous fait ainsi
entrer dans une ère de puissance
et de sophistication jamais
atteinte jusqu'alors pour un
appareil mobile, qui redéfinit
complètement l'utilisation d'un
téléphone portable. »

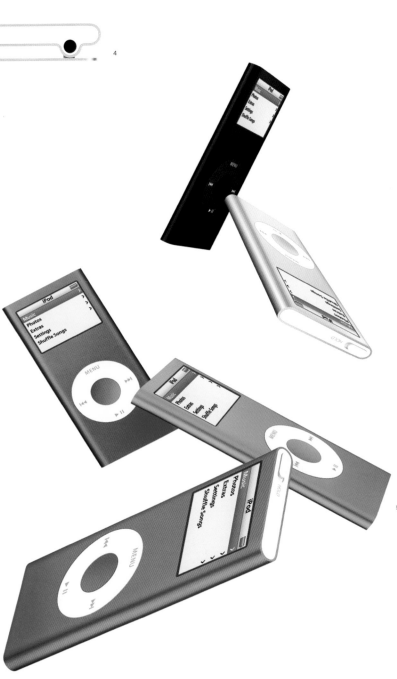

4
iPOD SHUFFLE
Second generation of the world's
smallest digital music player
with anodized aluminium
enclosure
2006

5
iPOD NANO
Second-generation digital music
player with anodized aluminium
enclosure that can hold up to
2,000 songs, up to 25,000
photos or a combination of both
2006

4

5

"We try to design and develop simple solutions
for extremely complex problems."

**JONATHAN IVE
& APPLE DESIGN TEAM**
Apple, Inc.
1 Infinite Loop
Cupertino
California 95014
USA
T +1 408 9961010
www.apple.com

**BIOGRAPHY
JONATHAN IVE**
1967 Born in London, England
1985–198 Studied art and
design at Newcastle Polytechnic
(now Northumbria University)
1989–1992 Partner, Tangerine
(design consultancy), London
1992 Moves to San Francisco
and joins the Apple Design
Team
1996 Director of Design,
Apple, Inc.
1998 Vice-President of Industrial
Design, Apple, Inc.
2005 Senior Vice-President of
Design, Apple, Inc.

RECENT EXHIBITIONS
2006 "Double Take", The
Museum of Modern Art,
New York; "Design Life Now,
National Design Triennial",
Cooper-Hewitt National Design
Museum, New York
2007 "Celebrating 25
Products", Design Museum,
London; "Scenes and Traces",
Stedelijk Museum, Amsterdam

RECENT AWARDS
2003 Designer of the Year,
Design Museum, London;
Royal Designer for Industry,
The Royal Society of Arts,
London

2004 Product Designer of the
Year, BluePrint magazine;
Benjamin Franklin Medal, The
Royal Society of Arts, London
2005 President's Medal, Royal
Academy of Engineers, London;
President's Medal, D&AD,
London
2006 CBE (Commander of
the British Empire) for services
to the design industry
2007 Winner – Product Design
Catagory, National Design
Awards, Cooper-Hewitt Nation-
al Design Museum, New York

Over the past four years Apple
products have also received

multiple gold awards from
D&AD (UK), Red Dot
(Germany), International Forum
Design (Germany), Good
Design Award (US), Industrial
Designers Society of America
(USA), Good Design Awards
(Japan)

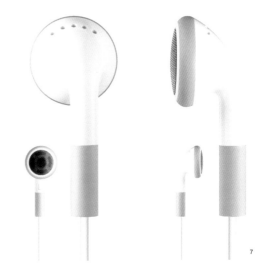

6
MACBOOK PRO
Notebook computer with
15" or 17" widescreen and
aluminium casing
2006

7
iPOD EARPHONES
Second-generation earphones for
use with iPod digital music player
2006

8
WIRELESS MIGHTY MOUSE
AA battery-powered wireless
mouse with tracking engine
based on laser technology
2006

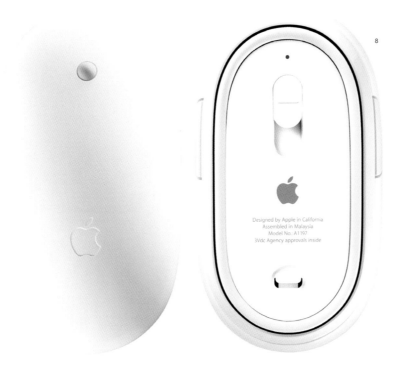

PATRICK JOUIN

"Don't repeat yourself... Don't get bored... Always be inventing... Go one better next time... Surprise yourself... Criticise... Start over again... Take your time... Never cheat... Listen... Discuss... Decide."

„Sich nicht wiederholen ... Sich nicht langweilen ... Immer etwas Neues erfinden ... Sich selbst übertreffen ... Sich überraschen ... Kritisieren ... Noch einmal von vorn anfangen ... Sich Zeit lassen ... Nie schummeln ... Zuhören ... Diskutieren ... Entscheiden ..."

«Ne pas se répéter... Ne pas s'ennuyer...Toujours inventer... Se dépasser... Se surprendre... Critiquer... Recommencer... Prendre le temps... Ne pas tricher... Écouter... Discuter... Décider.»

1

2

3

1–4
BLOW-UP
Series of four fluorescent ceiling
lights in rotational-moulded
polyethylene
2007
Client: Serralunga

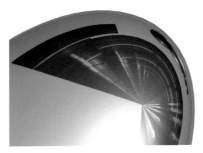

4

BLOW-UP LIGHTING SERIES
FOR SERRALUNGA, 2007

"Blow-up is a series of four swinging lights, the largest of which measures 1.8 metres in diameter. These impressive floating opaque discs of monolithic proportions contain a lighting appliance comprising 8 fluorescent spotlights that become apparent only when the light is switched on. A reflective film, either gold or silver, covers the cut surface of the module and creates a surprise effect, becoming transparent when the light shines through it. Whether lit or unlit, these innovative lights, produced by roto-moulding, occupy their space majestically, and with their size and lightness they outwit the laws of gravity."

„Die Blow-up-Serie besteht aus vier Pendelleuchten, deren größte 1,8 m im Durchmesser misst. Diese eindrucksvoll schwebenden opaken Scheiben mit ihren gigantischen Proportionen enthalten ein Beleuchtungsmodul aus acht Leuchtstoffstrahlern, die erst sichtbar werden, wenn man das Licht anmacht. Die Schnittfläche des Moduls ist mit einer reflektierenden Beschichtung in Gold oder Silber überzogen, die für einen Überraschungseffekt sorgt, weil sie plötzlich transparent wird und das Licht durchscheinen lässt. Ob im beleuchteten oder im unbeleuchteten Zustand, diese mittels Rotomoulding gefertigten innovativen Leuchten beherrschen den Raum auf majestätische Weise und überlisten mit ihrer Größe und Leichtigkeit die Gesetze der Schwerkraft."

« Blow-up est une collection de quatre lampes animées, dont la plus grande mesure 1,80 m de diamètre. Ces impressionnants disques opaques flottants aux proportions monolithiques contiennent une installation d'éclairage composée de 8 spots fluorescents qui n'aparaissent que lorsque la lampe est allumée. Un film réfléchissant, doré ou argenté, couvre la surface creuse du module pour créer un effet de surprise et devient transparent lorsqu'il est traversé par la lumière. Allumé ou éteint, ces luminaires novateurs, produits par rotomoulage, occupent majestueusement l'espace, tandis que leur taille et leur légèreté défient les lois de la gravité. »

5

5–6
THALYA
Single-form side chair in injection-moulded clear or translucent polycarbonate
2007
Client: Kartell

7–8
NIGHTCOVE
Sleep-improvement system that manages sleep environment and delivers sound and light programmes to enhance sleep quality
2007
Client: Zyken

6

7

8

"For the moment design is very chaotic,
because everything is permitted. After years of minimalism
and then the decorative desire following it,
we have now reached a mutually enriching coexistence
between the different camps."

PATRICK JOUIN
Agence Patrick Jouin
8, passage de la Bonne Graine
75011 Paris
France
T +33 1 55288920
E agence@patrickjouin.com
www.patrickjouin.com

BIOGRAPHY
1967 Born in Nantes, France
1992 Diploma of Industrial
Design, ENSCI-les Ateliers
1993–1994 Designer, Tim
Thom (Thomson Multimedia)
under the direction of Philippe
Starck
1995–1999 Designer, Philippe
Starck Office, Paris
1998 Founded Agence Patrick
Jouin, Paris
1998 Awarded "Carte Blanche"
fellowship by VIA, Paris
2001 Sanjit Manku joined
Agence Patrick Jouin, Paris
(becoming a partner in 2006)

2004 Founded a furniture
research studio in Paris

RECENT EXHIBITIONS
2003 Solo exhibition,
Maison & Objet, Paris
2004 "Solid", Galerie
Maisonneuve, Paris
2006 "Fear of Fredoom",
Droog Gallery, Amsterdam;
"Essences essentielles", Musée
des Beaux-Arts de Paris, Paris

RECENT AWARDS
2002 Innovation Prize,
Monoprix
2003 Designer of the Year,

Maison & Objet, Paris
2006 Best restaurant design
award, Travel + Leisure
magazine
2007 Créateur sans Frontière
(Designer without Borders),
Ministry of Foreign Affairs,
France; Innovation Prize,
Surface Magazine

CLIENTS
Alessi, Cassina, Fermob,
Da fact, Group Alain Ducasse,
Group Jacques Bogart,
Groupe Swatch, JC Decaux,
Kartell, Lexon, MGX, Renault,
Serralunga Starwood Capital,
Starwood Group, The Dorch-
ester Group, The New York
Palace Hotel, Van Cleef &
Arpels, YTL Corporation,
Zyken

SUNTAE KIM

"Mutual relations between environment and human, people and people, and user and object are flexible and variable. Among these relationships we can find useful and interesting aspects that we do not recognize, which I like to identify and express for the user's benefit. This gives another pleasure while simultaneously providing efficient functionality. These qualities are acquired through the observation of things happening in daily life, behaviour and habits of people, and surrounding objects. This is a beneficial experience and plays an important role in helping me solve problems that range from the personal to large systems. A sensitive and free approach, logical judgement, provision of solution measure, the valuable result completed by user; this is a design process. Pursuing a new thing in design is a process of rearranging both the necessary and the unnecessary sensuously. I arrange aesthetic and functional elements through this approach. I believe the results will improve the quality of life, especially personal life, and change our environment beautifully through the communication with users."

„Wechselseitige Beziehungen zwischen Umwelt und Mensch, Menschen und Menschen sowie Benutzer und Objekt sind flexibel und wandelbar. Unter diesen Beziehungen können wir nützliche und interessante, von uns unerkannte Aspekte entdecken, die ich gern identifiziere und für den Benutzer vorteilhaft zum Ausdruck bringe. Diese Eigenschaften kann man durch Beobachten von alltäglichen Dingen, von Verhalten und Gewohnheiten der Menschen und durch Betrachten von Objekten in unserer Umgebung erlangen. Für mich ist dies eine nützliche Erfahrung und eine wichtige Hilfe beim Lösen von Problemen. Ein sensibler und offener Ansatz, logisches Urteilsvermögen, das Bereitstellen einer Lösung und ein wertvolles Ergebnis, das erst vom Benutzer vervollständigt wird – das alles stellt den Gestaltungsprozess dar. Im Design etwas Neues zu entdecken bedeutet, dass man sowohl das Notwendige wie das Unnötige auf sinnliche Weise neu ordnet. Mit dieser Methode stelle ich die ästhetischen und funktionalen Elemente zusammen. Ich glaube, dass die Resultate die Lebensqualität – besonders die persönliche – verbessern und durch die Kommunikation mit den Benutzern unsere Umwelt schöner machen."

«Les relations qui se tissent entre environnement et humain, personne et personne, utilisateur et objet, sont souples et variables. Ces relations ont des aspects utiles et intéressants que nous ignorons le plus souvent et que j'aime identifier et exprimer pour l'utilisateur. Cette démarche permet de lui apporter un plaisir et une fonctionnalités supplémentaires. Ces qualités s'acquièrent grâce à l'observation de ce qui émaille la vie quotidienne, l'attitude et les habitudes des gens, les objets qui les entourent. Cette expérience, bénéfique, joue un rôle important dans mon travail parce qu'elle m'aide à résoudre les problèmes que posent les systèmes, qu'ils soient personnels ou plus larges. Une approche sensible et libre, une réflexion logique, des réserves de solutions possibles, le résultat adéquat validé par l'utilisateur ; voilà ce qu'est un processus de création de design. Pour faire des découvertes dans le design, il faut réorganiser voluptueusement nécessaire et superflu. J'assemble éléments esthétiques et fonctionnels selon ce principe. Je pense que la qualité de vie s'en voit améliorée, en particulier la vie personnelle, et que la communication avec les utilisateurs rend notre environnement plus beau.»

1

1–2
CLOVER BOWL
Fruit bowl in moulded,
beech-veneered plywood
2006
Client: BENTEK furniture

3

SUNTAE KIM
605-1602, Joonghung Village
Joong-dong, Wonmi-gu
Bucheon City 420-728
Korea
T +82 11 97700656
E info@suntaekim.com
www.suntaekim.com

BIOGRAPHY
1972 Born in Seoul, Korea
1996 Furniture Design
course, DIS (Denmark's International Study Program),
Copenhagen
1998 BFA Woodworking and
Furniture Design, Hongik
University, Seoul
2002 MFA Woodworking
and Furniture Design, Hongik
University, Seoul
2003 Began working as a freelance designer

RECENT EXHIBITIONS
2004 "Designers Planet",
Seoul; "TalentZone", Scandi-
navian Furniture Fair, Copen-
hagen
2005 "Salone Satellite", Salone
del Mobile, Milan; "Designers
Planet", Seoul
2006 "Seoul Living Design
Fair", Seoul; "Salone Satellite",
Salone del Mobile, Milan; "post
– MILAN", Seoul Arts Center
Hangaram Design Museum,
Seoul; "Seoul Design Festival",
Seoul

CLIENTS
American Hardwood Export
Council, BENTEK furniture,
Hongik University,
Hyundai-Kia Motor Company

3
FLYWOOD TABLE
Small table with removable
moulded, beech-veneered
plywood top supported on
stainless-steel base
2006
Client: BENTEK furniture

4–6
Y STOOL
Modular seating system based
on moulded, maple-veneered
plywood stool unit
2005
Client: self-produced prototype

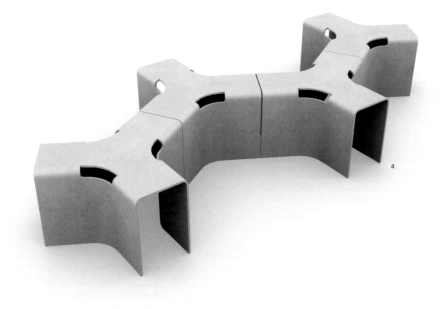

"Things communicate with us.
I listen to, observe
and rearrange them."

NIKOLA KNEZEVIC

"From the beginning of conscious existence, by shaping his surroundings, man has actually been shaping himself. As a result of his striving to explore and adjust, reform of the human environment became a faster process of evolution that is now running in both directions. Design is a creative act where all the creative potentials are focused on finding out about a specific need and ways for its satisfaction. To solve problems, the designer must be aware of and well acquainted with the multiple functional aspects of the object he is dealing with. Although industrial design leans and depends on industry and technology, it is increasingly becoming a tool for strong artistic expression as well as a stage for experimenting with diverse concepts and ideas. Multiplicity and accessibility of different production techniques open endless possibilities for sending out personal messages through a functional object, which thus becomes much more than just an object in space or a useful piece of material. Through that product the message becomes clearer, evolving to such a dominant force that it often blurs and obscures the main function. Complete interactivity between man and object provides us with the unique experience of feeling it with all our senses, and it thus becomes the ultimate art form."

„Der Mensch hat seit Beginn seiner bewussten Existenz seine Umgebung und damit auch sich selbst geformt. Sein Drang, zu forschen und anzupassen, hat die Veränderung seiner Umwelt vorangetrieben – ein evolutionärer Prozess, der heute in beide Richtungen verläuft. Design ist eine schöpferische Kunst, bei der das gesamte kreative Potenzial darauf ausgerichtet ist, ein bestimmtes Bedürfnis zu untersuchen und Befriedigungsmöglichkeiten dafür zu ermitteln. Um Probleme lösen zu können, muss der Designer die vielfältigen funktionalen Aspekte des Objekts, mit dem er sich beschäftigt, sehr genau kennen. Obwohl sich das Industriedesign auf die Industrie und Technik stützt und verlässt, wird es zunehmend auch zu einem überzeugenden künstlerischen Ausdrucksmittel und zu einem Experimentierfeld für verschiedenste Konzepte und Ideen. Die Vielzahl von Fertigungsverfahren und ihre Verfügbarkeit eröffnen unendlich viele Möglichkeiten, persönliche Botschaften durch ein funktionales Objekt zu vermitteln. So ist dieses viel mehr als nur ein Objekt im Raum oder ein nützliches Stück Werkstoff. Durch das Produkt wird die Botschaft klarer, wobei diese so dominant werden kann, dass die eigentliche Funktion dahinter verschwindet. Die vollkommene Interaktivität zwischen Mensch und Objekt verschafft uns die einzigartige Erfahrung, das Objekt mit allen unseren Sinnen wahrnehmen zu können, und wird dadurch zur ultimativen Kunstform."

« Depuis l'aube de son existence consciente, en façonnant son environnement, l'homme s'est en fait façonné lui-même. En conséquence de sa lutte pour explorer et s'adapter, l'homme a utilisé la réforme de son environnement pour évoluer plus vite, une stratégie qui se révèle aujourd'hui à double tranchant. Le design est un acte de création dans un monde où tout le potentiel créatif se concentre sur certains besoins et les moyens de les satisfaire. Pour résoudre les problèmes, le designer doit avoir une conscience et une connaissance aiguës des multiples aspects fonctionnels de l'objet auquel il travaille. Bien que le design industriel repose sur l'industrie et la technologie et qu'il en dépende, il devient de plus en plus un puissant outil d'expression artistique ainsi qu'une scène sur laquelle divers concepts et idées peuvent être manipulés. La multiplicité et l'accessibilité des techniques de fabrication ouvrent un champ infini de possibilités pour faire passer des messages personnels à travers un objet fonctionnel, qui devient ainsi bien plus qu'un objet dans l'espace ou un élément utile d'équipement. À travers ce produit, le message devient plus clair, d'une force si intense qu'il brouille et masque souvent la fonction principale de l'objet. Une complète interactivité entre l'homme et l'objet nous procure une expérience unique, celle de le ressentir avec tous nos sens, et c'est ainsi que l'objet de design devient l'ultime forme d'art. »

1
SOLAR STREET LAMP
Computer renderings of proposal for solar-powered public lighting
2003–2004
Client: self-generated concept

Solar street lamp

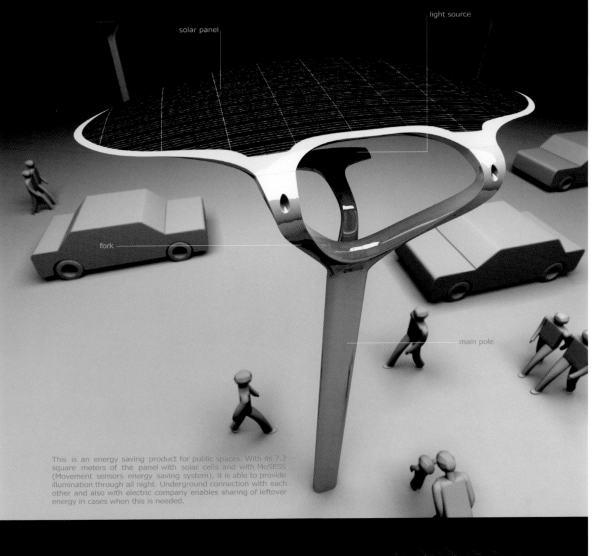

solar panel

light source

fork

main pole

This is an energy saving product for public spaces. With its 7.3 square meters of the panel with solar cells and with MoSESS (Movement sensors energy saving system), it is able to provide illumination through all night. Underground connection with each other and also with electric company enables sharing of leftover energy in cases when this is needed.

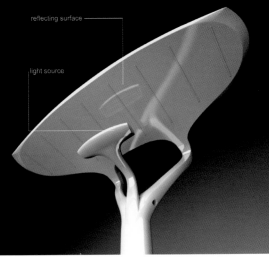

reflecting surface

light source

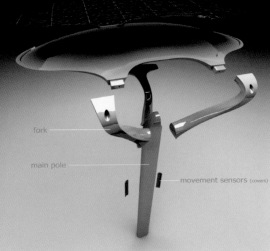

fork

main pole

movement sensors (covers)

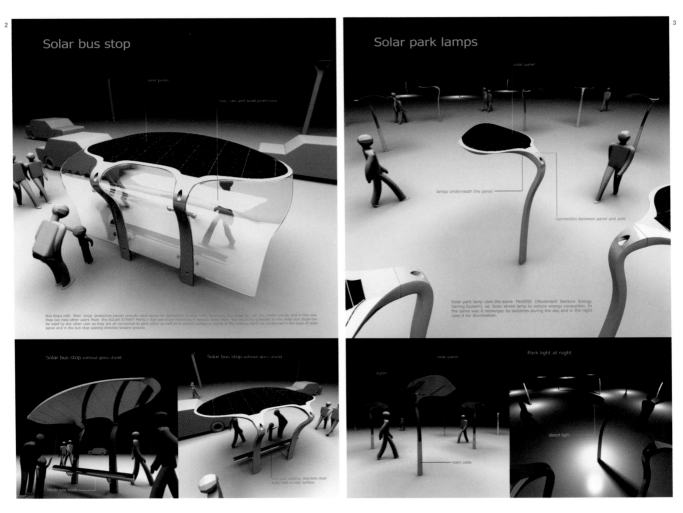

Solar bus stop

Solar park lamps

2
SOLAR BUS STOP
Computer renderings of
proposal for solar-powered
bus shelter
2003–2004
Client: self-generated concept

3
SOLAR PARK LAMPS
Computer renderings of
proposal for solar-powered
public lighting
2003–2004
Client: self-generated concept

4
SOLAR PHONE BOOTH
& ATM
Computer renderings of
proposal for solar-powered
phone booth and ATM machine
2003–2004
Client: self-generated concept

5
SOLAR STREET COUNTER
& NEWSSTAND
Computer renderings of
proposal for solar-powered
vending counter and newsstand
2003–2004
Client: self-generated concept

6
GALLION SERIES
Audio pre-amp and amplifier
with stainless-steel casing
2007
Client: Korato

1-5
SOLAR STREET CONCEPT,
2003-2004

"The Solar Street Concept comprises several energy saving
products made for public use in
public spaces. All the products
are made out of two different
modules (small and large solar
panels) and other elements that
form the whole object. The
clever movement sensor's energy-
saving system is incorporated to
save additional energy. Modular
solar cell panels provide the pos-

sibility to apply them on surfaces of any geometry whether
they are simple or organic. The
Solar Street objects are the direct
result of the combination of the
best constructional characteristics of organic forms needed to
make durable outdoor products
while meeting functional
requirements."

„Das Solar Street Concept
umfasst mehrere Energiesparele-
mente, die für die Verwendung
in öffentlichen Räumen vorgesehen sind. Alle Elemente beste-

hen aus zwei Modulen (kleinen
und großen Sonnenkollektoren)
und zusätzlichen Komponenten,
die das gesamte Objekt ergeben.
Intelligente Bewegungssensoren
werden eingesetzt, um weitere
Energieeinsparungseffekte zu
erzielen. Solarzellenmodule
haben den Vorteil, auf Flächen
mit unterschiedlichsten Geome-
trien einsetzbar zu sein, unabhängig davon, ob es sich um
einfache oder organische handelt. Die Objekte der Solar-
Street-Reihe machen sich die
hervorragenden Baueigenschaf-

ten organischer Formen zunutze,
die erforderlich sind, um haltbare Produkte für den Außenbereich zu generieren, und werden
auch den funktionalen Anforderungen gerecht."

« Le concept Solar Street comprend plusieurs produits économes en énergie destinés aux
lieux publics. Tous sont fabriqués à partir de deux modules
(des panneaux solaires petits et
grands) auxquels viennent se
greffer d'autres éléments. Le système d'économie d'énergie à

capteurs de mouvements est
incorporé de manière à ce que
l'appareil consomme encore
moins. Les panneaux modulaires
à photopiles peuvent être appliqués sur toutes les surfaces, que
leur géométrie soit simple ou
organique. Les objets Solar
Street découlent d'une combinaison des plus efficaces caractéristiques structurelles des formes
organiques, nécessaires pour réaliser des produits d'extérieur
durables qui remplissent aussi
leur rôle fonctionnel. »

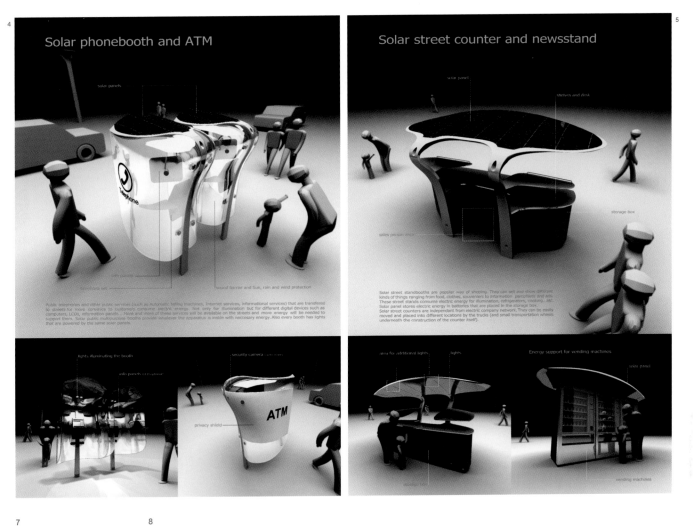

Solar phonebooth and ATM

solar panels

telephone set

info panels

sound barrier and Sun, rain and wind protection

Public telephones and other public services (such as Automatic telling machines, Internet services, informational services) that are transfered to streets for more convinice to tradesman's consumer energy. Not only for illumination but for different digital devices such as computers, LCDs, information panels... More and more of these services will be avaliable on the streets and more energy will be needed to support them. Solar public multipurpose booths provide whatever the apparatus is inside with neccesary energy. Also every booth has lights that are powered by the same solar panels.

lights illuminating the booth

info panels not optional

security camera

privacy shield

ATM

5

Solar street counter and newsstand

solar panel

shelves and desk

storage box

sales person area

Solar street standbooths are popular way of shoping. They can sell and show different kinds of things ranging from food, clothes, souveniers to information pamphlets and ads. These street stands consume electric energy for illumination, refrigerators, cooking...etc. Solar panel stores electric energy in batteries that are placed in the storage box. Solar street counters are independent from electric company network. They can be easily moved and placed into different locations by the trucks (and small transportation wheels underneath the construction of the counter itself).

area for additional lights

lights

Energy support for vending machines

solar panel

vending machines

7
AMPLIFIRE S01
Audio amplifier with wing-shaped profile and stainless-steel case
2005
Client: Korato

8
AMPLIFIRE G07
Audio amplifier with moulded plastic and stainless-steel case
2005
Client: Korato

6

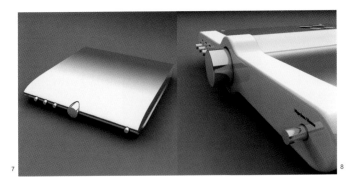

7

8

13
WATCH
Transparent LCD wristwatch
with polymer strap and battery
in buckle
2006
Client: self-generated concept

14
VIGO
Single-form moulded
carbon fibre side chair
2006
Client: Nikola Design &
Technologies

9–11
G3
Ultra-lightweight moulded
carbon fibre briefcase
2005
Client: Nikola Design &
Technologies

12
SHUTTLE TYPE 1
Ultra-lightweight moulded
carbon fibre backpack
2006
Client: Nikola Design &
Technologies

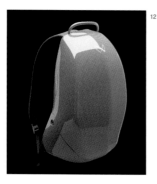

"Beauty is the depth of a surface."

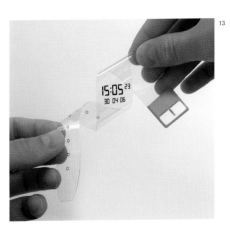

13

14

NIKOLA KNEZEVIC
Nikoladesign
Aleksinackih Rudara 28/34
11000 Belgrade
Serbia
T +381 64 2979079
E nikola.knezevic@nikolade-
sign.co.jp
www.nikoladesign.com
www.nikoladesign.co.jp

BIOGRAPHY
1973 Born in Belgrade, Serbia
1992 Studied at High School for Design, Belgrade
1998 BA Industrial Design, Faculty of Applied Art and Design, University of Art, Belgrade
1998 Founded Nikoladesign in Belgrade
2001 Assistant professor – industrial design course, Faculty of Applied Art and Design, University of Art, Belgrade
2003 Took Japanese Government's Ministry of Culture trainee programme in Tokyo
2004–2005 Worked as a freelance designer in London
2004 Co-founded Nikola Design & Technologies Inc., Tokyo with Misao Mizuno, Yoshimitsu Nakayama and Yuki Ogawa
2006 MA Industrial Design, Faculty of Applied Art and Design, University of Art, Belgrade

RECENT EXHIBITIONS
2004 "36th May Exhibition", Belgrade; "iF design exhibition", CeBIT, Hanover
2005 Solo exhibition, Museum of the 25th May (Museum of Yugoslavian History), Belgrade
2006 "37th May Exhibition", Belgrade

RECENT AWARDS
2003 Silver award, Osaka International Design Competition, Osaka; First Prize, Function Design Competition, Belgrade
2004 iF Award, International Forum Design Hanover; Award, Annual Design Review, I.D. Magazine; Grand Prix, 36th May Exhibition, Belgrade
2004 Honourable mention, Gyeonggi Design Competition, South Korea
2005 Museum of Applied Art and Design Award, Belgrade
2007 Belgrade Chamber of Commerce Design Award; Top Nomination, Index Award, Denmark

CLIENTS
B&W, Hewlett-Packard, IT Carozzeria, Korato, Polaroid, Sony, Toshiba

LAVERNIA CIENFUEGOS Y ASOCIADOS

"We are especially interested in design as a whole. We like to be involved in the design of products, packaging, corporate identity, catalogues, fair stands, websites – and to consider different aspects like marketing and communication that have a bearing on the project. In this way we are able to get efficient and strong design solutions. We don't have any preferences among our clients. But we prefer companies that are interested in design and bet on innovation and risk. We like to make a commitment with our clients, with their products, with their strategy. We try to simplify as much as we can in order to communicate a lot with just a few elements. In each project we are very interested in finding a concept within which to develop our work because we think that a good job always has to be based on a good initial idea. We like to look for new points of view, trying to get new ways to communicate."

„Wir sind besonders am Design in seiner Gesamtheit interessiert. Das umfasst die Gestaltung von Produkten, Verpackung, der Corporate Identity, von Katalogen, Messeständen, Websites – und Aspekte wie Marketing und Kommunikation, die das Projekt beeinflussen. Dadurch sind wir in der Lage, effiziente und überzeugende Designlösungen zu finden. Wir haben keine Präferenzen, was unsere Kunden betrifft. Am liebsten sind uns aber Unternehmen, die sich für Design interessieren und auf Innovation und Risiko setzen. Wir lassen uns gern auf unsere Kunden ein, auf ihre Produkte, auf ihre Strategie. Um mit wenigen Elementen viel auszudrücken, bemühen wir uns um weitestgehende Vereinfachung. Es ist uns ein besonderes Anliegen, für jedes Projekt ein Konzept zu erstellen, innerhalb dessen wir unsere Arbeit weiterentwickeln können, da wir der Ansicht sind, dass am Anfang jeder guten Arbeit eine gute Idee stehen muss. Wir machen uns auf die Suche nach neuen Standpunkten und versuchen, neue Kommunikationsformen zu entwickeln."

«Nous nous intéressons au design dans son ensemble. Nous aimons nous impliquer dans la création de produits, d'emballages, d'identités de marque, de catalogues, de stands de salons, de sites Internet – et prendre en compte tous les différents éléments qui influent sur les projets, comme le marketing et la communication. Nous parvenons ainsi à obtenir des solutions design efficaces et fortes. Nous ne préférons pas certains de nos clients aux autres. Mais nous préférons les entreprises qui s'intéressent au design et parient sur l'innovation et le risque. Nous aimons nous engager avec nos clients, pour leurs produits, dans leur stratégie. Nous essayons de simplifier les choses autant que possible afin de communiquer beaucoup avec peu d'éléments. Pour chaque projet, nous recherchons le concept au sein duquel nous allons travailler parce que nous pensons qu'un bon boulot doit toujours se fonder sur une bonne idée de départ. Nous aimons partir en quête de nouveaux points de vue, de nouvelles façons de communiquer.»

1

INGREDIENTES ACTIVOS: OLIGOSACARIDOS.
Aclarar abundantemente el cabello y cuero.

INGREDIENTES AQUA, SODIUM LAURETH SULFATE,
COCAMIDOPROPYL BETAINE, COCAMIDE DEA, POLY-
QUATERNIUM7, SODIUM CHLORIDE, PARFUM, PHE-
NOXYETHANOL, TRIDECETH-9, METHYLPARABEN, PEG-
5 ETHYLHEXANOATE, DISODIUM EDTA, IMIDAZOLIDIN-
YL UREA, BUTYLENE GLYCOL, GLYCERIN, ETHYLPARA-
BEN, ENTEROMORPHA COMPRESSA EXTRACT, PRO-
PYLPARABEN, CITRIC ACID, BUTYLPARABEN,
LIMONENE, ISOBUTYLPARABEN, LINALOOL.

geo

MADE IN SPAIN BY COSMÉTICOS PNB S.L.
C/ 3R024G/020 / 46185 VALENCIA
LOTE: VER BASE

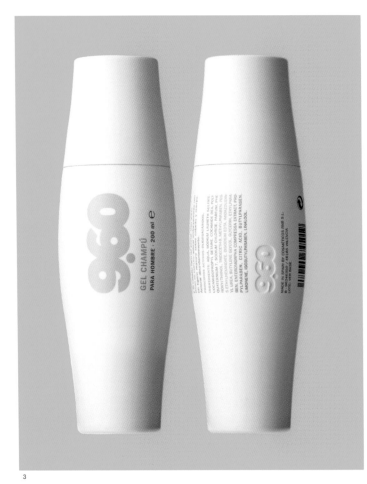

3

4

1–3

9.60 COSMETICS PACKAG-
ING FOR RNB LABORATO-
RIES, 2006

"9.60 is a mass-market range of
cosmetic products for men that
are exclusively distributed in
more than 1000 supermarkets of
the Spanish chain MER-
CADONA. This basic line of
cosmetics is related to concepts
such as being fit, practising
sport, performing a physical
exercise…The design of the

package tries to reinforce these
images. The name brings out the
idea of a sport record, and the
package makes reference to the
morphology of a muscle. All the
100 ml and 200 ml containers
were designed with an ergonomic shape and fabricated in flexible plastic so they are very resistant and can be easily carried in a
sports bag."

„9.60 ist eine Herren-Kosmetik-
serie für den Massenmarkt, die
exklusiv in den mehr als 1000

Supermärkten der spanischen
Ladenkette MERCADONA
vertrieben wird. Diese Basiskos-
metikserie nimmt Bezug auf
Begriffe wie Fitness, Sport, Training … Diese Assoziationen
sollen durch das Design der Verpackung noch verstärkt werden.
Der Name verweist auf eine
sportliche Rekordleistung, und
die Verpackung greift die Morphologie eines Muskels auf. Die
100-ml- und 200-ml-Behälter
haben eine ergonomische Formgebung und sind aus flexiblem

Kunststoff gefertigt, wodurch sie
sehr robust und problemlos in
der Sporttasche zu transportieren
sind."

« 9.60 est une gamme de produits cosmétiques grand public
pour hommes exclusivement dis-
tribuée dans les quelque 1000
supermarchés de la chaîne espagnole MERCADONA. Cette
ligne cosmétique simple est liée
à des concepts comme être en
forme, faire du sport, de l'exerci-
ce physique… Le design de

l'emballage tente de renforcer
cette image. Le nom rappelle
un record sportif et l'emballage
la morphologie d'un muscle.
Tous les flacons de 100 ml et
200 ml ont été dotés d'une forme ergonomique et fabriqués
en plastique souple afin d'être
très resistants et de pouvoir être
transportés facilement dans un
sac de sport. »

6–7
BONJOUR
Shower tray that can
incorporate standard-sized
shower stalls made of
Stonefeel (mineral resin)
2005
Client: Sanico

8
METRO
Chrome-finished brass water
faucet with integrated aerator
filter
2005
Client: Sanico

7

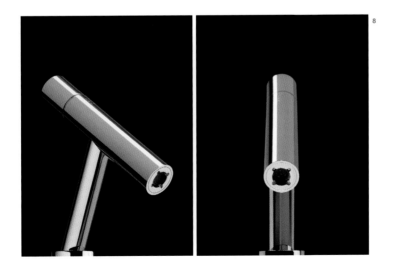

8

9

**LAVERNIA CIENFUEGOS
Y ASOCIADOS**

C/Félix Pizcueta 23
46004 Valencia
Spain
T +34 96 3522422
E lavernia@lavernia.com
E cienfuegos@lavernia.com
www.lavernia.com

DESIGN GROUP HISTORY

1995 Nacho and Associates
studio founded by Nacho
Lavernia in Valencia
2000 Alberto Cienfuegos
appointed partner and studio
name changed to Lavernia,
Cienfuegos y Asociados

**FOUNDERS' BIOGRAPHIES
NACHO LAVERNIA**

1950 Born in Valencia, Spain
1968–1972 Studied Interior
Design at Arts & Crafts School,
Valencia
1972–1974 Studied Industrial
Design at ELISAVA, Barcelona
1984–1989 Member of La Nave
– a Spanish multi-disciplinary
design collective
1989–1990 Studied
Management at La Universidad
Politécnica de Valencia
1989–1994 Art Director,
Gimeno & Lavernia studio

1995 Founded his own design
studio Nacho and Associates
1994–1995 Taught at the CEU
San Pablo University, Valencia
1992–1996 President of
ADCV (Asociación de
Diseñadores de la Comunidad
Valenciana)
1992–1996 President of the
Spanish Federation of Design
Associations (FESAD)
2000 Alberto Cienfuegos, who
had been working in the studio
from the beginning, became
partner and the name changed
to Lavernia Cienfuegos y Asociados

ALBERTO CIENFUEGOS

1972 Born in Granada, Spain
1990–1994 Studied Industrial
Design at CEU San Pablo
University, Valencia
1995–2000 Designer, Lavernia
& Asociados, Valencia

2000+ Partner, Lavernia
Cienfuegos y Asociados,
Valencia – working as art
director for industrial and
graphic design products
2000–2004 Taught at the CEU
San Pablo University, Valencia

RECENT EXHIBITIONS

2001 "Spanish Product Design
Exhibition", DDI Ministerio de
Economía, New Delhi
2002 "Pasión, Diseño Español",
Akademie der Künste, Berlin
2005 "Spain Color: Fresh Air in
Spanish Design", 100% Design,
Tokyo

RECENT AWARDS

2003 Delta Award, ADI-FAD
(Associació de Disseny Industrial del Foment de les Arts Decoratives), Spain
2005 Certificate of Typographic
Excellence, Art Directors Club

of New York; 2 x Design Plus
Awards, ISH, German Design
Council
2006 AEPD Award, AEPD
(Asociación Española de
Profesionales del Diseño), Spain
2007 Certificate of Typographic
Excellence, Art Directors Club
of New York; 2 x Design Plus
Awards, ISH, German Design
Council

CLIENTS

Antares/Flos, Auta, Babé,
Intermon Oxfam, Mercadona,
Paco Capdell, RNB, Sanico,
Sociedad Madrid 2012,
Tecno España

10

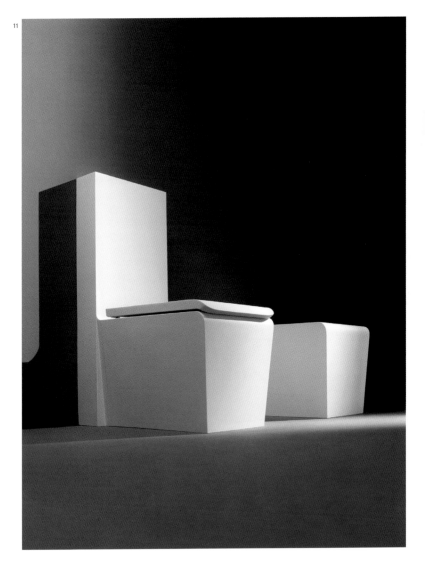

11

"To design is to look
in a different way."

9–10
PICTOS
Graphic signage system in
laser-cut stainless steel –
icons are self-adhesive
2005
Client: Sanico

11
TRANSIT
Lavatory and bidet made
of Stonefeel (mineral resin)
with porcelain interiors
2006
Client: Sanico

LEADING EDGE DESIGN

"Once, people could make all the daily items they needed, such as clothing, furniture and even houses, if they tried hard and had enough time. Today, however, no one in the world can make a cell phone from scratch. The amount of knowledge it would take to completely understand even the things we use in daily living goes far beyond what a single human being could possibly possess in his whole lifetime. The problem today is how to get something made that you want when there are basically too many domains of professional expertise for an individual to handle. I was once asked if there was something I was always careful about, to which I answered that I tried not to think of myself as an expert. If I try to build a leading edge product, while needing the help of various experts, I will proceed with the intention that I am going to design everything. It doesn't matter whether the person at the center of the creation is called a scientist or a designer. It's important that a coherent aesthetic sense runs through the entire development, from fundamental scientific research to the final form."

„Früher konnten die Menschen sämtliche Gegenstände des täglichen Gebrauchs wie Kleider, Möbel und sogar Häuser selbst herstellen, wenn sie sich anstrengten und genug Zeit hatten. Heutzutage ist niemand auf der Welt imstande, ein Mobiltelefon ganz allein zu bauen. Das Wissen, das erforderlich wäre, um auch nur die Dinge, die wir täglich verwenden, vollständig zu verstehen, übersteigt bei Weitem das, was ein einzelner Mensch im Laufe seines ganzen Lebens lernen kann. Heute besteht das Problem eher darin, die Herstellung von etwas, das man produzieren will, zu organisieren, weil eine für den Einzelnen unüberschaubare Menge von Fachkompetenzen involviert ist. Ich wurde einmal gefragt, ob es etwas gebe, worauf ich immer achte, und ich antwortete, dass ich versuche, mich nicht als Experten zu sehen. Wenn ich ein Spitzenprodukt herstelle, und dabei auf die Hilfe verschiedener Spezialisten angewiesen bin, wird mein Ziel die durchgehende Gestaltung sein. Es ist gleichgültig, ob man den Menschen, der im Zentrum des Schaffensprozesses steht, einen Wissenschaftler oder einen Designer nennt. Wichtig ist, dass der gesamte Prozess, von der wissenschaftlichen Grundlagenforschung bis zur endgültigen Form, von einem einheitlichen ästhetischen Empfinden geprägt ist."

« Autrefois, les gens pouvaient fabriquer tous les objets dont ils avaient besoin au quotidien, comme les vêtements, les meubles et même les maisons, s'ils avaient du courage et suffisamment de temps. Mais aujourd'hui, personne au monde ne peut fabriquer un téléphone portable à partir de rien. La somme de connaissances qu'exigerait une compréhension complète des objets que nous utilisons chaque jour dépasse largement ce qu'un seul être humain pourrait acquérir en y consacrant sa vie entière. Le problème est aujourd'hui de trouver comment obtenir que soit fabriquée une chose qui fait intervenir un nombre trop important de domaines d'expertise professionnelle pour un seul homme. On m'a une fois demandé s'il y avait une chose à laquelle j'étais toujours attentif, ce à quoi j'ai répondu que j'essayais de ne pas me considérer comme un expert. Si j'essaie de concevoir un produit novateur, tout en ayant besoin de l'aide de divers experts, mon intention, au fil du processus créatif, sera de tout designer. Peu importe que l'on qualifie la personne qui se situe au cœur de la création de scientifique ou de designer. Il est important qu'un sens esthétique cohérent serve de fil rouge au développement du projet, depuis la recherche scientifique fondamentale jusqu'à la forme finale. »

1
OXO KITCHEN TOOLS
Drawing of ladle and handle construction
2006
Client: OXO International

2
OXO KITCHEN TOOLS
Detail of serving tools' heads
2006
Client: OXO International

3
OXO KITCHEN TOOLS
Detail of precision tongs' grip
2006
Client: OXO International

4
OXO KITCHEN TOOLS
Detail of serving tools' grips
2006
Client: OXO International

3

4

5

5
OXO KITCHEN TOOLS
Daikon grater
2006
Client: OXO International

6
OXO KITCHEN TOOLS
Range of tools made of
stainless steel, Santoprene
elastomer, engineering plastic
and ABS resin
2006
Client: OXO International

1–6
OXO KITCHEN TOOLS FOR
OXO INTERNATIONAL, 2006

"These kitchen tools were
designed specifically for the
Japanese market in order to
meet the needs of the users
unmet by the original OXO
kitchen tools from the USA.
Japanese cooking often involves
lighter and more delicate manipulation of ingredients compared
to Western cooking. Part of the
reason for this is that Japanese
food is often cut into small
pieces so that one can eat with

chopsticks without having to cut
with a knife. Such differences
were considered in the development of the new OXO kitchen
tools. The product line also
includes more Japan-specific
products such as the Daikon
grater, which has been re-
engineered to surpass the performance of conventional
Japanese graters."

„Diese Küchenutensilien wurden
speziell für den japanischen
Markt gestaltet, um speziellen
Bedürfnissen Rechnung zu tragen, die von den aus den USA

stammenden OXO-Originalen
nicht erfüllt werden konnten. In
der japanischen Küche werden
die Zutaten oft sanfter und vor-
sichtiger als in der westlichen
Welt behandelt. Ein Grund
dafür ist unter anderem, dass
viele Lebensmittel in kleine Stücke zerteilt werden, um sie mit
Stäbchen essen zu können. Bei
der Entwicklung der neuen
OXO-Küchenutensilien wurden
diese kulturellen Unterschiede
berücksichtigt. Die Produktlinie
umfasst auch speziell auf Japan
ausgerichtete Produkte wie die
Raspel Daikon, eine Neuent-

wicklung, die den konventionellen japanischen Raspeln den
Rang ablaufen soll."

« Ces ustensiles de cuisine ont
été spécialement conçus pour le
marché japonais afin de combler
les attentes qui n'étaient jusqu'alors pas satisfaites par les
ustensiles originellement créés
par OXO pour les États-Unis.
La cuisine japonaise suppose
souvent une manipulation plus
légère et délicate des ingrédients
que la cuisine occidentale,
notamment parce que la nourriture japonaise est souvent cou-

pée en tout petits morceaux
pour qu'ils puissent être mangés
avec des baguettes sans avoir
recours à un couteau. De telles
différences ont été prises en
considération pour la conception
des nouveaux ustensiles OXO.
La gamme inclut aussi davantage
de produits spécifiquement japonais comme la râpe Daikon,
repassée entre les mains des
ingénieurs pour surpasser les
performances des râpes japo-
naises conventionnelles. »

6

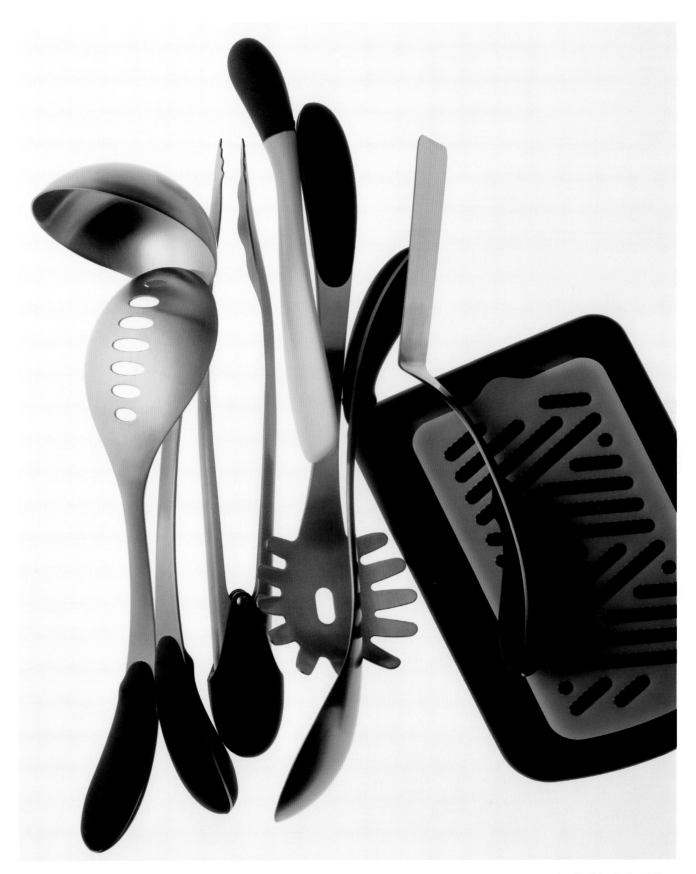

LEADING EDGE DESIGN

Leading Edge Design corp.
Naganumacho 104-2-1-7
Hachioji
Tokyo 192-0907
Japan
T +81 426 327932
E info@lleedd.com
www.lleedd.com

DESIGN GROUP HISTORY

1994 Founded by Shunji
Yamanaka in Tokyo, Japan

FOUNDER'S BIOGRAPHY
SHUNJI YAMANAKA

1957 Born in Tokyo, Japan
1982 Graduated from the Faculty of Engineering, University of
Tokyo
1982–1987 Worked as an
exterior designer for Nissan
Motor Co., Ltd.
1987 Began working as a
freelance industrial designer
1991–1994 Associate Professor,
Faculty of Engineering,
University of Tokyo
1994 Founded Leading Edge
Design in Tokyo

RECENT EXHIBITIONS

2001 "Worksphere", The Museum of Modern Art, New York
2002 "Robot Meme", National
Museum of Emerging Science
and Innovation, Tokyo, Japan
2003+ "Cyclops", Ars Electronica Center (permanently exhibited), Linz, Austria
2004 "Haptic" (Takeo Paper
Show 2004) Spiral Hall, Tokyo,
Japan
2005 "Move" (solo exhibition)
Spiral Hall, Tokyo, Japan
2006 "Nippon Design", Salon
du Meuble Paris 2006, Paris
2006 "Projections of Function"
(solo exhibition) AXIS Gallery,
Tokyo, Japan

RECENT AWARDS

2001 iF Award, International
Design Forum Hanover
2004 iF Award, International
Design Forum Hanover; The
Mainichi Design Award "2004
Designer of the Year", Mainichi
Newspaper, Tokyo
2006 2 x Gold Good Design
Awards, JIDPO (Japan Industrial
Design Promotion Organization); Good Design Award for
Ecology Design, JIDPO (Japan
Industrial Design Promotion
Organization)

CLIENTS

Arflex, Cannon,
East Japan Railway,
FX Palo Alto Laboratory,
Issey Miyake,
Japan Science and Technology,
Kokuyo, Mitsubishi Electric,
Nissan Motor, NTT DoCoMo,
OXO International,
Panasonic, Matsushita Electric,
Industrial, Seiko Instruments,
SUS Corporation,
Toyota Motor, Willcom

7

8
HALLUCIGENIA 01
Sketch of eight-wheeled vehicle
with detail of wheel module
2003
Client: self-produced prototype

7
HALLUCIGENIA 01
Robotic, eight-wheeled vehicle
concept study for the future of
automotive transportation.
Vehicle has independent control
of each of the wheels and
corresponding suspensions
to realize unconventional
maneuvers including diagonal
transition, rotation and
walking. 2003
Client: self-produced prototype

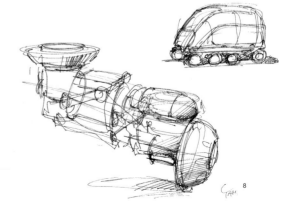

9–10
W-SIM
Modular cell phone system with its communication and software functions separated from the interface hardware. Its antenna, communication circuitry, address book data among other functions are all packed into a postage stamp-sized card called W-SIM. The card can be inserted into different interface hardware that typically has a keyboard and a display.
2005
Client: Willcom/Netibdex

10

9

"Beyond the boundary"

11
TT
Interface hardware for voice communication designed for use with a W-SIM card
2005
Client: Willcom/Netibdex

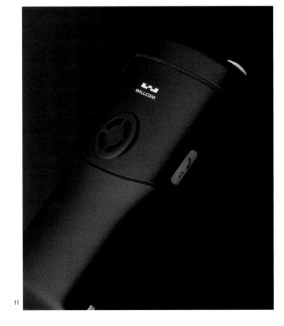

11

MATHIEU LEHANNEUR

"A few days ago I received an e-mail from Los Angeles. A woman diagnosed with bipolar disease three years previously was asking me if I could design one or more objects/systems to help her. Now on the mend, she wants to re-establish contact with her body, her sensations, her family and everything that makes up her immediate world: material and immaterial, visible and invisible, old relationships and perceptions. 'I've exhausted every resource here in LA, California and Florida.' I'm not sure yet how I can help; I need to know more about her. But what is certain is that she found it completely natural to contact me and allow design – in the widest sense – to fill the gaps which, traditionally, our discipline ignores."

„Vor einigen Tagen erhielt ich eine E-Mail aus Los Angeles. Eine Frau, bei der vor drei Jahren eine bipolare Störung diagnostiziert worden war, fragte mich, ob ich ein oder mehrere Objekte/Systeme gestalten könnte, um ihr zu helfen. Da es ihr inzwischen besser geht, möchte sie den Kontakt zu ihrem Körper, ihren Empfindungen, ihrer Familie und allem anderen wiederherstellen, was ihre unmittelbare Welt ausmacht: das Materielle und Immaterielle, das Sichtbare und Unsichtbare, die alten Beziehungen und Wahrnehmungen. ‚Ich habe alle Möglichkeiten hier in L. A., Kalifornien und Florida ausgeschöpft.' Ich weiß noch nicht, wie ich ihr behilflich sein kann, ich muss mehr über sie erfahren. Aber eines steht fest: Sie fand es vollkommen natürlich, sich an mich zu wenden und die leeren Stellen durch Design – im weitesten Sinn – ausfüllen zu lassen, obwohl diese normalerweise nicht von unserer Disziplin besetzt werden."

« J'ai reçu, il y a quelques jours, un mail de Los Angeles. Une femme diagnostiquée *bipolaire* depuis 3 ans, me demande si je peux lui concevoir un ou plusieurs objets/systèmes pour lui venir en aide. En voie de guérison, elle souhaite reprendre contact avec son corps, ses sensations, sa famille, et tout ce qui constitue son paysage immédiat : matériel et immatériel, visible et invisible, relationnel et perceptif. ‹ *J'ai épuisé toutes les ressources ici à Los Angeles, en Californie et en Floride.* › Je ne sais pas encore comment intervenir. Il me faut en apprendre davantage sur elle. Mais ce qui est sûr, c'est qu'il lui a semblé tout à fait naturel de s'adresser à moi et de permettre au design – au sens large – d'occuper les champs laissés libres et traditionnellement non dédiés à notre discipline. »

1

1–2
O
Oxygen generator for the home
in glass and aluminium
2006
Client: VIA

O OXYGEN GENERATOR
CONCEPT, 2006

"A veritable domestic breathing machine, O generates pure oxygen in the home. In big towns, oxygen levels are 90% lower than those required by our bodies under optimal conditions. Using an oximeter sensor, O constantly monitors the oxygen level in the air, and when it detects that this level is insufficient, it instantly activates the microorganisms it contains, Spirulina Platensis – a living organism with the highest yield of oxygen production – and a light that favours spirulin photosynthesis. This emits native oxygen, which is diffused into the surroundings. As soon as the air oxygen level has returned to optimum, the light and agitation are interrupted and the spirulin falls back to the bottom of the container. O will operate continuously on a day of high air pollution or during a party in an apartment. At present NASA is carrying out detailed studies on this subject, in connection with long-term trips for astronauts."

„O, eine richtige Heim-Atemmaschine, erzeugt reinen Sauerstoff für die Wohnung. In großen Städten ist der Sauerstoffgehalt der Atemluft häufig um 90 Prozent geringer als der Optimalwert, den unser Körper braucht. Ein Sensor misst ständig den Sauerstoffgehalt der Luft. Ist dieser zu niedrig, werden die im Glasbehälter eingeschlossenen Mikroorganismen – vor allem viel Sauerstoff produzierende Blaualgen des Stammes *Spirulina Platensis* – mittels Leuchtdioden zur Photosynthese angeregt. Der dabei erzeugte Sauerstoff wird an die Umgebung abgegeben. Sobald der Sauerstoffgehalt wieder optimal ist, werden die Beleuchtung und damit die Aktivität unterbrochen, und der Mikroorganismus fällt auf den Boden des Gefäßes zurück. Bei starker Luftverschmutzung oder beispielsweise während einer Party in der Wohnung bleibt O kontinuierlich aktiv. Derzeit untersucht die NASA dieses Konzept für Langzeitflüge im Weltraum."

« Véritable poumon domestique, O génère de l'oxygène pur dans la maison. Dans les grandes villes, l'air que nous respirons contient deux fois moins d'oxygène que le taux dont notre organisme aurait idéalement besoin. Grâce à un capteur d'oxymètre, O contrôle en permanence le taux d'oxygène dans l'air, et lorsqu'il détecte un niveau insuffisant, il active instantanément les micro-organismes qu'il contient, le *Spirulina Platensis* – un des organismes vivants qui produit le plus d'oxygène – ainsi qu'une lumière favorisant la photosynthèse de la spiruline. C'est ainsi que se génère de l'oxygène neuf, qui se diffuse dans l'environnement domestique. Dès que le taux d'oxygène dans l'air a retrouvé le niveau optimal, la lumière et l'agitation s'interrompent et la spiruline retourne se déposer au fond du récipient. O fonctionnera sans interruption un jour de forte pollution ou pendant une fête dans un appartement. La NASA poursuit actuellement des recherches détaillées sur ce sujet, en relation avec les voyages de longue durée des astronautes. »

3

3
AFTER THONET
Coat rack in bentwood for the Homme Collection for use in retail outlets
2005
Client: Yohann Serfaty

4–6
HOUSE 213.6
Modular dwelling system for
stray cats in rotational-moulded
polyethylene
2005
Client: Association
Chats Libres

5

4

6

MATHIEU LEHANNEUR
49, rue de Maubeuge
75009 Paris
France
T +33 8 71498877
E m@mathieulehanneur.com
www.mathieulehanneur.com

BIOGRAPHY

1974 Born in Rochefort, France
1994–2001 Studied industrial design at ENSCI (École Nationale Supérieure de Création Industrielle), Paris
2001 Began working as a freelance designer. Established his own studio in Paris
2002 Taught at ENSCI (École Nationale Supérieure de Création Industrielle), Paris
2004+ Post-graduate diploma Research Manager, Cité du Design, Saint-Étienne, France

RECENT EXHIBITIONS

2002 "International Design Biennale", Saint-Étienne, France
2003 "Non Standard Architecture", Georges Pompidou Centre, Paris; "Mosquito Bottleneck", Henry Urbach Architecture, New York; "Observeur du design", Cité des Sciences et de l'Industrie, Paris
2004 "International Design Biennale", Saint-Étienne, France; "Moulure utiles + Sacco + Ral 9006", CAC, Brétigny; "Appel d'Air", Now, Paris
2005 "SAFE", The Museum of Modern Art, New York; "Slim Retrospective", Resonnance, Lyon; "Domesticity, À Suivre…", Lieu d'art, Bordeaux
2006 "Bêtes de style", MUDAC (Musée de design es d'arts appliques contemporains), Lausanne; "L' Invenzione del quotidiano", Milan; "Elements", VIA, Milan and Paris

RECENT AWARDS

2000 Research Grant, ANVAR (Agencie Nationale de la Valorisation de la Recherche), Paris
2003 Research Grant, ANVAR (Agencie Nationale de la Valorisation de la Recherche), Paris
2006 Grand Prix de la Création, Paris; VIA Carte Blanche award

CLIENTS

Artemide,
Bangkok Museum/Thailand,
Cristofle, EDF, Flood/Paris,
Fondation Cartier pour l'art contemporain, FR66/Paris,
Issey Miyake Parfums,
MUDAM/Luxembourg,
Musée des Arts Décoratifs/Paris,
Paco Rabanne Parfums,
Palais de la Découverte/Paris,
VIA Y's Mandarina

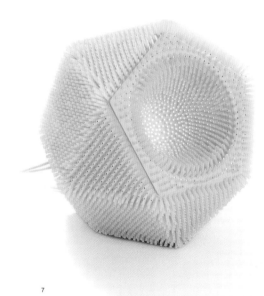

7

"What's visible is only a fraction of the world."

7–8
K
Daylight receiver/transmitter in aluminium, optical fibres, photoelectric cells and high-luminosity white LEDs for optimising biorhythms
2006
Client: VIA

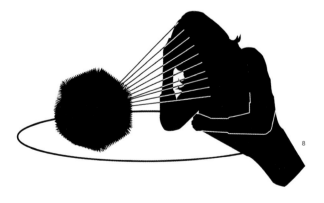

8

9
C°
"Intelligent" domestic infrared
heating unit in elastomer
with thermic camera and
shape-memory alloy that emits
localized infrared heat to
different body zones
2006
Client: VIA

10–11
dB
White noise diffuser in ABS
with mini speakers and electric
engine that automatically rolls
to source of unacceptable noise
and offsets it by continuously
emitting an equivalent intensity
of white noise
2006
Client: VIA

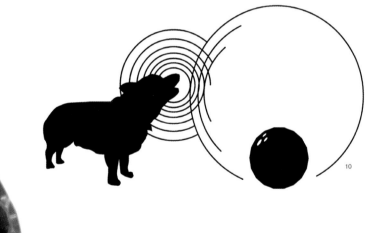

LIEVORE
ALTHERR
MOLINA

"Today's design does not just deal with functionality and the aesthetics of objects. Technology, the organisation of production, a perfect understanding of the markets it is focused towards, their modes of communication and distribution: these, amongst other factors, are what have led to design being considered a system of interacting disciplines rather than a specific discipline in itself... and having taken the above fully on board, all that remains is for us to devote ourselves to searching for the form that synthesises all this complexity and our own desires, just as an actor searches for the perfect gesture that says it all."

„Das heutige Design hat nicht nur mit der Funktionalität und Ästhetik von Objekten zu tun. Technologie, die Organisation der Produktion, perfekte Kenntnis der Zielmärkte, ihrer Kommunikations- und Distributionsweisen: Diese Faktoren haben unter anderen dazu geführt, dass Design eher für ein System von interagierenden Disziplinen gehalten wird als für eine eigenständige Disziplin ..., und da wir das selbst voll und ganz unterschreiben, bleibt uns nichts anderes übrig, als uns der Suche nach jener Form zu widmen, die eine Synthese dieser Komplexität und unserer eigenen Wünsche darstellt, so wie ein Schauspieler nach der perfekten Geste sucht, die alles auszudrücken vermag."

« Le design d'aujourd'hui ne s'intéresse pas seulement à la fonctionnalité et à l'esthétique des objets. La technologie, l'organisation de la fabrication, une parfaite connaissance des marchés dans lesquels ils s'inscrivent, leurs modes de communication et de distribution : en raison de ces facteurs, entre autres, le design est devenu un système de disciplines en interaction plutôt qu'une discipline en lui-même... Une fois tout ceci pris en considération, ce qui demeure est que nous devons nous consacrer à la recherche de la forme qui synthétise toute cette complexité et nos propres désirs, exactement comme un acteur recherche le geste parfait qui dit tout. »

1
LEAF 1804
Indoor/outdoor chaise longue in stove-enamelled metal rod
2005
Client: Arper

2
LEAF 1803
Indoor/outdoor lounge chair in stove-enamelled metal rod
2005
Client: Arper

3
LEAF 1802
Indoor/outdoor side chair in stove-enamelled metal rod
2005
Client: Arper

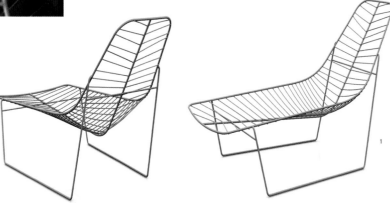

2

3

4

4
ZUMM
Wall cupboard in extruded
aluminium with sliding
tempered glass doors
2005
Client: Sellex

5–6
ZUMM
Residential and contract shelving
system in extruded aluminium,
detail of upright support tube
2005
Client: Sellex

6

5

7
CATIFA 70
Waiting chair with upholstered
polyurethane shell on aluminium
pedestal base, with matching
footstool
2007
Client: Arper

8
CATIFA 80
Lounge chair with upholstered
polyurethane shell on aluminium
pedestal base
2007
Client: Arper

7

"Indulgence is an important enough
function for us to want to satisfy it.
Endowing objects with sensuality is just
as noble as fulfilling a basic function
responsibly."

8

LIEVORE ALTHERR MOLINA

Lievore Altherr Molina s.l.
Plaça Berenguer 1, ático
08002 Barcelona
Spain
T +34 933 103292
E estudio@
lievorealtherrmolina.com
www.lievorealtherrmolina.com

DESIGN GROUP HISTORY
1991 Founded by Alberto
Lievore, Jeannette Altherr and
Manel Molina in Barcelona
1999 Received Premio Nacional
de Diseño (Spanish National
Design Award)

FOUNDERS' BIOGRAPHIES
ALBERTO LIEVORE
1948 Born in Buenos Aires,
Argentina
1970–1976 Studied Architec-

ture at la Facultad de Arquitec-
tura de Buenos Aires, Argentina.
1972 Founded Hipótesis
furniture showroom with its
own production facility
1977 Moved to Spain and
co-founded with Noberto
Chaves, Grupo Berenguer in
Barcelona (a design and architecture group, which later Jorge
Pensi and Oriol Pibernat joined)
1984 Established his own
product design office in
Barcelona

JEANNETTE ALTHERR
1965 Born in Heidelberg,
Germany
1985–1988 Studied Industrial
Design at Fachhochschule
Darmstadt, Germany
1989 Studied Product Design at
Escuela Massana, Barcelona and

began to collaborate with
Alberto Liévore

MANEL MOLINA
1963 Born in Barcelona,
Spain
1981–1984 Studied Interior
Design and Industrial Design at
Escuela de Arte y Diseño
(EINA), Barcelona
1985–1989 Freelance designer –
also worked with Miguel Milà
1987 Recieved "Nuevo Estilo"
(New Style) prize from
ADI/FAD

RECENT EXHIBITIONS
2003 "Exposición Premios
Nacionales de diseño",
Valencia, Barcelona; "The
World Best Design Exchange",
Korea
2004 "BIMM 2004",

Barcelona; "Décor Hàbitat",
Lleida, Spain
2005 "The World Best Design
Exchange", Korea; "100%
Design", Tokyo, London
2006 "100% Design", Tokyo

RECENT AWARDS
2003 Gold and Silver Delta
Awards, ADI-FAD (Associació
de Disseny Industrial del
Foment de les Arts Decoratives),
Spain; Gold Award, Neocon,
Chicago; Best of Competition
Award, Neocon, Chicago
2004 Premio AEPD Award,
AEPD (Asociación Española de
Profesionales del Diseño),
Spain; Jubiläums-Award, ZDF,
Germany
2005 Premio Oderzo Azienda e
Design, Città di Oderzo Unin-
dustria Treviso; New Classic

Prize, Schöner Wohnen, Ger-
many; iF Award, International
Forum Design Hanover; Gold
iF Award, International Forum
Design Hanover
2006 Best Outdoor Seat Award,
Wallpaper magazine
2007 Design Plus Award,
Ambiente, Frankfurt; iF Award,
International Forum Design
Hanover

CLIENTS
Andreu World, Arper, Arruti,
Bellato, Bernhardt, Casamilano,
Davis, Do+Ce, Dona, Emmebi,
Foscarini, Halifax, Metalarte,
Orizzonti, Perobell,
Santa & Cole, Segis, Sellex,
Sovet, Sunroller, Tacchini,
Tisettanta, Verzelloni, Vibia

LOT-EK

"LOT-EK is an ongoing investigation into the 'artificial nature', or the un-mappable outgrowth of familiar, unexplored, manmade and technological elements woven into the urban/suburban reality. LOT-EK is extracting from this artificial nature prefabricated objects, systems and technologies to be used as raw materials. LOT-EK is the random encounter with such objects, which are displaced, transformed and manipulated to fulfil program needs. LOT-EK is the dialogue that develops with the specific features of these already existing objects thus generating unexpected spatial/functional solutions. LOT-EK is rethinking the ways in which the human body interacts with products and by-products of the industrial/technological culture. LOT-EK is re-inventing domestic/work/play spaces and functions and questioning conventional configurations. LOT-EK is blurring the boundaries between art, architecture, entertainment and information."

„LOT-EK ist eine fortlaufende Untersuchung der ‚künstlichen Natur', das heißt der unüberschaubaren Auswüchse von bekannten, unerforschten, von Menschen gemachten technischen Elementen, die Teil der urbanen/vorstädtischen Realität sind. LOT-EK entnimmt vorgefertigte Objekte, Systeme und Technologien aus dieser künstlichen Natur und verwendet sie als Rohstoffe. LOT-EK ist die zufällige Begegnung mit solchen Objekten, die an einen anderen Ort versetzt, transformiert und manipuliert werden, um bestimmte Anforderungen zu erfüllen. LOT-EK ist der Dialog, der sich mit den Besonderheiten dieser bereits vorhandenen Objekte ergibt und der unerwartete räumliche/funktionale Lösungen hervorbringt. LOT-EK ist dabei, die Art und Weise, wie der menschliche Körper mit Produkten und Nebenprodukten der industriellen/technischen Kultur interagiert, neu zu überdenken. LOT-EK erfindet Haus-/Arbeits-/Spielräume und Funktionen neu und stellt konventionelle Strukturen infrage. LOT-EK verwischt die Grenzen zwischen Kunst, Architektur, Unterhaltung und Information."

«LOT-EK est une investigation en cours dans la ‹nature artificielle›, l'excroissance foisonnante d'éléments familiers ou inexplorés, artisanaux ou technologiques, qui sont imbriqués dans la réalité urbaine et suburbaine. LOT-EK extrait de cette nature artificielle des objets préfabriqués, des systèmes et des technologies qui sont utilisés comme matière première. LOT-EK est une rencontre de hasard avec de tels objets, qui sont déplacés, transformés et manipulés pour satisfaire des besoins de programmation. LOT-EK est le dialogue qui s'instaure grâce aux aspects particuliers de ces objets préexistants, de façon à susciter des solutions spatiales et fonctionnelles inattendues. LOT-EK repense les manières dont le corps humain interagit avec les produits et sous-produits de la culture industrielle et technologique. LOT-EK réinvente les espaces et fonctions domicile/travail/loisirs et remet en question les cadres conventionnels. LOT-EK estompe les frontières entre art, architecture, divertissement et information.»

1

2

1–7
CHK (CONTAINER HOME KIT), 2005

CHK™, Container Home Kit, combines multiple shipping containers to build modern, intelligent and affordable homes. 40-foot-long shipping containers are joined and stacked to create configurations that vary in size approximately from 1,000 to 3,000 square feet.
Each container is transformed by cutting sections of its corrugated metal walls. Joining the containers side by side, the cut-out layout allows for horizontal circulation expanding, at the same time, the width of the container to generate larger living spaces. Double height living rooms are created for the CHK loft model, for a more open layout. Incrementing the amount of containers allows the house to expand from a 1 bedroom to a 2, 3, and 4 bedroom home. CHK houses can be disassembled and reassembled anywhere.

Der Containerhaus-Bausatz CHK™ setzt mehrere Schiffscontainer zu modernen, intelligenten und preisgünstigen Häusern zusammen. 40-Fuß-Container werden miteinander verbunden und übereinander gestapelt, sodass variable Bauten mit einer Wohnfläche zwischen 90 und 280 qm entstehen. Jeder Container kann verändert werden, wenn man Teile seiner Wellblechwände entfernt. So kann der Raum horizontal erweitert werden, wenn die Container nebeneinander angeordnet sind, und der Bewegungsspielraum im Inneren durch geräumige Zimmer vergrößert werden. Das CHK-Loft-Modell zeichnet sich durch Wohnzimmer in doppelter Höhe und einen offenen Grundriss aus. Mit zusätzlichen Containern lassen sich weitere Zimmer anfügen. Die CHK-Häuser können abgebaut und an einem anderen Ort wieder aufgebaut werden.

CHK™, pour Container Home Kit, est une combinaison de divers conteneurs qui forment des habitations modernes, intelligentes et abordables. Des conteneurs maritimes de 12 m de long sont assemblés et empilés pour créer des configurations dont la surface varie, approximativement, de 90 à 280 m². Chaque conteneur est transformé par la découpe de parties de ses cloisons de métal ondulé. En joignant les conteneurs par les côtés, ces percées permettent une plus grande circulation horizontale tout en élargissant les pièces pour créer des espaces de vie plus vastes. Des salons à double hauteur sous plafond agrémentent le modèle CHK loft, pour un agencement plus ouvert. Augmenter le nombre de conteneurs permet de rajouter une, deux ou trois chambres à une habitation. Les maisons CHK peuvent aussi être démantelées et reconstruites ailleurs.

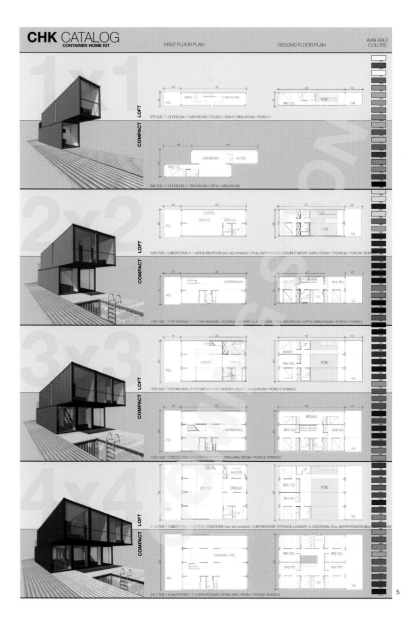

1–2
CONTAINERS
40-foot-long shipping containers used as basis of CHK (Container Home Kit) dwellings
2005

3
CHK 1X1
Computer rendering of single-unit Container Home Kit dwelling
2005

4
CHK 3X3
Computer rendering of triple-unit Container Home Kit dwelling
2005

5
CHK
Catalogue page showing
configuration and floor plans of
1x1, 2x2, 3x3 and 4x4 unit Container Home Kit dwellings
2005

6–7
CHK 3X3
Interior of triple-unit Container
Home Kit dwelling
2005

6

7

"Developing complex architecture
design by re-using already existing
industrial objects."

LOT-EK
55 Little West 12th Street
New York
New York 10014
USA
T +1 212 255 9326
E info@lot-ek.com
www.lot-ek.com

DESIGN GROUP HISTORY
1993 Founded by Ada Tolla and
Giuseppe Lignano in New York
City, USA

FOUNDERS' BIOGRAPHIES
ADA TOLLA
1964 Born in Potenza, Italy
1983–1989 Master's Degree in
Architecture and Urban Design,
Universita' di Napoli, Naples,
Italy
1990–1991 Post-graduate
studies in Architecture,
Columbia University, New York

GIUSEPPE LIGNANO
1963 Born in Naples, Italy
1983–1989 Master's Degree in
Architecture and Urban Design,
Universita' di Napoli, Naples,
Italy

1990–1991 Post-graduate
studies in Architecture, Columbia University, New York

RECENT EXHIBITIONS
2003 "MDU, Mobile Dwelling
Unit", Walker Art Center, Min-
neapolis; "MDU, Mobile
Dwelling Unit", Art Museum,
UCSB, Santa Barbara, CA;
"Crossed Lines – New Territo-
ries of Design", Center for Con-
temporary Culture, Barcelona;
"Concepts for the Snow Show",
Venice Architecture Biennale,
Venice; "American Pavilion",
São Paulo Architecture Biennal,
São Paulo, Brazil; "Strangely
Familiar", Walker Art Center,
Minneapolis; "Living in
Motion", Irish Museum of
Modern Art, Dublin

2004 "MDU, Mobile
Dwelling Unit", Whitney
Museum, New York; "Strangely
Familiar", Scottsdale Museum
of Contemporary Art (Arizona),
Musée de l'Ospice Comtesse
(Lille, France) and Carnegie
Museum of Art + Heinz
Architecture Center (Pitts-
burgh)
2005 CHK, School of Architec-
ture, Slocum Hall, Syracuse
University, NY; "Estrañamente
Familiares: Diseño e Vida
Cotia", MARCO (Museo de
Arte Contemporánea), Vigo,
Spain
2006 "X-Static Process" Steven
Klein's Madonna video portraits,
Louis Vuitton Store, Roppongi,
Tokyo; "X-Static Process"
Steven Klein's Madonna video

portraits, Gary Tatintsian
Gallery, Moscow
2007 "Theater For One",
Princeton University, New Jersey

RECENT AWARDS
2001 Finalist, National Design
Award, Cooper-Hewitt National
Design Museum
2002 Funding for the MDU
prototype, National Endowment
for the Arts Grant
2005 Best of Interactive Design
Category, Annual Design
Review, I.D. Magazine (with
Inbar Barak)

CLIENTS
Art Basel Miami, Bloomberg,
Sara Lee, Uniqlo USA

ROSS LOVEGROVE

"My path remains individual but I see an emerging possibility to break free conceptually and therefore aesthetically by embracing the full potential of our times and maybe with this will help define a new physicality in the objects and architecture that surrounds us. I am motivated by the need to remain relevant via contemporary process as well as remaining mindful that to be Human-centric one first needs to be Earth-centric. I know I have a skill to give form to the abstract nature of technology and through my research I see great potential to converge progressive manufacturing and materials technology to arrive at intelligent design which touches our soul with a new language that is economic, digital, lightweight and fluid."

„Mein Weg bleibt ein individueller. Aber ich sehe in zunehmendem Maß die Möglichkeit, konzeptionell und damit ästhetisch auszubrechen, indem man sich auf das gesamte Potenzial unseres Zeitalters einlässt und vielleicht dadurch eine neue, physische Präsenz in den uns umgebenden Objekten und Bauwerken definiert. Was mich motiviert, ist die Notwendigkeit, über einen zeitgenössischen Bezug relevant zu bleiben, ohne dabei die Tatsache zu vergessen, dass man zunächst auf die Erde bezogen sein muss, um auf die Menschen bezogen zu sein. Ich weiß, dass ich die Gabe habe, dem abstrakten Wesen von Technik eine konkrete Form zu verleihen, und durch meine Forschungen sehe ich ein großes Potenzial für die Annäherung an fortschrittliche Technologien im Bereich Herstellung und Material, um ein intelligentes Design zu erlangen, das unsere Seele mit einer neuen Sprache berührt, die ökonomisch, digital, leicht und fließend ist."

« Ma voie reste solitaire mais je commence à percevoir un moyen de nous libérer conceptuellement et donc esthétiquement en prenant à bras le corps tout le potentiel de notre époque : j'espère parvenir, grâce à cela, à définir une nouvelle présence physique des objets et de l'architecture qui nous entourent. Je suis motivé par la nécessité de rester pertinent dans le processus contemporain tout en gardant à l'esprit que pour se centrer sur l'Humain il faut d'abord se centrer sur la Terre. Je sais que j'ai la capacité de donner forme à la nature abstraite de la technologie et mes recherches m'ont confirmé l'importance d'une utilisation éclairée des technologies nouvelles en matière de fabrication et de matériaux pour parvenir à un design intelligent qui touche notre âme avec un nouveau langage économique, numérique, léger et fluide. »

1

"At first glance this table might appear to float like a black leaf elevated from the weight of gravitational forces, alert and strangely soft/ridged in form. This soft/ridged state is a unique condition that emulates the way that natural forms grow and evolve in space. It is a result of a constant search for evolutionary refinement, a trace of Immaculate Conception whereby total harmony between material, technology and form is the ultimate goal."

„Auf den ersten Blick könnte man den Eindruck bekommen, dass dieser Tisch wie ein von den Gravitationskräften losgelöstes schwarzes Blatt in der Luft schwebt, alert und mit seltsam weicher/geschwungener Form. Dieses Weich-/Geschwungensein ist ein einmaliger Zustand, der nachahmt, wie sich natürliche Formen im Raum entwickeln und ausbreiten. Es ist ein Ergebnis der ständigen Suche nach evolutionärer Verfeinerung, eine Ahnung von Unbefleckter Empfängnis, wobei die vollkommene Harmonie zwischen Material, Technologie und Form das höchste Ziel ist."

« À première vue, cette table semble flotter comme une feuille noire libérée de la gravité, alerte et étrange, à la fois lisse et ridée. Cet état lisse/ridé est un moyen unique d'imiter la manière dont les formes naturelles croissent et évoluent dans l'espace. Il résulte d'une quête constante de raffinement dans l'évolution, une touche d'Immaculée Conception par laquelle, objectif ultime, une harmonie totale entre matériau, technologie et forme peut être achevée. »

"Famous for what"?

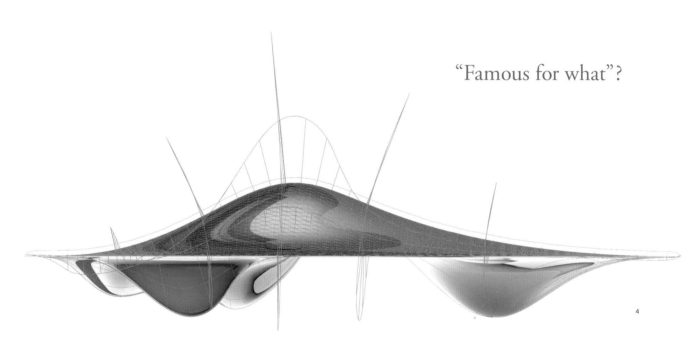

4

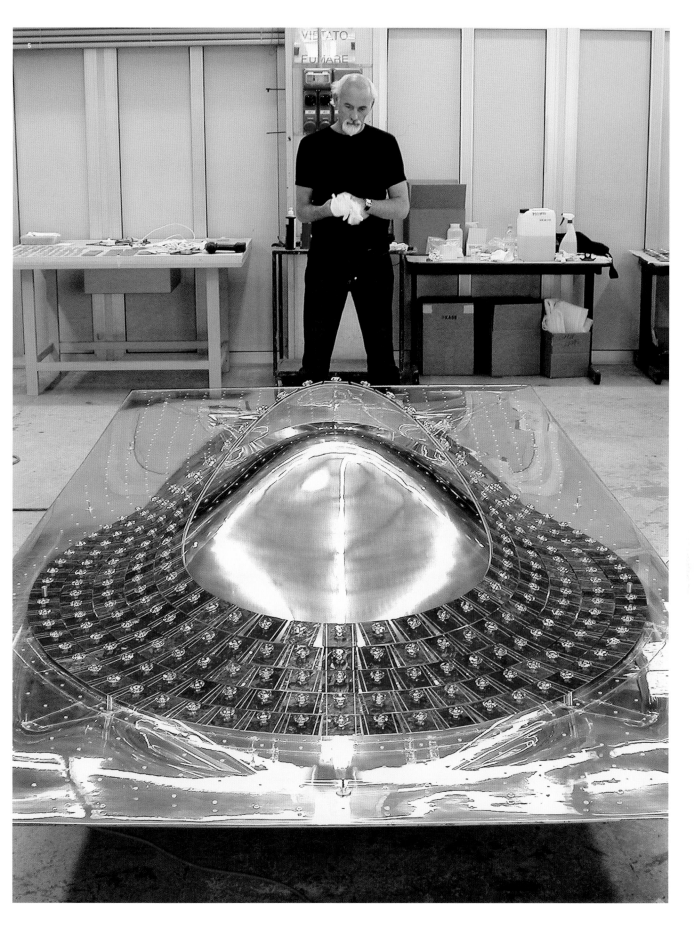

6–7
SUPERNATURAL ARMCHAIR
Wireframe and computer
analysis of Supernatural
Armchair structure
2007
Client: Moroso

6

7

8–9
SUPERNATURAL ARMCHAIR
Stackable indoor/outdoor
armchair in gas-assist injection-
moulded glass fibre reinforced
polyamide
2007
Client: Moroso

8

9

10
CRANBROOK PAVILION
Concept for a lightweight
pavilion to be used by the
Martha Graham Dance Com-
pany in the grounds of Cranbrook Academy of Art, constructed from three different
bladder-moulded carbon
composite modules
2006
Client: Cranbrook Academy
of Art/Max Protetch Gallery

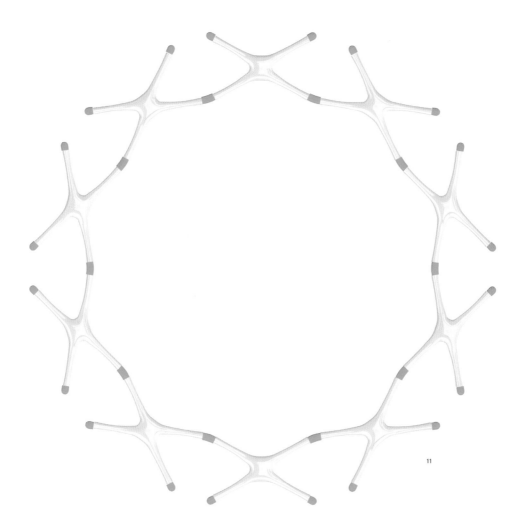

11

ROSS LOVEGROVE
Studio X
21 Powis Mews
London W11 1JN
United Kingdom
T +44 20 72297104
E studio@rosslovegrove.com
www.rosslovegrove.com

BIOGRAPHY
1958 Born in Cardiff, Wales
1980 BA (Hons) Industrial
Design, Manchester Polytechnic,
Manchester
1983 MA Industrial Design,
Royal College of Art, London
1983–1984 Designer, frog
design, Altensteig
1984–1987 In-house designer,
Knoll International, Paris
1990 Established his own design
office, Studio X in London

RECENT EXHIBITIONS
2001 "Material Transition",
Rheinauen Space, Cologne
2002 "Expanding the Gap",
Galerie Rendel & Spitz,
Cologne
2003 "De-light-ed by Corian",
Salone del Mobile, Milan
2004 "Designosaurs", Segheria,
Milan
2005 "Superliquidity", Le Bain
Gallery, Tokyo
2006 "Swarowski Crystal
Aerospace", Via Tortona, Milan
2007 "Endurance", Phillips de
Pury, New York; "MUON"
Sala del Cenacolo, Milan;
"Form Masters London/Milano,
Ross Lovegrove and Zaha
Hadid", Ospedale Maggiore,
Milan

RECENT AWARDS
2001 "Designer of the Year",
Architektur & Wohnen,
Hamburg
2002 "G" Mark Federal Design
Prize, Japan; Silver Award,
D&AD, London
2004 "Royal Designer for
Industry", The Royal Society of
Arts, London; Janus de l'Indus-
trie Award, Institut Français du
Design; Final Nomination for
the Prince Philip Design Prize
2005 World Technology Award
for 2005, Time magazine and
CNN

CLIENTS
Artemide, Knoll, Materialise,
Moroso, Serralunga, Swarovski,
VitrA, Yamagiwa

11
SYSTEMX
Modular hanging light system
in injection-moulded polycarbonate and aluminium with
curved fluorescent light tubes.
A single X-shaped module can
be configured to achieve ordered
geometries from modules of
2 to 3 up to large horizontal or
vertical planes of infinite
number relating to architectural
planes
2005
Client: Yamagiwa

12
SYSTEMX
Modular hanging light system
with optional light diffusing
or noise dampening inserts in
chromed or dark grey vacuum-
formed metalized acrylic
2005
Client: Yamagiwa

13
SYSTEMX
Engineering drawing of single
X-shaped light module
2005
Client: Yamagiwa

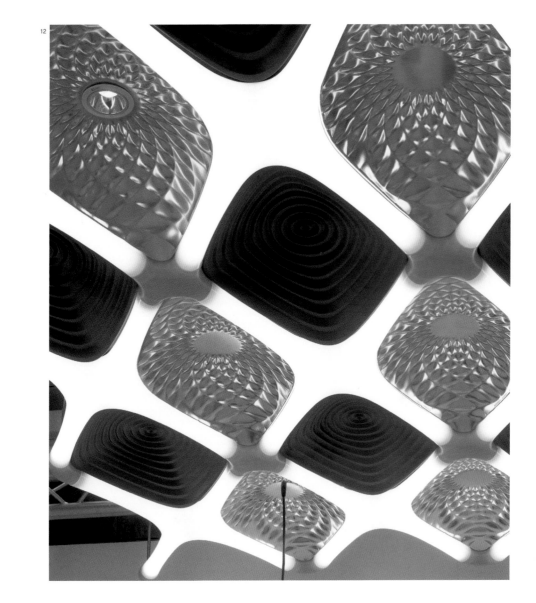

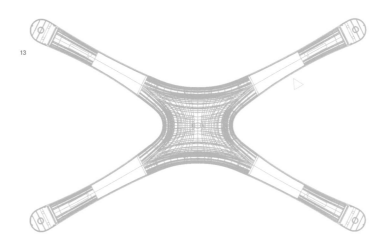

LUNAR DESIGN

"Our favourite products are those that stop you in your tracks. They are surprising. They have arisen from a creative individual's point of view and are objects of desire as much as they are objects of utility. Design has the ability to imbue products with traits that make people stop and think, behold or act. While all products have different proportions of these aspects, it's useful to consider them separately. Products make us think by surprising us through humour or by using metaphor to other familiar symbols. This aspect is at work in products that are anthropomorphic. Things that get us in the gut with their physical clarity or beauty make us want to behold them for that beauty. And products that delight us in the way that they work, the way they engage our use – those are products that invite us to act. The best products use these aspects to connect with us emotionally and contribute to our individual sense of meaning."

„Unsere Lieblingsobjekte sind solche, die jäh unsere Aufmerksamkeit erregen. Sie sind verblüffend. Sie sind aus der Sichtweise eines kreativen Individuums hervorgegangen und sind ebenso sehr Objekte der Begierde wie Objekte der Zweckmäßigkeit. Design hat die Fähigkeit, Produkte mit Eigenschaften zu versehen, die Menschen veranlassen innezuhalten und nachzudenken, zu betrachten oder zu handeln. Diese Aspekte sind in allen Produkten in unterschiedlichem Maß vorhanden, daher ist es hilfreich, sie getrennt zu betrachten. Produkte veranlassen uns zum *Nachdenken*, indem sie uns durch Humor oder die Verwendung von Metaphern für andere vertraute Symbole in Staunen versetzen. Dieser Aspekt kommt in anthropomorphen Produkten, also Dingen, denen menschliche Eigenschaften zugeschrieben werden, zum Tragen. Dinge, die uns durch ihre körperliche Klarheit oder Schönheit im Innersten bewegen, erwecken in uns den Wunsch, sie für diese Schönheit zu *betrachten*. Und Produkte, die uns in ihrer Funktionsweise erfreuen oder in der Art, wie sie uns zum Gebrauch einladen, sind Produkte, die uns zum *Handeln* auffordern. Die besten Produkte nutzen diese Aspekte, um sich auf emotionaler Ebene mit uns zu verbinden und zu unserem individuellen Gefühl von Sinnhaftigkeit beizutragen."

«Les objets que nous préférons sont ceux qui nous arrêtent dans notre course. Ils nous surprennent. Ils sont nés du point de vue créatif d'un individu et sont devenus des objets de désir autant que des objets utiles. Le design a la capacité d'imprégner les produits de traits qui vont pousser les gens à s'arrêter et à réfléchir, à regarder ou à agir. Les produits sont toujours porteurs de ces aspects, en proportions variées, mais il est utile de les considérer séparément. Les produits nous font *réfléchir* en nous surprenant grâce à l'humour ou à une métaphore d'autres symboles familiers. C'est notamment dans cette catégorie que se rangent les produits anthropomorphiques. Les choses qui nous frappent au cœur par leur clarté ou leur beauté physique nous donnent envie de les *regarder*. Et les produits qui nous ravissent par leur fonctionnement, la façon dont ils nous engagent à les manipuler – ceux-là invitent à *agir*. Les meilleurs produits ont recours à tous ces aspects pour nous toucher émotionnellement et venir enrichir notre perception individuelle du sens.»

1
NOVINT FALCON
Engineering rendering of computer game controller
2005
Client: Novint Technologies

2/4
NOVINT FALCON
New generation computer game controller that replaces a mouse or joystick and adds 3D touch to gaming
2005
Client: Novint Technologies

3
NOVINT FALCON
Sketch of computer game controller end effector
2005
Client: Novint Technologies

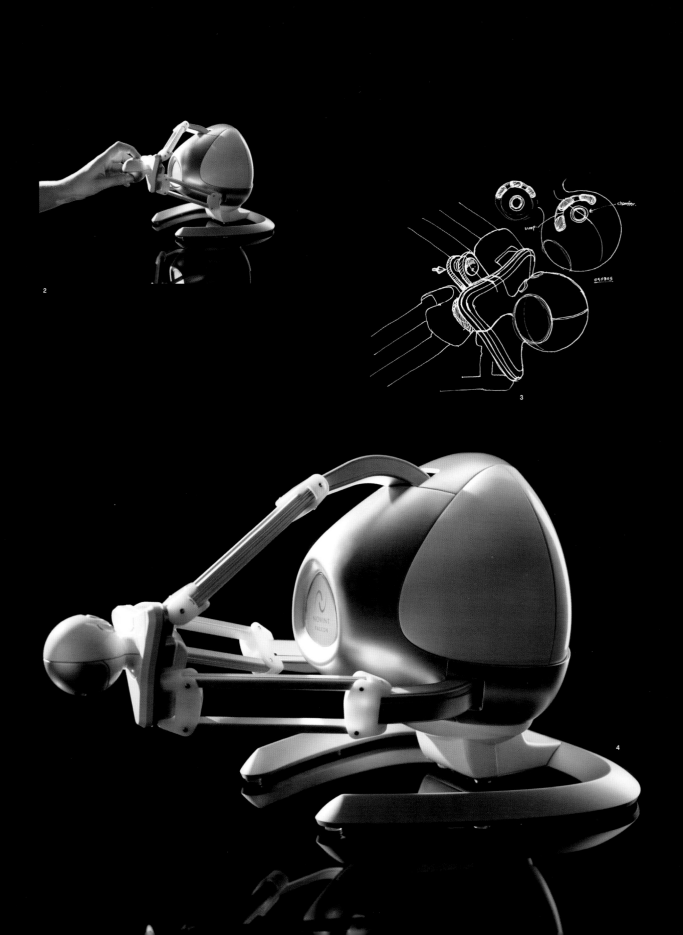

2

3

4

NOVINT FALCON GAME
CONTROLLER FOR NOVINT
TECHNOLOGIES, INC., 2005

The Novint Falcon, coupled
with the company's patented 3D
touch software, enables people
to experience a realistic sense of
touch on their computer, fundamentally transforming how they
play and interact. To bring the
Falcon's sophisticated level of 3D
touch technology to this consumer market, Lunar applied
their creativity and ingenuity to
solve key technical, aesthetic
and cost challenges. Based on
existing engineering Novint
licensed from Force Dimension,
a leading Swiss developer of
high-end haptic devices, Lunar
reinvented the technology's
robotics so it could be produced
within cost efficient manufactur-

ing processes that met Novint's
aggressive cost targets. The
resulting design delivers enriching tactile experiences for computer gamers at $200, less than a
percent of its commercial prede-
cessor. Lunar created a vortex-
like configuration and appearance to minimize size and also
make the device visually distinctive.

Der Novint Falcon Gamecon-
troller macht es in Verbindung
mit der patentierten 3D-Touch-
Software des Unternehmens
möglich, die Beschaffenheit vir-
tueller Objekte eines Computer-
spiels der Wirklichkeit entspre-
chend zu fühlen, wodurch sich
die Art, wie gespielt und interagiert wird, grundlegend verändert. Damit der Falcon mit
seiner raffiniert ausgeklügelten
3D-Touch-Technologie auch tat-

sächlich in diesem Sektor des
Konsumgütermarkts platziert
werden kann, haben die Designer von Lunar all ihre Kreativität und Erfindungsgabe darauf
verwandt, Lösungen für zentrale
technische, ästhetische und kos-
tenrelevante Probleme zu finden.
Basierend auf bereits vorhandener Technik – von Force Dimension, einem führenden Schweizer Entwickler von haptischen
leistungsstarken Eingabegeräten,
für Novint lizenziert – hat Lunar
die robotisierte Technologie neu
erfunden, sodass nunmehr in
kostengünstigen Herstellungsverfahren produziert werden
kann, was im Einklang mit
Novints aggressiven Kostenzie-
len steht. Das Design ist Ergebnis dieser Bemühungen und
bietet den Spielern für nur
100 Dollar, also für weniger als
ein Prozent des kommerziellen

Vorgängers, neue taktile Wel-
ten. Die Designer von Lunar
ließen sich bei der Gestaltung
des Gamecontrollers von Kreis-
strömungen und Wasserwirbeln
inspirieren, um das Gerät möglichst klein zu halten und gleichzeitig für ein markantes, unver-
kennbares Erscheinungsbild zu
sorgen.

Le Novint Falcon, associé aux
logiciels d'intéraction tactile en
3D brevetés par la compagnie,
permet aux joueurs de faire l'expérience d'une sensation réaliste
de toucher sur leur ordinateur et
transforme ainsi fondamentalement la façon dont ils jouent et
se comportent. Afin que le grand
public ait accès à la technologie
hautement sophistiquée et aux
compétences tactiles et tridimen-
sionnelles de Falcon, Lunar a
appliqué sa créativité et son

ingéniosité à relever des défis
techniques, esthétiques et finan-
ciers. À partir de la technologie
brevetée par Force Dimension,
important fabricant suisse de dis-
positifs haptiques haut-de-gam-
me, Lunar a réinventé les aspects
robotiques afin que sa production industrielle ait un rapport
coût-performance compatible
avec les objectifs drastiques de
Novint. L'objet de design qui en
résulte procure aux adeptes du
jeu sur ordinateur des expériences tactiles enrichissantes
pour 100 $, c'est-à-dire pour
cent fois moins cher que son
prédécesseur sur le marché.
Lunar a créé une configuration
et un habillage en tourbillon
pour en minimiser la taille et le
rendre reconnaissable visuelle-
ment.

5

CYBERKNIFE® ROBOTIC
RADIOSURGERY SYSTEM
Computer renderings of 4th
generation robotic radiosurgery
system
2005
Client: Accuray

TORTUGO
Computer renderings of media
player with integrated digital
camera for children aged four
to seven years
2005
Client: self-generated concept

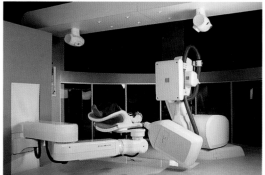

6

"We see design as the creative force of business,
answering three fundamental questions
that we apply to every challenge:
how will it be possible, what is different,
and why will people want it?"

7

8

9

10

MICROMEDIA PAPER
Sketches of micro digital
media display concept
2005
Client: self-generated concept

11

MICROMEDIA PAPER
Diagram showing functions of
micro digital media concept
2005
Client: self-generated concept

12

MICROMEDIA PAPER
Computer rendering of
inexpensive, wafer-thin,
trading-card sized digital media
concept for capturing photos,
music, video and other digital
information – a prediction of
how digital media technologies
may evolve within a decade
2005
Client: self-generated concept

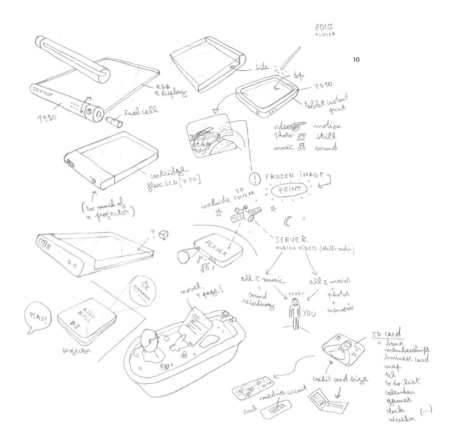

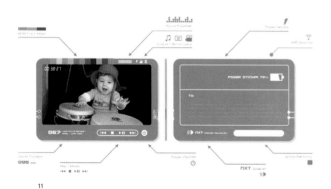

13

14

13–14
ULTRA II SD PLUS
Postage-stamp sized flash
memory card that plugs directly
into a USB slot without cables
or other gear
2005
Client: SanDisk

LUNAR DESIGN
541 Eighth Street
San Francisco
California 94103
USA
T +1 415 2524388
E talk@lunar.com
www.lunar.com

FOUNDERS' BIOGRAPHIES
JEFFREY SMITH
1953 Born in Springfield,
Illinois
1973–1977 Industrial Design,
University of Illinois
1978–1983 Project Manager,
GVO, Palo Alto, CA
1983–1984 Founding Principal,
Interform, Menlo Park, CA
1984 Co-founded Lunar
Design, Palo Alto, CA

GERARD FURBERSHAW
1952 Born in New York City,
New York
1970–1974 BS Architecture,
University of Southern
California
1977–1980 BS Industrial
Design, San José University

DESIGN GROUP HISTORY
1984 Founded by Jeffrey Smith
and Gerard Furbershaw in San
Francisco Bay Area, USA

1979–1983 Senior Industrial
Designer, GVO, Palo Alto, CA
1983–1984 Co-founded Interform, Menlo Park, CA
1984 Co-founded Lunar
Design, Palo Alto, CA

RECENT EXHIBITIONS
2003 "Inspiration + Perspira-
tion: Designed for Sports", San
Francisco Design Museum;
"National Design Triennial:
Inside Design Now", Cooper-
Hewitt National Design Muse-
um, New York; "37th Annual
Kite Festival – 100 Years of
Flight Exhibition", Smithsonian
Institution, Washington DC;
2005 "California Design
Biennial", Pasadena Museum
of California Art; "Fashion In
Motion", CTIA (Cellular
Telecommunications and
Internet Association), Las Vegas
2007 "Bay Area Design",
San Francisco Int. Airport

RECENT AWARDS
2005 Red Dot Award, Design
Zentrum Nordrhein Westfalen,
Essen; 2 x Good Design
Awards, Chicago Athenaeum;
Silver Industrial Design Excel-
lence Award, IDSA (Industrial
Designers Society of America);
USA; Scientistic Invitational
Award, IDSA (Industrial
Designers Society of America);
2 x Design and Engineering
CES Innovation Awards,
CES Consumer Electronics,
Las Vegas
2006 Silver and Bronze Indus-
trial Design Excellence Awards,
(Industrial Designers Society of
America); 4 x Design and
Engineering CES Innovation
Awards, CES Consumer
Electronics, Las Vegas
2007 4 x Design and Engineer-
ing CES Innovation Award,
CES Consumer Electronics, Las
Vegas; iF Award, International

Forum Design Hanover; 2 x
Good Design Awards, Chicago
Athenaeum; Silver and Bronze
Industrial Design Excellence
Awards, IDSA (Industrial
Designers Society of America

CLIENTS
Abbott Laboratories, Accuray,
Acuson, Apple Computer,
Becton Dickinson, BioSentient,
CardioVention, Cisco Systems,
Clorox, Dell, Farallon Medical,
Hamilton, Hewlett-Packard,
InFocus, Intel,
Johnson & Johnson/Lifescan,
Kimberly-Clark, LeapFrog,
Lumenis, Microsoft, Motorola,
Nike, Nova Cruz, Novint,
Oral-B, Palm, PepsiCo,
Polaroid, SanDisk, Segate,
SGI, Sony, Sun Microsystems,
Sunrise Medical, Vulcan, Xerox,
Yocum Photography

MARINE CURRENT TURBINES

"Our approach to design seeks innovative solutions based when possible on tried and tested components proven for other, analogous purposes. Marine Current Turbines Ltd is a technology development company that does exactly what it says on the label – we develop turbines for exploiting the kinetic energy in marine currents – that is mainly tidal currents but in some cases ocean currents. Because we are working in an unforgiving environment and seeking to develop entirely new technology, we are very conscious of risk. Therefore while obliged to take a certain amount of risk with elements of our design that are entirely unique, we seek wherever possible to use tried and tested components. For example while the rotor has to be an original novel design the generator it drives can be based on existing submersible generator technology. However even the rotor can use elements of wind turbine design methodology."

„Uns geht es im Design um die Entwicklung innovativer Lösungen, nach Möglichkeit ausgehend von Komponenten, die sich in analogen Anwendungen bereits bewährt haben. Marine Current Turbines Ltd. ist ein Unternehmen für Technologieentwicklung, das genau das tut, was sein Name sagt – wir entwickeln Turbinen zur Nutzung der kinetischen Energie von Meeresströmungen –, das heißt hauptsächlich von Gezeitenströmungen, aber auch von anderen ozeanischen Strömungen. Da wir in einer unerbittlichen Umgebung arbeiten und dabei sind, eine vollkommen neue Technologie zu entwickeln, sind wir sehr risikobewusst. Wir können es zwar nicht vermeiden, mit dem Einsatz der von uns selbst entwickelten, absolut einzigartigen Elemente ein gewisses Risiko einzugehen, verwenden aber erprobte Komponenten, wo immer sich die Möglichkeit dazu bietet. Während zum Beispiel die Neuentwicklung des Rotors unerlässlich ist, kann beim Generator, den der Rotor betreibt, auf die vorhandene Unterwassergeneratoren-Technologie zurückgegriffen werden. Aber auch beim Rotor können Elemente aus dem Design von Windkraftanlagen verwendet werden."

«Notre approche du design est une recherche de solutions innovantes fondées si possible sur des composants éprouvés et testés dans des situations analogues. La société Marine Current Turbines est une entreprise de développement technologique qui fait exactement ce qu'elle annonce – nous concevons des turbines pour l'exploitation de l'énergie cinétique des courants marins – c'est-à-dire principalement les marées mais parfois aussi les courants océaniques. Parce que nous travaillons dans un environnement impitoyable et tentons de développer des technologies entièrement nouvelles, nous sommes très conscients du risque que nous courons. C'est pourquoi, bien que nous soyons obligés de prendre certains risques avec des éléments de notre design qui sont totalement uniques, nous essayons autant que possible d'utiliser des composants testés et certifiés. Un exemple : si le rotor doit être à chaque fois une pièce unique, le générateur qui l'alimente peut être construit avec la technologie existante en matière de générateurs submersibles. Le rotor peut d'ailleurs lui aussi comporter des éléments hérités de l'énergie éolienne.»

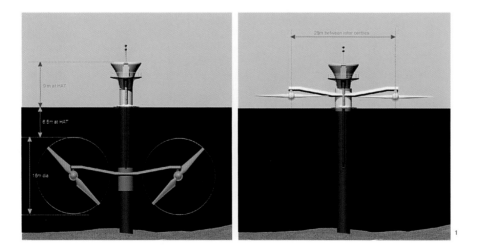

1
SEAGEN
Dimensioned drawing
of 1.2 MW tidal turbine
2006

2
SEAGEN
Computer rendering of
1.2 MW twin-rotor tidal turbine
2006

1–4/7
SEAGEN 1.2MW TIDAL TURBINE, 2006

"The Seagen 1.2MW tidal turbine system consists of twin rotors and power trains mounted on wing-like extensions either side of a monopile. The wing-like extensions form what is called the 'cross-arm', a continuous streamlined beam which surrounds a collar that fits concentrically around the pile and can be raised to slide up the pile so that the complete cross-arm and the rotors and powertrains at its tips can be positioned above sea level so as to allow ready access for maintenance purposes. This basic concept has been patented by MCT and we believe it represents possibly the most cost-effective and efficient means to extract energy from tidal flows."

„Das 1,2-MW-Gezeitenturbinensystem Seagen besteht aus zwei Rotoren und Generatoren auf flügelähnlichen Auslegern zu beiden Seiten eines Monopile genannten Pfeiler. Die Ausleger bilden den sogenannten Querarm, einen durchgehenden stromlinienförmigen Balken, der an einem Ring um den Pfeiler befestigt ist und entlang dem Pfeiler nach oben bewegt werden kann, sodass der gesamte Querarm mit den beiden Rotoren und Generatoren über den Wasserspiegel angehoben und für Wartungsarbeiten freigelegt werden kann. MCT hat dieses Grundkonzept patentieren lassen, und wir halten es für das kosteneffektivste und effizienteste System für die Energiegewinnung aus Gezeitenströmungen."

« Le système de turbine à marée Seagen 1.2 MW est constitué de rotors jumeaux et de trains de puissance montés sur des extensions aux allures d'ailes de part et d'autre d'un pilotis unique. Les ailes forment ce qu'on appelle le ‹ bras en croix ›, un barrot aérodynamique continu qui entoure un col qui vient s'encastrer concentriquement au pilotis et peut être surélevé afin que l'ensemble rotors-trains puisse glisser le long du pilotis jusqu'à dépasser le niveau de la mer et faciliter la maintenance du système. Ce concept fondamental a été breveté par MCT et nous pensons qu'il pourrait représenter le moyen le plus économique et efficace d'extraire de l'énergie des flux marins. »

3

"Running with the tide of renewable energy"

3
SEAGEN
Completed support pile for 1.2MW tidal turbine
2006

4
SEAGEN
Superstructure of 1.2MW tidal turbine under construction
2006

5–6
SEAFLOW
The world's first truly offshore tidal turbine (300kW) installed off Lynmouth in Devon, England
2003

7
SEAGEN
Computer rendering of 1.2MW tidal turbine superstructure
2006

4

5

6

MARINE CURRENT TURBINES

The Court
The Green
Stoke Gifford
Bristol BS34 8PD
United Kingdom
T +44 117 9791888
E info@marineturbines.com
www.marineturbines.com

COMPANY HISTORY

2000 Founded as an independent entity by Peter Fraenkel (b. 1942) and the company operated on a consultancy basis until the first full financing round when it was joined by Martin Wright in 2002.

RECENT EXHIBITIONS

2005 "Energy Ocean 2005", Washington DC
2006 "World Maritime Technology Conference & Exhibition", London; "Third Annual Wales Renewable Energy Conference", Cardiff

RECENT AWARDS

2005 Development grant from the UK Department of Trade and Industry

CLIENTS

EDF Energy (UK subsidiary of Electricité de France)

MARMOL
RADZINER PREFAB

"Marmol Radziner Prefab combines the efficiency of factory-built homes with the benefits of custom residential design. Our green homes are not a kit of parts – we build the prefab modules in our own factory and ship them complete with pre-installed interior and exterior finishes, flooring, appliances, and more. We can oversee the entire process, from design to delivery and installation, so no additional contractor is required. We create our prefab homes with the environment in mind and have designed them to achieve LEED certification. Through precise cutting and the ability to reuse and recycle excess materials, factory production reduces the vast majority of the waste associated with the traditional site-built construction process. Centralizing trades also minimizes vehicular emissions from travel to construction sites. For long-term sustainability, the module structures are made from recycled steel. The homes employ other green materials, such as Structural Insulated Panels (SIPs), FSC-certified wood, low VOC Green Seal paint, and solar panels. At the same time, floor-to-ceiling windows capture natural light, while expansive decks provide shade for passive cooling and promote the best of indoor/outdoor living."

„Marmol Radziner Prefab kombiniert die Effizienz fabrikfertiger Wohnhäuser mit den Vorteilen einer kundenspezifischen Wohnraumgestaltung. Unsere umweltfreundlichen Häuser sind keine Modellbaukästen. Vielmehr konstruieren wir die vorgefertigten Module in unserer eigenen Fabrik und liefern sie komplett mit ausgearbeiteten Innen- und Außenflächen, Fußbodenbelag, Haushaltsgeräten und mehr aus. Wir beaufsichtigen den gesamten Ablauf, vom Entwurf bis zur Lieferung und Installation. Daher ist kein zusätzliches Bauunternehmen erforderlich. Wir gestalten unsere Fertighäuser unter Einbeziehung ihrer Umgebung und haben sie so konzipiert, dass sie die LEED-Zertifizierung erhalten können. Durch präzises Zuschneiden und die Möglichkeit, überschüssige Materialien wiederzuverwerten oder zu recyceln, wird der Abfall in hohem Maß reduziert. Außerdem werden durch die Zentralisierung des Zuliefererverkehrs Fahrzeugabgase verringert. Die Modulkonstruktionen aus recyceltem Stahl sorgen für eine größere Nachhaltigkeit. Auch andere ökologische Materialien kommen bei den Wohnhäusern zum Einsatz, wie etwa Dämmplatten, FSC-zertifiziertes Holz, umweltfreundliche Lacke und Anstrichfarben sowie Solarzellen. Gleichzeitig fangen raumhohe Fenster das natürliche Licht ein, während große Balkonflächen für Schatten und Kühlung sorgen."

«Marmol Radziner Prefab combine efficacité les maisons préfabriquées et les avantages d'une architecture intérieure personnalisée. Nos maisons écologiques ne sont pas proposées en kit – nous construisons les modules préfabriqués dans notre propre usine et nous les expédions complets, avec les finitions extérieures et intérieures, revêtements de sol et autres éléments de décor pré-installés. Nous pouvons superviser l'ensemble de la chaîne de réalisation, de la conception à la livraison et à l'installation, afin qu'aucun autre intervenant ne soit nécessaire. Nous créons nos maisons préfabriquées avec un souci constant de préservation de l'environnement et veillons à ce qu'elles bénéficient du label LEED (Leadership in Energy and Environmental Design). Grâce à une découpe précise et à la possibilité de recycler et de réutiliser les chutes, notre chaîne de production réduit drastiquement la quantité de déchets par rapport aux techniques habituelles de construction in situ. Centraliser les activités minimise aussi la pollution liée au transport routier vers et depuis les sites de fabrication. Pour une durabilité à long terme, les structures du module sont composées d'acier recyclé. Nos maisons emploient d'autres matériaux écologiques, comme les panneaux de construction isolants (SIP), le bois certifié FSC, la peinture Green Seal à faible concentration en COV, et des panneaux solaires. Dans le même temps, les fenêtres qui s'étirent du sol au plafond capturent la lumière naturelle tandis que de vastes terrasses couvertes procurent une ombre reposante, pour créer les meilleures conditions de vie mêlant intérieur et extérieur.»

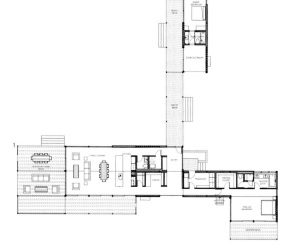

1
UTAH HOUSE 1
Floor plans of 2500 interior sq. ft./1720 deck sq. ft. prefabricated house
2006

2
UTAH HOUSE 1
2500 interior sq. ft./1720 deck sq. ft. two-bedroom, two-bathroom prefabricated house in Moab, Utah, with drawings of elevations
2006

UTAH HOUSE 1 MOAB,
UTAH, 2006

Designed for an active couple as
a vacation home, Utah House 1
celebrates nature through its
careful siting, emphasis on
indoor/outdoor living and integration of sustainable design.
Utah House 1 sits on an open,
hundred-acre site punctuated by
red rock formations and cliffs in
the arid desert of Moab, Utah.
The two-bedroom, two-bath
2500 sq. ft. home comprises five
interior and seven deck modules

and was entirely fabricated in
Marmol Radziner Prefab's own
factory. The home can be
shipped to a site complete with
pre-installed windows, doors,
cabinets, solar panels, appliances
and other interior and exterior
finishes.

Für ein aktives Paar als Ferien-
domizil konzipiert, erweist das
Utah House 1 der Natur Re-
verenz, indem seine Lage mit
Bedacht gewählt, besonderer
Akzent auf das Wohnen drinnen
und draußen gelegt und auf
umweltverträgliches Design

geachtet wurde. Das Utah
House 1 sitzt auf einem offenen,
von roten Felsen und Klippen
geprägten 40 ha großen Grundstück in der trockenen Moab-
Wüste in Utah. Das 230 qm
große Haus mit zwei Schlafzim-
mern und zwei Badezimmern
besteht aus fünf Innenraum-
und sieben Terrassen-Modulen
und wurde zur Gänze in der
Fabrik Marmol Radziner Prefab
vorgefertigt. Es kann komplett
mit eingebauten Fenstern,
Türen, Schränken, Sonnen-
kollektoren, Hauhaltsgeräten
und speziell ausgearbeiteten

Innen- und Außenflächen zum
jeweiligen Grundstück transportiert werden.

Conçue pour être la maison de
vacances d'un couple actif, la
Utah House 1 célèbre la nature
par son emplacement, l'accent
mis sur la vie en intérieur et en
extérieur, et l'intégration du
concept de design durable. La
Utah House 1 est posée sur un
vaste terrain ouvert de quarante
hectares ponctué de formations
et de falaises de roche rouge
dans le désert de Moab (Utah).
La maison de 760 m², dotée de

deux chambres et de deux salles
de bain, se compose de cinq
modules intérieurs et sept
modules en terrasses et a été
intégralement fabriquée dans
l'usine de Marmol Radziner
Prefab. Elle peut être livrée jusqu'à son terrain d'adoption totalement finie, ses fenêtres,
portes, rangements, panneaux
solaires, appareils électriques et
autres finitions intérieures et
extérieures pré-installées.

7

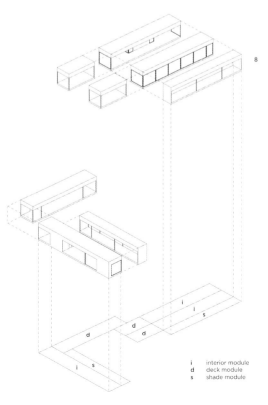

8

3–6
UTAH HOUSE 1
Construction process of 2500
interior sq. ft./1720 deck sq. ft.
two-bedroom, two-bathroom
prefabricated house in Moab,
Utah
2006

7
DESERT HOUSE
2100 interior sq. ft./2450 deck
sq. ft. two-bedroom,
two-bathroom prefabricated
house comprising four house
modules and six deck modules,
designed for principal
Leo Marmol and installed in
Desert Hot Springs, California
2004

8
DESERT HOUSE
Axonometric drawing of 2100
interior sq. ft./2450 deck sq. ft.
prefabricated house
2004

i   interior module
d   deck module
s   shade module

347

9
DESERT HOUSE
View of prefabricated
steel-framed deck and interior
modules of house: each module
is 12 ft. wide and can extend
up to 64 ft. in length
2004

10–12
MODEL 1
Views of 660 interior sq. ft./
360 deck sq. ft. one-bedroom,
one-bathroom prefabricated
house comprising one interior
module and one deck module
2005

13–15

MODEL 5

Views and floor plan of 1960 interior sq. ft./360 deck sq. ft. three-bedroom, three-bathroom prefabricated house comprising six interior/exterior deck modules

2005

MARMOL RADZINER PREFAB

12210 Nebraska Avenue
Los Angeles
California 90025
USA
T +1 310 6890089
info@marmolradzinerprefab.com
www.marmolradzinerprefab.com

COMPANY HISTORY

1989 Design-build architecture firm founded by Leo Marmol, FAIA, and Ron Radziner, FAIA in Los Angeles
1996 The firm began expanding its expertise to include prefabricated steel-frame construction in commercial projects
2005 The firm completed the first residential project made with prefabricated modules, the Desert House, located outside of Palm Springs, California
2006 The firm expanded its in-house cabinet and metal shops into a 65,000 square-foot factory for the production of prefab homes

FOUNDERS' BIOGRAPHIES
LEO MARMOL

1961 Born in Los Angeles
1987 Graduated from California Polytechnic State University – San Luis Obispo with a Bachelor of Architecture and Minor in Philosophy
1989 Founded Marmol Radziner + Associates

RON RADZINER

1960 Born in Los Angeles
1984 Graduates from California Polytechnic State University – San Luis Obispo with a Bachelor of Science in Engineering
1986 Master of Arts in Architecture, University of Colorado
1989 Founded Marmol Radziner + Associates

RECENT EXHIBITIONS

2006 "Some Assembly Required: Contemporary Prefabricated Houses," Walker Art Center (Minneapolis), Vancouver Art Gallery, Yale Art + Architecture Gallery, Los Angeles Museum of Contemporary Art, and National Building Museum (Washington DC); "Design-Build: Marmol Radziner + Associates," Rhode Island School of Design, Providence, Rhode Island

RECENT AWARDS

2006 Silver Award for Environments – IDEA (Industrial Design Excellence Awards), Industrial Designers Society of America/BusinessWeek; Design Honor Award, American Institute of Architects, Los Angeles; Merit Award, American Institute of Architects, Inland California Chapter; Honorable Mention, Magazine Annual Design Review, I.D. Magazine

"The building industry is very wasteful,
so we are working to create natural, modern homes
with a minimal environmental footprint."

16
CALIFORNIA HOUSE 3
3335 interior sq. ft./825 deck
sq. ft. three-bedroom,
three-bathroom prefabricated
house comprising eight interior/
exterior deck modules in Palm
Springs, California
2005

17
CALIFORNIA HOUSE 1
3200 interior sq. ft./1370 deck
sq. ft. three-bedroom,
two-bathroom prefabricated
house comprising ten interior/
exterior deck modules in
Malibu, California
2005

JEAN-MARIE MASSAUD

"My ambition is to propose brands, objects, architecture and scenarios that could influence our consumption pattern in a positive way. Groundbreaking and indispensable, these proposals aim at reconciling our desires with our responsibility as human beings. The goal is no longer to obtain appearance, status or simple possession. Instead, I aim to create a life experience that is fulfilling for the individual and that encompasses responsibility for the collectivity in harmony with our ecosystem. In contrast to the unavoidability of quantitative growth, this means a symbiosis between man, his creations and the environment, a symbiosis that I ceaselessly force myself to obtain, as a motor of innovation, an economic model and a life project. My approach as a designer is thus committed to the proposal of desirable and responsible projects in the service of life, *a human innovation*."

„Ich habe den Ehrgeiz, Marken, Objekte, Architektur und Szenarios vorzulegen, die unsere Konsumgewohnheiten positiv beeinflussen könnten. Diese neuartigen und dringend notwendigen Vorschläge verfolgen das Ziel, unsere Wünsche wieder in Einklang mit unserer Verantwortung als Menschen zu bringen. Es geht nicht mehr um Wirkung, Status oder einfach nur Besitz. Stattdessen möchte ich eine Lebenserfahrung ermöglichen, die für das Individuum erfüllend ist und der Verantwortung für die Gesamtheit in Harmonie mit unserem Ökosystem Rechnung trägt. Im Gegensatz zur Unvermeidbarkeit des quantitativen Wachstums bedeutet dies eine Symbiose zwischen dem Menschen, seinen Werken und der Umwelt, eine Symbiose, die ich mich bei allem zu erreichen zwinge, als Motor für Innovation, als Wirtschaftsmodell und als Lebensprojekt. Meine Haltung als Designer ist folglich der Entwicklung von sinnvollen und verantwortungsvollen Projekten im Dienste des Lebens, das heißt *einer humanen Innovation* verpflichtet."

«Mon ambition est de proposer des marques, des objets, une architecture et des scénarios qui puissent influencer nos schémas de consommation de façon positive. Révolutionnaires et indispensables, ces propositions ont pour but la réconciliation entre nos désirs et notre responsabilité d'êtres humains. L'objectif n'est plus d'obtenir l'apparence, le statut ou la simple possession. Je cherche au contraire à créer une expérience de vie qui comble l'individu et prenne en compte la collectivité, en harmonie avec notre écosystème. À la différence du caractère implacable de la croissance quantitative, cela signifie une symbiose entre l'homme, ses créations et l'environnement, une symbiose que je tente d'obtenir sans relâche, comme le moteur de l'innovation, un modèle économique et un projet de vie. Ma démarche de designer est ainsi vouée à la conception de projets utiles et responsables au service de la vie, *une innovation humaine*.»

1

3

1–6
MANNED CLOUD CRUISE
AIRSHIP CONCEPT FOR
ONERA, 2005

"Manned Cloud is an alternative project about leisure and travelling in all its forms, economic and experimental, with lightness, human experience and life scenarios being the guiding principles. The spiral of Archimedes is the driving force behind the airship, which takes the form of a whale gliding through the air. Manned Cloud is a hotel with 60 rooms and staffed by 150 people, which on a 3-day cruise at 170 km/h permits the exploration of the world without a trace: to re-experience travelling, timelessness and enhance the consciousness of the beauty of the world – and to experience spectacular and exotic places without being intrusive or exploitative. For me this project sums up a way of thinking that is crucial for tomorrow."

„Manned Cloud ist ein alternatives Projekt, das von Freizeit und Reisen in allen Formen handelt, dabei wirtschaftlich und experimentell ist und den Leitprinzipien Leichtigkeit und Gestaltung von menschlichen Erfahrungs- und Lebenswelten folgt. Die Formgebung des Luftschiffs, das wie ein durch die Luft gleitender Walfisch aussieht, ist bestimmt von der archimedischen Spirale. Manned Cloud ist ein Hotel mit 60 Zimmern, das zudem Platz für 150 Mitarbeiter hat. Bei 170 km/h kann man damit auf einer Dreitagesreise die Welt erkunden, ohne Spuren in ihr zu hinterlassen: Das bedeutet eine neue Reiseerfahrung, Zeitlosigkeit und bewussteres Wahrnehmen der Schönheit unserer Welt – und man kann spektakuläre, exotische Orte kennenlernen, ohne die Natur zu berühren oder zu beeinträchtigen. Für mich fasst dieses Projekt eine Einstellung zusammen, die für unsere Zukunft unumgänglich ist."

« Manned Cloud est un projet alternatif centré sur les loisirs et le voyage sous toutes ses formes, économique et expérimental, guidé par l'idée de légèreté, l'expérience humaine et les possibilités qu'offre la vie. Le dirigeable se meut par la force d'Archimède comme une baleine qui flotterait dans les airs. Manned Cloud est un hôtel de 60 chambres, où travaillent 150 personnes, qui partira pour des voyages de trois jours à 170 km/h au cours desquels les passagers pourront savourer le plaisir de découvrir le monde sans y laisser de traces, une nouvelle expérience du voyage, hors du temps, pour mieux prendre conscience de la beauté du monde, découvrir des lieux spectaculaires et exotiques sans intrusion ni exploitation. Pour moi, ce projet résume une façon de penser qui est capitale pour l'avenir. »

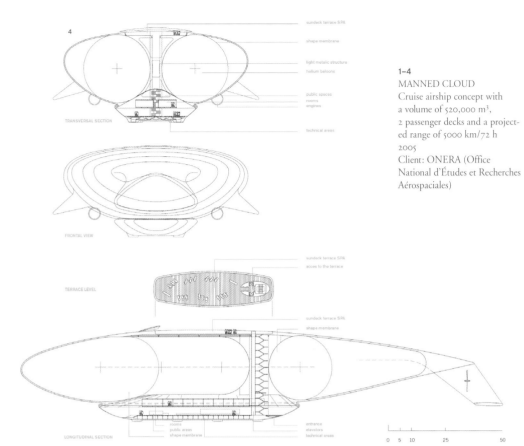

4

sundeck terrace SPA
shape membrane
light metallic structure
helium balloons
public spaces
rooms
engines
technical areas

TRANSVERSAL SECTION

FRONTAL VIEW

TERRACE LEVEL

sundeck terrace SPA
acces to the terrace

sundeck terrace SPA
shape membrane

LONGITUDINAL SECTION

rooms
public areas
shape membrane

entrance
elevators
technical areas

0 5 10   25   50

1–4
MANNED CLOUD
Cruise airship concept with
a volume of 520,000 m³,
2 passenger decks and a project-
ed range of 5000 km/72 h
2005
Client: ONERA (Office
National d'Études et Recherches
Aérospaciales)

5

6

5–6
MANNED CLOUD
Lounge interior of Cruise airship
concept
2005
Client: ONERA (Office
National d'Études et Recherches
Aérospaciales)

7

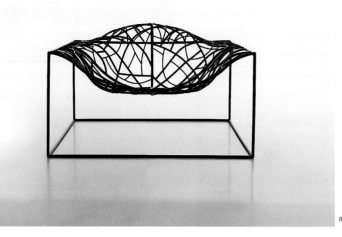

8

7–8
AD HOC
Armchair in enamelled steel
2007
Client: Viccarbe

9
MISSED TREE I AND II
Plant pots, one formed of a
single body and the other with
a branching element, made
of moulded polyethylene with
brushed steel bases
2007
Client: Serralunga

10
ASTON
Lounge chair and matching
ottoman with polyurethane
foam upholstery and swivell
pedestal bases in polished
or painted aluminium
2006
Client: Arper

9

"Create human fulfilment,
sense and harmony with our world."

10

11–14
AXOR MASSAUD
New generation water faucet
system for baths, showers and
washbasins
2006
Client: Hansgrohe

12

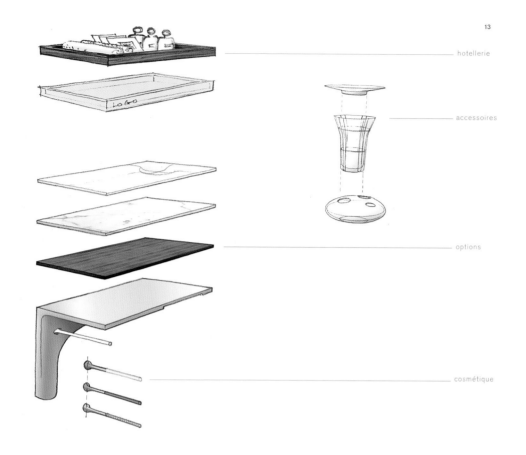

hotellerie

accessoires

options

cosmétique

15
VOLCANO STADIUM
45,000 seat, 130,000 m² football
stadium for the Chivas team in
Guadalajara, Mexico
2003–07
Client: Omnilife

16–19
VOLCANO STADIUM
Main entrance, plan view,
plan and elevation drawings
of football stadium
2003–07
Client: Omnilife

JEAN-MARIE MASSAUD
Studio Massaud
7, rue Tolain
75020 Paris
France
T +33 1 40095414
E studio@massaud.com
www.massaud.com

BIOGRAPHY
1966 Born in Toulouse, France
1985–1990 Studied Industrial
Design at ENSCI (École
Nationale Supérieure de
Création Industrielle), Paris
1991–1995 Collaborator and
associate at Marc Berthier's
Design Plan Studio (design,
urbanism and architecture)
1995 Received Carte Blanche
Scholarship, VIA Paris
2000 Co-founded with Daniel
Pouzet Studio Massaud in Paris

RECENT EXHIBITIONS
2005 "Human Nature", Time &
Style Existence Gallery, Tokyo
2007 "Massaud", Galerie VIA,
Paris

RECENT AWARDS
2001 Étoile APCI Observeur
du Design, Agence pour la
promotion de la création
industrielle, Paris
2002 Talents du Luxe award,
Paris
2004 APCI Observeur du
Design award, Agence pour
la promotion de la création
industrielle, Paris

2005 Designer de l'année,
Elle Décoration, France;
Best Eco Design,
Design Tide/AP Bank, Tokyo
2006 Elle Décoration Awards,
France and Italy; Designer of
the Year, Elle Decoration, Spain;
iF Award, International Forum
Design Hanover; APCI
Observeur du Design award,
Agence pour la promotion de
la création industrielle, Paris;
2007 Best Bed Award,
Elle Décoration International;
Best Sofa Award, The Wallpaper
Design Awards, UK; Créateur
de l'année, Salon du Meuble,
Paris

CLIENTS
Armani, Arper, Axor, Baccara,
B&B Italia, Cacharel,
Cappellini, Cassina, De Vecchi,
Dornbracht, E&Y, EMU,
Glas Italia, Habitat, Lancôme,
Lanvin, Lexon, Ligne Roset,
Liv'It, Magis, Mazzega,
Mizuno, Offecct,
Paloma Picasso, Poltrona Frau,
Porro, Serralunga, Time & Style,
Tronconi, Yamaha Offshore,
Väveriet, Yves Saint Laurent

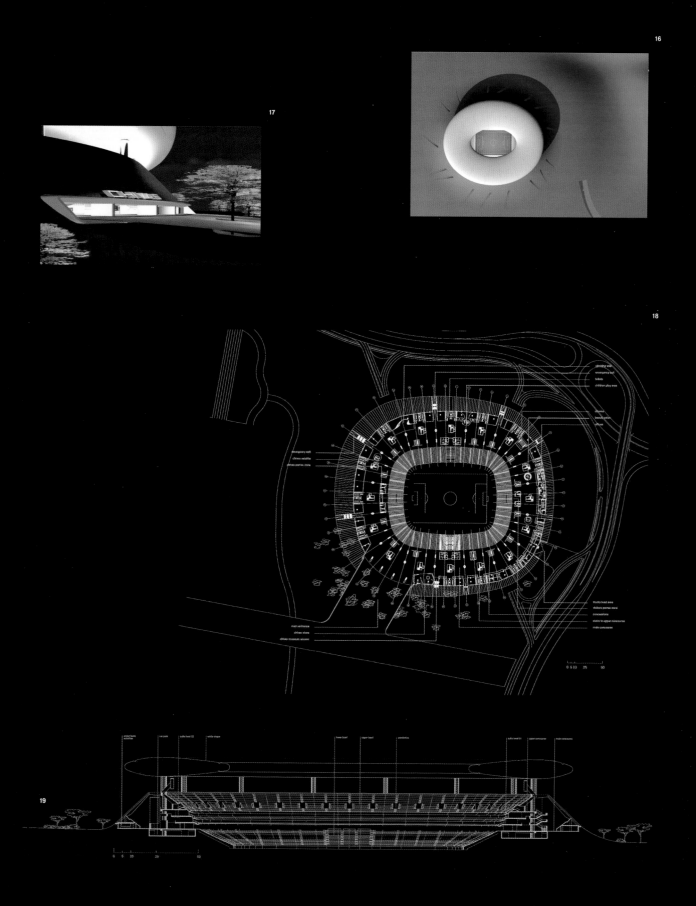

FREDRIK MATTSON

"Designing products is very much like raising kids. If you give them love and affection they will grow up to be strong, lovely persons with self-confidence. But if you treat them badly and without attention, you will end up with insecure and nervous kids. I try to raise my products with a lot of love and respect. I like them to be nice, not too loud, since I like to hang out with them for a long time."

„Produkte gestalten ist wie Kinder erziehen. Wenn man ihnen Liebe und Aufmerksamkeit schenkt, werden sie zu starken, angenehmen, selbstbewussten Menschen heranwachsen. Wenn man sie hingegen schlecht und nicht fürsorglich genug behandelt, hat man schließlich unsichere und nervöse Kinder. Ich bemühe mich, meine Produkte mit viel Liebe und Respekt entstehen zu lassen. Ich mag es, wenn sie nett und nicht zu laut sind, weil ich gern lange mit ihnen zusammen bin."

«Créer des produits a bien des choses en commun avec élever des enfants. Si vous leur donnez amour et affection, ils grandiront pour devenir des personnes fortes et agréables ayant confiance en elles. Mais si vous les traitez mal ou ne faites pas attention à eux, vous vous retrouverez avec des gamins angoissés et nerveux. J'essaie d'élever mes produits avec amour et respect. J'aime qu'ils soient sympathiques et pas trop bruyants, parce que j'aime passer beaucoup de temps avec eux.»

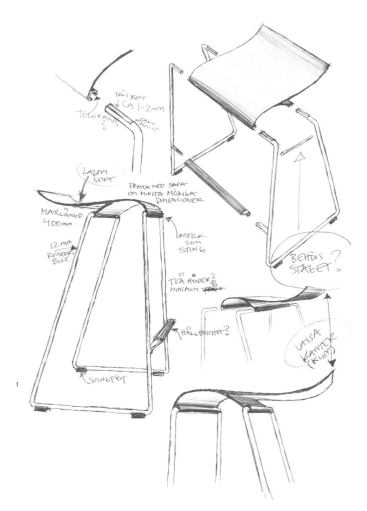

1–2
GECCO
Stackable barstool with anodized extruded aluminium seat and footrest, and stainless-steel legs (designed with Stefan Borselius)
2006
Client: Blå Station

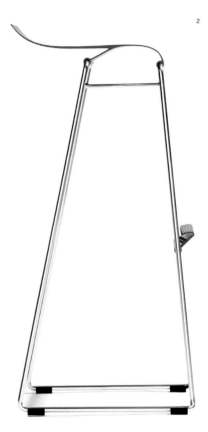

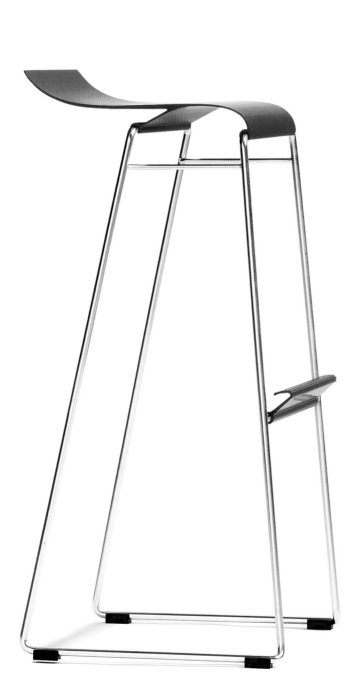

3

4

3–6
CHAIR 69
Stackable and linkable side chair
with single-form seat shell in
compression-moulded plywood
and legs in chromed tubular steel
2005
Client: Blå Station

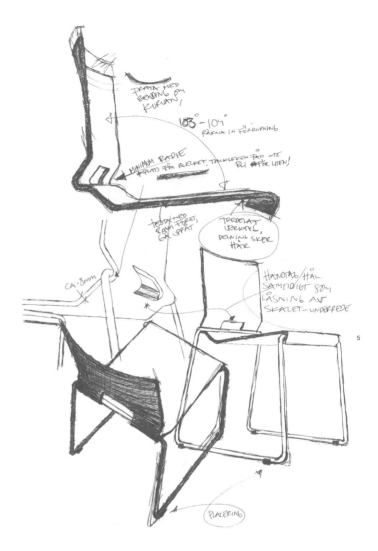

FREDRIK MATTSON
Fredrik Mattson Design
Stora Skuggans Väg 11
11542 Stockholm
Sweden
T +46 709 704354
E info@fredrikmattson.se
www.fredrikmattson.se

BIOGRAPHY

1973 Born in Malmö, Sweden
1995–1997 Studied Cabinet-making at FHS (Folkhögskola), Grebbestad
1997–2000 Studied Furniture Design at Stenebyskolan, Steneby
2000–2002 Studied Interior Architecture at Konstfack, Stockholm
2002 Founded own design studio Fredrik Mattson Design in Stockholm

RECENT EXHIBITIONS

2003 "Stockholm furniture fair", Stockholm; "Svezia Light", Palazzo Isimbardi, Milan; "Salone Del Mobile", Milan
2004 "Design in Sweden", Museum of London, London; "Stockholm Furniture Fair", Stockholm; "Salone del Mobile", Milan; Galerie Pascale Cottard-Olsson, Stockholm
2005 "40/4 forty years of forty/four", Svensk Form, Stockholm; "5 stolar", Galerie Pascale Cottard-Olsson, Stockholm; "H55/05 Allrum", Helsingborg, Sweden; "Salone Del Mobile", Milan; "Stockholm furniture fair", Stockholm; "Spectrum", London; "Made in Malmö", Form Design Center, Malmö, Sweden; "Vardagsrum", Helsingborg, Sweden; "Swedish Style", TownHouse 12, Milan
2006 "Allrum", Hotel de Ville, Paris; "Still Underground", Mornington Hotel, Stockholm; "Fjäll", Galerie Pascale Cottard-Olsson, Stockholm; "Salone del Mobile", Milan;
2007 "Stockholm furniture fair", Stockholm; Chairs, Furniture Fair Paris at VIA's stand, Paris

RECENT AWARDS

2002 Den Nordiska första St Johannis Logens Jubelfond, Sweden; Young Swedish Design Award, Svenska Form, Sweden
2003 Winner of the Elle Decoration International Design Award (EDIDA), Sweden; Architectural Review Award, London; Guldstolen (Golden chair) award, Sveriges Arkitekter (Swedish Association of Architects)
2004 Red Dot Award – "best of the best", Design Zentrum Nordrhein Westfalen, Essen, Germany; Architectural Review Award, London; Product of the year, Sköna Hem, Sweden; Nomination, FutureDesignDays Award, Sweden
2005 Forsnäsprize, Sweden; Pagrotskyrummet, Sweden
2006 Design S award, Sweden Design Award, Stockholm
2007 Red Dot Award, Design Zentrum Nordrhein Westfalen, Essen, Germany

CLIENTS

Atelje Lyktan, Blå Station, Brio, Gallery Pascal, PP Møbler, ZERO

7–9
FATBACK
Linkable easy chair and sectional sofa with fabric or leather-covered moulded polyurethane upholstery, an inner frame of steel and wood, and chromed steel legs
2006
Client: Blå Station

7

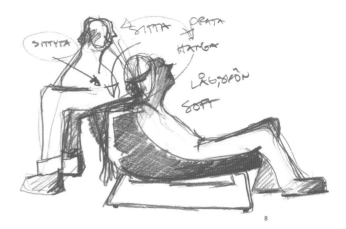

8

"Evolution,
Love
and Revolution"

9

INGO MAURER

"The most important factor in my work is the human being. Light is a service, it needs to match those who live and work with it. I hope that people enjoy my lights, that they feel better with my lamps. The emotional aspect of light, its influence on our feelings is so powerful, yet often disregarded. Design should not be placed on a pedestal, being misused just for the sake of one's ego. I try to create opportunities for the users, to participate whenever possible in the final design of my products. I think that is true not only of lighting but all product designs. Seen from the other side, the human being matters to me, too. One should feel the person behind the design. Spontaneity, a certain imperfection in contrast to slickness and flawlessness, an attitude neither rigid nor prim – that's what it is all about. Function? Yes, a product has to work well. Otherwise it's not really enjoyable. New technical developments provide solutions for previously unrealizable dreams; they constantly spark my interest and imagination – last but not least in the aesthetical sense. Still, the most beautiful light is the one coming from human hearts!"

„Der wichtigste Faktor bei meiner Arbeit ist der Mensch. Licht ist eine Hilfe, es muss den Menschen entsprechen, die damit leben und arbeiten. Ich hoffe, dass die Menschen meine Leuchten mögen und sich damit wohler fühlen. Der emotionale Aspekt von Licht, sein Einfluss auf unsere Gefühle ist so gewaltig und bleibt trotzdem oft unbeachtet. Design sollte nicht auf ein Podest gestellt und nur für das eigene Ego missbraucht werden. Ich versuche, den Benutzern die Chance einzuräumen, nach Möglichkeit am endgültigen Design meiner Produkte teilzuhaben. Das gilt, glaube ich, nicht nur für meine Leuchten, sondern für alle Produktdesigns. Umgekehrt ist mir auch der Mensch wichtig. Man sollte den Menschen hinter dem Design spüren. Spontaneität, eine gewisse Unvollkommenheit im Gegensatz zu Glätte und Makellosigkeit, eine Haltung, die weder starr noch steif ist – darum geht es. Funktion? Ja, ein Produkt muss gut funktionieren. Sonst hat man keine rechte Freude daran. Neue technische Entwicklungen liefern Lösungen für bisher unerfüllbare Träume. Sie stacheln ständig mein Interesse und meine Fantasie an – nicht zuletzt im ästhetischen Sinn. Dennoch, das schönste Licht leuchtet aus den Herzen der Menschen!"

« L'aspect le plus important de mon travail est l'être humain. La lumière est un service, qui se doit de répondre aux attentes de ceux qui vivent et travaillent avec elle. J'espère que les gens apprécient mes luminaires, qu'ils se sentent mieux grâce à eux. Le côté émotionnel de la lumière, la manière dont elle influe sur nos sentiments, est très puissant et pourtant souvent sous-estimé. Le design ne devrait pas être placé sur un piédestal ou mal utilisé pour le triomphe de l'ego. J'essaie de créer pour les usagers des occasions de participer, dès que possible, au design final de mes produits. Je pense que ceci ne s'applique pas seulement à la lumière, mais aussi à tous les produits du design. Je me place aussi de l'autre côté de la barrière, car l'être humain compte pour moi. Il faudrait savoir ressentir la personne derrière la création. La spontanéité, une certaine imperfection qui contraste avec le lisse et le sans défaut, une attitude qui n'est ni rigide ni guindée – voilà de quoi il s'agit. L'utile ? Oui, un produit doit bien fonctionner. Sinon il ne donne pas de réelle satisfaction. Les derniers développements techniques apportent des solutions à ce qui n'était jusqu'alors que des rêves irréalisables ; ces avancées attisent constamment ma curiosité et mon imagination – notamment dans un sens esthétique. Mais tout de même, la plus belle lumière, c'est celle qui sort des cœurs humains ! »

1

"Five per cent is the idea,
the rest is the path to the result:
long and exciting, now joyful,
now painful."

1
24 KARAT BLAU
Table and hanging light in
metal, plastic and gold leaf
(designed by Axel Schmid)
2005

2
L'ECLAT JOYEUX
One-off hanging light constructed of broken porcelain
plates and Chinese figurines
2005

3–4
SUSPENDED OLED
Experimental, one-off hanging
light that makes use of OLEDs
(organic light-emitting diodes)
currently being developed by
the German company Merck
2007

3

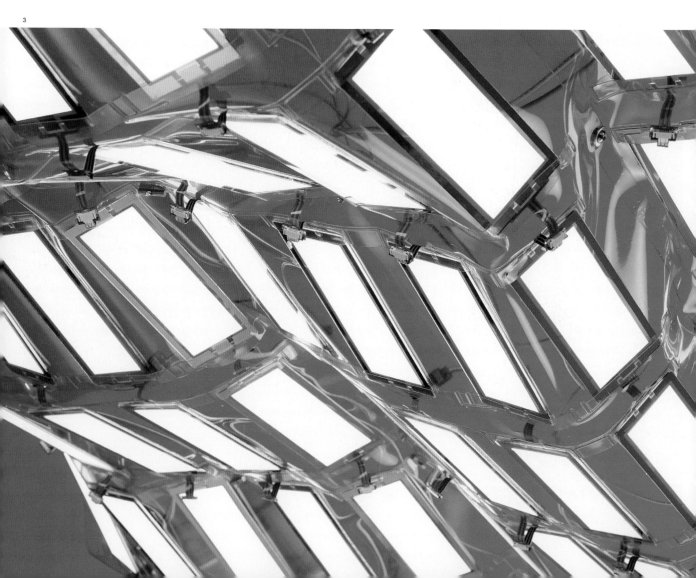

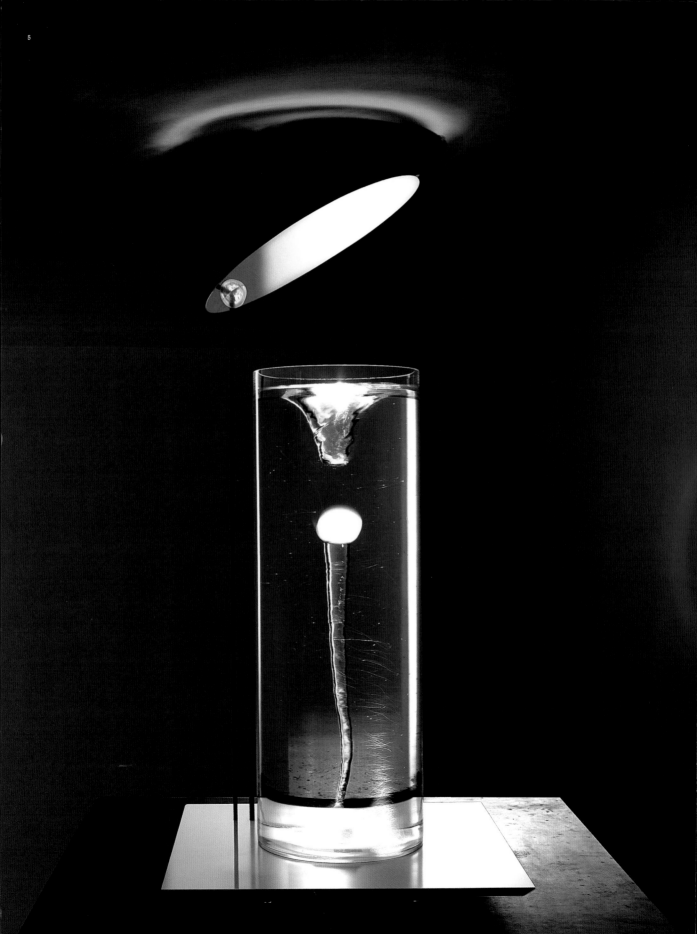

INGO MAURER

Ingo Maurer
Kaiserstraße 47
80801 Munich
Germany
T +49 89 3816060
E info@ingo-maurer.com
www.ingo-maurer.com

BIOGRAPHY

1932 Born on the island of Reichenau, Lake Constance, Germany

pre-1954 Trained as a typographer in Germany and Switzerland

1954–1958 Diploma in graphic design, Munich

1960–1963 Freelance designer, New York City and San Francisco

1963 Returned to Europe and settled in Munich

1966 Founded his own design/manufacturing company, Design M in Munich (later to become Ingo Maurer GmbH)

1986 Elected "Chevalier des arts et des lettres" by the Ministère de la Culture et de la Communication (French Ministry of Culture)

1998 Nominated "Designer of the Year" by Architektur & Wohnen magazine, Hamburg

2005 Elected Royal Designer for Industry, The Royal Society of Arts, London

2006 Doctorate (honoris causa) conferred by the Royal College of Art, London

RECENT EXHIBITIONS

2002–2006 "Ingo Maurer – Light – Reaching for the Moon" – travelling exhibition: Vitra Design Musem, Weil am Rhein; Dansk Design Center, Copenhagen; Beurs van Berlage, Amsterdam; La Grand Hornu, Hornu, Belgium; IVAm, Valencia, Spain; Tsukuba Museum of Art, Ibaraki, Japan; Tokyo Opera City Art Gallery, Tokyo: Sunotry Museum, Osaka, Japan

2004 "Brilliant", Victoria and Albert Museum, London; "Iluminar Design Da Luz 1920-2004", Museu de Arte Brasileira Fundação Armando Alvares Penteado, São Paulo

2006 "Le Mouvement des Images", Centre Georges Pompidou, Paris

RECENT AWARDS

2003 Georg Jensen Prize 2002, Georg Jensen Prize Committee, Denmark; 4th Oribe Award, Design Academy Division, Gifu Prefecture, Japan

2006 5th Abitare Il Tempo prize, Abitare Il Temp Fair, Verona, Italy

7

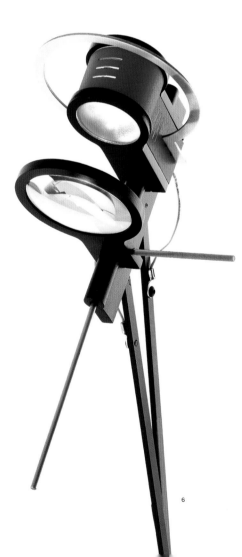

6

5

DELIRIUM YUM
Halogen table light in Corian, crystal glass, carbon fibre and silicon with external transformer – a magnetic field sets the bar on the bottom of the vase in rotation, the movement of which creates a vortex in the water (designed with Sebastian Hepting)
2006

6–7

HOT HOT
Continuously dimmable halogen floor light in steel and aluminium – the cone of the light is adjustable by means of a lens system
2006

ALBERTO MEDA

"The Design Process is not a linear process, it is not possible to plan it, it's a complex activity rather similar to a problem solving process of a reiterative nature, almost chaotic.... back and forth, left and right, guessing, testing, failing, changing, eliminating, finalizing and adding, frequently too late, many omissions.... for that very reason it is so fascinating and mysterious. I am interested personally in the world of technology, because it seems to me to be the contemporary expression of man's imaginative capability, of his ingeniousness fed by his scientific knowledge. Technology widens the scope of knowledge, but it is necessary to understand that technological development must no longer proceed without justification, without worrying about the meaning of its choices. Technology must be tamed in order to realize things that have the simplest possible relation with man, refusing the concept of technology-driven industrial goods without regard for human needs and with no communicative rationality. Technology is not an end in itself, but a means to produce simple things with cultural identity. It contains a paradox: the more technology is complex, the better it can produce objects with a simple, unitary, 'almost organic' image. I feel the necessity to produce things with a recognizable cultural quality, things that make 'sense', in addition to the 'shape', I mean design with a view to making products capable of solving unsolved problems in the direction of simplicity. Simplicity is not banal, it is a solved complexity and it is important to me because man has a biological need for simplicity, which is symmetric with his human complexity."

„Der Designprozess ist kein linearer Prozess, man kann ihn nicht planen, es handelt sich um eine komplexe Tätigkeit, die viel von einem iterativen, fast chaotischen Problemlösungsprozess hat ... hin und her, links und rechts, überlegen, testen, scheitern, verändern, aussortieren, abschließen und ergänzen, oft zu spät, viele Versäumnisse ... genau das macht ihn so faszinierend und geheimnisvoll. Ich selbst interessiere mich für die Welt der Technik, weil sie mir der zeitgemäße Ausdruck der menschlichen Vorstellungskraft und der aus wissenschaftlicher Erkenntnis gespeisten Erfindungsgabe zu sein scheint. Die Technik erweitert unser Wissensspektrum, aber es muss klar sein, dass der technische Fortschritt nicht mehr ohne triftige Gründe und ohne Nachdenken über die Konsequenzen weitergehen kann. Es ist notwendig, die Technik zu bändigen, um Objekte zu verwirklichen, die den denkbar einfachsten Bezug zum Menschen haben. Rein auf technischen Möglichkeiten beruhende Industrieerzeugnisse, die keine Rücksicht auf menschliche Bedürfnisse nehmen und keiner kommunikativen Vernunft folgen, sind abzulehnen. Die Technik ist kein Selbstzweck, sondern ein Mittel zur Herstellung einfacher Dinge mit einer eigenen kulturellen Identität. Aber je komplizierter die Technik, desto besser ist sie paradoxerweise geeignet, Objekte mit einer einfachen, einheitlichen, ‚beinahe organischen' Erscheinungsform zu ermöglichen. Ich halte es für notwendig, Gegenstände mit einer erkennbaren kulturellen Qualität zu erzeugen, Gegenstände, die zusätzlich zur ‚Form' einen ‚Sinn' haben, das heißt, man sollte Produkte so gestalten, dass sie sich zur Lösung ungelöster Probleme im Sinne von Einfachheit eignen. Einfachheit ist nicht banal, sie ist die Lösung von etwas Komplexem, und sie ist mir wichtig, weil der Mensch ein biologisches Bedürfnis nach Einfachheit hat, das symmetrisch zu seiner Komplexität ist."

« Le processus créatif n'est pas linéaire ; il est impossible de planifier cette activité complexe, assez semblable à un processus de résolution de problème, une approche réitérative, presque chaotique... d'avant en arrière, de droite et de gauche, à tâtons, à l'essai, échouer, changer, éliminer, finaliser et ajouter, souvent trop tard, de nombreux oublis... C'est justement pour ces raisons que c'est si fascinant et mystérieux. Personnellement, je m'intéresse au monde de la technologie parce qu'il m'apparaît comme l'expression contemporaine des capacités d'imagination de l'homme, de son ingéniosité nourrie de connaissances scientifiques. La technologie élargit le champ de nos connaissances, mais il est nécessaire de comprendre qu'elle ne doit plus progresser sans justification, sans se soucier de la signification de ses choix. La technologie doit être apprivoisée pour réaliser les choses qui auront le lien le plus simple possible avec l'homme, en refusant le concept de produits industriels induits pas la technologie sans égards pour les besoins humains et sans rationalité dans la communication. La technologie n'est pas une fin en soi, mais un moyen de produire des choses simples dotées d'une identité culturelle. Elle est porteuse d'un paradoxe : plus la technologie est complexe, mieux elle peut produire des objets ayant une image simple, cohérente, ‹ presque organique ›. Je ressens la nécessité de produire des choses qui ont une qualité culturelle reconnaissable, des choses qui ‹ font sens › et pas seulement ‹ forme › ; je considère le design comme une discipline permettant de résoudre les problèmes qui persistent. Qui dit simple ne dit pas banal, mais une complexité résolue et c'est important pour moi parce que l'homme a un besoin physiologique de simplicité, pour faire symétrie avec sa complexité d'homme. »

1–3
SOLAR WATER
DISINFECTION BOTTLE
Portable solar-powered water
disinfection bottle in bi-colour
blown injection-moulded PET
2006
Client: self-generated prototype

1

2

3

SOLAR WATER
DISINFECTION BOTTLE
(DESIGNED WITH FRANCIS-
CO GOMEZ PAZ), 2006

SODIS Solar Water Disinfection
is a simple, environmentally
sustainable, low-cost solution
for drinking water treatment at
household level for people consuming microbiologically con-
taminated raw water. SODIS
uses solar energy to destroy
pathogenic microorganisms
causing water-borne diseases and
improves the quality of drinking
water. The aim of this project
was to improve the SODIS
disinfection method while integrating a transport solution.
The new container, made of

PET and manufactured with a
bi-colour blown injection
moulding process, has a dual
face: one transparent for maximum UV-A ray collection, and
one black, which absorbs infrared
rays to augment the temperature. These 4 litre containers
have a high surface/thickness
ratio improving the performance
of solar water disinfection. The
reduced thickness also makes
transportation and storage
easier. A special handle also integrates the angular regulation in
order to improve sun exposure.

Die solare Trinkwasserdesinfektion SODIS ist eine einfache,
nachhaltige und preiswerte
Methode zur Aufbereitung von
mikrobiologisch kontaminiertem

Wasser in Privathaushalten.
Mittels Sonnenenergie werden
krankheitserregende Mikroorganismen zerstört und die Qualität des Trinkwassers verbessert.
Das Ziel dieses Projektes war,
die SODIS-Methode zu optimieren und eine transportable
Lösung zu finden. Der neue,
in einem Spritzgussverfahren aus
PET gefertigte Behälter hat zwei
verschiedene Seiten: Auf der
einen ist er transparent, um die
maximale Menge an UV-A-
Strahlung aufzunehmen, und
auf der anderen ist er schwarz,
um durch Absorption von Infra-
rotstrahlen die Temperatur zu
erhöhen. Das vorteilhafte Verhältnis zwischen Oberfläche und
Dicke dieser 4-Liter-Container
hat die Leistungsfähigkeit der

solaren Trinkwasserdesinfektion
erhöht. Die geringere Dicke
erleichtert den Transport und
die Lagerung. Ein integrierter
Spezialgriff ermöglicht die Auf-
stellung in dem für die beste
Sonneneinstrahlung erforder-
lichen Winkel.

La bouteille de désinfection
solaire de l'eau de SODIS est
une solution de traitement de
l'eau à la fois simple, écologiquement durable et peu coûteuse,
destinée à ceux qui ne peuvent
consommer qu'une eau non
potable. SODIS utilise l'énergie
solaire pour détruire les micro-
organismes pathogènes responsables des maladies liées à l'eau
contaminée et améliore ainsi la
qualité de l'eau domestique. Le

but de ce projet était d'améliorer
la méthode de désinfection
SODIS en y intégrant une solution de transport. Le nouveau
récipient, constitué de PET
(polyéthylène téréphtalate) bicolore moulé par injection-souf-
flage, a une surface duelle:
transparente pour une captation
maximale des rayons UV-A et
l'autre noire qui absorbe les
rayons infrarouges pour faire
monter la température. Ces
conteneurs de 4 litres ont un
rapport surface/épaisseur qui
améliore la performance de la
désinfection solaire de l'eau. La
finesse des parois facilite également le transport et le stockage.
Une poignée spéciale permet
aussi de l'incliner pour optimiser
son exposition au soleil.

"Man has a biological need for
simplicity, which is symmetric with his
human complexity."

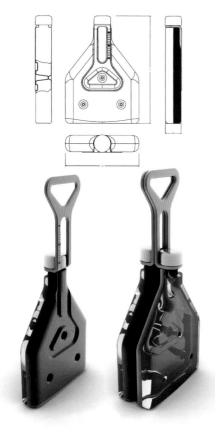

4
SOLAR WATER
DISINFECTION BOTTLE
Portable solar-powered water
disinfection bottle in bi-colour
blown injection-moulded PET
2006
Client: self-generated prototype

5–7
2941
Side chair in solid maple
2005
Client: Nextmaruni

ALBERTO MEDA
Alberto Meda Industrial Design
Via Savona 97
20144 Milan
Italy
T +39 02 42290157
E info@albertomeda.com
www.albertomeda.com

BIOGRAPHY
1945 Born in Lenno Tremezzina, Como, Italy
1969 MEng – Mechanical Engineering, Politecnico di Milano, Milan
1979 Began working as a freelance designer
1983–1987 Lecturer on industrial technology, Domus Academy, Milan
1995+ Lecturer, "Corso di Laurea di Disegno Industriale", Politecnico di Milano, Milan
1995–1997 Board Member of Designlabor Bremerhaven, Institut für System- und Produktgestaltung
2003+ Lecturer for design workshop, IUVA (Università Iuva di Venezia), Venice
2005 Nominated Royal Designer for Industry, Royal Society of Arts, London

RECENT EXHIBITIONS
2001 "Italia e Giappone Design come stile di vita", Pacifico Yokohama, Yokohama, Japan and Kobe Fashion Mart, Kobe, Japan

RECENT AWARDS
2001 Good Design Award, Chicago Athenaeum
2002 Red Dot Award, Design Zentrum Nordrhein Westfalen, Essen

2006 Design Plus Award, Ambiente, Frankfurt; Light of the Future Award, Light + Building, Frankfurt
2007 INDEX Award (Home category)

CLIENTS
Alessi, Alias, Arabia, Kartell, Luceplan, Nextmaruni, Olivetti, Vitra

8

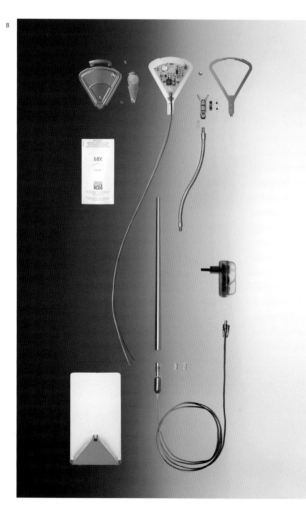

8–11
MIX
LED reading light with a lightweight frame – the light head is a sandwich construction made of two sheets of metal with the circuit combining the chip and LEDs in the middle.

A series of multicolour diodes produces an intense, warm light with very low energy consumption, only 5W (designed with Paolo Rizzatto)
2005
Client: Luceplan

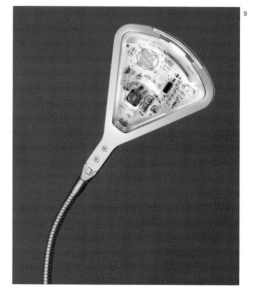

9

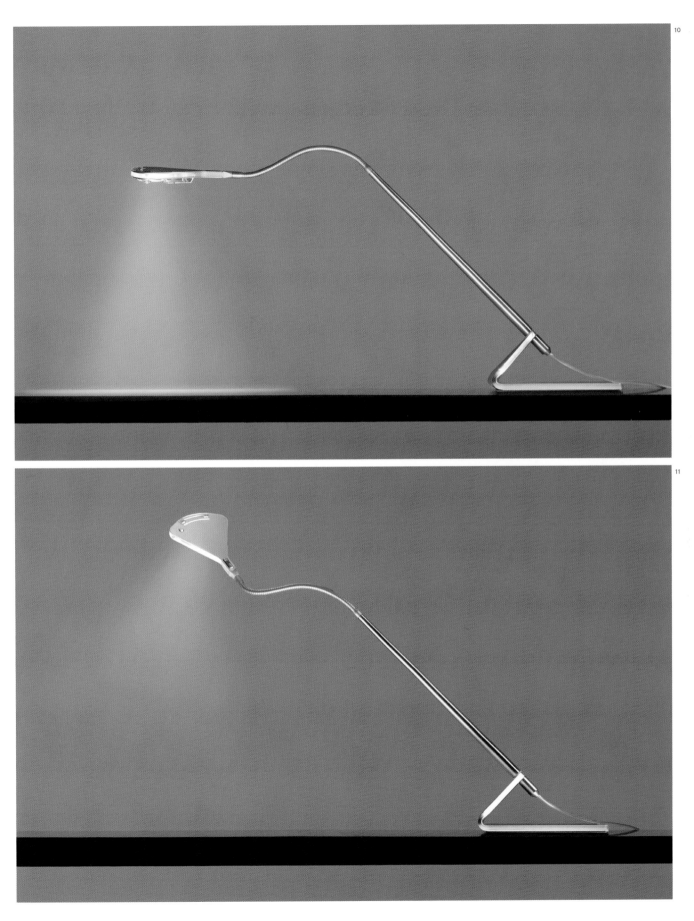

JASPER MORRISON

"There are better ways to design than putting a big effort into making something look special. Special is generally less useful than normal, and less rewarding in the long term. Special things demand attention for the wrong reasons, interrupting potentially good atmosphere with their awkward presence."

„Es gibt bessere Arten, Design zu gestalten, als etwas mit viel Aufwand ungewöhnlich aussehen zu lassen. Ungewöhnliches ist üblicherweise weniger nützlich als Gewöhnliches und langfristig weniger lohnend. Ungewöhnliche Gegenstände beanspruchen aus falschen Gründen Aufmerksamkeit und beeinträchtigen, weil sie aus dem Rahmen fallen, eine möglicherweise angenehme Atmosphäre."

« Il y a de meilleures façons de créer que de faire d'énormes efforts pour qu'une chose ait l'air spécial. Ce qui est spécial est généralement moins utile que la norme et moins gratifiant à long terme. Les choses spéciales réclament beaucoup d'attention pour de mauvaises raisons et brouillent une atmosphère potentiellement bonne de leur encombrante présence. »

1

2

1–3
MUSEUM PIECES FOR
GALERIE KREO, 2006

The Museum Pieces were
designed for an exhibition at
Galerie Kreo in Paris. The series
comprises 15 forms based on
antiquities photographed in

archaeological museums around
the world. The forms were
reconstructed as 3D data, cast
in resin by Davide Toppani, and
displayed in oak/glass vitrines
made by Michel Pinot.

Die Museum Pieces wurden für
eine Ausstellung in der Pariser

Galerie Kreo entworfen. Die
Reihe umfasst 15 Formen, die
nach Fotografien von Antiquitä-
ten aus archäologischen Museen
in der ganzen Welt gestaltet
wurden. Die Formen wurden
in 3-D-Daten umgesetzt, von
Davide Toppani in Harz gegos-
sen und in Vitrinen aus Eichen-

holz und Glas von Michel Pinot
ausgestellt.

Les « Pièces de Musée » ont été
créées pour une exposition à la
Galerie Kreo, à Paris. Cette série
comprend 15 objets copiant la
forme d'antiquités photogra-
phiées dans les musées archéolo-

giques du monde entier. Ces
formes ont été reconstituées en
trois dimensions sur ordinateur
puis moulées en résine par
Davide Toppani et présentées
dans des vitrines aux montants
de chêne réalisées par Michel
Pinot.

1–3
MUSEUM PIECES
Collection of 15 antique forms
cast in either black or white resin
and displayed in specially
made vitrines
2006
Client: Galerie Kreo
(limited edition of 12)

4
AIR–ARMCHAIR
Indoor/outdoor stacking chair
with arms in air-moulded
polypropylene with added
glass fibre
2006
Client: Magis

4

5

6

7

5–7
CARRARA TABLES
Collection of sixteen table
combinations in Carrara marble,
designed for a solo exhibition
at Galerie Kreo
2006
Client: Galerie Kreo
(limited editions of 6 and 12)

LOTUS
Moulded fabric or leather-
upholstered lounge chair
(with or without armrests)
with adjustable headrest and
polished aluminium base
2006
Client: Cappellini

10–12
POTS & PANS
Family of aluminium based,
pressed stainless-steel pots
and pans for domestic use
2006
Client: Alessi

"A good environment is probably
the result of a slow accumulation of
things which you like,
chosen for good reasons."

JASPER MORRISON
Office for Design
Jasper Morrison Ltd.
51 Hoxton Square
London N1 6PB
United Kingdom

Utilism Sarl
15, rue du Sentier
75002 Paris
France

T (UK) +44 20 77392522
T (F) +33 1 42211024
E mail@jaspermorrison.com
www.jaspermorrison.com

BIOGRAPHY
1959 Born in London, England
1979–1982 Studied furniture design at Kingston Polytechnic Design School, Greater London
1982–1985 MA Furniture Design, Royal College of Art, London
1984 Scholarship studies at Hochschule der Künste, Berlin
1986 Founded Office for Design in London
2003 Opened branch office of Office for Design in Paris
2005 Founded Super Normal with Naoto Fukasawa

RECENT EXHIBITIONS
2006 "Super Normal", Axis Gallery, Tokyo; "Museum Pieces", Galerie Kreo, Paris
2007 "Super Normal", Triennale, Milan

RECENT AWARDS
2001 Elected "Royal Designer for Industry", The Royal Society of Arts, London

CLIENTS
Alessi, Canon, Cappellini, Flos, FSB, Ideal Standard, Magis, Muji, Olivetti, Rowenta, Samsung Electronics, Sony, Vitra International

BRODIE NEILL

"Exploring design through the realm of digital technology allows for a response to the object, which is virtually simultaneous. As a designer, this offers the possibility of animating design, and freeing one's sense and sensibility of the potential of the design. Through the curvilinear shapes generated by computing technology, my work references organic forms, and is an evolution of the language of shape and form through contemporary techniques. As a designer, I feel it is essential to utilise the technology of the present in relation to design for the two to have a symbiotic relationship, influencing one another and determining new boundaries."

„Design mithilfe der digitalen Technologie zu erkunden, erlaubt eine Reaktion auf das Objekt, die praktisch simultan ist. Der Designer hat dabei die Möglichkeit, das Design zu animieren und die eigene Sinneswahrnehmung und Sensibilität losgelöst vom Potenzial des Designs einzusetzen. Durch die von der Computertechnologie erzeugten gekrümmten Formen nimmt meine Arbeit auf organische Gebilde Bezug und stellt eine Evolution der Formensprache mit heutigen Techniken dar. Als Gestalter halte ich es für essenziell, sich im Hinblick auf Design die Technologie der Gegenwart zunutze zu machen, da die beiden Bereiche in einer symbiotischen Beziehung stehen, in der sie sich gegenseitig beeinflussen und neue Grenzen definieren."

«Explorer le design grâce à la technologie numérique permet de fournir une réponse virtuellement simultanée à l'objet. Elle donne au designer la possibilité d'animer ses créations et de libérer ses sens et sa sensibilité des potentialités de ce design. À travers les formes curvilignes que génère la technologie informatique, mon travail se réfère aux formes organiques et fait évoluer le langage des formes grâce aux techniques contemporaines. En tant que designer, je pense qu'il est essentiel d'intégrer la technologie actuelle dans le processus créatif afin d'établir une relation symbiotique entre technique et design, où l'une influence l'autre pour déterminer de nouvelles frontières.»

1–3
E-TURN
Single-form bench in lacquered glass-reinforced polyester
2007
Client: Kundalini

1

E-TURN FOR KUNDALINI,
2006

E-turn is a sculptural bench entirely handmade in lacquered fibreglass that culminates from state-of-the-art 3D modelling. As the result of exploring an endless line in 3D space, E-Turn embodies a continuous morphing ribbon that twists and turns from seat to structure before overlapping and returning again in the configuration of a seat.

E-Turn, referring to eternity, dramatically transcends width and dimension as it wraps into its Möbius-like form. Overall the piece displays vibrant sections that emerge as quickly as they retreat making for dynamic formations from all angles.

E-Turn ist eine skulpturale, ganz von Hand gefertigte, lackierte Bank aus Glasfaser. Sie stellt eine Glanzleistung der neuesten Methoden im 3D-Modellieren dar. Durch Experimente mit einer endlosen Linie im dreidimensionalen Raum entstand ein beständig seine Gestalt wechselndes Band, das sich, von der Sitzfläche zur Struktur übergehend, dreht und wendet, ehe es sich überkreuzt und wieder als Sitzmöbel in Erscheinung tritt. Wie ein Möbiusband nimmt E-Turn, mit dem Namen auf die Ewigkeit verweisend, Gestalt an und löst damit alle Vorstellungen von Breite und Dimension auf. Die kraftvoll geschwungenen Linien des Objekts treten an manchen Stellen plötzlich in den Vordergrund, nur um sich gleich wieder zurückzuziehen, wodurch sich aus allen Perspektiven dynamische Formationen ergeben.

E-turn est un banc-sculpture entièrement réalisé à la main en fibre de verre laquée, un chef-d'œuvre ultime de modélisation en 3D. Parce qu'il explore une ligne infinie dans un espace en trois dimensions, E-Turn est comme un ruban en mutation perpétuelle qui se tord et ondule du siège au dossier avant de déborder et de virer à nouveau pour former l'assise. E-Turn, image d'éternité, défie les lois de la pesanteur et de l'équilibre en s'enroulant dans cette forme à la Moebius. Les sections animées du banc, qui émergent aussi si vite qu'elles s'escamotent, produisent une silhouette qui reste dynamique sous tous les angles.

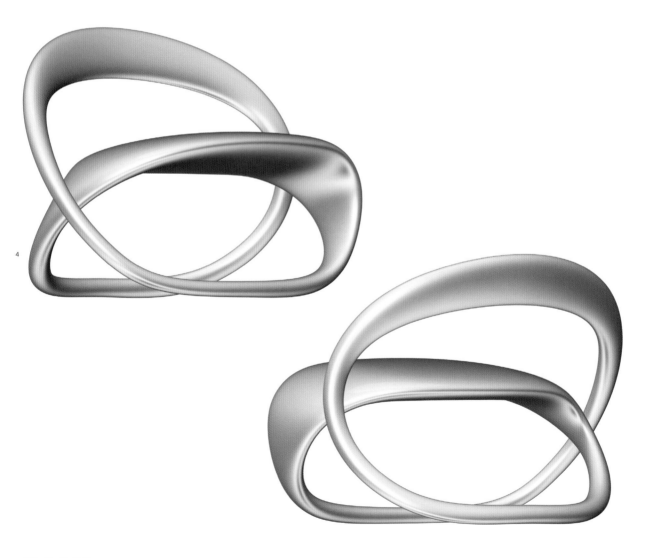

4

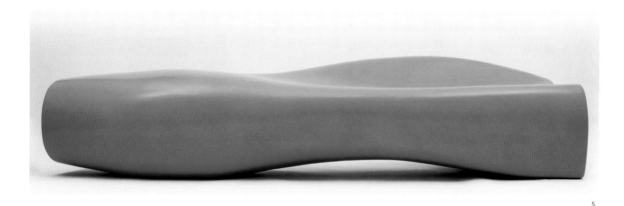

5

4
@ CHAIR
Single-form chair in lacquered glass-reinforced polyester
2007
Client: self-produced prototype

5
ML61K
Single-form bench in urethane-coated foam
2005
Client: self-produced prototype

6
MORPHIE
Wall light with two thermo-formed diffusers in translucent and transparent acrylic, fixed on a metal-coated structure with chrome-plated details
2006
Client: Kundalini

7
MOSES
Chaise longue configured of two morphing forms, the inner subtracted from the outer. The upholstered top surface contrasts with the smooth solid surface within.
2006
Client: self-generated concept

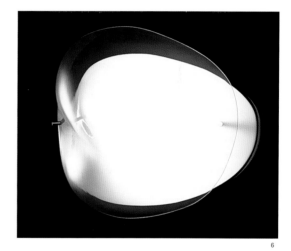

6

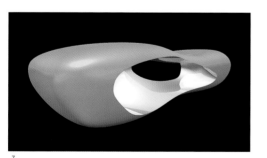

7

"… the full 360 degrees."

BRODIE NEILL
8-9 Rivington Place
London EC2A 3BA
United Kingdom
T +44 790 886 7431
E info@brodieneill.com
www.brodieneill.com

BIOGRAPHY
1979 Born in Tasmania, Australia
2001 BA Furniture Design, University of Tasmania
2004 MA Furniture Design, Rhode Island School of Design

RECENT EXHIBITIONS
2005 "Brodie Neill", Rubin Chapelle, New York; "Convergence", Oceanside Museum of Art, San Diego; "Semi Permanent", Lincoln Center, New York

2006 "Dieci Anni Luci Kundalini", Galeria Raas, Milan; "Conversation of Things New", Federation Square, Melbourne; "Brodie Neill", Adi Project Space, London
2007 "Brodie Neill", Rubin Chapelle, ICFF New York;

"Brodie Neill", Redchurch St., London

CLIENTS
Kundalini

NENDO (OKI SATO)

"There are so many small '!' moments hidden in our everyday. But we don't recognize them and even when we do recognize them we tend unconsciously to reset our minds and forget what we've seen. I believe these small '!' moments are what make our days so interesting, so rich. That's why I want to reconstitute the everyday by collecting and reshaping it into something that's easy to understand. I'd like the people who've encountered Nendo's designs to feel these small '!' moments intuitively. That's Nendo's job."

„Es sind so viele kleine ,!'-Momente in unserem Alltag verborgen. Aber wir erkennen sie nicht, und selbst wenn wir sie doch erkennen, neigen wir dazu, unbewusst unser Gedächtnis zurückzustellen und zu vergessen, was wir gesehen haben. Ich glaube, die kleinen ,!'-Momente sind das, was unsere Zeit so interessant, so reich macht. Deshalb will ich den Alltag rekonstruieren, indem ich diese Momente sammle und zu etwas umforme, das leicht verständlich ist. Ich möchte, dass die Menschen, die auf Nendos Designs stoßen, diese kleinen ,!'-Momente intuitiv wahrnehmen. Das zu erreichen ist Nendos Aufgabe."

« Il y a tant de petits moments ‹ ! › cachés dans notre quotidien. Mais nous ne les reconnaissons pas et même lorsque nous les reconnaissons nous avons tendance, inconsciemment, à les sortir de notre esprit et à oublier ce que nous avons vu. Je pense que ce sont ces petits moments ‹ ! › qui rendent nos journées si passionnantes, si riches. Voilà pourquoi je veux reconstituer le quotidien en collectant et transformant ces moments de façon à créer quelque chose qui soit facile à comprendre. J'aimerais que les gens qui ont croisé les créations de Nendo ressentent intuitivement ces petits moments ‹ ! ›. C'est le boulot de Nendo. »

1/3
TETRIS
Square table with a square section tubular iron frame, powder-coated in black or white, upper worktop and lower worktop in white or black lacquered MDF
2007
Client: De Padova

2
ISLAND TABLE
Composable coffee table formed by two elements of different dimensions and heights in laser-cut and folded metal plate, lacquered in white, black, cherry red, yellow or turquoise
2007
Client: Cappellini

2

3

TETRIS TABLE FOR
DE PADOVA, 2007

"The two table-tops inside the
frame of this coffee table are set
slightly apart, giving the slightest
feeling that something might
just be off, to those who notice.

„Die beiden im Rahmen dieses
Wohnzimmertisches eingelasse-

The variety of square planes
floating at different heights
creates a three-dimensional
space, and may just remind you
of the classic computer game
Tetris."

nen Tischplatten sind leicht versetzt, sodass man auf die Idee
kommen könnte, dass hier etwas
ein ganz klein wenig anders ist,
als es sein sollte, sofern man es
überhaupt bemerkt. Die Komposition der in verschiedenen
Höhen schwebenden quadrati-
schen Flächen schafft einen drei-

dimensionalen Raum, und man
fühlt sich dadurch möglicherweise an das klassische Compu-
terspiel Tetris erinnert."

« Les deux plateaux qui sur-
plombent le cadre de cette table
basse sont légèrement espacés, ce
qui donne à ceux qui y prennent

garde une subtile impression de
décalage. Les diverses surfaces
carrées qui flottent à différentes
hauteurs créent un espace tridimensionnel et rappelle aussi
le grand classique du jeu vidéo,
Tetris. »

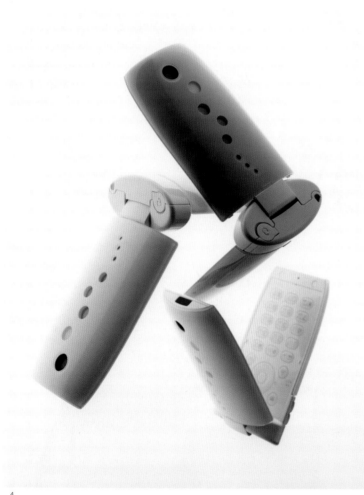

4

4–5
N702IS
Mobile phone based on the
form of a drinking glass, cast
in two layers of transparent
and coloured resins (designed in
collaboration with NTT
DoCoMo)
2006
Client: NEC

6–8
POLAR
Set of three nesting tables
with enameled steel frames
and clear glass tops with internal
polarizing film that produces
flower patterns when tables
are nested
2006
Client: Swedese

"Giving people a small '!'
moment."

5

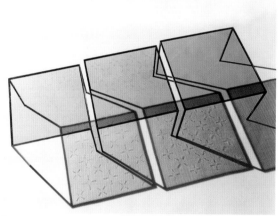

6

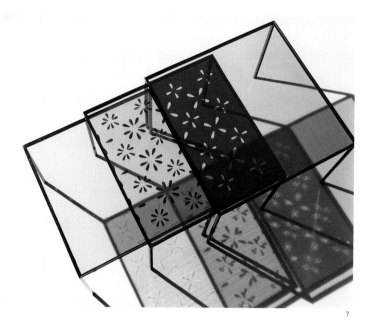

7

8

9

10

11

9–12
HANABI
Hanging light with shape-
memory alloy diffuser that
"blooms" when heated
by light bulb
2006
Client: self-generated concept

NENDO (OKI SATO)
Nendo
4-1-20-2A Mejiro Toshima-ku
Tokyo 171-0031
Japan

Via della Moscova 53
20121 Milan
Italy

T (J)+81 3 39545554
E info@nendo.jp
www.nendo.jp

BIOGRAPHY
1977 Born in Toronto, Canada
2000 BA Architecture, Waseda
University, Tokyo
2002 MA Architecture, Waseda
University, Tokyo
2002 Founded Nendo design
studio in Tokyo

RECENT EXHIBITIONS
2002 "Al(Pb)_lumi", Tokyo
Designers Block, Tokyo
2003 "Streeterior", Salone
Satellite, Salone del Mobile,
Milan; "Sinking about Furni-
ture", Tokyo Designers Week,
Tokyo
2004 "Furnature", Design Lab,
Paris
2005 "Furnature", Spin Off,
Cologne; "Furnature", Green
House, Stockholm; "Furnature",
Salone Satellite, Salone del
Mobile, Milan; "Tuyu Lounge",
Cibone, Tokyo, "Shanghai
Cool", Duolun Museum,
Shanghai; "Ama-Yado Lounge",
Design Tide, Tokyo
2006 "Bloomroom", Fuori
Salone – Zona Tortona, Milan;
"Bloomroom", Istitute Europeo
di Design, Madrid; "One per-
cent products", International
Furniture Fair Tokyo, Tokyo
2007 "Bloomroom", National
Art Center, Tokyo

RECENT AWARDS
2002 Gold Award, Koizumi
International Lighting Design
Competition for Students;
Award Winner, SD Review;
Frame Award for Installation,
Tokyo Designers Block; Design
Report Award Special Mention,
Salone Satellite, Milan Interna-
tional Furniture Fair; Guest
Award, JIDA Under30 Design
Competition, JIDA (Japan
Industrial Designers' Associa-
tion); Tokyo Designers Block
Award, Tokyo Designers Block;
Design Premio, Tokyo Design-
ers Week
2004 Rookie Award, JCD
Design Award, JCD (Japanese
Society of Commercial Space
Designers); Good Design
Award, JIDPO (Japan Industrial
Design Promotion Organiza-
tion); Japanese Nomination,
Elle Decoration International
Design Award

2005 Award for Excellence +
Special Mention, JCD Design
Award, JCD (Japanese Society
of Commercial Space Design-
ers); Grand Prix + 2 x Interior
Product Awards, JID Award
Biennal Silver Award, JID
(Japan Interior Designers'
Association)
2006 CS Design Award; Silver
Award + Special Mention, JCD
Design Award, JCD (Japanese
Society of Commercial Space
Designers)

CLIENTS
Cappellini, Cartier, De Padova,
Gebrüder Thonet, Kenzo, NEC,
Oluce, Swedese

MARC NEWSON

"I approach each design brief in exactly the same way .... I want to create something beautiful, to improve on what's already out there, to express order, and, most importantly ... simplicity. Then the process just kicks in and it becomes problem solving – and those problems are interesting to solve whether the object is a jet or a pair of shoes or a dish rack."

„Ich nähere mich jeder Designaufgabe auf die gleiche Art ... Ich möchte etwas Schönes hervorbringen, das Bestehende übertreffen, einen Ausdruck finden für Ordnung und am wichtigsten ... für Einfachheit. Dann setzt der Prozess ein, und ab da geht es um das Lösen von Problemen. Und es ist interessant, diese Probleme zu lösen, ganz gleich ob es sich bei dem Objekt um ein Düsenflugzeug, ein Paar Schuhe oder einen Geschirrständer handelt."

« J'approche chaque projet exactement de la même manière... Je veux créer quelque chose de beau, pour améliorer ce qui existe déjà, pour exprimer l'ordre et, surtout, la simplicité. Ensuite le processus est amorcé et il s'agit de résoudre des problèmes – des problèmes qui sont toujours intéressants, que l'objet soit un avion, une paire de chaussures ou un égouttoir à vaisselle. »

1

2

3

"Unexpected shapes, futuristic technology and a bit of whimsical fun. This is what Scope, the new Samsonite black label collection designed by Marc Newson, is all about. Functional, lightweight and mobile, the Scope collection includes two upright cases, a duffle bag, a shoulder bag, and a backpack, and comes in a bright palette of colours. Scope takes traditional, utilitarian luggage to the next level, combining futuristic elegance with technical precision. Scope is atypical, 'un-luggage' that merges function with stylish form."

„Außergewöhnliche Formen, futuristische Technologie und ein wenig Augenzwinkern. Genau darum geht es bei Scope, der neuen Kollektion, die Marc Newson für die Linie Samsonite Black Label kreiert hat. Die funktionale, leichte und mobile Kollektion umfasst zwei Upright-Modelle, eine Reisetasche, eine Schultertasche und einen Rucksack und ist in mehreren kräftigen Farben erhältlich. Mit der Kombination von futuristischer Eleganz und technischer Präzision stellt die Scope-Serie das traditionelle zweckmäßige Reisegepäck auf die nächste Stufe der Entwicklung. Scope ist atypisches Non-Gepäck, das Funktion mit stilvoller Form verbindet."

« Des formes inattendues, une technologie futuriste et un soupçon de fantaisie jouissive. Voilà ce qu'est Scope, la nouvelle collection label noir de Samsonite conçue par Marc Newson. Fonctionnelle, légère et mobile, la collection Scope se compose de deux valises droites, d'un sac de voyage, d'un sac à bandoulière et d'un sac à dos et existe dans une large palette de couleurs. Scope fait franchir une étape nouvelle à la bagagerie utilitaire traditionnelle en combinant élégance futuriste et précision technique. Scope est atypique, un anti-bagage qui mêle fonction et style. »

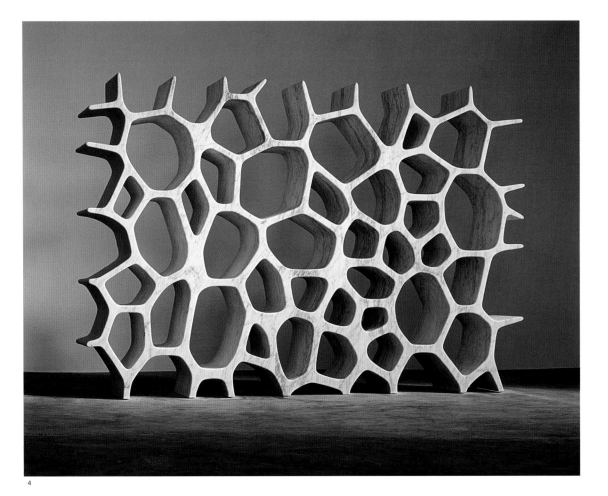

4

"Good design has always been about creating objects that stand the test of time … that have a sense of quality. This does not change – and is especially true now it feels like we live in a disposable age. It's all a matter of striving to improve the quality of things."

1–3
SCOPE
Luggage collection comprising five models with exteriors in expanded foam laminated with 600-denier polyester mesh and interiors in polyester
2005
Client: Samsonite

4
VORONOI
Freestanding shelf unit cut from a single block of white Carrara marble
2006
Client: Gagosian Gallery (limited edition of 8)

5
EXTRUDED CHAIR
Lounge chair cut from a single block of grey Bardiglio marble
2006
Client: Gagosian Gallery (limited edition of 8)

6
EXTRUDED TABLE 1
Side table cut from a single block of white Carrara marble
2006
Client: Gagosian Gallery (limited edition of 8)

7
EXTRUDED TABLE 2
Side table cut from a single block of grey Bardiglio marble
2006
Client: Gagosian Gallery (limited edition of 8)

5

6

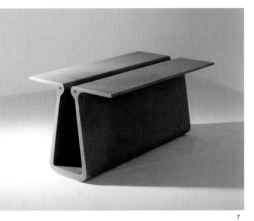

7

8
DOM PÉRIGNON
Champagne bucket in
polyurethane foam
2006
Client: Dom Pérignon

9
RANDOM PAK
Lounge chair in nickel-plated
metal with a mesh form that
has been "grown" using a series
of algorithms based on the
irregular Voronoi cell and
random close packaging
2006
Client: Gagosian Gallery
(limited edition of 10)

8

9

10
NIMROD
Lounge chair in blow-moulded
polyethylene with cushions in
expanded polyurethane
2003/07
Client: Magis

10

MARC NEWSON

Marc Newson Ltd.
175–185 Gray's Inn Road
London WC1X 8EU
United Kingdom

Nimrod Sarl
Group Marc Newson
19, rue Béranger
75003 Paris
France

T (UK) +44 20 72879388
T (F) +33 1 44788730
E pod@marc-newson.com
www.marc-newson.com

BIOGRAPHY
1963 Born in Sydney, Australia
1984 BA Jewellery & Sculpture,
Sydney College of Arts
c.1984 Awarded a grant from
the Australian Crafts Council
and staged an exhibition at the
Roslyn Oxley Gallery, Sydney
1987–1991 Lived and worked
in Tokyo, where Idée put his
designs into production
1991 Established his own design
studio in Paris
1993 Co-founded with Oliver
Ike the Ikepod Watch Company
1997 Moved to London and set
up Marc Newson Ltd.
2006+ Appointed Creative
Director of Qantas Airways
2006 Elected Royal Designer
for Industry by the Royal
Society of Arts, London
2007+ Adjunct Professor of
Design, Sydney College of Arts

RECENT EXHIBITIONS
2001 "Marc Newson: Design
Works", Powerhouse Museum,
Sydney
2003–2004 "Somewhere Totally
Else – The European Design
Show", Design Museum,
London
2004 "Kelvin 40 by Marc
Newson" (a concept jet),
Fondation Cartier pour l'art
contemporain, Paris; "Marc
Newson", Galerie Kreo, Paris
2004–2005 "Marc Newson",
Groninger Museum, Groningen,
and Design Museum, London
2007 "Marc Newson – New
Limited Edition Works",
Gagosian Gallery, New York

RECENT AWARDS
2000 Compasso d'Oro award,
ADI, Milan; Red Dot Award,
Design Zentrum Nordrhein
Westfalen, Essen

2001 Good Design Award,
Chicago Athenaeum; Short-
listed, Selfridges Design Award,
UK
2003 Australian Design Award,
Australia; 2 x Good Design
Awards, Chicago Athenaeum;
Elle Decoration Design Award,
UK
2004 Good Design Award,
JIDPO (Japan Industrial Design
Promotion Organization);
Honourable Mention –
Compasso d'Oro award, ADI,
Milan; Design & Decoration
Awards – best bathroom prod-
uct, UK; Bathroom & Kitchen
Magazine Product Innovation
Award, UK; Classic Design
Awards, Homes & Gardens with
Victoria and Albert Museum,
UK; Best New Restaurant
Design – Reader's choice, Time
Out Awards NY; L'Observateur
du Design award, Paris

2005 2 x Good Design Awards,
Chicago Athenaeum; SIFA
Award, Berlin
2006 Red Dot Award – "best
of the best", Design Zentrum
Nordrhein Westfalen, Essen

CLIENTS
Alessi, Azzedine Alaia,
B&B Italia, Cappellini,
Dom Pérignon, Flos,
Gagosian Gallery,
Grupo Hotelero Urvasco,
G-Star, Habitat, Ideal Standard/
American Standard, Idée Co. Ltd.,
Ikepod, Galerie Kreo, Magis,
Moroso, Nike Inc.,
Poltrona Frau, Qantas Airways,
Samsonite, Smeg,
Swarovski Optik, Target, Vitra

NICE CAR COMPANY

"NICE (No Internal Combustion Engine) is about freedom of choice. Our business is about offering a viable alternative to city transport ... it's about choosing a vehicle that lets you assert your individuality without compromising your social values. NICE challenges the perceptions of electric technology just being a fad, a short-term fashion accessory; this is a product with substance, the epitome of pioneering innovation for both the here and now, and our future. Clean and environmentally friendly technology combined within a modern, contemporary design allows the city dweller to experience a real improvement to their quality of life, with the sense of enrichment that comes with being a little more individual than the rest. NICE is all about simplicity. Functional yet stylish, it leads by example and is not afraid to make a statement. Designed for the urban lifestyle, NICE encourages a community spirit amongst the environmentally concerned population. It's not about your age or ethnic origin, it's about taking control and choosing the right transport. NICE cars for nice drivers."

„Bei NICE (No Internal Combustion Engine: kein eingebauter Verbrennungsmotor) steht die Wahlfreiheit im Vordergrund. Unser Unternehmen hat es sich zur Aufgabe gemacht, eine lebensfähige Alternative zum städtischen Verkehr anzubieten ... Es geht darum, ein Transportmittel zu wählen, das es erlaubt, die eigene Individualität zu behaupten, ohne Abstriche an den eigenen sozialen Werten zu machen. NICE stellt die Wahrnehmung von Elektrotechnologie als bloße Laune und kurzlebiges Modeaccessoire infrage. Es ist vielmehr ein Produkt mit Substanz, der Inbegriff einer bahnbrechenden Innovation sowohl für die Gegenwart wie für die Zukunft. Saubere und umweltfreundliche Technologie in Kombination mit einem modernen, zeitgemäßen Design verbessert die Lebensqualität der Stadtbewohner und bereichert die Menschen durch das Gefühl, ein wenig individueller zu sein als der Rest. Bei NICE dreht sich alles um Einfachheit. Funktional und trotzdem stilvoll geht das Unternehmen mit gutem Beispiel voran und hat keine Angst, ein Statement abzugeben. Für den urbanen Lebensstil konzipiert, fördert NICE den Gemeinschaftssinn der umweltbewussten Bevölkerung. Es geht nicht um Alter oder ethnische Herkunft, es geht darum, die Kontrolle zu übernehmen und das richtige Verkehrsmittel zu wählen. NICE-Autos für nette Fahrer."

« NICE (‹ No Internal Combustion Engine › : Moteur sans combustion interne), c'est une histoire de libre arbitre. Notre travail est de proposer une alternative viable au transport urbain... de choisir un véhicule qui vous laisse exprimer votre individualité sans compromettre vos valeurs sociales. NICE défie la conception selon laquelle la technologie électrique n'est qu'une tendance, un accessoire de mode à durée déterminée ; il s'agit d'un produit doté d'une substance, de la quintessence de l'innovation à la fois pour l'ici et maintenant et pour notre avenir. Une technologie propre et douce pour l'environnement combinée à un design contemporain permet au citadin de faire l'expérience d'une réelle amélioration de sa qualité de vie, du sentiment d'enrichissement qui vient de se montrer un peu plus individualiste. NICE, c'est une histoire de simplicité. Fonctionnel mais stylé, NICE fait la preuve par l'exemple et n'a pas peur de prendre position. Conçues pour un style de vie urbain, ses créations encouragent l'élaboration d'un esprit communautaire au sein d'une population concernée par les questions environnementales. Peu importent votre âge ou votre origine ethnique, il s'agit de prendre le contrôle et de choisir le bon mode de transport. Des voitures sympas pour des conducteurs sympas. »

1–2
MEGA CITY
Three-door, two-seat battery-powered 100% electric vehicle with body panels in non-dent ABS acrylic over an aluminium frame
2006

1

2

1–3

MEGA CITY ELECTRIC VEHICLE, 2006

The MEGA City is a pure electric vehicle, battery powered and able to travel at 40 mph. It has excellent acceleration and a range of up to 60 miles; ideal for use within metropolitan areas. With no need for petrol or diesel, the MEGA City immediately begins saving the user money – by plugging it in to any domestic electricity socket, it will provide motoring at less than 2 Euro cents per mile. Constructed of corrosion-proof, non-dent, 100% recyclable thermoplastic over a rugged advanced aluminium structure, it has undergone extensive crash testing to ensure passenger safety. The soft body panels and the absence of a hard engine underneath the bonnet additionally make the car a safer vehicle for other road-users and pedestrians. Quick, quiet and highly energy efficient, the MEGA City is one of the most environmentally friendly vehicles available today.

Das MEGA City nutzt als einzige Antriebseinheit einen Elektromotor, erreicht 65 km/h, beschleunigt exzellent und erzielt eine Reichweite von bis zu 97 km, ist also die ideale Lösung für den turbulenten Großstadtverkehr. Und eben weil das MEGA City kein Benzin oder Diesel benötigt, beginnen sich die Anschaffungskosten bereits zu rechnen, wenn es zum „Nachtanken" zu Hause an eine beliebige Steckdose muss – das Autofahren kostet so weniger als einen Cent pro Kilometer. Die Karosserie ist aus korrosionsbeständigem, stoßfestem, 100 Prozent recyclingfähigem Kunststoff, das Fahrgestell aus stabilem, hochwertigem Aluminium. Um die Sicherheit der Insassen zu gewährleisten, wurde das Elektroauto umfangreichen Crashtests unterzogen. Da die Karosserieteile relativ weich sind und unter der Haube kein schwerer Motor sitzt, sind aber auch andere Verkehrsteilnehmer und Fußgänger weniger gefährdet. Schnell, leise und überaus energieeffizient, ist das MEGA City eines der umweltfreundlichsten Fahrzeuge, das derzeit erhältlich ist.

La MEGA City est une voiture purement électrique, à pile, qui dépasse les 65 km/h. Son excellente accélération et son autonomie de 97 km la rend idéale pour les zones métropolitaines. Sans essence ni diesel, la MEGA City fait immédiatement économiser de l'argent à son propriétaire – il la branche sur n'importe quelle prise électrique domestique et se retrouve motorisé pour moins de 2 centimes au kilomètre. Constituée d'une structure en aluminium avancé recouverte d'un thermoplastique anticorrosion 100% recyclable, elle a subi d'intenses séries de crash testing pour assurer la sécurité de ses passagers. La souplesse du matériau utilisé pour l'habitacle et l'absence de moteur dur et lourd sous le capot rend également cette voiture plus sûre pour les autre usagers de la route et les piétons. Rapide, silencieuse et très économe en énergie, la MEGA City est un des véhicules les plus écologiques disponibles aujourd'hui.

"Our design is a statement of freedom, leading by example and having the confidence to make the right choice … contemporary design that reflects modern environmental attitudes … NICE design is all about simplicity, freedom and individuality."

3
MEGA CITY
Detail of interior
2006

4
MEGA MULTITRUCK
Detail of interior
2006

5
MEGA MULTITRUCK
Ultra-compact battery-powered 100% electric urban utility vehicle with body panels in non-dent ABS acrylic over an aluminium frame
2006

6
MEGA MULTITRUCK
Various configurations of urban utility vehicle, all of which are based on a patented aluminium ladder frame construction, utilizing cast cross members and weld-free assembly
2006

NICE CAR COMPANY
332 Ladbroke Grove
London W10 5AH
United Kingdom
T +44 20 89692200
E info@nicecarcompany.co.uk
www.nicecarcompany.co.uk

COMPANY HISTORY
2005 Founded by Julian Wilford and Evert Geurtsen in London
2006 Company and first product launched at the British International Motor Show, Excel, London, and company offices opened in Kensington, London

RECENT EXHIBITIONS
2006 "British International Motor Show", Excel, London; "Sustainable Energy", Olympia, London

2007 "Ecobuild, Cityscape and Regenex", Earl's Court, London; "Think Sustainability, Regeneration and Innovation", Excel, London

PATRICK NORGUET

"For me product design is a business – a fascinating and challenging business that is managed with financial constraints, rents and salaries to pay, delivery deadlines to meet, and clients to find and retain. If I had to define my work, it would be more specification design than discourse design. I personally would like to forget the vision of the shaman-designer who, by assiduously frequenting creative minds, is said to deposit the fruits of his visions in galleries and museums – the sacred temples of design. I have a vocational qualification in industrial draughtsmanship, lathing and milling, meaning I am a production-technology engineer. My trade is anchored – structured, even – by my knowledge of materials, production tools and manufacturing processes. I shifted from producing objects and staging exhibitions, more or less by chance, to shared encounters. A designer's contract with a company is primarily an exchange between two identities. The resulting object or exhibition cannot be boiled down to technical and commercial imperatives – for that, there are plenty of design agencies and in-house design offices. The problem with any new encounter is to build a lasting collaboration. To do this you have to start with the right product. It must correspond to the market and the production facilities. The show-object is never an end in itself but an essential professional tool enabling the switch from producing communication images to working as an industrial designer."

„Für mich ist Produktdesign ein Geschäft – ein faszinierendes und herausforderndes Geschäft, das unter finanziellen Zwängen geführt wird, mit Mieten und Gehältern, die zu zahlen sind, Lieferfristen, die einzuhalten sind, und Kunden, die man finden und halten muss. Wenn ich meine Arbeit definieren müsste, wäre es eher ein Design der Spezifikation als eines des Diskurses. Ich persönlich würde gern die Vorstellung eines Designer-Schamanen vergessen, von dem es heißt, dass er durch beharrliches Aufsuchen kreativer Geister die Früchte seiner Visionen in Galerien und Museen – den geheiligten Tempeln des Designs – unterbringt. Ich verfüge über berufliche Qualifikationen als technischer Zeichner, Dreher und Fräser, was bedeutet, dass ich Produktionstechniker bin. Mein Gewerbe ist verankert – ja sogar strukturiert – durch meine Kenntnisse von Materialien, Werkzeugen und Produktionsabläufen. Ich wechselte von der Herstellung von Objekten und der Gestaltung von Ausstellungen mehr oder weniger zufällig zu gemeinsamen Begegnungen. Der Vertrag eines Designers mit einer Firma ist hauptsächlich ein Austausch zwischen zwei Identitäten. Die daraus resultierenden Objekte oder Ausstellungen lassen sich nicht auf technische und kommerzielle Notwendigkeiten reduzieren – dafür gibt es genügend Designbüros und firmeninterne Designabteilungen. Das Problem bei jeder neuen Begegnung besteht im Aufbau einer dauerhaften Zusammenarbeit. Dazu muss man mit dem richtigen Produkt beginnen. Es muss mit dem Markt und den Produktionsmitteln korrespondieren. Das Schauobjekt ist niemals Selbstzweck, sondern ein wesentliches professionelles Werkzeug, mit dem sich der Wechsel von der Generierung von Kommunikationsbildern zur Arbeit als Industriedesigner bewerkstelligen lässt."

« Pour moi, la création de produit est un business – un métier fascinant et stimulant qui s'exerce avec des contraintes financières, des loyers et des salaires à payer, des délais de livraison à respecter et des clients à trouver et retenir. Si je devais définir mon travail, je parlerai davantage de création de précision que de création de discours. Je tiens personnellement à oublier la vision du designer-gourou qui, par la fréquentation assidue d'esprits créatifs, est élu pour exposer le fruit de ses visions dans les galeries et musées – les temples sacrés du design. J'ai une formation professionnelle et technique en dessin industriel, tour et crénelage, ce qui fait de moi un ingénieur en techniques de fabrication. Mon métier est ancré dans – et même structuré par – ma connaissance des matériaux, des outils de production et des procédés de fabrication. Je suis passé de la création d'objets et de l'organisation d'expositions, plus ou moins par hasard, aux rencontres croisées. Le contrat qu'un designer signe avec une entreprise est principalement un échange entre deux identités. L'objet ou l'exposition qui en résultent ne peuvent être réduits à des impératifs techniques et commerciaux – c'est pourquoi il existe tant d'agences de design et de bureaux d'étude internes. Le problème est de construire à chaque rencontre une collaboration durable. Pour y parvenir, il faut commencer par le bon produit. Il doit correspondre au marché et aux capacités de production. L'objet d'exposition n'est jamais une fin en soi mais un outil professionnel essentiel qui permet de passer de la production d'images de communication au travail réel de créateur industriel. »

1

1–2
NAO
Stool in solid wood, available in two heights, with natural or red, black or white lacquer finish
2006
Client: Silvera

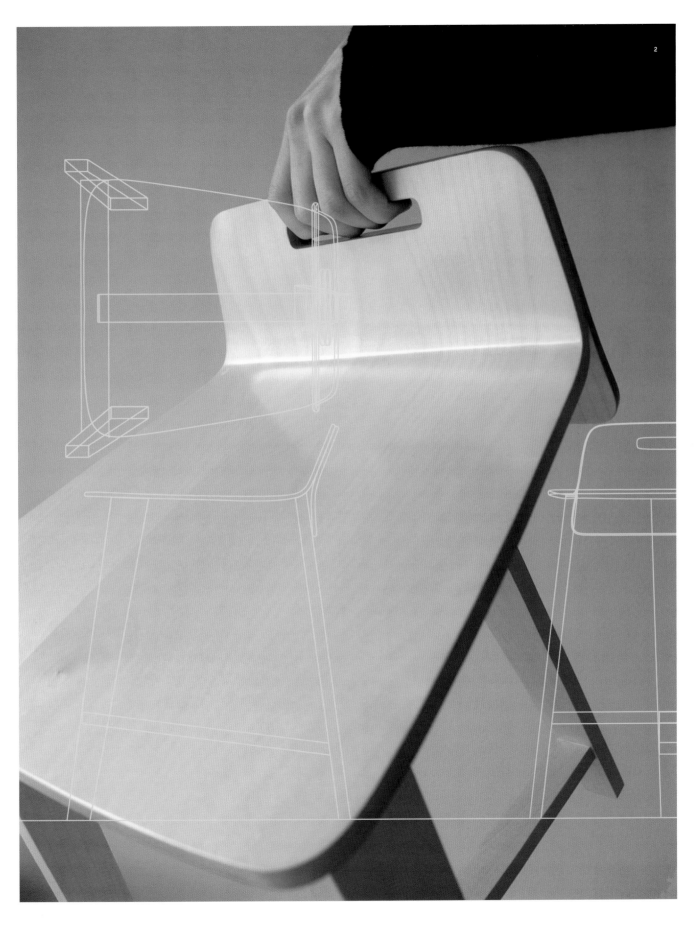

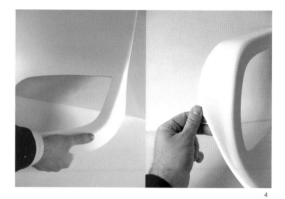

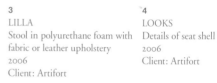

3
LILLA
Stool in polyurethane foam with
fabric or leather upholstery
2006
Client: Artifort

4
LOOKS
Details of seat shell
2006
Client: Artifort

PATRICK NORGUET
Studio Norguet
38, rue de Malte
75011 Paris
France
T +33 1 48072995
E patrick.norguet@wanadoo.fr
www.patricknorguet.com

BIOGRAPHY
1969
Born in Tours, France
1989–1993 Studied at École
d'ingenieur en productique,
Tours
1993–1996 Studied at ENSCI
(École Nationale Supérieure de
Création Industrielle), Paris
1996–1997 Head of visual
identity and merchandising,
Louis Vuitton, Paris
1998–1999 Worked as freelance
designer
2000 Founded his own design
studio Patrick Norguet Design
in Paris

RECENT EXHIBITIONS
2003 "Patrick Norguet",
Colette, Paris; "Patrick Nour-
get", Sentou/Artifort, Paris;
"La scène française du design",
Institut Français, Cologne;
"Habiter la Lumière", Centre
Culturel Français de Milan,
Milan; "Digital print", Abet
Laminati, Milan
2004 "Patrick Norguet",
Renault showroom, Paris
2005 "Designer of the Year –
Now: Patrick Nourget",
Maison & Objet, Paris;
"Designer's Days", Silvera,
Paris

2007 Scenography for
"Flaminia" exhibition in Milan

RECENT AWARDS
2004 International Design
Award, Elle Decoration, UK
2005 Designer of the Year –
Now 2005, Maison & Objet,
Paris; Distinction prize – design
section, Paris Capitale de la
Création
2007 Design Plus Award,
Ambiente, Frankfurt

CLIENTS
Artifort, Bernhardt Design,
Cappellini, DeVecchi, Flaminia,
frighetto, Group Accor, Lancel,
Lapalma, Nespresso, Petit
Bateau, Silvera Edition,
Thonet Vienna, Tronconi,
Van Cleef & Arpels, Veronese

"For me design means the moment of pleasure when one sits in an armchair designed equally well for the backside and the back as for the eye. The shared moment … the right moment."

5
BOSON
Lounge chair with outer seat shell in glass-reinforced polyester and inner shell in polyurethane foam with fabric upholstery, supported on a polished aluminium swiveling pedestal base
2005
Client: Artifort

6
LOOKS
Program of chairs with single-form injection-moulded thermoplastic seat shells and tubular metal bases
2006
Client: Artifort

5

6

OFFICE OF MOBILE DESIGN (OMD)

"Owning your own home is the American dream, but for many it's a compromised dream when the only affordable choice is a trailer. I design for people who like to live light. During my high school years I spent time on a kibbutz in Israel and also travelled with the Bedouin. From these formative experiences, I realized that the people who were the most creative and inventive were those who were bucking the system. I looked at low-tech systems and at high-tech communication devices, and at how young people stored their memories on their hard drive and didn't need to be surrounded by objects. I'm really a nomad and am comfortable with new situations. Through my designs I hope to reawaken the mid-20th century dream of moving homes and instant dwellings. My work incorporates prefabricated components and off-the-shelf parts and includes a model house erected this summer using eco-friendly bamboo and insulating polycarbonates. I try to promote a future of innovative materials that are light, strong and reusable. By developing smart buildings and new materials I hope to create work that responds to both the user and environmental demands. Dormant when not in use, but changing form and volume when occupied, these types of buildings have the potential to become viable and ecological alternatives to permanent buildings when planning cities in the near future."

„Ein eigenes Zuhause zu besitzen ist der amerikanische Traum, aber viele müssen Abstriche an diesem Traum machen, wenn die einzig finanzierbare Möglichkeit in einem Trailer besteht. Ich gestalte für Menschen, die gern mit leichtem Gepäck leben. Während meiner Highschool-Zeit habe ich eine Weile in einem Kibbuz in Israel verbracht und bin auch mit den Beduinen gewandert. Durch diese prägenden Erfahrungen habe ich erkannt, dass die kreativsten und erfindungsreichsten Menschen jene sind, die das System ablehnen. Ich untersuchte Low-tech-Systeme und Hightech-Kommunikationsmedien und die Art, wie junge Menschen heute ihre Erinnerungen auf der Festplatte speichern, ohne das Bedürfnis zu haben, sich mit Gegenständen zu umgeben. Ich bin im Grunde ein Nomade und fühle mich in neuen Situationen wohl. Durch meine Designs hoffe ich, den aus der Mitte des 20. Jahrhunderts stammenden Traum vom Wohnwagen und Fertighaus wiederzubeleben. In meiner Arbeit verwende ich vorgefertigte Bauteile und serienmäßig hergestellte Elemente, wie zum Beispiel bei einem Musterhaus aus umweltfreundlichem Bambus und isolierendem Polycarbonat, das letzten Sommer errichtet wurde. Ich engagiere mich für eine Zukunft innovativer Materialien, die leicht, stark und wiederverwendbar sind. Indem ich intelligente Gebäude und neue Materialien entwickle, hoffe ich, ein Werk zu schaffen, das sowohl auf die Benutzer wie auf ökologische Anforderungen eingeht. Diese Art von Gebäuden, die ruhen, wenn sie nicht in Gebrauch sind, aber im bewohnten Zustand Form und Volumen verändern, hat das Potenzial, für die Stadtplanung der nahen Zukunft eine lebensfähige und umweltfreundliche Alternative zu dauerhaften Gebäuden zu bieten."

« Le rêve américain est de posséder sa propre maison ; un rêve qui est compromis lorsque, comme pour de nombreuses personnes, la seule solution envisageable est une caravane. Je fais du design pour les gens qui aiment vivre léger. Quand j'étais au lycée, j'ai passé du temps dans un kibboutz en Israël et voyagé avec des Bédouins. Ces expériences formatrices m'ont fait comprendre que les personnes les plus créatives et inventives sont celles qui se rebiffent contre le système. J'ai étudié les systèmes rudimentaires et les outils de communication haute technologie, la façon dont les jeunes enregistraient leur mémoire sur leur disque dur et n'avaient plus besoin d'être entourés d'objets. Je suis profondément nomade et je me sens à l'aise dans les situations nouvelles. À travers mes créations, j'espère faire renaître le rêve du milieu du XXᵉ siècle des maisons mobiles et de l'habitat instantané. Mon travail incorpore modules préfabriqués et éléments tout faits et compte un prototype de maison érigé cet été, qui utilise du bambou écologique et des polycarbonates isolants. J'essaie de promouvoir des matériaux innovants légers, résistants et recyclables. En concevant des bâtiments intelligents et des matériaux nouveaux, j'espère répondre aux besoins du consommateur et de la planète. Dans un proche avenir, ce type de bâtiment, qui reste en sommeil lorsqu'il n'est pas utilisé mais change de forme et de volume quand il est occupé, pourrait devenir une alternative viable et écologique aux constructions permanentes dans les projets d'urbanisation. »

3

5

4

3–10/14
OMD PREFAB SHOWHOUSE VENICE, CALIFORNIA, 2006

"OMD's Prefab Showhouse, a development of the Portable House, exhibits the ideas of prefabrication, flexibility, portability and compact spaciousness. Its central kitchen/bath core divides and separates the sleeping space from the eating/ living space in a compact assemblage of form and function. The steel frame structure, measuring 12 x 60 feet, was trucked to its site and set on a temporary foundation. Its exterior is clad with metal siding and translucent polycarbonate panels, while its interior features a high sloping ceiling, a Boffi kitchen and bathroom, iPort sound system, flowing ventilation, radiant heat panels and a variety of sustainable floor and wall materials. Whether briefly situated on an urban lot, momentarily located in the open landscape, or positioned for a more lengthy stay, the Portable House accommodates a wide range of needs and functions."

„Im Muster-Fertighaus von OMD, einer Weiterentwicklung des Portable House, sind Ideen wie Vorfertigung, Flexibilität, Mobilität und kompakte Geräumigkeit sichtbar gemacht. Der aus Küche und Bad bestehende Block im Zentrum des Hauses trennt den Schlafbereich vom Ess-/Wohnbereich. Das 3,6 x 18,3 m große Stahlskelett wurde per LKW auf den Bauplatz transportiert und auf ein provisorisches Fundament gesetzt. Die Außenfassade besteht aus Metallverkleidungen und transluzenten Polycarbonat-Platten, während das Innere des Hauses durch hohe Decken, eine Küchen- und Badezimmerausstattung von Boffi, ein iPort-Sound-System, eine Belüftungsanlage, eine Wandheizung und verschiedene Boden- und Wandbeläge aus nachwachsenden Materialien gekennzeichnet ist. Egal, ob es kurzfristig auf einem Grundstück in der Stadt, vorübergehend in der offenen Landschaft oder irgendwo für längere Zeit aufgestellt wird, das Portable House vermag vielfältigen Bedürfnissen und Funktionen gerecht zu werden."

« La maison préfabriquée témoin d'OMD, née du développement de la ‹ Maison portable ›, met en scène les concepts de préfabrication, de flexibilité, de transportabilité et d'espace compact. Son cœur dédié à la cuisine et à la salle de bain sépare l'espace nuit de l'espace jour en assemblant de façon compacte forme et fonction. La structure extérieure en acier, qui mesure 3,65 m sur 18,3m, a été apportée par camion jusqu'au terrain choisi et installée sur des fondations temporaires. Sa coquille extérieure est habillée de métal et de panneaux de polycarbonate translucide tandis que l'intérieur présente un haut plafond incliné, une cuisine et une salle de bain signée Boffi, un système de sonorisation par iPort, une ventilation flottante, des panneaux radiants et des matériaux durables sur les murs et sols. Qu'elle soit posée en zone urbaine, momentanément installée en pleine nature ou positionnée en vue d'un séjour plus long, la Maison portable remplit une grande variété de besoins et de fonctions. »

6

7

8

"Be moved …
inventing and developing strategies for light,
smart, adaptive and ecologic architecture."

3–8
OMD SHOWHOUSE
Construction and installation
process of 720 interior sq. ft.
prefabricated house in Venice,
California
2006

9
OMD SHOWHOUSE
Drawings of elevations
2006

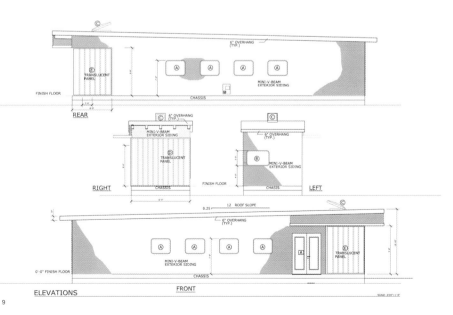

9

10

10
OMD SHOWHOUSE
Living area of 720 interior sq. ft.
prefabricated house in Venice,
California
2006

11
CAMARGO HOUSE
Exploded axonometric rendering
of 3550 interior sq. ft. two-story,
four-bedroom prefabricated
house
2007

14
OMD SHOWHOUSE
720 interior sq. ft. prefabricated
house (a development of the
OMD Portable House) based
on a single 12 x 60 ft. steel frame
module, in Venice, California
2006

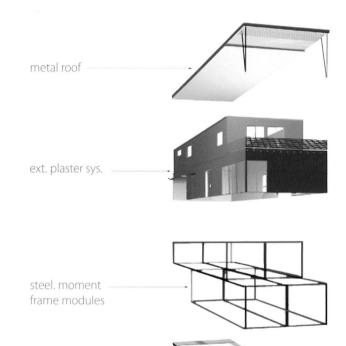

metal roof

ext. plaster sys.

steel. moment
frame modules

stem wall
foundation

11

12–13
SWELL HOUSE
Front and rear views of 3000
interior sq. ft. low-cost prefabricated house based on an "S"
modular structure
2006

12

13

14

OFFICE OF MOBILE DESIGN (OMD)

1725 Abbot Kinney Boulevard
Venice
California 90291
USA
T +1 310 4391129
E info@designmobile.com
www.designmobile.com

DESIGN GROUP HISTORY

1998 Founded by Jennifer Siegal in Venice, California

FOUNDER'S BIOGRAPHY JENNIFER SIEGAL

1965 Born in Manhattan, New York
1987 BA in Architectural Studies, Hobart and William Smith Colleges, Geneva; worked for Arcosanti, Cordes Junction, Arizona
1988 Worked for Skidmore, Owings and Merrill, San Francisco
1992–1993 Teaching Assistant, SCI-Arc, Los Angeles and Switzerland
1994 MArch, Southern California Institute of Architecture (SCI-Arc), Los Angeles
1994–1995 Worked for Hodgetts + Fung Design Associates, Santa Monica
1995–1996 Visiting Assistant Professor, Arizona State University, Phoenix
1996–1997 Assistant Professor, The University of North Carolina, Charlotte
1997–2006 Professor, School of Architecture and Design, Woodbury University, Los Angeles
2003 Loeb Fellow, Graduate School of Design, Harvard University, Cambridge, where she explored the use of intelligent, kinetic, and lightweight materials; Workshop Instructor, University of Minnesota Design Institute and Target Corporation, Minnesota

RECENT EXHIBITIONS

2002 "New Nomadism", Graduate School of Design, Harvard University
2003 "National Design Triennial: Inside Design Now", Cooper-Hewitt National Design Museum, New York; "Strangely Familiar: Design and Everyday Life", Walker Art Center, Minneapolis
2004 "Communities Under Construction", A + D Museum, Los Angeles
2006 "Mobile Living Exhibition", New York Design Week; "Rebuilding New Orleans", Ogden Museum of Southern Art, University of New Orleans
2007 "Reinventing the Globe: A Shakespearean Theater for the 21st Century", National Building Museum, Washington

RECENT AWARDS

2000 Faculty Design Award, ACSA; Collaborative Practice Award, ACSA
2003 Nomination, "America's Best and Brightest", Esquire Magazine; Emerging Voices, The Architectural League, New York; Honorable Mention, Samsung Art & Design Institute, Korea
2004 Residency, The Mac-Dowell Colony; Faculty Design Award, ACSA
2006 Julius Shulman Institute Fellowship, Woodbury University, Los Angeles; Infiniti Design Excellence Award

CLIENTS

California Institute of the Arts, Anna and Ricardo Carmargo, Carlson Hotels, Chinati Foundation, Chronicle Books, Cotsen Center for Puppetry and the Arts, Dwell, Frank Lloyd Wright Foundation, Häagen-Dazs, Marilyn and Harry Lewis, Pallotta TeamWorks, PIE.com, Popular Science, Richard Carlson, Scott Litt, Siegal Group, Smithsonian Cooper-Hewitt, National Design Museum, Todd Stevens, The Country School/North Hollywood, The History Channel, Toledo-Sherman, Wallpaper

ORA-ÏTO

"'Simplexity' is the art of making complicated things seem simple. It consists of developing a simple answer to a complex problem. To be simple, without being simplistic. This answer must inevitably integrate complex criteria. For a designer, 'Simplexity' consists of finding a solution, which integrates maximum complexity in the simplest envelope possible, to unite maximum constraints behind the most obvious façade of comprehension and utilization ... a 'Simplex' shape is a shape of simple appearance but which integrates an invisible complexity. The objective is to provide the user of an object a relationship deprived of all complication. The simpler an object is to use, the more the user's approach becomes intuitive, easy and natural. A 'Simplex' object presents a simple appearance that integrates its functionality intelligently. From a plastic and industrial point of view, it implies erasing maximum asperities of an object to make it more accessible. Nobody needs to add more complexity to their daily lives, but on the other hand everyone tries to find better solutions in order to simplify their life. 'Simplexity' is therefore a philosophical bias to a solid application: To make simpler that which is too complicated."

„'Simplexität' ist die Kunst, komplizierte Dinge einfach erscheinen zu lassen. Sie besteht aus der Entwicklung einer einfachen Lösung für ein komplexes Problem. Einfach sein, ohne vereinfachend zu sein. Diese Lösung muss zwangsläufig komplexe Kriterien einbeziehen. Für einen Designer besteht ‚Simplexität' darin, eine Lösung zu finden, die maximale Komplexität in eine möglichst einfache Hülle integriert, um ein Höchstmaß an Einschränkungen hinter der offenkundigen Fassade des Verständnisses und der Nutzung zu vereinen ... eine ‚Simplex'-Form ist eine Form der einfachen äußeren Erscheinung, die jedoch eine unsichtbare Komplexität enthält. Das Ziel ist, dem Nutzer eines Objekts ein Verhältnis bereitzustellen, das aller Komplikationen beraubt ist. Je einfacher der Gebrauch eines Gegenstandes ist, desto intuitiver, leichter und natürlicher wird der Zugang für den Benutzer. Ein ‚Simplex'-Objekt präsentiert eine schlichte Erscheinung, die ihre Funktionalität auf intelligente Weise integriert. Von einem formgebenden und industriellen Gesichtspunkt aus betrachtet, bedeutet das, möglichst viele Unebenheiten eines Objekts zu tilgen, um es zugänglicher zu machen. Niemand braucht noch mehr Komplexität im Alltag, vielmehr versucht jeder, bessere Lösungen zu finden, um sein Leben zu vereinfachen. ‚Simplexität' ist daher eine philosophische Neigung für eine praktische Anwendung: einfacher gestalten, was zu kompliziert ist."

«La ‹simplexité› est l'art de faire passer pour simple les choses compliquées. Elle consiste à élaborer une réponse simple à un problème complexe. Être simple, sans être simpliste. Cette réponse doit impérativement intégrer des critères complexes. Pour un designer, la ‹simplexité› consiste à trouver une solution qui intègre un maximum de complexité dans l'enveloppe la plus simple possible, unifier les contraintes maximales qui sous-tendent la façade de compréhension et d'utilisation la plus évidente... Une forme ‹simplexe› est une forme d'apparence simple mais qui intègre une complexité invisible. L'objectif est de procurer à l'utilisateur d'un objet une relation dépouillée de toute complication. Plus un objet est simple à utiliser, plus l'approche qu'en a l'utilisateur devient intuitive, facile, naturelle. Un objet ‹simplexe› est doté d'une fonctionnalité intelligemment intégrée à une apparence simple. D'un point de vue plastique et industriel, cela implique de gommer au maximum les aspérités d'un objet pour le rendre plus accessible. Personne n'a besoin de rajouter davantage de complexité à sa vie quotidienne; tout le monde cherche, en revanche, des moyens de se simplifier la vie. La ‹simplexité› est une façon philosophique de dire: rendre plus simple ce qui est trop compliqué.»

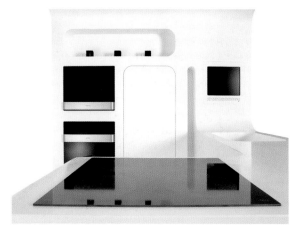

1

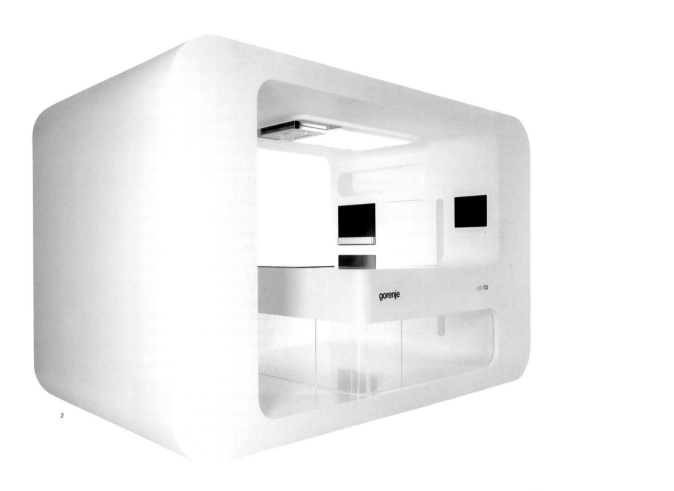

2

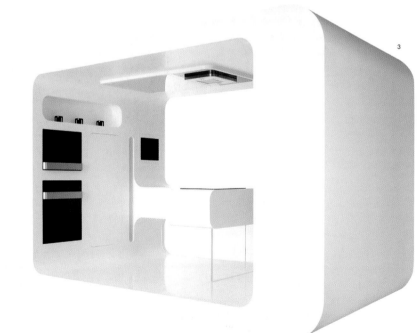

3

"'Simplex' is a neologism that combines two words – 'simple' and 'complex'."

4

1–3
FUTURISTIC KITCHEN
Modular kitchen, with numerous integrated appliances, manufactured in advanced composite
as a monolith that can be lifted and transported to desired location
2007
Client: Gorenje

4
TOYOTA DISPLAY STAND
Vehicle display stand for the Geneva Motor Show
2007
Client: Toyota

ORA-ÏTO
58, rue Charlot
75003 Paris
France
T +33 1 42460009
E info@ora-ito.com
www.ora-ito.com

DESIGN GROUP HISTORY
1998 Founded by Ito Morabito (alias Ora-Ïto) in Paris initially to create uncommissioned virtual products for real brands

BIOGRAPHY
ITO MORABITO
1977 Born in Paris, France
1996 Enrolled at the École de création et de design, Paris (now known as Creapole), however, dropped out after a few months – while there he met the shoe designer, Roger Vivier, for whom he created a 3D model of a dancing shoe
1998 Founded his own design brand/label – Ora-Ïto

RECENT EXHIBITIONS
2005 "Ora-Ïto Museum" installation/exhibition, Milan – organized in conjunction with Centre Georges Pompidou and the French Cultural Center of Milan

RECENT AWARDS
2001 Most Creative Artwork of the Year Award, Dazed & Confused magazine
2002 Oscar de L'Emballage award, French Institute for Packaging and Packing
2004 Red Dot Award, Design Zentrum Nordrhein Westfalen, Essen
2006 Janus de l'Industrie Award, Institut Français du Design

2007 Best Designer of the Year Award, Les Globes de Cristal, Art et Culture, Paris; "Best Stand Designer", Geneva Motor Show

CLIENTS
Adidas, Alfa-Romeo, Artemide, B&B Italia, Cappellini, Cartier, Centre Culturel France de Milan, Cindarella, Cortex, Danone, Davidoff, De Vecchi, Guerlain, Heineken, Hinda, IUM, Joop!, Kenzo, LaCie, Le Cabaret, Levi's, LG Electronics, L'Oréal Paris, L'Oréal Professionnel, Nike, Ogo, Pantone, Pechiney, Perrier, Pink TV, Pommery, Ravillon, Red Cross, Sagem, Smiley Licensing, Soma

Records, Sony Music, Swatch, Tarkett Sommer, T. Coin, Thierry Mugler, Toyota, Virgin, Vogue – Condé Nast, Wanadoo

5

5-6
AYRTON
Bed with structure in wood with
matt varnish surfaces and feet in
chromed steel
2007
Client: Frighetto

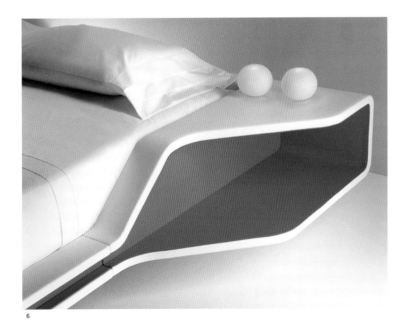

6

GIOVANNI PAGNOTTA

"A good friend once said to me, 'We are all carbon.' He was referring to my preoccupation with advanced composite technologies, and specifically carbon fibre—an obsession born of the possibilities locked within the complex composition of super materials. Designing chairs, tables, sofas, etc., doesn't feed my soul. We have millions of chairs; a few of them are quite good. We don't need more. What feeds my soul is the challenge of deciphering the secrets of a super material, and translating those discoveries into something unexpected and beautiful. When that special combination of material, idea, and execution comes together in perfect sequence, you have more than a chair, a table, a lamp, or a sofa. That is the Art of design, and it opens the door to solutions that transcend style and time. I truly believe what we create should be more than the person behind it. With that in mind, I maintain these objectives: go to bed with a clear conscience, wake up the next morning feeling good about what I've done, and try and be the hero my son believes I am."

„Ein guter Freund hat einmal zu mir gesagt: ‚Wir sind doch alle aus Kohlenstoff.' Er bezog sich damit auf meine Beschäftigung mit fortschrittlichen Verbundtechnologien, insbesondere Kohlenstofffaser – eine Obsession, entstanden aus den Möglichkeiten, die in der komplexen Zusammensetzung von Supermaterialien eingeschlossen sind. Das Gestalten von Stühlen, Tischen, Sofas etc. befriedigt meine Seele nicht. Wir haben Millionen von Stühlen, einige von ihnen sind ziemlich gut. Wir brauchen nicht noch mehr davon. Was meine Seele befriedigt, ist die Aufgabe, die Geheimnisse eines bestimmten Materials zu entschlüsseln und diese Entdeckungen in etwas Unerwartetes und Schönes zu übertragen. Wenn diese spezielle Kombination aus Material, Idee und Ausführung in perfekter Abfolge zusammenfindet, hast du mehr als einen Stuhl, einen Tisch, eine Lampe oder ein Sofa. Es ist die Kunst des Designs, und es öffnet die Tür zu Lösungen, die über Stil und Zeit hinausgehen. Ich glaube wirklich, was wir gestalten, sollte mehr sein als die Person dahinter. In diesem Sinne halte ich an diesen Zielen fest: mit reinem Gewissen ins Bett gehen, am nächsten Morgen mit gutem Gefühl aufwachen im Gedanken an das, was ich gemacht habe, und versuchen, der Held zu sein, den mein Sohn in mir sieht."

«Un bon ami m'a dit un jour : ‹Nous ne sommes que du carbone›. Il faisait référence à mon intérêt pour les technologies composites et en particulier pour la fibre de carbone — une obsession née des possibilités que renferme la composition complexe des super matériaux. Concevoir des chaises, des tables, des canapés, etc., ne me comble pas. Nous avons des millions de chaises, quelques-unes sont assez bonnes, inutile d'en avoir davantage. Ce qui me comble, c'est le défi de déchiffrer les secrets d'un matériau particulier et de traduire ces découvertes en quelque chose d'inattendu et de beau. Lorsque cette combinaison unique entre matériau, idée et exécution intervient de façon parfaitement orchestrée, on obtient bien davantage qu'une chaise, une table, une lampe ou un canapé. Voilà ce qu'est l'art du Design, qui ouvre la voie à des solutions qui transcendent style et époque. Je pense vraiment que ce que nous créons doit dépasser la personne qui en est à l'origine. Je garde ceci à l'esprit et je maintiens mes objectifs : aller me coucher la conscience claire, me réveiller le lendemain heureux de ce que j'ai accompli et tenter d'être le héros que mon fils croit que je suis.»

1

1
VORTICE LOUNGE
Single-form lounge chair in moulded carbon fibre with enamel finish on exterior surface
2006
Client: self-produced

2
VORTICE
Single-form side chair in moulded carbon fibre with enamel finish on exterior surface
2006
Client: self-produced

2

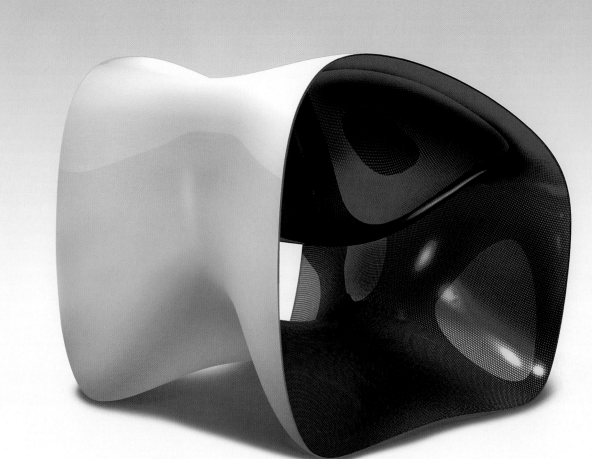

"Design keeps me up at night.
I always want more, never get enough,
and am often left thinking
'why do I put myself through this?'"

1–3
VORTICE CHAIRS, 2006

"With the Vortice chairs I wanted to create the thinnest material profile possible. My concerns were: ergonomics first, material efficiency of equal import, and line as the net result of that combination. The Vortice chairs are 100% solid carbon fibre. They have a cross sectional profile of just 2.15 millimeters, and weigh just under 4.0 kilo-grams. In addition, I wanted a system that would translate well to high production technology. The idea is to offer fibre-rein-forced injection molded versions of the carbon fibre counterparts. Beautiful can also be afford-able."

„Mit den Vortice-Stühlen wollte ich das dünnste Materialprofil entwickeln, das möglich ist. Mein Anliegen war: Ergonomie zuerst, Materialeffizienz ebenso hohe Priorität, und Linienfüh-rung als Nettoergebnis dieser Kombination. Die Vortice-Stühle bestehen aus 100 Prozent festem Carbonfaserkunststoff, haben aber ein Querschnittpro-fil von nur 2,4 mm und wiegen nur knapp über 4 kg. Außerdem ging es mir darum, ein System zu entwickeln, das sich leicht auf die Hochleistungstechnolo-gie übertragen lässt. Die Idee ist, eine faserverstärkte spritzgussge-formte Version der Carbonfaser-fassung anzubieten. Schönes kann auch erschwinglich sein."

« Avec les chaises Vortice, j'ai voulu créer un matériau aussi mince que possible. Je me suis concentré sur: l'ergonomie, la rentabilité du matériau et la ligne qui découle de cette com-binaison. Les chaises Vortice sont constituées à 100% de fibre de carbone solide, mais leur pro-fil ne mesure que 2,4 mm en coupe transversale et dépasse tout juste les 4 kilos. Je souhai-tais un système qui s'adapte bien aux techniques de la production de masse. L'idée est de proposer pour ces chaises des versions à fibre renforcée moulées par injection. Le beau peut aussi être abordable. »

GIOVANNI PAGNOTTA

143 Fremont Street A
Harrison
New York 10528
USA
T +1 914 3090720
E info@giovannipagnotta.com
www.giovannipagnotta.com

BIOGRAPHY

1964 Born in Morra De Sanctis, Avellino, Italy
1982–1986 BFA Environmental Design, Parsons School of Design, New York
1986–1989 MA Architecture, Yale University, New Haven
1989 Recipient of the Eero Saarinen Scholarship for design excellence at Yale University

RECENT EXHIBITIONS

2000 "Design Matters", Museum of Contemporary Art, Miami
2001 "Alumni Design", Yale University, New Haven; "TAG (ten avant-garde)", Surface Magazine exhibit, Salone del Mobile, Milan
2002 "Mood River", Wexner Center for the Arts, Ohio State University, Columbus; "Prototype", Issey Miyake, New York; "Prototype", Luminaire, Miami

RECENT AWARDS

2003 Design Distinction Award, Annual Design Review, I.D. Magazine
2004 Award, Annual Design Review, I.D. Magazine

CLIENTS

Artemide, de Sede, Herman Miller, Juventa, Pearl USA, Rezek, Tecno, Ycami

3
VORTICE LOUNGE
Single-form lounge chair in moulded carbon fibre with enamel finish on exterior surface
2006
Client: self-produced

4–6
XO
Series of side and lounge chairs in computer-milled, flat sheet carbon fibre that is bent into shape. High-strength aluminium brackets are used to buttress the supporting structure and wool felt is used to upholster the seats
2004–06
Client: self-produced

SATYENDRA PAKHALÉ

"Conception is the core of every single project but making it real is a challenge worth taking. Start every new project from scratch, just like a beginner. Explore the physical qualities and cultural associations of different materials. Link with the natural world, which is both metaphorical and concrete. Develop forms that have sensorial, symbolic and moral intent. Seek playfulness, craftsmanship, sustainability, technological rightness and obsessive prototyping. Generate a fusion between high and low, east and west, north and south, industrial and non-industrial, technological and humanist, ancient and contemporary; and a lot more. Reject all dogmas, isms and fixed notions and create with open-minded possibilities, which are free to respond to a range of physical and emotional needs. Merge sculpture with engineering. Retain a passion for making things, painting, sculpture, architecture and engineering. Regard the studio as part playground, part atelier, part personal museum, part fun home and part industrial design/architectural/engineering studio. Remember originality comes from the origin. Create work that is human."

„Konzeption bildet den Kern jedes einzelnen Projekts, aber es dann zu realisieren, ist eine Herausforderung, der es sich zu stellen lohnt. Beginne jedes neue Projekt ganz von vorn, genau wie ein Anfänger. Erkunde die physischen Eigenschaften und kulturellen Assoziationen unterschiedlicher Materialien. Trete in Verbindung mit der Natur, die sowohl metaphorisch als auch konkret ist. Entwickle Formen, die einen sensorischen, symbolischen und moralischen Zweck haben. Bemühe dich um Verspieltheit, Kunstfertigkeit, Nachhaltigkeit, technologische Verhältnismäßigkeit und obsessives Entwickeln von Prototypen. Bilde eine Verschmelzung von Hoch- und Alltagskultur, Ost und West, Norden und Süden, industriell und nicht industriell, technologisch und humanistisch, altehrwürdig und zeitgenössisch und vielem mehr. Verwerfe alle Dogmen, Ismen und starren Vorstellungen und schaffe Möglichkeiten, die uneingeschränkt auf eine große Bandbreite physischer und emotionaler Bedürfnisse antworten können. Verbinde Skulptur und Technik. Bewahre dir eine Leidenschaft für das Herstellen von Dingen, das Malen, Bildhauern, die Architektur und Technik. Betrachte das Studio als Spielplatz, Atelier, persönliches Museum, Vergnügungsort und Design-/Architektur-/Ingenieur-Büro. Vergiss nicht, Originalität kommt vom lateinischen ‚originalis‘ (ursprünglich). Schaffe ein Werk, das menschlich ist."

«La conception est au cœur de chaque projet, mais transformer une idée en réalité est un défi qui vaut la peine d'être relevé. Recommencer à zéro à chaque projet, comme un débutant. Explorer les qualités physiques et les correspondances culturelles de différents matériaux. Tisser des liens avec le monde naturel, qui est à la fois métaphorique et concret. Développer des formes dotées d'une intention sensorielle, symbolique et morale. Rechercher espièglerie, maîtrise des métiers, durabilité, rigueur technologique et obsession du prototype. Générer une fusion entre haut et bas, est et ouest, nord et sud, industriel et non-industriel, technologique et humaniste, ancien et contemporain; et bien plus encore. Rejeter tous les dogmes, doctrines et idées préconçues pour créer dans un champ ouvert de possibilités, libres de répondre à tout un éventail de besoins physiques et émotionnels. Fusionner sculpture et ingénierie. Conserver la passion de la fabrication des choses, de la peinture, de la sculpture, de l'architecture et de la technique. Considérer le studio comme un terrain de jeu, en partie atelier, en partie musée personnel, en partie maison pour rire et en partie bureau d'étude, d'architecture et de création. Se souvenir que l'originalité vient de l'origine. Créer un travail qui soit humain. »

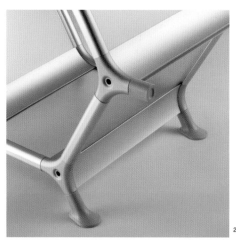

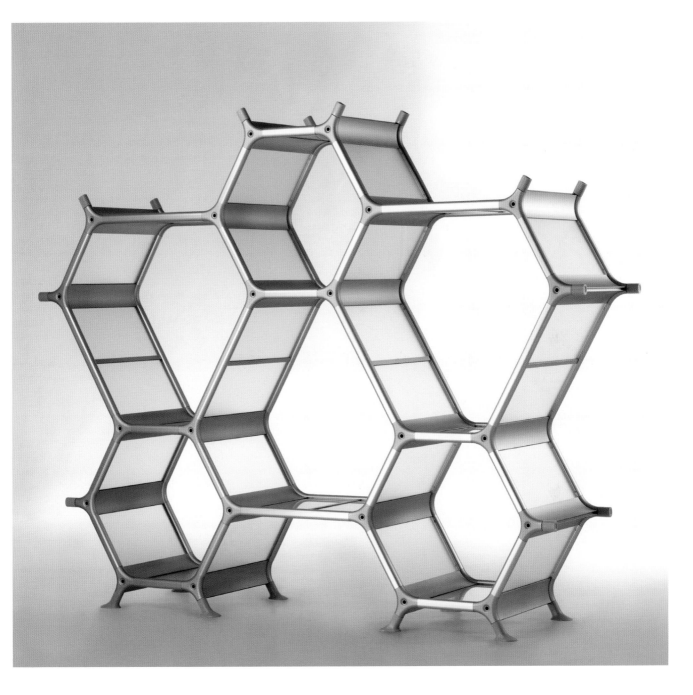

1–3
ALINATA
Freestanding modular shelving
system in extruded aluminium
with wood or glass panels that
allows endless combinations
2007
Client: Erreti

4
FLOWER OFFERING CHAIR
Chair in slip cast ceramic
2001–06
Client: Designer's Gallery
(limited edition of 7)

5
ADD–ON
Modular radiator system in
enameled metal available in
electric or hydraulic versions
2004
Client: Tubes

6
B.M. HORSE CHAIR
Chair in lost wax cast bronze
2000–07
Client: Designer's Gallery
(limited edition of 7)

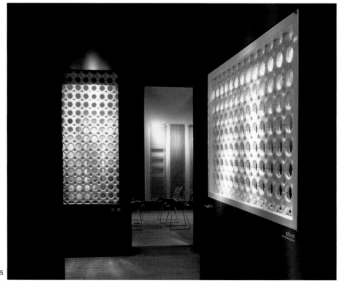

6

"Design is a universal poetry.
It is not a profession, but a way of life.
If one does not know how to idealize what
one does, then why do it? Why create?"

7
ADD–ON
Sketch of radiator system
module
2004
Client: Tubes

8
AMISA
Door handle in
chrome-plated die-cast brass
2004
Client: Colombo Design

9
PANTHER
Multichair with wood frame
and foam upholstery
2002–05
Client: Designer's Gallery
(limited edition of 7)

10–11
FISH CHAIR
Lounge chair in rotational-
moulded plastic with soft-touch
rubber coating on outer surface
2005
Client: Cappellini

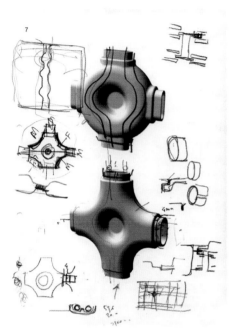

7

8

SATYENDRA PAKHALÉ

Atelier Satyendra Pakhalé
Zeeburgerpad 50
1019 AB Amsterdam
The Netherlands
T +31 20 4197230
E info@satyendra-pakhale.com
www.satyendra-pakhale.com

BIOGRAPHY

1967 Born in Washim, India
1985–1989 Bachelor of
Engineering, Visvesvaraya
National Institute of Technol-
ogy, Nagpur, India
1989–1991 Master of Design,
Industrial Design Centre, Indian
Institute of Technology,
Bombay, India
1992–1994 Adv. Product
Design, Art Center College
of Design (Europe),
La Tour-de-Pleiz, Switzerland
1993 Junior product designer,
frog design, Altensteig,
Germany
1995–1998 Senior product
designer, Philips Design,
Eindhoven
1998+ Principal designer,
Atelier Satyendra Pakhalé,
Amsterdam
2005+ Board of advisors,
Ambassadors Board, Design &
Technology community chain
mission, Eindhoven
2006+ Art-director and Head of
the Masters Program in Design
for Humanity at Design Academy Eindhoven

RECENT EXHIBITIONS

2003 "Design by Heart" (solo
exhibition), Otto 50 Gallery,
Bologna; "un:Usual by Satyen-
dra Pakhalé", Entrata Libera,
Milan; "RSVP", ICFF, New
York; "Design Mecca", Bijenkorf,
Maastricht; "Dutch Design en
Vitrine", Institut néerlandais,
Paris; "Via Milano 3", RAI,
Amsterdam; "Kalpa-Satyendra
Pakhalé", Galerie Tools, Paris
2004 "Normali Meraviglie",
curated by Arch. Alessandro
Mendini, Genoa; "Discovery",
Colombo design, Milan;
"MeToo – Magis", Milan design
week; "Add –On Radiator –
Tubes", Milan design week;
"150 Vases", MAC, Belgium
2005 "Satyendra Pakhale",
Future Design Days, Stockholm

2006 "Transformation: Nature
& Beyond", Material ConneX-
ion, New York; "Contemporary
Design – Designer's Gallery",
Galerie Gabrielle Ammann,
Cologne; "Design Miami/Basel
– Designer's Gallery", Galerie
Gabrielle Ammann, Cologne;
"NL- Lounge", the Ministry of
Foreign Affairs of the Nether-
lands, Dutch Embassy Berlin,
Germany; "Contemporary Edi-
tions – Ron Arad, Zaha Hadid,
Marc Newson & Satyendra
Pakhalé" – Design Miami/Basel,
Switzerland; "Gooood Food"
International Design Biennale,
Saint-Étienne
2007 "Satyendra Pakhalé",
Design Miami/Basel and
Designer's Gallery, Gabrielle
Ammann, Cologne; "A Dream
Come True", 10th Anniversary
Salone Satellite, Milan;
Centre Georges Pompidou,
Paris; FRAME @Colophon,
international magazine sym-
posium and exhibition, Luxem-
bourg

RECENT AWARDS

2001 Atelier grant, Sofa
Foundation, The Hague;
International Exhibition grant,
Mondriaan stitching,
Amsterdam
2002 Design Grant, The
Netherlands Foundation for
Fine Art, Architecture and
Design, Amsterdam
2003 Editor's Choice Award,
ICFF (International
Contemporary Furniture Fair),
New York

CLIENTS

Alessi, Bosa, Cappellini,
Colombo Design, CorUnum,
CRAFT, De Vecchi, Erreti,
Lille 3000, Magis,
Material ConneXion,
Moroso, Offecct, RSVP, SCA,
Tubes, Väveriet

PEARSONLLOYD

"The natural territory for our design practice lies within the commercial and industrial realities of mass production, where we believe the challenges and opportunities for the profession are at their most alive. We thrive on the restrictions imposed by product type, function, material, process, market, client and all else that defines the brief. Within this context, our practice has as much to do with observation and collation as with pure invention. In contrast, the opportunity to define new patterns of behaviour and types of product that is stimulated by the constantly developing socio-economic trends and technologies of today's global economy is one we embrace daily. At either end of the spectrum, our desire is to produce compelling solutions that are intelligent, appropriate and timeless, and contribute to what for us, is the still embryonic craft of industrial design."

„Das natürliche Terrain für unsere Designtätigkeit liegt im Rahmen der kommerziellen und industriellen Gegebenheiten der Massenproduktion, wo unserer Überzeugung nach die Herausforderungen und Möglichkeiten für den Berufsstand am größten sind. Wir wachsen mit den Einschränkungen, die uns durch Produktart, Funktion, Material, Fertigungsprozess, Markt, Auftraggeber und allen anderen Aspekten auferlegt werden und die die Aufgabenstellung definieren. In diesem Kontext hat unsere Vorgehensweise ebenso viel mit Beobachten und Vergleichen zu tun wie mit reiner Erfindung. Im Gegensatz dazu ergreifen wir täglich bereitwillig die Möglichkeit, neue Verhaltensmuster und Produkttypen zu definieren – ein Umstand, der durch die kontinuierliche Entwicklung sozioökonomischer Trends und Technologien der globalen Wirtschaft angeregt wird. An beiden Enden des Spektrums besteht unser Wunsch darin, überzeugende Lösungen zu finden, die intelligent, adäquat und zeitlos sind, und die einen Beitrag zu dem leisten, was für uns das noch unvollständig entwickelte Handwerk des Industriedesigns ist."

« Le territoire naturel de nos pratiques créatives se situe au sein des réalités commerciales et industrielles de la production en série, là où nous pensons que les défis et opportunités qui se présentent à la profession sont les plus vivaces. Nous profitons des restrictions imposées par le type de produit, sa fonction, le matériau, le processus de fabrication, le marché, le client et tout ce qui définit le projet. Dans ce contexte, notre travail tient autant de l'observation et de la collecte que de l'invention pure. Nous saisissons chaque jour l'occasion de définir de nouveaux modèles de comportement et de nouveaux types de produits, une opportunité qui naît des tendances socio-économiques et des technologies de l'économie mondialisée actuelle, en constante évolution. À chaque extrémité du spectre, notre désir est de produire des solutions incontestables qui soient intelligentes, appropriées et inusables et qui contribuent à ce qui, pour nous, est l'art encore embryonnaire de la création industrielle. »

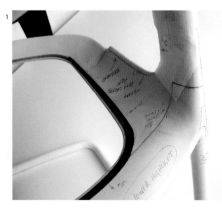

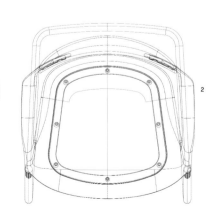

1–3
SOUL
Cantilever chair with injection-moulded seat, back and arms on a tubular steel frame
2006
Client: Allermuir

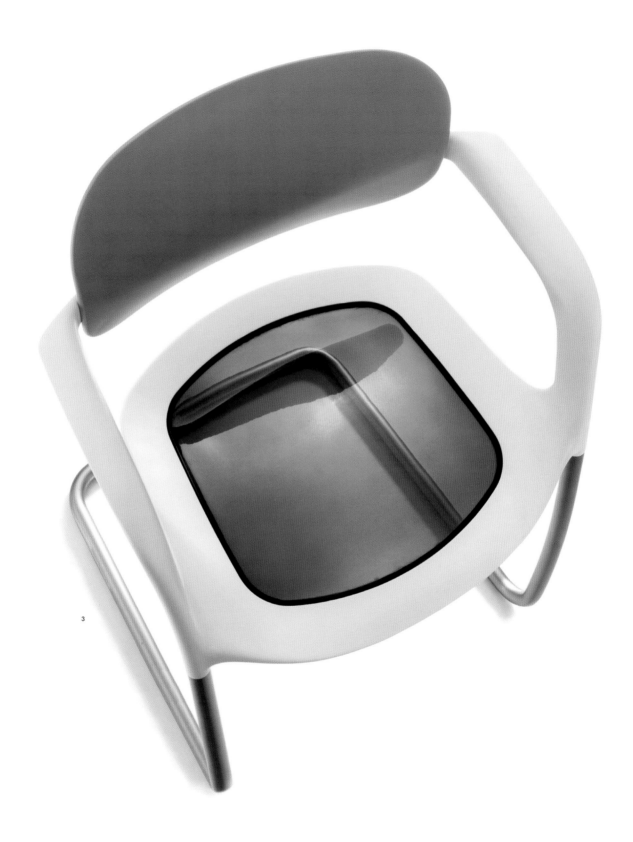

3

1–3
SOUL CANTILEVER CHAIR
FOR ALLERMUIR, 2006

"Soul is a cantilever chair that radically reinterprets an archetype that has remained unchallenged for eighty years. Using both computer modeling and hand carving, the structure and resulting form of this new cantilever chair has been reduced to its most elemental. A single plastic part simply plugs onto the steel frame, which for the first time terminates at the seat. The back and seat snap into the main plastic frame to complete the product."

„Soul ist ein Freischwinger, der einen seit 80 Jahren nicht hinterfragten Archetypus neu interpretiert. Die Struktur dieses Stuhles und seine sich daraus ergebende Gesamtform wurden durch Computermodelle und Handarbeit auf das Elementarste reduziert. Ein einziger Plastikkörper wird einfach auf den Stahlrahmen gesteckt, der mit dem Sitz abschließt. Die Rückenlehne und die Sitzfläche werden auf den Plastikkörper gedrückt, bis sie einschnappen – damit ist der Stuhl komplett."

« Soul est une chaise Cantilever qui réinterprète de façon radicale un archétype qui n'avait pas été retravaillé depuis quatre-vingts ans. Grâce à une utilisation de la modélisation par ordinateur et du façonnage manuel, la structure et la forme de cette nouvelle chaise Cantilever ont été réduites à leurs fondamentaux. Un unique élément en plastique vient simplement se caler contre le cadre d'acier qui, pour la première fois, se termine sous l'assise. Dossier et assise s'imbriquent simplement dans le principal cadre de plastique pour parachever la chaise. »

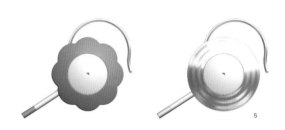

4–5
UNIVERSAL HEAR-RING
Hearing aid – a design proposal that repositions hearing aids within the culture of eyewear
2005
Client: experimental research project for the Royal National Institute for the Deaf

6
REVOLVE
Task light in white resin and polished chrome with a 330 degree pivoting head and stem, and flush circular switch
2007
Client: Bernhardt

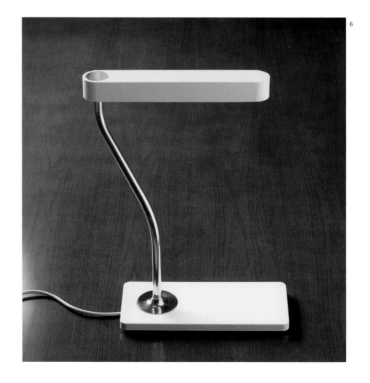

7

7
CONIC
Lounge chair with upholstered
moulded foam shell on a
polished chrome metal base
2006
Client: Allermuir

8
TWIST
Occasional table with a single
twisting surface in lacquered
or veneered MDF
2005
Client: Martinez Otero

8

PEARSONLLOYD

117 Drysdale Street
London N1 6ND
United Kingdom
T +44 20 70334440
E info@pearsonlloyd.com
www.pearsonlloyd.com

DESIGN GROUP HISTORY
1997 Founded by Luke Pearson and Tom Lloyd in London, England
1999 Won first prize in the "Millennium Street Furniture Competition", Westminster City Council, London

FOUNDERS' BIOGRAPHIES
LUKE PEARSON
1967 Born in Portsmouth, England
1991 BA Industrial Design, Central St. Martins College of Art and Design, London
1993 MA Furniture Design, Royal College of Art, London

TOM LLOYD
1967 Born in London, England
1991 BA Furniture Design, Nottingham Trent University, Nottingham
1993 MA Industrial Design, Royal College of Art, London

RECENT EXHIBITIONS
2003 "Mies meets Marx", The Geffrye Museum, London; "Home Time", British Council China, China
2004 "Au doigt et a la Baguette", École cantonale d'art de Lausanne, Milan; "Design UK", British Embassy, Tokyo
2005 "imm cologne"; "Salone del Mobile", Milan; "ISH", Frankfurt; "Design UK", British Embassy, Tokyo; "Spanish Design", Centre Georges Pompidou, Paris; "IFF", Valencia
2006 "Prima", London; "ICFF", New York; "Salone del Mobile", Milan
2007 "Salone del Mobile", Milan; "ICFF", New York; Neocon, Chicago

RECENT AWARDS
2003 Red Dot Award, Design Zentrum Nordrhein Westfalen, Essen; Baden-Württemberg International Design Award, DARC Baden-Württemberg; iF Award, International Forum Design Hanover; FX/Design Prima Award, FX Magazine, UK
2004 iF Award, International Forum Design Hanover; Design Award, Wallpaper magazine; Design Week Award, Design Week, UK; Gold Award – IDEA (Industrial Design Excellence Awards), Industrial Designers Society of America/BusinessWeek; Red Dot Award, Design Zentrum Nordrhein Westfalen, Essen; Red Dot Award – "best of the best", Design Zentrum Nordrhein-Westfalen, Essen; Award, Annual Design Review, I.D. Magazine; Silver award, D&AD Awards, UK; FX/Design Prima Award, FX Magazine, UK
2005 DBA Design Effectiveness Award, Design Business Association, UK; Silver nomination, D&AD Awards, UK
2006 iF Award, International Forum Design Hanover
2007 Design Distinction, Annual Design Review, I.D. Magazine; 2 x FX/Design Prima Awards, FX Magazine, UK; Neocon Gold and 2x Silver awards

CLIENTS
Artemide, Bernhardt, ClassiCon, Dune, Ettinger London, Ideal Standard, Knoll International, Kokuyo, Martinez Otero, Modus, Poltronova, Samas Roneo, Senator International/Allermuir, Sheffield City Council, South Yorkshire PTE, Steelcase, Tacchini, The Body Shop, Transport for London, Urban Splash, Victoria and Albert Museum, Virgin Atlantic Airways, Walter Knoll

9

ECONOMY CLASS SEAT
Airline seat with optimized ergonomics and passenger space
2006
Client: Virgin Atlantic Airways

10

PREMIUM ECONOMY SEAT
Airline seat that achieves substantial improvements in durability, whole life costs, maximization of passenger space and reduction of part numbers
2006
Client: Virgin Atlantic Airways

11–12
POLAR
Seating system with seats and
backs in differentiated density
foam filling on tubular steel
frames that can be combined to
create six sofa types
2006
Client: Tacchini

13
MP3
MP3 player that eases
navigation through simplified
form and graphics
2007
Client: Sirens

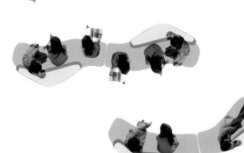

"Ours is the craft of mass-production
and a passion for what is yet to come …?"

PHILIPS DESIGN

"Philips Design is one of the largest and longest-established design organizations of its kind in the world. Part of Royal Philips Electronics, it is headquartered in Eindhoven, the Netherlands, with branch studios in Europe, the USA and Asia Pacific. Its creative force of some 450 professionals contains more than 30 different nationalities, embracing disciplines as diverse as psychology, cultural sociology, anthropology, and trend research in addition to the more 'conventional' design-related skills. The mission of these professionals is to create a harmonious relationship between people, objects and the natural/man-made environment. To realize this, Philips Design developed a unique methodology known as High Design. High Design is completely human-focused and research-based, and always uses a deep understanding of people's needs as the starting point for the design process. It also provides the framework for taking these insights and translating them into imaginative yet feasible solutions."

„Philips Design gehört weltweit zu den größten und ältesten Designzentren. Es ist Teil von Royal Philips Electronics und hat seinen Hauptsitz in Eindhoven/Niederlande mit Zweigniederlassungen in Europa, den USA und im asiatisch-pazifischen Raum. Sein Kreativteam umfasst mehr als 450 Spezialisten aus 30 verschiedenen Ländern und so unterschiedlichen Disziplinen wie Psychologie, Kultursoziologie, Anthropologie und Trendforschung, zusätzlich zu den eher konventionellen designspezifischen Branchen. Der Auftrag an diese Spezialisten ist, eine harmonische Beziehung zwischen Menschen, Objekten und der natürlichen/künstlichen Umwelt herzustellen. Um dieses Ziel zu erreichen, hat Philips Design eine einzigartige Methodik namens High Design entwickelt. High Design rückt ganz und gar den Menschen in den Mittelpunkt, basierend auf wissenschaftlicher Forschung. Der Ausgangspunkt für den Gestaltungsprozess ist dabei stets ein vielseitiges Wissen um die Bedürfnisse der Menschen. Darüber hinaus bietet High Design einen Bezugsrahmen, um diese Kenntnisse in fantasievolle und dennoch realisierbare Designlösungen zu übertragen."

« Philips Design est l'une des plus importantes et anciennes organisations de design de sa catégorie dans le monde. Elle fait partie de Royal Philips Electronics, siège à Eindhoven, aux Pays-Bas, et possède des studios en Europe, aux États-Unis et dans le Pacifique asiatique. Les quelque 450 professionnels qui constituent notre force créatrice sont d'une trentaine de nationalités différentes et spécialisés dans des disciplines aussi diverses que la psychologie, la sociologie culturelle, l'anthropologie et la recherche de tendance, en plus des métiers plus ‹conventionnels› du design. La mission de ces professionnels est de créer une relation harmonieuse entre les personnes, les objets et l'environnement naturel/construit. Pour y parvenir, Philips Design a élaboré une méthodologie unique connue sous l'appellation de *Haut Design*. Le *Haut Design* se concentre sur l'humain, se fonde sur la recherche et utilise toujours une profonde compréhension des besoins des gens comme point de départ de son processus créatif. Il apporte aussi un cadre dans lequel ces connaissances viennent s'inscrire et se traduire en solutions imaginatives mais réalisables. »

1

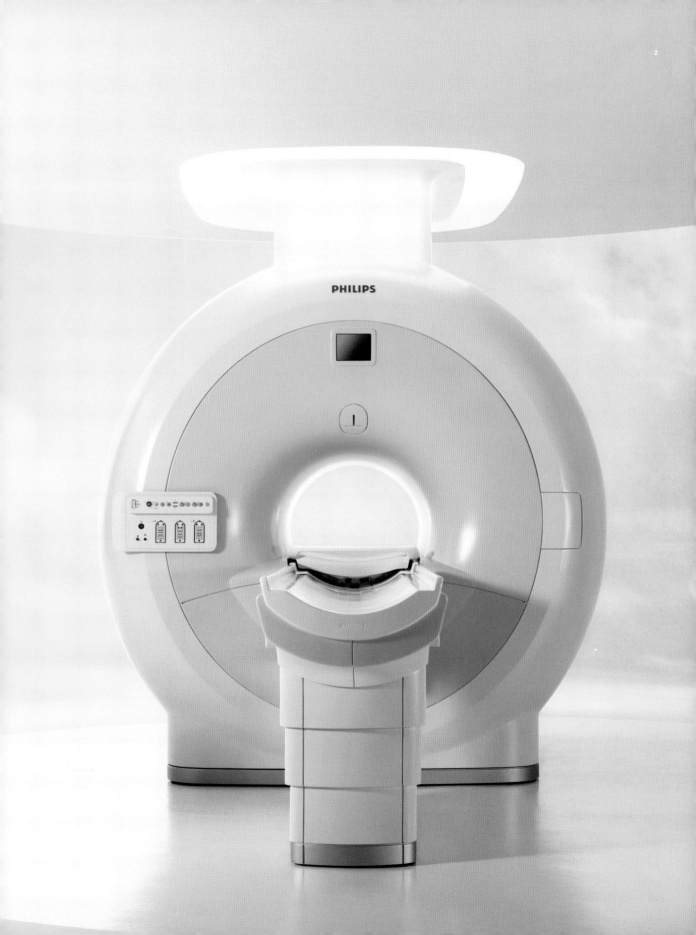

2

AMBIENT EXPERIENCE
DESIGN FOR HEALTHCARE,
2005

"Going for a brain scan can be a stressful experience. The Magnetic Resonance Imaging (MRI) equipment is imposing and patients are alone in the examination room while they're scanned. To improve the scanning experience for patients and clinicians, Philips has introduced the Ambient Experience for Healthcare. It's a truly significant step forward: a complete multimedia environment that adapts to suit individual patients and clinical staff. As soon as patients enter the MRI department they're automatically identified by the system and the environment changes to match their personal specifications. This means that a specific 'mood' can be selected which is stored on an RFID token, and this contains settings that influence the selection of music and images displayed as well as influencing the whole lighting and ambience."

„Sich einem Gehirnscanning zu unterziehen kann mit großer psychischer Belastung verbunden sein. Die für die Magnetresonanztomografie benötigte Apparatur ist imposant, und die Patienten bleiben während der Untersuchung allein im MRT-Raum. Um diese Situation so angenehm wie möglich zu gestalten, hat Philips für Healthcare das Konzept Ambient Experience entwickelt. Dieses komplette Multimedia-Environment, das auf den jeweiligen Patienten und das medizinische Personal abgestimmte Szenarien schafft, ist in der Tat ein großer Schritt vorwärts: Sobald die Patienten die MRT-Abteilung betreten, werden sie automatisch vom System identifiziert, und die Umgebung passt sich ihren individuellen Bedürfnissen an. Es kann also eine spezielle ‚Stimmung' gewählt werden, die zuvor auf einem RFID-System gespeichert wurde, wobei die Einstellungen nicht nur die Musikauswahl und Projektionen, sondern auch die gesamte Beleuchtung und das Ambiente steuern."

« Subir une scanographie cérébrale est une expérience pénible. L'équipement d'Imagerie à Résonnance Magnétique (IRM) est impressionnant et les patients se retrouvent seuls dans la salle pendant l'examen. Afin de le rendre plus agréable tant pour les patients que pour le personnel médical, Philips a créé ‹ l'Expérience ambiante pour soins médicaux ›. Il s'agit d'un important pas en avant : un environnement multimédia complet qui s'adapte à chaque client ainsi qu'à l'équipe médicale. Dès que les patients entrent dans le département d'IRM, ils sont identifiés par le système et l'environnement se modifie pour s'accorder à leurs particularités individuelles. Cela signifie qu'une ‹ humeur › spécifique peut être sélectionnée et entreposée sur un jeton RFID programmé pour diffuser certaines musiques et images, mais aussi des éclairages et des ambiances. »

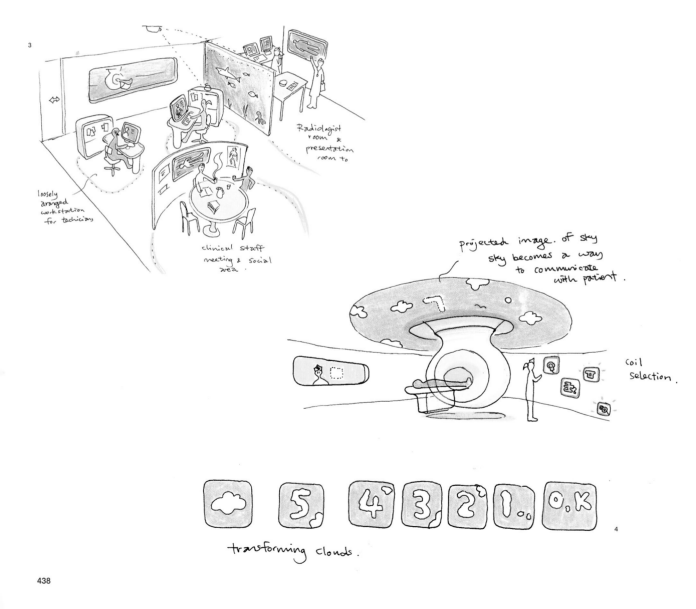

3

loosely
aranged
workstation
for technicians

clinical staff
meeting & social
area.

Radiologist
room &
presentation
room to

projected image. of sky
sky becomes a way
to communicate
with patient.

coil
selection.

transforming clouds.

4

5

1–2
AMBIENT EXPERIENCE
DESIGN FOR HEALTHCARE
Magnetic Resonance Imaging
(MRI) multimedia environment
2005

3–4
AMBIENT EXPERIENCE
DESIGN FOR HEALTHCARE
Sketches of Magnetic Resonance
Imaging (MRI) multimedia
environment layout
2005

6

5–6
CITY WING
Pedestrian lighting with
aluminium luminaire housing
and square mast that provides
uniform illumination on the
ground through new-generation
high-efficiency lens optics
combined with a mix of white
and amber LEDs
2005

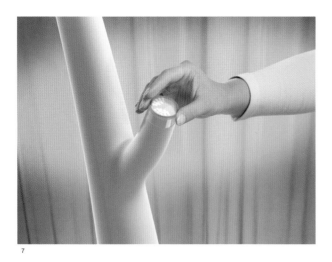

7

7–8
AIRTREE
Decorative domestic air purifier and humidifier that performs indoors the same function as biological trees. Design concept presented at the Philips Simplicity Event
2005

9–10
AIR SENSOR
Digital air sensor that provides a simple and instant method for determining outdoor air quality, day or night. Design concept presented at the Philips Simplicity Event
2005

8

"Design is about creating something
that is perceived by people as being ideal
and appropriate in all respects;
it will be seen as highly relevant and
meaningful and will improve
people's quality of life."

Stefano Marzano

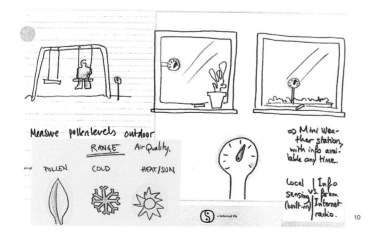

11

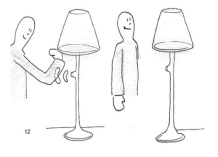

12

PHILIPS DESIGN
Building HWD–4
Emmasingel 24
Post Box 218
5600 MD Eindhoven
The Netherlands
T +31 202759000
E info.design@philips.com
www.design.philips.com

DESIGN GROUP HISTORY
Background: Philips Design is
a global design agency of Dutch
Philips Electronics
mid–1920s Louis Kalff
established, under the patronage
of Anton Philips, one of the
company's founders, the
Advertising Section of Philips
Netherlands (in-house design
studio)
1960s Philips' Board of
Management established
Industrial Design Bureau
headed by Rein Veersema
1969 In-house design studio
renamed Concern Industrial

Design Centre (CIDC) and
headed by Knut Yran
1980 Robert Blaich was
appointed Director of
CIDC
1991 Stefano Marzano
appointed CEO and Chief Creative Director of Philips Design

**CEO AND CHIEF CREATIVE
DIRECTOR'S BIOGRAPHY
STEFANO MARZANO**
1950 Born in Varese, Italy
1973 Doctorate in Architecture,
Politecnico di Milano, Milan
1973 Joined Philips Design team
working on projects with the
Major Domestic Appliances
division in Italy
1978 Design Leader for Data
Systems and Telecommunication
products, Philips Design,
Eindhoven
1982 Returned to Italy to
direct the Philips-Ire Design
Centre (Major Domestic
Appliances)

1989 Vice President of Cor-
porate Industrial Design for
Whirlpool International
(a joint venture of Whirlpool
and Philips)
1991+ CEO and Chief Creative
Director, Philips Design,
Eindhoven
1998+ Professor at the Domus
Academy in Milan and a
member of the Academy's
Strategic Board
2001+ Professor at the
Politecnico di Milano,
Faculty of Architecture
2005 Named one of the
"International Innovators of the
Year 2005" by BusinessWeek
magazine
2007+ Chairman of the
Supervisory Board for the
Faculty of Industrial Design at
the Technical University in
Eindhoven; Member of the
Design Management Institute
(Boston) Advisory Council;
Member of the Design Manage-

ment Advisory Panel of the
University of Westminster,
London

RECENT EXHIBITIONS
2007 "Design Experience 07",
Maastricht; "Opening Lighting
Exhibition", Netherlands
Architecture Institute (NAI),
Rotterdam

RECENT AWARDS
2004 3 x IDEA (Industrial
Design Excellence Awards),
Industrial Designers Society of
America/BusinessWeek;
Australian Design Award; 4 x iF
Awards, International Forum
Design Hanover
2005 3 x Hong Kong Awards for
Industries, Hong Kong; Red
Dot Award, Design Zentrum
Nordrhein Westfalen, Essen;
Design for Asia Award; Dutch
Design Prize; 4 x IDEA
(Industrial Design Excellence
Awards), Industrial Designers

Society of America/Business
Week; 2 x Good Design
Awards, The Chicago
Athenaeum; 12 x iF Awards,
International Forum Design
Hanover
2006 19 x iF Awards, Interna-
tional Forum Design Hanover;
2 x Red Dot Awards, Design
Zentrum Nordrhein-Westfalen,
Essen; 2 x Hong Kong Awards
for Industries, Hong Kong; 2 x
IDEA (Industrial Design
Excellence Awards), Industrial
Designers Society of
America/BusinessWeek;
Nominated, Design Manage-
ment Team of the Year, Design
Management Institute
2007 17 x iF Awards,
International Forum Design
Hanover

11–12
CHAMELEON
Lampshade that changes colour
to match whatever colour is
shown to it. Design concept
presented at the Philips Simplicity Event
2005

13–15
SINGAPORE LEARNING
CENTRE
Reception hub and chill-out
zone of Philips technical and
medical training centre that
features an open layout of
flowing spaces and dynamic
ambient lighting
2006

14

15

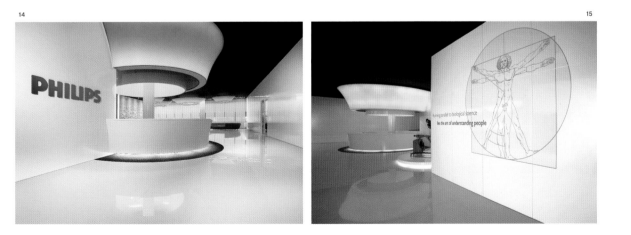

PHOENIX DESIGN

"We define our design philosophy as a frame of mind. One that not only encompasses ethics and aesthetics but also ergonomics, ecology and economy. We work together with manufacturers to develop a strategy. Instead of concentrating on one spectacular product, we focus on a product range that takes into account the needs of the consumer as well as the manufacturer's image and brand values. The defined goal of this strategy is to create products that have the potential to become bestsellers on international markets. Products created by us are not one-of-a-kind. And they never come with a particular designer's signature. They derive their unique character from skilled craftsmanship and visionary ideas influenced by people, environments and markets. Our philosophy manifests itself when a product is persuasive in its logic, when it transcends short-lived contemporary styles, and captivates with its magic."

„Wir definieren unsere Designphilosophie als eine Geisteshaltung. Eine, die nicht nur Ethik und Ästhetik umfasst, sondern ebenso Ergonomie, Ökologie und Ökonomie. Wir arbeiten zusammen mit Herstellern an der Entwicklung einer Strategie. Statt uns auf ein spektakuläres Produkt zu konzentrieren, liegt unser Fokus auf einem Produktsortiment, das sowohl den Bedürfnissen der Konsumenten wie dem Image und den Markenwerten des Herstellers Rechnung trägt. Erklärtes Ziel dieser Strategie ist es, Produkte zu gestalten, die das Potenzial haben, auf internationalen Märkten Bestseller zu werden. Die von uns entwickelten Produkte sind keine Unikate, und sie sind nie mit der Signatur eines bestimmten Designers versehen. Sie beziehen ihre Einzigartigkeit aus qualifizierter Handwerkstechnik und aus visionären Ideen, die von Menschen, Umwelt und Märkten beeinflusst sind. Unsere Philosophie manifestiert sich darin, dass ein Produkt durch seine Logik überzeugt, dass es über kurzlebige Moden hinausgeht und durch seine Magie bezaubert."

« Nous définissons notre philosophie créatrice comme un état d'esprit. Une perspective qui englobe non seulement éthique et esthétique mais aussi ergonomie, écologie et économie. Nous travaillons avec des fabricants pour développer une stratégie. Au lieu de nous concentrer sur un unique produit spectaculaire, nous concevons une ligne de produits qui prend en compte les besoins du consommateur ainsi que l'image du fabricant et les valeurs de la marque. Le but affiché de cette stratégie est de créer des produits capables de remporter un grand succès sur le marché international. Les produits que nous créons ne sont pas des modèles uniques. Et ils ne sont jamais porteurs d'une signature stylistique particulière. Ils tirent leur personnalité unique d'une connaissance expérimentée du métier et d'idées visionnaires nées sous l'influence de personnes, d'environnements et de marchés. Notre philosophie se manifeste lorsqu'un produit est intrinsèquement persuasif, lorsqu'il transcende les styles contemporains éphémères et captive par sa magie. »

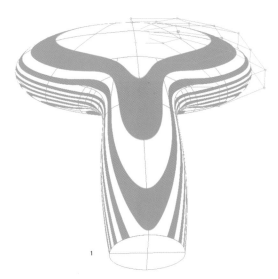

1

1–2
RAINDANCE AIR
Extra large handheld chrome showerhead integrating Rain AIR-Technology, rubit cleaning system and dirt filter
2005
Client: Hansgrohe

"Logic, Principles, Magic"

4

3

5

3
DOOR STATION
Surface-mounted door com-
munication/security station in
stainless steel with integral
camera
2006
Client: Gira

4
SMILE
Fountain pen for older children
with a plastic cap with three
movable rings that display
emoticons, which can be set in
the view window of the clip to
create small memos,
wish-lists, messages, etc.
2006
Client: Lamy

5
GIGASET SL550
Cordless telephone with integrated answering machine,
equipped with a computer
interface enabling rapid data
synchronization with a PC
2005
Client: Siemens

6
ASSIST
Remote control with aluminium
upper section and optimized
button spacing
2006
Client: Loewe

7
INDIVIDUAL
Family of televisions that
can change aspects of their
appearance to suit individual
tastes and décor – a variety of
differently coloured inlay panels
can be clipped on to the sides
of the TV
2005
Client: Loewe

PHOENIX DESIGN
Kölner Straße 16
70376 Stuttgart
Germany
T +49 711 9559760
E info@phoenixdesign.de
www.phoenixdesign.de

DESIGN GROUP HISTORY
1987 Founded by Andreas Haug
and Tom Schönherr in Stuttgart,
Germany

FOUNDERS' AND
PARTNERS' BIOGRAPHIES
ANDREAS HAUG
1946 Born in Heidenheim,
Germany
1966–1968 Trained and studied
technical-commercial theory at
Daimler-Benz, Stuttgart
1968–1972 Studied Design at
Staatliche Akademie der Bilden-
den Künste, Stuttgart under
Professor Klaus Lehmann
1972–1982 Designer/Partner,
Esslinger Design, Altensteig
1975–1982 Partner, Esslinger
Design, Altensteig
1982–1987 Partner/Vice President of Design, frog design,
Altensteig

TOM SCHÖNHERR
1954 Born in Stuttgart,
Germany
1976–1982 Studied Design at
Staatliche Akademie der Bilden-
den Künste, Stuttgart under
Professor Klaus Lehmann
1979–1982 Worked as an
independent designer under the
name of Duo Design
1982–1987 Designer,
frog design, Altensteig

RECENT AWARDS
2005 Good Design Award,
Chicago Athenaeum; "Focus"
award, Internationaler Design-
preis Baden-Württemberg,
Stuttgart; Red Dot Award,
Design Zentrum Nordrhein
Westfalen, Essen; Design Plus
Award, Ambiente, Frankfurt; iF
Award, Industrie Forum Design,
Hanover; iF Award China,
International Forum Design,
China; Design Award of the
Federal Republic of Germany,
German Design Council/ Rat
für Formgebung, Frankfurt
2006 Good Design Award,
Chicago Athenaeum; "Focus"
award, Internationaler Design-
preis Baden-Württemberg,
Stuttgart; Red Dot Award,
Design Zentrum Nordrhein
Westfalen, Essen; iF Award,
Industrie Forum Design,
Hanover; iF Award China,
International Forum Design,
China
2007 One Gold and 13 iF
Awards, Industrie Forum
Design, Hanover; Design
Award of the Federal Republic
of Germany, German Design
Council/ Rat für Formgebung,
Frankfurt; 8x Red Dot Award,
Design Zentrum Nordrhein-
Westfalen, Essen; Design Award
of the Federal Republic of Ger-
many, German Design Council

CLIENTS
Axor, BenQ-Siemens,
Duravit, Fuji Xerox/Japan,
Gira, Hansgrohe, Hirschmann,
Kaldewei, Lamy,
Laufen/Schweiz, Leonardo,
LG/Korea, Loewe, Miele,
NCR/USA, Pharo, Rösle,
Schock, Sharp/Japan,
Siemens, T-Mobile, Viessmann

POC

"POC is a Swedish company with the mission to do the best we can possibly do to save lives and to reduce injuries for skiers. In the process of developing products we need to establish a cross scientific platform to work from. Primarily, it's about understanding the most vital parts that need protection: the head and the spine. Furthermore it's about identifying the most appropriate materials, constructions and industrial opportunities, choosing the best to be implemented into our products, in order to optimize protection and performance. Then it's all about testing, refining, testing, refining ..."

„POC ist ein schwedisches Unternehmen, das sich zum Ziel gesetzt hat, das Bestmögliche zu tun, um Leben zu retten und Verletzungen im Skisport zu reduzieren. Dabei müssen wir im Produktentwicklungsprozess eine interdisziplinäre Plattform als Ausgangspunkt für unsere Arbeit schaffen. In erster Linie geht es darum, die wichtigsten Körperteilen zu kennen, die Schutz benötigen: den Kopf und die Wirbelsäule. Anschließend heißt es, die zweckdienlichsten Materialien, Konstruktionen und Produktionsmittel zu finden und für die Implementierung in unsere Produkte auszuwählen, um sowohl Schutz als auch Leistung zu optimieren. Und dann geht es nur noch darum, zu prüfen, zu verbessern, zu prüfen, zu verbessern ..."

« POC est une compagnie suédoise dont la mission est de faire tout son possible pour sauver des vies et réduire le nombre de blessés parmi les skieurs. Lorsque nous concevons un produit, nous travaillons à partir d'une plateforme scientifique transversale qu'il faut établir. Il s'agit d'abord de comprendre quels sont les points vitaux à protéger : la tête et la colonne vertébrale. Mais il s'agit aussi d'identifier les matériaux, les constructions et les possibilités industrielles les mieux adaptés, de choisir lesquels seront intégrés à nos produits, afin d'optimiser la protection et la performance. Tout n'est plus alors qu'essais, perfectionnement, essais, perfectionnement... »

1

2

3

1–4

SKULL COMP HELMET,
2006

POC's Skull Comp is the ultimate alpine ski-racing helmet. It combines a unique multi-layer shell with a patented Aramid-membrane penetration barrier, which cushions and reduces bounce, decreasing brain damage and neck injury as well as making the helmet dramatically lighter. The Skull Comp also features a special "snug fit" system of an inner core with extra padding. The result is an attractive-looking helmet with outstanding protective properties that also fits perfectly, with a secure grip but no pinching. It fits and feels like an injection-moulded ski boot.

Mit der Entwicklung des Skull-Comp-Helms für den alpinen Skirennsport hat das Unternehmen POC ein wahres Meisterstück vollbracht. Durch die Kombination einer einzigartigen, mehrschichtigen Schale und einer patentierten bruchsicheren Aramidmembran, die im Fall eines Sturzes den Aufprall dämpft, schützt dieser Helm Kopf und Nacken besser vor Verletzungen; dabei ist der Helm unglaublich leicht. Darüber hinaus hat der Skull Comp eine spezielle Auspolsterung, die für festen Sitz und Passgenauigkeit sorgt. Das Ergebnis ist ein ansprechender, eleganter Helm mit herausragenden schützenden Eigenschaften, der noch dazu wie angegossen sitzt, ohne zu drücken, und sich so angenehm trägt wie ein im Spritzgussverfahren hergestellter Skischuh.

Le Skull Comp de POC est l'ultime casque de ski de vitesse. Sa coquille multicouche unique, combinée à une barrière de protection enveloppée de toile Aramide, amortit les chocs et réduit le rebond, réduisant ainsi les risques de blessures cérébrales et cervicales tout en rendant le casque beaucoup plus léger. Le Skull Comp est également doté d'une enveloppe intérieure spécialement renforcée et ajustée, ce qui en fait un casque agréable à regarder et exceptionnellement protecteur qui s'adapte parfaitement au crâne sans le serrer de façon désagréable. Il apporte un aussi grand confort que des chaussures de ski moulées par injection.

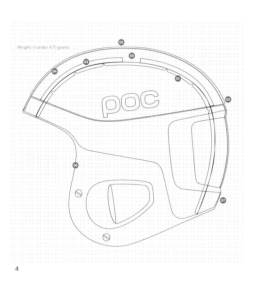

Weighs in under 475 grams

4

1

GOLD MEDAL WINNER
Julia Mancuso wearing a Skull Comp helmet in the Giant Slalom event at the 2006 Winter Olympics in Turin

2–4

SKULL COMP
Ski racing helmet with a multi-layer shell including a penetration barrier of ballistic Aramid and a slightly convex non-slip rubberized back panel to keep ski goggles in place
2006

5

IRIS COMP
Ski goggles that provide high-precision visibility and come with three interchangable lenses for different light conditions
2006

5

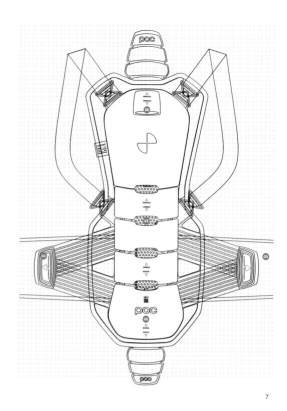

6–8
SPINE
Front and rear views of flexibly
jointed ski racing back protection system in injection-moulded
polypropylene, with optional
snap-on cervical and coccyx
shields
2006

9–10
TORSO ARMOR JACKET
Front and rear views of ski
racing underjacket with integrated, but individually detachable, back protection and shoulder and collarbone padding
2006

11
SKIN
One-piece ski racing suit made
of super-supple artificial fiber
with integrated padding
2006

12–13
PALM COMP
Anatomically shaped ski-racing
glove in leather with pre-curved
integrated protective panels
2006

POC
POC Sweden AB
Skogsövägen 22
13333 Saltsjöbaden
Sweden
T +46 8 7174050
E info@pocski.com
www.pocski.com

COMPANY HISTORY
2003 Founded by Stefan Ytter-
born (b. 1963) in Saltsjöbaden,
Sweden. Soon afterwards Jan
Woxing (b. 1962) and Fred
Wikström (b. 1970) joined and
became partners
2005 POC's first launch of
products at the ISPO trade fair
2005/2006 First season members of US Ski Team used POC
products, including Julia Man-

cuso, who won Olympic Gold
(Giant Slalom) in Turin while
wearing a POC helmet

RECENT EXHIBITIONS
2005 "ISPO", Munich
2006 "ISPO", Munich
2007 "Design S", Washington
DC; "ISPO", Munich; "SIA",
Las Vegas

RECENT AWARDS
2005 Swedish Outdoor Design
Award 2005, Jämtland Regional
Design Center; Brand New
Award, ISPO
2006 Gear of the Year award,
Ski Magazine; Winner, Sport
Design Award, Volvo Sports
Design Forum, Sweden;
Swedish Design Award, Adver-
tising Association of Sweden,
the Swedish Industrial Design

Foundation and Svensk Form
(the Swedish Society of Crafts
and Design)
2007 Gold Award, 2007 Design
Award of the Federal Republic
of Germany, German Design
Council/Rat für Formgebung;
Nomination, SportsDesign
Award, Volvo SportsDesign
Forum, Sweden

"It is all about relevance,
not forgetting that appearance
is relevant too."

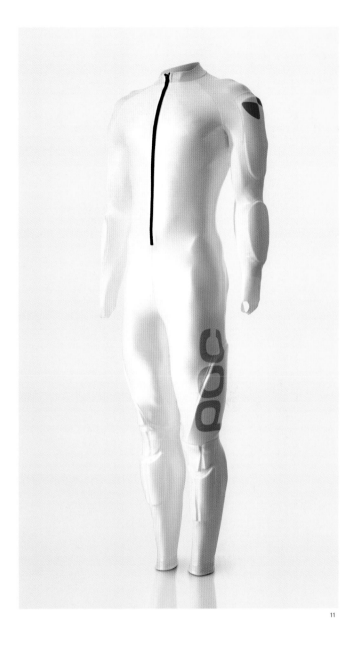

11

12

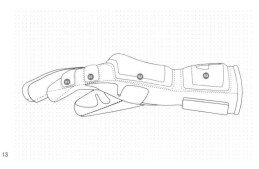

13

PORSCHE DESIGN STUDIO

"PORSCHE DESIGN was founded in 1972 by Ferdinand Alexander Porsche, the grandson of the Porsche founder Ferdinand Porsche. Until 1972 he was responsible for the design of the Porsche 911. His approach to design was closely associated with the Porsche philosophy, but also marked by the classic German design doctrine of the Bauhaus and Academy of Fine Arts in Ulm. Porsche sports cars are purist, technically precise and have traces of inventive talent with the aim of creating the best possible result – performance. Today, Porsche stands for luxury through purism instead of abundance. Emotionality is generated through practicality. Every detail and every concept follows a technical requirement. A further aspect of the Porsche tradition is the emphasis placed on the internal structural build-up of a product, instead of improving the exterior. PORSCHE DESIGN conceptualizes products from the inside out. Superficial design is avoided. Products with high internal quality, e.g. electronics, are supported through high quality materials on the outside. Materials acting as pure decoration are avoided. It is important here to find the fine borderline between 'added-on' materials as opposed to giving the product more quality and fascination. The styling of an individual product can therefore lie between classical and detail quality on the one hand and innovative standards coupled with concept quality on the other. PORSCHE DESIGN products are timeless and offer reliability and continuity to the user. This is achieved through their ease of maintenance, ageless styling, safety and solidity. The border between conceptual and experimental design is not crossed to avoid losing the sincerity and honesty that PORSCHE DESIGN portrays."

„PORSCHE DESIGN wurde 1972 von Ferdinand Alexander Porsche, dem Enkel des Porsche-Gründers Ferdinand Porsche ins Leben gerufen. Bis 1972 war er für das Design des Porsche 911 verantwortlich. Sein Designansatz war eng mit der Porsche-Philosophie verbunden, aber auch durch die klassische Gestaltungslehre des Bauhauses und der Ulmer Hochschule für Gestaltung geprägt. Sportwagen von Porsche sind puristisch, technisch präzise und zeugen von Erfindungsgabe, die eingesetzt wird, um das bestmögliche Resultat zu erzielen – Leistung. Heute steht Porsche für Luxus durch Purismus anstelle von Überfluss. Emotionalität wird durch Praktikabilität erzeugt. Jedes Detail und jede Konzeption entspricht einer technischen Anforderung. Ein weiterer Aspekt der Porsche-Tradition ist, dass besonderer Wert auf den Aufbau der inneren Konstruktion eines Produkts gelegt wird statt auf die Optimierung des Äußeren. PORSCHE DESIGN entwickelt Produkte von innen nach außen. Oberflächliches Design wird vermieden. Produkte mit hoher innerer Qualität, wie etwa die Elektronik, werden durch hochwertige äußere Materialien unterstützt. Vermieden werden Materialien, die lediglich als Dekoration dienen. Dabei ist es wichtig, die schmale Grenzlinie zu finden zwischen ‚zusätzlichen' Materialien und Materialien, die eingesetzt werden, um dem Produkt weitere Qualität und Faszination zu verleihen. Das Styling eines individuellen Produkts kann deshalb zwischen klassischer Qualität im Detail auf der einen Seite und innovativen Standards gepaart mit konzeptioneller Qualität auf der anderen Seite liegen. Produkte von PORSCHE DESIGN sind zeitlos und bieten dem Benutzer Zuverlässigkeit und Kontinuität. Das gelingt durch ihre mühelose Wartung und Pflege, ihre alterslose Formgebung, Sicherheit und Solidität. Die Grenze zwischen konzeptionellem und experimentellem Design wird nicht überschritten, um den Verlust von Aufrichtigkeit und Ehrlichkeit, die PORSCHE DESIGN ausstrahlt, zu vermeiden."

«PORSCHE DESIGN a été fondé en 1972 par Ferdinand Alexander Porsche, le petit-fils du fondateur de Porsche, Ferdinand Porsche. Il était jusqu'alors responsable du design de la Porsche 911. Son approche du design était étroitement liée à la philosophie Porsche, mais était aussi marquée par la doctrine allemande classique du Bauhaus et de l'Académie des Beaux-Arts d'Ulm. Les voitures de sport de Porsche sont puristes, techniquement précises et teintées d'un certain talent inventif dans le but de créer le meilleur résultat et la meilleure performance possibles. Aujourd'hui, Porsche est le symbole d'un luxe emprunt de purisme plutôt que d'abondance. L'émotion est provoquée par le caractère pratique. Chaque détail et chaque concept répond à un impératif technique. Un autre aspect de la tradition Porsche est l'importance accordée à la conception structurelle interne du produit plutôt qu'à l'amélioration de son aspect extérieur. PORSCHE DESIGN conceptualise des produits de l'intérieur à l'extérieur ; nous évitons le design superficiel. Des produits dotés d'une haute qualité interne, comme les produits électroniques, sont servis par des matériaux de haute qualité à l'extérieur. Nous évitons les matériaux qui ne seraient que pure décoration. Il est important, dès lors, de définir la mince frontière entre les matériaux ‹rajoutés› et le fait de donner davantage de qualité et de charme au produit. Le stylisme d'un produit individuel doit par conséquent se placer entre, d'un côté, la qualité classique jusque dans les détails, et de l'autre une rencontre entre innovation et rigueur conceptuelle. Les produits créés par PORSCHE DESIGN sont éternels et offrent au consommateur fiabilité et continuité, grâce à leur facilité d'entretien, à leur style sans âge, à leur sécurité et à leur solidité. La frontière entre design conceptuel et expérimental n'est pas franchie afin que soient conservées la sincérité et l'honnêteté qu'incarne PORSCHE DESIGN. »

1
NESPRESSO
Coffee-making machine in
brushed aluminium with digital
display and removable 1.2 litre
water tank
2005
Client: Siemens

2
XM
Tabletop radio with front-firing
loudspeakers and credit-card
sized remote control
2005
Client: Eton

3
P'3000 SERIES
Shake pen and ballpoint in
chromed metal and non-slip
natural rubber
2005
Client: Faber-Castell

4
SIEMENS HOME
APPLIANCES
Family of domestic appliances
in brushed aluminium, including
toaster, vacuum flask, cordless
kettle and Nespresso machine
2005
Client: Siemens

"Fascination through technical innovation, thoroughness and timelessness."

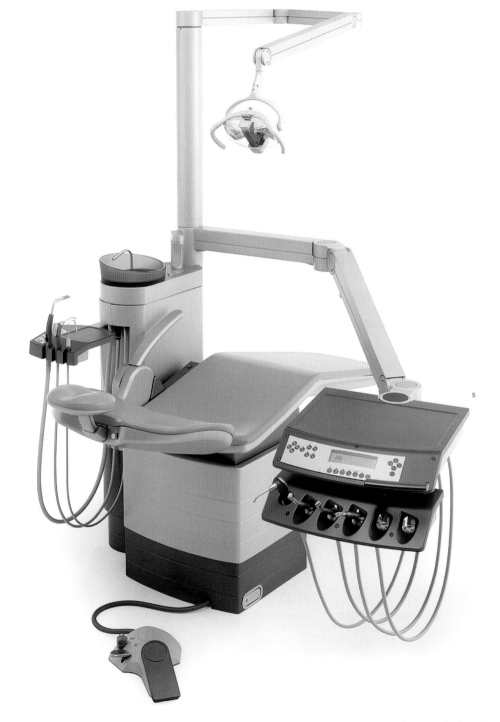

5
DENTAL TREATMENT UNIT
Dental treatment unit with high aluminium central column, to which all the rotating parts, such as the trays, arm systems and light unit are connected.
The table elements are made of a transparent synthetic material and the colour selection serves to promote a relaxing atmosphere
2005
Client: Morita

5

6

PORSCHE DESIGN STUDIO

Porsche Design GmbH
Flugplatzstraße 29
5700 Zell am See
Austria
T +43 6542 572270
E info@porsche-design.at
www.porsche-design.com

DESIGN GROUP HISTORY

1972 Founded by Prof.
Ferdinand Alexander Porsche in
Stuttgart
1974 Porsche Design Studio
moved to Zell am See, Austria
2003 Subsidiary of Porsche
Design Group

FOUNDER'S BIOGRAPHY

1935 Born in Stuttgart, Germany (son of Ferry Porsche and
grandson of Ferdinand Porsche)
1954 Apprentice, Bosch,
Stuttgart
1957 Studied at the Hochschule
für Gestaltung, Ulm
1958 Began working in the
Porsche design department
under Erwin Komenda
1961–1972 Headed the Porsche
auto design department
1972 Founded own design office
(Porsche Design Studio)

RECENT EXHIBITIONS

2000–2001 "Mensch Telefon",
Museum für Kommunikation,
Frankfurt
2001 "Design Austria.now"
travelling exhibition, Nagoya
Designzentrum, Japan
2002 "fahr!rad" ("Drive!
Wheel!"), Technisches Museum,
Vienna; "Design Austria.now",
Hong Kong
2002–2003 "Sammlung Kunst-
gewerbe und Design im 20.
Jahrhundert", Württembergi-
sches Landesmuseum, Stuttgart
2003 "Design Austria",
Kongresshaus, Zurich; "Design
Austria.now", Melbourne,
Brisbane
2004 "Design Austria", Galeria
und Octagon, Budapest;
"Design Austria.now", MAK,
Vienna

RECENT AWARDS

2004 Les Étoiles de l'Observeur
du Design, APCI (Agence pour
la promotion de la création
industrielle); Red Dot Award
and Red Dot Award – "best of
the best", Design Zentrum
Nordrhein-Westfalen, Essen
2005 Finalist, Corporate Design
Preis, Kommunikationsverband,
Stuttgart; ADC Deutschland
award, Art Directors Club
Deutschland; 3 x Red Dot
Awards and 1 x Red Dot Award
– "best of the best", Design
Zentrum Nordrhein-Westfalen,
Essen; 2 x iF Awards, Interna-
tional Forum Design Hanover;
Silver award, DDC Awards –
"Gute Gestaltung", Deutscher
Designer Club; 2 x Awards,
London International Award;
Designpreis des Landes Nord-
rhein-Westfalen – Ehrenpreis
Corporate Design, Design
Zentrum Nordrhein-Westfalen,
Essen; Finalist, Deutscher

Designer Club award, Deutscher
Designer Club; I.L.M. Award
2005, Messe Offenbach
2006 5 x iF Awards, Internation-
al Forum Design Hanover;
Red Dot Award – "best of the
best", Design Zentrum
Nordrhein-Westfalen, Essen;
Silver award, DDC Awards –
"Gute Gestaltung", Deutscher
Designer Club

CLIENTS

Self-production for Porsche
Design (e.g. Adidas,
Bosch-Siemens, Eterna, Eton,
Faber-Castell, Metano,
Navigon, Poggenpohl,
Rodenstock, Zumtobel)

Artemide, Boesendorfer,
Celda, Chroma, Fearless Yachts,
Grohe/Keramag, Kyocera,
Morita, Poltrona Frau,
SGP-Siemens

6
P'6910 INDICATOR
Wristwatch with case made of titanium and weight optimized rotor. The design consciously alludes to the Porsche Carrera GT sports car.
2005
Client: Eterna

7
P'5610 DRIVING SHOE
Driving shoe with asymmetrical tops and soles, which help boost performance and protect the foot during lateral movements. The extra-thin sole helps the driver feel the exact pressure on the pedals.
2005
Client: Adidas

8
P'9611 NAVIGATOR
Satellite navigation unit with pressure cast aluminium caps on the upper and lower sides
2005
Client: Navigon

9
P'7911 MULTIHAMMER
Power tool with aluminium and carbon casing. Its ergonomic form helps orientate the hands to the top to enable better control.
2005
Client: Metabo

KARIM RASHID

"I am interested in rethinking the banal, changing our commodity landscape and proposing new objects for new behaviours for diverse markets. I am interested in democratizing design and getting the public to live in the moment (not the past). I believe that design is extremely consequential to our daily lives where we impact physical, physiological and sociological behaviour, by setting up conditions of human experience. I am 'an artist of real issues'; everyday life mediates between industry and the user; between self-expression and desire, between production technologies and human social behaviour. Products and furniture must deal with our emotional ground, therefore increasing the popular imagination and experience. Industrial Design is a creative act, a political act, and a physical act. A socially interactive and responsible process that is greater than the physical form itself; its result is manifested in aesthetic forms. Design shapes our personal and commercial environments and has great significance for culture, for our evanescent public memory. I think the most important element is that I attempt to design objects, products and spaces that create a sense of well being, the energy of our time informs a heightened experience, increases pleasure, and that has some nuance of originality or innovation."

„Ich bin daran interessiert, das Alltägliche zu überdenken, unsere Warenlandschaft zu verändern, neue Objekte für neue Verhaltensweisen und vielfältige Märkte zu entwickeln. Ich bin daran interessiert, Design zu demokratisieren. Meiner Überzeugung nach ist Design äußerst folgenreich für unser Alltagsleben, denn wir beeinflussen als Gestalter das physische, physiologische und soziologische Verhalten, indem wir die Bedingungen für menschliche Erfahrung aufstellen. Ich bin ‚ein Künstler realer Themen'. Das Alltagsleben ist der Vermittler zwischen Industrie und Benutzer, zwischen Produktionstechniken und menschlichem Verhalten. Produkte und Einrichtungsgegenstände müssen sich mit unserem emotionalen Grundstock auseinandersetzen und folglich die allgemeine Vorstellungskraft und Erfahrung steigern und vermehren. Industrielle Formgebung ist ein kreativer Akt, ein politischer Akt und ein körperlicher Akt. Ein sozial interaktiver und verantwortungsvoller Prozess. Design gestaltet unsere persönliche und kommerzielle Umwelt und hat große Bedeutung für die Kultur, für unser vergängliches öffentliches Gedächtnis. Meiner Meinung nach ist der wichtigste Aspekt dabei, dass ich mich bemühe, Gegenstände, Produkte und Räume zu gestalten, die Wohlbefinden erzeugen. Die Energie unserer Zeit bildet ein erhöhtes Erlebnispotenzial, sie steigert den Genuss, und darin zeigen sich die Nuancen von Originalität oder Innovation."

« J'aime repenser la banalité, modifier notre paysage matériel, proposer de nouveaux objets pour de nouvelles attitudes et des marchés différents. J'aime démocratiser le design et encourager le public à vivre dans l'instant (et non dans le passé). Je pense que le design découle principalement de nos vies quotidiennes, de la façon dont nous modifions notre comportement physique, physiologique et sociologique pour faire avancer l'expérience humaine. Je suis ‹ un artiste de la réalité ›; la vie de tous les jours est un médiateur entre l'industrie et l'usager ; entre l'expression personnelle et le désir, entre les technologies de fabrication et le comportement social humain. Produits et meubles doivent être en lien avec notre terrain émotionnel afin de nourrir l'imagination et l'expérience populaires. Le design industriel est un acte créatif, un acte politique et un acte physique. Un processus social interactif et responsable qui dépasse la forme physique elle-même ; son résultat se manifeste sous une forme esthétique. Le design façonne notre environnement personnel et commercial et occupe une place significative dans notre culture, notre évanescente mémoire publique. Je pense que le plus important est que je tente de créer des objets, des produits et des espaces qui suscitent une impression de bien-être, porteurs de l'énergie de notre époque qui nourrit une expérience de plus en plus dense, qui augmentent le plaisir et sont doués d'une certaine originalité ou innovation. »

4

1
KIT 24
Computer rendering of 24-sided kit house
2006
Client: installation sponsored by *The Globe and Mail*

2
KIT 24
Computer rendering of 24-sided kit house, first floor
2006
Client: installation sponsored by *The Globe and Mail*

3
KIT 24
Computer rendering of 24-sided kit house, ground floor
2006
Client: installation sponsored by *The Globe and Mail*

4
KIT 24
24-sided kit house with exterior in painted aluminium panels
2006
Client: installation sponsored by *The Globe and Mail*

5
KIT 24
24-sided kit house, staircase leading to first floor
2006
Client: installation sponsored by *The Globe and Mail*

5

1–6
KIT 24 KIT HOUSE FOR THE EIGHTH ANNUAL INTERIOR DESIGN SHOW, TORONTO, 2006

Created specially for the eighth annual Interior Design Show in Toronto, Kit 24 is a house produced with simple, minimal parts and tooling. The environment comprises a few repeated elements that assemble a 24-sided house, but it is also intended as a metaphor for time and is based on a 24-hour day. Karim Rashid's aim was to show a contemporary approach to the idea of kit houses, a subject explored by architects and engineers for decades. His solution provides an interesting and artistic space for living inspired by technology, while also serving as a venue for his furniture designs.

Rashid schuf eigens für die achte Interior Design Show in Toronto das Fertighaus Kit 24, eine relativ schlichte Konstruktion aus minimalistischen Bauteilen, die mit einfachen Arbeitsgeräten montiert werden können. Ein paar Basiselemente fügen sich so zu einem 24-seitigen Environment zusammen, das überdies – vom 24-Stunden-Tag ausgehend – als Metapher für die Zeit steht. Karim Rashid wollte einen zeitgenössischen Ansatz für ein Thema präsentieren, das die Kreativen in Architektur und Bauwesen seit Jahrzehnten beschäftigt: die Idee des vorgefertigten Hauses oder des „Hausbaukastens". Seine Lösung sieht einen interessanten Wohnraum vor, der zugleich Kunstwerk ist, von Technologie inspiriert wurde und darüber hinaus auch als Schauraum für seine Möbeldesigns dient.

Spécialement créée pour le huitième salon annuel d'Architecture intérieure de Toronto, Kit 24 est une maison construite à partir d'éléments simples et minimalistes. L'environnement se constitue de quelques éléments qui sont répétés et assemblés entre eux pour former une maison à 24 facettes mais se veut aussi une métaphore du temps fondée sur la journée de 24 heures. L'objectif de Karim Rashid était de montrer comment aborder de façon contemporaine l'idée de la maison en pièces détachées, un sujet exploré depuis des décennies par architectectes et ingénieurs. Sa solution offre un espace de vie intéressant et artistique qui s'inspire de la technologie tout en servant d'écrin à ses créations de mobilier.

6

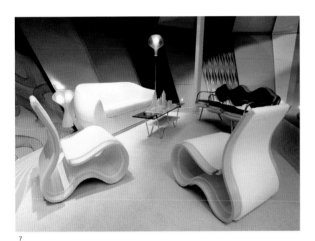

7

"Design is no longer a word or a profession,
it is a philosophy – a doctrine – a way of living,
a modus operandi, a way of being
and will one day be seamless with existence."

6
KIT 24
24-sided kit house
first floor bathroom
2006
Client: installation sponsored by
The Globe and Mail

7
KIT 24
24-sided kit house
ground floor living area
2006
Client: installation sponsored by
The Globe and Mail

8
KIT 24
24-sided kit house
ground floor
2006
Client: installation sponsored by
The Globe and Mail

8

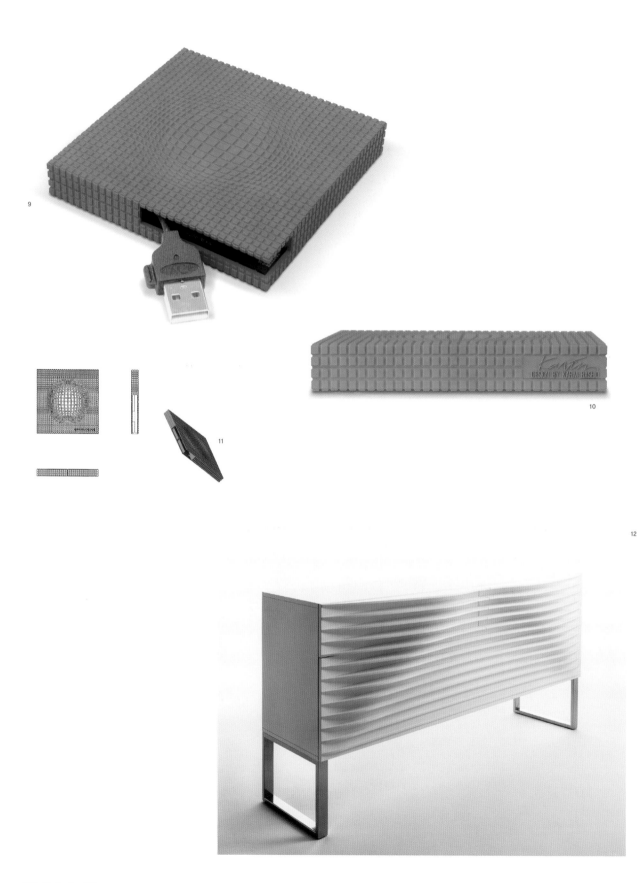

9

10

11

12

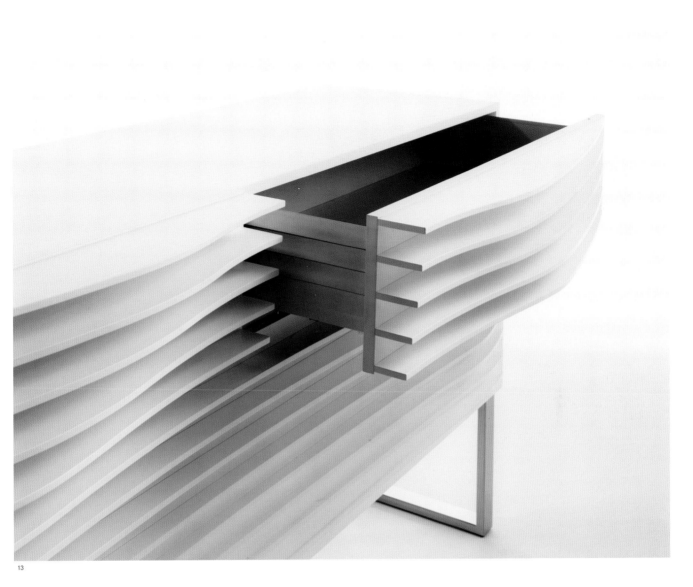

13

14

9–11
SKWARIM
60GB handheld portable hard
drive with an integrated hi-speed
USB 2.0 cable for instant
plug-and-play and a rubberized
external surface with an
embossed morphing grid
2005
Client: LaCie

12–14
TIDE
Sideboard in lacquered wood
with two drawers and a fall flap
on a varnished metal base
2006
Client: Horm

17–19
AXE LAB
Premium eau de toilette packaging in anodized aluminium
2006
Client: Axe

15

15–16
KONE
Cordless, battery powered
7.2 volt rechargeable hand-held
vacuum cleaner in injection-
moulded high-impact plastic
with an easy-empty bagless dirt
cup and soft tip that protects
delicate surfaces
2006
Client: Dirt Devil

16

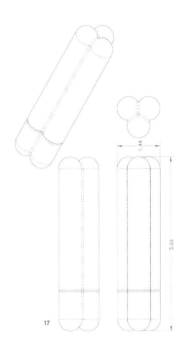

17

18

19

20

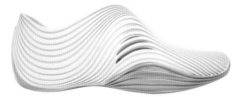

Vista Lateral

Vista Superior

21

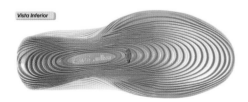

Vista Inferior

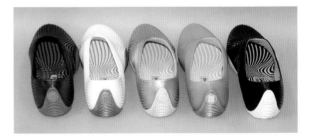

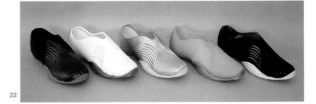

22

20–22
DYNAMIK
Slip-on sports loafer in
injection-moulded plastic
2006
Client: Melissa

23
CADMO
Halogen floor lamp with painted
steel body and a steel panel that
screens and releases a soft
indirect light upwards, together
with a diffused light along the
vertical aperture of the lamp
2006
Client: Artemide

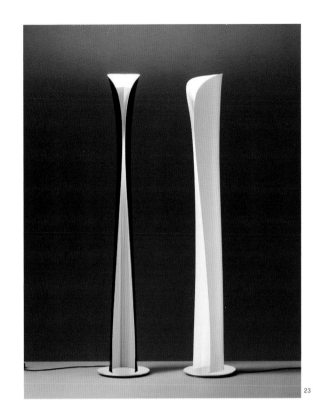

23

KARIM RASHID

Karim Rashid Inc.
357 West 17th St.
New York
New York 10011
USA
T +1 212 9298657
E office@karimrashid.com
www.karimrashid.com

BIOGRAPHY

1960 Born in Cairo, Egypt
(Canadian national)
1978–1982 BA Industrial
Design, Carleton University,
Ottawa
1981–1982 Designer, Mitel
Corporation, Kanata, Canada
1983 Post-graduate design
studies, Massa Lubrense, Italy
(sponsored by ADI/ISIA,
Rome)
1984 Designer, Rodolfo
Bonetto Industrial Design
Studio, Milan
1984–1991 Senior
designer/partner, KAN
Industrial Designers, Toronto
1985–1991 Senior designer/
co-founder, Babel Inc. & North
Studio, Toronto
1992 Founded Karim Rashid
Inc. in New York

1993–1995 Visiting Associate
Professor, Industrial Design
Dept., Pratt Institute, New York
1993+ Associate Professor,
Industrial Design Dept.,
The University of the Arts,
Philadelphia
2005 Honorary Doctorate of
Fine Arts from Corcoran College
of Art & Design; Published
"Digipop" book (a digital ex-
ploration of computer graphics)
at TASCHEN
2006 Honorary Doctorate,
Ontario College of Art and
Design, Toronto, Canada

RECENT EXHIBITIONS

2004 "Get Off", Museum of
Sex, New York
2005 "Safe: Design Takes on
Risk", The Museum of Modern
Art, New York; "Okso",
Tatintsian Gallery, Moscow;
"Extreme Abstraction", Albright
Knox, Buffalo, New York;
"Touch Me", Victoria and Albert
Museum, London; "Macro
Design Action Fun", Sandra
Gerring Gallery, New York;
"Super Design Action Fun",
Spazio Tashi Delek, Milan
2006 "Kairotics", Roma

Design ++, Rome; "Karim
Rashid", Price Tower Arts
Center, Bartlesville, OK;
"Karim Rashid", Philippine
International Furniture Show,
Manila, Philippines; "Karim
Rashid and Megan Lang", M
Modern Gallery, Palm Springs,
CA; "Kairotics", Townhouse
Gallery, Cairo

RECENT AWARDS

2006 Good Design Award,
Chicago Athenaeum; 100 Best
Design Products nomination,
Gioia Casa magazine, Italy; 4 x
Boutique Design Awards – Best
Use of Lighting, Best Use of
Space, Best Restaurant & Best
Flow; Nomination, APCI
Observeur du Design, Agence
pour la promotion de la création
industrelle, Paris; Pratt Legend
Award, Pratt Institute, Brook-
lyn; Housewares Design Award,
International Housewares
Association, USA; Bronze
Industrial Design Excellence
Awards, IDSA (Industrial
Designers Society of America);
Red Dot Award, Design Zen-
trum Nordrhein Westfalen,
Essen

2007 iF Award, International
Forum Design Hanover;
Honorable Mention, Annual
Design Review, I.D. Magazine;
Gold Award, NeoCon, Chicago;
3 X Awards, FiFi Awards, Fra-
grance Foundation, New York;
Product Design Finalist,
National Design Awards,
Cooper-Hewitt National Design
Museum, New York; 2 x Red
Dot Awards, Design Zentrum
Nordrhein Westfalen, Essen;
ADEX Award for Design
Excellence, Design Journal, San-
ta Monica

CLIENTS

Acme, Aisin Seiki, Alain Mikli,
Arena International,
Arnolfo di Cambio, Artbox,
Artemide, Bart, BDI,
Beauté Prestige International,
Benza, Biomega, Bitossi,
Bozart Toys,
Canada Post Corporation,
Cappellini, Carolina Herrera,
Cassabella, CNCP, ConEdison,
Contempo, Copco, Curvet,
Cybercouture, Danese,
David Design, Davidoff,
Decorum, Edra, Egizia,
Elika, Estée Lauder,

EXPO 86, Fabbian, Fasem,
Fauchon, Felice Rossi,
Feracchi Casa, Foscarini,
Frighetto, Gaia + Gino,
Galerkin, Georg Jensen,
George Kovacs,
Giorgio Armani,
Golay, Guzzini, Hanspree,
Herman Miller, Horm,
Idée Co. Ltd., IHW, Ioli,
Issey Miyake, Label, LaCie,
L'Art du Temps, Leeds,
Leonardo, Magis, Marburg,
Martinelli, Maybelline,
Method Home, M Glass,
Mikasa, Minka Group,
Mobilkom,
Morimoto Restaurant
My Hotel(s), Nambé, Natison,
Natuzzi, Nemo, Neverstop,
Nienkamper,
Normann Copenhangen,
OFFECCT, Offi, Prada,
Prescriptives, Pure Design,
Ralph Lauren, Ritzenhoff,
Ronson, Salviati, Sceye,
Semiramis Hotel, Serralunga,
Sony, Step, Taschen, Teppich
Timex, Tommy Hilfiger,
Totem, Toyota, Umbra,
Unilever, Wolf Gordon,
Yahoo!, Yves Saint Laurent,
Zeritalia, Zerodisegno

SEYMOUR-POWELL

"Seymourpowell thinks of the product itself and the brand as being inseparable parts of the whole. The term 'three-dimensional branding' has become an expression of this idea, because ultimately the product – what the customer sees, touches and uses in daily life – should be a constant reminder of the brand. This fundamental duality requires companies to have a deep understanding of, and connection with, the world of branding. Seymourpowell's track record and longevity is very much based on the company's record of successful, innovative consumer products for international markets, and this remains the centre of gravity of the consultancy, but the need to respond to ever changing client requirements and to constantly evolve the role of design is also key to the success of the business."

„Seymourpowell betrachtet das Produkt selbst und die Marke als untrennbare Teile eines Ganzen. Der Begriff ‚dreidimensionales Branding' ist zu einem treffenden Ausdruck für diese Idee geworden, weil letztendlich das Produkt, das die Kunden im Alltagsleben sehen, berühren und benutzen, fortwährend die Marke in Erinnerung rufen sollte. Diese grundlegende Dualität erfordert Unternehmen, die ein umfassendes Wissen von und eine enge Verbindung zu der Welt der Markenpositionierung haben. Die Leistungsbilanz und Langlebigkeit von Seymourpowell beruht in hohem Maß auf der langen Liste erfolgreicher, innovativer Konsumgüter für internationale Märkte, und das wird der Schwerpunkt unserer Beratungsfirma bleiben. Aber die Notwendigkeit, auf die sich stetig verändernden Kundenanforderungen zu reagieren und kontinuierlich die Rolle des Designs weiterzuentwickeln, ist ein weiterer Schlüssel zum Unternehmenserfolg."

«Seymourpowell considère la marque et le produit lui-même comme les parties inséparables d'un tout. Le terme de ‹marquage tridimensionnel› est devenu une expression de cette idée, parce que, au bout du compte, le produit – ce que le consommateur voit, touche et utilise dans la vie courante – doit servir à rappeler la marque. Cette dualité fonctionnelle exige des entreprises qu'elles aient une connaissance profonde du monde de l'identité de marque, et entretiennent des liens étroits avec lui. Le palmarès et la longévité de Seymourpowell se sont principalement construits sur des produits de consommation courante innovants qui ont eu du succès sur les marchés internationaux, ce qui reste le centre de gravité de notre carnet de commande, mais la nécessité de répondre aux exigences perpétuellement changeantes des clients et de faire évoluer constamment le rôle du design joue aussi un rôle capital dans le succès de notre affaire.»

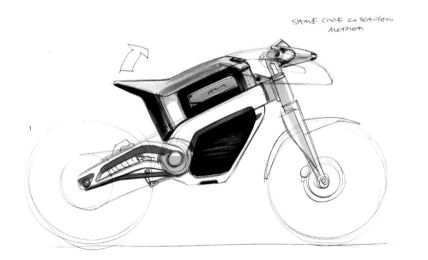

1
ENV
Drawing of fuel-cell motorcycle showing integration of Core hydrogen fuel cell
2005
Client: Intelligent Energy

2
CORE
Detachable hydrogen fuel cell with aluminium casing
2005
Client: Intelligent Energy

3–6
ENV
Fuel-cell motorcycle with
detachable Core hydrogen
fuel cell
2005
Client: Intelligent Energy

"To prove, through thoughts,
words and deeds, that design is about
'making things better for people
and business'."

7

1–6

ENV (EMISSIONS NEUTRAL VEHICLE) FOR INTELLI-GENT ENERGY, 2005

Designed and engineered from the ground up, the ENV is the world's first purpose-built, fuel cell motorbike. Nick Talbot of Seymourpowell comments, "When it came to designing the casing for the CORE we treated it as a standalone project, giving this radical fuel cell its due as a beautiful, valuable and useful energy resource. The CORE, which can be detached completely from the bike, is therefore designed to create interest as an enigmatic object. Although mostly encased in identical aluminium to the bike, of which it at first seems a completely integral part, the CORE is also part-covered on one plane in a micro-etched, textured and durable shell, in a pattern derived from brain coral. The pattern alludes to the fact that this is solid-state technology – but is also functional, in that the intricate patterns also disperse heat. We wanted this to be a finer and more beautiful object than, say, a diesel generator – and to make people look again at this new technology with a sense of wonder."

Das ENV ist das erste spezialgefertigte und völlig neu konzipierte Motorrad mit Brennstoffzellenantrieb. Nick Talbot, Chefdesigner von Seymourpowell, bemerkt dazu: „Als wir zur Ummantelung des CORE genannten Herzstückes des Fahrzeugs kamen, betrachteten wir dieses Gehäuse als ein eigenständiges Designprojekt, um die in ihrer Art einmalige Brennstoffzelle in gebührender Weise als einen schönen, wertvollen und nützlichen Energielieferanten zu würdigen. Die CORE-Brennstoffzelleneinheit, die komplett aus dem Bike herausgenommen werden kann, ist daher so gestaltet, dass sie als rätselhaftes Objekt Aufmerksamkeit erregt. Sie ist teils in Aluminium gehüllt, das auch beim Rahmen Verwendung findet, wodurch sie auf den ersten Blick ein integraler Bestandteil des Bikes zu sein scheint, teils ist sie von einer festen, langlebigen Schale umgeben, deren von Hirnkorallen inspirierte Oberflächenstruktur durch Mikroätzen entsteht. Das Muster spielt auf die Halbleitertechnologie an, die hier zum Einsatz kommt, ist aber auch funktional gestaltet, da durch die verschlungene Struktur Hitze abgeführt wird. Die CORE-Brennstoffzelleneinheit sollte ein eleganteres und schöneres Objekt als beispielsweise ein Dieselgenerator sein – sie sollte die Blicke auf diese neue Technologie lenken und alle, die sie betrachten, in Staunen versetzen."

Imaginée et élaborée des roues au guidon, l'ENV est la première moto au monde spécialement conçue pour carburer aux piles à combustible. Nick Talbot, de SeymourPowell, commente ainsi sa création : « Quand il s'est agi de concevoir le revêtement du CORE nous l'avons traité comme un projet à part entière pour donner à cette pile révolutionnaire une allure qui soit à la hauteur de son utilité en tant que source d'énergie. Le CORE, qui peut se détacher complètement de la moto, est par conséquent conçu comme un objet énigmatique qui attire la curiosité. Bien qu'en grande partie enrobé du même aluminium que la moto, dont il paraît à première vue faire partie intégrante, le CORE est aussi partiellement couvert, sur une de ses faces, d'une coquille microgravée, granitée et durable dont le motif est inspiré du corail du cerveau. Ce motif fait référence au fait qu'il s'agit de technologie à circuits intégrés tout en insistant sur sa fonctionnalité puisqu'il est aussi conducteur de chaleur. Nous voulions qu'il soit un objet plus réussi et plus beau que, disons, une pompe à essence – et que les gens se retournent sur cette nouvelle technologie avec un certain émerveillement. »

8

7–10
ENV
Front and rear views and details
of fuel-cell motorcycle
2005
Client: Intelligent Energy

9

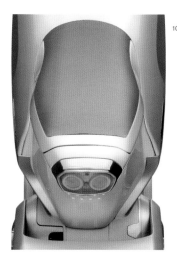

10

12–13
VIRGIN GALACTIC
SPACECRAFT INTERIOR
Concept commercial spacecraft
with interior designed to be
ultra-ergonomic to ensure
maximum comfort, space and
visibility for two pilots and six
consumer astronauts.
The seats can be moved into
a near horizontal angle allowing
the astronauts free movement
around the cabin
2006
Client: Virgin Galactic

11
LUX
Soap bar with organic and
sculptural form that has been
optimized for high-speed
manufacture
2005
Client: Unilever

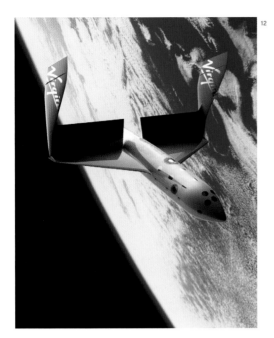

12

13

SEYMOURPOWELL

327 Lillie Road
London SW6 7NR
United Kingdom
T + 44 20 73816433
E design@seymourpowell.com
www.seymourpowell.com

DESIGN GROUP HISTORY
1984 Founded by Richard Seymour and Dick Powell in London
1989 Adrian Caroen joins practice
1994–1995 Nick Talbot and David Fisher join practice
1998 "Designs on your ..." television series for Channel 4
2000 "Better by Design" television series for Channel 4

FOUNDERS' BIOGRAPHIES
RICHARD SEYMOUR
1953 Born in Scarborough, England
1971–1974 BA (Hons) Graphic Design, Central St. Martin's College of Art and Design, London
1974–1977 MA Graphic Design, Royal College of Art, London
1977–1979 Freelance Art Director (for various Advertising Agencies), London
1979–1982 Creative Director of Blazelynn Advertising, London
1982–1983 Freelance Designer, London

1983 Formed Seymour-Furst
1984 Worked with Jonathan Miller on the TV commercial for "The Human Body"; Formed Seymourpowell with partner Dick Powell

DICK POWELL
1951 Born in Great Kingshill, England
1969–1970 Foundation Course at Farnham, West Surrey
1970–1973 BA Industrial Design, Manchester Polytechnic
1973–1976 MA Industrial Design, Royal College of Art, London
1976–1979 Formed CAPA Partnership
1980–1983 Freelance designer
1984 Formed Seymourpowell with partner Richard Seymour

RECENT EXHIBITIONS
2005 "100 % East", London Design Festival
2007 "Head Hand Heart", Petersfield, Hampshire

RECENT AWARDS
2003 Winner, DBA Design Effectiveness Awards; Short-listed, The Prince Philip Design Prize; Starpack Award, The Packaging Society; Winner – corporate film, Silver Screen Awards; Gerald Frewer Memorial Trophy, Institute of Engineering Design

2004 Joint Winner, Helen Hamlyn Awards
2005 Pro Carton Award, Pro Carton/ECMA; Bronze Award, Annual Design Review, I.D. Magazine; Homes & Gardens Awards; The Carmen's Company Award of Merit 2005, The Worshipful Company of Carmen; Finalist – Well-Tech Award for Innovation Technology and Sustainability; Winner – General Innovations Category, Popular Science Best of What's New 2005 Awards
2006 Finalist – Carton Board Packaging category, Outstanding Combination of Materials in Pack category, New Production Development through Packaging category, Packaging Awards; Finalist – Transport Category, First Choice Responsible Tourism Awards; Highly Commended – Industry Innovation Design Award, The East Journal Awards; Winner – DBA Design Effectiveness Awards; Winner – Consumer Products Category, Design Week Awards; Gold Medal, IDEA (Industrial Design Excellence Awards), Industrial Designers Society of America/BusinessWeek
2007 Gold Winner, EID (Excellence in Design) Awards, Appliance Design

CLIENTS
Addis, Aqualisa, Barclays, Bell Helicopters Textron, Birdseye, BMW, Bombardier, British Army, Cadbury Schweppes, Calor, Cambridge Audio, Canon, Casio, Cathay Pacific, Charnos, Coffee Nation, Day Son & Hewitt, Dell, Diageo, Dockers, Dr Martens, Dove, Dualit, Duracell, Durex, Ford, General Motors, Goodwood, Guinness, Hasbro, Hewlett Packard, Honda, Huntleigh Healthcare, Intelligent Energy, Jaguar, JCB, Knorr, Lever Faberge, LG Electronics, Lufthansa Technik, Mercury Appliances, Midland Mainline, Minolta, Mission, MZ Motorcycles, NCR, Nokia, Panasonic, Philip Morris, Pizza Express, Renault, Rexona, Roland, Rowenta, Saitek, Samsung, Shell, Shimano, Stannah, Tefal, Toshiba, TOTO, Tumi, Unilever, Vaseline, Virgin Galactic, Volvo, Waterman, Yamaha

FUMIE SHIBATA

"I am dedicated to producing real home products for the present age. As consumers, we all live with the items in our home in the same way as we live with our roommates, partners or family members. My aim is to find out the real functionality required of the items we surround ourselves with in our modern lives. I try to go beyond basic specifications and look at the emotional factors of how we relate to the items in our personal space, and how they provide us with both comfort and care, and then I give shape to items that embody these characteristics. I attempt to rethink the attitude of simply replacing the items around us with newer versions that have higher specifications, and instead try to focus on bringing objects into our lives that we really need."

„Ich habe mich der Produktion realer Haushaltsprodukte für das gegenwärtige Zeitalter verschrieben. Als Konsumenten leben wir alle mit den Gegenständen in unserem Zuhause, genauso wie wir mit unseren Mitbewohnern, Partnern oder Familienmitgliedern leben. Mein Ziel ist es, die wahre Funktionalität von Gegenständen herauszufinden, mit denen wir uns in unserem modernen Leben umgeben. Ich versuche, über die grundlegenden Spezifikationen hinauszugehen und betrachte die emotionalen Aspekte unserer Beziehung zu den Gegenständen in unserem persönlichen Umfeld und die Art, wie sie uns Trost spenden und Fürsorge bieten. Dann verleihe ich Gegenständen eine Form, die diese Merkmale verkörpert. Ich versuche, die Haltung zu korrigieren, mit der wir die Gegenstände in unserer Umgebung einfach durch neuere Versionen mit mehr Spezifikationen ersetzen, und konzentriere mich stattdessen darauf, Objekte in unser Leben zu bringen, die wir wirklich brauchen."

« Je me consacre à la conception de produits ménagers réellement adaptés à l'époque moderne. En tant que consommateurs, nous cohabitons tous avec les objets de notre maison comme nous cohabitons avec nos colocataires, partenaires ou parents. Mon objectif est de découvrir les fonctionnalités dont doivent réellement être dotés les objets dont nous nous entourons dans nos vies modernes. J'essaie de dépasser les spécificités traditionnelles et de prendre en compte les facteurs émotionnels de notre relation avec les objets qui peuplent nos espaces personnels ainsi que la manière dont ils nous procurent à la fois confort et soin ; je façonne ensuite des accessoires qui incarnent ces caractéristiques. Je tente de repenser l'attitude qui consiste à simplement remplacer nos outils quotidiens par des versions plus récentes et plus performantes, en essayant plutôt de faire entrer dans nos vies des objets dont nous avons vraiment besoin. »

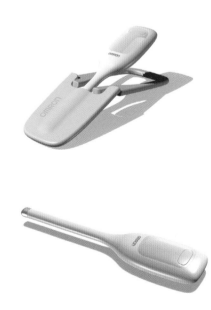

1

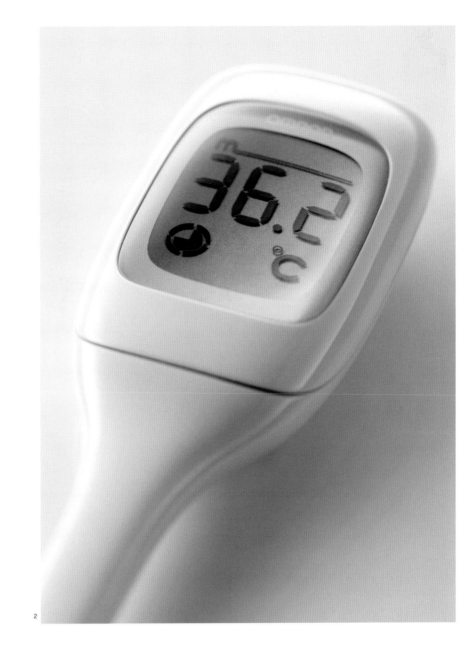

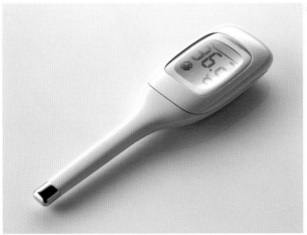

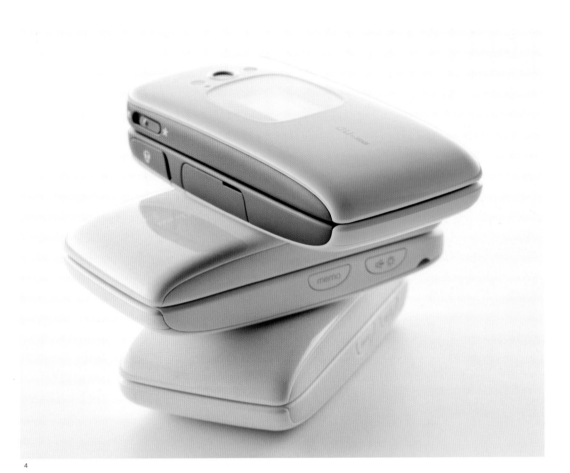

4

"Approach: Reconstruct the basic functions of household items and search for new standards."

1–3
MC-670-E (i-TEMPO)
Digital thermometer with an easy-to-read LCD display and a flat tip that allows users to hold it comfortably
2004
Client: Omron Healthcare

4–5
SWEETS PURE
Mobile phone with smooth texture and high-gloss finish featuring a camera, email and GPS system
2006
Client: au by KDDI

5

6

7

8

6
ZUTTO
Coffee maker in
brushed aluminium
2004
Client: Zojirushi

8
ZUTTO
Electric rice cooker in
brushed aluminium
2004
Client: Zojirushi

7
ZUTTO
Electric kettle in
brushed aluminium
2004
Client: Zojirushi

FUMIE SHIBATA
Design Studio S
4-2-35-301 Roppongi
Minato-ku
Tokyo 106-0032
Japan
T +81 3 34797113
E info@design-ss.com
www.design-ss.com

BIOGRAPHY
1965 Born in Yamanashi
Prefecture, Japan
1986–1990 Studied industrial
design at Musashino Art
University
1990–1993 Designer, Toshiba
Design Center, Tokyo
1994 Established own design
office, Design Studio S in Tokyo
2003+ Judge of Good Design
Award, Japan
2006+ Part-time Lecturer of
Product Design Course at Tama
Art University

RECENT EXHIBITIONS
2006 "Takeo Paper Show
2006", Spiral Hall, Tokyo;
"Real" (Solo exhibition), Matsuya Ginza Design Gallery,
Tokyo

RECENT AWARDS
2000 Good Design Award,
JIDPO (Japan Industrial Design
Promotion Organization),
Tokyo
2003 Good Design Award,
JIDPO (Japan Industrial Design
Promotion Organization),
Tokyo

2004 Good Design Award,
JIDPO (Japan Industrial Design
Promotion Organization),
Tokyo
2005 Good Design Award,
JIDPO (Japan Industrial Design
Promotion Organization),
Tokyo
2006 Good Design Award,
JIDPO (Japan Industrial Design
Promotion Organization),
Tokyo
2007 Gold iF Award, Interna-
tional Forum Design Hanover

CLIENTS
Benesse, Combi,
Iwatani International,
KDDI, Kinto,
Kobayashi Pharmaceutical Co.,
Konica Minolta, LG Electronics,
Matsushita Electric Industrial Co.,
Miyoshi Soap Corp,
OKA Co.,
Omron Healthcare Co.,
Shachihata, Shiseido,
Zojirushi

JENS MARTIN SKIBSTED

"We at Skibsted use design as a marketing tool, creating radically new concepts for clients, hopefully Instant Icons. An Instant Icon is a new product, which somehow transcends ordinary product types. It has an immediate emotional appeal and tells a story you really want to hear. Instant Icons were key in generating PR value exceeding 136 million USD for the luxury brand Biomega. The pull effect of an Instant Icon is dramatically superior to a traditional marketing approach. We apply the thinking of motion pictures, fashion and branding to the world of industrial design. The need to differentiate and be innovative has probably never been greater than today. Companies invest huge sums in innovation. However, research from Doblin Group tells us that up to 96% of all industrial innovations fail. Part of the reason for this lack of efficiency is that companies often have the wrong approach. The great potential today lies in applying the right amount and right type of innovation for the right thing, not in reinventing the wheel. At Skibsted Ideation we will work with existing product portfolios in order to reposition brands. Through Micro-innovation we rewire and remix existing features in playful and even groundbreaking ways to create cost effective emotional appeal and just cooler products for our clients. Specifically, we have a long track record with urban mobility. Urban Mobility is about commuting effectively and in style within the city environment. Being active in the city challenges your equipment in new ways. When you get off your bike and walk, in and out of an air-conditioned environment or a steaming subway, you need to counter moisture and temperature. On your bike you are constantly accelerating and braking between the lights. In short, a whole host of new bi-polar functionalities are needed. This is where Urban Mobility sets in and becomes the answer as the aesthetic choice."

„Wir von Skibsted setzen Design als Marketinginstrument ein und erarbeiten radikal neue Konzepte für Klienten, aus denen hoffentlich Instant Icons werden. Instant Icon ist ein neues Produkt, das gewöhnliche Produkttypen übertrifft. Es hat eine unmittelbar wirksame emotionale Anziehungskraft und erzählt eine Geschichte, die man wirklich hören möchte. Instant Icons waren der Schlüssel für einen mehr als 136 Millionen Dollar umfassenden PR-Wert der Luxusmarke Biomega. Die Erfolgsrate von Instant Icon im Hinblick auf Schaffung von Verbrauchernachfrage ist einer traditionellen Marketingstrategie bei Weitem überlegen. Wir wenden die Denkart von Film, Mode und Branding auf die Welt des Industriedesigns an. Unternehmen investieren riesige Summen in Innovation. Eine von Doblin Group durchgeführte Untersuchung verrät uns jedoch, dass bis zu 96 Prozent aller industriellen Innovationen fehlschlagen. Ein Grund für die mangelnde Effizienz ist, dass Unternehmen oft einen falschen Zugang haben. Heutzutage liegt das große Erfolgspotenzial im richtigen Maß und der richtigen Art von Innovation für die richtige Sache und nicht darin, dass man das Rad neu erfindet. Wir von Skibsted Ideation arbeiten mit bestehenden Produkt-Portfolios, um Marken neu zu positionieren. Mittels Mikroinnovation überarbeiten wir auf spielerische und sogar revolutionäre Weise bestehende Merkmale oder kombinieren sie neu, um einen kosteneffizienten emotionalen Reiz und einfach coolere Produkte hervorzubringen. Speziell im Bereich urbane Mobilität können wir eine hohe Erfolgsbilanz vorweisen. Urbane Mobilität dreht sich darum, effizient und stilvoll innerhalb des Stadtgebiets zu pendeln. Der Anspruch auf aktives Stadtleben ist eine neue Herausforderung für die eigene Ausrüstung. Steigt man von seinem Fahrrad ab und geht in eine klimatisierte Umgebung oder in eine dampfende U-Bahn hinein, muss man sich gegen Feuchtigkeit und Temperaturschwankungen wappnen. Auf dem Fahrrad muss man zwischen den Ampeln abwechselnd beschleunigen und bremsen. Kurz: Es wird eine ganze Palette neuer bipolarer Funktionsmerkmale benötigt. Hier setzt urbane Mobilität an und bietet eine Antwort als ästhetische Wahl."

Chez Skibsted, nous utilisons le design comme un outil marketing en créant pour nos clients des concepts nouveaux et, avec un peu de chance, des Icônes de l'Instant. Une Icône de l'Instant est un produit nouveau qui parvient à transcender la typologie classique du produit. Elle exerce une séduction émotionnelle immédiate et raconte une histoire que vous avez réellement envie d'entendre. Les Icônes de l'Instant ont été décisives dans la création d'une visibilité qui a permis à la marque de luxe Biomega de générer plus de 136 millions de dollars de profits. Le pouvoir d'attraction d'une Icône de l'Instant est spectaculairement supérieur à celui d'une approche commerciale traditionnelle.

Nous appliquons les stratégies du cinéma, de la mode et de la musique au monde du design industriel. Le besoin de se différencier et d'innover n'a sans doute jamais été aussi important qu'aujourd'hui. Les entreprises investissent des sommes énormes dans l'innovation. Une étude du Doblin Group révèle pourtant que 96 % des innovations industrielles échouent. Ce manque d'efficacité est en partie dû au fait que les entreprises abordent souvent le problème sous le mauvais angle.

Il est aujourd'hui capital de décider quelle quantité et quel type d'innovation appliquer à quoi, au lieu de réinventer la roue. Chez Skibsted Ideation, nous travaillons avec des portfolios de produits existants afin de repositionner les marques. Grâce à la micro-innovation, nous reconnectons et remixons les modèles existants de façon ludique et même révolutionnaire afin de créer une attirance émotionnelle renouvelée et, tout simplement, des produits plus frais pour nos clients. Nous avons plus précisément une longue expérience de la mobilité urbaine. La Mobilité Urbaine, c'est se connecter avec efficacité et élégance avec l'environnement urbain. Être actif dans la ville met au défi notre équipement de façon nouvelle. Lorsque nous descendons de vélo pour marcher, que nous entrons et sortons d'un environnement climatisé, nous devons combattre l'humidité et la chaleur. Sur un vélo, nous passons notre temps à accélérer ou à freiner entre deux feux. En bref, il faut instaurer tout un nouvel éventail de fonctionnalités bipolaires. C'est ici que la Mobilité Urbaine entre en scène et devient une réponse esthétique.

Wheelbase 1000 mm
Chainstay 400 mm
Seattube ø 35
Seattube length 500 mm c to top

2

Cross-section of extruded seat and chainstay (ideal)   Rear and front forepost   Extruded seatstay bridge

Folded frame

3

BOSTON BIKE FOR
BIOMEGA, 2005

"Unfasten the heavy-gauge cable that serves as the down tube to fold the Boston bike in half for carrying on cramped subway cars or storing in closet-sized studio apartments. When out and about, the same wire serves as a lock – just secure it around a sturdy object on the sidewalk. Should the cord be cut, the frame won't stay in riding position, rendering the bike as spineless as the thief trying to snatch it."

„Löst man das dicke Drahtseil, das als unteres Rahmenrohr dient, kann man sein Boston in der Mitte zusammenklappen, um es in überfüllten U-Bahn-Wagen zu transportieren oder in winzigen Einzimmerwohnungen zu verstauen. Ist man jedoch damit unterwegs, kann dasselbe Seil als Schloss verwendet werden – man muss es nur um einen festen Gegenstand auf dem Gehsteig schlingen. Sollte dieses Drahtseil durchgeschnitten werden, wäre das Rad nicht mehr fahrtüchtig und so rückgratlos wie die Person, die es sich schnappen wollte."

« Détachez le câble d'écartement transversal ultrarésistant pour plier le vélo Boston et l'embarquer dans un wagon de métro bondé ou le ranger dans un coin de chambre de bonne. Lorsqu'il est de sortie et de balade, le même câble sert de cadenas – il suffit de l'enrouler autour d'un objet urbain fixe. S'il était sectionné, le cadre ne pourrait plus rester en position active et le vélo se retrouverait aussi pantelant que son agresseur. »

1–3
BOSTON BIKE
Semi-folding, single-speed bicycle for everyday riding with an 18" aluminium frame, unique integrated locking system and twin disc brakes
2005
Client: Biomega

4–5
BOSTON BIKE
Details of semi-folding bicycle frame hinge lock and front disc brake
2005
Client: Biomega

4

5

6–8
PUMA UM
Bike-riding shoe with reflective
side panels and integrated elastic
bicycle clip
2005
Client: Puma

JENS MARTIN SKIBSTED
Skibsted Ideation A/S
Skoubogade 1,1
1158 Copenhagen K
Denmark
T +45 70 229900
E info@skibstedid.com
www.skibstedid.com

BIOGRAPHY

1970 Born in Sønderborg,
Denmark
1990 Co-founded AV-ART
arts association
1992–1994 Professional
diploma/equivalent to BA/
Film-making, ESEC, Paris
1994–1998 BA Philosophy,
Copenhagen University
1998 Co-founded Biomega
in Copenhagen
2000 Professional diploma
in Project Management,
University of California,
Berkeley
2003 Published his own
collection of poems "Kavesom"
2004 Co-founded Actics
(an ethical consultancy)
in Copenhagen
2005 Founded his own design
consultancy, Skibsted Ideation
in Copenhagen

RECENT EXHIBITIONS

2004 "Dreams on Wheel",
Danish Design Center, Copen-
hagen; "De Industrielle Ikoner –
Design Danmark", Det danske
Kunstindustrimuseum;
"Designbody", Trapholt
Museum, Denmark
2005 "Taipei International
Cycle Show 2006", Taipei;
"InterBike", Las Vegas; "Bio-
mega for PUMA", Museum
of Modern Art, San Francisco
2006 "Taipei International
Cycle Show 2006", Taipei;
"Premium Fashion Fair", Berlin;
"Danish Design", Rocket
Gallery, London; "Honey, I'm
home", Danish Design Center,
Copenhagen; "SAFE: Design
takes on Risk", Museum of
Modern Art, New York
2007 "Biennale for Art of
Crafts and Design 2007",
Trapholt and Koldinghus,
Denmark; "Magisk Design –
produkter der har ændret vores
liv", Danish Design Center,
Copenhagen; "Taipei Interna-
tional Cycle Show 2007",
Taipei; Museum of Modern Art,
San Francisco; "INDEX:Award
exhibition", Kgs. Nytorv,
Copenhagen; "[Skibsted's]
Micro-Innovation, Danish
Design Center, Copenhagen

RECENT AWARDS

2004 Winner of Best Bike
award, Wallpaper magazine
2005 Certificate of Excellent
Design Distinction – Consumer
Products, Annual Design
Review, I.D. Magazine
2005 Design Distinction –
Consumer Products, Annual
Design Review, I.D. Magazine
2007 Top Nominee,
INDEX:Award, Copenhagen

CLIENTS

Biomega, Copenhagen City
Center, Danfoss Bionics,
Formation, Georg Jensen,
Lightyears, Mater, Okiedog,
Openphace, Puma, Saab,
StressO, Volkswagen, Zio & Zia

9

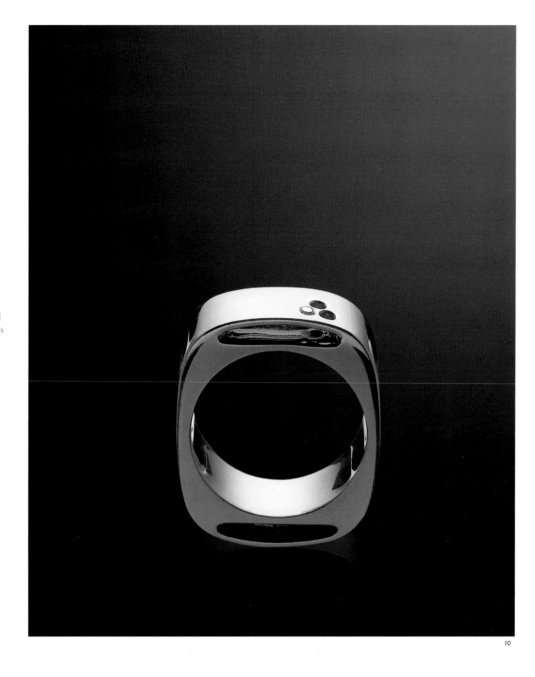

9
SIDEON
Series of cutlery in stainless steel
with integral chopstick-type rests
that enable utensils to stand on
edge so as to minimize contact
with potentially dirty surfaces
2006
Client: Mater

10
TOM
Man's ring in sterling silver
that makes reference to
mechanical design, rather than
high jewellery
2006
Client: Georg Jensen

10

"I believe that the right idea will drive the entire design process.
I believe that in the future great designers will be idea-driven shape-shifters
(like Madonna or Christina Aguilera are in music today)."

SMART DESIGN

"We live in a time of readily available technology, advanced manufacturing methods, and CAD design tools that enable designers to conceive just about anything. Sure we could make it – but should we? This is the question design must increasingly answer. In the past, designers simply presented options to their clients for consideration. Today we must go beyond the constraints of the immediate project to answer bigger questions in guiding our clients to relevant solutions. In many ways we know more than they do when it comes to improving the world through the things we create. To do so, designers need to embrace a broader perspective that anticipates the context of people using the design: how the design will perform over time, its environmental impact, and the business model that enables its viability. Without fully considering this broader perspective in the design process, design itself can become the problem – not the solution."

„Wir leben in einer Zeit schnell und leicht verfügbarer Technologien, innovativer Herstellungsmethoden und computergestützter Designwerkzeuge, die es Gestaltern ermöglichen, sich so ziemlich alles auszudenken und zu entwerfen. Sicher könnten wir es machen – aber sollten wir auch? Das ist die Frage, die Design in zunehmendem Maß zu beantworten hat. In der Vergangenheit haben Gestalter ihren Kunden einfach Optionen zur Auswahl präsentiert. Heute müssen wir über die Grenzen eines konkreten Projekts hinausgehen, um größere Fragen zu beantworten und dabei unsere Kunden zu relevanten Lösungen zu leiten. In vielerlei Hinsicht wissen wir mehr als sie, wenn es darum geht, die Welt durch die Dinge, die wir schaffen, zu verbessern. Zu diesem Zweck müssen sich Designer auf eine breitere Perspektive einlassen, eine, die den Kontext berücksichtigt, in dem die Menschen das Design benutzen: Wie gut wird das Design im Laufe der Zeit funktionieren, wie werden seine Auswirkungen auf die Umwelt und das Unternehmensmodell sein, das seine Existenz ermöglicht? Wenn diese breitere Perspektive nicht vollständig in den Gestaltungsprozess integriert ist, wird möglicherweise das Design selbst zum Problem – nicht zur Lösung."

« Nous vivons à l'époque de la technologie à portée de main, des méthodes de fabrication perfectionnées et des outils de création assistée par ordinateur qui permettent aux designers de concevoir quasiment tout. Bien sûr qu'on peut le faire. Mais le doit-on ? C'est la question à laquelle le design va de plus en plus être obligé de répondre. Dans le passé, les designers se contentaient de proposer des options à la bienveillance de leurs clients. Aujourd'hui, nous devons dépasser les contraintes du projet immédiat pour répondre à des questions plus vastes et guider nos clients vers des solutions pertinentes. Nous en savons souvent bien plus qu'eux sur les moyens de faire avancer le monde grâce aux choses que nous créons. Les designers doivent donc embrasser une perspective plus ouverte, qui anticipe la façon dont les gens utiliseront l'objet de design : la façon dont le design se comportera dans le temps, son impact environnemental et le modèle commercial qui permet sa viabilité. Si l'on ne prend pas en considération cette perspective dans le processus créatif, alors le design lui-même risque de devenir le problème – et non la solution. »

1

2

3

4

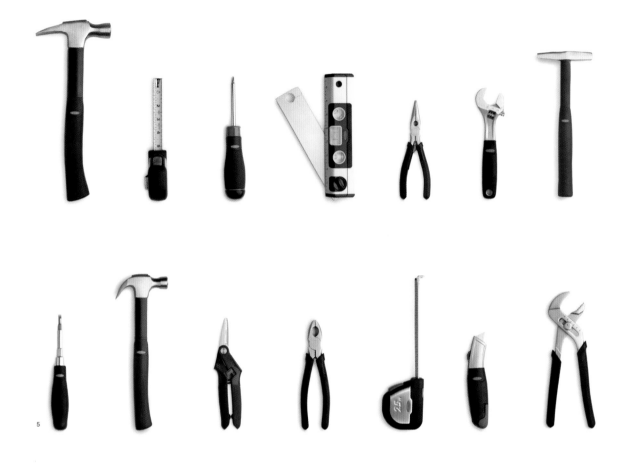

5

1–5

OXO HARDWARE HAND
TOOLS FOR OXO, 2005

"For OXO's new line of hardware hand tools Smart Design
needed to create innovative
products that would appeal to
a broad audience, particularly
women, but also get a thumbs-
up from the experts who shop
and work at Lowe's. The do-it-
yourselfers we interviewed liked
innovation, but they also wanted
a hammer to look like a hammer.
So we designed a line of over
twenty clearly recognizable tools
that are loaded with new user
benefits. For example, the tape
measure has a thumb break to
slow down the tape retraction,

and the utility knife has an internal cartridge that presents itself
with the pull of a lever for safe
and convenient blade storage
and replacement. Like all OXO
products, the tools are ergonomic, durable and of superior quality."

„Bei der Konzipierung von
OXOs neuer Handwerkzeug-
Produktlinie sah sich Smart
Design vor die Aufgabe gestellt,
innovative Arbeitsgeräte zu
entwickeln, die nicht nur eine
breite Zielgruppe, insbesondere
Frauen, ansprechen, sondern
auch die Experten, die bei Lowe's
einkaufen und arbeiten, über-
zeugen würden. Die Heimwer-

ker, die wir befragten, waren
Innovationen nicht abgeneigt,
legten jedoch Wert darauf, dass
ein Hammer auch wie ein Hammer aussieht. Wir gestalteten
daher eine Produktlinie mit über
20 Werkzeugen, die eindeutig
identifizierbar sind, aber allen,
die sie benutzen, viele neue
Vorteile bieten. So hat beispielsweise das Maßband eine Art
‚Daumenbremse', um das Ein-
ziehen des Bandes zu verlang-
samen. Das Mehrzweckmesser
wiederum ist zur Aufbewahrung
der Klingen mit einem praktischen Innengehäuse ausgestattet,
das sich mittels eines Hebels
entriegeln und öffnen lässt und
ein sicheres Auswechseln der

Klingen gewährleistet. Wie alle
OXO-Produkte sind auch diese
Werkzeuge ergonomisch gestaltet, extrem langlebig und von
herausragender Qualität."

« Pour la nouvelle ligne d'outil-
lage léger OXO, Smart Design
devait créer des produits novateurs qui séduiraient un large
public, en particulier les femmes,
mais serait aussi salué par les
experts qui consomment et travaillent chez Lowe. Les bricoleurs
que nous avons interrogés appré-
ciaient l'innovation, mais ils
souhaitaient aussi qu'un marteau
ressemble à un marteau. Nous
avons donc conçu une gamme
d'une vingtaine d'outils claire-

ment reconnaissables bourrés
de nouveaux avantages pour leur
utilisateur. Le mètre à ruban est
par exemple doté d'un frein au
pouce qui permet de ralentir sa
rétraction, et le cutter renferme
une cartouche à laquelle on
accède par un effet de levier
afin d'assurer un rangement et
un remplacement sûr des lames.
Comme tous les produits OXO,
ces outils sont ergonomiques,
durables et de qualité
supérieure. »

1
OXO HARDWARE HAND
TOOLS
Adjustable 6-inch wrench in
drop-forged corrosion-resistant
chrome nickel steel with soft,
non-slip contoured handle
2005
Client: OXO International

2
OXO HARDWARE HAND
TOOLS
16-ounce rip claw hammer
with a reinforced fibreglass
core and a soft, non-slip handle,
which helps reduce vibration
to the hand
2005
Client: OXO International

3
OXO HARDWARE HAND
TOOLS
Ratcheting screw driver with
Quick Draw Bit Carriage
containing six different bits and
three-sided Trilobal® grip,
which allows greater comfort
and torque
2005
Client: OXO International

4
OXO HARDWARE HAND
TOOLS
Utility knife with an internal
cartridge that presents itself
with the pull of a lever for safe
and convenient blade storage
and replacement
2005
Client: OXO International

5
OXO HARDWARE
HAND TOOLS
14 examples from a series of
22 hand tools, all based on the
principles of Universal Design
2005
Client: OXO International

6
OXO GOOD GRIPS
Wire cheese slicer in die-cast
zinc with a soft, non-slip handle
and replaceable stainless steel
wires
2006
Client: OXO International

7–8
OXO GOOD GRIPS
Flame, stain, steam and heat
resistant (600°F) 100%
high-grade silicone oven mitt
and trivet/pot holder
2005
Client: OXO International

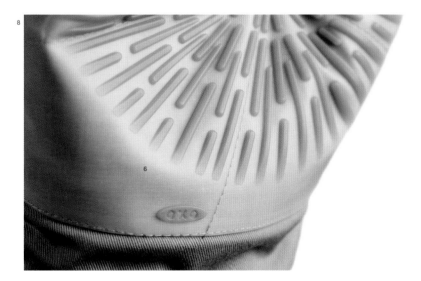

SMART DESIGN
601 W 26th St, Suite 1820
New York
New York 10001
USA
T +1 212 8078150
E info@
smartdesignworldwide.com
www.smartdesignworldwide.com

DESIGN GROUP HISTORY
1978 Founded by
Davin Stowell in New York
2001 Opened sister office in
San Francisco; other partners:
Tom Dair, Greg Littleton
and Clay Burns
2005 Opened sister office in
Barcelona

**FOUNDER'S BIOGRAPHY
DAVIN STOWELL**
1953 Born in Corning, New
York
1971–1976 BA Industrial
Design, Syracuse University,
New York
1976–1978 Worked as con-
sultant to Corning Glass
Works

RECENT EXHIBITIONS
2003 "National Design
Triennial – Inside Design Now",
Cooper-Hewitt National Design
Museum, New York
2007 "Bay Area Design", San
Francisco Airport Museums,
San Francisco, California; "Taxi
07", Design Trust for Public
Spaces, New York International
Auto Show, New York

RECENT AWARDS
2004 2 x Gold and 3 x Silver
Industrial Design Excellence
Awards, IDSA (Industrial
Designers Society of America);
2 x HOW International Design
Annual Awards, Chicago; Gold
Medical Design Excellence
Award; 7 x Good Design
Awards, Chicago Athenaeum
2005 3 x Silver Industrial Design
Excellence Awards, IDSA
(Industrial Designers Society of
America); Gold Medical Device
Excellence Award, MD&DI
(Medical Device & Diagnostic
Industry) magazine; 2 x HOW
International Design Annual
awards, Chicago; 2 x CES Inno-
vation Awards; 2 x Good Design
Awards, Chicago Athenaeum
2006 Award, Annual Design
Review, I.D. Magazine; 3 x
Housewares Design Awards,
International Housewares Asso-
ciation; CES Innovation Award,
CES Consumer Electronics,
Las Vegas; 6 x Good Design
Awards, Chicago Athenaeum
2007 3 x iF Awards, International
Forum Design Hanover; 2 x
Red Dot Awards, Design
Zentrum Nordrhein-Westfalen,
Essen; Design Week Award,
London; 2 x Silver and 1 x
Bronze Industrial Design
Excellence Awards, IDSA
(Industrial Designers Society
of America); Finalist, National
Design Awards, Cooper-Hewitt
National Design Museum, New
York

CLIENTS
Acer, Becton Dickinson, Burton,
Cisco Systems, Coca-Cola,
Corning, ESPN, Estée Lauder,
General Motors, HBO,
Hewlett-Packard, Imation, Issey
Miyake, Johnson & Johnson,
Kellogg's, Lexar Media, LG
Electronics, Microsoft, National
Geographic, OXO International,
Samsung, Shell, simplehuman,
Starbucks, Techtronics Indus-
tries, Timberland, Timex,
Toshiba, Toyota, Vicks, World
Kitchen, WOVO, XM Satellite
Radio, Yahoo!

9

"Design possibilities are endless;
meaningful solutions are few."

9
NYC TAXI
Taxi concept and graphics
designed in conjunction with
other New York based design
firms for the Taxi 07 exhibit
2007
Client: self-generated concept

10
POUR & STORE WATERING
CANS
Eight, three and one litre
watering cans with soft, non-slip
handles and spouts that rotate
toward the body for easier filling
and space-efficient storage
2005
Client: OXO International

10

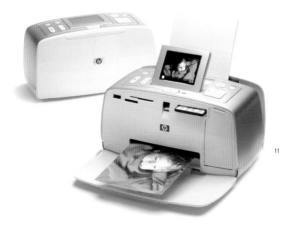

11–12
HP PHOTOSMART 375
PHOTO PRINTER
The first truly portable photo
printer on the market,
the Photosmart 375 is
battery-driven and prints 4x6-
inch images – no PC or external
power source is required
2004
Client: HP

11

13–14
MICROSOFT VISTA
User-friendly structural
packaging in impact-resistant
plastic
2006
Client: Microsoft

12

13

14

SONY DESIGN TEAM

"The expressions, 'Do what has never been done before' and 'Always stay one step ahead' have underscored our corporate philosophy since the very beginning, and have always represented the backbone of Sony's design philosophy of building high-performance, easy-to-use and beautiful products with a distinctive Sony flair. **Originality**: Sony Design continuously strives to create something original that becomes the world standard. Sony Design's originality lies in innovations that fulfill people's latent desires. For us, human-focused design is the foundation for creating something original. **Lifestyle**: People often note that the Sony Walkman® changed their lives. In reality, the Walkman's success can be credited to the basic human demand for a 'music on the go' lifestyle. The Walkman touched the hearts of people by making it possible to take their music with them and access it on demand. The Walkman story is a perfect example of what it takes to create consumer lifestyle changes—a product must strike a universal, heart-touching chord with people everywhere. **Functionality**: When Sony Design was established in 1961, its Black & Silver design language elevated Sony's image. The idea is to do away with excessive ornamentation and accentuate a powerful, high performance, professional feel through the use of simple, cool colors and materials. **Usability**: It all starts with the principle of carefully listening to the user's needs. Every aspect of Sony Design considers the needs of people who use our products. This includes everything from the shape of each button and dial, the position of every switch, to the interface design. We carefully observe the conditions under which the product is operated and pursue continuous improvement. Our products are not only functional, but also give full expression to the beauty of functionality."

„Die Redensarten ‚Tun, was noch nie zuvor getan wurde' und ‚Immer einen Schritt voraus sein' haben von Anfang an unsere Unternehmensphilosophie auf den Punkt gebracht und waren immer Hauptbestandteil der gestalterischen Grundsätze von Sony. Diesen Grundsätzen folgend haben wir leistungsstarke, benutzerfreundliche und schöne Produkte mit dem charakteristischen Sony Touch entwickelt. **Originalität:** Sony Design ist kontinuierlich bestrebt, etwas Originelles zu schaffen, das zum Weltstandard wird. Die Originalität von Sony Design liegt in Innovationen, die die verborgenen Bedürfnisse von Menschen erfüllen. Für uns ist ein auf den Menschen ausgerichtetes Design die Grundlage, um Originalität zu schaffen. **Lifestyle:** Viele stellen fest, dass der Sony Walkman ihr Leben verändert hat. In Wirklichkeit lässt sich der Erfolg des Walkmans durch das menschliche Bedürfnis nach einem ‚Music to Go'-Lifestyle erklären. Der Walkman berührte die Herzen der Menschen, weil er es ihnen ermöglichte, ihre Musik mitzunehmen und sie zu hören, wann immer sie wollten. Die Walkman-Story zeigt beispielhaft, was erforderlich ist, um eine Veränderung im Lebensstil der Konsumenten zu bewirken – ein Produkt muss bei allen Menschen weltweit eine universelle zu Herzen gehende Saite berühren. **Funktionalität:** Als Sony Design 1961 gegründet wurde, wertete sein von Schwarz und Silber gekennzeichneter Designstil das Image von Sony auf. Die Idee ist, auf überflüssige Ornamentierung zu verzichten und einen kraftvollen, leistungsstarken, professionellen Eindruck durch die Verwendung schlichter, kühl-sachlicher Farben und Materialien zu verstärken. **Zweckmäßigkeit:** Alles beginnt mit dem Prinzip, Aufmerksamkeit für die Bedürfnisse der Konsumenten zu zeigen. Sony Design trägt in allen Aspekten den Bedürfnissen der Menschen, die unsere Produkte benutzen, Rechnung. Das umfasst jedes Detail, von der Formgebung der Knöpfe und Regler, über die Position der Schalter bis zum Interface Design. Wir beobachten sorgfältig die Bedingungen, unter denen die Produkte bedient werden, und nehmen kontinuierlich Verbesserungen vor. Unsere Produkte sind nicht nur funktional, sondern verleihen auch der Schönheit von Funktionalität vollkommenen Ausdruck."

« Les expressions ‹ Fais ce qui n'a jamais été fait › et ‹ Garde toujours une longueur d'avance › ont défini notre philosophie d'entreprise depuis le tout début et ont toujours constitué la colonne vertébrale de la conception du design par Sony : concevoir de beaux produits hautement performants et faciles à utiliser grâce au flair qui fait la spécificité de Sony. **Originalité :** Sony Design tente perpétuellement de créer une chose originale qui deviendra une norme mondiale. L'originalité de Sony Design réside dans des innovations qui comblent les désirs secrets des gens. Pour nous, un design anthropocentrique est à l'origine de la création d'une chose originale. **Style de vie :** Les gens disent souvent que le Walkman Sony a changé leur vie. En réalité, le succès du Walkman peut être mis au crédit de la demande des hommes de vivre ‹ en musique ›. Le walkman a touché les gens au cœur en leur permettant d'emporter leur musique avec eux et d'y avoir accès à la demande. L'histoire du Walkman illustre parfaitement la manière dont les habitudes des consommateurs peuvent être modifiées — un produit doit toucher la corde sensible de personnes dans le monde entier. **Fonctionnalité :** Quand Sony Design a été créé en 1961, son lexique Noir & Argent a exalté l'image de Sony. L'idée est de se débarrasser des ornements superflus pour accentuer l'impression de performance et de professionnalisme à travers l'utilisation de couleurs et de matériaux froids. **Utilité :** Tout part du principe d'écouter attentivement les désirs du consommateur. Chaque aspect du design Sony tient compte des besoins de nos acheteurs, de la forme de chaque bouton à la localisation de chaque commutateur en passant par l'interface. Nous observons de près les conditions dans lesquelles le produit est utilisé et sommes perpétuellement à la recherche de perfectionnements possibles. Non seulement nos produits sont fonctionnels mais ils expriment pleinement la beauté de la fonctionnalité. »

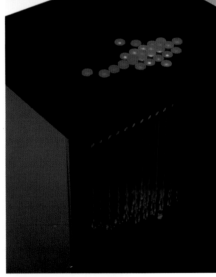

2
HDR-HC1 HANDYCAM®
2.8MP Digital High Definition
Camcorder
2005

3–4
LUMEN (PROTOTYPE)
Display that conveys a sense of
touch – applicable as an equip-
ment interface or for communi-
cation through conveyed images
and forms
2004
(Collaboration between Sony
Creative Center and Sony CSL)
Client: Sony Computer
Entertaiment Inc.

5
PSP-1000
Handheld Entertaiment System
PSP® (PlayStation® Portable)
with high-resolution LCD
widescreen
2004
Client: Sony Computer
Entertaiment Inc.

"Designing products
that touch tomorrow."

6

VAIO®, TYPE U/UX SERIES
Micro Personal Computer
VAIO® with LCD touch screen
and hidden keyboard
2006

7

Z610/W850 WALKMAN® +
MPS-60/K800 CYBER-SHOT™
(from left to right) Clam-shell
mobile phone; mobile phone
with an advanced digital music
player, large touch screen and
portable speakers; 3G mobile
phone with camera and music/
video player
2006
Client: Sony Ericsson Mobile
Communications AB

SONY DESIGN TEAM
Creative Center
Sony Corporation
1-7-1 Konan Minato-ku
Tokyo 108-0075
Japan
www.sony.net/design
www.sony.co.jp/design/

DESIGN TEAM HISTORY
1961 Design Group of Sony
Corporation was established in
Toyko
2005+ Masao Morita, SVP,
Corporate Executive has been
heading the Creative Center
of the Sony Corporation

RECENT EXHIBITIONS
2000 "Digital Dreams", AXIS
Gallery, Tokyo and Asia &
Pacific Trade Center, Osaka
2007 "Sony Design x Master
Craft Lombardia", Sony Build-
ing Tokyo and Piazza Mercardi 2
Milan

RECENT AWARDS
2005 Gold Award, IDEA
(Industrial Design Excellence
Awards), Industrial Designers
Society of America/Business
Week; Design for Asia Award,
Hong Kong Design Center
2006 iF Gold Award and iF
Award, International Forum
Design Hanover; Good Design
Gold Prize and Good Design
Award, JIDPO (Japan Industrial

Design Promotion Organiza-
tion); Red Dot Design Award,
Design Zentrum Nordrhein-
Westfalen, Essen; Silver Award,
IDEA (Industrial Design Excel-
lence Awards), Industrial
Designers Society of
America/BusinessWeek; Japan
Commendation for Invention,
Japan Institute of Invention and
Innovation; Award, Japan
Packaging Competition (JPC),
Japan Packaging Institute; Japan
Package Design Awards, Japan
Package Design Association;

Japan Manual Award, Japan
Manual Board
2007 6 x Red Dot Design
Awards, Design Zentrum
Nordrhein-Westfalen, Essen;
iF Award, International Forum
Design Hanover; Good Design
Award, JIDPO (Japan Industrial
Design Promotion Organiza-
tion)

PHILIPPE STARCK

"Today 'the environment' is all the rage, the current buzzword. Ecology has been hijacked as yet more fodder for cover stories of magazines and political debate. Ever better informed, each of us has a chance to regain some control over Mankind's destiny instead of drifting with market forces. Faced with an array of ecological threats, we have to take a long-term view of production in terms of the evolution of our civilisation – do our best with the minimum of materials in order to reach the goal signposted by our history: dematerialisation. With this in mind I have developed alternative means of travel – including hydrogen-powered bicycles – which satisfy the requirement to reduce usage of materials and employ them intelligently in a structured programme for urban transport. The utilisation and transformation of natural resources are also important ecological commitments: water purification plants, for example, or tuneful wind-turbines that temper energy production with a little poetry. The search for new technologies represents a response to our real requirements and not to those created by mercenary multinationals to whom every passing fashion is a commercial bonus. For instance, hydrogen cars offer a natural solution to our obvious transport problems. It is also vital to recognise the role of those synthetic materials whose technical, practical, economic and ecological advantages sometimes far outstrip those of natural ones. They are also in line with today's growing insistence on longevity. Modern product design demands built-in durability to counter abuses of recycling incompatible with the logic of sustainable development. This idea of sustainability is implicit in any stand on environmental protection: a new relationship is needed between Man, production and goods. This I attempted to initiate in my Good Goods catalogue back in 1998. We have to break out of the trend-driven cycle directly responsible for consumption and over-consumption and move to researching justifiable products that answer our true needs. In this way, working together, we can create the market of tomorrow: a market based on morality."

„Heute ist ‚die Umwelt' der letzte Schrei, das aktuelle Modewort. Die Ökologie wird in Geiselhaft genommen, um als unerschöpfliches Futter für Titelgeschichten in Zeitschriften und politische Debatten zu dienen. Jeder von uns ist immer besser informiert und hat die Möglichkeit, etwas Kontrolle über das Schicksal der Menschheit zurückzugewinnen, statt sich willenlos mit den Kräften des Marktes treiben zu lassen. Konfrontiert mit einer wahren Phalanx von ökologischen Bedrohungen müssen wir die Produktion im Sinne der Weiterentwicklung unserer Zivilisation einer langfristigen Betrachtung unterziehen – mit einem Minimum an Materialaufwand unser Bestes tun, um das von unserer Geschichte vorgegebene Ziel zu erreichen: die Entmaterialisierung. Mit dieser Absicht habe ich alternative Transportmittel entwickelt – einschließlich mit Wasserstoff betriebene Fahrräder –, die der Notwendigkeit entsprechen, den Materialverbrauch zu reduzieren, und die auf intelligente Weise für ein systematisch aufgebautes Programm des städtischen Transportwesens einzusetzen sind. Die Suche nach neuen Technologien stellt eine Antwort auf unsere realen Bedürfnisse dar und nicht auf jene, die von profitgierigen Multis erzeugt wurden, für die jede vorübergehende Modeerscheinung einen wirtschaftlichen Nutzen bringt. So bieten etwa Wasserstoffautos eine natürliche Lösung für unsere augenscheinlichen Verkehrsprobleme. Ebenfalls entscheidend ist, die Bedeutung jener synthetischen Materialien zu erkennen, deren technische, praktische und ökologische Vorteile manchmal die von natürlichen bei Weitem übertreffen. Die Idee der Nachhaltigkeit ist in jeder Position zum Umweltschutz enthalten: Eine neue Beziehung zwischen Mensch, Produktion und Waren ist erforderlich. Wir müssen aus dem trendbesessenen Kreislauf, der unmittelbar für Verbrauch und übersteigerten Konsum verantwortlich ist, ausbrechen und uns auf die Entwicklung vertretbarer Produkte verlegen, die unseren wahren Bedürfnissen entsprechen. Auf diese Weise und indem wir zusammenarbeiten, können wir einen Markt von morgen schaffen: einen Markt, der auf Ethik beruht."

Aujourd'hui, le mot environnement est devenu à la mode, tendance. L'écologie est devenue un chapitre comme les autres dans les débats politiques ou la une des magazines. De plus en plus informés, nous avons tous la possibilité de reprendre en main le destin de l'espèce humaine plutôt que de se laisser aller aux mécanismes du marché mercantile. Face aux multiples dangers écologiques, notre obligation de production pour l'évolution de notre civilisation doit s'inscrire dans la durée : faire le mieux avec le minimum de matière afin d'aller dans le sens de notre Histoire : la dématérialisation.

J'ai ainsi développé différents moyens de transports – par exemple des vélos motorisés à l'hydrogène – qui répondent à ce devoir de réduction de la matière et son utilisation intelligente pour un programme de déplacement urbain. L'utilisation et la transformation des matières naturelles sont également un des actes écologiques importants : telle la station de purification d'eau ou les éoliennes musicales qui apportent aussi un peu de poésie à la transformation de l'énergie. La recherche de nouvelles technologies répond à nos réels besoins et non à ceux créés par la vénalité des multinationales dont le phénomène de mode et démode est un des outils complices. Par exemple, la voiture à hydrogène s'imposera naturellement comme une des solutions évidentes de transport. Rendons également leur noblesse aux matières synthétiques qui permettent des accomplissements techniques, pratiques, économiques et écologiques qui dépassent parfois de loin celles des matières naturelles. L'engagement pour la protection de notre environnement implique la notion de pérennité : il doit apparaître une nouvelle relation entre l'Homme, la production et l'objet ; ce que j'ai tenté d'initier avec mon catalogue Good Goods déjà en 1998. Il faut s'extraire du cycle des modes qui sont un réel incitateur à la consommation et la surconsommation et aller vers la recherche de produits justes qui correspondent à nos réels besoins. Ainsi, nous créerons ensemble le marché de demain, le futur marché moral.

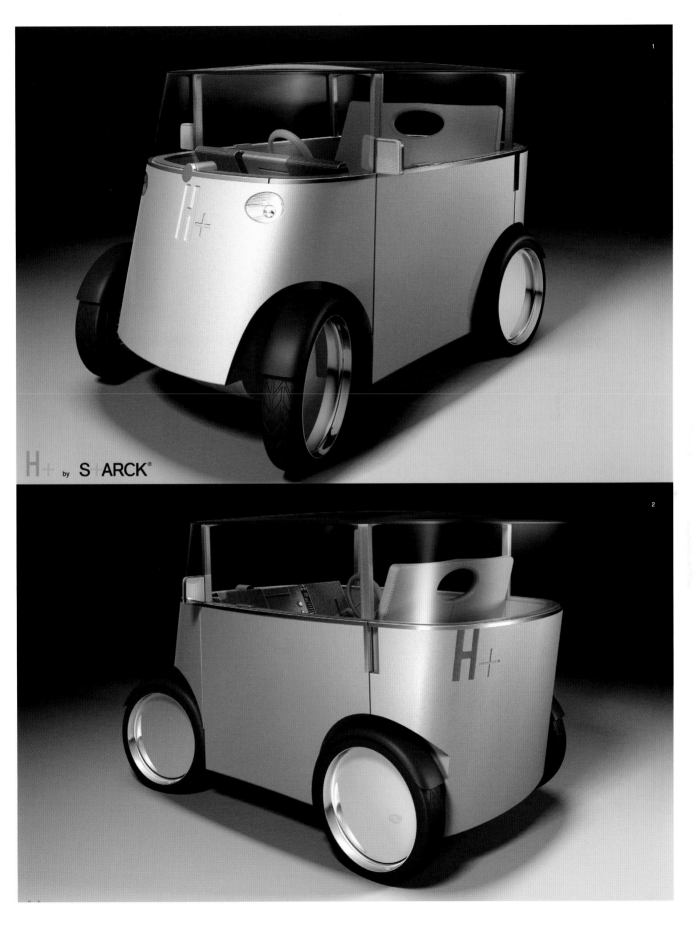

H+ by S ARCK®

"Today electrical and soon hydrogen powered, this car is part of a programme for creativity and high technology for the democratization of ecology. This vehicle, of low cost, features a new technology of production and moulding: the main body is one monobloc of polyurethane. Suspension, engine and brakes are in the wheels."

„Heute mit Elektro- und bald schon mit Wasserstoffantrieb, entstammt dieses Auto einem Kreativitäts- und Hochtechnologie-Programm zur Demokratisierung der Ökologie. Dieses – kostengünstige – Fahrzeug entsteht in einem neuen Produktions- und Formgebungsverfahren: Korpus und Gestell sind ein einziger, kompakter Block aus Polyurethan. Radaufhängung, Motor und Bremsen sind in den Rädern."

« Aujourd'hui électrique et bientôt propulsée à l'hydrogène, cette voiture fait partie d'un programme mêlant créativité et technologie pour la démocratisation de l'écologie. Ce véhicule, peu coûteux, bénéficie d'une technologie de fabrication et de moulage nouvelle : la carrosserie est un bloc autoportant en polyuréthane. Suspensions, moteur et direction sont dans les roues. »

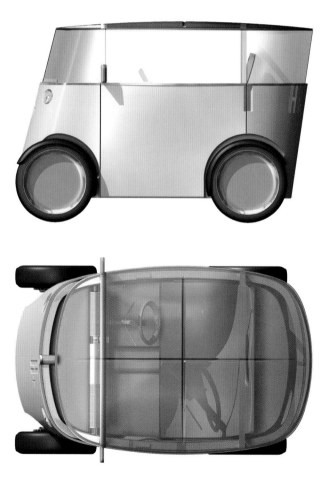

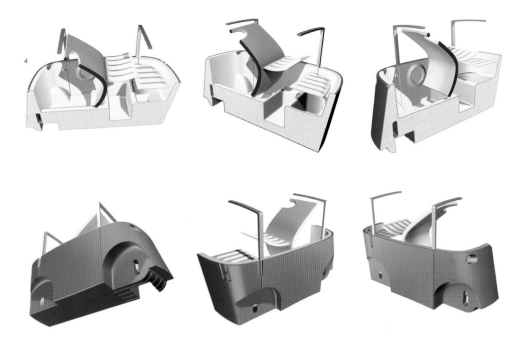

4

1–3
H+
Low-cost hydrogen fuel cell
powered car with main body
in a single polyurethane
monobloc moulding
2003
Client: self-generated concept

4
H+
Details of hydrogen fuel
cell powered car's main body
and chassis
2003
Client: self-generated concept

5
CUBE
Water-purification station
on a river near Beijing that
distributes free drinking water
2004
Client: self-generated concept

5

"Industrial Design: a political
engagement, the democratization of design."

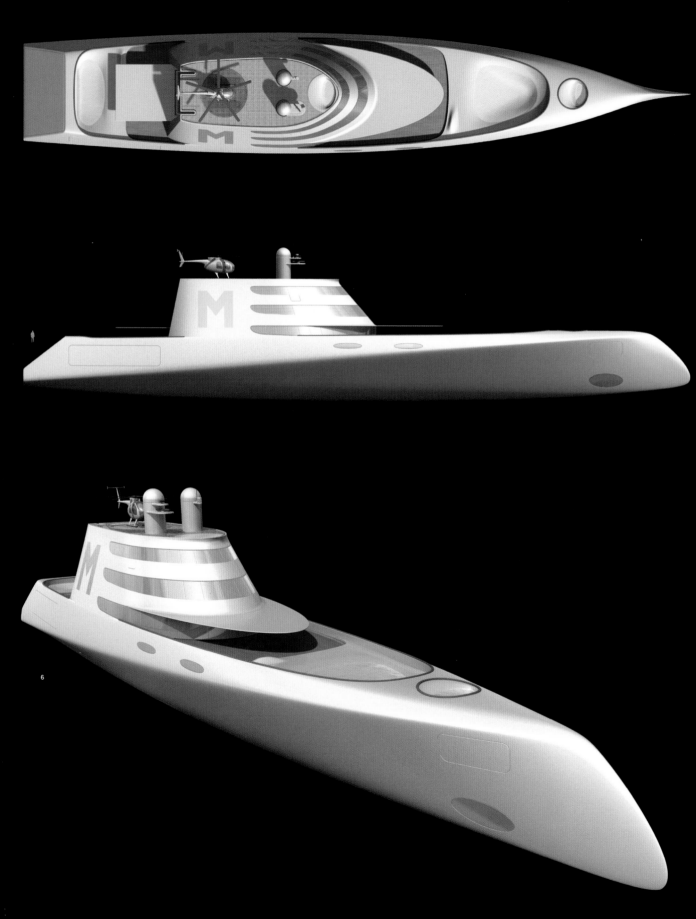

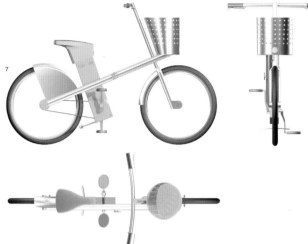

6
BATEAU M
120 meter mega yacht with a
revolutionary shaped hull that
creates no wave at 25 knots.
2003
Client: self-generated concept

7–8
VELO ELECTRIQUE
Electric bicycle for rental use in
cities with a minimal/reduced
structure that is resistant to
vandalism and optimized for
intensive operation
2002
Client: Self-generated concept

PHILIPPE STARCK
18/20, rue du Faubourg
du Temple
75011 Paris
France
T +33 1 48 07 54 54
E projects@starcknetwork.com
www.philippe-starck.com

BIOGRAPHY
1949 Born in Paris
1968 Studied at École Nissim
de Camondo de Paris
1979 Established Starck Products
1982 Redesigned the private
apartment of the French president at the Palais de l'Élysée,
Paris
1983 Established Ubik
agency
Present+ Visiting professor at
the Domus Academy, Milan
and École Nationale des Arts
Décoratifs de Paris

RECENT EXHIBITIONS
2003 "Philippe Starck", Centre
Georges Pompidou, Paris, and
Groninger Museum, Groningen,
The Netherlands; Design
Museum, London, and
Museum of Modern Art,
New York

RECENT AWARDS
2000 Chevalier de l'Ordre
National de la Légion
d'Honneur, France
2001 Pratt Institute Black
Alumni Award, USA; Compasso
d'Oro award, ADI, Milan
2003 Best Boat of the Year,
Monaco Show Boats
2004 Lucky Strike Designer
Award, Raymond Loewy
Foundation
2006 Prix Madrid Créatividad

CLIENTS
Aprilia, Baccarat, Cassina,
Driade, Eurostar, Flos, Fossil,
Kartell, Microsoft, Mikli,
Oregon Scientific, Puma,
Target, Thomson, Virgin
Galactic, XO

SWE DES

"We firmly believe that creating new ideas for a global market is not a process purely revolving around maths and science. Today it's more than ever about the ability to imagine, inspire and connect with the hearts and minds of an audience. We try to achieve this by identifying new ideas and opportunities through observing and revealing people's latent needs and desires and transforming these into new solutions that serve and support people in their daily lives. For us this ambition means finding ways to preserve the relevance and delight of an original idea from concept generation to the factory output. A process, we hope in the end will create something that reflects character and identity, adding value aside from price or features logic – and maybe even something that can bring a smile to the face of a viewer."

„Wir sind der festen Überzeugung, dass das Entwickeln neuer Ideen für einen globalen Markt kein Prozess ist, der sich nur um Mathematik und Wissenschaft dreht. Vielmehr geht es heute mehr als je zuvor um die Fähigkeit zur Imagination und zur Inspiration sowie um die Kunst, sich mit den Herzen und Köpfen eines Publikums zu verbinden. Wir versuchen, das zu leisten, indem wir die latenten Bedürfnisse und Wünsche der Menschen beobachten und aufzeigen und dadurch neue Ideen und Möglichkeiten ermitteln, um diese Erkenntnisse in neue Designlösungen zu übertragen, die den Menschen in ihrem Alltagsleben nützen und helfen. Für uns bedeutet dieses Ziel, Methoden zu finden, um die Relevanz und die Freude einer originellen Idee von der Planungsphase bis zur Fabrikation zu bewahren. Ein Prozess, von dem wir hoffen, dass er am Ende etwas entstehen lässt, das Charakter und Identität ausstrahlt, das unabhängig von Preis oder Funktionslogik einen besonderen Wert darstellt – und vielleicht sogar ein Lächeln auf das Gesicht des Betrachters zaubert."

«Nous sommes persuadés que créer des idées nouvelles pour un marché mondial n'est pas une démarche qui tourne uniquement autour des maths et de la science. Aujourd'hui plus que jamais il s'agit avant tout d'imaginer, d'inspirer et d'entrer en contact avec les cœurs et les esprits d'un public. Nous tentons d'y parvenir en identifiant de nouvelles idées et de nouvelles possibilités grâce à l'observation et à la mise au jour des besoins et désirs latents du public, que nous transformons en nouvelles solutions qui accompagneront et assisteront les gens au quotidien. Pour nous, cette ambition exige de trouver des moyens de préserver la pertinence et le charme de l'idée originale, de la conception à la sortie d'usine. Nous espérons qu'au bout du compte cette démarche créera une chose dotée de caractère et d'identité, d'une valeur qui ne dépende ni du prix ni des caractéristiques techniques – et peut-être même une chose qui puisse faire sourire celui qui la regarde.»

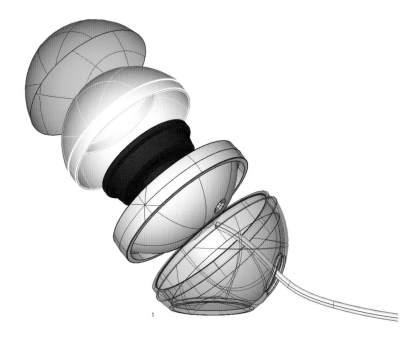

1–3
BOCCIA
Speaker system for mobile
phones powered by four AAA
batteries
2007
Client: IMEGO

1

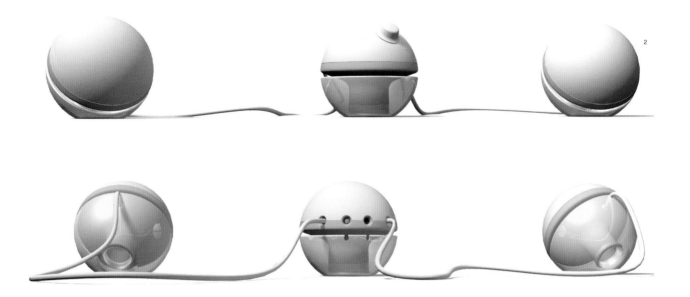

2

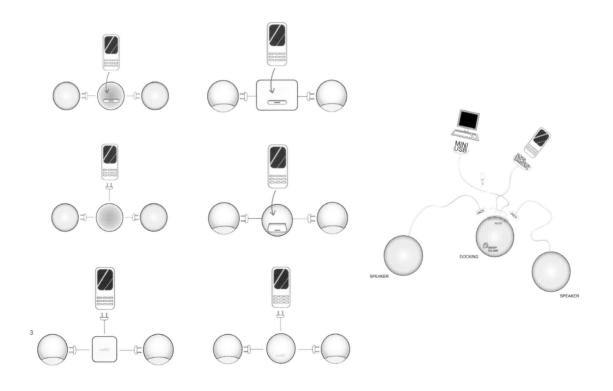

3

1–3

BOCCIA MOBILE PHONE
SPEAKER SYSTEM FOR
IMEGO, 2007

"The Boccia is a speaker system
that works across all mobile
phone platforms. It is based
on three main design features:
portability and compactness;
cross platform cell phone use;
and intuitive cable management.
An integrated design process led
to the Boccia's distinct construc-

tion and shape and made it
possible not only to coil up any
excessive cable, but also enhance
the sound quality and bass
depth within the same design.
It charges your phone and runs
on 4 AAA batteries – this is a
speaker system for the summer's
outgoing music listener."

„Dieser Satz Boccia-Kugeln ist
tatsächlich ein Lautsprechersystem, das mit den unterschiedlichsten Handy-Plattformen

kompatibel ist. Das Design
basiert auf drei zentralen Kriterien: Mobilität und Kompaktheit, systemübergreifende Einsatzmöglichkeiten und intuitive
Verkabelung. Ein Designprozess, der all diesen Aspekten
Rechnung trug, hatte Klarheit
in Struktur und Form zum
Ergebnis und ermöglichte es, in
ein und demselben Design nicht
nur dem Kabelsalat den Kampf
anzusagen, sondern auch die
Tonqualität zu verbessern und

die Bässe zu akzentuieren. Boccia lädt das Telefon auf und läuft
mit vier AAA-Batterien – kurz:
ein Lautsprechersystem für alle,
die im Sommer ihre Musik gern
draußen hören."

« Le Boccia est un système d'en-
ceintes qui fonctionne avec tous
les téléphones portables. Il a été
conçu autour de trois compétences : portabilité et compacité ;
utilisation possible sur tous les
supports de téléphonie mobile

et gestion intuitive des fils. La
construction et la forme distinc-
tives du Boccia découle d'un
processus créatif intégré qui
permet non seulement de rem-
bobiner la longueur de fil inutile
mais aussi d'améliorer la qualité
du son et la profondeur des
basses dans un design minima-
liste. Il recharge votre portable
et fonctionne avec des piles
4 AAA – ce sont des baffles pour
l'estivant amateur de musique
en extérieur. »

"Preserving the delight
of an original idea."

4–5

SEMI-POWERED BIKE
Research project bicycle that is
partially powered by a hydrogen
fuel-cell engine
2004
Client: Aprilia

6

6–7
JIVE BOX
iPod loudspeaker docking
station with patterned textile
covering and remote control
2006
Client: Plastoform/Logic 3

5

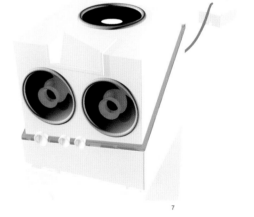

7

SWE DES

Sweden Design
Unit 129 1/F, Innocentre
72 Tat Chee Avenue
Kowloon Tong
Hong Kong
T +852 27769050
E info@swedendesign-hk.com
www.swedendesign-hk.com

FOUNDER'S BIOGRAPHY
JOHAN PERSSON

1971 Born in Gothenburg,
Sweden

DESIGN GROUP HISTORY

2004 Founded by Johan
Persson in Hong Kong (SWE
DES brings together the multi-
disciplinary expertise of three
of Sweden's leading design con-
sultancies: No Picnic, Ergono-
midesign and Lundberg Design)

1999 BA Industrial Design,
Umea University, Sweden
2001 MFA Industrial Design,
Konstfack (University College
of Art, Craft and Design),
Stockholm – won scholarship
for Best Graduating Industrial
Design Project
Post–2001 Executive
Program, Nordic Brand
Academy, Stockholm Uni-
versity, Stockholm and post-
graduate design management

course at Konstfack,
Stockholm
2005+ Part-time teacher
and invited lecturer at Konstfack, Stockholm and Hong
Kong Polytechnical University,
School of Design

RECENT EXHIBITIONS

2004 "Företagsminnen",
Stockholm City Museum,
Stockholm
2006 "The Design of Swedish

Innovations", BODW, Hong
Kong

CLIENTS

Aprilia, Electrical Electronics,
Imego, Innovation Technology
Company, Kerry Logistics,
Plastoform

TEAGUE

"We believe that great design relies on collaborative thought processes. Drawing strength from mutual trust as well as diverse perspectives, rich in heritage and experience, we ensure that our work remains relevant, impactful and representative of contemporary culture. At its core, design is a cerebral activity based on thoughtful, intelligent analysis of the broad context in which products will exist. Our collaborative, analytical approach assures the integrity of our work, allowing us to create products and experiences that are as necessary as they are desirable. We design with an explicit purpose, to enhance people's lives and to act as a powerful contributor to business success."

„Wir glauben, dass großes Design sich auf gemeinschaftliche Denkprozesse stützt. Indem wir unsere Stärke aus dem gegenseitigen Vertrauen ebenso wie aus unterschiedlichen Perspektiven, einem reichen Erbe und Erfahrungsschatz beziehen, stellen wir sicher, dass unsere Arbeit bedeutsam, wirkungsvoll und für die zeitgenössische Kultur repräsentativ bleibt. In seinem Kern ist Design eine intellektuelle Aktivität, die auf einer durchdachten und intelligenten Analyse des breiteren Kontextes, in dem das Produkt bestehen soll, beruht. Unser kollektiver, analytischer Zugang sichert die Integrität unserer Arbeit und ermöglicht uns, Produkte und Erlebnisse zu gestalten, die gleichermaßen notwendig wie reizvoll sind. Unser Design entsteht mit der expliziten Absicht, das Leben der Menschen zu bereichern und einen nachhaltigen Beitrag zum Unternehmenserfolg zu leisten."

«Nous pensons qu'un design de qualité repose sur des cheminements de pensée basés sur la collaboration. En tirant notre force de la confiance mutuelle et de la diversité des perspectives riches en expériences et en souvenirs qu'elle offre, nous nous assurons que notre travail reste pertinent, frappant et représentatif de la culture contemporaine. Fondamentalement, le design est une activité cérébrale qui se construit sur une analyse profonde et intelligente du contexte dans lequel nos produits iront s'inscrire. Notre approche collective et analytique assure l'intégrité de notre travail et nous permet de créer des produits et des expériences qui sont aussi nécessaires que souhaitables. Notre design a l'objectif précis de donner du relief à la vie des gens et de contribuer largement au succès commercial des entreprises.»

1–2
TOUCHSMART
All-in-one multimedia PC with integrated 19-inch touch screen, 320GB hard drive and integrated 1.3-megapixel WebCam with array microphone for easy video conferencing
2006
Client: Hewlett-Packard

1

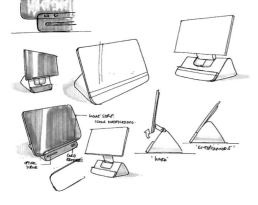

2

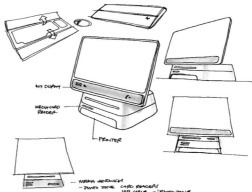

HP TOUCHSMART PC FOR
HEWLETT PACKARD, 2006

"The HP TouchSmart PC
enables 'walk-up computing',
the ability to quickly and easily
access digital content wherever
life happens in the home. It's
an all-in-one, touch-screen PC.
With one touch, families can
check weather or e-mail, leave
notes for each other, manage
daily schedules, or watch a show
– all through HP SmartCenter.
With an adjustable 19" widescreen BrightView LCD display
this PC provides one-touch
entertainment options including
digital photos, radio, TV,
movies, music and Web. The

space-saving, clutter-free design
makes it easy to place almost
anywhere in the home. Plus, the
wireless keyboard and mouse
store in a hideaway bay when
not in use. An integrated soft
dock and convenient connection
ports easily connects a printer to
the PC for on-the-spot photo
printing."

„Der HP TouchSmart PC er-
möglicht 'Walk-up computing',
das heißt, er erlaubt es, schnell
und unkompliziert dort auf
digitale Inhalte zuzugreifen,
wo sich das Leben zu Hause
gerade abspielt. Er ist nämlich
ein Alles-in-einem-Touchscreen-
PC: Durch Berührung mit dem
Finger können die Familienmit-

glieder das aktuelle Wetter ab-
fragen, E-Mails abrufen, sich
gegenseitig Nachrichten hinterlassen, die täglichen Termine
verwalten oder fernsehen –
und all das mit der HP-eigenen
SmartCenter-Software. Mit
einem höhenverstellbaren
19"-BrightView-LCD-Display
im Breitbildformat bietet dieser
PC auf Fingerdruck viele Unter-
haltungsmöglichkeiten, darunter
Digitalfotos, Radio, TV, Filme,
Musik und Internet. Dank des
platzsparenden, reduzierten
Designs kann das Gerät ohne
Probleme fast überall im Haus
aufgestellt werden. Wenn das
Keyboard und die Mouse,
die beide kabellos sind, nicht
gebraucht werden, lassen sie

sich in einem dafür vorgesehe-
nen Platz unter dem Rechner
verstauen. Und für den Foto-
druck an Ort und Stelle kann
der PC über einen integrierten
Docking-Anschluss auch noch
rasch mit einem Drucker verbunden werden."

« Le PC HP TouchSmart autorise ‹ l'informatique mobile ›, la
capacité d'accéder rapidement
et facilement à un contenu
numérique où que la vie nous
appelle dans la maison. Il s'agit
d'un PC tout-en-un à écran tactile. En touchant simplement
l'écran, les membres de la famille
peuvent consulter la météo ou
leurs mails, se laisser des messages les uns aux autres, gérer

leurs emplois du temps ou regarder un spectacle – le tout grâce
au HP SmartCenter. Son grand
écran BrightView LCD ajus-
table de 19" est enrichi d'options
interactives de divertissement
parmi lesquelles la photo numérique, la radio, la télévision, le
cinéma, la musique et l'Internet.
Le gain d'espace et le décloison-
nement qui caractérisent son
design permettent de le placer
n'importe où dans la maison. De
plus, le clavier et la souris sans
fil se rangent dans une anse esca-
motable lorsqu'ils ne servent pas.
Un plateau intégré sous l'écran
offre un accès aisé aux ports de
connection pour pouvoir impri-
mer une photo contenue dans le
PC à la minute. »

"Great design relies on collaboration
to produce relevant and thought provoking
work that ultimately enriches people's lives
and benefits our core culture."

3

5

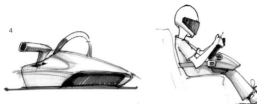

4

3

FIRST-CLASS IFE SYSTEM
REMOTE
Remote control handset with a
tub & lid construction that
provides all-in-one access to
almost any in-flight entertainment device or system including
on-demand video, games, audio,
Internet, passenger reading
light and seat recline
2005
Client: Panasonic

4–6

XBOX 360 WIRELESS
RACING WHEEL
Computer gaming racing wheel
in moulded rubber and plastic
with aluminium accents that
provides a uniquely authentic
racing experience via "rumble"
and "force-feed back" features
2006
Client: Microsoft

6

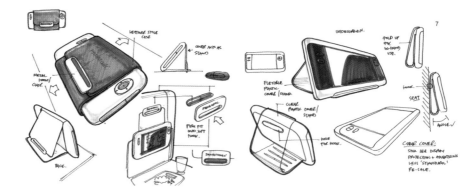

7–9
EXPRESS PMP
Hand-held, in-flight entertainment system with wide-screen and rubber "savegrip" that delivers audio, video, games and information to passengers on demand
2005
Client: Panasonic

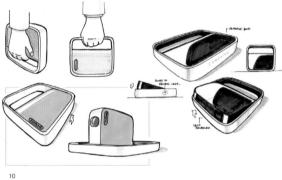

10

12

**10–12
PORTABLE DIGITAL
PROJECTOR**
Compact and ultra-portable
digital projector (no larger than
a digital camera) in aluminium
with an LED-powered display,
folding case and rechargeable
batteries
2005
Client: Samsung

TEAGUE

2727 Western Avenue
Number 200
Seattle
Washington 98121
USA
T +1 206 8384200
E info@teague.com
www.teague.com

DESIGN GROUP HISTORY
1926 Founded in New York City
by industrial design pioneer,
Walter Dorwin Teague. A true
visionary, designing at the height
of the machine age, Teague
forged a path for a company
dedicated to cultural innovation
and intelligent design with the
express goal of creating products
and experiences that enhance
our daily lives

2004 John Barratt, joins the
Teague team as president and
CEO

RECENT AWARDS
2006 DMI (Design Manage-
ment Institute) Design Manage-
ment Team of the Year Award,
Boston; Excellence Award,
IDEA (Industrial Design
Excellence Awards), Industrial
Designers Society of America/

BusinessWeek; 3 x Red Dot
Awards, Design Zentrum
Nordrhein-Westfalen Essen;
3 x Good Design Awards,
Chicago Athenaeum; 3 x IDSA
(Industrial Designers Society
of America) Awards - NWDI
(Northwest Design Invitational);
4 x iF Awards, International
Forum Design Hanover
2007 3 x iF Awards, International
Forum Design Hanover

CLIENTS
Amp'd Moble, Boeing,
Hewlett-Packard, Huawei,
Intel, Microsoft, Nike, Oster,
Panasonic, Precor, RadioFrame,
Rockwell Collins, Samsung,
Starbucks, Thales, Xbox,
ZF Marine

TESLA MOTORS

"Headquartered in Silicon Valley, California, Tesla Motors designs and builds high-performance, highly efficient, 100% electric sports cars – with no compromises. Tesla Motors cars combine style, acceleration, and handling with advanced technologies that make them among the quickest and the most energy-efficient cars on the road. By manufacturing cars that people passionately love to own and drive, we are confident that we can offer cars that are competitive on features, performance, value, and style, with the best of what is available on the market. By providing consumers with a highly desirable alternative to combustion engine vehicles at a competitive price point, we believe that we have the business model to support Tesla's becoming a viable mainstream automotive manufacturer. As Tesla Motors blossoms into a large scale manufacturer, we will both be doing our part to help reduce pollution and reliance on foreign oil, as well as inspiring others to follow our lead."

„Tesla Motors, mit Hauptsitz im kalifornischen Silicon Valley, entwirft und konstruiert leistungsstarke, hoch effiziente, 100-prozentig elektrische Sportautos – ohne Kompromisse. In Tesla-Motors-Autos vereinigen sich Stil, Geschwindigkeit und Handling mit modernster Technologie, die sie zu den schnellsten und energiesparendsten Autos auf der Straße macht. Wir produzieren Autos, die Menschen leidenschaftlich gern besitzen und fahren, und sind daher zuversichtlich, Fahrzeuge anbieten zu können, die im Hinblick auf Funktion, Leistung, Wert und Stil mit dem Besten konkurrieren können, was es derzeit auf dem Markt gibt. Wir bieten Konsumenten zu einem wettbewerbsfähigen Preis eine äußerst attraktive Alternative zu Fahrzeugen mit Verbrennungsmotoren und glauben, über das Unternehmensmodell zu verfügen, mit dem sich Tesla zu einem lebensfähigen, den Geschmack einer großen Mehrheit ansprechenden Automobilhersteller gestalten lässt. Während sich Tesla Motors zu einem Großhersteller entwickelt, werden wir unseren Teil dazu beitragen, sowohl die Umweltverschmutzung wie auch die Abhängigkeit von ausländischem Öl zu reduzieren, und andere dazu anzuregen, unserem Beispiel zu folgen."

«Installé dans la Silicon Valley, en Californie, Tesla Motors conçoit et construit des voitures de sport hautement performantes et économiques, 100% électriques – et sans compromis. Les voitures de Tesla Motors combinent style, vitesse d'accélération et maniement de technologies avancées qui les classent parmi les automobiles les plus rapides et économiques sur le bitume. En fabriquant des voitures que les gens aiment passionnément posséder et conduire, nous sommes convaincus de pouvoir créer des voitures compétitives en matière d'accessoires, de performance, de valeur et de style, en utilisant ce qui existe de meilleur sur le marché. En proposant aux consommateurs une alternative très séduisante aux voitures dotées de moteurs à combustion à un prix compétitif, nous pensons avoir en main le modèle de développement commercial nécessaire pour faire de Tesla un important constructeur automobile viable. À mesure que Tesla Motors s'épanouit pour devenir un constructeur majeur, nous prendrons nos responsabilités, à la fois pour aider à réduire la pollution et la dépendance envers le pétrole étranger et pour encourager les autres à suivre notre exemple.»

1

3

1–8
TESLA ROADSTER, 2004-06

With a top speed of 130 mph (210 km/h) and zero-to-60 mph (100 km/h) acceleration in about 4 seconds (better than a Lamborghini Murciélago) the Tesla Roadster is the ultimate electric vehicle. This extraordinary performance is delivered via a 3-phase, 4-pole electric motor, which produces a maximum output of 185k W at 13,500 rpm. The Roadster is also incredibly efficient – it offers double the efficiency (85 to 95%) of popular hybrid cars, while generating one-third of the carbon dioxide. Against other sports cars it is six times as efficient and produces one-tenth the pollution, all while achieving the same performance and acceleration. The Roadster's battery pack, one of the largest and most advanced in the world, is its biggest innovation. Using proprietary Lithium ion battery technology, the batteries can be fully charged from completely flat in under four hours, and can store enough energy for the car to travel 200 miles (320 km) without recharging – something no other production electric vehicle in history can claim.

Mit einer Spitzengeschwindigkeit von 210 km/h und einer Beschleunigung auf 100 km/h in etwa vier Sekunden (rasanter als der Lamborghini Murciélago) ist der Tesla Roadster die Sensation unter den Elektroautos. Diese außergewöhnliche Performance beruht auf einem dreiphasigen, vierpoligen Elektromotor, der mit einer maximalen Leistung von 185 kW bei bis zu 13 500 Umdrehungen pro Minute kräftig aufdreht. Der Roadster ist auf unglaubliche Effizienz getrimmt – er ist doppelt so effizient (85 bis 95 Prozent) wie die beliebten Hybridfahrzeuge, die Kohlendioxidemission liegt aber um zwei Drittel niedriger. Im Vergleich zu anderen Sportwagen ist er sogar sechsmal effizienter und emittiert nur ein Zehntel der umweltbelastenden Schadstoffe, kann jedoch mit der gleichen Performance und Beschleunigung aufwarten. Die bemerkenswerteste Innovation ist allerdings der Batterieblock, einer der größten und modernsten der Welt. Zum Einsatz kommen handelsübliche Lithium-ionenbatterien, die in weniger als vier Stunden komplett aufgeladen werden können und so viel Energie speichern, dass man mit einer vollen Ladung 320 km weit fahren kann – was in der Geschichte des Elektroautos bisher noch mit keinem anderen Modell möglich war.

Avec une vitesse de pointe de 210 km/h et une accélération à 100 km/h en environ 4 secondes (mieux qu'une Lamborghini Murciélago), le Roadster de Tesla est le véhicule électrique suprême. Ses performances exceptionnelles sont atteintes grâce à un moteur électrique triphasé quadripolaire qui produit un rendement maximum de 185 kW à 13 500 tr/min. Le Roadster est aussi incroyablement économe en énergie – deux fois plus (85 à 95%) que les voitures hybrides traditionnelles, tout en générant trois fois moins de dioxyde de carbone. Son rendement est six fois supérieur à celui des autres voitures de sport tandis qu'il produit une pollution dix fois moindre, tout en étant aussi performante et nerveuse. La batterie du Roadster, une des plus grosses et perfectionnées du monde, représente sa principale innovation. Elle utilise des batteries lithium-ion qui peuvent être intégralement rechargées en quatre heures et emmagasiner suffisamment d'énergie pour propulser la voiture sur 320 km – ce dont aucune autre voiture électrique au monde ne peut se prévaloir.

"Burn rubber, not gasoline."

1–3
ROADSTER
2-seat, open-top, rear-drive high-performance electric roadster with a carbon-fibre body and 4 second zero-to-60 mph acceleration
2004–06

4
ROADSTER
Detail of electric roadster's central console with two-speed shifter and cabin heating and cooling controls

5
ROADSTER
Detail of electric roadster's two-toned leather-trimmed interior

4

5

6

7

8

6
ROADSTER
Detail of electric roadster's
charging interface

7
ROADSTER
Detail of roadster's 3-phase,
4-pole electric motor, which
produces a maximum output
of 185k W at 13,500 rpm and
weighs about 70 lbs

8
ROADSTER
Schematic of electric roadster
showing position of motor

TESLA MOTORS
1050 Bing Street
San Carlos
California 94070
USA
T +1 650 4134000
E dvespremi@teslamotors.com
www.teslamotors.com

COMPANY HISTORY
2003 Founded by engineers
Martin Eberhard and Marc
Tarpenning in San Carlos,
California
2006 Public debut of Tesla's
first model, the Roadster
2007+ Tesla employs more than
170 people worldwide, with

offices in Michigan, Taiwan,
and the UK. The primary
investor in Tesla Motors is Elon
Musk, the founder of PayPal
and SpaceX.

RECENT EXHIBITIONS
2006–2007 Various launch
events throughout the USA

RECENT AWARDS
2006 "Best Cars 2006" Award,
"New car that best lived up to
the Hype" category, Forbes
Magazine; Nominated, "Best
Inventions 2006 – Transportation Invention", TIME magazine; Breakthrough Award 2006,
Popular Mechanics magazine;

Environmental Leadership
Award, Global Green USA
2007 People's Choice: Most
Exciting 2007 Car Launch,
Car Domain

DANNY VENLET

"Although I'm generally considered to be a Belgian designer, I think my work is actually infused with the typical Australian laidback spirit – open, direct, freewheeling and relaxed. My work is wide-ranging: from mobile office chairs, ice-coolers and showers, to interiors for private mansions, bars and showrooms as well as exhibition design. Each project has a playfulness, which is expressed in clear simple outlines and fresh colours. The 'Gestalt' (form or shape) of my designs is centred on the concept of playfulness, which in turn is linked to the idea of mind-games in which I continuously question and undermine given ideas about form, materials, scale, or the use of space and objects. This way of working ensures surprising results: the office chair that has the look of an over-sized baby-crawler or my shower that has the water fountain coming from the bottom rather than the top. My discreet, flexible, but topsy-turvy world is really an exercise in relativity, inviting the user to become a homo ludens – not boisterous and arrogant, but peaceful and humble, and with the perspective of a child, for whom anything remains possible."

„Obwohl ich im Allgemeinen als belgischer Designer betrachtet werde, glaube ich, dass meine Arbeit eigentlich vom typisch australischen Geist der Relaxtheit geprägt ist – offen, direkt, sorglos und entspannt. Mein Betätigungsfeld ist weit gespannt: von Bürostühlen, Kühlboxen und Duschen über Inneneinrichtungen für Privatvillen, Bars und Schauräumen bis zu Ausstellungen. Jedes Projekt hat eine gewisse Verspieltheit, die sich in klaren, einfachen Linien und kräftigen Farben ausdrückt. Die *Gestalt* meiner Designs gründet sich auf das Konzept der Verspieltheit, das wiederum mit der Idee von Gedankenspielen verknüpft ist, in denen ich permanent bestehende Vorstellungen von Form, Material, Größenordnung oder der Verwendung von Raum und Objekten hinterfrage. Diese Arbeitsweise sorgt für überraschende Resultate: der Bürosessel, der aussieht wie ein überdimensionierter Strampelanzug für Babys, oder meine Dusche, bei der der Wasserstrahl von unten und nicht von oben kommt. Meine unaufdringliche, flexible, aber auf den Kopf gestellte Welt ist im Grunde eine Übung in Relativität und lädt den Benutzer dazu ein, zum *homo ludens* zu werden – nicht lärmend und arrogant, sondern friedlich und bescheiden und mit der Perspektive eines Kindes, für das alles möglich ist."

«Bien que je sois généralement considéré comme un designer belge, je pense que mon travail est en fait imprégné d'un esprit peinard typiquement australien – ouvert, franc, insouciant et relax. Mon champ de création est vaste: chaises de bureaux à roulettes, glacières, douches, décoration intérieure de résidences privées, de bars et de salons de présentation ainsi que conception d'expositions. Chaque projet est teinté d'une espièglerie qui s'exprime par des contours clairs, des configurations simples et des couleurs fraîches. La *Gestalt* (la forme) de mes créations s'élabore en fonction de ce concept d'espièglerie, lui-même lié à l'idée des jeux psychologiques grâce auxquels je remets continuellement en doute les idées préconçues sur la forme, le matériau, l'échelle ou l'utilisation de l'espace et des objets. Cette façon de travailler débouche sur des résultats surprenants: la chaise de bureau qui ressemble à une poussette géante ou ma douche dont l'eau sort par le bas au lieu de jaillir par le haut. Mon univers, discret et souple mais à la pointe, procure une expérience de la relativité, invite l'utilisateur à devenir un *homo ludens* – non pas tapageur et arrogant, mais humble et pacifique, comme un enfant, pour qui tout demeure possible.»

1–2
Q
Outdoor stool in two heights with abrasion- and tear-resistant synthetic fabric covering on a galvanized and aluminium-coated base
2006
Client: Viteo Outdoors

3

DANNY VENLET
Marcqstraat 24
1000 Brussels
Belgium
T +32 2 2233828
E office@venlet.net
www.venlet.net

BIOGRAPHY

1958 Born in Victoria, Australia (of Dutch parents)
1978 Studied computer programming at Brussels University
1979–1983 Degree in Interior Architecture (with Distinction) at Sint Lukas Institute of Architecture and Visual Arts, Brussels
1988 Worked with Neil Burley on a number of projects
1988–1990 Worked with Marc Newson on a number of projects
1989–1990 Founded Daffodil Design in Sydney, Australia, with Marc Newson and Tina Engelen
1991 Opened his own studio, Venlet Interior Architecture in Brussels
1998–2003 Part-time tutor, Sint Lukas Institute of Architecture, Ghent
2003–2004 Part-time tutor, Insitut Supérieur d'Architecture Saint Luc, Liège
2002–2007 Part-time tutor, Sint Lukas Institute, Brussels

RECENT EXHIBITIONS

2002 "Interieur 2002", Kortrijk, Belgium; "Design Biennale", Saint-Étienne, France
2003 "Mobiliers 3", La Châtaigneraie, Wallonia, Brussels; "Trademart", Brussels Design District; "Acqua-da-bere", Triennale, Milan
2004 "Design from Flanders", State of Design Festival, Melbourne; "Triënnale Vormgeving", Ghent; "Salone del Mobile", Milan; "Interieur 2004", Kortrijk; "Art Brussels Illy", Brussels
2005 "Red Dot Exhibition", Design Zentrum Nordrhein Westfalen, Essen; "Kölner Messe", Cologne; "(Im)perfect by Design", Brussels; "Design Biennale", Saint-Étienne, France; "Salone del Mobile", Milan
2006 "Danny Venlet", Viteo, Milan; "Salone del Mobile", Milan
2007 "Red Dot Exhibition", Design Zentrum Nordrhein Westfalen, Essen; "Kölner Messe", Cologne; "Design Biennale", Saint-Étienne, France; "Salone del Mobile", Milan

RECENT AWARDS

2002 Good Design Award, The Chicago Athenaeum
2003 Verlicht Award – Light Award, Knokke Belgium; Red Dot Award, Design Zentrum Nordrhein Westfalen, Essen; Henri van de Velde Jury Award and Henri van de Velde Public Award, Brussels
2005 Red Dot Award, Design Zentrum Nordrhein Westfalen, Essen
2006 Red Dot Award, Design Zentrum Nordrhein Westfalen, Essen; Discovery Prize, Maison & Objet, Paris
2007 Gold iF Award, International Forum Design Hanover

CLIENTS

Bulo, Coro Italia, Dark, Extremis, Illy, Mini, Musée de Sport/Paris, Naked, Red Cross, Stad Brussel/City of Brussels, Timberland, UEFA, Viteo

3
DISH
Upholstered polyester sectional
sofa
2005
Client: Naked

4
D2V2
Hanging light in translucent
polyethylene with coloured light
tubes or filters, and dimmable
TL lamps
2005
Client: Dark

5–6
RED CROSS "TERRORISM"
INSTALLATION
Element of interactive installation comprising various cases
containing multi-media presen-
tations of terrorist attacks
2005
Client: Red Cross/Album SPRL

"Design is more than form
and function … it's a way of life."

CLEMENS WEISSHAAR & REED KRAM

"Every new project presents an entirely new set of conditions and characters. And a new learning process. Our clients are as diverse as possible: from century-old porcelain-maker Nymphenburg to multi-national financial powerhouse PriceWaterhouseCoopers. The differences, and even contradictions, between the projects force us to develop very case-specific approaches and attitudes. While developing solutions we engage in a candid and exhaustive analysis of the precise conditions for each project. This results in a logic according to which we manipulate these conditions, engage latent potentials in order to achieve a desired effect. The end result may then be a strategy, a piece of software, a process, a product or a space."

„Jedes neue Projekt stellt eine vollkommen neue Konstellation von Bedingungen und Charakteren dar. Und einen neuen Lernprozess. Unsere Klienten sind so verschieden wie nur möglich: vom jahrhundertealten Porzellanhersteller Nymphenburg bis zum multinationalen Finanzoberligisten PriceWaterhouseCoopers. Die Unterschiede und sogar Widersprüche zwischen den Projekten zwingen uns, sehr fallspezifische Herangehensweisen und Positionen zu entwickeln. Während wir Lösungen ausarbeiten, widmen wir uns einer unvoreingenommenen und gründlichen Analyse der genauen Bedingungen für jedes Projekt. Das resultiert in einer Logik, der gemäß wir diese Konditionen ändern und verborgene Potenziale aktivieren, um den gewünschten Effekt zu erzielen. Das Endergebnis kann dann eine Strategie, eine Software, ein Herstellungsverfahren, ein Produkt oder ein Raum sein."

«Chaque nouveau projet comporte un jeu totalement neuf de restrictions et de personnages. Et un nouveau processus d'apprentissage. Nos clients sont aussi variés que possible : du fabricant de porcelaines centenaire Nymphenburg à la multinationale financière PriceWaterhouseCoopers. Les différences, et même les contradictions, entre les projets nous obligent à concevoir nos stratégies au cas par cas. Tout en façonnant les solutions, nous nous engageons dans une analyse candide et exhaustive des contraintes spécifiques à chaque projet. Grâce à cette démarche, nous manipulons ces contraintes avec logique et laissons apparaître les potentiels latents pour obtenir l'effet souhaité. Le résultat de ce processus peut dès lors être aussi bien une stratégie qu'un logiciel, un mode de fabrication, un produit ou un espace. »

1–2
BREEDING TABLES
Table in laser-cut,
CNC brake-bent powder-coated
mild steel
2004–2005
Client: self-produced
and Moroso

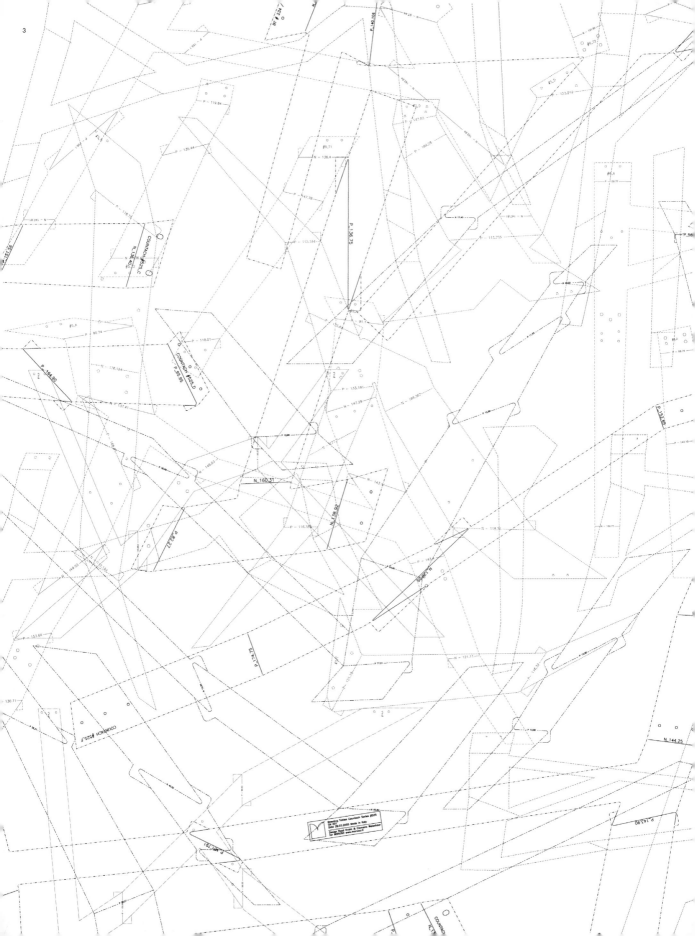

2

1–5

BREEDING TABLES FOR MOROSO AND SELF-PRODUCTION, 2004-05

The main idea behind the Breeding Tables has to do with process rather than product – namely, the use of custom computer code to generate an infinite number of different tables. The term "breeding" bundles several concepts central to the project. Each of the Breeding Tables is "bred" according to algorithmic presets and stands equal and individual. There is no longer an ultimate product. The issue of the distinction between the original and its copy becomes irrele-vant. Each table is representative of an algorithmic model and simultaneously in its uniqueness, a model for further objects of its "species". In tune with contem-porary production facilities and conditions, the Breeding Tables stand for a new form of integrat-ed product and process develop-ment – and thus for a new way of thinking about design.

Der grundlegende Gedanke, der die Gestaltung der Breeding Tables, also der „gezüchteten Tische" bestimmte, orientiert sich mehr am Prozess denn am Produkt – es geht nämlich darum, mithilfe eines speziellen Computerprogramms eine un-begrenzte Anzahl unterschied-licher Tische zu produzieren. Das Wort „gezüchtet" bündelt mehrere zentrale Ideen dieses Projektes: Ein jeweils mit unter-schiedlichen Daten gefütterter Algorithmus „züchtet" unter-schiedliche Tische, die alle Teil einer Produktserie und Unikat zugleich sind. Das endgültige Produkt gibt es nicht mehr. Das Problem, zwischen dem Original und seiner Kopie zu unterschei-den, wird irrelevant. Jeder Tisch repräsentiert einen Algorithmus und ist in seiner Einzigartigkeit doch wieder ein Modell für wei-tere Objekte seiner „Spezies". In Einklang mit zeitgemäßen Produktionsmöglichkeiten und -bedingungen, stehen die Bree-ding Tables für einen neuen, ganzheitlichen Zugang zur Pro-dukt- und Prozessentwicklung – und somit für eine neue Art, Design zu interpretieren.

La principale idée qui sous-tend ces Breeding Tables est davan-tage de l'ordre du processus que du produit – plus précisément, l'utilisation de codes informa-tiques personnalisés pour géné-rer un nombre infini de tableaux différents. Le terme « breeding » (reproduction, élevage, surrégé-nération) rassemble plusieurs concepts fondamentaux pour le projet. Chacune des Breeding Tables est « reproduite » selon des programmations algoryth-miques tout en demeurant sem-blables les unes aux autres mais personnelles. Il n'y a plus de pro-duit « fini ». Le problème de la distinction entre l'original et sa copie devient obsolète. Chaque tableau est représentatif d'un modèle algorythmique et, tout en étant unique, est aussi un modèle pour de futures objets de la même « espèce » que lui. En harmonie avec les installa-tions et les capacités industrielles contemporaines, les Breeding Tables incarnent une nouvelle forme de produit intégré et de développement de procédés – et donc une nouvelle façon de pen-ser le design.

3

BREEDING TABLES
Cutting patterns of table bases from the initial two series of tables
2004–2005
Client: self-produced and Moroso

4

BREEDING TABLES
Variables diagram of the Breeding Tables software – the variables define the "genetic code" of each table
2004–2005
Client: self-produced and Moroso

5

BREEDING TABLES
Process diagram illustrating the software and hardware manufacturing steps
2004–2005
Client: self-produced and Moroso

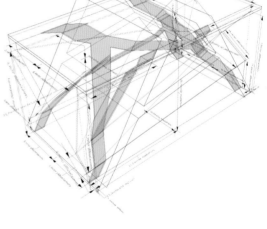

4

DIGITAL

(1) INPUT
(2) GENETIC ALGORITHM
(3) GENETIC ALGORITHM
(4) CONSTRUCTION SURFACES
(5) STRUCTURE EXTRACTION
(6) 2D LASER GEOMETRY

PHYSICAL

(7) LASER CUTTING
(8) BENDING
(9) ASSEMBLY
(10) COMPLETE TABLES

5

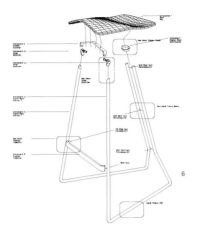

6–7
TRITON
Bar stool with seat in injection-moulded ABS on a chrome-plated steel base
2007
Client: Classicon

8
TRITON
Drawings of bar stool seat
2007
Client: Classicon

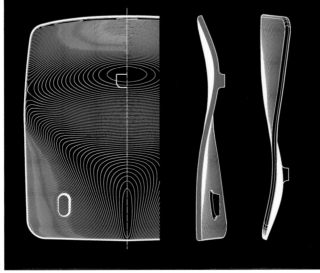

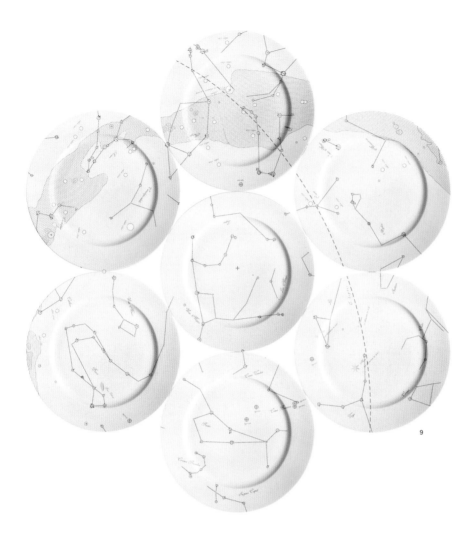

9–10
MY PRIVATE SKY
Set of seven hand-made and
hand-painted porcelain dinner
plates – a computer program
calculates the constellation
pattern on plates according
to customer's place and date
of birth
2007
Client: Nymphenburg (limited
edition of 100 sets)

11
ALPINE
Side chair with transparent
polycarbonate legs locked firmly
in a moulded single-form
composite plastic seat
2002/07
Client Moroso

9

"There is no specific ideology,
philosophy or method behind
our work."

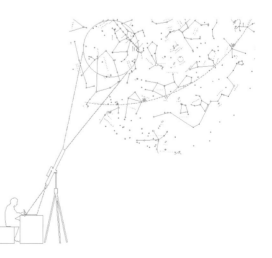

10

11

CLEMENS WEISSHAAR & REED KRAM

Kram/Weisshaar North
Katarina Bangata 52
11639 Stockholm
Sweden

Kram/Weisshaar South
Blumenstraße 28/2
80331 Munich
Germany

T (SE) +46 86428960
T (D) +49 89 55276781
E office@kramweisshaar.com
www.kramweisshaar.com

FOUNDERS' BIOGRAPHIES
CLEMENS WEISSHAAR

1977 Born in Munich
1994–1995 Metalworking apprenticeship in Munich
1995–1997 BA (Hons) Product Design, Central St. Martins College of Art and Design, London
1996–1999 Designer, Konstantin Grcic Industrial Design, Munich
1999–2002 Established and headed own studio, Clemens Weisshaar Industrial Design, London/Munich
2002 Co-founded Kram/Weisshaar in Munich and Stockholm

REED KRAM

1971 Born in Ohio, USA
1989–1993 Bachelor of Science and Engineering, Duke University, Durham, USA
1994–1995 Video game apprenticeship, San Francisco
1996–1998 MSAS Media Design, Massachusetts Institute of Technology, Cambridge. Aesthetics and Computation Group, MIT Media Laboratory with John Maeda
1999–2002 Established and headed own studio, Reed Kram Design, Copenhagen/Stockholm
2002 Co-founded Kram/Weisshaar in Munich and Stockholm

RECENT EXHIBITIONS

2001 "PRADA Works in Progress", Fondazione Prada, Milan; "Stealing Eyeballs", Kunsthaus & Museum in Progress, Vienna
2003 "Architecture, Media, Industrial Design for PRADA", Ospedale degli Innocenti, Florence
2004 "Content", Nationalgalerie, Berlin
2005 "La Raccolta", Spazio Krizia, Milan; "Jung & Deutsch", Goethe-Institut Berlin and Tokyo
2006 "Breeding Tables", Tank, Design Museum, London
2007 "30-Year Anniversary show of the Permanent Collection", Centre Georges Pompidou, Paris

RECENT AWARDS

2006 Studio selected as one of 100 "Germans of the Future" by the federal initiative "Land of Ideas"

CLIENTS

ACNE Art & Industry, Artek, Authentics, BMW Group, Centre Georges Pompidou, Classicon, Merten, Messe Frankfurt, Moroso, OMA/AMO (Rem Koolhaas), Porzellan-Manufaktur Nymphenburg, Prada, PriceWaterhouseCoopers, Svensk Form

HANNES WETTSTEIN

"Hannes Wettstein develops and realises lighting and furniture designs; he undertakes architectural projects in both the public domain and the private sector and always seeks the ideal combination of technology and form in his creations. However, his attention is centred on the development process rather than the design. His interest lies as much in interaction, dialogue and producing results with consummate ease as in the product itself. As an intermediary between architects, engineers, manufacturers and customers, he concentrates and transforms their combined knowledge. A design always emerges after consideration of the balance between contextual associations, customer's demands and production requirements. That is why Hannes Wettstein and his team develop a design language for each client, the equivalent of a brand image, that pointedly expresses this kind of brand culture or makes an important contribution to allowing it to come into being. Innovative technology – and also the transfer of knowledge from areas outside design – are crucially important for this. A design for a chair may be realised with the help of technology used in the construction of racing cars, while the archetypal use of an innovation in lighting technology will be in a lighting object. So, together with his team, Hannes Wettstein goes deeply into formal, philosophical, socio-cultural and economic questions and answers them with pure, functional and authoritative designs – in both the development of products and the design of rooms."

„Hannes Wettstein entwickelt und realisiert Leuchten- und Möbeldesigns; er verfolgt architektonische Projekte im öffentlichen Raum sowie in Privatbereichen und sucht in seinem Schaffen stets nach der idealen Verbindung von Technologie und Form. Dabei steht nicht die Formgebung im Vordergrund, sondern der Entwicklungsprozess. Wettsteins Interesse gilt der Interaktion, dem Dialog und dem spielerischen Generieren von Resultaten ebenso wie dem Produkt selbst. Als Vermittler zwischen Architekten, Ingenieuren, Herstellern und Kunden bündelt er das gemeinsame Wissen und setzt es um. Eine Form entsteht immer unter Berücksichtigung des Gleichgewichts von kontextuellen Zusammenhängen, den Anforderungen eines Kunden und den Produktionsbedingungen. Deshalb entwickeln Hannes Wettstein und sein Team für jeden Auftraggeber eine Formsprache, die der Kultur einer Marke entspricht, diese pointiert ausdrückt oder maßgebend dazu beiträgt, eine solche Markenkultur überhaupt entstehen zu lassen. Zentral ist dabei ein innovativer Technologie- und Wissenstransfer auch aus designfremden Bereichen. Ein Entwurf für einen Stuhl kann seine Materialisierung etwa mithilfe einer Technologie finden, die bei der Herstellung von Rennwagen zur Anwendung kommt – umgekehrt erlangt eine Innovation in der Beleuchtungstechnologie ihre archetypische Umsetzung in einem Leuchten-Objekt. So geht Hannes Wettstein zusammen mit seinem Team den formalen, philosophischen, soziokulturellen und ökonomischen Fragen auf den Grund. Und beantwortet sie mit funktionalem, purem und entschiedenem Design – in der Produktentwicklung genauso wie in der Gestaltung von Räumen."

«Hannes Wettstein conçoit et réalise des luminaires et du mobilier; il supervise des projets architecturaux dans le domaine public comme dans le secteur privé et recherche toujours dans ses créations la combinaison idéale entre technologie et forme. Il concentre toutefois davantage son attention sur la mise au point technique que sur le design. Il s'intéresse autant à l'interaction, au dialogue et à la production de résultats avec une aisance consommée qu'au produit lui-même. Intermédiaire entre les architectes, les ingénieurs, les fabricants et les consommateurs, il concentre, combine et transforme leurs connaissances. Une création n'émerge qu'après qu'ait été pris en considération l'équilibre entre associations contextuelles, demande des consommateurs et contraintes de production. C'est pourquoi Hannes Wettstein et son équipe conçoivent un vocabulaire stylistique pour chaque client, l'équivalent d'une identité de marque, qui exprime ostensiblement la culture de la marque ou contribue à lui permettre d'exister. Les technologies innovantes – tout comme le transfert de connaissances de secteurs jusque-là extérieurs au design – sont d'une importance cruciale. Une chaise peut être conçue avec l'aide des technologies utilisées dans la construction de voitures de course et les innovations dans les techniques d'éclairage sont naturellement utilisées pour la conception d'un luminaire. C'est ainsi que, avec son équipe, Hannes Wettstein s'implique profondément dans les questions formelles, philosophiques, socioculturelles et économiques et y répond par des créations pures et fonctionnelles qui font autorité – à la fois dans la conception des produits et dans le design des espaces.»

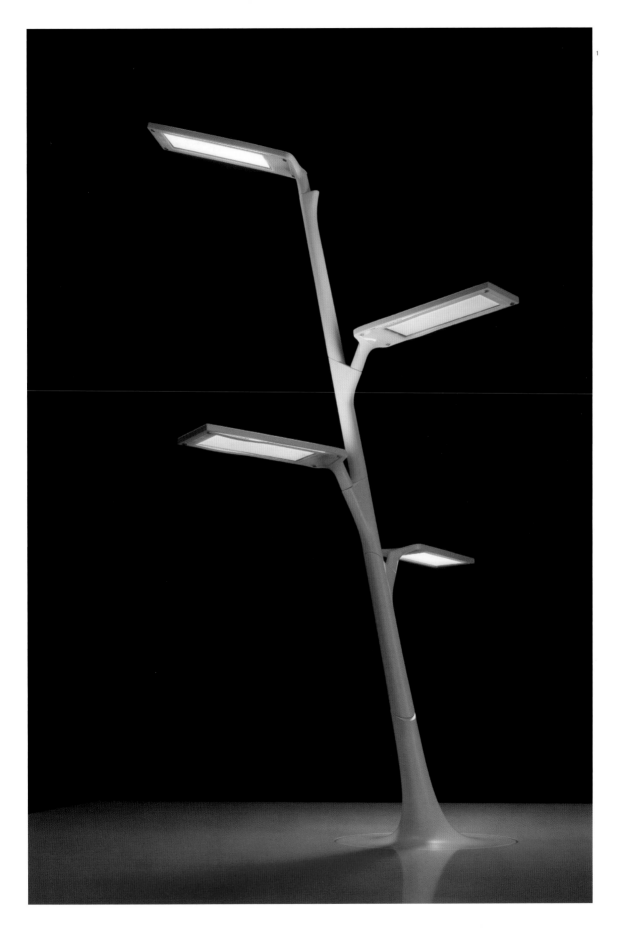

1–2
OLED LIGHT OBJECT FOR
MERCK, 2006

Light, durable, energy-saving
and versatile in its application,
Hannes Wettstein's OLED light
object is a synonym for a completely new generation of lumi-
naries. With this design he has
combined what is, in terms of
technology, currently the most
innovative light source with a
biomorphic shape: a branch or
plant stem. In the manner of a

branch that sprouts buds, an
atmospheric light unfolds on
this object both upwards and
downwards. Wettstein has
merged the OLEDs seamlessly
with the luminaire sail, which
can be horizontally tilted thanks
to a snap-in device. The body
of the light object is made of
plastic and is characterized by
a porcelain-like finish.

Leicht, langlebig, energiesparend
und vielseitig in der Anwendung, wird das OLED – das

derzeit vom technologischen
Standpunkt innovativste Leucht-
mittel – vom Designer Hannes
Wettstein in eine biomorphe
Form gefasst. Sein „Leucht-
zweig" ist somit ein Synonym
für eine vollkommen neue
Generation von Leuchten und
Lichtobjekten. So wie auf einem
Zweig Knospen und Blätter
sprießen, treibt sein Objekt ein
atmosphärisches Licht aus, das
nach oben und nach unten
strahlt. Wettstein hat die OLEDs
nahtlos mit den stilisierten Blät-

tern oder „Lichtflügeln" ver-
schmolzen, die ihrerseits mit
einem Schnappverschluss befestigt und horizontal gedreht
werden können. Das Lichtobjekt
ist aus Kunststoff und zeichnet
sich durch eine porzellanartige
Oberfläche aus.

Léger, durable, économe en
énergie et polyvalent, l'objet
lumineux OLED de Hannes
Wettstein symbolise une nouvelle génération de luminaires.
Grâce à son design et à ses quali-

tés techniques, il est aujourd'hui
la source lumineuse biomorphique la plus innovante puisqu'il
ressemble à un arbrisseau. À la
manière d'un rameau sur lequel
poussent des bourgeons, une
lumière atmosphérique éclot de
l'objet par en haut et par en bas.
Wettstein a fusionné en douceur
structure et surfaces lumineuses,
et les OLEDs peuvent aussi être
fixés horizontalement. Le support est fait d'un plastique qui se
caractérise par sa finition rappe-
lant la porcelaine.

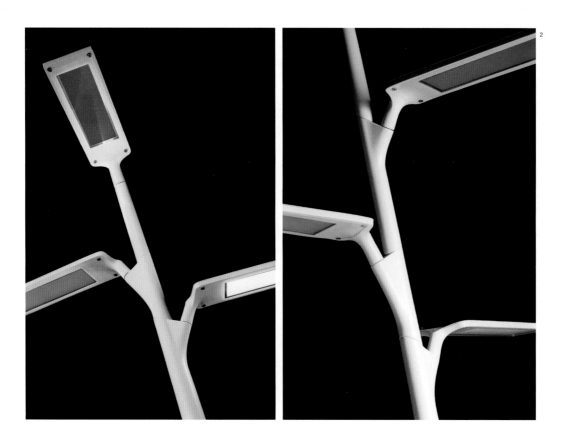

1–2
OLED
Multi-branch luminaire with
plastic body and OLED light
sources
2006
Client: Merck

3–4
TOTOTO
Indoor/outdoor, stackable
monobloc armchair in injection-
moulded polypropylene
2007
Client: Max Design

3

4

"The methodology of our design process is the constant factor in our work."

5

6

HANNES WETTSTEIN

Hannes Wettstein
Seefeldstrasse 303
8008 Zurich
Switzerland
T +41 44 4212222
E info@hanneswettstein.com
www.hanneswettstein.com

BIOGRAPHY

1958 Born in Ascona, Switzerland
1974–1978 Draughtsman apprenticeship specializing in building construction
1982–1988 Freelance designer, Büro für Gestaltung, Zurich
1989 Foundation of the "Diesseits" edition (limited edition and one-off pieces)
1989–1991 Partner and head of 3D sector, Design Agency, Erlenbach, Switzerland
1990–1995 Guest lecturer: Gerrit Rietveld Academie Amsterdam, Netherlands; Fachhochschule, Hanover, Germany; F.F.I.Basel, Switzerland; Piccola scuola di design Milano, Milan; Centro Europeo di Design Milano, Milan
1991+ Founder and owner, zed.design network, Zurich
1991–1996 Lecturer, Swiss Federal Institute of Technologie (ETH), Zurich
1994–2001 Professor at the Hochschule für Gestaltung, Karlsruhe, Germany
2002 Lecturer, Hochschule für Gestaltung und Kunst, Zurich

RECENT EXHIBITIONS

2002 "Diva", Molteni, Torlonia, Italy
2004 "white eclectic", Designmai, Berlin; "endless", Pro Helvetia, Schweizerische Kulturstiftung (Arts Council of Switzerland)
2005 "whiteball", Stylepark, imm Cologne

RECENT AWARDS

2000 Good Design Award, Chicago Athenaeum
2001 Red Dot Award, Design Zentrum Nordrhein Westfalen, Essen
2002 iF Award, International Forum Design Hanover
2003 Goldener Hase award, Zurich; iF Award, International Forum Design Hanover
2004 Compasso d'Oro award, ADI, Milan; Good Design Award, Chicago Athenaeum
2005 2 x Red Dot Awards, Design Zentrum Nordrhein Westfalen, Essen; Design Plus Award (Material Vision 05), Ambiente, Frankfurt; iF Award, International Forum Design Hanover; Design Preis Schweiz, Design Center, Langenthal
2006 Red Dot Award, Design Zentrum Nordrhein Westfalen, Essen; Nomination, "neue Klassiker", Schöner Wohnen; Gold award, Promax/BDA World Awards, New York; FX Award - Public or Leisure Furniture, FX Magazine

CLIENTS

Airport Frankfurt/Main, Arflex, Artemide, Avantgarde Acoustic, Baleri, Belux, BMW, Bosch, Brionvega, Bulo, Carl Zeiss, Cassina, Convention Point, Zurich, Dada, Desalto, Dietiker, ENIA, EST, Extremis, Feller, Fotomuseum Winterthur, Fraport, Grand Hyatt Berlin, Hasselblad, Horgenglarus, IB Office, Interna, JAB, Kanton St. Gallen, Keramag, KPMG, Kurz, KWC, La Clinic Montreux, Lamy, Matsushita, Max Design, Merck, Molteni, Nemo, Neuco, Novartis, Pallucco, Pastoe, Philips, Piega, Revox, Sanitas Troesch, SBB, Schock, Schweizer Fernsehen, Shimano, Similor Kugler, Sony, Steiner, Stylepark, Sulzer, Swiss Embassy Madrid, Swiss Embassy Teheran, Swiss Embassy Washington, Tumi, UBS, Ventura, Victorinox, Vitra, Wirz Werbung Zurich, Wittmann, Wogg, Zai

5
VICTORY FL 8 /10X32 T
Light, compact and ergonomic
binoculars, entirely rubberized
and waterproof to 400 mbar
2005
Client: Carl Zeiss Sports Optics

6
VELA
Indoor/outdoor armchair with
a tubular stainless steel frame
and seat and back in raw rope
and pvc rope
2005
Client: Accademia

7
OPTICAL 03
Halogen floor light with
methacrylate diffusers and
polished aluminium frame –
the diffusers can be rotated
360 degrees and are lined with
OLF (optical lighting film),

which creates reflections and
projects the light uniformly
without glare
2004
Client: Pallucco Lighting

TOKUJIN YOSHIOKA

"To me, design is not making but creating. It is not about explaining with words but feeling it. Design is attractive because it cannot be fully expressed with words ... creating something that has never existed before requires a great effort, as much as a mother gives birth to her children. Good design makes it possible to bring joy and surprise to many people of all ages, beyond language, race and nationality. It can also bring happiness, making one's life change magically. Dealing with objects too often involves arranging what already exists. Creating a 'new' thing, that is to say, an 'original design', requires innovation on many levels and should ultimately move people. In my approach to design I attempt to stimulate one's consciousness – to set the user's senses free. In the future, design will be less about the physicality of objects and more about their sensual excitement."

„Für mich besteht Design nicht im Machen, sondern im Erschaffen. Es geht nicht darum, es mit Worten zu erklären, sondern darum, es zu fühlen. Design ist attraktiv, weil man es nicht ganz in Worte fassen kann ... Etwas zu gestalten, das es noch nie zuvor gegeben hat, verlangt eine große Anstrengung, vergleichbar der Anstrengung einer Mutter bei der Geburt ihres Kindes. Gutes Design macht es möglich, vielen Menschen jeden Alters Freude zu bereiten und sie in Staunen zu versetzen, unabhängig von Sprache, Ethnie und Nationalität. Es kann auch ein Glücksgefühl erzeugen und das eigene Leben auf magische Weise verändern. Wenn man beruflich mit Objekten zu tun hat, heißt das allzu oft, lediglich neu zusammenzustellen, was es bereits gibt. Einen ‚neuen' Gegenstand zu kreieren, also ein ‚ursprüngliches Design', erfordert Innovation auf vielen verschiedenen Ebenen und sollte letzten Endes die Menschen emotional berühren. Bei meinem Ansatz von Design strebe ich danach, das Bewusstsein der Benutzer anzuregen – ihre Sinne freizusetzen. In Zukunft wird es beim Design weniger um die physikalische Beschaffenheit von Objekten und mehr um ihre sinnliche Spannung gehen."

«Selon moi, le design n'est pas faire mais créer. Il ne s'agit pas de l'expliquer avec des mots mais de le ressentir. Le design est attrayant parce qu'il ne peut pas être totalement exprimé avec des mots... Créer quelque chose qui n'a jamais existé auparavant exige de gros efforts, autant qu'il en faut à une mère pour donner naissance à ses enfants. Un bon design permet d'apporter joie et surprises à un grand nombre de gens de tous âges, par-delà les langues, les races et les nationalités. Il peut aussi apporter le bonheur, changer la vie des gens de façon magique. S'occuper d'objets suppose trop souvent d'accommoder ce qui existe déjà. Créer une chose ‹nouvelle›, c'est-à-dire un ‹design original›, suppose d'être novateur à bien des niveaux et finira un jour par émouvoir les gens. Dans mon approche du design, je tente de stimuler les consciences – de libérer les sensations des usagers. Dans l'avenir, le design accordera moins d'importance à la présence physique des objets et davantage à la stimulation sensorielle qu'ils provoquent.»

2

1–2
MEDIA SKIN
Mobile telephone with flip-style cover over the keypad, 131 mega pixel CMOS camera and the world's first 260K colour QVGA organic EL main display
2007
Client: KDDI
CORPORATION

1–4

MEDIA SKIN MOBILE PHONE FOR KDDI, 2007

"I wanted to create a mobile phone that people would wonder why it had never existed before. This is not a designer's mobile phone; rather it is a mobile phone that is closer to contemporary art. In other words, Media Skin is not about form but is intended as something people can feel with their bodies and souls. How long each day are we in physical contact with our mobile phones? A mobile phone is one of the closest products to us. Media Skin was designed to go beyond an object and to become part of one's self. It is a new type of mobile phone, which assimilates with our body, as smooth as a person's second skin. It has real texture and the form contrasts beautifully with the user. Media Skin transcends utility and provides a rich experience with a new feeling, like we get when appreciating a beautiful work of contemporary art."

„Ich wollte ein Mobiltelefon so gestalten, dass sich alle fragen würden, warum es das denn nicht längst gibt. Also nicht wieder ein Mobiltelefon eines Designers, sondern eher ein Handy, das fast schon ein moderner Kunstgegenstand ist. Mit anderen Worten: Das Media Skin behandelt nicht das Thema Form, sondern soll ein Objekt sein, das emotional berührt, das mit dem Körper und der Seele gefühlt wird. Wie lange kommt unser Körper jeden Tag mit dem Mobiltelefon – einem der am meisten benutzten Gegenstände – in Berührung? Das Media Skin geht jedoch über den Gegenstand hinaus und wird Teil des Menschen, der es besitzt. Es ist ein neuer Typ von Mobiltelefon, das sich unserem Körper anpasst und so weich ist wie eine zweite Haut. Seine Struktur kann gefühlt werden, und seine Form kontrastiert wunderbar mit dem Menschen, der es benutzt. Das Media Skin transzendiert somit den Begriff der Nützlichkeit und vermittelt uns reiche Erfahrungen, neue Gefühle und die Schönheit eines zeitgenössischen Kunstwerks."

« Je souhaitais créer un téléphone portable dont les gens se demanderaient pourquoi il n'a pas été inventé plus tôt. Ce n'est pas un téléphone de designer, il s'agit plutôt d'un portable qui confine à l'art contemporain. En autres termes, Media Skin n'est pas affaire de forme mais de ce que les gens peuvent ressentir avec leurs corps et leurs esprits. Combien de temps passons-nous chaque jour en contact physique avec notre téléphone portable? Il fait partie des objets que nous touchons le plus au cours d'une journée. Media Skin a été conçu pour transcender l'objet et devenir une part d'individualité. Il s'agit d'une nouvelle espèce de téléphone, qui apprivoise le corps avec la douceur d'une seconde peau. Il est doté d'une réelle texture et sa forme contraste magnifiquement avec son utilisateur. Media Skin dépasse l'utile pour procurer une expérience riche et une sensation nouvelle, semblable à celle que nous éprouvons face à une belle œuvre d'art contemporain. »

3

MEDIA SKIN

Tokujin Yoshioka Design

4

3–4
MEDIA SKIN
Mobile phone with different
colours and textures – the
orange and white models feature
paint made with silicon particles
for a smooth texture, while the
black model is made with a
soft-feel paint that includes
special urethane particles to
provide a rubber-like texture
2007
Client: KDDI
CORPORATION

5–6
TEAR DROP
Halogen table/floor light in glass
and aluminium
2007
Client: Yamagiwa

5

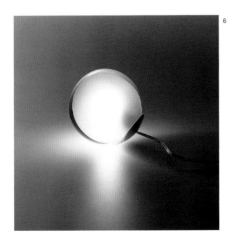

6

"To create a new 'origin of design'
that has never existed."

7

8

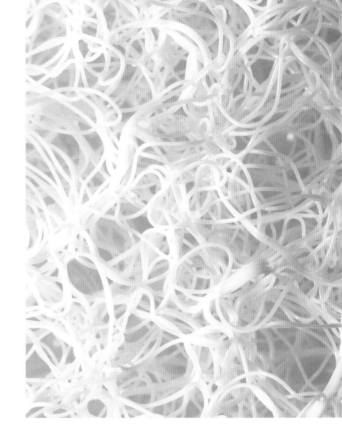

9

7
PANE
Single-form armchair in moulded translucent polyester elastomer fibres
2006
Client: self-generated prototype

8
PANE
Sequence showing manufacturing process of chair – a semi-cylindrical block of fibres is rolled, inserted into a paper tube, and by baking it in a kiln at 104 degrees C, the fibres memorize the shape of the mold
2006
Client: self-generated prototype

9
PANE
Detail of chair's translucent polyester elastomer fibres

TOKUJIN YOSHIOKA

Tokujin Yoshioka Design
9-1 Daikanyama-cho
Shibuya-ku
Tokyo 150-0034
Japan
T +81 3 54280830
E tyd@tokujin.com
www.tokujin.com

BIOGRAPHY
1967 Born in Saga Prefecture, Japan
1986 Graduated from Kuwasawa Design School, Tokyo
1987–1988 Worked briefly in the design office of Shiro Kuramata in Tokyo
1988–1991 Designer, Miyake Design Studio, Tokyo – in charge of shop design
1992 Began working as a freelance designer

2000 Established his own design office, Tokujin Yoshioka Design in Tokyo

RECENT EXHIBITIONS
2004 "Air du Temps", Maison Hermès, Tokyo
2005 "Stardust", Swarovski Crystal Palace, Tokyo, Milan
2006 "Tokujin Yoshioka – Super Fiber Revolution", AXIS; "Tokujin Yoshioka x Lexus L-finesse" – Evolving Fiber Technology, TOYOTA, Milan

2007 "Tokujin X Moroso", Moroso, Milan

RECENT AWARDS
2001 "The Coming Designer for the Future" Award, Architektur & Wohnen, Hamburg
2002 Mainichi Design Award 2001, Japan
2005 Talents du Luxe award, Salon du Meuble, Paris
2007 Encouragement Prize, Agency for Cultural Affairs, Government of Japan

CLIENTS
Audi, Bang & Olufsen, BMW, Driade, Hermès, Issey Miyake, KDDI, Moroso, Muji, Nissan, NTT-X, Peugeot, RMK Isetan, Suqqu, Swarovski, Toyota, Vitra, Yamagiwa

YOUMEUS

"People need more than just solutions; they need to be engaged on an emotional level. If a consumer is moved emotionally by a product or service, they will continue to use it. This can only be achieved if the product is conceived as a whole on all levels from the beginning. We believe that at the heart of any design project the process involves designing for people and not trying to make any grand statements or to follow a stylistic only approach. Any piece of design work we do comes about by understanding people, what they need, what they want and how they want to feel. True design is when an object and people are unified in harmony to form an exceptional product or service experience. Inspired strategic product design on a client level acts in much the same way as a well illustrated road map that helps the motorist in unfamiliar territory. It clearly informs and enables our clients to choose which routes are the most relevant, in order to get from where they are to where they need to be. Unfortunately many companies think that designers are people you bring in at the latter stages of product development to make their ideas 'look good'. Companies who use designers at the early stages, to help plan and define their business strategy are the ones who have learnt that it takes more than elegant looking case work to build brand loyalty."

„Menschen brauchen mehr als nur Lösungen; sie müssen sich auf einer emotionalen Ebene angesprochen fühlen. Werden Konsumenten emotional von einem Produkt oder einer Dienstleistung berührt, werden sie weiterhin davon Gebrauch machen. Das kann nur erreicht werden, wenn das Produkt von Anfang an ganzheitlich konzipiert wird. Wir glauben, dass der eigentliche Kern jedes Designprojekts darin liegt, für Menschen zu gestalten und nicht irgendwelche hochfliegenden Statements abzugeben. Jede unserer gestalterischen Arbeiten entsteht dadurch, dass wir verstehen: Menschen und das, was sie brauchen, was sie wollen und wie sie sich fühlen möchten. Wahres Design entsteht, wenn sich ein Objekt mit Menschen harmonisch zu einem außergewöhnlichen Produkt oder einer besonderen Serviceerfahrung verbindet. Ein hervorragendes strategisches und kundenorientiertes Produktdesign funktioniert ganz ähnlich wie eine anschauliche Straßenkarte, die dem Reisenden auf unbekanntem Terrain weiterhilft. Es informiert unsere Klienten und ermöglicht ihnen zu entscheiden, welche Wege am geeignetsten sind, um dorthin zu gelangen, wo sie hinwollen. Leider glauben viele Unternehmen, Designer seien Leute, die man zu den letzten Phasen der Produktentwicklung heranzieht, damit sie ihre Ideen ‚gut aussehen' lassen. Dagegen haben Unternehmen, die bereits in den frühesten Stadien Designer einsetzen, verstanden, dass es mehr als elegant aussehender Fallstudien bedarf, um Markentreue aufzubauen."

«Les gens recherchent plus que des solutions; ils ont besoin d'être stimulés émotionnellement. Si un consommateur est ému par un produit ou un service, il continuera à l'utiliser. Cette émotion ne peut être atteinte que si le produit est conçu comme un tout, dès le début. Nous pensons qu'il faut placer l'utilisateur au cœur de tout projet de design, et non de grandes déclarations ou une approche purement stylistique. Chacune des pièces que nous concevons naît de notre compréhension des gens, de leurs besoins, de leurs désirs et des sensations qu'ils recherchent. Le vrai design est atteint lorsque l'objet et la personne s'harmonisent pour former un produit ou un service exceptionnel. Une présentation intelligente du projet aux clients doit agir de manière similaire, tout comme une carte routière illustrée aide le motard sur un trajet inconnu. Elle informe clairement nos clients et leur permet de choisir quelles routes sont les plus pertinentes pour aller de l'endroit où ils sont à celui qu'ils veulent atteindre. De nombreuses entreprises pensent malheureusement que les designers ne doivent intervenir que dans les dernières étapes de la conception du produit pour ‹mettre en valeur› leurs idées. Les entreprises qui ont recours aux designers dès le démarrage d'un projet, pour participer à la planification et à la définition de leur stratégie commerciale, ont compris qu'il faut plus qu'un joli emballage pour construire la fidélité à une marque.»

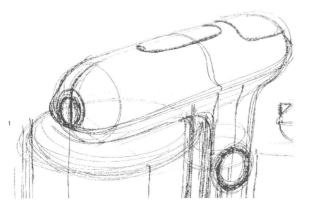

1

"The kMix food mixer project encompassed: branding, naming, visual identity, industrial design, packaging design and sales and marketing tools aimed at helping Kenwood engage with the consumer in new and exciting ways. We achieved this by controlling the whole product experience. With an over-saturated marketplace it was obvious that we could not just develop a product that competed on function and price alone. We needed to create a new definition of what value means and to do it in the spirit of the brand. Where 'Old luxury' values anchor themselves to solid production qualities, our focus on kMix was 'New luxury', which invests in intangibles. They include the magic and experience of the brand. As well as product development our work included the identification and creation of various consumer touch-points to make every point of interaction with the product and the brand behind it delightful."

„Unsere gestalterische Arbeit beim Küchenmaschinenprojekt kMix umfasste: Branding, Naming, visuelle Identität, Industriedesign, Verpackungsdesign sowie Verkaufs- und Marketing-Tools, die Kenwood dabei unterstützen sollten, den Konsumenten auf eine neue und aufregende Art für sich zu gewinnen. Wir erreichten diese Ziele, indem wir das Produkt von Anfang an als Ganzes konzipierten. Es war natürlich klar, dass wir für einen übersättigten Markt nicht einfach nur ein Produkt entwickeln konnten, das sich von vergleichbaren Produkten der Mitbewerber nur durch Funktion und Preis unterscheidet. Wir mussten neu definieren, was Wert oder Nutzen bedeutet, und wir mussten das im Geist der Marke tun. Während sich ‚alter Luxus' an Produkteigenschaften wie Gediegenheit und Zuverlässigkeit verankert, fokussierten wir bei kMix einen ‚neuen Luxus', der in immaterielle Werte investiert und auch Magie und das Erleben der Marke umfasst. Neben der Produktentwicklung beinhaltete unsere Arbeit die Identifizierung und gestalterische Umsetzung verschiedener emotionaler Attribute, um jeden Aspekt der Interaktion mit dem Produkt und der Marke, die dahinter steht, zu einem wunderbaren Erlebnis zu machen."

« Le projet de mixeur alimentaire kMix a intégré identité de marque, dénomination, identité visuelle, design industriel et conception d'emballage ainsi que stratégie commerciale et outils marketing, afin d'aider Kenwood à établir avec le consommateur une relation nouvelle et excitante. Nous y sommes parvenus en gardant le contrôle de toute la création du produit. Sur un marché sursaturé, il était évident que nous ne pouvions créer un produit qui ne soit compétitif qu'en termes de fonctions et de prix. Il nous fallait créer une nouvelle définition de la valeur tout en respectant l'esprit de la marque. Tandis que les valeurs du ‹ vieux luxe › se fondent sur de solides capacités de production, pour le kMix nous nous sommes concentrés sur le ‹ nouveau luxe ›, qui s'investit dans l'intangible, tient compte de la magie de la marque et de son expérience. Outre la conception du produit en lui-même, notre travail a aussi consisté à identifier et créer les détails qui accrocheraient le consommateur en rendant merveilleux chaque aspect de son interaction avec le produit et la marque. »

3

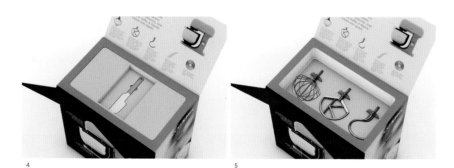

4   5

"Trends informed
user-centric design."

1–3
KMIX
All metal food mixer with
stainless steel bowl
2007
Client: Kenwood

4–5
KMIX
Food mixer packaging
showing spatula, beater, whisk
and dough tool accessories
2007
Client: Kenwood

6
HAND-HELD POWERED
KITCHEN TOOLS
Computer renderings of hand
blender, hand whisk, electric
knife and electric can opener all
with soft textured grips for easy
operation and comfort
2004
Client: Kenwood

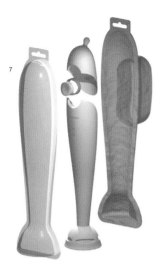

7

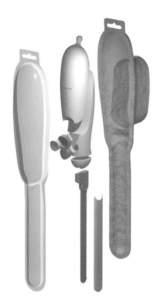

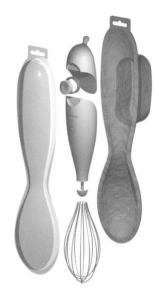

9

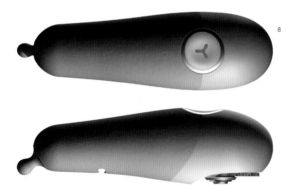

8

7
HAND-HELD POWERED
KITCHEN TOOLS
Exploded computer renderings
of hand blender, electric knife
and hand whisk
2004
Client: Kenwood

8
HAND-HELD POWERED
KITCHEN TOOLS
Computer renderings of electric
can opener
2004
Client: Kenwood

9
HAND-HELD POWERED
KITCHEN TOOLS
Electric knife and hand whisk
with optional hanging hooks for
wall mounting or hanging from
a rail
2004
Client: Kenwood

10
WATER FILTER
Water filter in injection-moulded plastic with replaceable filter
cartridge
2004
Client: Kenwood

YOUMEUS
109 Westbourne Studios
242 Acklam Road
London W10 5JJ
United Kingdom
T +44 20 75247540
E mail@youmeusdesign.com
www.youmeusdesign.com

DESIGN GROUP HISTORY
2003 Founded by Chris
Christou in London

FOUNDER'S BIOGRAPHY
CHRIS CHRISTOU
1972 Born in Harrow, Middle-
sex, England
1991–1994 BA (Hons) Product
Design, Ravensbourne College
of Design and Communication,
Kent

1994–2000 Designer, kdo,
Basingstoke
2000–2003 Founded his own
design practice, Future Creative
in London

RECENT EXHIBITIONS
2007 "The Art of Living",
Maison & Objet, Paris

RECENT AWARDS
2001 Winner of Glassware
category and Winner of kitchen
tool category, Annual Design
Review, I.D. Magazine

CLIENTS
British American Tobacco,
Compaq, DeLonghi, Kenwood,
Motorola, NEC,
Procter & Gamble, Sony,
Vodafone

MICHAEL YOUNG

"It seems that over the last ten years design has grown tremendously but a lack of industrial consumption in Europe has forced the profession into two fields: design decoration (of which the Netherlands seems guilty) and industrial design. It would be too bold to say the former is superficial but Europe seems to be bursting with un-necessary things now, whilst in the same breath complaining about China's over-productivity (which it imports). For me, working now in Asia is the superior option since it is not ego driven, the future scope is simply inspiring and healthier."

„Der Bereich Design ist im Laufe der letzten zehn Jahre scheinbar enorm gewachsen, aber ein Mangel an Konsum von Industriegütern in Europa hat den Berufsstand in zwei Betätigungsfelder gezwungen: dekoratives Design (woran offenbar die Niederlande schuld sind) und industrielles Design. Es wäre kühn, zu behaupten, Ersteres sei oberflächlich, aber Europa scheint vor überflüssigen Dingen zu bersten, während es sich gleichzeitig über Chinas Überproduktivität beklagt (die importiert wird). Für mich bedeutet meine jetzige Tätigkeit in Asien die bessere Wahl, da man hier nicht so Ich-besessen und das zukünftige Betätigungsfeld einfach inspirierender und gesünder ist."

« Le design semble avoir pris une place croissante ces dix dernières années mais, dans le même temps, une faible consommation industrielle en Europe a poussé la profession dans deux directions : le design décoratif (dont sont apparemment responsables les Pays-Bas) et le design industriel. Il serait exagéré de dire que le premier est superficiel, mais l'Europe semble aujourd'hui sur le point d'exploser tant elle est remplie d'objets non nécessaires, tout en se plaignant, dans un même souffle, de la surproduction chinoise (qu'elle importe). Pour moi, travailler en Asie aujourd'hui est l'option ultime puisque la société n'y est pas menée par l'ego et que ses perspectives d'avenir sont tout simplement plus enthousiasmantes et plus saines. »

1

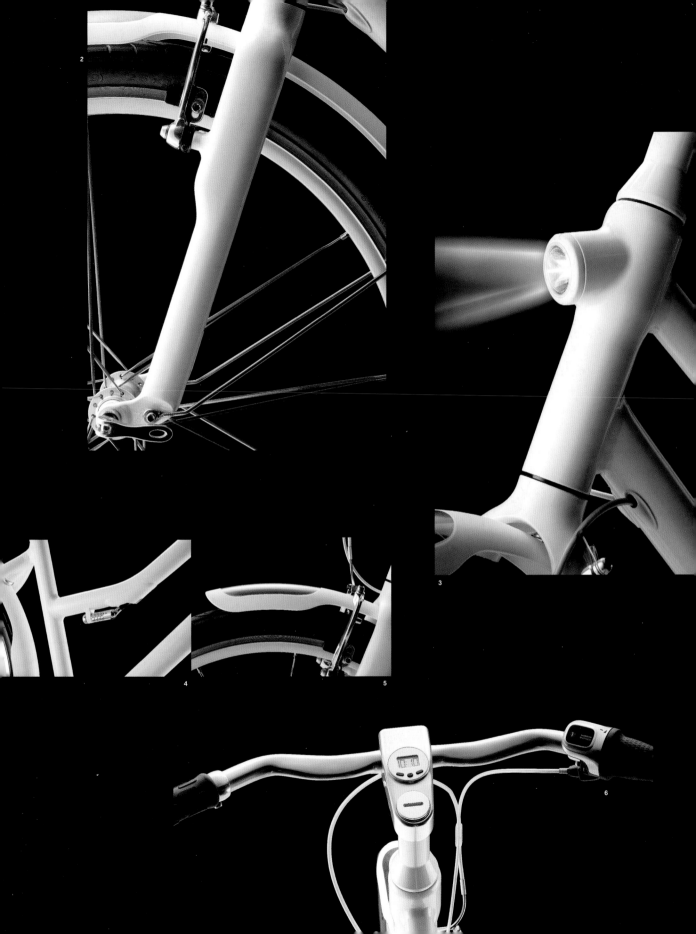

1–6

CITY STORM BICYCLE FOR
GIANT, 2006

"The aim of this project was not only to make a more functional city bike but also one that could be emotionally compelling and communicate to consumers who might demand a more design-related option. In terms of design I decided that in order to please a global market and broad age group we needed to maintain a classical frame construction and use that to build in fresh design aspects. We considered these design aspects 'demands' and listed them very clearly to understand what might be needed in the city. I then calculated how these could be integrated into real working details. The four aspects of the City Storm that distinguish it from other city bicycles are: integrated design elements, the touch points, its functionality and, of course, my design language."

„Dieses Projekt zielte darauf ab, nicht nur ein funktionelleres Fahrrad zu entwickeln, sondern ein Citybike, das auch jene Konsumenten emotional ansprechen würde, die sich bei der Produktwahl vielleicht mehr von gestalterischen Kriterien leiten lassen. Was das Design betrifft, habe ich mich dafür entschieden, eine klassische Rahmenkonstruktion beizubehalten – allein schon um einen globalen Markt und eine breite Altersgruppe zufriedenzustellen – und davon ausgehend neue gestalterische Aspekte einfließen zu lassen. Wir betrachteten diese gestalterischen Aspekte als ‚Ansprüche' und haben sie aufgelistet und definiert, um zu verstehen, was in der Stadt gebraucht werden könnte. Ich habe mich dann damit beschäftigt, wie sie funktional gestaltet und in das Fahrrad integriert werden könnten. Die vier Aspekte des City Storm, die es von anderen Citybikes unterscheiden, sind integrierte Designelemente, die emotionalen Attribute, seine Funktionalität und natürlich meine Designsprache."

« Le but de ce projet était de créer un vélo urbain qui soit non seulement plus fonctionnel mais qui puisse aussi émouvoir et entrer en communication avec les personnes séduites par une option de transport plus design. Afin que ce design attire un public international et de tous âges, j'ai jugé qu'il fallait conserver la construction classique et l'agrémenter d'innovations. Nous avons dressé une liste exhaustive de ces ‹ contraintes › pour comprendre de quel vélo un citadin a besoin. J'ai ensuite calculé comment ces compétences pourraient être intégrées à l'objet. Les quatre aspects qui distingue le City Storm des autres vélos de ville sont: des éléments de design intégrés, ses points de contact, sa fonctionnalité et bien sûr mon vocabulaire créatif personnel. »

7

1–6
CITY STORM
Bicycle for city use with
enclosed chain guard and
integrated lock, headlight,
rear light and digital clock
2006
Client: Giant

7–8
WRITING DESK
Desk with drawer in aluminium,
composite wood and linoleum
2005
Client: Established & Sons

8

9

9–10
SOFT CAPACITIVE MOUSE
IGNITION
Soft cordless computer mouse in
a variety of colours
2006
Client: Logitech

10

MICHAEL YOUNG
Michael Young
G/f No.1 New Street
Sheung Wan
Hong Kong
T +852 28030344
E info@michael-young.com
www.michael-young.com

BIOGRAPHY
1966 Born in Sunderland,
England
1988–1989 Art Foundation
Course, Sunderland Polytechnic
1989–1992 BA (Hons)
Furniture and Product
Design, Kingston University,
London
1990–1993 Worked at Tom
Dixon's Space Studio, London
1994 Received a Crafts Council
Bursary and commenced a series
of one-man shows in Paris,
Germany, Tokyo and Kyoto
1995 Established MY- 022 Ltd
design office in London
1995–2005 Michael Young
Studios, London/Iceland/Hong
Kong
2002 Guest of Honour, Kortrijk
Design Biennale

RECENT EXHIBITIONS
2000 Installation for Magis,
Palermo
2001 "Mirrors", Galerie Kro,
Paris
2003 "Early Paradise",
Mandarina Duck, Milan
2004 Installation for Dupont,
100% Design, London
(in collaboration with Katrin
Olina)
2005 Group exhibition,
Established & Sons, Milan
2006 "Crossovers", Pearl Lam
Contrast Gallery, Shanghai
2007 "100% Design Tokyo",
Tokyo (creative director)

CLIENTS
Artemide, Asahi,
Beauté Prestige International,
Cappellini, Danese,
Dupont Corian, Dupont SGX,
Established & Sons,
Eurolounge,
E&Y, Georg Jensen, Giant,
Idée, Kro, Kuro Music,
Kymco, Lacoste,
Laurent Perrier,
Magis, MK Maeda, Nokia,
Passanha Olive Oli, PQI,
Radio Shack, Rosenthal,
Sawaya & Moroni, Schweppes,
SMAK Iceland, Swedese

"I'm an industrial optimist,
perhaps a romantic."

11

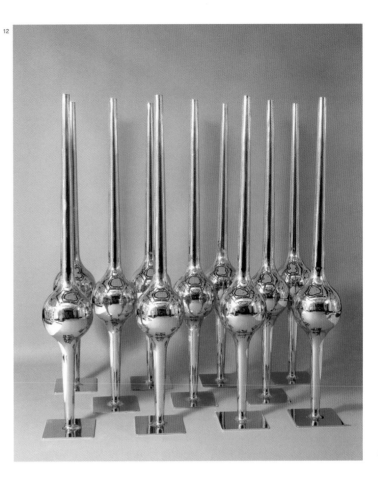

11
KURO NEO
MP3 player for use with the
Kuro peer-to-peer file-sharing
network that comes with 512MB
of flash memory, while also
featuring an SD memory card
slot so users can expand their
storage capacities
2005
Client: Kuro

12
SUPER STEEL STICKS
Installation of silver-mirrored
objects for the "Crossovers:
Beyond Art and Design"
exhibition in Shanghai
2006
Client: Pearl Lam Contrast
Gallery

13
SCHWEPPES PREMIUM
BARWARE
Drinking glasses and dual
function swizzle sticks/muddlers
in stainless steel
2006
Client: Schweppes

14
SCHWEPPES PREMIUM
BARWARE
Ice bucket and tongs in stainless
steel and plastic ice tray
2006
Client: Schweppes

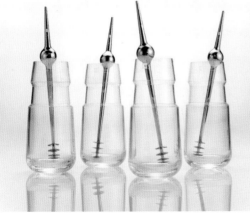

CREDITS

Paris / Zyken, Paris (photo: Grégoire Alexandre) **p.286–289** © Suntae Kim, Bucheon City, Korea **p.290–295** © Nikola Knezevic, Belgrade **p.296–303** © Lavernia Cienfuegos y Asociados, Valencia **p.304–309** © Leading Edge Design, Tokyo (photos: Yukio Shimizu) **p.310** © (*portrait*) Mathieu Lehanneur, Paris (photo: Cécile Fricker) **p.311** © Mathieu Lehanneur, Paris (photo: Véronique Huyghe) **p.312–313** © Mathieu Lehanneur, Paris **p.314–315** © Mathieu Lehanneur, Paris (photos: Véronique Huyghe) **p.316–317** © Lievore Altherr Molina, Barcelona / Arper SpA, Monastier (Treviso) Italy **p.318** © Lievore Altherr Molina, Barcelona / Sellex SA, Irun, Spain **p.319** © Lievore Altherr Molina, Barcelona / Arper SpA, Monastier (Treviso) Italy **p.320–323** © LOT-EK, New York **p.324** © (*portrait*) Ross Lovegrove, London (photo: John Ross) **p.324–326** © Ross Lovegrove, London **p.327** © Ross Lovegrove, London (photo: Pierre Jusselme) **p.328–332** © Ross Lovegrove, London **p.333** © Ross Lovegrove, London (photo: John Ross) **p.334–339** © Lunar Design, San Francisco **p.340–343** © Marine Current Turbines Limited, Bristol **p.344–346** © Marmol Radziner Prefab, Los Angeles **p.347** © Marmol Radziner Prefab, Los Angeles (photo: David Glomb) **p.348–349** © Marmol Radziner Prefab, Los Angeles (photo: Benny Chan) **p.350–351** © Marmol Radziner Prefab, Los Angeles **p.352** © (*portrait*) Jean-Marie Massaud, Paris (photo: Mario Pignata Monti) **p.352–355** © Jean-Marie Massaud, Paris **p.356** © Jean-Marie Massaud, Paris / Viccarbe Hábitat s.l., Valencia, Spain **p.357** © (*top*) Jean-Marie Massaud, Paris / Serralunga srl, Biella, Italy **p.357** © (*bottom*) Jean-Marie Massaud, Paris / Arper SpA, Monastier (Treviso) Italy **p.358–359** © Jean-Marie Massaud, Paris / Hansgrohe AG, Schiltach, Germany **p.360–361** © Jean-Marie Massaud, Paris **p.362–367** © Fredrik Mattson, Stockholm / Blå Station, Åhus, Sweden **p.368–373** © Ingo Maurer, Munich (photos: Tom Vack) **p.375–376** © Alberto Meda and Franciso Gomez Paz, Milan **p.377** © Alberto Meda, Milan **p.378–379** © Alberto Meda, Milan / Luceplan, Milan (photos: Miro Zagnoli) **p.380** © (*portrait*) Jasper Morrison, London (photo: momoko, Japan) **p.380–381** © Jasper Morrison, London (photos: Morgane Le Gall) **p.382** © Jasper Morrison, London / Magis, Motta di Livenza, Italy **p.383** © Jasper Morrison, London (photos: Morgane Le Gall) **p.384** © Jasper Morrison, London (photos: Studio one) **p.385** © Jasper Morrison, London (photos: André Huber) **p.386–387** © Brodie Neill, London (photos: Simon Murrell) **p.388** © Brodie Neill, London **p.389** © (*top*) Brodie Neill, London (photo: Sari Goodfriend) **p.389** © (*middle*) Brodie Neill, London / Kundalini, Milan **p.389** © (*bottom*) Brodie Neill, London **p.390** © Nendo (Oki Sato), Tokyo / De Padova, Milan **p.391** © (*top*) Nendo (Oki Sato), Tokyo / Cappellini, Mariano Comense (Como) Italy **p.391** © (*bottom*) Nendo (Oki Sato), Tokyo / De Padova, Milan **p.392–395** © Nendo (Oki Sato), Tokyo (photos:

Masayuki Hayashi) **p.396** © (*portrait*) Marc Newson, London (photo: David Bailey) **p.396–397** © Marc Newson, London / Samsonite Corporation, Denver **p.398–399** © Marc Newson, London (photos: Lamay Photo / Courtesy Gagosian Gallery, New York) **p.400** © (*top*) Marc Newson, London (photos: Jean-Luc Viardin) **p.400** © (*bottom*) Marc Newson, London (photo: Lamay Photo / Courtesy Gagosian Gallery, New York) **p.401** © Marc Newson, London / Magis, Motta di Livenza, Italy **p.402–405** © NICE Car Company Ltd., London **p.406–409** © Patrick Norguet, Paris **p.410–415** © OMD Corp., Venice, California **p.416–417** © Ora-Ïto, Paris / Gorenje, Velenje, Slovenia **p.418** © Ora-Ïto, Paris / Toyota Motor Corporation, Tokyo **p.419** © Ora-Ïto, Paris / Frighetto, Vicenza, Italy **p.420–423** © Giovanni Pagnotta, Harrison, New York **p.424–425** © Satyendra Pakhalé, Amsterdam / Erreti Srl, Ravenna, Italy **p.426** © (*top*) Satyendra Pakhalé, Amsterdam (photo: European Ceramic Work Center, The Netherlands) **p.426** © (*bottom*) Satyendra Pakhalé, Amsterdam / Tubes, Resana (TV) Italy **p.427** © Satyendra Pakhalé, Amsterdam **p.428** © (*left*) Satyendra Pakhalé, Amsterdam **p.428** © (*right*) Satyendra Pakhalé, Amsterdam / Colombo Design SpA, Terno d'Isola (BG) Italy **p.429** © (*top + middle*) Satyendra Pakhalé, Amsterdam **p.429** © (*bottom*) Satyendra Pakhalé, Amsterdam / Cappellini, Mariano Comense (Como) Italy **p.430** © PearsonLloyd, London **p.431** © PearsonLloyd, London / Allermuir, Lower Darwen, Lancashire **p.432** © (*top*) PearsonLloyd, London **p.432** © (*bottom*) PearsonLloyd, London / Bernhardt Design, Lenoir, North Carolina **p.433** © (*top*) PearsonLloyd, London / Allermuir, Lower Darwen, Lancashire **p.433** © (*bottom*) PearsonLloyd, London / Martinez Otero S.L., Pontevedra, Spain **p.434** © PearsonLloyd, London / Virgin Atlantic Airways Ltd., Crawley, West Sussex **p.435** © (*top + middle*) PearsonLloyd, London / Tacchini Italia srl, Baruccana di Seveso (Milan) Italy **p.435** © (*bottom*) PearsonLloyd, London / Siren Inc., Japan **p.436–443** © Philips Design, Eindhoven, The Netherlands **p.444–447** © Phoenix Design, Stuttgart **p.448** © (*left*) photo: Agence Zoom, France **p.448** © (*right*) POC Sweden AB, Saltsjöbaden, Sweden **p.449–453** © POC Sweden AB, Saltsjöbaden, Sweden **p.454–459** © Porsche Design GmbH, Zell am See, Austria **p.460** © (*portrait*) Karim Rashid, New York (photo: Milovan Knezevic) **p.460–465** © Karim Rashid Inc., New York **p.466** © (*top + middle*) Karim Rashid Inc., New York / LaCie USA, Hillsboro, Oregon **p.466** © (*bottom*) Karim Rashid Inc., New York / Horm, Azzano Decimo, Italy **p.467** © Karim Rashid Inc., New York / Horm, Azzano Decimo, Italy **p.468** © Karim Rashid Inc., New York / Royal Appliance Mfg. Co., Glenwillow, Ohio **p.469** © Karim Rashid Inc., New York / Axe, Unilever plc, London **p.470** © Karim Rashid Inc., New York **p.471** © Karim Rashid Inc., New York / Artemide, Pregnana Milanese (MI) Italy **p.472–479** © Seymourpowell, Lon-

don **p.480–483** © Design Studio S, Tokyo **p.485–486** © Skibsted Ideation A/S, Copenhagen / Biomega, Copenhagen **p.487** © Skibsted Ideation A/S, Copenhagen / Puma AG, Herzogenaurach, Germany **p.488** © Skibsted Ideation A/S, Copenhagen / Mater A/S, Copenhagen **p.489** © Skibsted Ideation A/S, Copenhagen / Ibsen & Co., Copenhagen **p.490–493** © Smart Design, New York (photos: Claudia Christen) **p.494** © (*top*) Smart Design, New York **p.494** © (*bottom*) Smart Design, New York (photo: Claudia Christen) **p.495** © (*top + middle*) Smart Design, New York (photos: Davin Stowell) **p.495** © (*bottom*) Smart Design, New York **p.497** © Sony Computer Entertainment Inc., Tokyo **p.498** © (*top + middle*) Sony Corporation, Tokyo **p.498** © (*bottom*) Sony Computer Entertainment Inc., Tokyo **p.499** © (*top*) Sony Corporation, Tokyo **p.499** © (*bottom*) Sony Ericsson Mobile Communications AB, London **p.500–505** © Philippe Starck, Paris **p.506–507** © Swe Des, Hong Kong **p.508** © Swe Des, Hong Kong (photo: Kent Johansson) **p.509** © (*top + lower right*) Swe Des, Hong Kong **p.509** © (*lower left*) Swe Des, Hong Kong (photo: Kent Johansson) **p.510–515** © Teague, Seattle, Washington **p.516–521** © Tesla Motors, San Carlos, California **p.522–525** © Venlet Interior Architecture, Brussels **p.526** © (*portrait*) Clemens Weisshaar, Munich (photo: Matthias Ziegler) **p.526** © (*portrait*) Reed Kram, Stockholm (photo: Skogquist) **p.526** © Kram/Weisshaar, Munich (photo: Florian Böhm) **p.527** © Kram/Weisshaar, Munich (photo: Frank Stolle) **p.528–530** © Kram/Weisshaar, Munich **p.531** © Kram/Weisshaar, Munich (photo: Matthias Ziegler) **p.532** © Kram/Weisshaar, Munich **p.533** © Kram/Weisshaar, Munich (photo: Florian Böhm) **p.535–536** © ZED AG, Zurich / Merck KGaH, Darmstadt, Germany **p.537** © ZED AG, Zurich / Max Design, Bagnaria Arsa (UD) Italy **p.538** © (*top*) ZED AG, Zurich / Carl Zeiss Sports Optics GmbH, Wetzlar, Germany **p.538** © (*bottom*) ZED AG, Zurich / Potocco SpA, Manzano (Udine) Italy **p.539** © ZED AG, Zurich / Pallucco Lighting, Milan **p.540** © (*portrait*) Tokujin Yoshioka, Tokyo (photo: Tomoki Futaishi) MISSING **p.540–542** © Tokujin Yoshioka, Tokyo **p.543** © (*top*) Tokujin Yoshioka, Tokyo / Yamagiwa Corporation, Tokyo (photos: Masayuki Hayashi) **p.544–545** © Tokujin Yoshioka, Tokyo **p.546–551** © Youmeus, London **p.552–p.553** © Michael Young, Hong Kong **p.554** © Michael Young, Hong Kong / Established & Sons, London **p.555** © (*top*) Michael Young, Hong Kong / Established & Sons, London **p.555** © (*middle + bottom*) Michael Young, Hong Kong **p.556** © Michael Young, Hong Kong **p.557** © (*top*) Michael Young, Hong Kong / Pearl Lam Contrast Gallery, Shanghai **p.557** © (*middle + bottom*) Michael Young, Hong Kong / Cadbury Schweppes plc, London

ABOUT THE AUTHORS
IMPRINT

Charlotte and Peter Fiell are leading authorities on 20th and 21st century design and have written numerous books on the subject, including *1000 Chairs, Design of the 20th Century, Industrial Design A-Z, Scandinavian Design, Designing the 21st Century, Graphic Design for the 21st Century, 1000 Lights* and *Contemporary Graphic Design*, all published by TASCHEN. In addition, they edited TASCHEN's *Decorative Art* series and the twelve-volume *Domus 1928-1999*. The Fiells are based in London and can be contacted at: fiell@btinternet.com

Charlotte und Peter Fiell sind führende Experten für Design des 20. und 21. Jahrhunderts mit zahlreichen einschlägigen Buchpublikationen, darunter *1000 Chairs, Design des 20. Jahrhunderts, Industriedesign A-Z, Scandinavian Design, Designing the 21st Century, Graphic Design for the 21st Century, 1000 Lights* und *Contemporary Graphic Design*, die alle bei TASCHEN erschienen sind. Sie haben für TASCHEN die *Decorative-Art*-Serie und die neue zwölfbändige Ausgabe *Domus 1928-1999* herausgegeben. Sie wohnen in London und können unter fiell@btinternet.com kontaktiert werden.

Spécialistes du design des XXe et XXIe siècles, Charlotte et Peter Fiell ont écrit de nombreux livres sur ce sujet, notamment *1000 Chairs, Design of the 20th Century, Design Industriel A-Z, Design Scandinave, Designing the 21st Century, Graphic Design for the 21st Century, 1000 Lights* et *Contemporary Graphic Design*, tous publiés chez TASCHEN. Ils ont également conçu la collection *Decorative Art* et la nouvelle collection *Domus 1928-1999* de TASCHEN, en douze volumes. Les Fiell travaillent à Londres et peuvent être contactés à l'adresse : fiell@btinternet.com

To stay informed about upcoming TASCHEN titles, please request our magazine at www.taschen.com/magazine or write to TASCHEN, Hohenzollernring 53, D-50672 Cologne, Germany, contact@taschen.com, fax: +49-221-254919. We will be happy to send you a free copy of our magazine, which is filled with information about all of our books.

© 2007 TASCHEN GmbH
Hohenzollernring 53, D–50672 Köln
www.taschen.com

Design: *Sense/Net, Andy Disl* and *Birgit Reber*, Cologne
Editorial coordination: *Jutta Hendricks*, Cologne
Production: *Ute Wachendorf*, Cologne
German translation: *Karin Haag, Brigitte Rapp, Friederike Kulcsar*, Vienna
French translation: *Alice Petillot*, Charenton-le-Pont

Printed in Italy
ISBN 978-3-8228-5267-5

COVER:
ZAHA HADID
Vortexx
Suspended ceiling light, 2005
Client: Sawaya & Moroni

© Zaha Hadid, London /
Sawaya & Moroni, Milan /
Zumtobel Lighting GmbH &
Co. KG, Lemgo, Germany

BACK COVER:
TOKUJIN YOSHIOKA
Media Skin
Mobile telephone, 2007
Client: KDDI
CORPORATION

ENDPAPERS:
ROSS LOVEGROVE
Technical drawing of
Ginko Carbon Table,
2007